China, the United States, and 21st Century Sea Power

Defining a Maritime Security Partnership

edited by Andrew S. Erickson,
Lyle J. Goldstein, and Nan Li

NAVAL INSTITUTE PRESS
Annapolis, Maryland

Naval Institute Press
291 Wood Road
Annapolis, MD 21402

Library of Congress Cataloging-in-Publication Data
China, the United States, and 21st-century sea power : defining a maritime security
partnership / edited by Andrew S. Erickson, Lyle J. Goldstein, and Nan Li.
     p. cm.
  Includes bibliographical references and index.
    ISBN 978-1-59114-243-0
  1. Sea-power—History—21st century. 2. Naval strategy—History—21st century.
3. United States—Military relations—China. 4. China—Military relations—United
States. 5. United States—History, Naval—21st century. 6. China—History, Naval—
21st century. I. Erickson, Andrew S. II. Goldstein, Lyle. III. Li, Nan, 1956-
  V25.C45 2008
  359'.03—dc22
                              2010022124
Printed in the United States of America on acid-free paper

14 13 12 11 10   9 8 7 6 5 4 3 2
First printing

Contents

Andrew S. Erickson and Lyle J. Goldstein

Introduction:
In the Same Boat Together

DURING JUNE 2009, four People's Liberation Army (PLA) Navy doctors flew to Tumaco, Colombia, to spend a week aboard the USNS *Comfort*, where they learned how the U.S. Navy promotes goodwill by delivering high quality and efficient medical care to parts of the world that are in need. No doubt this quite remarkable step in building a U.S.–China maritime partnership was a direct result of the March 2009 visit to Qingdao by chief of naval operations (CNO) Admiral Gary Roughead, in which he participated in the sixtieth anniversary of the PLA Navy and toured its first purpose-built hospital ship, the Type 920 *Daishandao/Peace Ark* (岱山岛号, AHH 866). CNO Roughead's visit, like that of the four PLA Navy doctors to USNS *Comfort*, suggests a strong commitment on both sides of the Pacific to seizing opportunities to share best practices and develop new areas for cooperation in support of global development and security. As the first of what will reportedly be annual international deployments, *Peace Ark* is slated to call on ports in the Middle East and Africa in 2010.[1]

Nevertheless, CNO Roughead's attendance at the PLA Navy's sixtieth anniversary celebrations was very nearly derailed by the "*Impeccable* incident" of 8 March 2009, in which a group of Chinese enforcement vessels and fishing trawlers harassed the surveillance ship USNS *Impeccable* then operating some seventy-five miles south of Hainan Island. Many have cited this incident as the most serious crisis in U.S.–China military relations since the "EP-3 incident" of 1 April 2001. Moreover, tensions have also been building over enhanced Chinese capabilities in a variety of areas, ranging from new submarines to antisatellite weapons to the potential for an antiship ballistic missile. CNO Roughead's decision to attend the PLA Navy celebration just a month after the *Impeccable* incident was a definite signal at the most senior U.S. military levels that this most crucial bilateral military relationship would not be permitted to drift in a dangerous direction. Indeed, President Barack Obama had underlined in the immediate aftermath of the *Impeccable* crisis "the importance of raising the level and frequency of the U.S.-China military-to-military dialogue in order to avoid future incidents."[2] Rather than simple idealism, this approach signaled in fact a new realism: the understanding that global security now depends on a working partnership between the U.S. and Chinese armed forces. While such a partnership could have an impact on various aspects of global security, this partnership is especially crucial in the maritime realm, where both nations share a core interest in protecting the global maritime trading system. This volume is intended to be a guidebook for practitioners—for those charged with the difficult task of building and nurturing the nascent Sino-American maritime partnership, which is beset with challenges, yet holds enormous promise.

This book is the result of the U.S. Naval War College's China Maritime Studies Institute's third annual conference, "Defining a Maritime Partnership with China," held in Newport, Rhode Island on 5–6 December 2007. The conference featured seven delegates from the People's Republic of China (PRC), who represented some of China's leading universities in the maritime domain. The Chinese delegation included PLA Navy rear admiral Yang Yi, then director of the Institute of Strategic Studies at China's National Defense University. American participants included representatives from the U.S. Pacific Fleet and other relevant fleet commands as well as the State Department and the Department of Homeland Security.

Despite recent turbulence in U.S.–China military-to-military relations, conference participants reaffirmed that the United States and China have substantial shared interests that could enable extensive bilateral U.S.–China maritime security cooperation. The goal of the conference was to foster dialogue between Chinese and American experts on potential areas of cooperation among our nations' respective maritime services. Attendees agreed that a strong foundation for maritime partnership exists in the increasingly robust commercial relationship but that the military side of the partnership lags well behind. The conference focused on determining which areas might be fruitful for more extensive U.S.–China maritime cooperation.

Conference Findings

The conference reached six major conclusions:

- Economic cooperation provides a durable foundation for enhanced partnership between the United States and China on the world's oceans since the health of the global system relies on secure and stable sea-lanes.

- Although barriers still exist that prevent a robust U.S.-Chinese partnership to maintain security at sea, there has been some impressive success in creating new forms of collaboration in search and rescue as well as in fisheries enforcement.

- China's cautiously positive reaction to the new U.S. Maritime Strategy suggests possibilities for expanding cooperation in humanitarian assistance and disaster relief operations, maritime environmental issues, energy security, counterterrorism, and professional military education (PME).[3] Further discussions with respect to international legal authorities will be required to find ways to cooperate that take into account each country's perspective.

- Beijing's growing capabilities and presence on the seas will make maritime collaboration and crisis management procedures with Washington both more feasible and more essential.

- The sensitive Taiwan issue, differences over definitions and appropriate prioritization of transparency, and a paucity of mutual trust remain fundamental limiting factors for expanded military and maritime cooperation.

- To enhance maritime cooperation, political leaders in Washington and Beijing must create sufficient political and institutional space for maritime and naval professionals to structure cooperation. They must also resist the temptation to use maritime cooperation to "score points" in the various political controversies that will inevitably affect this complex bilateral relationship. Indeed, repeated suspensions of the bilateral military relationship during 2008–10 have severely hampered the development of long-term cooperative efforts.

The Vibrant Maritime Commercial Partnership

Both the United States and China are vital participants in, and beneficiaries of, the global system, particularly the global economy.[4] This creates a fundamental imperative for transparent, mutually beneficial cooperation based on equality and reciprocity. Both states are major forces in global international trade, of which 80 percent is seaborne. The United States is China's most significant export destination. Recent statistics reveal that about 16 million shipping containers enter U.S. ports annually, and Chinese ports handle as much as 40 percent of world container volume. The interconnections between the two economies are vast in scope. As demonstrated clearly by the global financial crisis of 2008–10, a crisis in one economy inevitably has adverse effects on the other. Rear Admiral Yang Yi characterized this close economic relationship as "mutually assured dependence."

The Container Security Initiative (CSI) represents a major success in U.S.–China maritime cooperation that has flowed directly from this intensive economic interaction. Beijing has moved rapidly to ensure that its major ports are compliant with new post-9/11 practices for ensuring the security of containerized cargo. As U.S. Customs Commissioner Robert Bonner recently noted, "Due to the continued support of CSI by [PRC] Minister Mu Xinsheng, U.S. borders are more secure and efficient." Economic partnership between the United States and China is also based on common structural features between the two economies. Both economies are extremely dependent on the reliable and efficient seaborne transport of energy. This shared interest creates a wide range of opportunities for enlarging maritime cooperation. Five of the world's ten largest ports are in China, and China has the world's second-largest merchant marine (with many other Chinese-owned vessels sailing under foreign flags). In addition, there is increasing convergence in the two states' preferences with respect to the balance of port-state rights versus flag-state rights. It is therefore essential that the military and security partnership develop in a manner that complements these larger trends. Indeed, the financial cooperation that has underpinned efforts in Beijing and Washington to limit the global financial crisis and its aftereffects over the course of 2007–10 needs to take into account the close relationship between the global economy and maritime security that protects the world's trading networks.

Significant Search and Rescue Successes

Beijing's interest in maritime search and rescue has increased substantially in recent years. The tragic loss of 291 Chinese lives when the ferry *Dashun* caught fire and sank within sight of shore in 1999 served as a stark symbol of China's deficiencies in this area. Thanks to a major effort in this domain, according to Captain Bernard Moreland, former Coast Guard Liaison Officer Beijing, "Less than 10 years after the Dashun tragedy, China has a fully operating professional maritime search and rescue capacity." The China Rescue and Salvage Bureau claims to have saved or assisted 3,849 persons in 2006. Beijing is looking to improve coordination for maritime rescue among the many relevant agencies, including the PLA Navy.

The PLA Navy and the U.S. Navy collaborated in a series of small-scale search-and-rescue exercises during 2006. There has also been robust U.S. Coast Guard (USCG) engagement with Chinese maritime authorities. Visits by USCG cutters have created opportunities for "several days of professional exchanges culminating in demonstrations of practice boarding scenarios," Captain Moreland elaborated. Fisheries cooperation has been extensive as well, and there have also been "U.S. and Chinese maritime command centers [coordinating] control of ships [and] aircraft . . . in real-time 24 hour operations to save lives." The USCG's AMVER search-and-rescue system was critical to saving the lives of nineteen sailors of the *Unicorn Ace*, which sank in the South China Sea in March 2007. In July 2007 thirteen Chinese sailors were rescued from *Hai Tong 7*, three hundred miles northwest of Guam, with the pivotal involvement of both U.S. Navy and USCG assets. Beijing is eager to expand cooperative initiatives with the USCG.

Prospects for Joint Disaster Relief Operations

Having overcome major reservations, stated Su Hao of China Foreign Affairs University, "the Chinese government [now] views [humanitarian operations] as an important part of international security cooperation." The emphasis of the new U.S. Maritime Strategy on disaster relief offers opportunities for the United States and China to cooperate and build mutual trust. As Zhuang Jianzhong of Shanghai Jiao Tong University states, much more can be done to address "common challenges and common security threats such as . . . bird flu, climate change and tsunamis." Rear Admiral Yang Yi pointed out that possibilities will materialize as China increases its capabilities in this area, drawing on extensive PLA experience with domestic disaster relief. Indeed, the tragic 12 May 2008 Wenchuan earthquake and 14 April 2010 Yushu earthquake, in addition to other major internal relief operations in China during the last few years, have served to reinvigorate the PLA's long tradition in this area.

The experiences in the relief efforts following the 26 December 2004 Indian Ocean tsunami provide another relevant example. Dr. Michael J. Green, Center for Strategic and International Studies, observed that "the 2004 tsunami led to unprecedented cooperation among Asia Pacific navies, centered on the U.S.-Japan-India-Australia Regional Core Group"—maritime forces that were already accustomed to working together and thus could assemble and interoperate rapidly. This episode made "China aware of the limitations of its navy's capacities to deliver [assistance and aid], compared with the U.S. Navy." Su Hao judged that China's "navy [is] not only facing traditional security threats, it must [now] deal with maritime disasters, humanitarian crises, and other non-traditional security threats." "The PLA Navy could gain experience and build confidence in the region by exercising with the U.S. and other navies to be better prepared for operations in response to future humanitarian crises," added Michael J. Green. Peter A. Dutton, Naval War College, maintained that "cooperation in humanitarian relief operations seems a very real possibility for the near future, and exercises to practice for instance a medical relief operation could be fruitful and non-threatening." Rear Admiral Eric A. McVadon, USN (Ret.), judged that China's new landing platform dock, as well as a new class of hospital ship, suggests that the PLA Navy may now have the requisite capabilities to participate in major maritime international disaster relief operations in the future. In Dr. Su's evaluation, "Humanitarian assistance . . . could create good conditions for Chinese-American maritime cooperation in the long run." Rear Admiral Yang Yi suggested that an exchange of specialists as well as certain war-gaming techniques could be undertaken as first steps in cooperative disaster relief efforts.

Maritime Cooperation in Other Regional Settings

China, with its rapid economic and maritime development, is playing an increasingly significant role in East Asia and beyond. Naval War College president (2004–8) Rear Admiral Jacob Shuford, USN, cited China's contribution to the Six Party Talks as an example. When considering the tragic 26 March 2010 sinking of Republic of Korea Navy ship *Cheonan* on the South Korean side of the disputed northern limit line in the Yellow Sea, coordination by the U.S. and Chinese navies to limit regional disputes seems all the more important. But such maritime cooperation need not be limited to East Asia. As Shen Dingli of Fudan University noted, "the world is finding China everywhere, and China is finding itself involved everywhere." Rear Admiral Yang Yi stated that "China's interests around the world are continually expanding . . . [and Beijing] should use its own power and provide the world with more 'public goods.'"

In East Asia, however, Michael J. Green maintained, some of China's maritime neighbors are anxious and so "are engaged in pronounced *internal* balancing (increasing naval capabilities) in response to China's growing capabilities," and there is even more widespread "evidence of *external* balancing (alignment) to ensure that a stable equilibrium is maintained." Despite such concerns, "all of the maritime powers in Asia seek closer cooperation, confidence-building and mutual transparency with the PLA Navy" and "all of the powers seek a stable U.S.–China relationship." Moreover, as Dr. Zhu Huayou of the National Institute for South China Sea Studies observed, "the United States serves as an important driver for the rapid growth of the ASEAN economy. . . . The ultimate settlement and management of [Southeast Asia regional security] issues cannot be achieved without Sino-U.S. cooperation, especially Sino-U.S. maritime cooperation." Under the aegis of the International Maritime Organization, the United States and China have already undertaken joint research investigating the handling of oil spills as well as the upgrading of navigation aids in the Strait of Malacca. Beijing is also discovering some of the costs of its growing international profile. In Ethiopia, nine Chinese workers were killed when the Ogaden National Liberation Front attacked an oil facility in 2007. Chinese have also been victims of terrorism in Pakistan, such as when a bus of Chinese engineers was recently bombed and three Chinese workers were shot dead in Baluchistan. Cooperation in such regions as South Asia might be bilateral or, more likely, multilateral. In the view of James R. Holmes and Toshi Yoshihara, Naval War College, "conditions are auspicious for shaping a mutually beneficial maritime relationship among India, China, and the United States." Insofar as both Washington and Beijing have common interests in promoting stability and combating these types of terrorist activities, maritime cooperation in a variety of regions may be increasingly feasible.

The Next Steps in Maritime Educational Cooperation

Understanding the differences and similarities in U.S. and Chinese PME, observed Nan Li, Naval War College, "may help to explore the possibilities of future maritime cooperation between the U.S. and China." Yet "except for occasional exchanges of short visits to each other's naval schools by higher-ranking officers, no institutionalized, longer-term exchange programs exist between American and Chinese naval education systems," even though such exchanges are already occurring between Chinese and Japanese maritime services. Although less sensitive cooperation areas, including civilian academic conferences and exchanges, can be augmented immediately, robust ties between relevant PME institutions should build on this foundation, potentially focusing on short courses for students. Rear Admiral Yang Yi emphasized that academic exchanges could additionally facilitate explanation of all aspects of the new U.S. Maritime Strategy to Chinese officials and subject matter experts.

Mutual discussion of nonsensitive linguistic, curricular, and technical elements (e.g., best practices and simulation techniques) could further cooperation possibilities. Despite some key differences in educational methods and organization, Nan Li elaborates, "issues such as coastal waters security, maritime search and rescue, countering terrorism and piracy, countering weapons of mass destruction (WMD) proliferation by sea, maritime humanitarian assistance and disaster relief, maritime quarantine of diseases, peacekeeping and international law and the Law of the Sea Convention have become common subjects of study for both American and Chinese naval education." Thus, "cooperation on noncompetitive issues may lay the interactive and cognitive basis for further joint efforts to mitigate the consequences of maritime and naval competition." Such institutional relationships among naval research and educational centers will help to build up a group of academic and operational experts (including PME students) who are comfortable with and may advocate forcefully for enhanced U.S.–China maritime partnership in spite of the many challenges that this partnership is bound to confront.

Convergent and Divergent Legal Perspectives

The legal sphere is a major mechanism to strengthen maritime security cooperation between the United States and China. In the opinion of Guifang (Julia) Xue, Ocean University of China, "regarding law of the sea issues [and despite its status as a nonsignatory], the United States is . . . full of vigor as a world leader." Now Beijing is endeavoring to be more proactive: "[Compared to its previously limited actions,] China now attends more international forums, signs more statements, and conducts more consultations on law of the sea issues with its maritime neighbors." One noteworthy area of U.S.–China cooperation resulting from common legal norms is the series of anti-driftnet fishing enforcement operations that have involved the USCG and the PRC Fisheries Law Enforcement Command (FLEC) for more than a decade now. FLEC ship riders on USCG cutters, working in tandem FLEC cutters as well as other nations' assets, have been able to significantly increase enforcement of the UN resolution against driftnet fishing on the high seas. Although the USCG started fisheries cooperation with China in the mid-1990s, including driving cutters around with Chinese agents and sharing "fisheries intelligence" at conferences, there was an exponential jump in effectiveness recently because the real-time communications channels came into place for effective international operational coordination of cutters, agents, airplanes, and intelligence.[5] In the experience of Captain Moreland, intelligence and reconnaissance suddenly became actionable; operational resources could be coordinated (e.g., China got cutters under way on short notice to support USCG seizures).

American delegates at the conference emphasized that Chinese participation in the Proliferation Security Initiative (PSI) would be wholly consistent with international legal norms. As Rear Admiral Yang Yi emphasized, this was a point that Chinese presenters were reluctant to embrace, insisting that further UN mandate might be required. However, Shen Dingli did say that he had recommended to the Chinese government that China join PSI. Elaborating further on Beijing's view of the Law of the Sea, Julia Xue observed that "China has not been entirely satisfied with the Law of the Sea Convention." Specifically, she noted that Chinese domestic law does not recognize the right of innocent passage for warships. While acknowledging that the Chinese law on innocent passage does not comply with the text of the UN Convention on the Law of the Sea (UNCLOS), she stated that it is based on long-standing Chinese tradition. Additionally, "China found itself disadvantaged in enjoying full entitlement [to its exclusive economic zone] under the Law of the Sea." The March 2009 *Impeccable* incident brought to light the rather stark differences between Beijing and Washington concerning the issue of permissible military activities in exclusive economic zones. Legal aspects of China's 2008 counterpiracy deployment to the Gulf of Aden are likewise suggestive of differences in perspective.[6] What can be said definitively at this point is that the law provides a reasonable forum for civilized states to present alternative interpretations. Such disagreements may in fact reflect the strength of institutions to limit conflict by facilitating compromise among the major powers.

New Areas for Cooperation

There is already a strong record of Sino-American cooperation in the domain of search and rescue. Prospects for broader disaster relief cooperation are promising, as are expanded educational initiatives and regional maritime security cooperation. Several other ideas raised by conference participants also deserve limited mention in this summary. Participants agreed, for instance, that maritime energy transport was a strong potential area for cooperation. The two governments have already agreed to coordinate strategic petroleum reserve policies for mutual benefit. Gabriel B. Collins of the Naval War College suggested, "There are certainly frictions that will be associated with China's rise as an energy consumer. . . . Yet now is the time to engage China on the maritime energy security issue in the hope of positively influencing its behavior and policy choices for the benefit of all." Indeed, it is not surprising that nascent maritime cooperation between China and the United States has begun to develop within the Gulf of Aden counterpiracy mission, as noted by CNO Roughead in Qingdao during April 2009. At considerable distance from the sensitive flashpoints of East Asia, the Gulf of Aden may function in the near term as a strategic cooperation zone for the U.S. and Chinese navies. A related fruitful area of cooperation might be studying the maritime implications of ongoing climate change. Polar research is also said to be a promising subject, as demonstrated by USCG Vice Admiral Charles Wurster's recent visit to the Polar Research Institute of China. With respect to maritime counterterrorism cooperation, Paul J. Smith, Naval War College, added, "China . . . is confronting a nascent, yet burgeoning challenge of terrorism and political violence, similar to what has plagued the United States." Beijing and Washington could together form "a powerful bulwark against militant extremism and the instability that it promotes." Finally, some participants in the conference called on Beijing and Washington to establish more bilateral and multilateral forums focused on maritime cooperation. For instance, it was suggested that the United States and China already have an important strategic economic dialogue, but they might also form a "strategic maritime dialogue" or alternatively a "northeast Asia maritime security forum."

China's Rapid Naval Modernization

Conference participants generally agreed that China's naval modernization was primarily focused on the Taiwan contingency. As Jin Canrong, Renmin University, explained, "The Taiwan issue is the dominant factor that drives the modernization of China's navy. This is the only factor that can lead China into an unlimited arms race." In this regard, Rear Admiral Yang Yi said that "the strategic intention of the United States . . . is not transparent in many aspects." Shen Dingli offered: "no sovereign government could fail to prepare for the worst-case situation. When all peaceful means have been tried and have failed, China either needs to honor its deterrence or accept a political fiasco." Shortly after the late 2007 conference, however, the election of Ma Ying-jeou as president of Taiwan on 22 March 2008 did pave the way for much enhanced stability in the cross-strait relationship. Although the issue of arms sales from the United States to Taiwan has taken a toll on U.S.–China military relations during 2008–10, it seems that the chances of conflict are much reduced, causing many Chinese and American naval strategists to think anew about other missions and new possibilities for cooperation.

Indeed, conference participants discussed Chinese naval capabilities "beyond Taiwan," including sea lines of communication defense and regional security collaboration. The twenty or more roles and capabilities that were discussed suggest a broadening and deepening of China's maritime strategic missions. The United States and China clearly need to engage in more complete exchanges on these issues, but they may remain constrained by differing definitions of transparency and national security.

One American presenter was strongly critical of Beijing's blue water naval aspirations, asserting that China's rapid naval modernization represented folly motivated above all by Chinese nationalism rather than rational national security requirements. Several Chinese presenters said that China would not challenge U.S. naval supremacy. As Jin Canrong explained, "China will never compete with the U.S. for naval power leadership. One reason is that China basically is a land power. . . . In modern world history . . . land powers like France, Germany and the Soviet Union . . . all failed when they tried to seek sea power leadership."[7] Many Chinese presenters registered concerns that recent U.S. deployments in East Asia might be directed against China.

Nevertheless, there was general agreement among both Chinese and American participants that China's navy would increase its capabilities significantly, and would undertake other missions (aside from preparing for a Taiwan scenario). Shen Dingli observed that "new threat perceptions . . . and expanding [requirements] for sea-lane protection, have . . . combined to provide the Chinese Navy with missions commensurate with [its] new power." Jin Canrong stated, "Today China's navy has no blue water reaching capability at all. So, to increase the capability to protect China's overseas interests is an important part of China's future national security strategy." A central theme of this conference was the imperative to consider how expanding Chinese maritime capabilities, including naval forces, might support a broader maritime cooperation agenda.

Initial Reactions to America's New Maritime Strategy

"A Cooperative Strategy for 21st Century Seapower," which was presented by the chief of naval operations and the commandants of the U.S. Marine Corps and U.S. Coast Guard at the International Seapower Symposium in Newport, Rhode Island, on 17 October 2007, was warmly endorsed by several Chinese participants. In the assessment of Rear Admiral Shuford, "The Chinese were explicit in their recognition that they are 'stakeholders' in the system, that they have relied on the U.S. Navy to preserve it, and that they have a responsibility to contribute more. They are very interested in a dialogue with us to better understand key concepts in the new strategy." Zhuang Jianzhong said that he "fundamentally agreed with the content of the New Maritime Strategy." Rear Admiral Yang Yi also praised the strategy: "The Thousand Ship Navy [concept] serves many . . . Chinese and U.S. interests. It is congruent with China's goal of pursuing a harmonious world." It may serve as "a possible 'test-bed' for [bilateral] military cooperation," particularly in the areas of humanitarian assistance and disaster relief.

Chinese participation, on a case-by-case basis, may hinge on adherence to the following principles, according to Rear Admiral Yang: "all activities should be strictly within the framework of U.N. authorization and consistent with international laws; the sovereignty and territorial integrity of other countries must be respected and the use of force in order to intervene in a country's internal affairs shall be avoided; the target of activity should be non-traditional security threats such as terrorism, religious extremism and national separatism." Having read the entire Maritime Strategy carefully, and praising most of its content, Rear Admiral Yang Yi raised specific concerns about the section "Deter Major Power War," stating that the U.S. approach here could "backfire" because it would make China feel targeted. To address these and other concerns, Rear Admiral Shuford suggested that workshops be held in which three major subject areas could be addressed: the Maritime Strategy; approaches to identify and overcome internal institutional and cultural barriers (working across governmental agencies) to effectively addressing maritime security missions; and models and lessons learned in working in ad hoc maritime coalitions. The current U.S. Maritime Strategy, emphasizing as it does the maintenance of the global trading system that has benefited no state more than China, certainly lays down a positive framework to undertake enhanced maritime cooperation between Washington and Beijing.

The Imperative for Crisis Management

In the view of many conference participants, military partnership is grossly lagging and creates a serious potential for miscalculation wherein unplanned actions at the tactical level create strategic setbacks for both countries. In a similar vein, Rear Admiral Yang Yi added, "contact between the two navies [is increasing]. If the two are in a state of serious mutual distrust, 'incidents' will never cease to crop up." There is an increasing possibility of misperceptions (potentially exacerbated by cultural and linguistic differences) transforming tactical incidents into major crises. Unfortunately, in the opinion of Michael J. Green, "the U.S. and China are not much better prepared to respond to an incident than in 2001" because the existing 1998 Military Maritime Consultative Agreement (MMCA) merely provides for an annual meeting. "The agreement on a hotline may prove easier to implement and test than the MMCA, but it is prone to bureaucratic delay and cannot replace well rehearsed rules-of-the road in theater." Yet, as David N. Griffiths of Dalhousie University emphasizes, "China and the United States cannot afford to leave incident management to chance or instinct. The stakes are too high." A single mishandled incident could unintentionally undo years of painstaking progress in building U.S.–China maritime cooperation. Indeed, the *Impeccable* incident of March 2009 appears to have left many deep scars on the relationship, just as CMSI conference participants had anticipated.

Much discussion at the conference focused on creating significantly more routine exchanges at all levels within the military bureaucracy as one approach to help address this liability. In an era of advanced communications and sensing technology, a robust "risk management mechanism" that facilitates early, real-time tactical communication between military platforms as well as between operational headquarters would greatly further a larger effort to improve bilateral communications and crisis management. It should be coupled with more frequent meetings (particularly among apolitical military professional operators behind closed doors and among their civilian counterparts) and perhaps some form of after-incident review process and confidence building measures. This would hardly be unprecedented, as there are numerous historical and current models to draw upon.

Impediments to Enhanced U.S.–China Maritime Cooperation

There remain significant political, cultural, and practical obstacles to enhanced Sino-American maritime cooperation. Chinese participants concurred that Washington's continuing support for Taipei (e.g., arms sales) remains the most significant barrier to enhanced bilateral cooperation. Rear Admiral Yang Yi explained, "Needless to say, the Chinese and American armies are both making military preparation for worst-case scenarios in the Taiwan Strait. So, at present, it is unrealistic for the PLA and the U.S. military to engage in substantial military cooperation." And there are political reservations on the U.S. side as well. As Michael J. Green observed, "While there is renewed momentum in U.S.–China maritime cooperation, reciprocity is falling short of expectations."

A significant cultural divide between the United States and China is a reflection of the states' very different modern histories. The United States has been a major world maritime power for more than a century. By contrast, China is a new maritime power that has suffered major predations by hostile foreign powers originating from its maritime flank. This may explain, in the view of Peter A. Dutton, Beijing's very slow transition away from a "coastal state" mentality to a "maritime power" mentality. As David N. Griffiths pointed out at the conference, even language can have a complicated impact on discussions of future cooperation, since in Chinese the word for "security" (安全) is also the same word for "safety," and so may have a rather different connotation in the Chinese context.

There is also a variety of impediments to enhanced maritime cooperation. There are major resource limitations on both sides. For example, the USCG apparently must turn down many engagement opportunities with China because it does not have adequate resources to respond to all Chinese requests for cooperative activities. Likewise, China seems for now to still lack some critical assets (e.g., large helicopters) for major offshore disaster relief operations. There are organizational problems as well—for example, the bewildering number of Chinese organizations involved in search-and-rescue operations. Finally, there are also some major differences in the organization of maritime and naval education systems in each country; these might pose further challenges to building cooperative relationships.

Despite these major impediments, however, it is certainly worth considering how the improved cross-strait situation since 2008, coupled with new cooperation-oriented platforms such as hospital ships as well as new outward initiatives such as the Gulf of Aden counterpiracy mission may, taken in the aggregate, have opened a significant "window of opportunity" for enhanced U.S.–China maritime cooperation.

Organization of This Book

The first section of this volume surveys the stakes that the United States and China share in the global maritime commons. In his opening chapter on China's maritime development, Zhuang Jianzhong emphasizes that Beijing intends to pursue both a full range of development and security interests at sea and cooperation with other stakeholders such as the United States. Zhuang is heartened at the truly unprecedented cooperative language of the new U.S. Maritime Strategy and is waiting to see how it will be implemented in practice. Gabriel B. Collins then deploys detailed figures and statistics to demonstrate the critical importance of the global maritime commons to China's economic development, as exemplified by the PLA Navy's counterpiracy deployment to the Gulf of Aden. Collins suggests a variety of specific ways in which the United States can help to further integrate China into the international maritime system and ensure that its core interests are recognized there. David N. Griffiths concludes the section with a thought-provoking primer on military-to-military relationships, their challenges, and their important contributions to peace and stability. Griffiths suggests that a professional gathering of sailors and other maritime specialists can often find agreement and rules of the road where their political counterparts cannot.

The second section considers the understudied subject of maritime domain awareness, or how the oceans can best be monitored and managed in support of a robust U.S.–China maritime partnership. Andrew S. Erickson, Naval War College, examines the CSI, its genesis, and its practice and value in the United States and China. Erickson concludes that CSI has succeeded by linking robust economic and security interests, introducing new technologies and commercial opportunities, facilitating access to the U.S. market, and allowing for true reciprocity. Paul J. Smith then explores how China's vulnerability to terrorism has increased with its international profile and human footprint. He shows that the United States and China have substantial shared interests in this area, and that their collaboration has deepened, particularly since 11 September 2001. In subsequent chapters, Lyle J. Goldstein, Naval War College, and Captain Bernard Moreland discuss a wide spectrum of cooperative opportunities in the civil maritime governance domain. Goldstein offers a detailed analysis of the five major Chinese organizations responsible for maritime enforcement, their respective roles, and their prospects for eventual consolidation. He finds that in addition to strengthening China's maritime claims and furthering China's growing soft power, China's civil maritime organizations, like the USCG, can serve "as a kind of buffer between states in crisis, circumventing the intensification of crises that may result from rapid naval deployments." Drawing largely on his personal experience as Coast Guard liaison officer at the U.S. Embassy in Beijing, Moreland details the rationale for, and accomplishments of, bilateral civil maritime cooperation. He demonstrates that, thanks to the relatively less sensitive nature of maritime law enforcement, the United States and China have achieved far more in this area than they have thus far in the naval dimension.

The third section covers both maritime legal issues and humanitarian operations. The first two contributors offer Chinese and U.S. viewpoints on important aspects of the Law of the Sea. Julia Xue details the differing legal perspectives that China and the United States have concerning the Law of the Sea and observes the divergent strategic interests and national histories from which these perspectives emerge. Nonetheless, Xue is optimistic that China and the United States will find ways to overcome these differences because the nations share too many common concerns to allow "obstacles to stand in the way of cooperation." Indeed, Xue notes, as major powers China and the United States have a "common responsibility" to cooperate to achieve peace and development. Peter A. Dutton assesses Chinese decisions to either participate in or opt out of four major maritime security initiatives—PSI, CSI, Combined Task Force 150, and counterpiracy operations—in light of normative international law interpretations and unique Chinese legal perspectives. His chapter concludes that U.S.–China cooperation must respect both nations' sovereign interests and legal perspectives, but that cooperation can be achieved based on independent, coordinated action that allows each participant the freedom to define the scope of authorities it views as legitimate to employ. Su Hao then turns to humanitarian assistance and search and rescue, which are assuming increasing importance in China as new missions for the PLA Navy. Su believes that this could be a good area for collaborative efforts with the United States in the future. Rear Admiral Eric A. McVadon, USN (Ret.), offers a historically informed *tour d'horizon* of U.S.–China cooperation concerning humanitarian assistance and disaster relief. He addresses obstacles to maritime security cooperation, including the *Impeccable* incident, but is optimistic that cooperative efforts can facilitate broader strategic understanding on the high seas. Lyle J. Goldstein and William S. Murray then introduce an understudied and thought-provoking topic: international efforts to rescue submarines in distress. They acknowledge that there are security concerns on all sides but argue forcefully that increased Chinese participation under the aegis of the International Submarine Escape and Rescue Liaison Office would be a valuable confidence-building measure whose advantages would outweigh any costs. Andrew S. Erickson concludes the section with another somewhat unorthodox topic: the prospects for joint U.S.–China naval efforts to combat avian influenza. Noting the clear existence of a common enemy and robust medical infrastructure in both militaries, Erickson contends that such cooperation is an idea whose time has come.

The fourth section provides a regional context for U.S.–China efforts. Here Michael J. Green draws on his considerable policy experience to assess the responses of China's neighbors to its naval development and cooperation with the United States. He emphasizes that the two nations need to work harder to "insulate maritime cooperation from capricious political retaliation, to test and strengthen agreements like the MMCA, and to increase reciprocity." Dr. Wu Shicun, National Institute for South China Sea Studies, offers a broad overview of China's interests and maritime claims in the South China Sea region. While discussing candidly strategic differences, he sees substantial room for cooperation between China, the United States, and other nations in the region against such nontraditional security threats as terrorism, piracy, and transnational crime. Zhu Huayou then discusses in detail the cooperation in the South

China Sea to date and outlines potential areas for future initiatives, including efforts to combat proliferation of weapons of mass destruction, environmental pollution, and challenges to sea-lane security. James R. Holmes and Toshi Yoshihara conclude the section with an analysis of the prospects for cooperation among the United States, China, and India in the Indian Ocean. This "strategic triangle" of great power relations, they argue, has the potential either to further regional security or to destabilize the region, depending on how it is handled by the parties involved.

The fifth section concludes the volume by assessing the prospects for maritime security cooperation between the two nations in the future. Nan Li initiates this discussion by comparing U.S. and Chinese naval education systems. He finds that the Chinese Navy has defined nontraditional security-related nonwar naval operations as a major driver of China's naval modernization, which addresses major concerns shared by the U.S. Navy. Growing similarity, familiarity, and shared concerns may open windows of opportunity for U.S.–China naval education cooperation; this in turn may help to enhance confidence building and improve crisis management. Andrew S. Erickson then examines Chinese assessments of the new U.S. Maritime Strategy. He finds that the strategy's emphasis on conflict prevention echoes many elements of Chinese strategic culture and doctrine; the avowed objective of securing the global maritime commons is highly compatible with China's strategic interests; and the new emphasis on humanitarian operations, especially, offers opportunities for bilateral cooperation to build mutual trust. Chinese analysts are heartened by the strategy's new rhetoric, and encouraging progress has been made in bilateral maritime cooperation already. But at the higher levels of China's military and civilian government, officials believe that the ball is in Washington's court, and they are waiting for concrete actions on the part of the United States. Yu Wanli, Peking University, reviews China's maritime development, which he believes to be moderate and constrained, and its influence by the United States. He concludes optimistically that "China's national strategy . . . and the stakeholder relations between China and the U.S. call for the two navies to strengthen bilateral exchanges and joint actions in areas such as sea rescue and anti-piracy operations." Rear Admiral Yang Yi concludes the volume by offering a Chinese naval perspective on maritime security cooperation between China and the United States. He points out that without increased efforts at communication and joint exercises between the two militaries, growing U.S. focus on East Asia and China's naval development will lead to increased incidents that are in neither side's interest. He therefore advocates for "gradual trust-building [to] reduce suspicions and misjudgment. It means an exploration in selective and incremental engagement." China will thus decide whether to participate in global maritime partnership activities on a case-by-case basis in accordance with its own principles and national interests. This candid and realistic assessment offers reason for cautious optimism, and Rear Admiral Yang's participation in the conference and this volume is itself a very positive and encouraging step in the building of more robust maritime relations between the United States and China.

This book contains chapters that were not presented at the conference but were deemed to be of sufficient importance to demand inclusion. It must be emphasized that the views expressed in the introduction and these chapters are those of the authors alone and in no way represent the official policies or estimates of any organization of the governments of the United States or the People's Republic of China. This volume has been compiled on the principle of academic freedom; no one associated with it, including the editors and contributors, should be construed in any way to endorse any ideas other than his or her own.

The Larger Perspective

The Wenchuan earthquake of 12 May 2008, which killed more than sixty-nine thousand Chinese citizens and devastated communities across Sichuan province, reminds us that some of the greatest threats to human security do not stem from international relations but *can* be addressed by them. In this light, it was heartening to see both China's own robust efforts, many involving the PLA, and offers of assistance from governments around the world, including that of the United States. In response to Chinese requests, for instance, U.S. military aircraft delivered supplies from Hawaii to Chengdu. "The members of U.S. Pacific Command [PACOM] offer our sincere condolences to the citizens of the People's Republic of China who have been affected by this recent earthquake," stated Admiral Timothy Keating, commander, U.S. Pacific Command. "We will continue to provide any assistance we can to minimize their suffering and loss of life."[8] This tragedy only reinforces our determination to work with Chinese scholars and maritime policymakers to help mitigate the effects of natural and other disasters everywhere around the world in the future.

An encouraging step toward this larger goal is currently being taken in the Gulf of Aden, where, as this volume went to press, PLA Navy ships were escorting merchant vessels from China and other countries as part of a UN-sanctioned counterpiracy effort. Since 26 December 2008 China's navy has dispatched twelve ships in five task forces to the pirate-infested waters near Somalia. As of 20 March 2010 PLA Navy forces have escorted 1,768 ships in 179 convoys. Sixteen PLA Navy operations have rescued 10 Chinese and 13 foreign-flagged vessels from pursuit by pirates.[9] As of 25 December 2009, 3,300 PLA Navy personnel had participated, and 405 foreign vessels had been escorted.[10]

This is part of a growing pattern of contributions to international security in which, in fulfillment of President Hu Jintao's fourth new mission for the PLA—namely, to "play an important role in maintaining world peace and promoting common development"[11]—China has dispatched UN peacekeepers at levels that periodically lead the permanent members of the Security Council (and now total more than fifteen thousand on eighteen UN missions).[12] The United States, in accordance with its new Maritime Strategy, has welcomed China's efforts in the waters off Somalia as an example of cooperation that furthers collective security. On 18 December 2008 at the Foreign Press Center in Washington, Admiral Keating vowed to "work closely" with the Chinese flotilla and to use the event as a potential "springboard for the resumption of dialog between People's Liberation Army (PLA) forces and the U.S. Pacific Command forces." "This augurs well for increased cooperation and collaboration between the Chinese military forces and U.S. . . . . forces," he stated.[13] On 1 November 2009, Rear Admiral Scott Sanders, commander, Combined Task Force-151, visited his counterpart, Rear Admiral Wang Zhiguo, aboard the PLA Navy frigate *Zhoushan* (hull 529). "As a partner in maritime security, we have worked with China on a tactical level in order to prevent piracy . . . off the coast of Somalia," Sanders stated. "Having the opportunity to sit down and share views with Adm. Wang was an invaluable experience. The cooperation between our nations continues to pay big dividends."[14] In January 2010 Chinese media confirmed that China may assume the rotating chairmanship of the Shared Awareness and Deconfliction (SHADE) meetings, a multinational effort to coordinate counterpiracy efforts among organizations operationally, and on the water tactically.[15] Captain Chris Chambers, director of Combined Maritime Forces operations, described this as "a very positive development." He added, "There has been major progress in communication and co-operation with navies that once didn't really speak to each other. . . . It will open the door for other independent nations to come in."[16]

We hope that this volume will help policymakers on both sides of the Pacific to chart a course for enhanced U.S.–China maritime cooperation sufficiently compelling to weather occasional storms of bilateral discord. In the words of Sun Zi, the United States and China are "crossing the river in the same boat, and should help each other along the way" (同舟共济). Global security for the twenty-first century and beyond can, and indeed perhaps must, be built upon such a solid and significant foundation.

Notes

1. Senior Captain Duan Zhaoxian, Assistant Chief of Staff, PLA Navy, presentation in "Session 5: Humanitarian Assistance and Disaster Relief," Maritime Security Challenges Conference 2010, Maritime Forces Pacific, Canadian Navy, Victoria, British Columbia, 29 April 2010.

2. "The President Meets with Chinese Foreign Minister Yang Jiechi," *The White House Blog*, 12 March 2009, http://www.whitehouse.gov/blog/2009/03/12/president-meets-with-chinese-foreign-minister-yang-jiechi.

3. For further analysis of PLA Navy counterpiracy deployments, see "A Cooperative Strategy for 21st Century Seapower" (Washington, DC: U.S. Chief of Naval Operations and the Commandants of the U.S. Marine Corps and U.S. Coast Guard, 17 October 2007), http://www.navy.mil/maritime/MaritimeStrategy.pdf.

4. The following sections address major themes of the 2007 conference and draw on direct statements of the delegates as much as possible. The conference proceedings are cited as "Defining a Maritime Security Partnership with China," Third annual conference, China Maritime Studies Institute, U.S. Naval War College, 5–6 December 2007.

5. Captain Moreland adds, "U.S., Japan, Russia, and Canada have been flying maritime surveillance flights for years, and sharing the sighting reports weeks or months afterwards through conferences and diplomatic channels."

6. For further details, see Andrew S. Erickson, "Chinese Sea Power in Action: The Counter-Piracy Mission in the Gulf of Aden and Beyond," in Roy Kamphausen and David Lai, eds., *The PLA at Home and Abroad—Assessing the Operational Capabilities of China's Military* (Carlisle, PA: U.S. Army War College, 2010).

7. For further analysis of this timely subject, see Andrew S. Erickson, Lyle J. Goldstein, and Carnes Lord, eds., *China Goes to Sea: Maritime Transformation in Comparative Historical Perspective* (Annapolis, MD: Naval Institute Press, 2009).

8. Jim Garamone, "U.S. Sends Relief Supplies to China," *American Forces Press Service*, 18 May 2008, http://www.defenselink.mil/news/newsarticle.aspx?id=49920.

9. "Sailing into the Storm: International Praise for Chinese Escort Fleets Protecting Merchant Ships against Somali Pirates," *Beijing Review*, 19 April 2010, http://bjreview.com.cn/quotes/txt/2010-04/19/content_264275.htm.

10. Li Xiaokun and Peng Kuang, "Anti-Piracy Special: Calming Troubled Waters," *China Daily*, 29 December 2009.

11. Introduced by Hu at an expanded Central Military Commission conference on 24 December 2004, the first three missions are to serve as an "important source of

strength" for the Chinese Communist Party (CCP) to "consolidate its ruling position"; to "provide a solid security guarantee for sustaining the important period of
strategic opportunity for national development"; and to "provide a strong strategic support for safeguarding national interests." "Earnestly Step up Ability Building
within CPC Organizations of Armed Forces," 解放军报 [*Liberation Army Daily*], 13
December 2004, available at www.chinamil.com.cn.

12. Lü Desheng, "PLA Contributes a Lot to UN Peacekeeping Operations," *Liberation
Army Daily*, 26 April 2010, http://eng.chinamil.com.cn/news-channels/china-mili
tary-news/2010-04/26/content_4194204.htm.

13. Donna Miles, "U.S. Welcomes Chinese Plans to Fight Piracy, Admiral Says,"
American Forces Press, 18 December 2008, http://www.defense.gov/news/newsarticle.
aspx?id=52386.

14. "CTF-151 Commander Visits Chinese Counter-Piracy Flagship," U.S. Naval Forces
Central Command Public Affairs, 2 November 2009, http://www.centcom.mil/en/
news/ctf-151-commander-visits-chinese-counter-piracy-flagship.html.

15. "Principled Consensus on Escort Missions Reached between China, EU, NATO, CMF,"
Xinhua, 30 January 2010, http://www.gov.cn/english/2010-01/30/content_1523729.
htm; and "Chinese Fleet Protects Merchant Ships," Ministry of the National Defense
People's Republic of China, 25 January 2010, http://eng.mod.gov.cn/Video/2010-01/25/
content_4120288.htm.

16. Greg Torode, "China to Lead Anti-Piracy Patrols: PLA Navy Officials Agree to
Expanded Role Coordinating International Efforts off Somalia," *South China Morning
Post*, 28 January 2010.

China, the United States, and 21st Century Sea Power

PART I

China, the United States, and the Global Maritime Commons

Zhuang Jianzhong

China's Maritime Development and U.S.–China Cooperation

How Do Maritime Issues Fit into China's Overall Development Strategy?

As China's president, Hu Jintao, explained in his report at the recent 17th Party Congress, "The strategic development goal of China right now is to build a moderately prosperous society in all aspects."[1] To achieve this goal, by 2020 China will increase its per capita gross domestic product (GDP) to four times that of the year 2000.[2] China's long-term goal, to be achieved by 2050, is to transform China into a mid-level developed country. President Hu stated, "We have made progress toward the goal of building a moderately prosperous society in all aspects set at the 16th Congress, and we will continue to work hard to ensure its attainment by 2020."[3]

In terms of national defense, President Hu emphasized that "to strengthen national defense and the armed forces occupies an important place in the overall arrangements for the cause of socialism with Chinese characteristics. Bearing in mind the overall strategic interests of national security and development, we must take both economic and national defense development into consideration and make our country prosperous and our armed forces powerful while building a moderately prosperous society in all aspects."[4] He added, "We must implement the military strategy for the new period, accelerate the revolution in military affairs with Chinese characteristics, ensure military preparedness, and enhance the military's capacity to respond to various security threats and accomplish diverse military tasks. We are determined to safeguard China's sovereignty, security and territorial integrity and help maintain world peace."[5]

With regard to naval development, according to China's defense white paper of 2006, "the navy is working to build itself into a modern maritime force of operation consisting of combined arms with nuclear and conventional means of operations." Moreover, "the navy is endeavoring to build mobile marine troops capable of conducting operations under conditions of information, and strengthen its overall capacity of operation in coastal waters, joint operations and integrated maritime support."[6]

President Hu Jintao remarked in 2007 that "to develop maritime issues is one of strategic tasks to boost our national economic development," and he stressed on many occasions the importance of developing China's ocean economy.[7] The oceans are of extreme importance to China's peaceful development in a multitude of areas. It is not enough to rely on land for the supply of food; China must also obtain food from the sea. The oceans are also an important source of energy. China imports half of its oil from abroad, and the proportion of imported oil will only increase in the future. In addition, more than 60 percent of the oil China imports comes via sea-lanes. China is facing environmental challenges and resource shortages. The oceans are a critical medium for communications; telephone and Internet cables run along the seabed. As a major country, China also explores the two polar regions and outer space. China even has rich culture buried in the seabed in the form of archaeological heritage. These are just a few examples of how essential the maritime dimension is to Chinese civilization and national development.

Most importantly, the reunification and the integrity of our territory remain unfulfilled, and most of the key areas are situated in the East China Sea, South Sea, and Taiwan Strait. Also, as we assume increasing international responsibilities, we need more sea-projection capability to send the rescue and humanitarian forces and forces on antiterrorism and antipiracy missions. China's recent deployment of its naval ships against pirates in Gulf of Aden is an example of these missions. It is thus abundantly clear that ocean strategy is an indispensible part of China's overall national development strategy.

Still, it must be emphasized that China is pursuing a peaceful policy; we are going along a peaceful development road, and we are promoting the development of a harmonious world of lasting peace and common prosperity. Our maritime strategy must be subordinate to our overall national strategy. We can only build a relatively moderate People's Liberation Army Navy to defend our coast areas, not a blue water navy or a strong sea power to control the sea as the United States does. Regarding maritime issues, we should uphold a concept of peaceful use of ocean resources and harmonious joint use of these resources. We should oppose sea hegemony and promote common development. These new concepts of maritime strategy should be in line with our overall peaceful development strategy, and not the reverse. We should build harmonious oceans and a harmonious world.

What Are the Main Factors Driving China's Maritime Development?

The first driving factor in China's maritime development is the new realization of the importance of oceans. It is now common consensus worldwide that the twenty-first century is a maritime century. Under the driving forces of economic globalization and integration, everything in today's world has something to do with the oceans. International politics, international economics, military activities, and scientific research are all closely related to the oceans. There are three phases in mankind's ocean views: the first phase is in the earlier stage of capitalism, when the ocean became the main venue of the capitalist expansion to find colonies and accumulate capital. The ocean played a major role in accelerating industrial civilization. In the later part of the twentieth century came another leap in mankind's ocean views. With the development of ocean technology and exploration, the oceans themselves have changed from being merely the venues and passages to the outside world to being new rich resources for development as well. With the signing of the United Nations Convention on the Law of the Sea (UNCLOS) in 1982, almost all countries link their economic development with coastal areas and use the maritime economy to support their economic development. The so-called Blue Demarcation Movement (a widespread effort by coastal states to demarcate maritime claims) is a prime example. Now in this new age of transforming from industrial civilization to information civilization, the oceans have become a new area and new space of mankind's existence and sustained development as well as the new area and new height for seizing strategic advantage. China too has recognized this transformation and has raised maritime consciousness greatly.

The second force promoting awareness of the oceans' new role and significance is the new maritime development strategy of many developed countries. Many Western countries have established new maritime development strategies in rapid succession, thus entering a new stage of development. For instance, the United States emphasizes sustainable maritime development, enhances administration of ocean resources, develops further the maritime technology industry and ocean thermal energy, and explores seabed minerals. Russia is also establishing a new maritime strategy of strengthening its navy, commercial relations, and scientific research ships in order to improve its comprehensive maritime strength. The other maritime countries such as Japan, the Republic of Korea, and India are likewise in the process of establishing their respective new maritime development strategies with the goal of rapidly becoming sea powers. These developments represent another driving force for China to have its own strategy.

The third driving factor in maritime development is China's own requirements. China is a maritime country with a long coastline of about eight thousand miles. China has the largest population in the world but has limited land resources. The ocean is definitely the choice for sustained development. Building a strong maritime country is an objective need for both our economic construction and our national security. Becoming a sea power generally means having a comprehensive capacity to explore and develop one's ocean economy, to find and utilize maritime resources and have a sea-controlling capacity, and it means being able to take the best advantage of one's power to safeguard national interests and security. Strictly speaking, China is a land country, not a sea power, and we are far behind the Western sea powers. We are not even among the big five: the United States, United Kingdom, European Union, Japan, and the Republic of Korea. So being a sea power is not compatible with our country's position in the world. For instance, the value our total maritime economy production in 1978 was 6 billion RMB; in 2005 it was 1,700 billion RMB. It only accounts for 2.6 percent of total GDP; by comparison, South Korea's maritime economy occupies 7.8 percent of GDP.

As we all know, a complete maritime strategy covers many fields, including maritime resources, maritime engineering, maritime industry, maritime environment, maritime security, maintenance of maritime rights, maritime transportation, maritime law enforcement, and international maritime cooperation. In all these aspects, China is only at the beginning. We must raise our maritime consciousness, accelerate our maritime development, establish a new strategy, and aim at becoming a maritime country at the earliest opportunity.

What Is the Role of Maritime Policy in China's New Global Diplomacy?

In his report at the 17th Party Congress, President Hu Jintao stated that "the world today is undergoing tremendous changes and adjustments. Peace and Development remain the main themes of the present era, and pursuit of peace, development and cooperation has become an irresistible trend of the times." He added, "We maintain that the people of all countries should join hands and strive to build a harmonious world of lasting peace and common prosperity."[8] Personally, I think that this is the key to our new global diplomacy.

To build a harmonious world, we also need a harmonious ocean, which is one component of a harmonious world. The oceans became an arena for nations to interact with each other when the human society entered a certain stage. If we look back at the five thousand years history of ocean development and usage, and the five hundred years of cooperation and competition, we can see that oceans in peace or in turbulence have been a barometer indicating the state of major power relations. The history of ocean development could be considered, in a certain sense, one of great power competition. Those countries that are stronger will control the oceans. Portugal became a sea power at the time of the sixteenth century, and then the sixteenth century witnessed Portuguese hegemony. The seventeenth century was dominated by Dutch sea power. The eighteenth century saw French sea power politics. The nineteenth century saw the never-fallen flags of the British on the oceans, and U.S. aircraft carriers cruised the high seas in the twentieth century. History tells us that the international community needs stable, harmonious great-power relations. So whether the sea is tranquil or stormy is really an important indicator of great power relations.

China's maritime policy is dedicated to building a harmonious ocean and peaceful seas, which includes several aspects. We will carry out policies of peaceful use of ocean space and proper development of ocean resources, work hard to protect the ocean environment, and promote secure and sustained stewardship of the oceans for mankind.

Land resources are diminishing, and some of them are even approaching exhaustion, but there are still rich stockpiles of ocean resources. So we should have a joint maritime policy of proper usage of ocean resources along with a scientific development concept to achieve a win-win result. We should also fight against exclusive, predatory, and aggressive exploitation. I think this maritime policy will contribute to building a harmonious and friendly ocean.

"To shelf disputes for common development" is an important maritime policy concept put forward by Deng Xiaoping. There are many disputes in sea territories and demarcations of the exclusive economic zone between China and neighboring nations. Our new diplomacy stresses that we should still carry out the Five Principles of Peaceful Coexistence and resolve disputes through consultation and negotiation.[9] In April 2007, Chinese premier Wen Jiabao, in his speech to the Japanese Diet, introduced a new maritime initiative between China and Japan, stating that "with regard to the issue of the East China Sea, our two countries should follow the principles of shelving differences and seeking joint development, and conduct active consultation so as to make substantive progress towards peaceful settlement of the differences and make the East China Sea a sea of peace, friendship and cooperation."[10] I think this initiative has created a new mode of resolving maritime disputes and has contributed to our overall peaceful new diplomacy of building a harmonious world.

To abide by the international law is one of our maritime policies. UNCLOS, which took effect in November 1994, marked the establishment of a legal system of rules and regulations concerning the oceans, and it serves as a catalyst in creating a fair and just international oceanic order. China signed the convention and maintains that the international community should strictly observe the convention in order to protect rights and solve disputes, for it reflects the common interests of majority countries and peoples. In December 2002 China signed an agreement with Vietnam on the delimitation of sea territory of the Beibu Gulf. This represents an application of UNCLOS in resolving maritime delimitation disputes. We think that to improve the legal system, to increase cooperation in maritime legislation, and to strengthen the role of the international community in handling crises, conflicts, and maritime environmental protection is the key to maintaining oceanic harmony and furthering world harmony.

How Could China–U.S. Maritime Cooperation Facilitate Maritime Security and Development?

Why should the United States and China cooperate in maritime affairs? The answer is that we have a common goal and shared interests. The common goal is that both the United States and China want to maintain peace and stability in the Asia-Pacific region, and our shared interests are development and prosperity. We also have common challenges and common security threats such as piracy, smuggling, terrorism, avian influenza, climate change, and natural disasters.

The biggest issue is how to view the development of a modern Chinese navy. Many of us know that we are facing common traditional and nontraditional security threats and the common task of development. But not all of us know that cooperation is absolutely necessary, and some even doubt the feasibility and possibility of cooperation. Some even think that a strong Chinese navy is a threat to the U.S. Navy. I do not know how strong our navy is now, but I can tell you that China is still a land power, not a sea power as the United States is. China's navy is not qualified to be called a blue water navy because we have no aircraft carriers. U.S. naval superiority plays a key role in the Pacific area.

As defined in the Party Congress report, and as a service of the PLA, China's navy will fulfill two tasks. One is to safeguard sovereignty, security, and territorial integrity of China. The other is to help maintain world peace. So the building up of the Chinese navy is mainly to prevent Taiwan from declaring independence, but we are trying to solve the issue primarily by peaceful means. To help maintain world peace, we will not challenge the U.S. leading role in East Asia. On the contrary, we want to cooperate with the United States on securing the commerce and sea lines of transportation, especially for energy security. Here I find a minor change of wording to be highly significant. In the 2006 Defense White Paper, we used the phrase "playing a major role in maintaining world peace and promoting common development," while in the Party Congress report we use the even more defensive phrase "help maintain world peace."[11] In the white paper we simply say that the PLA Navy's task is to strengthen its overall capabilities of operations in coastal areas. For all these reasons, China's defensive posture is not threatening to the United States.

The Taiwan issue will be another obstacle to our cooperation. This problem is China's internal problem but has some international implications. Taiwan could still become a hot spot for U.S.–China confrontation even though Chen Shuibian is no longer in a position to pursue reckless moves toward independence. At the same time, we are sending peaceful signals to the Taiwan people, and we hope the United States and China can jointly curb any steps to change the status quo. A war in the Taiwan Strait could be avoided if the United States and China would cooperate, if we really want to maintain peace and stability across the Strait, if we uphold the main themes of peace and development, if you abide by the 8.17 communiqué of reducing arms sale to Taiwan, if the United States does not want to shed the blood of your young sons and daughters for Taiwan independence.

U.S.–China maritime cooperation is not only about traditional sea operational activities such as search-and-rescue exercises, joint exercises, or humanitarian operations. It is also about maintaining regional security on the Korean peninsula (e.g., through the Six Party Talks), across the Taiwan Strait, and in the Strait of Malacca and Indian Ocean. U.S.–China maritime cooperation could also be in such nontraditional security areas as the new thousand-ship navy initiatives (raised by then-CNO Admiral Michael Mullen and now known as the Global Maritime Partnership), the Proliferation Security Initiative, and the Container Security Initiative. U.S.–China maritime cooperation could and should be in the broad and wide-ranging areas of common development. A small sample of potential areas includes maritime warming, sea energy, wind energy, fishing, seabed mining, oceanographic research activities, joint research in Antarctica, coast guard law enforcement, and even tourism.

My Personal Views on the New U.S. Maritime Strategy

The recent promulgation of the new U.S. Maritime Strategy is good news. The title is positive, as is its stress on cooperation with other nations.

A New Attitude Toward Collective Cooperation

I like the title "A Cooperative Strategy for 21st Century Seapower" very much. I have studied several U.S. military strategies in the past and have never come across a strategy that uses the word "cooperative." It is truly unique and typifies the special characteristics of this strategy. In its introduction, the strategy says "maritime forces will be employed to build confidence and trust among nations through collective security efforts that focus on common threats and mutual interests in an open, multipolar world."[12] This sentence exemplifies the new views of U.S. maritime commanders on today's world, their new approaches to solving these problems, and the new attitude toward dealing with other nations. It is widely recognized that we are living in a new century; we face many new challenges and we have many common threats as well as common interests, so we are linked together and we stress collective and collaborative partnerships. Cooperation is really the key word for today's world in this new epoch.

A New Realization of Today's World

As the strategy says, the world is an open and multipolar world. With globalization and recent innovations in communications and the Internet, the world is becoming increasingly open and instantaneously interconnected. There are emerging new powers such as China, India, Brazil, and many others. Today's world is therefore "an open multipolar world," not a unipolar or a bipolar world as some think. Undoubtedly, the United States is a dominant country, but it cannot abandon or ignore others in maintaining peace and prosperity in the world. In the words of the strategy itself, "No one nation has the resources required to provide the safety and security throughout the entire maritime domain. Increasingly, governments, non-governmental organizations, international organizations, and the private sector will form partnerships of common interest to counter these emerging threats."[13] Never before in any official U.S. document, let alone in any military strategy, have I seen today's world described as being multipolar, or seen this concept being linked to the function of nongovernment organizations and private sector's function. It is really a very advanced idea.

A Stress on Fostering and Sustaining Cooperative Relationships

The strategy says that "although our forces can surge when necessary to respond to crises, trust and cooperation cannot be surged. They must be built over time so that the strategic interests of the participants are continuously considered while mutual understanding and respect are promoted."[14] I think that this is the right way to foster cooperative relationships. No friendship can be built overnight; rather, it must be fostered over a long period of time and through ups and downs. U.S. establishment of trust and confidence with China requires time and patience, for we are two very different countries with different political systems and ideology.

The Good Initiative of Global Maritime Partnership

The strategy states that "the Global Maritime Partnership Initiative seeks a cooperative approach to maritime security, promoting the rule of law by countering piracy, terrorism, weapons proliferation, drug trafficking and other illicit activities."[15] After I read some relevant materials on the initiative, and after the discussions with some navy officials, especially with Admiral Eric McVadon, I find it to be a good approach as the documents says: "The Global Maritime Partnership initiative will serve as a catalyst for international interoperability in support of cooperative maritime security."[16] Now the U.S. side should explain the initiative in detail and have more exchanges of views with relevant partners.

A Key to Success in Any Military Strategy: To Prepare the People

The strategy clearly recognizes that "as it has always been, these critical tasks will be carried out by our people."[17] The relevant parties in this case include not only U.S. sailors, marines, coast guardsmen, and junior and senior leaders, but also the other peoples with which the U.S. develops partnerships. The strategy elaborates: "If we are to successfully partner with the international community, we must improve regional and cultural expertise through expanded training, education, and exchange initiatives."[18] As Andrew Erickson has written, "The new U.S. Maritime Strategy contains a variety of crucial elements that could facilitate enhanced cooperation with China." But there are still some misunderstandings and suspicions, so "the key for the United States will be to attempt to convince China that the goals and intentions of the new strategy are real and not, as many in China fear, merely 'window dressing' or a disguise for a 'containment.'"[19] I think that such explanation and enhanced understanding are necessary in the form of academic exchanges and seminars such as the conference that produced this volume. Only through repeated briefings to the senior leaders of PLA and extensive exchanges with Chinese scholars could these misunderstandings disappear gradually. Of course, the most important thing is the actions of the United States, for actions speak louder than any words. The explanation and implementation of the new U.S. Maritime Strategy will take considerable effort and time to accomplish.

Notes

1. Hu Jintao, "Report at the 17th Party Congress," 15 October 2007, http://www.china.org. cn/english/congress/229611.htm.

2. Ibid., Part 1.

3. Ibid.

4. Ibid., Part 9.

5. Ibid.

6. Information Office of the State Council, People's Republic of China, "China's National Defense in 2006," 29 December 2006, Part 4, available at www.china.org.cn.

7. Quoted in Xu Ganchu, "On Harmonious Oceans as a Component of a Harmonious World," Pacific Forum 2007, 18 May 2007, Shanghai, China.

8. Hu, "Report at the 17th Party Congress," Part 11.

9. China's Five Principles of Peaceful Coexistence are (1) mutual respect for each other's territorial integrity and sovereignty; (2) mutual nonaggression; (3) mutual noninterference in each other's internal affairs; (4) equality and mutual benefit; and (5) peaceful coexistence.

10. "Speech by Premier Wen Jiabao of the State Council of the People's Republic of China at the Japanese Diet: For Friendship and Cooperation," 13 April 2007, Ministry of Foreign Affairs, People's Republic of China, http://www.fmprc.gov.cn/eng/wjdt/zyjh/ t311544.htm.

11. Information Office, "China's National Defense in 2006," Part 2; and Hu, "Report at the 17th Party Congress."

12. "A Cooperative Strategy for 21st Century Seapower" (Washington, DC: U.S. Chief of Naval Operations and the Commandants of the U.S. Marine Corps and U.S. Coast Guard, 17 October 2007), http://www.navy.mil/maritime/MaritimeStrategy.pdf, 3.

13. Ibid., 5.

14. Ibid., 5.

15. Ibid., 9.

16. Ibid., 14.

17. Ibid., 15.

18. Ibid.

19. Andrew S. Erickson, "New U.S. Maritime Strategy: Initial Chinese Responses," *China Security* 3, no. 4 (Autumn 2007): 43.

Gabriel B. Collins

China's Dependence on the Global Maritime Commons

CHINA'S GROWING RELIANCE ON THE SEA poses a formidable twenty-first-century diplomatic and security challenge. This could trigger confrontation between major maritime powers if badly managed, or could align mutual interests in secure maritime activities and enhance cooperation if managed adeptly.

Introduction

China's dependence on the global maritime commons is growing rapidly. Ships bring oil and other key raw materials into China and carry finished goods out to overseas markets. Secure sea-lanes are thus vital to China's economy and, by extension, its national security. While most trade activity is entirely private and commercial in character, the growing importance of maritime trade to China's economy is attracting high-level political attention. Chinese strategists debate vigorously whether China should be a "land power" or whether it should explicitly position itself as a "maritime power."[1] The outcome of these debates will have meaningful strategic consequences for maritime stakeholders worldwide.

High-ranking government officials are involved in these exchanges, as evidenced by State Oceanic Administration head Sun Zhihui's March 2008 call for China to develop a stronger popular "maritime consciousness" commensurate with its growing interests at sea.[2] If China's population comes to recognize more broadly that a secure maritime commons is fundamental to continued economic prosperity, stronger pressures could arise for naval development aimed at "upholding" Chinese maritime interests. Some Chinese thinkers support the concept of "comprehensive sea power," under which a country must build a strong maritime commercial and intellectual foundation before it can become a true naval power.[3]

This chapter will analyze China's growing dependence on the global maritime commons and the ways in which this might affect Chinese naval development. It will also attempt to identify opportunities for cooperation resulting from shared interests among China and other major maritime powers. It will address the following questions:

- How does China's maritime economy fit into its overall national economy as well as the global economy?

- What is China's emerging attitude toward dependence on seaborne resource imports, and what are possible implications of measures that Beijing might use to protect its interests in the global maritime commons?

- How might China's maritime development facilitate U.S.–China cooperation?

China's Maritime Economy

China is unique because, while historically described as a "continental power," it is proving to have a wide range of legitimate commercial maritime interests. It will be fascinating to see how China's growing commercial maritime interests might shape its naval development. In this sense, China's maritime development path will be very different from that of other "continental" nations that have previously endeavored to become maritime powers. The Soviet Union and Wilhelmian Germany built their navies first and then promoted commercial maritime development.

The Soviet and German relationship between commercial maritime interests and naval development was based on a "push" from the state, rather than a "pull" in which commercial interests led the way and then the state stepped in to create the capacity to protect these new commercial maritime interests. China is following a different path, which is marked by an emphasis on commercial maritime development, with naval development trailing behind.

That said, commercial operators in China often have close ties to the Chinese Communist Party and could lobby for increased PLA Navy power to uphold sea-lane security for their shipping operations. Commercial lobbying by shippers (many of whom had served in the Imperial Navy), after all, helped shape Japan's post–World War II sea-lane security doctrine.[4]

Many top Chinese shipping executives have occupied, and in some cases continue to occupy, high-level political positions in conjunction with their business roles. For example, Dr. Qin Xiao, chairman of China Merchants Group, is a member of the 10th Chinese People's Political Consultative Conference and served as a deputy to the 9th National People's Congress.[5] China's shipping industry certainly has the aggregate financial clout to justify an important political role. As it continues to grow, the industry's location along China's populous, politically influential east coast, its growing ranks of workers, and its contribution to national and local coffers may give it more political influence. If China's shipping industry continues to generate large profits and tax revenue, the industry's political weight may become commensurate with that of the highly influential Chinese oil and gas industry, which has shown an ability to shape national policies in its own interest.[6]

If China continues to expand its naval forces, the drivers will be a mix of seeking status in the international community and needing to defend economic interests, but the single most prominent element will be that Beijing's cadres are struggling to keep up with China's dynamic commercial mariners. In this sense, China's maritime and naval development path may better approximate the successful path of the United States than the failed efforts of the USSR, Meiji Japan, or pre–World War I Germany. Indeed, some analysts closely examine the growth of the United States as a naval power, noting that its expanding maritime trade interests after the Civil War conferred economic advantages and that the U.S. Navy's share of the federal defense budget more than doubled as the Navy became the world's third-largest naval force.[7]

China already depends heavily on the global maritime commons.[8] In 2006 China's maritime industry accounted for $270 billion in economic output, equal to roughly 10 percent of China's national gross domestic product (GDP), and employed nearly 30 million people.[9] "Direct" maritime industrial activities in China include port operation, shipbuilding, ship repair, manufacture of ship subcomponents, and fishing. Chinese seaborne trade is expected to reach $1 trillion annually by 2020, much of which will be carried on Chinese-built, -owned, and -operated merchant vessels.[10]

Unlike Japanese- and U.S.-controlled merchantmen, Chinese long-distance shipping increasingly flies the People's Republic of China (PRC) flag. This is due to a combination of security and commercial concerns. With regard to oil shipments, state flagging raises the stakes for any outside power that might interdict China-bound tankers because interfering with these vessels would be an act of war. From the commercial perspective, ships built in China that are funded by Chinese state banks must by law be PRC-flagged.[11] Figure 1 shows merchant fleet total size and proportion of state-flag vessels in the Japanese, PRC, and U.S.-controlled merchant fleets, which are among the world's largest.

Figure 1. Total Merchant Fleet Size and Proportion of State-flagged Vessels

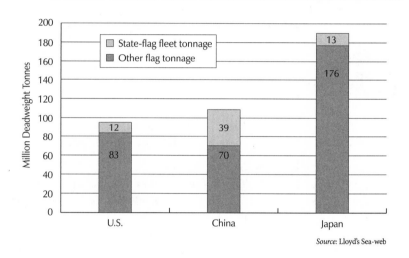

Source: Lloyd's Sea-web

Chinese shipping companies are rapidly expanding their fleets, and Chinese shipyards are seeking to become world leaders. The PRC central government recently affirmed shipbuilding as a "strategic industry" in need of "special oversight and support."[12] The industry's growth has been explosive. From producing only 220,000 deadweight tons of commercial shipping in 1980, Chinese shipyards launched more than 13 million tons of new ships in 2006 and aim to produce 50 million tons annually by 2011, according to the State Council.[13] As of mid-2010, the Chinese and South Korean shipbuilding industries (which together produce 90 percent of world ships by volume) had been for a more than a year waging a tug-of-war for the title of world's largest shipbuilder.[14] It is not a surprise that the Chinese shipbuilding industry is now on a level with South Korea's in terms of ship orders secured, but Chinese yards' steady gains in the battle for market share also reflect rising competitiveness in terms of volume and value. Figure 2 shows PRC shipbuilding industry growth, and figure 3 shows the rapid rise in China's merchant marine over the past twenty years.

As figure 2 illustrates, Chinese shipbuilders have major competitive advantages in building tankers and bulk carriers, which also happen to be the primary ship types needed by shipowners who wish to capitalize on China's explosive bulk commodity demand growth. Leading seaborne bulk commodity imports to China include crude oil, iron ore, coal, and grain.

Figure 3 treats merchant marine growth as a useful proxy for China's rapidly expanding presence and interests in the global maritime commons. One factor to note while comparing figures 2 and 3 is that while China has experienced rapid parallel growth in its shipbuilding industry and merchant marine, only about 20–25 percent of the ships currently under construction in Chinese yards are being built for Chinese shipowners. The balance is aimed at foreign ship buyers from "traditional" ship-owning countries including Greece, Norway, Germany, and the United States.

China's Dependence on Seaborne Resource Imports

China relies on the sea both to bring in resources and to get finished goods to market. It depends on maritime transportation for 90 percent of its overall imports and exports, and for 40 percent of its oil imports.[15] In 2009 China imported an estimated 630 million tons of iron ore, more than 4 million barrels/day of crude oil, 130 million tons of coal, significant amounts of nonferrous metals such as copper and aluminum, and large amounts of timber. Imports in 2009 equaled roughly $921.5 billion, most of which came by sea.[16] Chinese exports in 2009, most of which also traveled by sea to China's key export partners (the European Union, the United States, and Japan), totaled nearly $1.2 trillion. By way of comparison, the United States imported $1.4 trillion in goods by sea and exported roughly $995 billion worth, and Japan imported approximately $491 billion worth of goods and materials while exporting $516 billion worth of finished goods.[17] Table 1 shows key Chinese seaborne imports in terms of volume, value, sources, and key chokepoints that shipments must pass through.

China's dependence on maritime commerce, and its potential to cooperate with other nations to secure it, has been underscored by the Chinese navy's ongoing deployments to protect Chinese and foreign vessels against piracy in the Gulf of Aden. They have made the area safer from Somali piracy, thus

Figure 2. Chinese Shipbuilding Industry Growth (2007 data)

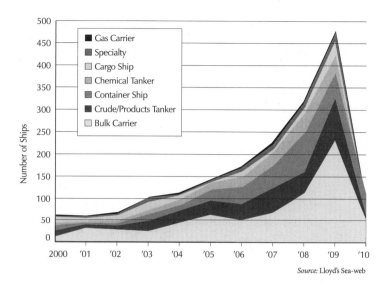

Source: Lloyd's Sea-web

Figure 3. China's Merchant Marine Growth (2007 data)

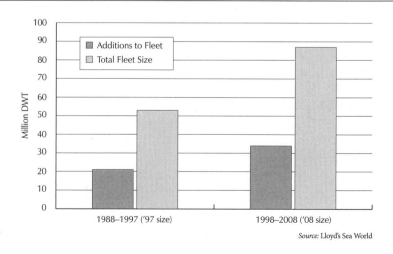

Source: Lloyd's Sea World

Table 1. China's Maritime Resource Dependency: Raw Numbers

Resource	Annual Volume	Dollar Value	Primary Sources	Choke Points along Route
Energy Resources				
Crude oil	204 Million Tonnes (MT)	$119 billion (est.)*	Angola, Iran, Saudi Arabia, Russia	Hormuz, Malacca
Oil products/ petrochemicals	37 MT	$25 billion	Singapore, Middle East	Malacca, Hormuz
Liquefied natural gas	5.5 MT	-	Australia, spot cargoes from Algeria, Oman, Nigeria	Makassar, Hormuz, Malacca, Lombok
Coal	130 MT	$10.9 billion	Indonesia, Australia	Makassar, Lombok
Minerals				
Iron ore	630 MT	~$50.4 billion**	Australia, Brazil	Malacca, Makassar, Lombok

Sources: China Statistical Yearbook; Reuters; General Administration of Customs; *China Daily*.
 * Crude oil import value calculation assumes an average landed cost of $80/bbl and an average
   of 7.3 bbl/ton.
** Based on average landed cost of near $80/ton.

benefitting both the international system and Chinese trade and energy interests. Security of the sea lines of communication (SLOC) around the Horn of
Africa is especially critical since China imports 16 percent of its overall energy
(including one-third of its oil), as well as numerous strategic resources critical
to manufacturing, from Africa. China is the EU's second-largest trading partner, the EU is China's largest, and much of their trade transits via container
ship the Red Sea as well as the Indian Ocean, where 40 percent of the vessels
transiting the Indian Ocean are Chinese.[18]

Maritime Dependence: Geostrategic Perceptions

Chinese authors across the board note that the vast majority of key seaborne
raw material inputs must pass through the Malacca Strait as well as the Strait of

Hormuz in the case of oil and future liquefied natural gas (LNG) shipments.[19] Japan and other regional importees face the same challenge. Yet while China does not have the same degree of relative maritime import reliance as Japan, it also sees itself as being more geographically constrained. Whereas Japan has unfettered access to the Western Pacific from its eastern ports, Chinese analysts believe that China is "hemmed in" by a "first island chain" composed of the Philippines, Ryukyus, Japanese home islands, and Kurile Islands in the north, as well as a "second island chain" composed of the Mariana Islands and centered on Guam.[20]

Although Chinese thinkers are likely speaking about the island chains' constraining effect on the ability of the PLA Navy to break out into the open ocean during wartime, similar constraints could also bottle up key commercial shipping during crisis times if an opponent set up blockades of key passages. Because many egress and ingress routes for Korean and Japanese ports could bypass a contingency inside the first island chain, Chinese analysts may be convinced that they could be at a strategic disadvantage since shipping originating from or headed into any Chinese port must first transit the first island chain. Map 1 shows the Pacific island chains as conceived by Chinese analysts.

Sea-Lane Security: Threats, Capabilities, and Countermeasures

Chinese views on what constitutes the most acute maritime security threats have been evolving rapidly. From 1840 and 1949, by Chinese analysts' count, their country suffered 479 violations of its sovereignty, 84 of which were considered "large scale."[21] Nearly all of these assaults came by sea. Indeed, Chinese naval policy through the Mao and early Deng eras was driven largely by an intense desire to ward off any attempts at invasion. Today, however, maritime threats to China no longer take the form of invasion but rather of hostile powers and substate actors having the potential ability to interdict Chinese maritime trade.

Now Chinese analysts see upholding sovereignty (e.g., vis-à-vis Taiwan), maritime disputes with neighbors, and piracy and military blockade by hostile outside powers as the key threats to China's maritime security interests.[22] China needs steady seaborne resource supplies to sustain its economy, half of its claimed maritime territory lies in disputed zones, and, unlike Japan, it does not have a strong outside ally to help ensure its shipping security. Thus, in Chinese eyes, China needs a strong stand-alone naval capability to safeguard its interests and make its maritime diplomacy credible.[23]

Map 1. China's Island Chains

Note: The "Island Chains" concept has never been defined officially or depicted graphically by the People's Liberation Army Navy, or any other element of China's government. It is therefore depicted notionally and must be interpreted with caution.

Source: The dimensions of the "Island Chains" outlined here are derived from Zu Ming, "A Schematic Diagram of the U.S. Naval Forces Deployed and System of Bases in the Western Pacific," *Naval & Merchant Ships*, no. 2 (January 2006): 24.

Table 2. Comparative Dependence on the Global Maritime Commons

	China	Japan	United States	Germany
Mineral import dependency	High	High	Low	Low
Energy import dependency	High (>50%)	Very high (>90%)	High (>60%)	Low (<25%)
Food supply from sea (food imports + fishing)	Medium (substantial proportion of seafood raised by aquaculture)	High	Low	Low
Ability to project power into global maritime commons	Limited regional	Limited regional	Global, unconstrained	Very limited regional

One key question that permeates the entire sea-lane protection debate in China is, what does sea-lane protection actually mean? Peacetime and wartime sea-lane protection are two completely different undertakings. During peacetime, the main threats are nonstate actors, weather, and collisions with other vessels or grounding. During wartime, state-flagged belligerent ships on the high seas, or private ships that appear poised to enter or leave belligerent ports are at risk of attack by the warring parties' armed forces.

Insofar as shipping protection is concerned, China may choose between two primary paths. The first entails continuing reliance on international ship operators carrying cargoes that, like oil, are often bought and sold while still at sea. In East Asia, until these vessels come within several hundred miles of the Chinese coast, it would be very difficult to selectively interdict them based on knowledge of their final destination. Most importantly, by the time ships have entered the zone in which it is clear they are bound for a Chinese port, they are well within range of existing Chinese aerial and naval platforms, which could defend them from a blockader. Thus, so long as it relies primarily on multinational, convenience-flagged shipping for key resource imports, the PLA Navy can, in its current form, substantially safeguard China-bound vessels.

The second course of action appears to have growing support within China.[24] It involves PRC-based shipping companies operating vessels flying the PRC flag.[25] While state-flagging merchant vessels raises the stakes for a blockader by making interdiction an act of war against the flag state, it also clearly marks the vessel's likely destination. This would be especially true during a time of crisis, when state-flagged ships might be requisitioned by the flag-state government. Removing the "veil of deniability" offered by using multinational shippers requires that the flag state have a long-range naval force capable of defending its shipping from possible blockades or other interference. Shipping protection requirements, along with national pride, could thus become key drivers of the PLA Navy's incremental transition to a blue water force.

Yet the PLA Navy would face enormous challenges if it were to attempt shipping escort missions of significant scale—beyond the historical 26 December 2008 counterpiracy deployment of three vessels to the Gulf of Aden to more widespread, comprehensive, high-end coverage. The PLA Navy would need dozens of dedicated warships and auxiliary vessels to operate thousands of miles from the Chinese coast for extended periods to conduct such an operation. Once these vessels left their home ports, they would risk attack from a range of highly lethal aerial, surface, and subsurface enemy assets. Setting combat attrition aside, the sheer logistics of sustaining such an operation would likely render it infeasible, particularly when one considers the warship employment opportunity cost, because escort missions pull ships away from the battle that triggered the threat to Chinese shipping in the first place. Table 3 (below) shows the force strength that Japan's Maritime Self-Defense Force (MSDF) felt it needed to protect shipping up to one thousand nautical miles from the home islands and compares that force strength with today's PLA Navy assets that might have a role in sea-lane security missions.

It seems that China might do well to rely on non-state-flagged shipping and build a naval capability sufficient to protect shipping from the southern entrance to the South China Sea onward to China. First, given the fungible nature of the global oil trade and tendency for cargoes to be bought and sold on the high seas, all that a potential blockader would know when a tanker left Hormuz and headed east is that the oil was headed for one of dozens of potential Asian buyers.[26] Second, the political ramifications of China deploying warships far afield and acquiring the basing infrastructure and access necessary to support them would be highly provocative to other major powers. Finally, the physical and operational realities of sustaining naval operations more than fifteen hundred miles from home port is a barrier that the PLA Navy will not likely be able to surmount for some time to come.

To put the demands of long-range shipping protection in perspective, according to the leadership of the U.S. Navy of the 1970s, even the highly capable U.S. Navy of that time would have likely been unable to sustain shipping protection in the Atlantic and Indian oceans against Soviet forces.[27] In 1970 U.S. Navy

Table 3. Comparison of Past and Potential Future East Asian Sea-Lane
       Protection Forces

Japanese MSDF Force Structure Proposal 1976		Current Chinese PLA Navy Force Structure	
Destroyers	60	Advanced destroyers/ Frigates	40 (est).
Diesel submarines	16	Advanced diesel submarines	32
Nuclear attack submarines	0	Nuclear attack submarines	5 (est.)
ASW patrol aircraft	100	ASW patrol aircraft	None yet
Air defense fighters	120 (10 squadrons)	Air defense aircraft	~275* (est.)
Early warning aircraft	24 (2 squadrons)	Early warning aircraft	Unclear (4 KJ-2000, at least 3 Y-8 variants are in Chinese military possession)

* These are the SU-27/J-11s, J-10s, SU-30MKKs, and J-8Ds of the PLAAF and PLANAF.
Sources: Graham, *Japan's Sea Lane Security: 1940–2004*, 136; SinoDefense.com; 2010 Department of Defense China Military Power Report.

vice admiral T. F. Caldwell noted that even a highly capable force supported by nuclear attack submarines would have trouble conducting shipping protection against a capable foe, and in 1975, Chief of Naval Operations Admiral James Holloway supported this view, stating that the U.S. Navy could not guarantee the security of oil shipping from the Persian Gulf if a major war erupted.[28]

With respect to Malacca Strait security, relying on non-state-flagged shipping to carry resource imports may be a more effective policy for the PRC than building a state-flagged fleet along with the naval forces and basing infrastructure necessary to protect it. The nature of the oil market makes a distant blockade of the Malacca Strait very difficult (unless China state-flags its oil tankers). Thus, the real threats to shipping through Malacca are pirates, terrorists, and the collision and grounding risk that comes with the strait's rising ship traffic volumes. These issues are all best dealt with "capacity building" measures aimed at improving the ability of the Indonesian and Malaysian governments to solve these problems from the grassroots level on up. Such measures might include providing training to regional police forces and coast guards, building a regional vessel tracking network, and promoting economic development that gives would-be pirates and terrorists other opportunities. Steaming warships (whether American, Chinese, Indian, or Japanese) through the strait would have little ability to effectively resolve piracy, terrorism, or physical navigational problems.

Maritime Dependence: Energy Import Security

China's growing seaborne oil and gas imports are the focal point in the discussion of Chinese maritime resource security concerns. Although oil accounts for a smaller portion of total energy consumption in China than in the United States or other Western economies (~22% vs. ~40% in the West), the fact is that in today's world oil has virtually no feasible large-scale substitutes as a transportation fuel. An oil supply cutoff could therefore have substantial effects on China's economic growth, which depends on well-functioning internal transportation networks. Chinese industry could still function on a crisis footing because it is predominantly powered by coal, but it would be difficult to move raw materials and finished goods if there were a serious shortage of gasoline and diesel fuel. Chinese analysts see the economic injury resulting from an oil supply disruption as a factor that would directly affect national security.[29]

Energy security threat perspectives found in Chinese open-source literature depend upon analyst affiliations. Market analysts and energy company researchers often hold very different views than security analysts do. Market and commercial analysts in China are most concerned with the adverse effects that energy price volatility can have on China's economy (and, by extension, the country's comprehensive national power). Chinese energy articles authored by security analysts tend to focus very heavily on the possibility of a maritime energy blockade, which they fear Japan, India, or the United States could impose. Such an event would be "disastrous for China" and must be avoided or deterred.[30]

The United States is seen as having the most influence on Chinese maritime security, and Japan is seen as the most threatening country to China's maritime interests, likely in part due to tensions over the East China Sea.[31] A particularly insightful analysis in the October 2006 issue of 现代舰船 (Modern Ships) articulates a three-point maritime energy-security strategy for China, which may reflect the approach taken by the Chinese naval community to the energy question: "[China] must view things from the perspective of keeping [an outside power] from cutting its oil supply lines. Concretely speaking, this entails making [the outside power] not willing to cut China's oil supply lines, not able to do so, and not daring to do so."[32]

The first two parts of this statement (unable and unwilling to cut oil supply lines) stem from the reality that the global oil market is highly flexible and can effectively work around most natural and man-made disruptions. Oil is carried on ships that may be owned by national or private oil companies, or on private shippers that may be flagged in a large number of jurisdictions for tax and regulatory purposes and that may be crewed by a wide range of nationalities. Moreover, in normal commerce, traders may buy and sell an oil cargo at sea multiple times between the port of loading and the final customer who takes delivery. This flexible, unpredictable, and wonderfully effective oil supply chain would make a distant maritime oil blockade both very difficult to accomplish and harmful to the economies of all oil consumers, thus bringing significant international pressure on any blockader to end things quickly.

The third part of the statement (not daring to blockade) would require China to have a credible naval force that could inflict sufficient injury on a would-be blockader to induce it to refrain from such actions. China's current naval platform acquisition programs appear primarily focused on creating the ability to deal with regional contingencies—first and foremost a Taiwan crisis. Were the PLA Navy to pursue a longer-distance force capable of blue water energy SLOC protection (this would be needed to defend PRC-flagged tankers in a future crisis), there would be significant lead time, and several indicators would alert outsiders that something was afoot. Figure 4 elaborates on barometers of possible blue water navy construction.

The indicators shown in figure 4 will not all occur simultaneously. Some programs, such as diesel and nuclear submarine construction and improvement of ship repair capability, continue to move ahead rapidly. Others, such as the aircraft carrier and sustained PLA Navy deployments, are much more nascent or have not yet begun in earnest.

Based on the Chinese sources the author has read to date, the predominant line of thought appears to be that China's main strategic energy SLOC security option for the next few years is to maintain good relations with the United States and free ride on U.S. naval protection of key energy supply routes. Looking beyond five years, Chinese energy import needs are likely to continue rising, which may drive stronger calls for creating an independent energy-SLOC-protection capacity. Yet even if hawkish factions win the energy-SLOC security debate, the PLA Navy will still face a long and expensive road to acquiring such capabilities.

Figure 4. Barometers of Chinese SLOC Protection Intent

Energy SLOC Protection?

- Construction and deployment of additional nuclear attack submarines with significant demonstrated ASW capabilities
- Construction of aircraft carriers
- Establishment of shipyards dedicated to military ship production
- Expansion of PLAN auxiliary fleet, particularly long-range, high-speed oilers and replenishment ships
- Development of the ability to conduct sophisticated repairs to ships remotely—either through tenders or overseas repair facilities
- Aquisition of reliable overseas bases (e.g., in the Indian Ocean)
- Deployment of a substantial portion of PLAN forces at all times to achieve high levels of presence and readiness
- Maturation of advanced levels of PLA doctrine, training, and human capacity

Source: Figure from Erickson and Collins, "China's Maritime Evolution," 47–75.

Large capital blue water programs such as a significantly expanded nuclear-powered attack submarine force or the construction of carriers are extremely expensive and will create substantial internal and external political problems. Internally, there will likely be a significant intraservice competition for funding, but externally, such moves may reinforce the worst fears of other regional powers such as Japan and the Southeast Asian countries. These nations might then alter their postures in the region, which could raise tensions and erase any security gains that having blue water naval capability might have otherwise brought Beijing.

Indeed, East and Southeast Asia are already on the verge of becoming a naval "armed camp" as South Korea and the Southeast Asians all substantially enhance their naval capabilities. A 2007 report by the Australian Strategic Policy Institute notes that Indonesia, Malaysia, Singapore, and South Korea all plan to expand their submarine fleets from now until 2016, with total regional additions of fifteen or more hulls in the next ten years, equivalent to roughly half of China's current modern diesel submarine inventory.[33] An emphasis on shared economic interests and political dialogue may be more effective to safeguard the maritime commons than unchecked naval buildup would be.

Securing Maritime Transit: Shared Means to a Common End

The realities discussed earlier strongly support a multilateral cooperative approach to SLOC security in the Asian region. A strategic motive for engaging the issue promptly is that there is now a window of opportunity to exert a proactive shaping influence on China as it becomes a key regional and global maritime player. Decisions made in the next few years will lead to path dependence in many cases as investments are made and vested internal interests arise within China's defense establishment. Only by engaging now can the United States and others signal that we welcome China's role in the world and that we want mutually beneficial relations, rather than a twenty-first-century containment system.

An immediate reason for promoting a cooperative approach to SLOC security is that regional spillover effects are likely if one power (for instance, China) takes a host of unilateral measures to secure international sea-lanes upon which it relies. Under such conditions, it is likely that Japan and other regional players would follow suit. Indeed, well-informed Japanese have told this author that Japan is considering state-flagging of vessels carrying LNG to Japan.[34] Vietnam is also entering the game, as Petro Vietnam recently signed a deal for fifteen very large crude oil carriers, all of which are likely to be state-flagged.[35]

A secure maritime environment facilitates trade and prosperity because more than 75 percent of global trade travels by sea.[36] Global maritime trade has burgeoned over the past three hundred years in part because, except during major interstate wars, there has generally been a power or concert of powers capable of ensuring freedom of navigation. Indeed, Pax Britannica at sea helped facilitate the round of globalization that swept the world in the late nineteenth century and helped the United States rise to global prominence. Similarly, Pax Americana at sea has underpinned the rapid global trade growth of the post–World War II era.

While one or two major navies have dominated the seas for much of the past two hundred years, a more diverse maritime power structure is materializing as India, China, and other powers leverage their economic growth and enhance their commercial and military presence at sea. As the new global maritime security architecture takes shape, questions arise concerning the confluence of old and new. On one hand, the existing global maritime system involves globalized shipping lines that are often effectively stateless operating in seas secured by a U.S. Navy presence. On the other hand, the rising maritime powers, led by China, increasingly rely on maritime resource imports to power their economic growth; they distrust U.S. sea control and are beginning to build state-flagged merchant fleets that could be requisitioned during times of crisis and legally escorted by their growing naval forces.[37]

The new U.S. Maritime Strategy reflects the world's growing multipolarity at sea and could mark a major historical inflection point in the evolution of the global maritime security structure. Pax Americana at sea may gradually be replaced by a much more cooperative system. Such a structure reflects two key realities. First, the U.S. maritime services may be increasingly hard-pressed to single-handedly uphold security of the global maritime commons. Second, the Maritime Strategy provides room and flexibility to accommodate rising naval powers and integrate them into a new maritime security structure if each side can summon the political will.

One way to build the political will is to start with lower-level cooperation on discrete issues of shared interest that can be used to build trust and institutional bonds that can survive high-level leadership changes and other buffeting forces. The following section will examine the potential for building a U.S.–PRC energy port security best practices exchange mechanism.

Possible U.S.–PRC Maritime Energy Security Cooperation

Both the United States and China rely heavily on maritime oil, gas, and refined product imports, and both share the need for a stable and secure maritime environment for energy transport. The PRC is relatively "new" as a major energy importer (it only became a net oil importer in 1994) but has a long and rich history of coastal shipping and now is home to some of the world's busiest international ports. Thus, as a long-standing maritime energy importer, the United States has expertise to share and the PRC, given its location in a high ship-traffic region, could share expertise in water traffic management.

The first cooperative maritime energy security activities might focus on exchanging best practices for securing LNG shipments and facilities in Chinese coastal waters. Reasons for the narrow initial focus on LNG include the facts that

- China is new to the LNG market, and relevant U.S. agencies can offer significant expertise in securing LNG shipments and facilities in coastal areas.

- LNG is increasingly important to China's energy security but does not yet have the strategic importance (and commensurate political sensitivity) that seaborne oil shipments do.

- U.S.–PRC bilateral activities are politically and diplomatically simpler than sea-lane security operations in Malacca or other areas where outside parties would be heavily involved.

- Energy-related activities of this type typically fall under coast guard jurisdiction, and coast guard–coast guard ties are simpler to manage than navy–navy ties.[38]

- U.S.–PRC coast guard cooperation is already on solid footing.

- Energy transport and facility security cooperation would focus on combating nonstate threats. Thus, cooperation would enhance national security and build trust without appreciably boosting the other side's military capability and intelligence.

- Both the U.S. and PRC coast guards bring discrete sets of expertise and experience to the table, creating natural complementarity that makes best practices exchanges meaningful.

The United States Coast Guard (USCG) has substantial experience protecting LNG and tanker loading operations and facilities. In the wake of the 9/11 attacks, the USCG stepped up its port security operations and learned how to foster public and private partnerships, helping it secure some of the world's busiest energy ports, most notably the Port of Houston.[39] This experience would be valuable in advising Chinese security services as they work to formulate the most effective facilities protection plans.

The Coast Guard's energy security experience spans the globe. USCG units have successfully protected Iraq's Persian Gulf oil export facilities for more than three years, developing a wealth of experience and combat tested techniques that could be usefully shared with Chinese border security forces. The USCG's maritime security response teams and maritime safety and security teams are trained to operate in high-threat areas and deploy anywhere in the United States within twelve hours.[40] If the USCG helped to train China Maritime Safety Administration teams with similar capabilities, this would enhance Chinese seaborne energy import security and perhaps even bolster bilateral trust concerning energy security issues. This is an important point since the majority of threats to seaborne energy shipments come from nonstate actors.

Maritime energy security cooperation can build on the precedent established by the six-year-old North Pacific Coast Guard Forum, which brings civil maritime forces from Japan, Russia, Korea, China, Canada, and the United States together to cooperate on regional maritime issues. Russia held the forum's annually rotating presidency in 2007. This presented an ideal moment to begin discussions on bilateral and multilateral maritime energy security collaboration. Existing fisheries enforcement agreements between the United States and other Pacific coast guards may provide a starting point for energy security cooperation in the North Pacific.[41]

Bilateral Benefits of LNG Security Cooperation

For cooperation to be sustainable and successful, it is important to be candid and realistic. Focusing on mitigating and deterring nonstate threats to LNG shipping will begin as a politically (as opposed to commercially) driven enterprise aimed at building trust between the United States and China in the maritime energy security arena. That said, once the program is under way, it could bring very tangible benefits and high returns on diplomatic and political investment to Beijing and Washington. LNG security cooperation could provide a cornerstone upon which to build broader maritime energy cooperation that in the future could move farther offshore and incorporate elements of cooperation that are currently too sensitive to be politically feasible. These might include joint sea-lane patrols in the South China Sea and Malacca Strait area under the auspices of a multilateral force that might include Japanese, Indian, and Southeast Asian assets.

The program could also provide a lever to promote broader working level cooperation that would help create institutional bonds that might transcend leadership changes and shifting political winds on either side. At the intellectual level, exchanging best practices could bring gains at a relatively low "cost," both in terms of monetary and additional manpower expenditures. Computer-based distributed gaming and simulation could facilitate "maintenance" of cooperation from each side's home base, thus reducing the financial and logistical costs of continual travel. Student exchanges between the U.S. Coast Guard Academy and Chinese Maritime Safety Administration educational institutions would also facilitate movement toward the broader goal of building trust and institutionalizing bonds between American and Chinese maritime security forces.

With regard to physical exercises, existing Coast Guard port calls in China could add vessel security exercises to their China visit agendas if the USCG, China Maritime Safety Administration (MSA), and other Chinese maritime security players can reach agreement on the issue.[42] Certain additional assets might have to be moved in-theater for such exercises, but costs would be reduced compared to implementing training and exchange programs not able to build on existing physical and institutional infrastructure. Figure 5 depicts the author's perception of where U.S.–PRC maritime security cooperation currently stands in comparison to U.S. maritime security ties with a range of other key partners.

Figure 5. U.S.–PRC Comparative Maritime Security Cooperation Levels

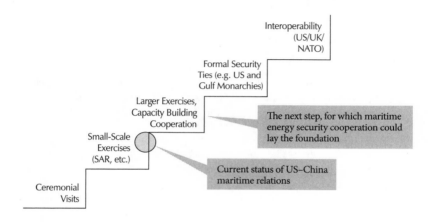

Conclusion

China's increasing reliance on the global maritime commons for resource inputs and for moving finished goods to market is an irreversible trend that Beijing is now coming to grips with. China's choices on how to deal with its dependence on the global maritime commons will shed light on Beijing's broader worldview; as such, the issue should be taken very seriously. China now stands at a strategic crossroads with respect to how it will manage security issues associated with its rising dependence on the maritime commons. Decisions made now—such as the pursuit of a state-flagged oil tanker fleet— will have repercussions for decades to come. Thus, now is the time for the United States and other major global maritime stakeholders to engage with China and attempt to proactively shape policies and decisions in a peaceful, mutually beneficial direction.

Understanding China's maritime interests both quantitatively and qualitatively and the historical experiences that shape Chinese views on these issues is the first step in formulating an effective engagement policy. Subsequent steps entail identifying discrete areas for PRC maritime energy security cooperation with outside partners and then working to make these activities the cornerstone of a broader maritime security partnership. Following such a path of turning rhetoric into concrete action can help China, the United States, and other maritime stakeholders work together to resolve and avoid problems in ways that provide maximum mutual benefit.

Notes

1. 孙培松 [Sun Peisong], "中国利益重心到底在哪" ["Where is the Center of Gravity of China's Maritime Interests?"], 世界论坛网 [*World Forum*], 10 December 2007, http://www.wforum.com/gbindex.html. See also 叶自成 [Ye Zicheng], "中国巨龙站起来了: 中国军方指向天空和大海!" ["China Has Stood Up in a Big Way: China's Military Moves Toward the Sky and the Great Ocean!"], *Sina.com*, 15 November 2007, blog.sina.com.cn/s/blog_4d96dead01000chu.html.

2. 孙志辉 [Sun Zhihui], "提高海洋意识, 繁荣海洋文化" ["Raising Maritime Consciousness, Enriching Maritime Culture"], 国家海洋局党组书记 [Secretary of National Maritime Affairs Leading Group], 中国海洋报 [*China Maritime Report*], 6 March 2008.

3. 杨明杰 [Yang Mingjie, ed.], 海上通道安全与国际合作 [*Sea Lane Security and International Cooperation*] (Beijing: 时事出版社 [Current Affairs Publishing House], 2005), 366.

4. Euan Graham, *Japan's Sea Lane Security 1940–2004: A Matter of Life and Death?* (New York: Routledge, 2006), 102. See also Andrew Erickson, review of ibid. in *Naval War College Review* 60, no. 1 (Winter 2007): 153–54.

5. China Merchants Group Web site, http://www.cmhk.com/en/management/default.htm.

6. Erica Downs, Brookings Foreign Policy Studies Energy Security Series, "China," December 2006, http://www.brookings.edu/~/media/Files/rc/reports/2006/12china/12china.pdf.

7. 曹文振 [Zao Wenzhen], 经济全球化时代的海洋政治 [*Maritime Politics in the Era of Economic Globalization*] (Qingdao: China Ocean University Press, 2006), 261.

8. For the purposes of this analysis, "global maritime commons" means those maritime zones that are beyond national jurisdiction and where the activities of non-flag-state vessels cannot typically be regulated. This includes areas beyond the twelve-nautical-mile territorial waters of a country as well as key international passageways such as the

straits of Malacca and Hormuz. See Stuart Kaye, "Threats from the Global Commons: Problems of Jurisdiction and Enforcement," *Melbourne Journal of International Law* 8, no. 1 (2007): 185–97.

9. C. Bert Kruk, "Recent and Expected Developments in Ports, Maritime Transport, and Trade," The World Bank, May 2007, http://www.temsb.com/assets/thai07/CBertKruk. pdf.

10. 徐起 [Xu Qi], "21世纪初海上地缘战略与中国海军的发展" ["Maritime Geostrategy and the Development of the Chinese Navy in the Early 21st Century"], 中国军事科 学 [*China Military Science*] 17, no. 4 (2004): 75–81, trans. Andrew Erickson and Lyle Goldstein, *Naval War College Review* 59, no. 4 (Autumn 2006): 46–67.

11. Author's interviews with shipowner, Hong Kong, February 2008.

12. "China to Limit Foreign Investment in Shipyards," *Shanghai Daily*, 19 September 2006, http://www.shanghaidaily.com/article/?id=292385&type=business.

13. Derived from new construction and order book statistics in Lloyd's Register, Fairplay, Ltd., Register of Ships, Sea-web database, http://www.sea-web.com.

14. Keith Wallis, "South Korea Yards Win 51% of Global Ship Orders," *Lloyd's List*, 16 April 2010, http://www.lloydslist.com/ll/news/south-korea-yards-win-51-of-global-ship-orders/ 20017768482.htm;jsessionid=46F9D73E9EF9DF07604F0F9063525D27.5 fa4e8cc80be35e2653c9f87d8b8be45bf6ba69a.

15. For further details, see Andrew S. Erickson, "Multinational Coordination with China's Counter-Piracy Task Force," Paper presented at the Chinese and American Approaches to Non-Traditional Security: Implications for the Maritime Domain conference, Naval War College, May 4–5, 2010.

16. CIA World Factbook—China, https://www.cia.gov/library/publications/the-world-factbook/geos/ch.html.

17. Ibid.

18. This paragraph draws on Andrew S. Erickson, "Chinese Sea Power in Action: the Counter-Piracy Mission in the Gulf of Aden and Beyond," in Roy Kamphausen and David Lai, eds., *The PLA at Home and Abroad—Assessing the Operational Capabilities of China's Military* (Carlisle, PA: U.S. Army War College, 2010).

19. See, for example, 李兵 [Li Bing], "国际战略通道研究" ["International SLOC Research"] (PhD diss.,中共中央党校 [Chinese Communist Party Central Party School], 1 May 2005), 355.

20. 刘华清 [Liu Huaqing], 刘华清回忆录 [*The Memoirs of Liu Huaqing*] (Beijing: People's Liberation Army, 2004), 437; cited in Andrew Erickson and Andrew Wilson, "China's Aircraft Carrier Dilemma," *Naval War College Review* 59, no. 4 (Autumn 2006): 44.

21. Yang, *Sea Lane Security and International Cooperation*, 358.

22. Ibid., 363.

23. Zao, *Maritime Politics*, 362.

24. Peng Cuihong, "China Must Carry 60% of Seaborne Oil Imports on Local Shippers," Xinhua Financial Network News, 14 June 2007; "More Oil Tankers Taking to the Sea," *China Daily*, 14 June 2007.

25. See Andrew Erickson and Gabriel Collins, "Beijing's Energy Security Strategy: The Significance of a Chinese State Owned Tanker Fleet," *Orbis* (Fall 2007): 661–80.

26. For more information on possible Chinese responses to a maritime energy embargo, see Gabriel Collins and William Murray, "No Oil for the Lamps of China?" *Naval War College Review* 62, no. 2 (Spring 2008): 79–95.

27. Graham, *Japan's Sea Lane Security*, 109.

28. Ibid.

29. Yang, *Sea Lane Security and International Cooperation*, 15; and Andrew Erickson and Lyle Goldstein, "Gunboats for China's New 'Grand Canals'? Probing the Intersection of Beijing's Naval and Energy Security Policies," *Naval War College Review* 62, no. 2 (Spring 2009): 43–76.

30. 陈安刚, 武明 [Chen Angang and Wu Ming], "马六甲: 美国觊觎的战略前哨" ["Malacca Strait: The U.S. Covets a Strategic Outpost,"], 现代舰船 [*Modern Ships*] (December 2004): 13.

31. See Andrew Erickson, "Can China Become a Maritime Power?" in Toshi Yoshihara and James Holmes, eds., *Asia Looks Seaward: The Emerging Dynamics of Regional Sea Power* (Westport, CT: Praeger Security International, 2008), 109–10.

32. This section draws heavily on Gabriel Collins, Andrew Erickson, and Lyle Goldstein, "Chinese Naval Analysts Consider the Energy Question," in Collins, Erickson, Goldstein, and William Murray, eds., *China's Energy Strategy: The Impact on Beijing's Maritime Policies* (Annapolis, MD: Naval Institute Press, 2008), 299–335, esp. 325–26.

33. Andrew Davies, "The Enemy Below: Anti-Submarine Warfare in the ADF," Australian Strategic Policy Institute, Special Report, February 2007, 22, http://www.aspi.org.au/publications/publication_details.aspx?ContentID=116&pubtype=0.

34. Author's interviews, Tokyo, April 2007.

35. "Vietnam Oil Giant to Establish Oil Tanker Fleet," *People's Daily Online*, 2 March 2007, http://english.peopledaily.com.cn/200703/02/eng20070302_353730.html.

36. Victor Renuart and Dane Egli, "Closing the Capability Gap: Developing New Solutions to Counter Maritime Threats," *Naval War College Review* 61, no. 2 (Spring 2008): 15–24.

37. See Erickson and Collins, "Beijing's Energy Security Strategy," 661–80.

38. For simplicity and space reasons, I refer to both U.S. and PRC "coast guards," but the reality is that while the USCG is a unified force, the PRC Maritime Safety Administration, State Oceanic Administration (SOA), and other maritime security agencies outside the PLA Navy are actually quite balkanized. Chinese authors refer to "five dragons stirring up the sea" when they discuss their maritime law enforcement agencies. For more on the Chinese maritime law enforcement services, see Lyle Goldstein, "China: A New Maritime Partner?" U.S. Naval Institute *Proceedings* 133, no. 8 (August 2007): 26–31.

39. D. Hauser, "Port Coordination in the Largest U.S. Petrochemical Complex: A Public/ Private Partnership," *Proceedings of the Marine Safety Council* 63, no. 1 (Spring 2006): 55–59.

40. Aaron C. Davenport, "Maritime Security and Safety Teams: A Force for Today," *Proceedings of the Marine Safety Council* 63, no. 1 (Spring 2006): 83–86.

41. John Davis, "How International Enforcement Cooperation Deters Illegal Fishing in the North Pacific," *Economic Perspectives: An Electronic Journal of the U.S. Department of State* 8, no. 1 (January 2003): 11–13, http://www.scribd.com/doc/29180991/Over-Fishing-a-Global-Challenge.

42. For more on China's coast guard structure, see Goldstein, "China: A New Maritime Partner?"

David N. Griffiths

Challenges in the Development of Military-to-Military Relationships

MARITIME OPERATIONS ARE COMPLEX, demanding, and highly technical, and they sometimes take place where the political environment can be as volatile as the natural environment. Above all, maritime operations are a human endeavor, which means that mistakes and misunderstandings are inevitable. For that reason, when military forces of are operating in proximity to one another, it is clearly in the national interest of all parties to have in place a well-established and proven risk management mechanism that will avoid unwanted incidents or, if the unplanned happens, that will mitigate and manage the negative effects. Great nations such as China and the United States cannot afford to leave incident management to chance or instinct. The stakes are too high.

Introduction

In 1998 the governments of China and the United States signed an agreement between the two defense departments titled "Establishing a Consultation Mechanism to Strengthen Military Maritime Safety," colloquially known as the Military Maritime Consultative Agreement (MMCA). Three years later, on 1 April 2001, a Chinese F-8 interceptor and a U.S. Navy EP-3 electronic surveillance aircraft collided over the South China Sea, resulting in the loss of the F-8, the death of its pilot, and an emergency landing by the American aircraft on Hainan with the subsequent diplomatic and intelligence embarrassment. Clearly, in this case the MMCA consultation mechanism had failed to "strengthen military maritime safety."

It is highly unlikely that the young pilots of these two aircraft had taken off that day intending to create such a tragedy. It is even less likely that either government had intended to create a deliberate diplomatic furor. An accident just happened, as these things do in the complex and demanding environment of modern maritime operations. The problem is that such unintended consequences can bring nations to the brink of crisis, sometimes to the detriment of carefully crafted plans and policies of their political leadership. The challenge, therefore, is to establish effective risk management mechanisms to ensure that unintended incidents are avoided or managed safely, and that intended incidents resulting from deliberate policy decisions unfold as intended, send clear signals to the other party (or parties), and are managed through effective communication mechanisms so that the event can be brought to a satisfactory conclusion.

Warships and military aircraft of the two nations are continuing to interact beyond the limit of territorial seas but within areas of national strategic concern. In March 2009, for example, a running confrontation occurred between the USNS *Impeccable* and a number of Chinese vessels, resulting in considerable diplomatic and political fuss. The effectiveness of the 1998 MMCA therefore needs to be examined, not just in a bilateral perspective but also within the volatile regional context.[1] This chapter explores four questions posed by the conference organizers:

- What can history teach about patterns of military-to-military interactions, and what are the most successful examples of confidence-building measures (CBMs)?

- What are the challenges and opportunities offered by navy-to-navy relationships in particular?

- How should the MMCA be evaluated in the China–U.S. context?

- What can be done to move navy-to-navy activities toward concrete and significant results for the broader bilateral relationship?

What Can History Teach about Patterns of Military-to-Military Interactions, and What Are the Most Successful Examples of Confidence-Building Measures?

History offers policymakers a rich and invaluable source of ideas and lessons, but these must be used with care. As one distinguished historian has cautioned, "History is not a recipe book; past events are never replicated in the present in quite the same way."[2] Throughout much of history, military-to-military relationships have generally taken the form of posturing in peacetime and combat in war. Nonetheless, in the maritime domain, seafarers share a long history of a common culture and, indeed, of mutual understanding and cooperation. With that in mind, four examples can illustrate the sort of lessons that history suggests to those aiming to enhance mutual confidence on military matters.

Perceptions and Misperceptions

There are all kinds of theories to explain impersonal social or historical forces driving nations into that least desirable of military-to-military interactions—war. And yet, as Dr. John Stoessinger concludes from the eight case studies in his book *Why Nations Go to War*, "it was *people* who actually *precipitated* wars" (his italics).[3] Furthermore, despite what history books usually suggest, leaders rarely take that irrevocable step as a result of cold, dispassionate strategic calculation. More often, suggests Stoesssinger, "the most important single precipitating factor in the outbreak of war is misperception."[4]

One lesson that history can teach us, then, is that security is about the actions of people, individually and in groups, and not of inexorable and impersonal forces. In that context, misperception is everyone's mutual enemy.

Maritime Confidence-Building Experience

Addressing misperceptions is, of course, a core function of confidence building, which explains why it has become such a growth industry in an era of mass destruction. Nonetheless, it is worth noting that the history of confidence building stretches back well before the advent of nuclear weapons. It also has a significant maritime heritage. Formal and tacit agreements for the conduct of vessels at sea have been a norm on the world's oceans from time immemorial: there are records of maritime law in the Mediterranean dating to the fourth century BCE, just as well-developed Indo-Pacific maritime trade had evolved its own body of customs of behavior on the other side of the globe.[5] More recently, one of the earliest examples of a recognizable information exchange CBM was part of an agreement on naval arms limitation on the Great Lakes between

Canada and the United States. The Rush-Bagot postwar agreement of 1817 still remains in force after 190 years and was, for example, invoked by Canada in the 1960s when the United States considered deploying ballistic missiles afloat in the Great Lakes, and again as recently as 2006 when the U.S. Coast Guard announced that it would mount machine guns on its cutters.[6]

A second lesson that history can teach is that sailors have a lot of institutional experience in confidence building, although most individuals may not be aware of it. This suggests that some education may be in order.

Prevention of Incidents at Sea

Arguably one of the most successful of all CBMs has been the 1972 agreement for prevention of incidents at sea (INCSEA) between the United States and then–Soviet Union.[7] This agreement is one of the most enduring and resilient of CBMs, still in force today after more than thirty-five years. Furthermore, the nature of this bilateral agreement is so demonstrably successful that it has been adopted, adapted, and become the inspiration for a wide variety of bilateral and multilateral arrangements of varying effectiveness worldwide. Not all resulted in formally signed agreements, but most at least increased mutual understanding and reduced misperceptions.[8]

Russia and Others. The original 1972 prototype was adapted by eleven other nations to establish navy-to-navy dialogue with the Soviet Union, and later Russia. In the case of Japan and South Korea, these agreements were negotiated and signed after the Cold War was over (1993 and 1994, respectively), demonstrating that the value of the idea goes much deeper than simple conflict prevention between potential adversaries. A similar agreement was also concluded between Poland and West Germany as the Cold War was ending in 1990.

Greece and Turkey. The U.S.–USSR agreement was inspiration for a 1983 Memorandum of Understanding (MOU) and subsequent "Guidelines for the Prevention of Accidents and Incidents on the High Seas and International Airspace" between Greece and Turkey. Although lacking the real-time tactical communications and annual consultation provisions of the prototype, this arrangement did illustrate the virtue of creative thinking in addressing specific mutual problems by agreeing to be particularly diligent about incident avoidance during the peak tourist season.

Middle East. INCSEA was one of two elements in the maritime dimension of the Middle East Peace Process in 1993–95, the other being cooperative search and rescue. Although the operational experts achieved a mutually acceptable draft agreement, the political process collapsed before it could be submitted for political-level consideration. Nonetheless, the effort was not wasted because the process had brought former combatants together in a three-year joint problem-solving process that did much to improve mutual understanding as well as to lay foundations for some discreet cooperation at sea that continued long after the political environment had again become confrontational.[9]

UN and CSCE Multilateral Proposals. In 1989 Sweden submitted a working paper to the UN disarmament commission proposing a multilateral agreement for the prevention of incidents at sea. Nothing came of it for a number of reasons, mostly related to the difficulties inherent in a multilateral arrangement's unsuitability for dealing with sensitive bilateral issues. Russia made a similar proposal to the Conference on Security and Cooperation in Europe (CSCE) in 1990 but that too went nowhere for similar reasons.

Western Pacific. The Western Pacific Naval Symposium produced a Code for Unalerted Encounters at Sea (CUES) in 2000. It incorporates elements of the original INCSEA wording but goes far beyond the classic simplicity of a straightforward incident avoidance mechanism by adding tactical maneuvering and signaling instructions, reproducing elements of North Atlantic Treaty Organization (NATO) procedures that were declassified after the Cold War to encourage cooperative multinational maritime operations among like-minded states. The effectiveness of this hybrid approach remains to be analyzed in the public domain.

Malaysia and Indonesia. Because of the same limitations on multilateral arrangements that the Swedish proposal encountered, Malaysia and Indonesia found it necessary to supplement the multilateral CUES process with the parallel development of their own bilateral "MALINDO [Malaysia-Indonesia] Prevention of Incidents at Sea Cooperative Guidelines." This was signed by the respective naval commanders in Jakarta in 2001. More complex than the classic INCSEA model but much simpler and focused than CUES, this arrangement is an interesting example of a carefully staffed and functional adaptation of the INCSEA concept to address very different circumstances.

India and Pakistan. In 1999 the foreign ministers of India and Pakistan signed an MOU in Lahore to "conclude an agreement on prevention of incidents at sea in order to ensure safety of navigation by naval vessels, and aircraft belonging to the two sides." While little was happening on the official front afterward, academic work by retired senior officers from both countries has studied the principles, practice, and international experience in detail.[10] Official negotiations are now reportedly ongoing.

China and the United States. The 1998 "Agreement between the Department of Defense of the United States of America and the Ministry of National Defense of the People's Republic of China on Establishing a Consultation Mechanism to Strengthen Military Maritime Safety," or Military Maritime Consultative Agreement (MMCA), was much more diplomatic in nature and tone than the classic INCSEA model, minimizing the role of operational experts and containing no provision for real-time tactical communication, as tragically highlighted by the 2001 mid-air collision off Hainan. While annual meetings are useful to discuss incidents, they are not much help when events are unfolding rapidly on, over, or under the sea.[11]

Dangerous Military Activities Agreements. In addition to these naval-oriented arrangements, the INCSEA experience has also inspired several examples of broader bilateral dialogue involving all branches of the armed forces called Dangerous Military Activities Agreements. This demonstrates how—as is often the case in confidence building—maritime initiatives offer opportunities to create new precedents in an arena that is governed by long traditions and established law of the sea, and therefore are often less sensitive than along land boundaries.

◆ ◆ ◆

The many lessons offered by these examples can be (and are) the subject of entire seminars and workshops. For purposes of this discussion, however, the important point is that the successful variants were those that focused on operational risk management rather than on creating diplomatic documents. This is crucial because it allows incidents to be treated as mutual problems to be resolved in private, rather than as treaty violations to be protested in public. More important perhaps, in each case the process brought together human beings who had previously dealt with each other as impersonal occupants of fighting machines.

A third lesson that history teaches us is that the INCSEA experience offers many useful suggestions for ways to create innovative and tailor-made (or "sailor-made," as one Russian commentator put it[12]) ways to prevent or mitigate the effects of incidents. Before suggestions can be applied, however, they have to be identified and analyzed, which suggests that preservation of institutional memory and education of negotiators is a prerequisite to moving forward.

Confidence Building or Measure Creating?

James Macintosh is a Canadian academic who, after many years of analyzing and categorizing CBMs, concluded that a focus on producing measures is misleading and can be counterproductive. The process, he says, is most important. Too often political leaders commit themselves to creating CBMs and then, if negotiations do not result in a "measure," they are left announcing failure. Macintosh has argued for a "transformation view" of confidence building, undertaken by policymakers "with the minimum, explicit intention of improving at least some aspects of a suspicious and traditionally antagonistic security relationship."[13] Arguing the case in detail is beyond the scope of this discussion, but it is sufficient to observe here that successful relationships do not necessarily rely on documentation.[14] As Ken Booth said about arms control, "a formal treaty is to arms control what marriage is to love: it dramatizes, formalizes, constrains and solidifies a relationship, but is by no means necessary for its realization."[15]

A fourth lesson that history teaches us is that effective confidence building should not necessarily be focused on production of a "measure." Rather, it should focus on the dynamic process of transforming a security relationship from a flawed present to a more stable and less risky future.

What Are the Challenges and Opportunities Offered by Navy-to-Navy Relationships in Particular?

In the jargon of social science, those of all nationalities who go to sea can be described as an "epistemic community"—that is, a transnational group of specialists who share a common professional culture that transcends national or racial background. This is a particularly potent advantage of navy-to-navy relationships. The history of INCSEA-related confidence building is full of anecdotes about naval officers achieving levels of understanding that were almost unimaginable to diplomats. After one very sensitive consultation following a serious incident between U.S. and Soviet ships, a State Department advisor to the subsequent navy-to-navy consultation said that he was "utterly amazed at the frankness, professionalism, and objectivity of the exchanges during the sessions, in contrast to the normal diplomatic intercourse between the two countries."[16] That single comment encapsulates nicely the opportunities suggested by the difference between the navy-to-navy INCSEA model and more traditional politically dominated approaches to confidence building. What, then, are the challenges facing those who wish to build on the INCSEA experience? In the case of the United States and China, three stand out.

Establishing "Political Space"

The military is an instrument of the state, custodian of the national armory, and steward of some of the government's most sensitive security concerns. Furthermore, in most advanced societies, the military is firmly subordinate to civilian leadership. Consequently, any suggestion of an independent role can (and should) be viewed with justifiable suspicion in political and diplomatic circles. Before any substantive navy-to-navy dialogue can take place, therefore, the respective political authorities must not only grant permission but also be confident that the interaction will be a substantial asset to the national security interest. Fortunately, that is not a difficult case to make since unintended incidents between armed forces are clearly not in anyone's national interest. The business of government is to manage events and minimize risk, so no political leader wants a situation where an honest misjudgment by a junior officer at sea may create a counterproductive international political problem at an inopportune moment. The challenge, therefore, is for political leaders to understand the unique nature and advantages of the INCSEA approach of frank and open mutual problem solving, and then to define what Dr. Peter Jones calls the "political space" within which naval professionals are free to deal with technical matters candidly and honestly. A fundamental lesson from thirty-five years of INCSEA experience is that political posturing has no place inside a professional incident management forum.

Developing a Common Language

Once the military professionals arrive in the same room and are ready to discuss issues frankly, openly, and honestly, another challenge arises: language. Some ideas simply cannot be translated precisely, and experience has shown that when this is not recognized and addressed, much confusion can follow. In English, for example, the word "security" has a different sense than "safety." This distinction can be important: in a Track Two Middle East forum some years ago, discussion of security issues had to be avoided because they were too sensitive to be allowed within the authorized "political space," but the humanitarian business of safety, such as marine search and rescue, was perfectly acceptable.[17] In Chinese, however, the same word is customarily used to translate both, with the characters suggesting a more harmonious and less militant tone for "security" than the common usage in Western militaries. That word, "an quan," consists of two characters: 安 ("an," meaning peace), the character for which combines the characters for "woman" and "roof"; and 全 ("quan," meaning "complete" or "perfect"), which combines the characters for "joined" and "work." While Americans may hear in the word "security" a robust sense of stronger defense mechanisms, their Chinese counterparts may picture a more harmonious home-like environment in which defenses should be unnecessary. It is important to make the effort to explore these often subtle differences because some can have operational implications. In another Middle East experience, difficulties once arose over use of the word "surveillance," which in English describes a legitimate, overt activity but in Arabic translation carries the nefarious implication of covert spying.

We also need to understand each other's cultural paradigms if we are to communicate effectively. This sensitive issue needs to be approached with caution because differences can be overplayed as well as underestimated. Nonetheless, studies in cultural psychology have suggested significant differences between typical Asian and Western thought processes. Richard Nisbett, for example, has made a strong case that Western modes of thought with their ancient Greek philosophical roots are linear, categorical, and analytical while Asian approaches tend to be more cyclical, contextual, and holistic; that Westerners focus on contracts while Asians value relationships; and that Westerners stress abstract reason while Asians stress interpersonal reasonableness.[18] If this is true, then the implications for military-to-military dialogue need to be explored and understood. Conversely, arguments for a unique "Asian way" that is fundamentally different from Western thinking can also be exaggerated and even exploited for political purposes. Our cultural modes of thought may be different, but we are all human. As Chris Patten has argued, "decency is decent everywhere; honesty is true; courage is brave; wickedness is evil; the same ambitions, hopes and fears crowd around and result from similar experiences in every society."[19] Understanding our differences and celebrating our common humanity is key to building resilient relationships that are sustainable in stormy times as well as during sunny periods.

Transforming the Security Relationship

Too often in military discourse, security is defined solely in terms of armed capability; of defenses, barriers, shields, and weapons. The problem with this chimeric goal of absolute control over events is that it depends on the certainty of prevailing over adversaries. But real and enduring security is not a matter of achieving control because, even if that were achievable, more control by one adversary necessarily means less control by the other. This zero-sum thinking not only becomes a never-ending circle but also increases the risk of misunderstanding. Whatever political leaderships may be thinking, it is vital that their military subordinates share a professional relationship of mutual respect and understanding so that unintended consequences of military actions do not damage the national interest. In most English-language dictionaries, "security" is defined not in terms of control but of confidence. Security

> means having confidence that one will wake up safely in the morning, go about one's business in peace and raise one's family in prosperity and happiness. Maritime security means confidence that legitimate trade will flow predictably and unhindered; that the sea remains, in Mahan's famous phrase, a "great common" and not an avenue for attack. It means that the ocean's resources upon which we all depend can be used responsibly and safely, and that the life support system that it represents remains functional. Armed force is an important and irreplaceable element in the establishment of confidence since it is a guarantor against threats by perverse human beings. . . . Nonetheless, it is only one element, and not the entire answer.[20]

Even in an adversarial relationship, there should be mutual confidence that each side is an honorable and rational actor. Salvador de Madariaga famously said: "Nations don't distrust each other because they are armed; they are armed because they distrust each other."[21] Trust, or confidence, should therefore be the core concern of any relationship between representatives of armed forces that must interact when implementing national security policy.

Many commentators use Samuel Huntington's "clash of cultures" paradigm to suggest that intercultural conflict is inevitable, but they fail to note that the title of his original 1993 article was a question, not a statement.[22] Huntington developed the thesis further in his subsequent book and concluded not that cross-cultural clash is inevitable but that the real clash will be "between Civilization and barbarism."[23] The United States and China have much in common in a world that allows much of its security agenda to be driven by a relatively small percentage of bigoted, humorless, misogynistic, religion-abusing, criminal zealots. Business people enjoying a drink in Shanghai, young women having their nails manicured after school in trendy Beijing salons, or poor peasant farmers in central China are all allies with their counterparts in Los Angeles, Washington, and Mississippi in the campaign for civilization, notwithstanding disagreements between their governments on many other issues. The sad reality is that the United States and China will continue to have substantial government-to-government disputes for the foreseeable future. Nonetheless, the twenty-first century is too complicated a time to afford the luxury of clinging to outdated security paradigms. It is in the national interest for governments to enable those who are entrusted with armed force to find common ground to manage their professional interactions professionally, safely, and responsibly. During an unlikely standoff in which Canadian and Spanish warships found themselves confronting each other over a fisheries dispute in 1994–95, despite fiery political and media rhetoric on both sides, "a Canadian Admiral and his Spanish counterpart were almost constantly in contact reviewing the situation and it was extremely unlikely that the two forces would have ever traded fire over the issue."[24] In fact, both admirals and both commanding officers knew each other personally through NATO interaction. This does not imply that anything happened contrary to government direction—on the contrary, it meant that both navies were able to implement the intended policies of their respective governments responsibly, safely, and without misunderstanding or mishap.

How Should the Maritime Incidents at Sea Mechanism Be Evaluated in the China–U.S. Context?

In good flying weather on a pleasant April morning in 2001, with an agreement in place between two defense departments to "strengthen military maritime safety," what ought to have been a routine Chinese interception of an American reconnaissance aircraft went horribly wrong.[25] The Chinese pilot was killed and the American crew of twenty-four, after making a forced landing at the Lingshui Air Base in Hainan, was interrogated during a tense period of what Gries and Peng call "apology diplomacy" that finally resulted in a peculiar letter from the U.S. ambassador saying that the president and secretary of state were "sorry" for the loss of the pilot, and that the EP-3 entered Chinese airspace and landed without verbal clearance. The president and secretary of state then made it abundantly clear to the public that this did not imply any acknowledgment of U.S. fault. Meanwhile, the incident generated a political storm in both countries that, in the United States, for example, led to debates over issues ranging from the scale of future arms sales to Taiwan to support for China's accession to the World Trade Organization.[26]

The Hainan incident is an excellent case study not only of the strengths and limitations of consultation compared to incident-prevention mechanisms but also of the wider considerations discussed earlier, which suggests two questions. First, what does it tell us about issues of culture and language in a U.S.–China context, and second, what difference might it have made if the MMCA had included some of the more successful elements of INCSEA-like arrangements?

Two National Narratives

Reviewing what both sides said about the incident illustrates the misperception challenge well.[27] The United States was conducting what any Western nation would recognize as overt surveillance, but in Chinese eyes, this was perfidious spying. To Americans it was obvious that the aircraft was in legal airspace since international law does not prohibit military flights over an exclusive economic zone (EEZ), but Chinese observed that the United States was violating the spirit, if not the letter, of the law and was being hypocritical since it has an air defense identification zone off its own coast extending well beyond its own EEZ. The United States objected strenuously about China claiming the right to examine the crippled EP-3 in Hainan while the Chinese noted that when a Soviet defector flew a MIG-25 into Japan in 1976, U.S. Air Force technicians from the Foreign Technology Division dismantled the aircraft and returned it in packing crates.[28] The almost universal focus in the United States was on the issue of air-to-air interceptions and previous recorded experience with this particular pilot who, this time, made a fatal mistake resulting in an American crew being held hostage for the sake of a hollow face-saving apology. Chinese discourse was more contextual, with this being seen as just one of many aspects of a long U.S. pattern of intelligence-gathering and intimidation in the air and on the sea, stretching back to humiliating gunboat diplomacy in the nineteenth century. The U.S. discourse was full of commentary on the perfidy and hegemonic ambitions of China. Chinese discourse was full of commentary on the perfidy and hegemonic ambitions of the United States. In fact, as Gries and Peng have argued, both sides made equally valid arguments within their own cultural context but also exhibited many cultural similarities. The important lesson, they point out, is that "a Sino-American relationship devoid of mutual trust becomes a volatile powder keg. Once 'they' cease to be human, the psychological foundation for violence is laid."[29]

INCSEA Implications

Although the MMCA contains nothing that would have helped once this situation began to develop, the incident could have been avoided through good airmanship and existing procedures. There is, after all, a lot of global experience with air-to-air interceptions and even an international manual governing interception of civil aircraft, the principles of which would presumably be equally applicable to a military transport or reconnaissance aircraft.[30] Nonetheless, if an INCSEA-like arrangement had been in place, a more precise and positive mechanism would have been available to prevent the incident or, if that had failed, contribute to crisis resolution in the short term and improved "military maritime safety" in the longer term.

What difference might it have made if, instead of the MMCA, China and the United States had created an INCSEA-like arrangement in 1998?[31]

- The pilots did not communicate other than hand signals from the Chinese pilot, the meaning of which were unclear to U.S. crew. With an INCSEA-like agreement in place, working radio frequencies and call signs could have been available, and special codes could have been used to bridge the language barrier to express intention or concern.

- Neither operational headquarters ashore was able to relay real-time incident-resolution messages through national authorities to the other nation. With an INCSEA-like agreement in place, at very least there could have been urgent communication using established channels through attachés.

- After the incident was over, there was no forum for, or tradition of, candid consultation in which the facts of the case could be laid on a table so that both sides could establish, privately and without political posturing, what happened and how to prevent it from happening again. With an INCSEA-like arrangement in place, an annual or specially convened consultation could have done just that. It is interesting to note that although it seems clear that the immediate cause of collision was pilot error on the part of the interceptor, the unconvincing counteraccusations against the American pilot all appear to have originated from China's civilian diplomatic community rather than from the defense establishment, which suggests political posturing rather than factual analysis.[32] It would seem that the professionals would have had no problem going behind closed doors and taking a mutual approach to incident and risk management.

What Can Be Done to Move Navy-to-Navy Activities toward Concrete and Significant Results for the Broader Bilateral Relationship?

The evidence indicates that the current MMCA is inadequate for effective incident management at sea. The MMCA would therefore make an excellent starting point for transforming the bilateral military-to-military relationship by drawing on the lessons of INCSEA principles, practices, and experience worldwide to revisit the MMCA in a spirit of mutual problem solving. To do that, the three challenges and opportunities described earlier would need to be addressed.

Political Space

Addressing the political space should not be a major problem in the United States since the precedent is well established, although it may be necessary to refresh institutional memories about the spirit and traditions that underlie the text and the interesting innovations elsewhere. In China there may be a need to educate senior decision makers on the positive contribution that an INCSEA-like arrangement could make to national security as a risk-reduction tool.

Mutual Understanding

Separate from but complementary to an INCSEA-like process, it might be useful to consider an interactive academic and social program to foster a common understanding of language and cultural factors that may impact on security dialogue. Both sides might benefit much by learning from the other.

Relationship Building

No matter how tense the political relationship may become at times, the interests of peace and security are best met by defining appropriate political space within which those who actually implement national policy at sea can discuss privately, frankly, and honestly (within the constraints of security) how to minimize and mitigate the inherent risk that comes with naval operations.

Conclusion

Junior military officers such as China's Wang Wei and his wingman, and America's lieutenant Shane Osborn and his crew of twenty-three, are decent, honest, and professional people. Nevertheless, the tactical level mishaps that can happen to the best of them should not plunge political leaders into unexpected state-to-state confrontation because they lack a robust and effective incident management mechanism.

History teaches us that the human element is fundamentally important in international relations, and mutual misunderstanding is one of the greatest risks. Reducing misperception is a core function of confidence building, and that is something with which sailors have had centuries of experience. The best example of a modern CBM is the concept of navy-to-navy agreements for prevention of incidents at sea, an innovative, resilient, adaptable, and proven mechanism that has been adopted and adapted to a wide variety of circumstances. Successful examples have transformed relationships from uncertainty and suspicion to understanding and clarity.

The shared professional culture of the international naval community offers a powerful opportunity to improve security relationships between nations. For this to happen, however, there are three challenges and opportunities to consider. First, political leadership must recognize that navy-to-navy interaction is a vital national interest, not a security threat, and then must grant their military experts sufficient "political space" within which to conduct their professional, technical business free of political posturing. Second, the military professionals must develop a common understanding of their differing languages and culture so that communication is clear and mutual understanding is achieved. Third, this process can, and should, lead to a fundamental transformation of the relationship—not of political policies but of the way that the professional armed forces implement those policies to achieve the political intent.

The Military Maritime Consultation Agreement between the United States and China was a good start on confidence building but, in its present form, is an inadequate measure for preventing incidents and does not contain the relationship-transforming elements that could make it far more relevant and useful. After more than a dozen years, numerous potentially hazardous incidents, and one death, it is time to reevaluate it in the light of INCSEA experience worldwide to better serve the interests of both parties. With the right "political space" and a commitment to better mutual understanding, the two great nations can transform their security relationship at sea.

Notes

1. For implications of the *Impeccable* incident on themes discussed in this chapter, see David N. Griffiths, "Sino-American Maritime Confidence Building: Paradigms, Precedents and Prospects" Naval War College *China Maritime Study* 6 (forthcoming 2010), http://www.usnwc.edu/Research---Gaming/China-Maritime-Studies-Institute/Publications.aspx.

2. Gerda Lerner, *Why History Matters: Life and Thought* (New York: Oxford University Press, 1997), 204.

3. John G. Stoessinger, *Why Nations Go to War*, 8th ed. (Boston: Bedford/St. Martin's, 2001), xv.

4. Ibid., 255.

5. To explore the history further, see Edgar Gold, *Maritime Transport: The Evolution of International Marine Policy and Shipping Law* (Lexington, MA: D. C. Heath and Company, 1981); and Li Qingxin, *Maritime Silk Road*, trans. William W. Wang (Beijing: China Intercontinental Press, 2006).

6. For a history of the Rush-Bagot agreement, see B. O'Neill, "Rush-Bagot and the Upkeep of Arms Treaties," *Arms Control Today* 21, no. 7 (September 1991): 22. The 2006 discussions about arming U.S. Coast Guard cutters was reported by the Canadian Broadcasting Corporation in "U.S. Puts Machine-Guns in Coast Guard Vessels," 15 March 2006, http://www.cbc.ca/canada/story/2006/03/15/coastguard-060315.html.

7. For details, see "United States/Russian Federation Incidents at Sea and Dangerous Military Activities Agreements," OPNAVINST T 5711.96C, 10 November 2008, http://doni.daps.dla.mil/Directives/05000%20General%20Management%20Security%20and%20Safety%20Services/05-700%20General%20External%20and%20Internal%20Relations%20Services/5711.96C.pdf.

8. The author and his colleague, Dr. Peter Jones from the University of Ottawa, have been personally involved in a number of the examples described here, and have been researching the issues and conducting INCSEA seminars and consultations worldwide for more than a decade, most recently in Shanghai, China, in October 2007. They are currently producing an annotated compendium of selected source documents, which they hope to publish in both English and Chinese in early 2008. By far the best description of the original U.S.–USSR agreement and some of the subsequent variations is David F. Winkler, *Preventing Incidents at Sea: The History of the INCSEA Concept* (Halifax, NS: Centre for Foreign Policy Studies, Dalhousie University, 2008).

9. Described in detail in Peter Jones, "Maritime Confidence-Building Measures in the Middle East," in *Maritime Confidence Building in Regions of Tension*, Report No. 21, ed. Jill R. Junnola, 57–73 (Washington, DC: The Henry L. Stimson Center, May 1996).

10. "Confidence and Cooperation in South Asian Waters," Dalhousie University Web site, http://centreforforeignpolicystudies.dal.ca/events/marsec_CCSAW.php.

11. For details, see "Agreement between the Department of Defense of the United States of America and the Ministry of National Defense of the People's Republic of China on Establishing a Consultation Mechanism to Strengthen Military Maritime Safety." Published online by the Federation of American Scientists at www.fas.org/nuke/control/sea/text/us-china98.htm.

12. Bakhtiyar Tuzmukhamedov, "'Sailor-Made' Confidence-Building Measures," in *Maritime Security: The Building of Confidence*, ed. Jozef Goldblat (New York: United Nations Institute for Disarmament Research, 1992).

13. James Macintosh, *Confidence Building in the Arms Control Process: A Transformation View*, Arms Control and Disarmament Studies, No. 2 (Ottawa: Department of Foreign Affairs and International Trade, Non-Proliferation, Arms Control and Disarmament Division, 1996), 63.

14. For further discussion, see David N. Griffiths, "Confidence Building at Sea," in *Canadian Gunboat Diplomacy: The Canadian Navy and Foreign Policy*, eds. Ann

L. Griffiths, Peter T. Haydon, and Richard H. Gimblett (Halifax: Dalhousie University, Centre for Foreign Policy Studies, 1998), 313–33.

15. Ken Booth, "Disarmament & Strategy" in *Contemporary Strategy*, eds. Baylis et al., (London: Croon Helm, 1975 [1981 reprint]), 107.

16. Winkler, *Preventing Incidents at Sea*, 179.

17. The forum was the Maritime Safety (MarSaf) Colloquium described in Dalia Dassa Kaye, *Talking to the Enemy: Track Two Diplomacy in the Middle East and South Asia* (Santa Monica, CA: RAND Corporation, 2007), 45–46.

18. See Richard E. Nisbett, *The Geography of Thought* (London: Nicholas Brealey Publishing, 2005); Gregory Kulacki, "Lost in Translation," *Bulletin of the Atomic Scientists* 62, no. 3 (May–June 2006): 34–39; and Gregory Kulacki, "Chinese Perspectives on Transparency and Security," 13 January 2003, Nuclear Weapons & Global Security Web site, www.ucsusa.org/global_security/china/chinese-perspec tives-on-transparency-and-security.html.

19. Chris Patten, *East and West* (Toronto: McClelland & Stewart Inc., 1998), 140.

20. David N. Griffiths, "Maritime Security, Terrorism and the 'New Economy,'" in *Ocean Yearbook*, Volume 19, eds. Aldo Chircop and Moira L. McConnell (Chicago: University of Chicago Press, 2005), 292.

21. Salvador de Madariaga, *Morning without Noon* (Farnborough, Hampshire: Saxon House, 1974), 48.

22. See Samuel P. Huntington, "The Clash of Civilizations?" *Foreign Affairs* (Summer 1993): 22–49.

23. Samuel P. Huntington, *The Clash of Civilizations and the Remaking of World Order* (New York: Simon & Schuster, 2003), 321.

24. Laura J. Higgins, *Canadian Naval Operations in the 1990s: Selected Case Studies*, Maritime Security Occasional Paper No. 12 (Halifax: Dalhousie University, Centre for Foreign Policy Studies, 2002), 118.

25. For an American account, see Bill Gertz, "The Last Flight of Wang Wei," *Air Force Magazine*, July 2001, 51–53.

26. CRS Report for Congress, "China-U.S. Aircraft Collision Incident of April 2001: Assessments and Policy Implications," updated 10 October 2001 (Washington: Congressional Research Service, Library of Congress), www.fas.org/sgp/crs/row/ RL30946.pdf.

27. For a Chinese perspective, see for example Ji Gioxing, "Rough Waters in the South China Sea: Navigation Issue Confidence-Building Measures," *Asia Pacific Issues*, no. 53 (Honolulu: East-West Center, August 2001). The U.S. perspective is well summarized in the CRS Report for Congress. For discussion of the cultural similarities and differences between the two, see Peter Hays Gries and Kaiping Peng, "Culture Clash? Apologies East and West," *Journal of Contemporary China* 11, no. 30 (2002): 173–78.

28. John E. Jessup, *An Encyclopedic Dictionary of Conflict and Conflict Resolution, 1945–1996* (Westport, CT: Greenwood Press, 1998), 357.

29. Gries and Peng, "Culture Clash?" 178.

30. International Civil Aviation Organization, *Manual Concerning Interception of Civil Aircraft*, ICAO Document 9433, 2nd ed., 1990. The CRS Report for Congress (p. 18) suggests that the Chinese pilot should have followed the *International Flight Information Manual*, which has details on "International Interception Procedures" and "Intercept Pattern for Identification of Transport Aircraft" but—notwithstanding the "international" in the title—that is a U.S. publication issued by the Federal Aviation Administration, not an international document.

31. Event descriptions are compiled from a variety of the references cited for this chapter.

32. It is interesting to note that the Web site of the Chinese embassy in Washington still posted a section dedicated to the incident six years later. It has since been removed.

PART II

Maritime Domain Awareness

Andrew S. Erickson

The Container Security Initiative and U.S.–China Relations

IN MARCH 2004 A SHOCKING EXPLOSION rocked Port Ashoda, Israel. Two suicide bombers who had stowed away in the false compartment of a shipping container had detonated their weapons when discovered by guards before they could target the port's fuel depot.[1] Although ten people were killed in this tragedy, it was not the first time that terrorists had attempted to exploit the mobility and anonymity of shipping containers, and it will not be the last.[2] In a future incident, the damage could be far greater and far more wide-ranging.

With the rise of globalization and the consequent benefits for economic growth, maritime security is more important for the survival and prosperity of nations than ever before: "90% of world trade and two-thirds of . . . petroleum are transported by sea."[3] With East Asia's developing market of nearly 2 billion people, its disproportionate number of major commercial ports, and its status as both a conduit for and a source of much of world trade and energy transport, East Asia (with China at its core) is central to this process. Ports in mainland China, Hong Kong, and Taiwan account for more than 42 percent of U.S.-bound cargo.[4]

The region's future depends on the security of its sea-lanes. Yet a variety of nonstate forces—piracy, smuggling, accidents, and even potentially maritime terrorism—threaten to impede or even disrupt the functioning of this vital system. It is difficult to conceive of an area in which the United States and China have more shared interests in, and could derive more benefits from, security cooperation. Progress in seaborne container security, in turn, could build confidence and what Carla A. Hills, vice chairman of the Council on Foreign Relations, terms "habits of cooperation" that could bolster the other bilateral and multilateral initiatives outlined in this volume.[5]

Given its great dependence on container shipping amid the dangers of the post-9/11 world, the United States has established the Container Security Initiative (CSI) to safeguard seaborne container trade. In June 2002 U.S. Customs invited China to join CSI, and the process was completed the following year.[6] This chapter examines the CSI's vital contribution to East and Southeast Asian supply chain security and China's vital role therein. This chapter demonstrates that

- The United States and China are both vital contributors to, and beneficiaries of, CSI.

- CSI has succeeded by linking robust economic and security interests, introducing new technologies and commercial opportunities, facilitating access to the U.S. market, and allowing for true reciprocity.

- CSI cooperation has expanded rapidly and has inspired other programs.

- The major obstacles to bilateral maritime cooperation in this arena are the complexity, cost, and time-consuming implementation of effective initiatives.

Rationale for the Container Security Initiative (CSI)

An important security measure with particular significance for Asia, which boasts thirteen of the world's top twenty container shipping ports, is the Container Security Initiative (CSI, 集装箱安全倡议).[7] CSI was introduced by the U.S. Customs Service in January 2002 following the 11 September 2001 terrorist attacks. Containerized cargo security's importance for economic development and stability, particularly in East Asia, is readily apparent as Table 1 (below) indicates. Of central significance to the economic interests of the United States, its East Asian trading partners, and indeed the world, is the security of "megahubs," which can accommodate the sixty-foot drafts of the largest container ships. Seven of these deep-water ports (Singapore, Shanghai, Hong Kong, Ningbo, Guangzhou, Kaohsiung, and Yokohama) are in East and Southeast Asia, the location of the majority of global container trade. More are under development as the region's ports are improved at a staggering rate.

Intra-Asian transport reached 28.3 million twenty-foot container equivalent units (TEUs) in 2007. Here, "out of the 20 busiest container trade routes 11 involve Greater China as origin or destination [and represent] 37.6 percent of world volumes."[8] Trans-Pacific stood at 20.6 million TEUs, and Asia-Europe at 18.6 million TEUs.[9]

Table 1. World's Top 15 Ports by Container Traffic, 2008

Rank	Port	Country/Economy	TEUs
1	Singapore	Singapore	29,918,200
2	Shanghai	P.R. China	28,006,400
3	Hong Kong	S.A.R. China	24,494,229
4	Shenzhen	P.R. China	21,416,400
5	Busan	South Korea	13,445,693
6	Dubai Ports	United Arab Emirates	11,827,299
7	Ningbo	P.R. China	11,226,000
8	Guangzhou	P.R. China	11,001,400
9	Rotterdam	Netherlands	10,783,825
10	Qingdao	P.R. China	10,024,400
11	Hamburg	Germany	9,737,110
12	Kaohsiung	Taiwan	9,676,554
13	Antwerp	Belgium	8,662,891
14	Tianjin	P.R. China	8,502,700
15	Port Kelang	Malaysia	7,973,579

Source: "World Port Ranking—2008," American Association of Port Authorities, http://aapa.files.cms-plus.com/Statistics/WORLD%20PORT%20RANKINGS%2020081.pdf.

Note: Xiamen ranked twenty-second, Dalian twenty-third, and Lianyungang thirty-fifth.

Containers transport nearly 90 percent of global trade annually—a total of 153 million TEUs in 2008 (a 7 percent increase over 2007).[10] The world's 20 megahub container ports send nearly 68 percent of the 5.7 million containers entering the United States by sea annually on 214,000 vessels at 301 distinct entry ports.[11] This is part of a larger pattern in which seaborne trade, which accounts for 80 percent of all international trade, has increased an estimated 4.1 percent (in 2004), and 3.6 percent (in 2005 and 2006).[12] From 1982–2005, global container trade grew 3.5 times faster than global gross domestic product, and 40 percent faster than overall global trade; every year since 2003, it has averaged double-digit growth. While global economic conditions may reduce the growth rate, international trade remains significant and environmental concerns may further favor seaborne trade.[13]

This burgeoning trade imposes tremendous traffic and processing burdens on container ports. Large ships carrying as many as eight thousand containers transport nearly half of incoming trade (by value), 40 percent overall, to the United States' 360 commercial ports; this percentage is even higher in Japan, Singapore, and the United Kingdom. U.S. ports received 9.8 million containers from 611 ports in fiscal year 2008;[14] in 2004 seaborne containers also transported one-quarter of U.S. imports ($423 billion) and one-sixth of U.S. exports ($139 billion).[15] More than 600 foreign seaports in approximately 170 countries export products to the United States. The largest 80 of these countries send 95 percent of all containers to the United States.[16] Sixteen million shipping containers arrived in U.S. ports in 2005.[17] During that fiscal year, U.S. Customs and Border Protection processed 20 million sea, truck, and rail containers entering the United States and 29 million of its trade entries.[18]

Like that of the United States, China's economy is critically dependent on container traffic. In 2006 China had $974 billion in exports, 21 percent ($250 billion) of which went to the United States and 9.5 percent of which went to Japan. China imported $777.9 billion worth of goods that year.[19] In 2009 China shipped $1.2 trillion in goods overseas, thereby becoming the world's largest exporter.[20] Logistical and commercial imperatives meant that the vast majority of goods by volume, and a substantial majority by value, travel by sea. Empty containers constantly enter China's major ports—which are nearing 100-million-TEU capacity[21]—and full ones are shipped out, many through just-in-time supply chains, so China, like the United States, has to have complete confidence in the safety of containers coming from other nations. With logistics accounting for 18 percent of GDP, double that of most developed economies, and port development under way at a speed and scale unequaled anywhere else in the world, China has both reason and ability to keep its container security cutting edge.[22]

Given this tremendous reliance, disruption of trade by terrorist activities involving shipping containers could be disastrous. To grasp the challenge inherent in safeguarding container shipments, note the sheer scale of Denmark's $145-million *Emma Maersk*. With a length of 1,302 feet and width of 207 feet, *Emma Maersk* is larger than a U.S. Navy aircraft carrier, yet it has far fewer personnel (thirteen versus five thousand) and can cross the Pacific at 27 knots. It carries 15,000 containers, or 123,200 tons of cargo. Now consider that Maersk operates 550 container ships.[23] To be sure, the world's 12 million containers are carried in groups of 3,000 or less on many of the world's 4,600 container ships, but the value is still higher than for most cargo ships. For U.S. maritime trade, they represent 11 percent of tonnage but 66 percent of value. To this tremendous volume is added a large number of logistical steps divided among many locations. Typically loaded in one or more of many remote company warehouses, a container may contain goods from several customers. Its progress from exporter to freight forwarder to land transporter to customs broker to customs inspector to port operator to feeder ship/ocean carrier to final port of entry is tracked by as many as forty documents and can range as far as nine thousand miles in as few as sixteen days. Safeguarding such a long and complex process is truly monumental in its challenges, but so are the interests at stake.[24]

Not to be underestimated is the indirect economic damage that could also result from containerized terrorism. According to a 2002 report by Booz, Allen and Hamilton, which was cited by the U.S. Government Accountability Office (GAO) in its 2003 Container Security Report, if searching for an undetonated weapon of mass destruction were to require the closure of a single U.S. seaport for twelve days, economic costs could reach $58 billion, or $4.8 billion per day.[25] In 2002 a Brookings Institution study suggested that a detonation in a similar single-port scenario could cause $1 trillion in economic damage by triggering trade restrictions.[26] The U.S. Department of Homeland Security already spends roughly $140 million annually on CSI, in part to reduce the possibility of such a scenario erupting.[27] A strike by the International Longshore and Warehouse Union in 2002 provided a real-life example of the costs of port disruption, as twenty-nine West Coast ports were closed for ten days and thirty to forty vessels were unable to be unloaded at any point.[28] Perishable goods were spoiled and shippers and exporters suffered huge losses for an estimated cost of $2.4 billion per day ($19.4 billion in total).[29]

Clearly, China's economy would be negatively impacted by any disruption in imports from the United States, the destination of $250 billion of Chinese exports in 2006, or 21 percent of China's total for that year.[30] This danger can be seen broadly in the impact of the recent U.S. recession on Chinese manufacturing. Even a delay in the shipment of preordered goods increases prices and decreases consumption, thereby harming Chinese exports. Better container monitoring can also reduce the smuggling and corruption tendencies that threaten ports around the world. For instance, in 1998 then-premier Zhu Rongji declared, "It is necessary to . . . equip all ports with a container perspective monitoring system . . . so as to enhance anti-smuggling combat capability."[31] There is therefore a major economic and security rationale for cooperation in this area. As one Chinese port industry veteran adds, "By joining CSI, we can learn from the United States' advanced container security management experience, which is definitely something positive for domestic enterprises."[32]

CSI Procedures

Under CSI, officials are deployed overseas to work in cooperation with their host nation counterparts at the fifty-eight CSI ports that supply 86 percent of container cargo to the United States.[33] U.S. Customs and Border Protection officers are stationed in overseas locations that ship a number of containers above a certain threshold, where they engage in reciprocal information exchange.[34] This is in complete accordance with utmost respect for host nations' sovereignty.

Cooperation in law enforcement is usually much easier for nations to achieve than is military cooperation, especially against mutual threats. U.S. officers from the Immigration and Naturalization Service as well as from the Drug Enforcement Administration have worked successfully in foreign ports for years.[35] As has been widely reported in China's official media, CSI partner nations may also send officers to U.S. ports to monitor containers destined for their own nations' ports.[36] Japan and Canada have already done so at multiple locations.

To enter CSI, participants first conduct a thorough analysis of port infrastructure vulnerabilities (including personnel integrity) and address any outstanding problems. Then, to ensure the security of container shipping, CSI participants use a four-part process—all based on best practices and coordinated with U.S. Customs and Border Protection:

1. Identify and target containers that risk facilitating terrorist activities by using intelligence, standardized information, risk management, and automated targeting tools. To support this process, "exports destined for or transiting through the U.S. . . . must be compliant with the U.S. 24-hour rule, which requires 14 data elements [e.g., ports of loading and discharge] to be reported 24 hours prior to loading aboard a vessel destined for the U.S."[37]

2. Prescreen at-risk containers at the earliest stage possible, ideally at the port of departure, before they arrive at ports in participating member nations.

3. Employ sophisticated nonintrusive inspection (NII) detection technology (e.g., radiation detection devices as well as X-ray and gamma ray machines) to rapidly prescreen at-risk containers bound for ports in participating member nations with minimal disruption to trade movement while physically inspecting if necessary.

4. Introduce containers that are more secure and that more clearly reveal any tampering that they might have encountered.[38]

In Hong Kong, for example, shipping lines presend information to a port terminal owner's computer system. Hong Kong Customs receives the same information and detains and inspects containers selectively based on assessment of relative risk. For example, when there was a bombing in Colombo, Sri Lanka, containers from that port were subjected to additional scrutiny. Inspectors watch for abnormal movements of certain commodities. Perishable coconuts stored in port for five days, for instance, triggered inspection and were revealed to conceal drugs. There are multiple layers of security procedures. Employees have different levels of security access, and port exit gates will not open unless authorized. There is strong incentive for shippers to police themselves because they pay for any costs associated with delays.[39] Given that the United States has decided to mandate a high level of container inspection, CSI compliance actually makes cargo shipping to the United States more efficient.

Participating East and Southeast Asian Nations

With the tremendous concentration of container ports in East and Southeast Asia, it is both natural and fortunate that CSI has made great inroads there. For a list of currently operational ports in the region, see table 2.

All the nations and entities listed in table 2 have played a critical role in furthering CSI's coverage, and they deserve great recognition for their many efforts in this regard. For the purposes of this chapter, however, it is necessary here to focus on the implementation of CSI in China.

China

With its rapid manufacturing-based economic growth, China has already had a major impact on global container trade. Beijing's active participation has been and will be essential to the success of CSI. With six of the world's top fifteen container ports, mainland China processes a tremendous volume of containerized exports.[40] In 2004 Chinese ports handled roughly one-quarter of global container traffic that year and (when including that of the Hong Kong

Table 2. CSI Ports in East and Southeast Asia

Location of Port	Port Facility	Date Joined
Mainland China	Shanghai	28 April 2005
	Shenzhen	24 June 2005
Hong Kong	Hong Kong*	5 May 2003
Taiwan	Kaohsiung	25 July 2005
	Chi-Lung	25 September 2006
Singapore	Singapore*	10 March 2003
Japan	Yokohama	24 March 2003
	Tokyo	21 May 2004
	Nagoya	6 August 2004
	Kobe	6 August 2004
South Korea	Busan*	4 August 2003
Malaysia	Port Klang	8 March 2004
	Tangjung Pelepas	16 August 2004
Thailand	Laem Chabang	13 August 2004

* Also participates in Secure Freight Initiative

Source: "CSI Fact Sheet," U.S. Customs and Border Protection, 2 October 2007, http://www.cbp.gov/xp/cgov/trade/cargo_security/csi/ports_in_csi.xml .

S.A.R.) nearly 40 percent of world container volume. China's ports have had the world's largest cargo and container throughput since 2002, when China overtook the United States. In 2007 China exported 114.76 million TEUs; the projection for 2008 is between 137–39 million TEUs. Mainland Chinese ports handled their 100 millionth container in November 2007. Annual growth is 25–35 percent, and roughly half of the containers transiting Pacific sea-lanes are from China. For statistics from 2006–9 and projections for 2010–11, see table 3.

Mainland China has two of the world's top ten container shipping companies (China Ocean Shipping Company, COSCO, 中国远洋, and China Shipping Container Lines, 中国集装箱运输股份), and Taiwan has one (Evergreen Marine Corporation, 长荣海运). China also manufactures 90 percent of world containers. State-owned COSCO has more than 130 vessels (with a capacity of 320,000 TEU).[41] Table 4 shows how China's top shipping companies compare with other world leaders.

Table 3. Recent and Projected Container Throughput for Mainland China and Its Top 9 Major Ports (in millions of TEU)

Port	2006	2007	2008	2009	2010*	2011*
Shanghai	21.71	26.15	28.01	25.00	27.65	29.04
Shenzhen	18.47	21.10	21.42	18.25	19.93	20.92
Guangzhou	6.60	9.26	11.00	11.19	14.00	N/A
Ningbo-Zhoushan	7.07	9.43	10.93	10.50	10.00	N/A
Qingdao	7.70	9.46	10.02	10.26	12.00	N/A
Tianjin	5.95	7.10	8.50	8.70	12.00	N/A
Xiamen	4.02	4.63	5.04	4.68	10.00	N/A
Dalian	3.21	3.81	4.53	4.55	8.00	N/A
Lianyungang	1.30	2.00	3.00	3.02	3.4	N/A

* Estimate.

Note: Zhongshan was China's tenth-largest port in terms of annual TEU throughput from 2006–7; since 2008, Suzhou has held that position.

Source: Projections for 2010–11 for Shanghai and Shenzhen from 撰文, 余黄炎 [Zhuan Wen and Yu Huangyan], "全球集装箱港口行业动态—多数港口第三季度吞吐量无明显回升" ["Global Container Port Industry Trends—No Significant Rebound in the Third Quarter for Most Ports"], 中国港口 [*China Ports*] 11 (November 2009): 48. Projections for 2010 for all ports besides Shanghai and Shenzhen as well as 2009 data from "2009年1-12月全国规模以上港口国际标准集装箱吞吐量前10名" ["International Standard Container Throughput for the Top Ten National Ports, January–December 2009"], 1 February 2010, 交通运输部 [Ministry of Transport and Communications], http://www.61226122.com/CSD3.0/profession/detail.jsp?articleid=68587. Data for 2008 from Matt Schiavenza, "An Uncertain Year for China's Ports? The Latest Throughput Figures to Date," *China Intelligence Online*, 11 September 2009, http://www.chinaintelligenceonline.com/News/2009/09/11/something-else-about-something. Data for 2007 from 撰文, 杨震宁 [Zhuan Wen and Yang Zhenning], "加快发展国际集装箱海铁联运的研究" ["Research on Accelerating the Development of International Sea-Rail Intermodal Transport"], 中国港口 [*China Ports*] 1 (January 2009): 19. Data for 2006 from 中国港口协会研究中心 [China Port Association Research Center], "2008年中国港口集装箱运输预测" ["2008 Container Transport Forecast for Chinese Ports"], 中国港口 [*China Ports*] 185, no. 11 (November 2007): 27. Data checked against "China," *Lloyd's List Ports of the World 2010*, vol. 1 (London: Informa Maritime and Professional, 2010), 221–300.

China's rapid port development and economic growth will probably only increase its portion of global container trade.[42] China's policy of deliberately distributing shipping among its different ports (as opposed to the more market-driven approach used in Western economies) may offer additional opportunities for security regulation. Beijing may be able to allocate container traffic in a way that facilitates focus on the most at-risk containers while allowing the others to be processed more rapidly.

Table 4. Top 10 Container Shipping Companies in Order of TEU Capacity (March 2009)

Company	TEU capacity	Market share (%)	Number of ships	Market share (%)
A. P. Moller-Maersk Group	2,031,886	15.5	539	8.91
Mediterranean Shipping Company S.A.	1,469,865	11.20	425	7.03
CMA CGM Group	988,141	7.50	378	6.25
Evergreen Marine Corporation	624,536	4.80	176	2.91
Hapag-Lloyd	488,135	3.70	128	2.12
COSCO Container Lines	485,796	3.70	148	2.45
American President Lines (APL)	473,170	3.60	131	2.17
China Shipping Container Line (CSCL)	450,928	3.40	143	2.36
NYK Line	433,000	3.30	119	1.97
Hanjin-Senator	378,282	2.90	91	1.50
World Fleet Capacity	13,108,859	100	6,048	100

Source: John Konrad, "Container Shipping Companies—The Ten Largest Visualized," *gCaptain*, 7 March 2009, http://gcaptain.com/maritime/blog/the-ten-largest-container-shipping-companies-visualized/.

President Jiang Zemin's announcement at a 25 October 2002 meeting with President George W. Bush in Crawford, Texas, that China would join CSI and his subsequent strong support represented a major step forward for global container security.[43] "I am very pleased that the Chinese government has agreed in principle to join with the United States in the Container Security Initiative," U.S. Customs commissioner Robert C. Bonner responded. "We will be working with the appropriate Chinese government officials to implement the program as quickly possible. This is an important step, not only for the protection of trade between the U.S. and China, but for the protection of the most critical component of the world trading system as a whole—containerized cargo."[44] In January 2003 General Administration of Customs (GAC) deputy director Sheng Guangzu proposed a set of technical conditions. In early June 2003 presidents Bush and Hu met in Evian, France, to approve a "declaration of principles."[45] On 29 July 2003 China formally joined CSI when Commissioner Bonner and Mu Xinsheng, China's commissioner of GAC, signed a declaration of principles in Beijing.[46]

Hong Kong

The Hong Kong S.A.R.'s proactive participation in both CSI and the Secure Freight Initiative (for which it became a Phase 1 port in July 2007) has been an extremely welcome development; Hong Kong currently ranks first in terms of the volume of both shipments and containers exported to the United States.[47] In 2004 the U.S. received $43.4 billion containerized imports from Hong Kong.[48] In fiscal year 2006, Hong Kong sent 11.48 percent of its 1,333,812 shipments (in 948,876 containers) to the United States, which represented 9.28 percent of all shipping containers the United States received that year.[49] Moreover, 90 percent of Hong Kong's shipments are themselves transshipments, making their safety all the more important to verify.[50]

Recognizing the importance of its trade with the United States, Hong Kong has taken a proactive approach from the start.[51] "As the world's busiest container port, we consider it is our responsibility to work with the international community to safeguard the global maritime trading system from the potential risks facing all of us," declared Secretary for Commerce, Industry, and Technology Henry Tang in 2002.[52] U.S. officials enjoy excellent cooperation with their counterparts in Hong Kong, which has been described by Customs and Border Protection (CBP) Commissioner Bonner as "a model for CSI ports throughout the world."[53] Previously paper-based, Hong Kong Customs and Excise used the implementation of CSI to develop and refine a cutting-edge electronic targeting system/database. It paid for the system and purchased rights to manifest data (e.g., bills of lading and Automated Targeting System [ATS] data for U.S.-bound containers). It implemented twenty-four-hour advanced notice for targeted containers.[54] Although it is not one of the three locations required to implement 100 percent scanning under the October 2006 Security and Accountability for Every Port (SAFE) Ports Act, the Modern Terminal in Hong Kong is nevertheless scanning all U.S.-bound containers that it processes in order to "help determine the impact of scanning at large volume ports." In addition to NII equipment for imaging, and radio-frequency identification (RFID) for tracking, the Modern Terminal employs such technologies as radiation portal monitor and radiation isotope identification device systems to detect radiation.[55] The results are sent to the CSI team on site and the U.S. National Targeting Center for analysis.[56]

Mainland China

Beijing's accession to CSI has been followed with the participation of two high-volume mainland ports. "We appreciate the continued support of CSI by President Hu Jintao," Commissioner Bonner stated. "The CSI security blanket is now expanding and strengthening as it encompasses the ports of Shanghai and Shenzhen."[57] The inclusion of these ports is logical: both in the top four globally in container throughput, they are China's largest by that measure and are located in regions that have the most international trade.

On 28 April 2005, U.S. Customs and Border Protection Commissioner Bonner and Minister Mu announced that the port of Shanghai would become operational in CSI.[58] "China and the U.S. have great prospects for anti-terrorism cooperation, and both sides' efforts in strengthening cooperation in container security is a good example," Minister Mu declared in a written statement. "The China-U.S. cooperation on CSI that has been launched in Shanghai is a good start for cooperation between customs authorities in China and the U.S."[59] Shanghai has particular significance for container security. Targeted by Chinese authorities to become the world's largest port by 2010, with a major role in "international container transshipment," the port is competing strongly with Singapore for that position.[60] Experts assess that the port retains significant growth potential.[61] In 2008 Shanghai International Port Group, which operates the port's public terminals, unveiled the Shanghai-Savannah Express Trade Lane Project in partnership with the Georgia Ports Authority. This innovative project uses active RFID-based electronic seals (e-seals) from Savi Networks to track containers traveling between Shanghai and Savannah, Georgia.[62] An expert from the Ministry of Communications emphasizes, however, that even as more of Shanghai's forty-two terminals reach technological levels comparable to those of Hong Kong, security remains important.[63]

On 24 June 2005 Minister Mu and Commissioner Bonner announced that the Port of Shenzhen would officially become operational within CSI as well. The Port of Shenzhen comprises three major container ports (Yantian, Shekou, and Chiwan, which contribute more than 98 percent of the port's throughput), the new Da Chan Bay facility, which started operation in December 2007, and several smaller facilities. The main facilities, which serve international vessels, are all CSI-compliant.[64] Bonner applauded the efforts of his Chinese counterpart,

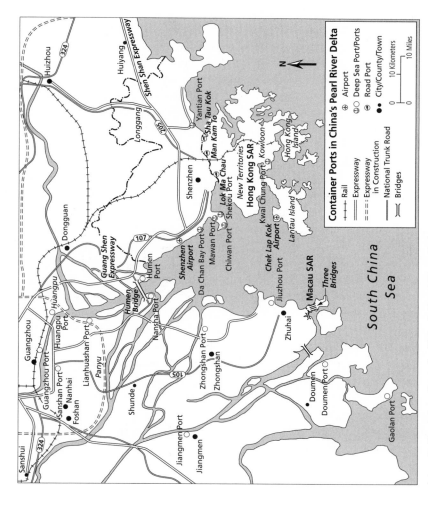

Map 1. Container Ports in China's Pearl River Delta

declaring: "Due to the continued support of CSI by Minister Mu Xinsheng, U.S. borders are more secure and more efficient."[65] For a map that shows the ports of Shenzhen, Hong Kong, and surrounding facilities, see map 1 (previous page).

Given the tremendous scale of China's shipping industry and the nation's significant technical capacity, it is not surprising that CSI has attracted much attention and research.[66] Recognition of the importance of maritime antiter-rorism appears to be increasing in China.[67] Local officials are working to raise awareness about the need to follow regulations and prevent human smuggling and other threats to port security.[68] Chinese attention to nontraditional security threats appears to have prompted a variety of unprecedented maritime safety exercises.[69] U.S. and Chinese customs have also cooperated in bilateral exercises.[70] Gong Zheng, vice-minister of China Customs, has stated that "China Customs will make every effort to facilitate global trade [to] ensure its security."[71] Yet, according to a Hong Kong columnist, some CSI-related activities "cannot be done on the mainland by Chinese authorities."[72]

It is hoped that more Chinese ports will enter CSI in the near future because there is significant and growing container activity beyond Shanghai and Shenzhen. The ports of Xiamen and Fuzhou, for instance, already send significant exports to the United States.[73] The Ninth Five-Year Plan called for additional container wharfs to be constructed in Dalian, Tianjin, Qingdao, and Ningbo by 2010.[74] These and other ports are developing rapidly and will likely continue to do so.[75] For example, Central Party School vice president Zhang Zhixin has stated: "We are pursuing a strategy of . . . build[ing] Qingdao into a north China international shipping center. By 2002, our port handling capacity will reach 85 million tons, with our container handling capacity reaching 28 million standard containers, to make Qingdao an international container transfer hub port, with overall port technology and management up to advanced world standards."[76] Dai Xianglong, mayor of Tianjin Municipality, has declared: "In the construction of the Tianjin Port, it is necessary to . . . build it into a big and modern international deep-water port with a handling capacity of 170 million tonnes and a volume of goods transported by containers of 6 million standard containers."[77]

Broader Impact of CSI around the World

In addition to securing the world's major seaports, CSI increasingly serves as a model for security cooperation in general. In June 2002, all 161 member nations of the World Customs Organization (WCO) adopted the Resolution on Supply Chain Security and Trade Facilitation, which assists with development of programs for their ports modeled on CSI. A subsequent WCO task force devised

- An amended WCO data Model and a list of twenty-seven essential data elements for identification of high risk consignments;

- Customs guidelines for Advance Cargo Information (ACI Guidelines) to enable the advance (pre arrival) electronic transmission of customs data. (Title of these guidelines has recently been changed to "Integrated Supply Chain Management Guidelines" (ISCM Guidelines);

- WCO high-level guidelines for Cooperative Arrangements between Members and private industry to increase supply chain security and facilitate the flow of international trade; and

- A new International Convention on Mutual Administrative Assistance in Customs Matters to assist members in developing a legal basis to enable the advance electronic transmission of customs data.[78]

The G8 has adopted a similar resolution.[79] An agreement signed by the European Union and the Department of Homeland Security on 22 April 2004 envisions the spread of CSI throughout the European Union.[80] A European Commission statement immediately following the agreement, signed by U.S. Homeland Security secretary Tom Ridge and Irish minister of finance Charlie McCreevy on behalf of the EU emphasized the following:

> The Commission fully shares U.S. concerns about improving cargo security and considers that the most effective means to meet these concerns is by co-operation at EU level with the U.S. The new agreement is based on the principle that substantially greater security of legitimate trade can be achieved through a system where the customs authority of the importing country works collaboratively with customs authorities involved in earlier parts of the supply chain to use timely information and inspection technology to target and screen high-risk containers before they are shipped from their ports or places of loading or transshipment.[81]

Clearly the CSI model has broad applicability to enhancing the security of global seaborne trade. But more work is needed because many critical ports are not yet covered (e.g., in mainland China).[82]

Related Programs

The U.S. government and relevant international organizations have initiated several other programs that complement and supplement CSI; China participates in many of these. U.S. Customs and Border Protection is responsible for the U.S. Customs Trade Partnership against Terrorism (C-TPAT) and the National Targeting Center (NTC). The Export Control and Related Border Security Assistance Program (EXBS) and the Megaports/Secure Freight Initiative are run by the departments of State, Energy, and Homeland Security to counter nuclear proliferation. In the international arena, the International Maritime Organization runs the International Ship and Port Facility Security (ISPS) Code, the World Customs Organization is responsible for the SAFE framework of standards, and the International Organization for Standardization (ISO) promotes a variety of other standards. The U.S. Coast Guard plays a major role in supporting all these initiatives for the United States. In keeping with its growth over the past three decades as a major trading nation, China is involved in many of these programs. The following is a selective overview of relevant initiatives and Beijing's involvement in them.

International Organization for Standardization

The ISO, which promulgates standards designed to standardize processes and ensure quality control, is a nongovernmental organization with government and private-sector personnel from 157 nations.[83] It has developed an ISO 28,000 supply-chain security standard. It can be used to certify that a port is in compliance with relevant practices in such areas as "financing, manufacturing, information management and the facilities for packing, storing and transferring goods between modes of transport and locations."[84] "Trouble tickets" are issued for specific areas that need improvement. A port with a poor security reputation can solicit an audit and, if the results are favorable, can petition relevant organizations to upgrade its status (e.g., Lloyd's of London for insurance premiums). While neither the United States nor China might be expected to have such a problematic port themselves, as major importers they are both more secure because of efforts to bring such ports up to standard.

International Ship and Port Facility Security

Beijing joined the International Maritime Organization (IMO) in 1974. Developed by the U.S. Coast Guard under Admiral James Loy in 2001, the ISPS was adopted by 148 members of the IMO in 2002 for implementation by 1 July 2004 following advocacy by the U.S. delegation. An amendment to the Safety of

Life at Sea Convention, SOLAS (1974)/(1987), ISPS establishes minimum mandatory requirements for the security of port facilities and ships over 500 gross tons at different security levels as well as suggestions concerning their implementation and dissemination of relevant information.[85] This risk management mechanism provides the basis for awarding International Ship Security Certificates.[86] It must be emphasized, however, that the IMO lacks the power to penalize violators directly; rather, it relies on market forces to reward safe practices.[87]

The United States met its obligations under ISPS by enacting the Maritime Transportation Security Act, with the U.S. Coast Guard responsible for oversight and implementation.[88] As required by the IMO by 1 July 2004, China's Ministry of Communications designated 620 port facilities as needing ISPS statements of compliance.[89] Under ISPS reciprocal exchanges, the Chinese also inspect U.S. ports. The International Labor Organization and IMO code of practices complement ISPS by regulating "the security of the greater port area and the persons who work in the port."[90]

U.S. Coast Guard Programs

The U.S. Coast Guard promotes the use of best practices to help further port security and thereby keep cooperating ports off its Port Security Advisory.[91] At Modern Terminals, Ltd., Hong Kong, for instance, each ship security officer (or person designated by the master) must work with a port facility security officer (or designated terminal security officer) to complete a ship/terminal security checklist.[92] This is particularly useful because it applies not only to ships but also to barges, which are not covered by ISPS because they do not normally engage in ocean transit but in East Asia may nevertheless engage in cross-border trade. As part of a program with reciprocal visits to Charleston, South Carolina, and New York City, the USCG International Port Security Liaison visited China in 2005 and 2006 to observe ISPS implementation.[93] At the Shekou Container Terminals in mainland China, containers suspected of being used for human smuggling are subjected to carbon dioxide and temperature monitoring as well as visual inspection.[94] At Yantian International Container Terminals, China, a camera-monitored electronic gangway gate allows only those with Frontier Inspection Bureau–issued electronic cards to enter and exit ships.[95]

The Megaports/Secure Freight Initiative

The Megaports Initiative is a Department of Energy/National Nuclear Security Administration program to protect the United States from nuclear and radiological threats at seaports. It is being implemented in various stages in twelve countries with an addition at eighteen ports. Following the signing of a bilateral memorandum in May 2007, two Chinese ports are in the process of becoming involved.[96] A product of this initiative, as required by the U.S. Safe Ports Act, is the Secure Freight Initiative. Initiated officially on 7 December 2006 in cooperation with the Department of Homeland Security, the Secure Freight Initiative supplements CSI by screening a greater portion of containers, even those not predetermined to be of high risk, with the goal of identifying radiological hazards.[97] It therefore integrates sophisticated scanning technology (e.g., nuclear detection devices) into selected operations at selected ports and subport terminals.[98] This offers the CSI team data beyond bills of lading. In fiscal year 2006, the six ports under evaluation handled more than 10 percent (nearly 1.2 million) of U.S.-bound shipments.[99] Three East Asian ports— Singapore's Brani Terminal, South Korea's Gamman Terminal (in Busan), and Hong Kong—are participating in the Secure Freight Initiative.

Export Control and Related Border Security Assistance Program (EXBS)

The State Department's International Security and Nonproliferation Bureau runs the EXBS program to prevent the proliferation of weapons of mass destruction. Agencies in the Department of Homeland Security such as the Coast Guard and Customs and Border Protection assist with implementation. As part of this program, for instance, Malta's major transshipment port received X-ray equipment to improve cargo screening.[100] In conjunction with its support of the UN Conventions on Terrorism/International Convention for the Suppression of Acts of Nuclear Terrorism, China is participating in EXBS.[101] In cooperation with the Department of Energy's International Nonproliferation Export Control Program (INECP), EXBS has sponsored events in Shanghai and Dalian to train "Chinese frontline Customs enforcement officials and technical experts responsible for interdicting illicit shipments of WMD-related, 'dual-use,' strategic commodities."[102] In January 2008 representatives from Chinese ministries participated in an EXBS-sponsored "industry-government forum." Also in conjunction with EXBS, the INECP program is collaborating with the China Atomic Energy Authority (CAEA) within the CAEA-DOE Peaceful Uses of Nuclear Technology framework on the development of technical guides on nuclear and nuclear dual-use materials, equipment, and technology. As this chapter went to press, State Department officials envisioned a variety of follow-on activities to increase the capacity of Chinese industry and law enforcement officials to review export license applications and to select and investigate illicit shipments. These include training

Chinese Customs officers at the port of Charleston, South Carolina, and help-ing China to develop an industry "internal control program."[103]

National Targeting Center

Established on 21 October 2001 in Reston, Virginia, the NTC coordinates the integration and sharing of information among a variety of agencies, which have representatives on site.[104] NTC has more than sixty on-site employees, forty-six of whom currently work as "targeters" who examine data, assisted by the Automated Targeting System (ATS), for links to terrorists. NTC plays an important role in CSI.[105]

U.S. Customs Trade Partnership against Terrorism

The Customs Trade Partnership against Terrorism Program (C-TPAT), initiated in 2002, employs U.S. supply chain security specialists who work directly with companies to ensure supply chain security by maintaining twenty-four-hour advance notification. In return for complying with C-TPAT measures, participants benefit from reduced inspections, priority processing, and even potentially the allowance for some self-policing as part of the CBP Importer Self-Assessment program.[106] Starting in 2008 U.S. CBP has assisted China Customs in completing two rounds of joint supply chain security vali-dation visits.[107]

Self-Policing

The institutions and procedures discussed earlier have created incentives for ports and shippers to engage in proactive security measures. Pilot initia-tives include the use of such tracking technologies as radio-frequency identifi-cation (RFID) and global positioning systems. Dubai Ports World, for instance, has invested $300 million to better secure its forty-two terminals worldwide using X-ray, radiation, and optical container recognition, including in China, in addition to significantly upgrading infrastructure there.[108]

Challenges to U.S.–China Cooperation in CSI

As this book went to press, the global economic slowdown was still affecting container trade, but the overall scale remains significant, and there are already signs of recovery.[109] Global container traffic is forecast to grow by 8.6 percent in 2010, and throughputs at Chinese ports in particular are returning to pre-downturn levels.[110] Potential security threats have not abated, however. CSI therefore remains relevant, and the United States and China should work hard to ensure its continued success.

Despite CSI's great achievements to date, its further implementation faces a variety of challenges. To maximize chances of success in the future, it is important to address these issues frankly to see how they might be resolved or at least mitigated. A number of Chinese concerns have been addressed already, according to one source: "Some of the issues were clarified in the form of annex to the 'declaration of principles' through bilateral negotiations; some are unresolved, pending consultations on details when the US evaluation team is in China, following the signing of the 'declaration of principles.'"[111]

Nations have different conditions, national interests, and perceptions of what priorities should drive shared security initiatives. This raises the question of the extent to which container security should be linked to other issue areas. Some governments may view the problem of achieving container security in a specific, technical sense while others may insist on addressing larger political and institutional factors that they perceive as being essential to further progress. The question of how to balance the investment of scarce economic and political resources in preparations designed to prevent or mitigate high-risk, low-probability events and low-risk, high-probability events will pose a constant challenge for counterterrorism policy formulation and international cooperation and coordination. Six related challenges are addressed below.

Loopholes and Vulnerabilities

CSI should not be viewed as a panacea. Some experts have voiced concerns that CSI designation of a container as safe could give a false sense of security.[112] Certain ports are known to harbor corruption and organized crime. The electronic targeting system is only as good as the data being inputted, which are subject to both malfeasance and human error.[113] Documents such as bills of lading can contain inaccurate information and even be forged.[114] Even scanning may not be a panacea because harmful items might be disguised (e.g., with lead shielding, in the case of radioactive materials) or otherwise concealed.[115] Detection technologies have different levels of error, and there has not been a unified performance standard.[116] It might be possible to "launder" a container through transshipment from an underregulated port, to sneak in unauthorized contents, or even (in theory, at least) to tamper with a container en route. Also, even if a WMD attack or other port disruption occurred in another country, it could still have a terrible impact on the United States' supply chains and economy.[117] Finally, ship-borne containers—while highly vulnerable—are only one potential means of transporting a dirty bomb or other threatening devices.[118]

It is noteworthy, for instance, that while foreign vessels weighing more than three hundred gross tons must provide ninety-six hours' notice before entering U.S. waters, vessels under three hundred gross tons receive far less scrutiny.[119] It was reported in 2002 that less than 10 percent of noncommercial private vessels in U.S. waters were inspected by Customs.[120] The fact that Columbian drug smugglers already operate submersibles capable of carrying up to ten tons of cocaine, for instance, is worrisome indeed.[121] While security officials must work vigilantly to minimize these possibilities, however, the existing imperfect system is certainly preferable to the previous absence of one. And by significantly increasing the difficulty to shipping dangerous or unauthorized goods, CSI has already created a powerful deterrent effect.[122]

Sovereignty and Legal Issues

Some nations are reluctant to engage in activities that they worry may compromise their sovereignty. Scholars at the China Institutes of Contemporary International Relations, for instance, lump CSI together with other "new international multilateral security mechanisms" promoted by the United States "as the leading authority in the institution of international organizations' regulations." "The new regulations advocated by the United States clash seriously with existing international guidelines, especially with the principles of national sovereignty. The backdrop of counter-terrorism affords these proposals with a degree of rationality, so the U.S. is pushing for them more than ever and an increasing amount of countries are joining."[123]

Perhaps because of such sensitivities, the purpose and procedures of CSI have been misrepresented. An Internet weekly affiliated with the Chinese Communist Party Central Committee's China Youth League, for instance, has claimed that "to a host country, experienced special agents and intelligence experts coming from the United States stationed in its ports are . . . of potential threat. . . . No one can guarantee that they will not 'hunt rabbits while cutting grass' [搂草打兔子] when they are engaged in collecting anti-terrorism intelligence."[124] But unarmed and lacking arrest powers, foreign officers stationed in host country ports conduct themselves strictly in accordance with CSI guidelines and bilateral agreements, with local law being the deciding factor. Because these personnel are essentially law enforcement officials, and not military officials, they can more easily share relevant information, which is related strictly to law enforcement activities. In fact, in multiple rounds of consultation, the Chinese team reportedly negotiated vigorously to make sure that the agreement was advantageous for China. According to one source, by following the basic principle of "putting ourselves first, turning it to our advantage, dealing with them cleverly, and submitting to the overall interests," [以我为主, 为我所用, 巧妙周旋, 服从大局] China appropriately controlled the progress of negotiations and consultations and managed to obtain some results that were favorable to us. This was somewhat different from the "declarations of principles" signed by other countries, which were roughly the same in content and contained broad principles. On some rather sensitive issues, China consistently refrained from committing itself too easily, leaving room for future in-depth consultations. These issues included the diplomatic immunity for members of the U.S. CSI teams stationed in China.[125]

It has been reported, moreover, that the "declaration of principles" negotiated by the United States and China for CSI implementation specifies that "neither party may access the other party's customs computer system or database and any data required by either party shall be provided in accordance with the scope and method agreed between the two parties. More importantly, the data provided by either party to the other party may not be used for any purpose other than those expressly specified in the latter's request."[126] Specifically, the "declaration of principles," Article 1, annex, states that

> the U.S. side must respect the sovereignty of China. Any personnel sent by the U.S. CBP to the Chinese ports for the purpose of implementing the CSI must strictly abide by the pertinent laws and regulations of China and the pertinent provisions of its customs and other departments and work under the framework of the bilateral CSI arrangements. These personnel deployed by the United States shall not perform any enforcement acts and, therefore, may not carry weapons and have no right to detain either cargo or personnel.[127]

Moreover, China does not allow U.S. technicians direct access to its ports. (Chinese inspectors offer X-ray images to U.S. counterparts, who can then request a more thorough examination by the Chinese.) While reciprocal inspection ability is offered under CSI, China has reportedly not requested it thus far.[128]

A related possibility is that Chinese policymakers believe that their nation's own growing network of port security regulations and domestic discussion of related issues already provides sufficient safeguards.[129] On a similar note, some Western scholars interpret recent U.S. efforts to enhance such nonproliferation regimes as CSI as a fundamental reformulation of the process of development of international law of the sea from "multilateral, negotiated consensus" to "cooperative unilateralism."[130]

Regulatory Burden

There are expenses and potential delays associated with complying with security regulations. The prevailing U.S. view is that these are the price of safeguarding international security, for which all nations are responsible, as well as the cost of access to the lucrative U.S. market. Representatives of U.S. factories based in China with whom the author spoke wished the system could be more flexible but did not feel that it unduly harmed their exports to the United States.[131] Technology- and trade-focused nations such as Singapore seem to share this view in many ways. It is the view of some observers in Asia, however, that there is a "widespread belief that the CSI is designed to serve U.S. interests by shifting the terrorism threat elsewhere. As it is a bilateral measure, the CSI is difficult to enforce, but the U.S. nonetheless applies subtle pressure on ports and shipowners by dictating that cargo from countries outside the initiative be subjected to more thorough checks, often leading to long delays in processing."[132] In response to concerns that cargo flow in participating ports would be reduced, China has apparently stipulated that cargo reinspection should not be requested unless substantial new information surfaces.[133]

One Chinese view (as expressed to author) is that container security is a U.S. Homeland Security issue. By this logic, the United States has more ability to afford security upgrades than does China and should therefore bear the cost.[134] A similar debate is taking place among the U.S. federal, state, and local governments as well as the maritime industry.[135] Presumably, there is a parallel debate in China. Here it is important to realize that costs of operation will ultimately be passed on to U.S. consumers regardless of which procedures are followed. On a related note, there have reportedly been disagreements concerning who should pay for various exchanges and who should attend them (specialists versus more senior bureaucrats with less involvement in the specific subject matter area).[136]

While it is understandable that nations will have different views and interests, one must ask where there is a more concrete basis (in both economic and national security terms) for bilateral and multilateral cooperation than in the field of container security. If the United States and China cannot achieve robust, broad-based cooperation here, where can they do so? It is hoped that, just as the United States tolerates large trade deficits with China (however grudgingly) in part because its consumers benefit from China's production of affordable consumer goods, China will continue to be proactive in increasing container security standards because it is in its own national interest to continue to export large amounts of goods to the U.S. market expeditiously.

Scanning Systems

A fourth challenge concerns national and commercial interests in different detection technologies and systems. The United States, China, and Europe each have major companies seeking to have their own technology selected for use. Within the United States, different companies are lobbying Congress to adopt their system. While this competition over commercial standards is likely to cause complications, it is important to note that China stands to benefit significantly from the sale of its scanning technology around the world as its private corporations increase container security in every region. China's state-owned Nuctech Co. Ltd. (威视股份), for instance, is a leader in scanning technology and already dominates Asian markets.[137]

Nuctech, which originated from Qinghua University, was founded in 1997. Nuctech has developed a wide variety of products, including a fast scan container/vehicle inspection system. It holds 90 percent of China's domestic market and has been selected to provide security scanners for China's 147 airports. It has exported more than 220 system sets to more than sixty countries and regions worldwide.[138] Nuctech's foreign clients include Australian Customs. In February 2006 "Nuctech's new X-ray scanners were installed in the Dublin port at a cost of €3 million ($4 million) to assist on the inspection of containers and commercial vehicles."[139] As part of a program to improve Suriname's port security and infrastructure, Nuctech set up a container scanner in its main port, Nieuwe Haven (Paramaribo), in January 2009.[140] Supported by a $3.2 million loan, this effort will speed the port's container processing.[141]

Hualixing Sci-Tech Development Co. Ltd., China (HLX), has also entered the global scanning market. In 2005 National Logistics Cell, the Pakistan army transport wing, received a five-year contract to be HLX's sole agent in Pakistan, with responsibility for sales promotion in the Middle East.[142] In 2006 China agreed to provide Cambodia with an HLX THSCAN mobile container scanning system.[143]

Port Infrastructure

Nations have different levels and ages of port infrastructure and consequent ability to implement scanning equipment and procedures at affordable cost. Smaller, older European ports, for example, tend to be at a disadvantage vis-à-vis their Asian counterparts, including some of the newest, largest in capacity yet relatively compact, and most efficient in the world.[144] This factor works in China's favor because China has some of Asia's foremost container ports and is rapidly upgrading related infrastructure.[145] In 2006, for instance, Beijing announced a $242 million plan to develop 28,000 km of railroads by 2020, which will help better service ports.[146]

New Requirements

Additional security regulations may be issued by such bodies as the U.S. Congress. An ambitious measure thus passed under the 9/11 Commission Act of 2007 mandating 100 percent scanning of containers before their arrival in U.S. ports now appears both politically and economically unrealistic, and implementation has already been postponed until at least July 2014 while the issue is studied further.[147]

Before 2001, 2–4 percent of containers entering the United States were physically inspected by U.S. Customs.[148] Currently, 86 percent of containers entering the United States come from CSI ports.[149] On 9 January 2007 U.S. House Resolution 1 (PL110-53) was passed by an overwhelming majority.[150] HR 1 amended the SAFE Ports Act to mandate a 100 percent container-scanning requirement by 2012.[151] Section 501 of the bill would "prohibit cargo shipping containers from entering the United States unless they have been sealed and scanned with imaging and radiation-detection equipment." Specifically, the U.S. Department of Homeland Security "would promulgate standards for scanning equipment and for container seals that could detect breaches in containers after they have been scanned. The new requirements would become effective within three years (for containers loaded in countries that originate more than 75,000 '20-foot equivalent' containers) and within five years (for countries originating a smaller volume of container shipping traffic)."[152]

This legislation built on Section 232 of the October 2006 Security and Accountability For Every Port (SAFE) Ports Act (Public Law 109-347), which "also requires DHS to ensure all containers have been scanned before they arrive in the United States . . . as soon as possible—and establishes several conditions for the scanning system, including the requirement that it does not significantly affect trade capacity and the flow of cargo at foreign or U.S. ports." From November 2007 to May 2009, the Department of Homeland Security ran a pilot program at three ports (in Southampton, United Kingdom; Puerto Cortés, Honduras; and Port Qasim, Pakistan) as well as a more limited feasibility study in South Korea, Singapore, and Oman. These programs were run under the Secure Freight Initiative, which had cost U.S. taxpayers $100 million as of December 2009.[153] They covered less than 1 percent of U.S.

container exports to the United States in 2005, yet no port achieved more than 86 percent scanning. Rain in Southampton and heat at Port Qasim rendered scanners dysfunctional on a regular basis.[154] In fiscal year 2007 alone, the U.S. departments of Homeland Security and Energy were projected to spend $60 million on radiation-detection and imaging equipment, additional personnel, and necessary computer systems and infrastructure for these programs.

According to the U.S. Congressional Budget Office (CBO), the Department of Homeland Security would have to spend $160 million from 2008–12 to meet H.R. 1's container security–related requirements, an increase over the gradually growing sum that it would otherwise spend. The CBO estimates that

> most of these amounts would be used to hire, equip, train, and support an additional 300 to 400 DHS employees in the United States and at foreign ports to review container scans and enforce the law's requirement that containers be sealed and scanned . . . much of the estimated funding would be used to develop guidelines and regulations . . . and to coordinate the development of sealing technology with private industry and foreign ports. Also, funds would be used to help foreign ports develop scanning systems and procedures and to develop software to be used by DHS to monitor scans and seal integrity.

Roughly $2 million would be spent at each of the largest foreign container ports serving the U.S. market "to review ship manifests, screen selected containers, inspect high-risk cargoes, and assist foreign ports with security measures." These estimates assume that

> the cost of acquiring, installing, and maintaining the systems necessary to comply with the act's requirements would be borne by foreign ports in order to maintain trade with the United States. Industry experts have estimated that up-front costs to acquire and deploy the necessary scanning and detection equipment for the [large] foreign ports that ship the vast majority of containers entering the United States would be about $1.5 billion over three years . . . [although] some larger ports may receive federal assistance such as that provided by the pilot program under Public Law 109-347, at an estimated cost of up to $10 million per port.

For estimated costs to the U.S. government associated with container scanning requirements associated with H.R. 1, see table 5.

Table 5. Hypothetical Budgetary Effects of H.R. 1, Scanning Containers in Foreign Ports Subcomponent

Fiscal Year, in Millions of Dollars

	2007	2008	2009	2010	2011	2012
Estimated authorization level	$10	$15	$30	$40	$45	$45
Estimated outlays	$2	$10	$25	$35	$45	$45

Source: "H.R. 1: Implementing the 9/11 Commission Recommendations Act of 2007, as passed by the House of Representatives on January 9, 2007," *Congressional Budget Office*, 2 February 2007, http://www.cbo.gov/ ftpdoc.cfm?index=7780&type=0&sequence=0.

As the CBO acknowledges, "imposing such a mandate could affect the efficiency of the international transportation system and thus have broad economic implications." This legislation, Homeland Security Secretary Janet Napolitano herself acknowledges, would impose $8 million in shipping costs for each of the 2,100 shipping lanes at the more than 700 ports that ship to the United States.[155]

In addition, the private sector would develop standardized seals that would then be used to secure containers prior to their shipment to the United States. While such seals are projected to cost approximately $30 to $45 per container, the overall expense is indicated by the fact that 10 million maritime containers were forecast to enter U.S. ports in 2010 alone.

Regardless of the exact details in practice, this departure from the previous doctrine of risk management may cause increased expenses, shipping delays, and foreign opposition. A key challenge is maintaining high container through-put if scanning of every container is required—a port the size of Hong Kong's processing three thousand boxes per day, for instance, would lose 750 hours, or 4.5 weeks, of productivity off of the current timetable, if it took 15 minutes to scan each box.

Another problem has been identified by the U.S. Government Accountability Office: at least some other nations would want to the United States to scan 100 percent of goods coming to their ports from the United States.[156] An American port security expert told the author that Singapore wanted precisely such reciprocity, and that he saw no evidence of U.S. congressional officials being attuned to this or prepared to address it.[157]

As this volume went to press, it seemed highly unlikely that 100 percent scanning would be funded sustainably or implemented. Given the likely reluctance of politicians to abandon anything that promises (at least on paper) to protect the United States from future terrorist attacks, the law seems unlikely to be reversed in the near future. Further extensions are possible. Eventually, however, the law may be subtly recast to make its implementation far more realistic. One source reportedly told *Fairplay* that the mandate to scan 100 percent of containers or "[physically inspect] with a technological device" will be replaced with a mandate to screen them, or engage in "non-physical analysis of a box's manifest."[158] Such an approach would seem far more realistic and grounded in security and commercial realities. We must accept that there is no such thing as absolute security and then work to reduce the risk of serious disasters, all the while keeping our efforts in the context of larger interests and priorities.

While these challenges are significant and will require substantial effort to mitigate, it is important to remember that CSI was never designed as a one-size-fits-all solution to address all maritime security concerns. Its strength lies in its specificity. While vital, it is merely one component of a broader array of complementary initiatives.

Conclusion

The Asia-Pacific region boasts increasing maritime commerce but faces growing unconventional security threats. A wide variety of bilateral and multilateral maritime security cooperation initiatives that recognize both the gravity of extant threats and the interests of those responsible nations involved (e.g., CSI and global maritime partnerships) can help provide a set of frameworks for collective security. CSI, in particular, has enjoyed great success thus far. It is important to consider how the CSI experience might be used to inform and strengthen other maritime security initiatives. Following are some of the lessons from CSI to date.

- Measures that allow for true reciprocity are more likely to be accepted.
- Linking robust economic and security interests appeals to the interest of many nations.
- Access to the U.S. market is highly valued regardless of the international political atmosphere.
- Incorporation of new technologies allows for new capabilities and new incentives.

- Despite these positive factors, implementation of effective security initiatives will still be complex, expensive, and time consuming.

- They must therefore be employed judiciously, with maximum effectiveness and efficiency in mind.

In addition to CSI's success thus far, there are other positive indications that analysts in China increasingly seek cooperative solutions to maritime security concerns. Establishing specific security measures, such as CSI, offers prospects for increasing trust, fostering goodwill, and enhancing maritime security in East Asia. The United States and China, as the world's largest developed and developing nations, respectively, as well as two major Pacific powers, have a critical role to play in this process. Effective bilateral communication in this regard will maximize prospects for positive results. According to Yang Mingjie, director of the Arms Control and Security Studies Division, China Institute of Contemporary International Relations,

> In view of the fact that counterterrorism will become the primary concern of U.S. national security in the coming period, and in the view of Americans counterterrorism and anti-proliferation are two sides of the same coin, counterterrorism and anti-proliferation will become two major contents of Sino-U.S. relations. On the counterterrorism issue, the United States hopes . . . that China will cooperate with its counterterrorism actions in a number of specific fields, especially in certain counterterrorism measures related to economic issues, such as . . . container security at ports. . . . Due to the changes in the international situation, China's status, and the international community's ardent strategic expectations of us, we will naturally consider things from new angles when analyzing the security environment confronting us.[159]

An analyst at the Chinese Academy of Social Sciences Asia-Pacific Institute assesses that "cooperation in nontraditional security fields" such as container security "can promote bilateral understanding and lay the foundation for higher-level cooperation."[160]

Beyond the specifics of bilateral cooperation, important questions need to be addressed by all Asia-Pacific maritime stakeholders in the future: How have nonstate threats combined to form a new challenge to international maritime commerce and security? What is the nature and level of the threat? Will the maritime realm be a continued target for terrorism? How will the national interests of regional states be safeguarded? Are the international responses and reforms accomplishing what they set out to do? Finally, what are the specific implications for East Asia? Each nation will have its own interests and priorities, but it will be important to reach a common understanding on these broader issues.

One issue that all parties can agree on already is that the multiple, complex security challenges that confront the region call for cooperative security measures that are no less sophisticated than the threats that they are designed to address. As former U.S. chief of naval operations (now Chairman of the Joint Chiefs of Staff) Admiral Michael Mullen has emphasized,

> Today's reality is that the security arrangements and paradigms of the past are no longer enough for the future. And today's challenges are too diverse to tackle alone and require more capability and resources than any single nation can deliver. Our level of cooperation and coordination must intensify in order to adapt to our shared challenges and constraints. We have no choice in this matter because . . . no nation today . . . can go it alone, especially in the maritime domain. There is no inherent conflict between a country's national interests in maritime security and the greater security of the global commons. They are mutually reinforcing and inextricably linked—they are two sides of the same coin in today's globalized world.[161]

Notes

The views expressed in this draft paper are solely those of the author as a private individual. This study is based only on publicly available sources and does not represent the official position or analysis of the U.S. Navy or any other organization of the U.S. government. The author thanks Peter Dutton; Lyle Goldstein; Captain Bernard Moreland, USCG; William Murray; Erik Tiemroth; Andrew Winner, and several anonymous interviewees for their invaluable insights. Lieutenant Commander Brendan Kettner, USCG, provided particularly detailed information and suggestions as well as permission to cite a valuable student paper that he wrote as a student at the U.S. Naval War College, "Port Security Status and Implementation in Chinese Ports," 30 May 2008.

1. Robert Block, "Security Gaps Already Plague Ports," *Wall Street Journal*, 23 February 2006, available at http://online.wsj.com.

2. Less than one month after 11 September 2001, an Egyptian al-Qaeda operative was apprehended while in a shipping container destined for Canada. He was equipped with a satellite phone, laptop, maps, and security badges for various airports, and had an airplane engine maintenance school certificate. Graham Allison, *Nuclear Terrorism: The Ultimate Preventable Catastrophe* (New York: Times Books, 2004), 110.

3. "A Cooperative Strategy for the 21st Century Seapower," U.S. Chief of Naval Operations and the Commandants of the U.S. Marine Corps and U.S. Coast Guard, 17 October 2007, http://www.navy.mil/maritime/MaritimeStrategy.pdf, 5. While statistics vary to some extent, at least 80 percent of world trade by volume is transported by sea. The percentage may differ with respect to value because airfreight can move small-sized, high-value, time-sensitive freight such as electronics.

4. Interview, Hong Kong, February 2008.

5. Carin Zissis, "Hills: U.S.-Chinese Relations Need 'Habits of Cooperation,'" *Council on Foreign Relations*, 10 April 2007, http://www.cfr.org/publication/13021/hills.html?brea dcrumb=%2Fbios%2F3373%2Fcarla_a_hills.

6. Wang Xiangwei, "China to Study U.S. Customs Plan," *South China Morning Post*, 19 July 2002, OSC# CPP20020719000105.

7. Congressional Budget Office (CBO), "The Economic Costs of Disruptions in Container Shipments," 29 March 2006, 1.

8. "Global Container Trade in Recovery Mode," *Emirates Business 24-7*, 24 March 2010, http://www.zawya.com/Story.cfm/sidZAWYA20100324044619.

9. "Trade," Container Shipping Information Service, previously available at http://www. shipsandboxes.com/eng/factsandfigures/didyouknow/?ParentID=1686012568.

10. A 20-foot equivalent unit is the standard container size, 20 feet long (6.09 meters), 8 feet wide (2.4 meters), and 8 feet 6 inches high (2.6 meters), set by the International Organization for Standardization (ISO). "Dry Cargo Containers," *World Shipping Council*, http://www.worldshipping.org/about-the-industry/containers/dry-cargo-containers.

11. "China Joins the U.S. in Container Security Initiative," U.S. Customs and Border Protection, 25 October 2002, http://www.cbp.gov/xp/cgov/newsroom/news_releases/archives/legacy/2002/102002/china_joins_csi_1025.xml.

12. "Hong Kong Trails Singapore in 2005 Container Volume," *Bloomberg*, 16 January 2006, available at http://www.bloomberg.com; UNCTAD, *Review of Maritime Transport 2006*, p. x, cited in Michael Grubb and Gabriel Collins, *A Comprehensive Survey of China's Dynamic Shipbuilding Industry: Commercial Development and Strategic Implications*, Naval War College *China Maritime Study* 1 (August 2008), 47.

13. The average container ship emits 40 times less carbon dioxide than a large cargo aircraft and more than 3 times less than a large truck, even though it carries far more freight. Shipping a given volume by container is 2.5 more times as energy efficient as by train and 7 times as energy efficient as by truck. "Low Environmental Impact," World Shipping Council, http://www.worldshipping.org/benefits-of-liner-shipping/low-envi ronmental-impact.

14. "Container Security Initiative Fact Sheet," U.S. Customs and Border Protection, 27 March 2008, http://www.cbp.gov/xp/cgov/newsroom/fact_sheets/trade_security/csi.xml.

15. CBO, "The Economic Costs," 1.

16. CBO, "H.R. 1: Implementing the 9/11 Commission Recommendations Act of 2007, as Passed by the House of Representatives on January 9, 2007," 2 February 2007, http://www.cbo.gov/ftpdoc.cfm?index=7780&type=0&sequence=0.

17. Ibid.

18. "Container Security Initiative 2006–2011 Strategic Plan," U.S. Customs and Border Patrol, Office of Policy and Planning and Office of International Affairs, Container Security Initiative Division, August 2006, http://www.cbp.gov/linkhandler/cgov/trade/cargo_security/csi/csi_strategic_plan.ctt/csi_strategic_plan.pdf, 5.

19. Of China's 2006 imports, 14.6 percent were from Japan, 11.3 percent from South Korea, and 7.5 percent from the United States. "China," *CIA World Factbook*, https://www.cia.gov/library/publications/the-world-factbook/geos/ch.html.

20. Denise Tsang and Toh Han Shih, "Mainland Records Strong Growth in Exports, Imports," *South China Morning Post*, 11 February 2010, 3.

21. "Coastal Take-off," *China Economic Review*, June 2008, 15.

22. *China Logistics Development Guide 2010—The State of the Industry* (Research and Markets, March 2010), http://www.researchandmarkets.com/reportinfo.asp?report_id=1208903&t=e&cat_id=.

23. "A New Maritime Strategy for Twenty-First-Century National Security: Final Report," Institute for Foreign Policy Analysis and International Security Studies Program of the Fletcher School, 2007, xii.

24. John F. Frittelli, "Port and Maritime Security: Background and Issues for Congress," Congressional Research Service, 27 May 2005, 3, 8.

25. Other estimates have produced rates of $1–2 billion per day. For official purposes, the U.S. government assumes a cost of $1 billion per day, with a 1 percent probability of occurrence, to estimate a "cost avoidance benefit of $9.4 million per year." See "Container Security Initiative 2006–2011 Strategic Plan," 31.

26. Frittelli, "Port and Maritime Security," 11.

27. CBO, "H.R. 1."

28. Interview, Hong Kong, February 2008.

29. Steven S. Cohen, "Economic Impact of a West Coast Dock Shutdown," Berkeley Roundtable on the International Economy, University of California, Berkeley, January 2002, 12.

30. "China," *CIA World Factbook*, https://www.cia.gov/library/publications/the-world-factbook/geos/ch.html.

31. Zhu Rongji, "Unify Thinking, Strengthen Leadership, and Swiftly and Sternly Crack Down on the Criminal Activities of Smuggling—Speech at the National Conference on the Work of Cracking Down on Smuggling," as published in *Qiushi* [*Seeking Truth*], no. 17 (1 September 1998); Xinhua, 31 August 1998, OSC# FTS19980902000993.

32. Feng Qing, "Shanghai and Shenzhen Join 'Antiterror Treaty' for Container Shipping," *Shiji Jingji Baodao*, 4 August 2003, OSC# CPP20030808000066.

33. Department of Homeland Security, "Container Security Initiative Ports," http://www.dhs.gov/xprevprot/programs/gc_1165872287564.shtm.

34. Lieutenant Commander Brendan Kettner, USCG, "Port Security Status and Implementation in Chinese Ports," unpublished paper, 30 May 2008, 12.

35. Russell Barling and Louis Beckerling, "HK Must Join U.S. Customs Plan," *South China Morning Post*, 10 September 2002, OSC# CPP20020910000064.

36. "China, U.S. Strengthen Anti-Terrorism Cooperation in Container Security," Xinhua, 29 July 2003, OSC# CPP20030729000135.

37. For Chinese analysis of how to minimize costs imposed by this rule, see 李沅涛 , 张维竞 [Li Yuantao and Zhang Weijing], School of Naval Architecture, Ocean and Civil Engineering, Shanghai Jiao Tong University, "美国集装箱安全倡议的装船实践" ["Practicing Loading under the U.S. Container Security Initiative"], 世界海运 [*World Shipping*], no. 2 (April 2005): 18–19, http://scholar.ilib.cn/A-sjhy200502008.html; 许路, 陈春峰 [Xu Lu and Chen Chunfeng], 美国海关24小时舱单申报规定剖析与应对方案 ["An Analysis of U.S. Customs' 24 Hour Manifest Report Provision and Plan of Response"], 集装箱化 [*Containerization*], no. 5 (2003): 32–33, 15.

38. Unless otherwise specified, information in this paragraph is derived from "CSI in Brief," U.S. Customs and Border Protection, 20 March 2008, http://www.cbp.gov/xp/cgov/trade/cargo_security/csi/csi_in_brief.xml.

39. Information in this paragraph derived from author's interview, Hong Kong, February 2008.

40. "World Port Ranking—2008," *American Association of Port Authorities*, http://aapa.files.cms-plus.com/Statistics/WORLD%20PORT%20RANKINGS%2020081.pdf.

41. COSCO Today Web site, http://www.cosco.com/45years/en/today1.htm.

42. See Andrew S. Erickson and Gabriel B. Collins, "China's Maritime Evolution: Military and Commercial Factors," *Pacific Focus* 22, no. 2 (Fall 2007): 47–75.

43. Yang Guoqiang and Liao Zhenyun, "Jiang Zemin Attends Informal Leaders' Meeting of the Asia Pacific Economic Cooperation Forum," Xinhua, 27 October 2002, OSC# CPP20021027000030; and "Jiang Zemin Calls China 'Victim' of Terrorism, Supports APEC Security Initiatives," Xinhua, 27 October 2002, OSC# CPP20021027000029.

44. Quoted in "China Joins the U.S. in Container Security Initiative."

45. Feng, "Shanghai and Shenzhen Join 'Antiterror Treaty.'"

46. "China Signs Declaration of Principles with Container Security Initiative to Target and Pre-Screen Cargo Destined for U.S.," U.S. Customs and Border Protection, 29 July 2003, http://www.cbp.gov/xp/cgov/newsroom/news_releases/archives/cbp_press_releases/072003/07292003.xml.

47. "Hong Kong to Scan U.S.-Bound Goods for Radiation as Part of Secure Freight Initiative," U.S. Customs and Border Protection, 27 July 2007, http://www.cbp.gov/xp/cgov/newsroom/news_releases/archives/2007_news_releases/072007/07272007_2.xml.

48. This represented 10 percent of overall containerized imports and 3 percent of total imports. CBO, "Economic Costs of Disruptions," 1.

49. Primary exports to the United States include electrical machinery and appliances, textiles, apparel, footwear, watches, clocks, toys, plastics, precious stones, and printed material. "Port at a Glance: Hong Kong (Modern Terminal)," U.S. Customs and Border Protection, October 2007. For Hong Kong's latest throughput statistics, see "Port and Maritime Statistics," Marine Department, Government of the Hong Kong Special Administrative Region, http://www.mardep.gov.hk/en/publication/portstat.html#1.

50. CBO, "Economic Costs of Disruptions," 1.

51. "Changing the Rules," *South China Morning Post*, 24 September 2002, OSC# CPP20020924000100.

52. "HK Shares APEC Goal to Fight Terrorism," Xinhua, 24 October 2002, OSC# CPP20021024000116.

53. "Xinhua Cites Robert Bonner's Comments on U.S.-HK Container Security Initiative," Xinhua, 1 August 2003, OSC# CPP20030801000169. For a similarly positive appraisal, see "U.S. Trade Official Visits HK Customs Department," Xinhua, 14 November 2003, OSC# CPP20031114000140; and "U.S. Diplomat Highlights Importance of HK Economy," Xinhua, 20 February 2003, OSC# CPP20030220000188.

54. Interview, Hong Kong, February 2008.

55. 张传龙 [Zhang Zhuanglong], "现代化港口及RFID的应用" ["Hong Kong's Modern Port and the Use of RFID"], 中国港口 [*China Ports*] 189, no. 3 (2008): 45–46.

56. "Port at a Glance: Hong Kong (Modern Terminal)."

57. "China Signs Declaration of Principles."

58. "Ministry of Foreign Affairs Spokesman Qin Gang Answers Journalists' Questions at Routine News Conference on 28 April," Ministry of Foreign Affairs of the People's Republic of China, 28 April 2005, available at http://www.fmprc.gov.cn, OSC# CPP20050428000166; and Liang Chao, "Terror Threat Spawns Co-Operation," *China Daily*, 28 April 2005, OSC# CPP20050428000015.

59. "China Implements Container Security Initiative at Port of Shanghai to Target and Pre-Screen Cargo Destined for U.S.," U.S. Customs and Border Protection, 28 April 2005, http://www.cbp.gov/xp/cgov/newsroom/news_releases/archives/2005_press_releases/042005/04282005.xml.

60. Choe, "Asian Ports Struggle"; "Firmly Take the Road of Scientific Development, Accelerate the Realization of the 'Four Firsts,' and Strive To Create a New Situation in Making Shanghai the 'Four Centers' and a Modern International Socialist Metropolis—Report at the Ninth Shanghai Municipal CPC Congress" delivered by Xi Jinping, secretary of the Shanghai Municipal CPC Committee on 24 May 2007, *Jiefang Ribao*, 30 May 2007, http://epaper.jfdaily.com/html/2007-05/30/content_25002351.htm, OSC# CPP20070530332008. "Shanghai Port by Numbers," *China Economic Review*, June 2008, p. 11. For an estimate that Shanghai surpassed Singapore in 2009 in terms of TEU throughput, see "The World's Record-Breaking Container Ports," *Ship Technology*, 28 January 2010, http://www.ship-technology.com/features/feature75321/.

61. 金志伟 [Jin Zhiwei], "提高上海港集装箱集疏运能力的建议和对策" ["Recommendations and Measures for Increasing the Dredging and Transport Capacity of the Port of Shanghai"], 中国港口 [*China Ports*] 185, no. 11 (2007): 25–27.

62. "上海港首次开通集装箱电子标签中美航线" ["The Port of Shanghai Initiates the First Container Radio Frequency Identification for the China-U.S. Route"], 中国港口 [*China Ports*] 189, no. 3 (2008): 47; and Beth Bacheldor, "Pilot Project Tracks Cargo from Shanghai to Savannah," *RFID Journal*, 12 June 2007, http://www.rfidjournal.com/article/articleview/3398/1/1/definitions_off.

63. 彭传圣 [Peng Zhuansheng], 交通部水运科学研究院 [Ministry of Communications Water Transport Science Research Office], "上海与香港和国外大型集装箱码头生产率比较" ["A Comparison of the Throughput of Large-Scale Container Ports in Shanghai, Hong Kong, and Overseas"], 中国港口 [*China Ports*] 187, no. 1 (2008): 29.

64. Interview, Hong Kong, January 2008. Other Port of Shenzhen facilities include Mawan, Dongjiaotou, Fuyong, Xiadong, Shayuchong, and Neihe. "Brief Introduction of Shenzhen Port," Shenzhen Port Web site, http://www.szport.net/. It was unclear from interviews and the Port of Shenzhen Web site whether the smaller facilities (which may not serve international shipping) were within CSI.

65. "Container Security Initiative Port of Shenzhen, China, Is Operational: Port of Shenzhen Will Target and Pre-Screen Cargo Destined for U.S.," U.S. Customs and Border Protection, 24 June 2005, http://www.cbp.gov/xp/cgov/newsroom/news_releases/archives/2005_press_releases/062005/06242005.xml.

66. See, for instance, 吴文一 [Wu Wenyi], "集装箱安全倡议 (CSI) 对货运行业的影响及应对策略" ["The Impact of CSI on the Cargo Transport Industry and Suggested Countermeasures"], 水运管理 [*Shipping Management*], no. 1 (2004): 13–14, http://scholar.ilib.cn/A-sygl200401005.html; 朱立志 [Zhu Lizhe], "中美贸易对集装箱运输的影响" ["The Impact of Trade between China and the U.S. on Container Transport"], 中国远洋航务 [*Maritime China*], no. 1 (2004), http://scholar.ilib.cn/A-zgyyhwgg200401031.html; 黄春杨, 徐海蓉 [Huang Chunyang and Xu Hairong], "美国'集装箱安全计划'及其最新进展" ["The Latest Evolution of the U.S. Container Security Initiative"], 世界海运 [*World Shipping*], no. 2 (2003), http://scholar.ilib.cn/A-sjhy200302010.html; 木谷 [Mu Gu], "中美之间的集装箱运输" ["Container Transport between China and the U.S."], 中国水运 [*China Water Transport*], no. 9 (2003), http://scholar.ilib.cn/A-zgsy200309004.html; and 廖一帆 [Liao Yifan], "美国CSI对我国集装箱运输影响初步评估及对策" ["Evaluation and Countermeasures Concerning the Impact of the U.S. CSI on China's Container Transport"], 水运管理 [*Shipping Management*], no. 1 (2003), http://scholar.ilib.cn/A-sygl200301004.html.

67. See, for example, 张丽娜 [Zhang Linuo], "海上反恐与国际海运安全制度的新发展" ["Maritime Anti-Terrorism and Recent Developments in the International Marine Transportation Security System"], 中国水运 (学术版) [*China Water Transport*], no. 1 (2007), http://scholar.ilib.cn/A-zgsy-xsb200701111.html; 王飞 [Wang Fei], "反恐时代的美国'港口安全'政策—信息革命下的安全对策" ["The Policies of U.S. 'Port Security' in the Age of Anti-Terrorism and Information Revolution Safety Measures"], 信息化建设 [*Informatization Construction*], no. 4 (2006), http://scholar.ilib.cn/A-xxhjs200406018.html; and 俞成国, 李大泽 [Yu Chengguo and Li Daze], "关于加强海上反恐保安措施的几点思考" ["Thoughts on Strengthening Maritime Security Counter-Terrorism Measures"], 中国航海 [*China Navigation*], no. 2 (2003).

68. 周卫 [Zhou Wei], "浙江省港口设施保安履行国际公约的措施和建议" ["Measures and Recommendations to Ensure Public Safety and Fulfill International Conventions at Port Facilities in Zhejiang Province"], 中国港口 [*China Ports*] 184, no. 10 (2007): 49–50; and 周火星 [Zhou Huoxing], 厦门港务控股集团有限公司 [Xiamen Port Affairs Stock Group Corporation], "浅析厦门港反偷渡工作" ["A Brief Analysis of Xiamen Harbor Anti-Stowaway Work"], 中国港口 [*China Ports*] 186, no. 12 (2007): 40–41.

69. See, for example, 远宣 [Yuan Xuan], "实施国际保安规则预防突发恐怖袭击中国海事局，中远集团举行超大油轮反恐演习" ["China's First Anti-terrorism Drill Involving an Oil Tanker with a Loading Capacity of 300,000 Tons—Launched Jointly by the China Maritime Safety Administration and COSCO"], 中国远洋航务 [*Maritime China*], no. 7 (2004), http://scholar.ilib.cn/A-zgyyhwgg200407005.html.

70. "中美"集装箱安全倡议"合作启动" ["Cooperation between the U.S. and China Begins on the Container Security Initiative"], 物流技术 [*Logistics Technology*], no. 5 (2005): 107.

71. "China Customs Promoting Trade Security, Facilitation," Xinhua, 14 May 2006, OSC# CPP20060514052006.

72. See, for example, Shen Xuhui, "Mystery of Kitty Hawk, Role of Hong Kong," *Yazhou Zhoukan [Asiaweek*], no. 48 (9 December 2007): 38, OSC# CPP20071205710012.

73. 吴燕子，朱云海 [Wu Yanzi and Zhu Yunhai], "聚焦海峡西岸集装箱运输" ["Focusing Container Transport on the West of the (Taiwan) Strait"], 中国港口 [*China Ports*] 187, no. 1 (2008): 33–34.

74. "Outlines of the Ninth Five-Year Plan for National Economic and Social Development and the Long-Term Target for the Year 2010 of the People's Republic of China," Adopted on 17 March 1996 by the Fourth Session of the Eighth National People's Congress, Xinhua, 18 March 1996, OSC# FTS19970417001884.

75. "Marine Freight Volume and Turnover Volume, 2005" and "International Standardized Containers Handled at Principal Seaports by Regions," in 国家海洋局 [State Oceanic Administration, ed.], 中国海洋统计年鉴2006 [*China Maritime Statistical Yearbook 2006*] (Beijing: 海洋出版社 [China Ocean Press], 2006), 127, 131; 侯丹伶 [Hou Danling], "把脉中国集装箱运输业发展—专访交通部水运科学研究院副院长兼总工程师费维军" ["The Future Development of China's Container Transport Industry—An Interview with Mr. Fei Weijun, Deputy Director-General and General Engineer of the Ministry of Communications' Scientific Institute for Waterborne Transport"], 中国海事 [*China Maritime*], no. 1 (2008): 18–20.

76. "Excerpts of Speeches at Theoretical Forum on 'Outreach' Open Strategy (1)," *Zhongguo Dangzheng Ganbu Luntan* [China Party and Government Official Forum], 6 June 2000, 11–25, OSC# CPP20000703000161.

77. "Government Work Report Delivered by Dai Xianglong at the First Session of the 14th Tianjin Municipal People's Congress on 18 January 2003," *Tianjin Ribao*, available at http://www.tianjindaily.com.cn, 27 January 2003, OSC# CPP20030128000052.

78. "What Is the ISPS Code?" International Maritime Organization, http://www.imo.org/Newsroom/mainframe.asp?topic_id=897#blacklist.

79. "Container Security Initiative Fact Sheet," U.S. Customs and Border Protection, 2 October 2007, www.cbp.gov/linkhandler/.../csi/csi_fact_sheet.../csi_fact_sheet.doc.

80. Ibid.; and "European Community and U.S Customs and Border Protection Adopt Measures to Strengthen Maritime Container Security," Background Note, http://ec.europa.eu/taxation_customs/resources/documents/IP_04_1360_Background_note_en.pdf.

81. "EU Welcomes Signature with U.S. of Agreement Expanding Customs Cooperation to Trade Security," News Release no. 56/04, 22 April 2004, http://www.eurunion.org/News/press/2004/20040056.htm.

82. See, for example, John Haveman, Ethan Jennings, Howard J. Shatz, and Greg C. Wright, "The Container Security Initiative and Ocean Container Threats," Public Policy Institute of California Working Paper No. 4, 2006, http://papers.ssrn.com/sol3/papers.cfm?abstract_id=889469#PaperDownload.

83. Kettner, "Port Security Status," 7–8.

84. "ISO/PAS 28000:2005," International Organization for Standardization, "Specification for Security Management Systems for the Supply Chain," http://www.iso.org/iso/catalogue_detail?csnumber=41921.

85. For discussion of applications to China, see 王敬涛 [Wang Jingtao], "加强国际危规培训，保障港口生产安全—山东省港口‘国际危规培训’须上一个新台阶" ["Strengthen International Danger Regulations Training, Ensure the Safety of Port Production—'International Danger Regulations Training' Must Reach a New Level in the Ports of Shandong Province"], 中国港口 [*China Ports*] 183, no. 9 (2007): 48.

86. As part of its Global Integrated Shipping Information System, the IMO's ISPS Code Database provides information concerning whether a given port has an approved port facility security plan. A specific measure with which container ships must comply is the Ship Security Alert System. This antipiracy and antiterrorism system notifies the flag state of a ship if it "is under threat or has been compromised" without giving any indication on board or alerting ships or coastal states in the vicinity. See "Guidance for the Ship Security Alert System (SSAS)," Commandant, U.S. Coast Guard, 1 March 2004, http://www.uscg.mil/directives/ci/3000-3999/CI_3120_3.pdf.

87. Moreover, while ISPS complements CSI, it is not a substitute: "For measures to be applied for container security, it is important to put in place the necessary measures for shippers and container packers to secure the 'real content' of containers. This area is beyond the scope of IMO and necessary measures have been under consideration at the World Customs Organization (WCO)." "What Is the ISPS Code?" International Maritime Organization, http://www.imo.org/Newsroom/mainframe.asp?topic_id=897#blacklist.

88. Kettner, "Port Security Status," 4.

89. "Port Facilities," available at the International Maritime Organization Web site, www.imo.org.

90. Kettner, "Port Security Status," 7.

91. For the latest port security advisory to date, see http://homeport.uscg.mil/cgi-bin/st/portal/uscg_docs/MyCG/Editorial/20080318/Port%20Security%20Advisory%20(3-08).pdf?id=3df04b27e046ef81e6ce85626a069dc3a1ee6bc2.

92. "Best Practice: Ship/Terminal Security Checklist," U.S. Coast Guard Homeport Web site, http://homeport.uscg.mil/cgi-bin/st/portal/uscg_docs/MyCG/Editorial/20070213/BP05-DF,%20Hong%20Kong,%20Ship-Terminal%20Security%20Checklist.pdf?id=4d6e5bebdb6fd9bcb968348d939326960d3de6eb.

93. Kettner, "Port Security Status," 10.

94. "Best Practice: Targeting Shipping Containers Suspected of Being Used for Human Smuggling," U.S. Coast Guard Homeport Web site, http://homeport.uscg.mil/cgi-bin/st/portal/uscg_docs/MyCG/Editorial/20080116/BP43%20-%20AC%20Suspicious%20Containers_2.pdf?id=aeb3bd2ff775a28c364a6a39c7fbe12153d495de.

95. "Best Practice: Electronic Gangway Gate," U.S. Coast Guard Homeport Web site, http://homeport.uscg.mil/cgi-bin/st/portal/uscg_docs/MyCG/Editorial/20080116/BP42%20-%20AC%20Electronic%20Gangway%20Gate_2.pdf?id=5bd83a5056c176c7f94f3b968b443c255ec7389b.

96. American Chamber of Commerce, People's Republic of China, "China, U.S. Finish Technical Talks on Mega-Port Initiative," http://www.amcham-china.org.cn/amcham/show/content.php?Id=2431&menuid=&submid=&PHPSESSID=cfd71f52bfb99; "U.S. and the People's Republic of China Cooperate on Detecting Illicit Shipments of Nuclear Material Will Help Thwart Attempts to Smuggle Material for Nuclear Weapons and 'Dirty Bombs,'" 22 November 2005, National Nuclear Security Administration Web site, http://nnsa.energy.gov/news/1180.htm; and "NNSA's Second Line of Defense Program," February 2010, NNSA Web site, http://www.nnsa.energy.gov/news/2299.htm.

97. "DHS and DOE Launch Secure Freight Initiative," 7 December 2006, U.S. Department of Homeland Security Web site, http://www.dhs.gov/xnews/releases/pr_1165520867989.shtm.

98. "Secure Freight Initiative," Department of Homeland Security Web site, http://www.dhs.gov/xprevprot/programs/gc_1166037389664.shtm#content.

99. Dannielle Blumenthal, "CBP Kicks off Secure Freight Initiative," *U.S. Customs and Border Protection Today*, April/May 2007, http://www.cbp.gov/xp/CustomsToday/2007/apr_may/secure.xml.

100. "The EXBS Program," U.S. Department of State Web site, http://www.state.gov/t/isn/ecc/c27911.htm.

101. "International Convention for the Suppression of Acts of Nuclear Terrorism," 13 April 2005, United Nations Web site, http://untreaty.un.org/cod/avl/ha/icsant/icsant.html.

102. Patricia McNerney, Principal Deputy Assistant Secretary, International Security and Nonproliferation, "China's Nonproliferation Practices," Statement before the U.S.-China Economic and Security Review Commission, Washington, D.C., 20 May 2008, http://merln.ndu.edu/archivepdf/china/State/105084.pdf.

103. Ibid.

104. These include the Federal Bureau of Investigation Countererrorism Watch, Transportation Security Administration, Federal Air Marshals, the U.S. Coast Guard, and the U.S. Food and Drug Administration's Prior Notice Center, which is charged with implementing the Public Health Security and Bioterrorism Preparedness and Response Act of 2002.

105. The following is an example of NTC operations: "As part of CSI, the NTC is participating in a prototype program with the government of New Zealand to target shipments prior to their lading. The shipment is examined in New Zealand using nonintrusive inspection technology. Using imaging software, the images of the examina-

tion are relayed to the NTC and personnel in New Zealand and at the NTC decide jointly if there are any anomalies." "National Targeting Center Keeps Terrorism at Bay," U.S. Customs and Border Protection Today (March 2005), http://www.cbp.gov/xp/CustomsToday/2005/March/ntc.xml.

106. Tier 2 status is contingent on meeting minimum security criteria; Tier 3 status, on exceeding minimum security criteria and adopting best practices. "C-TPAT Overview," U.S. Customs and Border Protection, 13 December 2007; and Frittelli, "Port and Maritime Security," ii.

107. "CBP Conducts Second Round of C-TPAT Validations in China—China, United States Cooperation Continues to Validate 15 C-TPAT Companies," U.S. Customs and Border Protection, 17 November 2008, http://www.cbp.gov/xp/cgov/newsroom/news_releases/archives/2008_news_releases/nov_2008/11172008_5.xml.

108. "DP World Invests 300 Million Dollars in Port Security," Xinhua, 20 October 2007, OSC# CPP20071020968098.

109. See, for instance, Bouko de Groot, "Recovery Rises in the East," Fairplay, 28 January 2010, 28–29; John Gallagher, "Cautious Optimism for U.S. Box Market," Fairplay, 28 January 2010, 14–15.

110. "China's Container Throughput Experienced a Substantial Growth," Transport Weekly, 8 March 2010, http://www.transportweekly.com/pages/en/news/articles/69923/; "Box/Supply Demand Gap Narrowing," Fairplay, 4 March 2010, 9; Toh Han Shih, "Shanghai, Shenzhen Ports End Year Well; Throughput Returns to Pre-Crisis Levels," South China Morning Post, 9 January 2010, 3.

111. Feng, "Shanghai and Shenzhen Join 'Antiterror Treaty,'" 108; and "100% Scanning Does Not Equate to 100% Security, According to Esteemed Port of Hamburg Executive," An Exclusive Interview with Dr. Jurgen Sorgenfrei, Chairman, Maritime & Border Security News, no. 7 (20 December 2007).

112. Stephen Flynn, America the Vulnerable: How Our Government Is Failing to Protect Us from Terrorism (New York: Harper Collins, 2004), 107.

113. Qiu Yongzheng, "If a Nuclear Bomb Is Put in a Container; China and USA to Send Special Agents," Qingnian Cankao [Elite Reference], 13 August 2003, OSC# CPP20030814000055.

114. Erin G. Lambie, "Container Security Initiative," U.S. Naval War College, 30 May 2007, unpublished paper.

115. GAO Report to Congressional Requesters, "Container Security: A Flexible Staffing Model and Minimum Equipment Requirements Would Improve Overseas Targeting and Inspection Efforts," GAO-05-557, April 2005, 24–25, http://www.gao.gov/new.items/d05557.pdf.

116. Lambie, "Container Security Initiative," 10.

117. Paul W. Parfomak and John Frittelli, "Maritime Security: Potential Terrorist Attacks and Protection Priorities," Congressional Research Service, 9 January 2007, 18–19.

118. Lambie, "Container Security Initiative," 13.

119. Allison, Nuclear Terrorism, 116.

120. Columbian vice admiral Edgar Cely is concerned that FARC guerillas "could use the craft to transport arms and explosives in an attack on a port," and has been quoted as saying, "Anything could be aboard those things." Hugh Bronstein, "Colombian Smugglers Take Cocaine under the Waves," 26 June 2003, http://www.reuters.com/articlePrint?articleId=USN17363654.

121. Interviews, Hong Kong, February 2008.

122. "The Impact and Effect of Terrorism and the War against Terror," chapter 3, in *Guoji Zhanlue yu Anquan Xingshi Pinggu 2004–2005 [Review of the International Strategic and Security Situation, 2004–2005]* (Beijing: Shishi Chubanshe, 2005), OSC# CPP20070110320003.

123. Qiu, "If a Nuclear Bomb."

124. Feng, "Shanghai and Shenzhen Join 'Antiterror Treaty.'"

125. Ibid.

126. Ibid.

127. Interview, Guangzhou, December 2006.

128. See, for example, "海上交通安全" ["Maritime Transportation Security"], in 中国海洋年鉴2007 [*China Ocean Yearbook 2007*], 中国海洋年鉴编纂委员会 [ed. China Ocean Yearbook Compilation Committee] (Beijing: 海洋出版社 [China Ocean Press], 2007), 184–88; and 沈跃, 胡铁军 [Shen Yue and Hu Tiejun], "港口应构建安全防护体系" ["Ports Must Construct and Build Security Protection Systems"], 中国港口 [*China Ports*] 183, no. 9 (2007): 49–50.

129. For details on Chinese port security regulations, see Kevin Cullinane and Teng-Fei Wang, "Port Governance in China," in Mary R. Brooks and Kevin Cullinane, eds., *Devolution, Port Governance and Port Performance*, Vol. 17, Research in Transportation Economics Series (Stamford, CT: JAI Press, 2007), 331–356; Wen Jie Wang et al., "RFID Implementation Issues in China: Shanghai Port Case Study," *Journal of Internet Commerce*, 5, no. 4 (December 2006): 89–103; and James J. Wang et al., "Port Governance in China: A Review of Policies in an Era of Internationalizing Port Management Practices," *Transport Policy*, 11, no. 3 (July 2004): 237–50.

130. The author thanks Peter Dutton for this point. See Kerry L. Nankivell, "The Container and Proliferation Security Initiatives: A First Look," *CANAPS Bulletin* 41 (May 2004): 6; and David Rosenberg and Christopher Chung, "Maritime Security in the South China Sea: Coordinating Coastal and User State Priorities," *Ocean Development & International Law* 39 (2008): 51–68.

131. Interviews, Shanghai, April 2008.

132. Alan Boyd, "Asian Ports Still Open to Terror," *Asia Times Online,* 11 May 2007, http://www.atimes.com, OSC# CPP20070511715033.

133. Feng, "Shanghai and Shenzhen Join 'Antiterror Treaty.'"

134. Interview, Shanghai, July 2007.

135. Frittelli, "Port and Maritime Security," 15–16.

136. Interview, Guangzhou, December 2006.

137. John W. Miller, "New Shipping Law Makes Big Waves in Foreign Ports," *Wall Street Journal*, 25 October 2007; and "Nuctech Beefs up Security," *China Daily*, http://www.chinadaily.com.cn/en/doc/2003-12/18/content_291196.htm.

138. "同方威视技术股份有限公司" ["Nuctech Company Limited"], 中国港口 [*China Ports*] 184, no. 10 (2007): inset advertisement.

139. Shu-Ching Jean Chen, "China's First Son Keeps Low, Goes Global," *Forbes*, 13 December 2006, http://www.forbes.com/facesinthenews/2006/12/13/hu-haifeng-china-markets-equity-cx_jc_1213autofacescan02.html.

140. "Container Scanner Funded by China Officially Handed over to Suriname," Embassy of the People's Republic of China in Suriname, 16 January 2009, http://sr.china-embassy.org/eng/sbgxyw/t532584.htm.

141. "Suriname: Chinese Investments to Improve Port Security, Infrastructure," Bridgetown CMC (Caribbean Media Corporation), 27 December 2007, OSC# LAP20071227950002.

142. Ikram Hoti, "NLC Becomes Sole Agent for Chinese Anti-Smuggling Scanners," *The News*, 6 September 2005, OSC# SAP20050906000041.

143. "Full Text of Joint Communique between Chinese, Cambodian Governments," Xinhua, 8 April 2006, OSC# CPP20060408057007.

144. Miller, "New Shipping Law."

145. See, for example, 徐鹏 [Xu Peng], "加快发展天津港集装箱海铁联运的必要性和可行性" ["The Necessity and Feasibility of Accelerating Development of Tianjin Container Port Sea and Rail Transportation"], 中国港口 [*China Ports*] 186, no. 12 (December 2007): 19–21; 傅海威 [Fu Haiwei], "宁波港集装箱腹地拓展的现实与展望" ["The Current Situation and Outlook for the Regional Container Expansion of the Port of Ningbo"], 中国港口 [*China Ports*] 183, no. 9 (September 2007): 32–34; and 吕霞 [Lu Xia], "珠江港口群集装箱码头发展态势及对策" ["The Development Situation and Measures for Container Terminals in the Pearl River Port Cluster"], 中国港口 [*China Ports*] 183, no. 9 (September 2007): 31, 37.

146. "Taking a Toll—Logistics Firms Are Upbeat at the Prospect of a 'Super-Ministry' Cutting Away the Industry's Red Tape," *China Economic Review* (June 2008): 8.

147. R.G. Edmonson, "100 Percent Stalled," *Journal of Commerce*, 14 December 2009, http://www.safeports.org/news/100-percent-stalled.

148. Marc Thibault, "The Response of the U.S. Maritime Industry to the New Container Security Initiatives," *Transportation Journal* (Winter 2006): 2.

149. "Container Security Initiative Fact Sheet," 27 March 2008, 2, http://www.cbp.gov/xp/cgov/newsroom/fact_sheets/trade_security/csi.xml.

150. HR 1 passed by 371–40 (with 22 not voting) in the House of Representatives and by 85–8 (with 7 not voting) in the Senate. "Final Vote Results for Roll Call 757," U.S. House of Representatives, 2007, http://clerk.house.gov/evs/2007/roll757.xml; and "On the Conference Report (H.R. 1, Conference Report)," U.S. Senate Roll Call Votes 110th Congress—1st Session, U.S. Senate, http://www.senate.gov/legislative/LIS/roll_call_lists/roll_call_vote_cfm.cfm?congress=110&session=1&vote=00284.

151. "H.R.1: Implementing Recommendations of the 9/11 Commission Act of 2007 (Enrolled as Agreed to or Passed by Both House and Senate)," Library of Congress, http://frweb gate.access.gpo.gov/cgi-bin/getdoc.cgi?dbname=110_cong_bills&docid=f:h1enr.txt.pdf.

152. Unless otherwise specified, all data in this section are derived from "H.R. 1: Implementing the 9/11 Commission Recommendations Act of 2007, as passed by the House of Representatives on January 9, 2007," Congressional Budget Office, 2 February 2007, http://www.cbo.gov/ftpdoc.cfm?index=7780&type=0&sequence=0.

153. Greg Miller and John Gallagher, "U.S. Relents on 100% Scanning," *Fairplay*, 10 December 2009, 14.

154. Ibid., 15.

155. Mike Frassinelli, "N.J. Sen. Robert Menendez Urges Full Scan of Cargo Entering U.S. Ports," *Star-Ledger*, 4 March 2010, http://www.nj.com/news/index.ssf/2010/03/menen dez_pushing_for_full_scan.html.

156. "Supply Chain Security: Feasibility and Cost-Benefit Analysis Would Assist DHS and Congress in Assessing and Implementing the Requirement to Scan 100 Percent of U.S.-Bound Containers" (Washington, DC: U.S. Government Accountability Office, October 2009), http://www.gao.gov/new.items/d1012.pdf.

157. Interview, April 2010.

158. Greg Miller and John Gallagher, "U.S. Relents on 100% Scanning," *Fairplay*, 10 December 2009, 15.

159. Yang Mingjie, "Changes in the Environment Resulting from Stressing Antiterrorism," Paper presented at the third academic symposium of the Contemporary International Relations Experts Forum held 5 November 2002; "Assessing China's International Environment," 现代国际关系 [*Contemporary International Relations*], no. 11 (20 November 2002): 15–16, OSC# CPP20021206000161.

160. Cao Xiaoyang, "An Analysis of U.S.-China Security Cooperation," *Dangdai Yatai* [*Contemporary Asia-Pacific*] (15 July 2007): 55, OSC# CPP20070907329001. For a similar correlation, see Qiu Huafei, "The Development Trend in Sino-U.S. Strategic Relations in the New Century," *Shehui Kexue* (20 February 2006): 18–26, OSC# CPP20060314329001; Yu Donghui, "Before the Meeting between Chinese and U.S. Heads of State Is Held, Zhou Wenzhong Says the Common Interests of China and the United States Are Overriding," *Zhongguo Xinwen She* [*China News Service*] (2 September 2005), OSC# CPP20050902000030; Wang Baofu, "Feeling Secure— China and the United States Cooperating in Anti-Terrorism," *Beijing Review* (16 September 2004), OSC# CPP20040916000058; and Wang Faen, "Premier Wen Jiabao's Visit to the United States Will Promote Sino-U.S. Mutual Understanding and Trust— Interviewing PRC Ambassador to the United States Yang Jiechi," Xinhua, 6 December 2003, OSC# CPP20031206000065.

161. Michael Mullen, "Remarks as Delivered for the 17th International Seapower Symposium," Naval War College, Newport, RI, 21 September 2005, http://www.navy.mil/ navydata/cno/mullen/speeches/mullen050921.txt.

Paul J. Smith

China's Power Ascendancy and the Global Terrorism Burden
Opportunities for U.S.–China Cooperation

Introduction

On 18 October 2008, nine Chinese oil workers employed by the China National Petroleum Corporation (CNPC) were kidnapped in the Southern Kordofan state of Sudan. The kidnappers, believed to be members of a local militia, reportedly demanded a share of the region's oil profits. However, the kidnappers later told a Saudi Arabian newspaper that "we don't have any material demands. We want Chinese companies to leave the region immediately because they work with the government."[1] In a subsequent interview a militia spokesman reported that the organization had decided to kidnap Chinese workers because "China supports the Khartoum government militarily and helps it marginalize our region."[2]

In subsequent days, what had originally begun as a kidnapping incident quickly deteriorated into something much more tragic as news emerged that five of the nine Chinese being held had been killed by the kidnappers. Some media reports suggested that the Chinese were killed in the context of a botched rescue operation involving Sudanese security forces. There was also speculation—strongly denied by Chinese officials—that Chinese security forces had participated in the attempted rescue operation.[3] In the end, however, Chinese foreign minister Yang Jiechi noted that "it is one of the most serious killing cases of overseas Chinese workers in recent years and we are very shocked by it."[4] Later the Chinese foreign ministry expressed "strong indignation and condemnation for the inhumane terrorist deed" by kidnappers who had attacked the unarmed Chinese workers.[5]

Yet, as horrific as this case was, it mirrored a series of similar incidents that China has endured around the world as a result of the country's increased overseas presence and economic activism. As a rising economic and political power, China is recognizing that its heightened profile around the world is exposing it to potential violence generated by terrorists, criminals, and others seeking to pursue various political or economic agendas.

In recent years, Chinese-registered maritime vessels have been attacked by maritime pirates operating off the coast of Africa. This led to an unprecedented decision in December 2008 by the Chinese government to deploy naval vessels to that region, far beyond China's territorial waters. Similarly, rising terrorist or criminal violence directed at Chinese interests around the world is generating increased consternation in Beijing and may lead to a more vigorous Chinese response—including enhanced diplomatic and military measures—in the years and decades ahead.

China's Rise and Terrorist Violence

The rise of the People's Republic of China is considered one of the most important geopolitical events of the early twenty-first century. Deputy Secretary of State John Negroponte recently told a meeting of the U.S.-Asia Pacific Council that "China's rise is one of the major events of our time. It is a growing player in the international community, and we are encouraging China to play a responsible and constructive role."[6] Moreover, a recent report by the National Intelligence Council stated that "few countries are poised to have more impact on the world over the next 15–20 years than China. If current trends persist, by 2025 China will have the world's second largest economy and will be a leading military power."[7]

Yet, like many major powers before it, China has begun to realize that a rising and robust commercial and political profile in countries throughout the world sometimes carries a violent price tag. This lesson was especially apparent in February 2006 when the bodies of three Chinese engineers, who had been shot while on assignment in southwest Pakistan, were returned to China.

In a somber ceremony held in China, Vice Governor Wen Haiying stated that "the death of the Chinese engineers in the terrorist attack in Pakistan had [stirred] a wave of deep shock and grief among [the] 64 million people [of Anhui] Province."[8]

The attack highlighted several important facts regarding Sino-Pakistan relations. First, China—or Chinese state entities or private companies—has deployed hundreds of technicians, engineers, and other workers to Pakistan. Second, some of these workers had been threatened or attacked (and sometimes killed) by criminals, militants, or terrorists. Third, in light of the historically close relationship that has flourished between China and Pakistan, the attacks are viewed with increasing alarm. The culmination of attacks recently prompted Beijing to urge Pakistan to increase the safety of Chinese workers in the country.

But the attack was by no means isolated. In July 2007 a bus full of Chinese engineers was bombed in the southwestern province of Baluchistan. None of the Chinese was killed, although a number of police officers on detail to protect the Chinese were.[9] On 8 July 2007 three Chinese workers were shot dead in Peshawar. A year earlier, in February 2006, militants shot and killed three Chinese engineers in the town of Hub. In October 2004 two Chinese engineers were kidnapped, and in May 2004 three Chinese were killed in a car bomb attack.

China has also witnessed rising violence toward its citizens and companies in Africa. In April 2007 nine Chinese oil workers were killed in Ethiopia when militants associated with the Ogaden National Liberation Front launched a raid on an oil facility. In Zambia, where China has been blamed by local politicians for "exploitation" and transforming the country into a "dumping ground," Chinese shopkeepers were forced in 2006 to barricade their shops against gangs of looters in Zambia's capital, Lusaka.[10] In Nigeria five Chinese telecommunications workers were abducted in the Niger Delta by unidentified armed men believed to be linked to the Movement for the Emancipation of Niger Delta.[11] In Niger a Chinese uranium company executive was taken hostage. The executive, Zhang Guohua, was reportedly abducted by members of the local Tuareg tribe "who were upset at the company's policy of employing people from the capital rather than locals."[12]

In other parts of the world, too, China has witnessed rising violence directed toward its nationals or other economic interests. In Afghanistan eleven Chinese construction workers were killed when their construction site was raided by militants operating near Kunduz.[13] According to reports, the militants attacked a compound where the Chinese workers were sleeping and opened fire. In June 2005 a bus carrying Chinese nationals was attacked in northern Kyrgyzstan, although none of the bus occupants was killed. In still another case, a group of nineteen Chinese businessmen traveling from Bishkek to China in early 2003 was less fortunate; all nineteen were killed when their bus was attacked by "unidentified men armed with Kalashnikov assault rifles."[14] In June 2002 Chinese diplomat Wang Jianping, who worked at the Chinese embassy in Bishkek, was gunned down as he was riding in his car along a street in the Kyrgyz capital.

Overall, the rising violence directed at Chinese overseas has prompted at least one Chinese company, CNPC, to adopt new measures in an effort to mitigate the risks. In a recent forum with its employees, CNPC admitted that its "vast investments overseas have made it vulnerable to terrorist attacks."[15] In total, the company has projects in more than twenty-nine countries, and it provides engineering services in an additional forty-four countries.[16] Of these, the company has identified eighteen "high-risk" countries where the potential for militant attacks is significantly elevated. One measure being considered is to raise the number of local workers in its various projects, to as much as 90 percent of the workforce in certain high-risk locations.[17]

Domestically, China considers the Xinjiang Uighur Autonomous Region (XUAR), home to roughly 8 million non-Han Uighurs and other minorities, to be its gravest and most direct terrorism-related security challenge.[18] Beijing is particularly concerned with Xinjiang's Uighur population, which is ethnically Turkic and has diaspora linkages throughout Central Asia. On 5 July 2009 a major riot involving Uighurs and ethnic Han Chinese erupted on the streets of Xinjiang's regional capital, Urumqi, resulting in nearly two hundred deaths. Beijing responded with a massive security crackdown, including subsequent prosecutions of nearly two hundred individuals accused of instigating or participating in the violence. In February 2010 the Chinese government announced plans to recruit five thousand special police officers for Xinjiang in order to prevent any future riots. Overall, the July 2009 incident highlighted the persistently sensitive and precarious state of Han-Uighur relations in Xinjiang. It was likely a major factor in the near doubling of Xinjiang's public security budget in 2010 to $423 million.[19]

A small minority of Uighurs has engaged in violent attacks that can be properly characterized as terrorism on Chinese interests throughout the country. An instance of such violence occurred on 7 March 2008, when a China Southern Airlines jet took off from Urumqi (capital of the northwest XUAR) at about 10:35 a.m. and headed toward Beijing. About two hours later, the plane made an emergency landing in Lanzhou, capital of neighboring Gansu

Province. Investigators would later report that a nineteen-year-old female ethnic Uighur had attempted, with the assistance of a male collaborator, to set fire
to the airplane while in flight. The airline's crew was able to subdue the woman
in a timely manner. The Chinese government later characterized the attempted
attack as "organized and premeditated."[20]

Beijing also disclosed that it had disrupted similar plots emanating from
Xinjiang, some of which had been directed against the summer Olympic
Games and others focused solely against Chinese government targets within
Xinjiang.[21] One of these occurred in early August 2008 when Xinjiang-based
militants attacked a division of police officers, in front of the Yijin Hotel in
the city of Kashgar, killing sixteen of the police officers and injuring sixteen
others. The attackers not only reportedly threw homemade explosives but also
"hacked the policemen with knives."[22] In another attack on 10 August 2008, a
group of fifteen militants (including a fifteen-year-old girl) attacked a police
station in Kuqa county, Xinjiang, by crashing an explosives-laden vehicle into
it; one person was killed and five were injured. Police shot eight of the suspects and captured two others, and another two of the militants blew themselves up.[23] Two days later, attackers leaped from a vehicle and stabbed civilian
guards at a roadside checkpoint in Yamanya town (near Kashgar), resulting in
three deaths.[24]

Beijing has long associated unrest within Xinjiang with its campaign
against the "three evils," namely terrorism (恐怖主义), separatism (分裂主义),
and extremism (极端主义).[25] Among other things, Beijing has claimed that
there were "300 Uighurs in Afghanistan in late 2001 [a number later reduced
to 100] and that all Uighur separatists in Xinjiang were linked to al Qaeda."[26]
In January 2002 the Information Office of China's State Council issued a report
titled "East Turkistan Terrorist Forces Cannot Get Away with Impunity." The
report stated over a long period of time (particularly since the 1990s) "the 'East
Turkistan' forces inside and outside Chinese territory have planned and organized a series of violent incidents in the Xinjiang Uighur Autonomous Region
of China and some other countries."[27] The report asserted that from 1990 to
2001, East Turkistan terrorists inside and outside of China were responsible for
more than two hundred terrorist incidents in Xinjiang "resulting in the deaths
of 162 people of all ethnic groups, including grass-roots officials and religious
personnel, and injuries to more than 440 people."[28]

In addition, Beijing accused the East Turkestan Islamic Movement
(ETIM), in particular, of having ties with Osama bin Laden and the larger al-
Qaeda organization (including allegations that ETIM received funding and
training from al-Qaeda).[29] This charge was denied by the ETIM leader, Hasan

Mahsum, although he acknowledged (prior to his assassination by Pakistani security forces in December 2003) that some ETIM members had trained or fought with al-Qaeda forces in Afghanistan.[30] Beijing has blamed a number of attacks outside of China on East Turkistan militants, including the attack in Afghanistan that killed eleven Chinese workers and the attacks against Chinese engineers in Pakistan.

Great Power Status and the Terrorism Burden: Will the American Experience Apply to China?

Although China may view attacks against its interests with alarm, in many respects, such attacks can also be viewed as a reflection of China's growing power and international success. In other words, terrorists—whether domestic or international—may target Chinese interests because China increasingly matters on the world stage. Terrorists typically have limited means and expose themselves to significant risks; thus, their choice of target must be particularly meaningful or effective. "As purposeful activity, terrorism is the result of an organization's decision that it is a politically useful means to oppose a government."[31] Moreover, terrorism should be viewed as a tactic or strategy of compulsion: weaker nonstate actors seek to use terrorist tactics to compel a more powerful state to change or abandon its policies or objectives.[32] As practitioners of psychological warfare, terrorists seek to undermine their enemies' sense of peace, order, and stability.[33]

In some respects, China's experience may reflect that of the United States, particularly as the latter emerged as a global power in the early twentieth century. It could be argued, as has Randall Woods, that the United States was once a "third-rate power, considered to have little influence in the councils of the world."[34] However, the Spanish-American War (declared in 1898) and its aftermath marked the United States' arrival as a nascent global power. Moreover, with its emerging world power status, the United States also learned that global power prestige not only attracted the attention of other major powers but also of militants and terrorists who had alternative ideas about how the international system should be ordered.

In September 1901 the assassination of President William McKinley by Leon Czolgosz, a twenty-eight-year-old self-described anarchist, reminded Americans their country was not immune to the wave of anarchist terrorism that had swept across Europe and parts of the United States from the late nineteenth to the early twentieth century. That same month, an obscure militant group in Macedonia, the Internal Macedonian Revolutionary Organization, kidnapped Ellen M. Stone, an American Congregationalist missionary. During the six months of her captivity, Theodore Roosevelt's administration was forced to wrestle with complicated and uncharted issues related to the legal status of Americans kidnapped abroad, including whether the federal government should negotiate and whether a ransom should be paid, among other questions. Overall, the kidnapping of Miss Stone "introduced the United States to twentieth-century international terrorism and in so doing provided the Republic with one of its first lessons in the limitations of great power status."[35]

The "Miss Stone Affair" would be a portent of future terrorism to come, particularly as American economic and political power began to reach across the globe. Following World War II, American influence in the Middle East—and particularly Saudi Arabia—increased steadily, particularly as reliance on oil imports grew. In the 1950s "American capital became predominant in the oil industry, and the United States became the major guardian of Western strategic and political interests."[36] By the 1970s relations between the United States and Saudi Arabia were so close that European countries feared that separate deals between the two countries (and also the United States and Iran) "would give the United States a privileged position in the marketing of oil from those countries and, in a time of scarcity, ensure that its needs are met, if necessary, at the expense of Europe."[37]

As American involvement in the Middle East grew in the mid- to late twentieth century, American interests were increasingly targeted by discontented groups and individuals. By 1974 Arab militants were singling out American targets in the region—including banks, airlines, commercial firms, and embassies—for bombing or urban guerrilla attacks.[38] The 1979 Iranian revolution and the U.S. embassy hostage crisis in Tehran in the same year were historic turning points for anti-American violence and terrorism in the Middle East. As Barry Desker argues, Iran's successful establishment of a purist Islamic theocracy "inspired a new sense of confidence in the power of Islamic identity and the strength of Islam to mobilize the masses."[39] In addition, the Iran experience galvanized Saudi Arabia "to aggressively promote Wahabi beliefs in competition with Iran."[40]

On 29 September 1982 the United States deployed U.S. military forces to Lebanon as part of a multinational force composed of U.S., French, Italian, and ultimately, British forces.[41] A key purpose of the multinational force was to assist the Lebanese Armed Forces in establishing sovereignty over the Beirut area.[42] On 18 April 1983, however, militant Islamist forces bombed the U.S. embassy in Beirut. Six months later, on 23 October 1983, a large truck laden with more than twelve thousand pounds of TNT crashed through a perimeter of the multinational force compound at Beirut International Airport and struck the U.S. Marine Corps battalion landing team headquarters and detonated, killing 241 American service members.[43] U.S. officials, who had believed that American forces would be viewed by the local population as neutral and impartial, quickly realized that they were perceived as pro-Phalangist (referring to a largely Christian political party in Lebanon) and anti-Muslim.

In the 1990s militant Islamist groups targeted the United States because of its vast and intrusive influence over the Middle East, particularly in its core country (from an Islamic point of view), Saudi Arabia. The substantial American military buildup in Saudi Arabia prior to the first Gulf War (1990–91) greatly angered a number of religious militants, including Osama bin Laden, particularly after the U.S. military failed to withdraw completely from the country after the conclusion of the war. Perhaps as a result of this resentment, in November 1995 militants detonated a car bomb in Riyadh, Saudi Arabia, killing 7 individuals, including 5 U.S. military personnel. In June 1996 a fuel truck bomb exploded outside a U.S. Air Force facility (the Khobar Towers apartment complex) in Dhahran, Saudi Arabia, killing 19 U.S. military personnel. On 7 August 1998 terrorists associated with the Saudi Arabia–rooted al-Qaeda organization simultaneously bombed the U.S. embassies in Nairobi, Kenya, and Dar es Salaam, Tanzania, killing more than 260 people.

As the American experience has demonstrated, the ascendancy to great power status and worldwide influence has entailed significant terrorism burdens. Moreover, U.S. policies in the twentieth century (e.g., Vietnam War, pro-Israeli posture, stationing military forces in Saudi Arabia) have added to the "political oxygen" that has stimulated anti-American terrorism in Europe, the Middle East, Latin America and other regions. Since the late 1960s, the United States has been the "preferred target, the victim of approximately one-third of international terrorist attacks over the past 30 years."[44]

China's Terrorism Vulnerabilities and Responses

In contrast with the United States' experience, it might be reasonably argued that China's foray into the realm of great power status will evoke less terrorist violence. China's foreign policy and global reach are far less "transformational."[45] That is, Chinese leaders often claim that they are interested only in business or commercial relations, not the internal political circumstances or human rights conditions within the countries with which Chinese entities conduct business.

Moreover, many Chinese scholars and analysts attribute contemporary terrorism to American power and the various "contradictions" (矛盾) inherent in the practice of global politics, namely "power politics" (强权政治) and the power structure of the international system. Following the 9/11 attacks, a prominent scholar with the Chinese Institute of Contemporary International Relations stated: "Destructive anti-American terrorism is essentially a product of the American pursuit of power politics and the contradictions inherent within the processes of globalization."[46]

By contrast, the Chinese government has placed a great priority on cultivating "soft power" in Asia and throughout the world in an attempt to promote a benign image regarding its economic and political rise.[47] Speaking to a group at Moscow State Institute for International Relations, Chinese president Hu Jintao assured his audience that "though China will grow rich and strong in the future, it will never seek hegemony, it will never be expansionist, and it will always remain a staunch force protecting world peace and promoting development in common."[48] In addition, China has historically pursued a more pro-Arab stance in the Middle East; thus it is less likely to be tied to some of the anti-American (or anti-Israeli) sentiment that has underpinned terrorism directed at the United States.[49]

However, as comforting as this reasoning may be, there are certain limitations to this logic that must be considered. First, China's chief terrorism vulnerability, as for many great powers that preceded it, lies in its ability—within an increasingly globalized economy—to reach out and penetrate various states, many of which are insecure, weak, or plagued with various ethnic or governance challenges. A 2004 U.S. National Intelligence Council report described globalization—defined essentially as growing flows of commerce, trade, and people—as "an overarching 'mega-trend,' a force so ubiquitous that it will substantially shape all the other major trends in the world of 2020."[50] Yet, as the same report warned, globalization will have winners and those countries that are left behind. Moreover, those countries (and individuals) not benefiting from globalization will likely resent the circle of winners, of which China is likely to be part.

As China's economy grows and reaches across the globe—in some cases displacing local industries or stimulating layoffs of local workers—China is likely to emerge as the new and, in some cases, resented "face" of globalization. Displaced and vengeful workers in countries affected by Chinese economic penetration will view China as the economic culprit behind their woes. China's challenges may be particularly acute within developing countries in which Chinese infrastructure development, investment, trade, and resource acquisition have enriched urban elites while leaving the poor in the provinces behind. In addition, the rural poor may view Chinese investment actions as threatening to the cottage industries on which they depend for their livelihood and as damaging to the natural environment. From a strategic perspective, China will most likely be unable to hide from its dominant position in the globalization process. Thus, notwithstanding China's global "soft power" strategy, which is generally targeted toward national leaders and other elites, anti-Chinese sentiment may grow among nonstate actors (or among opposition political parties within various countries in which China is active) who are not beneficiaries of Chinese commercial activities or development.

Currently, China's global drive for energy supplies and other resources serves as a key underlying motive for an increased presence around the world. According to one assessment, the most significant influence on twenty-first-century global energy markets is likely to be the rise of two key players: China and India.[51] For its part, China is increasing its dependence on foreign oil, which has grown from 6.3 percent (of total oil consumption) in 1993 to 30 percent in 2000 and 46 percent in 2004; the trend is expected to continue.[52] Based on current projections, China's crude oil imports are expected to double by the year 2020.[53] Such dependence has driven Chinese companies, both state and private, to oil-rich countries throughout the world, some of which are socially volatile or politically unstable.

For example, China's drive for energy security has led to a much more profound economic and political presence in the Middle East, a source, ideologically and functionally, of much terrorist violence during the past century. The Middle East in general supplies 47 percent of the crude going to China. According to the International Energy Agency, China may consume the equivalent of Saudi Arabia's entire expected production of crude by 2015 if the current pace of Chinese economic growth continues.[54] Not surprisingly, Saudi–China relations are growing stronger. Upon assuming the throne, Saudi Arabian king Abdullah chose China to be the first country in which to conduct his first official state visit. Moreover, Saudi Arabia has become China's largest trading partner in the Middle East, with total two-way trade exceeding USD$40 billion in 2008.[55]

China's relationship with Iran is also strong and growing. The country is emerging as one of Beijing's top suppliers of crude oil. In December 2007 the Chinese firm Sinopec signed a $2 billion deal over Iran's Yadavaran oil field. The Chinese government made it clear that the deal was commercial in nature, signed under the "principle of equality and mutual benefit" and "should not invite the interference of the U.S. government."[56] China is also reaching out to Iraq. China and Iraq have recently engaged in negotiations on a $1.2 billion deal, originally signed in 1997 under the Saddam Hussein regime, to allow CNPC to develop the al-Ahdab oil field, which is estimated to hold oil reserves of 1 billion barrels.[57] More recently, CNPC also entered into two other major Iraqi oil deals: Rumaila (November 2009) and Halfaya (January 2010).[58]

As commercial interests grow between Beijing and Middle Eastern countries, it will most likely lead to a greater Chinese commercial (and potentially military) presence, thus attracting the attention of terrorist organizations. First, if Beijing is seen as favoring key factions or elements within countries (such as in the fractured Iraqi state), it could lead to dissatisfaction among groups or factions who feel left out, which could then manifest in violence.

Moreover, China could also become susceptible to charges or themes that al-Qaeda has leveled against the United States and other oil-consuming countries. For example, Osama bin Laden has urged Arab governments to preserve oil as "a great and important economic power for the coming Islamic state."[59] Al-Qaeda often speaks of Middle Eastern oil as having been "stolen" and, directing its wrath toward Middle Eastern regimes, exhorts its followers "to not allow the thieves ruling [Muslim] countries to control this oil."[60] Finally, China could find itself increasingly at odds with one of al-Qaeda's most persistent grievances: pervasive foreign presence and influence within the Middle East. A recent U.S. congressional study summarized al-Qaeda's (and affiliated groups') strategic goals as relating to two key themes: expelling foreign forces and influences from Islamic societies and establishing an Islamic state governed by Sharia law.[61]

China's Vulnerability Outside of the Middle East

In addition to the Middle East, China is also potentially exposed to terrorist violence through its increased involvement in Africa, a continent that remains a key focus in Beijing's energy and natural resource acquisition activities. Africa's natural wealth makes the continent "an inviting target for the attentions of the People's Republic of China, whose dynamic economy . . . has an almost insatiable thirst for oil."[62] Angola, for example, constitutes China's third-largest source of crude.[63] Other countries, such as Sudan and Nigeria, offer significant opportunities for Beijing to satisfy (or at least diversify) its growing energy demand.

Nevertheless, China's increasing energy- and natural resource–driven involvement in Africa could have manifold consequences for terrorism or criminal violence, particularly as the scale of mutual trade and investment grows in the years and decades ahead. Although it would be too simplistic to assert that increased economic activity between China and African countries necessarily and automatically translates into increased terrorist violence, it does increase China's vulnerability. Reflecting what appears to be a wave of growing suspicion directed at Beijing, one African business analyst writing for a major African wire service noted that "this wild Dragon [China] has tasted and discovered that Africa is really sumptuous. . . . Enter the Dragon—the latest colonial master—ravaging Africa from Sudan through Nigeria to Angola, trailing the aroma of oil."[64]

In African countries with weak, factionalized government structures, China's practice of favoring certain dominant parties or factions within governments may result in dissatisfaction by out-of-power groups (political parties or private individuals) who may feel excluded or marginalized by such arrangements. Such groups or individuals may express their anger by resorting to political violence. Similarly, China's practice of shipping arms to client states—most recently Zimbabwe in 2008—may lead to anti-Chinese sentiment, particularly among those groups against which these arms may be used.

Another area of the world that may expose China to terrorist violence is Central Asia, a region of the world known for its abundant energy supplies. Following the end of the Cold War, China has increasingly viewed Central Asia within the prism of its "western development strategy" ("西部大开发战略") China has launched a number of ambitious pipeline projects in Central Asia to diversify both the sourcing and importation of oil and gas supplies. Beijing has shown particular interest in Kazakhstan, with which it shares a 1,533-km-long border and from which it already receives its oil through a long 1,200-km pipeline.[65] In January 2010 CNPC announced that the Sino-Kazakh crude oil pipeline had delivered 20.39 million tons of crude oil since it started operations in July 2006.[66] Most recently, major Chinese and Uzbek energy firms established a joint venture to build a gas pipeline between Uzbekistan and China.[67] In Kyrgyzstan, Chinese companies are exploring potential oil and natural gas sources in the southern part of the country.[68]

Pipelines connecting Central Asian states to China may traverse areas with known or suspected terrorist threats, potentially rendering Beijing vulnerable to terrorist or criminal violence in this region. Central Asia hosts a number of extremist or terrorist organizations that operate in Uzbekistan, Kazakhstan, Kyrgyzstan, and Tajikistan, although the threat level varies according to the country (and even regions within countries). For example, some countries, such as Kazakhstan, have a relatively mild threat while other countries (Uzbekistan, Kyrgyzstan, and Tajikistan, for example) are far more vulnerable.

Central Asia is particularly important to China because of its cultural and geographic connections to Xinjiang (Xinjiang Uighur Autonomous Region, XUAR). The XUAR has been home to various branches of Turkic people, including Uzbeks, Tatars, Kyrgyz, Kazaks, and Uighurs, who have comprised "the single most numerous ethnic group in Xinjiang based on common Turkic ancestry and rich Uighur language."[69] One of Beijing's concerns has been that the rise of independent Central Asian states could revive or bolster separatist sentiment in Xinjiang. Indeed, some Chinese officials have feared that the establishment of Central Asian states may trigger among Muslims in Xinjiang a growing identification with their Pan-Turkic roots and their affiliation with the larger Islamic world.[70] Moreover, cross-border trade and migration between Xinjiang and Kazakhstan, Kyrgyzstan, Afghanistan, and Pakistan "has resulted in greater interaction among the Xinjiang people and their counterparts in Central Asia, Turkey, Pakistan and Saudi Arabia."[71]

Beijing depends on its influence with Central Asia—and particularly Kazakhstan and Kyrgyzstan—to manage Uighur separatism. "Both of these states have substantial Uighur minorities and Beijing is keen to prevent them from supporting the aspirations of the Uighurs in XUAR in any way."[72] However, Uighur dissatisfaction is probably motivated more by Beijing's policies rather than subversive activities among the Uighur diaspora. One source of friction is Uighur resentment of Beijing's policy of promoting Han immigration into Xinjiang.[73] In addition, there is a persistent economic gap between Uighurs and the majority Han population that sustains Uighur unease and dissatisfaction. Consequently, Uighurs maintain a strong perception that they are the underprivileged ethnic group in Xinjiang.[74]

In addition to ethnic persecution, Uighurs have long felt that Xinjiang is being exploited for Beijing's energy requirements. According to Gardner Bovingdon, "the mining and export of Xinjiang's oil and gas by an almost entirely Han workforce and according to Beijing's dictates instead of through explicit bargaining all increase Uighurs' sense that their region's resources are being expropriated."[75] Such sentiments will likely increase in the future as Xinjiang is increasingly used as an entry point for energy supplies (oil and natural gas) traversing Central Asia, via Xinjiang toward China's interior.

As in Central Asia, China is also exposed to potential terrorist violence in South Asia. This vulnerability is perhaps most acute in Pakistan, a country that hopes to become an energy and trade conduit that links China to important oil-exporting states in the Middle East. In a February 2006 interview, former president Pervez Musharraf stated: "We are interested in setting up a trade and energy corridor for China."[76] Pakistan views the development of Gwadar

Port as the key node linking African, Iranian, and other Middle Eastern oil to China via Pakistan's Karakoram Highway, which links Pakistan to China's Xinjiang Province.[77] Gwadar's primary purpose, according to one analyst, is to "build a direct thoroughfare to China over land, to connect China with oil-producing countries in the Middle East and Central Asia via Pakistan through a network of railways and highways."[78] However, Gwadar Port is located in Pakistan's restive western province of Baluchistan. Chinese construction activities in Gwadar have inflamed the low-grade insurgency in Baluchistan that has been directed against the Pakistani government since at least 2002. The displacement of local residents away from the port area, the influx of non-Baloch immigrants into the region, and the increased Pakistani army presence (associated with Gwadar port-building activities) have all inflamed what was already a relatively tense security environment.[79] As a result, Chinese personnel and other interests have been targeted, particularly as Balochi militants view the Islamabad-Beijing link as a critical but vulnerable lifeline for the Pakistani regime. In March 2010 Pakistan's prime minister, Syed Yusuf Raza Gilani, told visiting Chinese officials that he hoped their two countries could "fast track" infrastructure projects, including upgrading the Karakoram highway, and that his government would accord "highest priority" to the protection of Chinese workers engaged in these projects within Pakistan.[80]

The 9/11 Effect on Sino-American Relations

On 11 September 2001, the United States suffered an unprecedented terrorist attack that killed more than three thousand individuals and caused more than $500 billion in destruction. It was an attack, moreover, that led to a substantial reordering of U.S. foreign and domestic policies. Almost immediately after the attack, Chinese leaders offered support and condolences to the United States and expressed a willingness to cooperate in Washington's international campaign against terrorism. This was remarkable since relations between the two countries had been somewhat tense and unfriendly until that point. China's goodwill toward the United States was reciprocated by American leaders. At an Asia Pacific Economic Cooperation forum meeting held in Shanghai in October 2001, President Bush referred to China as a "great power" that had stood "side by side with the American people."[81] China quickly repositioned some of its policies to coincide with American counterterrorism objectives.

For Beijing, the fight against terrorism was an ongoing challenge that was rooted in the persistent extremist threat associated with the restive northwestern XUAR. Since 1996, China had confronted a rising challenge of extremist or separatist violence emanating from that part of the country. Moreover, the year 1996 was also significant in that the "Shanghai Five"—which would eventually evolve into today's Shanghai Cooperation Organization (SCO)—held its first meeting. The SCO would provide an important instrumental (and psychological) framework on which future transregional military cooperation would be based.

Although not the sole purpose of the SCO, counterterrorism has played a major—if not the primary—rationale for the organization's continued evolution. At its inaugural meeting in June 2001 in Shanghai, SCO members signed the Shanghai Convention on Combating Terrorism, Separatism and Extremism.[82] The convention, known in Chinese as "打击恐怖主义, 极端主义, 分裂主义上海公约," states that the six signatory parties are "firmly convinced that terrorism, separatism and extremism . . . cannot be justified under any circumstances, and that the perpetrators of such acts should be prosecuted under the law."[83] Moreover, Beijing has strongly pushed the counterterrorism agenda in light of internal challenges (e.g., in Xinjiang) and was instrumental in the creation of a new counterterrorism center—the Regional Anti-Terrorist Structure—that was originally planned to be located in Bishkek, Kyrgyzstan, but later was moved to Tashkent, Uzbekistan.

From a strategic perspective, the SCO has evolved into a mechanism for greater political integration among participant states to counter the threat of terrorism and crime within participant states. In a recent assessment of the SCO, Russia's foreign ministry recently stated that "the themes of counteracting terrorism, extremism and transfrontier crime are firmly established in [the SCO's] agenda."[84] This was particularly apparent in the wake of the twin suicide bombings of the Moscow subway system in March 2010. In addition to stating that his government "resolutely condemns the terror attacks" in Moscow, Chinese foreign ministry spokesman Qing Gang urged increased cooperation against the "three evils" [terrorism, separatism, and extremism] within the context of the SCO.[85]

Moreover, the SCO has provided a framework on which a number of counterterrorism-themed military exercises have been based. In 2007 SCO members held their first joint military exercise (involving all members) in Russia—known as Peace Mission 2007—which was directed against terrorism (this followed a similar exercise in 2005). After this exercise, the SCO secretary-general, Bolat Nurgaliyev, announced that this SCO would be holding regular antiterror exercises.[86] In July 2009, roughly 2,600 Chinese and Russian troops participated in "Peace Mission 2009," which once again was organized around an antiterrorism theme. For China, the SCO has provided a mechanism through which it can develop its special force and expedition-ary capacity. In September 2006, for instance, China and Tajikistan held joint military exercises designed with terrorism in mind. China has held numerous counterterrorism military exercises with Pakistan as well. In December 2007, under the aegis of counterterrorism, China and India completed their first-ever counterterrorism exercise. The joint exercise was based on a fictional sce-nario in which an unnamed terrorist organization had established a base along the border between the two countries. Overall, the various military exercises have given Chinese security forces extensive experience in the types of military conflict that Chinese analysts believe are (and will remain) paramount in the twenty-first century, namely localized conflicts, terrorism, and transnational crime.[87]

A Convergence of Interests?

China and the United States, as fellow permanent members of the UN Security Council, have common interests in countering terrorism. Both countries are stakeholders and beneficiaries of the current international trading system, a system that would likely be devastated by another large-scale terrorist attack, particularly if it involved weapons of mass destruction (WMD).

In addition, the leaders of both countries have acknowledged publicly that China and the United States have an enduring interest in countering interna-tional terrorism. In 2003 a high-ranking Chinese foreign ministry official told a crowd in Los Angeles that the "Chinese people will stand firmly on the side of the American people in the war against terrorism because we understand China is also a victim of terrorism."[88] In addition, the official noted that, at various lev-els, China and the United States have cooperated on different aspects of terror-ism, including sharing intelligence and addressing terrorism finance.[89] Similarly, Vice President Dick Cheney echoed this cooperative spirit in 2004 when he told an audience at Shanghai's Fudan University that "since my country was attacked on September 11th, 2001, the United States and China have worked together to apprehend terrorists and to prevent them from killing more innocent people."[90] According to one Chinese writer, such cooperative spirit on both sides would seem to reflect the idea that great powers can often subdue traditional geopoliti-cal rivalries in the face of larger, common threats such as terrorism.[91]

Simultaneously, the United States and China have an interest in promot-ing or maintaining stability in various parts of the world, such as Central Asia, Africa, and South Asia, which are sometimes sources of terrorism and political violence. For instance, Chinese engagement in Africa may arrest certain countries' slide toward state weakness or failure. Similarly, China's engagement with Pakistan may also serve U.S. interests. Pakistan, China, and the United States have been engaged in a triangular relationship—with both congruent and divergent interests and objectives—since the 1960s. Pakistan played a major role in facilitating the opening of diplomatic relations between Washington and Beijing in the early 1970s.[92] Moreover, both Beijing and Washington have courted Pakistan for decades for various geopolitical reasons, offering financial aid, armaments, and a variety of security guarantees or reassurance.

Because Pakistan is currently viewed as a potential new base for al-Qaeda, from which it may seek to influence future developments in Afghanistan and elsewhere, the United States and China would seem to have common interests in strongly engaging with Islamabad to subdue any potential terrorism threat.[93] Moreover, Washington may discover that Beijing may actually have greater influence within Pakistan, which regularly proclaims China to be its most reliable partner. When President Asif Ali Zardari found that his country needed outside financial assistance in late 2008, he arranged a four-day trip to China to focus on "trade and economic ties."[94] Such partnership potentially gives China an effective foundation to urge Pakistan to reduce militancy and extremism (and its official support of the same). This is perhaps why India has sought, in the wake of the Mumbai attacks of November 2008, to leverage Chinese influence over Pakistan as a way of putting pressure on Islamabad to take measures "so that cross-border terrorism against India ends."[95]

However, terrorism (or counterterrorism) does not occur within a vacuum. It exists within and is shaped by the larger international political environment. Moreover, cooperation between states—particularly major powers—is shaped by larger geopolitical contexts. Chinese-American cooperation over terrorism, particularly in the long term, will depend on how the two powers manage their evolving relationship. Moreover, they will have to address certain differences in the way that each considers the problem of contemporary terrorism, including the question of whether counterterrorism campaigns should be waged primarily by military force or other means.[96]

One of these key differences lies in how each country perceives the "root cause" of contemporary terrorism. According to one perspective that can be found throughout China, al-Qaeda and aligned movements have been able to feed upon the political oxygen provided by anti-American sentiment (produced by unpopular U.S. policies), which can be found abundantly throughout the Middle East.[97] The U.S.-led war in Iraq (March 2003 to the present) has clearly added to this pervasive anti-American sentiment, according to some

Chinese analysts.[98] Although most individuals in this region, it can safely be argued, do not approve of al-Qaeda's methods, they nevertheless sympathize with the larger anti-American theme of Islamist terrorists. The persistent presence of anti-American sentiment in this region helps to explain "why Arab support for the war on terrorism has been relatively limited."[99]

In contrast to the Chinese view, the official American narrative regarding the causes of terrorism has traditionally focused on problems of governance, particularly the absence of democracy in certain parts of the world. For instance, the 2006 National Security Strategy linked terrorism to such problems as political alienation, grievances that can be blamed on others, subcultures of conspiracy (and misinformation) and ideologies that justify murder.[100] In addition, the administration of President Barack Obama believes that terrorism is rooted in extremist ideologies and propaganda, which can be defeated "in the battle of ideas by returning to an American foreign policy consistent with America's traditional values."[101]

Notwithstanding their occasional political differences, the United States and China clearly have more in common than not with regard to international terrorism. This perhaps explains why the United States was so keen on providing counterterrorism aid, technology, and assistance prior to and during the 2008 Olympic Games in Beijing.[102] In fact, FBI director Robert Mueller commented that he hoped that Sino-American counterterrorism cooperation would continue well past the Olympic Games.[103]

Political leaders in Washington and Beijing are recognizing that in a post-9/11 era, terrorism emerging anywhere in the international system is likely to have destructive effects throughout the globe. Moreover, both countries are acknowledging the value of cooperation, both on a bilateral as well as multilateral basis, in mitigating the threat of terrorism. In his July 2009 address to the U.S.–China Strategic and Economic Dialogue, President Barack Obama listed terrorism (among other transnational challenges) as a key area for U.S.–China cooperation: "Through continued intelligence-sharing, we can disrupt terrorist plots and dismantle terrorist networks," the president stated.[104] In addition, Deputy Assistant Secretary of State David Shear told U.S. congressional leaders in January 2010 that the United States regularly engages with its Chinese counterparts on the subject of terrorism "both at senior levels and at the working level through a counterterrorism working group."[105]

Clearly, both the United States and China seek to cultivate and maintain a stable and increasingly prosperous international system, not simply out of altruistic motivation but due to the fact that the economies of both countries are deeply embedded in a globalized international system. Each would suffer substantially in the event of a major terrorist attack—such as one conducted with WMD—which would almost invariably disrupt, at least temporarily, a substantial portion of the global economy. For this reason, U.S. officials welcomed Chinese president Hu Jintao's comments in April 2010, which clarified China's opposition to nuclear proliferation and nuclear terrorism and urged enhanced international cooperation to promote nuclear security.[106]

Conclusion

China's economic and political rise is one of the most significant geopolitical transitions of the early twenty-first century. With its rising economic and political clout, China is increasingly establishing a presence in almost every region of the world. However, like great powers before it, China is discovering that sometimes its presence may not be completely welcome. In certain extreme cases, China is reaping the violent side effects of its emerging great power status.

China's encounter with terrorism would appear, at least to some extent, to echo the experience of the United States, as the latter enjoyed the benefits and burdens associated with its rising political and military status. However, due to its unique economic circumstances and political history, China's experience will likely be markedly different.

Perhaps the more interesting and important question relates to the likelihood of viable and sustained U.S.–China cooperation against international terrorism. As major players and beneficiaries within an increasingly globalized international system, both the United States and China are ideally positioned to foster global security by cooperating against international terrorism. Such a cooperative posture would also be useful in mitigating other transnational or nontraditional security challenges, including international crime, climate change, proliferation of nuclear weapons, maritime piracy, and pandemics, among similar issues.[107] However, such cooperative spirit is also contingent on the ability of the two countries to prevent geopolitical antagonisms from undermining what would otherwise be a powerful bulwark against militant extremism and the instability that it promotes.

Notes

Special thanks to Andrew Erickson and Amy Chang for helpful comments and suggestions. I would like to acknowledge the generous financial support of the U.S. Naval War College Foundation's endowment to the John Nicholas Brown Chair of Counterterrorism, which funded research in China and Singapore. Portions of this essay are derived from a separate article, "China's Economic and Political Rise: Implications for Global Terrorism and U.S.-China Cooperation," *Studies in Conflict and Terrorism* 32, no. 7 (July 2009): 627–45.

1. "Sudan Kidnappers Want Chinese Oil Firms Out: Report," Agence France Presse, 24 October 2008.

2. "Sudan: Rebel Says Chinese Hostages Moved to Area Government Forces Cannot Reach," *BBC Monitoring Middle East-Political*, 26 October 2008.

3. "Sudanese Army Accused of Killing Chinese Hostages," *BBC Monitoring Middle East-Political*, 1 November 2008.

4. "China Urges Sudan to Ensure Safety of Chinese Personnel," Xinhua General News Service, 28 October 2008.

5. "China Condemns 'Inhumane Terrorist' Killings in Sudan," Agence France Presse, 28 October 2008.

6. Transcript of remarks by Deputy Secretary of State John Negroponte to the U.S.-Asia Pacific Council (as released by the U.S. State Department), Washington, DC, Federal News Service, 11 April 2008.

7. "Global Trends 2025: A Transformed World" (Washington, DC: National Intelligence Council, November 2008), 29.

8. "Shehzad Waseem Hands over Bodies of Chinese Engineers," *Balochistan Times*, 18 February 2006.

9. "Twelve Killed in Attack on Chinese Convoy in Pakistan," *BBC Monitoring International Reports*, 19 July 2007.

10. David Blair, "Rioters Attack Chinese after Zambian Poll," *The Daily Telegraph* (London), 3 October 2006, 17.

11. "Five Telecoms Workers Abducted in Niger Delta," *AFX-Asia*, 5 January 2007.

12. Scott McDonald, "China Says Uranium Executive Taken Hostage in Niger," The Associated Press, 9 July 2007.

13. "Afghanistan: 11 Chinese Dead on Building Site," *ANSA English Media Service*, 10 June 2004.

14. "Murderers of 19 Chinese Citizens Identified—Kyrgyz Interior Ministry," [AKI Press News Agency, Bishkek, in Russian 3 July 2003], *BBC Monitoring Central Asia Unit*, 3 July 2003.

15. Terry Wang, "China National Petroleum Corp. (CNPC) Will Employ a Greater Proportion of Local Workers," *China Energy Weekly*, 17 December 2008.

16. Ibid.

17. Ibid.

18. 罗海龙 [Luo Hailong], "恐怖主义对中国国家安全战略的影响" ["The Strategic and National Security Effects of Terrorism on China"], 石家庄铁道学院学报 (社会科学版) [*Journal of Shijiazhuang Railway Institute* (Social Sciences)], no. 6 (2008): 24.

19. Malcolm Moore, "China to Double Security in Xinjiang," *The Telegraph*, 14 January 2010, http://www.telegraph.co.uk/news/worldnews/asia/china/6988844/China-to-double-security-in-Xinjiang.html.

20. "China Focus: Suspect Confesses to Terrorist Attempt on China Flight," Xinhua Economic News Service, 27 March 2008.

21. "China Reveals It Has Foiled Two Terror Plots," *Straits Times* (Singapore), 10 March 2008.

22. "Xinjiang Terrorists Suspected in Deadly Attack against Chinese Policemen," *BBC Monitoring Asia Pacific-Political*, 4 August 2008.

23. Bill Savadore, "Uygur Bombers Included Teenage Girl, Authorities Say; 15-Year-Old among Group Linked to Attacks in Xinjiang," *South China Morning Post*, 12 August 2008, 6.

24. Audra Ang, "2 Chinese Policemen Killed, 7 Wounded in Xinjiang," Associated Press Worldstream, August 28, 2008.

25. June Teufel Dreyer, "China's Vulnerability to Minority Separatism," *Asian Affairs*, 38, no. 2 (Summer 2005): 69–85.

26. Gaye Christoffersen, "Constituting the Uighur in U.S.-China Relations: The Geopolitics of Identity Formation in the War on Terrorism," *Strategic Insight*, 2 September 2002.

27. "Full Text of 'East Turkistan' Terrorist Forces Cannot Get Away with Impunity," Xinhua General News Service, 21 January 2002.

28. Ibid.

29. 李健和 [Li Jianhe], 王存奎 [Wang Cunkui], 梅建明 [Mei Jianming], 马振超 [Ma Zhenchao], 翟金鹏 [Zhai Jinpeng], "当代恐怖主义的特征与发展趋势" ["The Character and New Tendency of Contemporary Terrorism"], 中国人民公安大学学报(社会科学版) [*Chinese People's Security University, Social Sciences Edition*], no. 3 (2008): 2–3.

30. Erik Eckholm, "China Muslim Group Planned Terror, U.S. Says," *New York Times*, 31 August 2002, A5.

31. Martha Crenshaw, "The Causes of Terrorism," *Comparative Politics* 13, no. 4 (July 1981): 385.

32. Martha Crenshaw, "Why America? The Globalization of Civil War," *Current History* 100, no. 650 (December 2001): 425.

33. Peter R. Neumann and M. L. R. Smith, "Strategic Terrorism: The Framework and Its Fallacies," *Journal of Strategic Studies* 28, no. 4 (August 2005): 576.

34. Randall B. Woods, "Terrorism in the Age of Roosevelt: The Miss Stone Affair, 1901–1902," *American Quarterly* 31, no. 4 (Autumn 1979): 478.

35. Ibid., 479.

36. Charles Issawi, "Oil and Middle East Politics," *Proceedings of the Academy of Political Science* 31, no. 2 (December 1973): 119.

37. Ibid.

38. Joseph Fitchett, "Terrorists Blast U.S. Mideast Sites," *Christian Science Monitor*, 20 December 1974, 1.

39. Barry Desker, "The Jemaah Islamiyah (JI) Phenomenon in Singapore," *Contemporary Southeast Asia* 25, no. 3 (2003): 491–92.

40. Ibid., 492.

41. "Report of the DOD Commission on Beirut International Airport Terrorist Act, October 23, 1983" (Washington DC: Department of Defense, 20 December 1983), 2–3.

42. Ibid.

43. Ibid.

44. Crenshaw, "Why America?" 425.

45. The U.S. State Department under the administration of President George W. Bush pursued a policy of "transformational diplomacy." See "Testimony of Howard J. Krongard, Inspector General, U.S. Department of State and Broadcasting Board of Governors, House Committee on Government Reform, Subcommittee on National Security, Emerging Threats and International Relations," 18 October 2005, http://oig.state.gov/documents/organization/55371.pdf.

46. 王在邦 [Wang Zaibang], "世界三大主要矛盾及其变化" ["Three Key Global Contradictions and Transformations"], 现代国际关系 [*Contemporary International Relations*], no. 9 (2006): 15–16.

47. Thomas Lum, Wayne Morrison, and Bruce Vaughn, "China's 'Soft Power' in Southeast Asia," *CRS Report for Congress* (Washington DC: Congressional Research Service, 4 January 2008), 1–10.

48. "Text of Hu Jintao's speech at Moscow State Institute for International Relations," *World News Connection*, 23 May 2003.

49. Nigel Disney, "China and the Middle East," *MERIP Reports*, no. 63 (December 1977): 3–18.

50. "Mapping the Global Future: Report of the National Intelligence Council's 2020 Project" (Pittsburgh, PA: U.S. Government Printing Office, December 2004), 10, http://www.foia.cia.gov/2020/2020.pdf.

51. Joseph A. Stanislaw, "变革中的能源格局: 21世纪的最大挑战" ["Key Transformations in Energy Structures: The Most Significant Challenge of the 21st Century"], 能源安全 [*Energy Security*], no. 7 (2008): 3.

52. Xu Yi-Chong, "China's Energy Security," *Australian Journal of International Affairs* 60, no. 2 (June 2006): 270.

53. Gabriel Collins, "China's Refining Expansion to Reshape Global Oil Trade," *Oil & Gas Journal*, 18 February 2008, 22.

54. "China Could Consume Saudi Arabian Oil Output by 2015: IEA," *Platts Oilgram News* 85, no. 218 (5 November 2007): 3.

55. "Saudis, China Agree to Boost Trade Despite Petrochemicals Dispute," *Oil Daily*, January 12, 2010.

56. "China Stands by Iran Deal," *International Oil Daily*, 13 December 2007.

57. "China-Iraq Renegotiating Al-Ahdad Oil Field," *Middle East and Africa Oil and Gas Insights*, 1 April 2008.

58. Victor Wang, "CNPC Wins New Iraqi Oil Contract," *China Energy Weekly*, 3 February 2010.

59. Christopher M. Blanchard, "CRS Report for Congress: Al Qaeda: Statements and Evolving Ideology," (Washington, DC: Congressional Research Service, 9 July 2007), 15.

60. Ibid.

61. Ibid.

62. "Testimony of Dr. J. Peter Pham, before the Committee on Foreign Relations, Subcommittee on Africa and Global Health," *Africa News*, 3 August 2007.

63. Winnie Lee, "Saudi Arabia is China's Top Crude Supplier," *Platts Oilgram Price Report* 85, no. 193 (5 October 2007): 8.

64. Adeniyi Ologunleko, "Nigeria; How Sincere Is China's Rapport with Country?" *Africa News*, 2 January 2009.

65. Gawdat Bahgat, "Central Asia and Energy Security," *Asian Affairs* 37, no. 1 (March 2006): 14.

66. Victor Wang, "Sino-Kazakh Pipeline Pumps 20.39 mln Tons of Oil," *China Energy Weekly*, 27 January 2010.

67. "Uzbekistan, China Team Up for Gas Pipeline Construction," *The Times of Central Asia*, 18 April 2008.

68. "Chinese Company Starts Prospecting for Oil, Gas in Kyrgyz South," [Text of report by Kyrgyz news agency Kabar], reported in *BBC Monitoring Central Asia Unit*, 11 January 2008.

69. Abanti Bhattacharya, "Conceptualising Uighur Separatism in Chinese Nationalism," *Strategic Analysis* 27, no. 3 (July–September 2003): 359.

70. Ibid., 372.

71. Ibid.

72. "Xinjiang," *Jane's Sentinel Security Assessment—China and Northeast Asia*, 20 April 2006.

73. Bhattacharya, "Conceptualising Uighur Separatism," 359.

74. Herbert S. Yee, "Ethnic Relations in Xinjiang: A Survey of Uighur-Han Relations in Urumqi," *Journal of Contemporary China* 12, no. 36 (August 2003): 444.

75. Gardner Bovingdon, *Autonomy in Xinjiang: Han Nationalist Imperatives and Uighur Discontent* (Washington, DC: East-West Center, 2004), 47.

76. Qin Jize, "Musharraf Offers Transit Facilities," *China Daily*, 22 February 2006, OSC# CPP20060222052003.

77. "Pakistan, China to Discuss Road Projects," *Lahore Daily Times*, 16 March 2006, OSC# SAP20060316037004.

78. Xie Yanjun and Ji Ge, "Open Sesame: Weighing Pros and Cons of 'Energy Corridor' between China and Pakistan," *21 Shiji Jingji Baodao* [*21st Century Economic Herald*], 24 February 2006, OSC# CPP20060303058012.

79. "Sino-Pakistan Port Ripples Surface Tension," *Jane's Foreign Report*, 29 March 2007.

80. "PM: Pakistan Welcomes Chinese Involvement in Gawadar, Says Gilani," Pakistan Newswire, 30 March 2010.

81. "Jiang and Bush Try for a Fresh Start," *Financial Times*, 20 October 2001, 5.

82. The original six SCO members (as of 2001) included the Republic of Kazakhstan, the People's Republic of China, the Kyrgyz Republic, the Russian Federation, the Republic of Tajikistan, and the Republic of Uzbekistan. For an understanding of the key rationale for the SCO, see 杨明杰 [Yang Mingjie], "推进反恐要超越冷战思维" ["Countering Terrorism Requires Overcoming the Cold War Mentality"], 现代国际关系 [*Contemporary International Relations*], no. 9 (2006): 19.

83. The full text of the Shanghai Convention on Combating Terrorism, Separatism and Extremism is available at http://english.scosummit2006.org/en_bjzl/2006-04/20/content_87.htm.

84. Statement of the Ministry of Foreign Affairs of the Russian Federation, "The Asia Pacific Dimension of Russian Foreign Policy: Unity of Bilateral Relations and Multilateral Diplomacy Asia-Pacific Region—Challenges and Opportunities," States News Service, 31 December 2008.

85. "China Condemns Moscow Bombings—Diplomat," *Russia and CIS Diplomatic Panorama*, 30 March 2010.

86. "Shanghai Group to Hold Regular Anti-Terror Drills," *BBC Monitoring Asia Pacific-Political*, 29 February 2008.

87. "Agency Reviews China's Joint Military Exercises in 2007," *BBC Monitoring International Reports*, 26 December 2007.

88. He Yafei, "China-United States Relations: Potential Foes or Partners," *Vital Speeches of the Day* 70, no. 2 (1 November 2003): 49.

89. Ibid.

90. "Remarks by Vice President Dick Cheney regarding U.S.-China Relations, Fudan University, Shanghai, People's Republic of China," Federal News Service, 15 April 2004.

91. Gong Yutao makes the point that the 9/11 incident and its aftermath created an international political environment that allowed Russia to tolerate (at least temporarily) U.S. military presence in Central Asia. See 宫玉涛 [Gong Yutao], "'9-11' 事件以来大国关系调整的特点" ["The Character of Changing Great Power Relationships since the '9-11' Incident"], 学术探索 [*Academic Exploration*], no. 4 (2008): 19.

92. William J. Barnds, "China's Relations with Pakistan: Durability amidst Discontinuity," *China Quarterly*, no. 63 (September 1975): 464.

93. Statement of Peter Bergen, Schwartz Senior Fellow, New America Foundation, Committee on House Select Intelligence, *CQ Congressional Testimony*, 9 April 2008.

94. "Zardari for Long Term Economic Cooperation with China," Pakistan Newswire, 23 October 2008.

95. "Chinese Foreign Minister Likely to Visit India Next Week-Agency," *BBC Monitoring South Asia-Political*, 3 January 2009.

96. 庞中英 [Pang Zhongying], "滥用反恐及其后果" ["The Consequences of Indiscriminate Counterterrorism"], 现代国际关系 [*Contemporary International Relations*], no. 9 (2006): 22.

97. Author's interviews in People's Republic of China, July 2007. See also 杨明杰 [Yang Mingjie], "恐怖主义根源探析" ["A Probing Analysis of the Sources of Terrorism"], 现代国际关系 [*Contemporary International Relations*], no. 1 (2002): 54–62.

98. 李伟 [Li Wei], "国际恐怖与反恐怖斗争的错位" ["International Terrorism and the Incorrect Approach to Fighting Terrorism"], 现代国际关系 [*Contemporary International Relations*], no. 9 (2006): 23–24.

99. Stephen Walt, "Beyond bin Laden: Reshaping U.S. Foreign Policy," *International Security* 26, no. 3 (Winter 2001–2): 60.

100. "The National Security Strategy of the United States" (Washington, DC: The White House, 2006), 10.

101. "The Agenda: Homeland Security," White House home page, http://www.whitehouse.gov/agenda/homeland_security/.

102. Bill Gertz, "U.S. to Lend Sensitive Security Gear; Fears Raised over China's Use of Equipment," *Washington Times*, 5 June 2008, A01.

103. Stephanie Ho, "VOA News: FBI Chief Impressed with Beijing Olympics Security," *US Fed News*, 30 January 2008.

104. "Remarks by President Barack Obama to the U.S.-China Strategic and Economic Dialogue," Ronald Reagan Building and International Trade Center, Washington, DC, 27 July 2009.

105. "Testimony of David Shear, Deputy Assistant Secretary of State for East Asian and Pacific Affairs, before the Hearing of the House Armed Services Committee, Subject: China—Recent Security Developments," Federal News Service, 13 January 2010.

106. "China Opposes Nuclear Proliferation, Nuclear Terrorism: President Hu," Xinhua General News Service, 2 April 2010.

107. Yang Mingjie, "Countering Terrorism," 21.

Lyle J. Goldstein

Improving Chinese Maritime Enforcement Capabilities

Challenges and Opportunities

IN AN AGE OF DELICATE MANEUVERING among the great powers, coast guards have taken a new leading role on the world stage. When Washington wanted to demonstrate conviction and bring supplies to beleaguered Georgia without escalating already simmering tensions around the Black Sea, the *Dallas*, a large U.S. Coast Guard cutter, was quickly dispatched. This trend has long been visible in Asia. Tokyo's most extensive use of deadly force in the post-war era was an action by the Japan coast guard against a North Korean surveillance vessel. More recently, a Japan coast guard cutter sank a Taiwan fishing vessel in a collision near the disputed Senkaku/Diaoyu islands in the East China Sea, prompting a relatively serious diplomatic incident. Meanwhile, these most powerful coast guards are spawning imitators. India, for example, announced a bold new purchase of long-range patrol aircraft for its coast guard in the fall of 2008. South Korea's improving coast guard, meanwhile, invited foreign reporters to tour in the vicinity of islands that are administered by South Korea but claimed by Japan, accompanying the visit with belligerent rhetoric.[1]

Against this background, but also given the wide consensus that the rise of China is one of the most important phenomena for international security in the twenty-first century, it is especially curious that almost nothing is known about the organization, capabilities, service culture, and prospects for China's coast guard. While the Japan coast guard has appropriately drawn the recent attention of scholars in the field, China's developments in this regard have been neglected despite ample available source material in Chinese.[2] Notably, a leading expert on China's "frontier defense" recently observed that his own work "examines only China's approach to securing its land borders. . . . Future research should study China's approach to maritime defense."[3] Of course, there has been considerable scholarly attention to Chinese naval development, and this is wholly appropriate.[4] Interest in Chinese naval development has grown even more intense since the unprecedented dispatch of a small Chinese naval task force to combat piracy in the Gulf of Aden during January 2009. Most studies of Chinese naval development previously tended to focus on off-shore and high-intensity combat scenarios, including submarine operations, amphibious operations, extended sea-lane defense, power projection, and nuclear deterrence. The widely noted 8 March 2009 incident involving the surveillance vessel USNS *Impeccable* and Chinese maritime enforcement vessels (alongside Chinese fishing boats) has also increased the salience of understanding China's nonmilitary maritime enforcement capabilities. Although new attention is now focused on the international piracy issue, coastal defense issues, especially questions related to so-called nontraditional security, have not been adequately explored in the Chinese maritime context. If Chinese perceptions with respect to coastal management and monitoring, port security, narcotrafficking, environmental protection, and search and rescue are poorly understood outside of China, then cooperation among the maritime powers of East Asia may well remain underdeveloped. The unprecedented December 2008 deployment of the Chinese Navy to join other navies in the Gulf of Aden in counterpiracy operations is unquestionably a major step in the right direction. But much more can and should be done to find common ground with China in countering nontraditional threats.

Today China remains relatively weak in the crucially important middle domain of maritime power, between commercial prowess and hard military power, which is concerned with maritime governance—enforcing its own laws and assuring "good order" off its own coasts.[5] Despite major improvements over the last decade, China's maritime enforcement authorities remain balkanized and relatively weak—described in a derogatory fashion by many Chinese experts as five "dragons stirring up the sea."[6]

In Northeast Asia, China's weak maritime enforcement capacities are the exception, especially when compared to the coast guard capacities of the United

States or Japan. Indeed, the latter's forces were recently described as almost, though not quite, a second navy for Tokyo.[7] China's relative weakness in this area is a mystery that forms the central research question of the present study. This condition of relative weakness is outlined in the first section. The second section describes and analyzes the current situation of each of the five most important bureaucratic agencies responsible for maritime enforcement and governance in China today. The third section of this chapter raises the question of what relationship these entities and any future unified Chinese coast guard would have with the Chinese navy. Before turning to implications and prospects, the fourth section delves into a variety of macro explanations for the weakness of China's coast guard entities today. Finally, the last section elaborates on three possible strategic implications of enhanced Chinese coast guard capabilities. This study draws on hundreds of Chinese-language sources, interviews in China, and especially upon a highly detailed and remarkably candid survey published in 2007 and authored by Professor He Zhonglong and three other faculty members at the Border Guards Maritime Police Academy in Ningbo.[8]

The continuing evolution of Chinese coast guard entities into more coherent and effective agents of maritime governance presents both a challenge and an opportunity for security and stability in East Asia. Enlarged capacities will naturally result in more stringent enforcement of China's maritime claims vis-à-vis its many neighbors. However, a more benign result is potentially that enhanced Chinese capacities in maritime governance may result in Beijing's greater willingness to assist in supporting global maritime safety and security norms as a full-fledged and vital "maritime stakeholder."

Relative Weakness in a Strong Neighborhood

The weaknesses in China's coast guard capacities are amply evident to Chinese maritime analysts. These capacities are viewed as being disproportionately small given the scale of China's maritime development. He Zhonglong and his colleagues write: "Our current maritime law enforcement forces . . . are not commensurate with our status and image as a great power."[9] They elaborate: "Currently, among maritime enforcement ships, the vast majority consists of small patrol boats of less than 500 tons, and the number of ship-borne helicopters is such that these forces cannot meet the requirements of comprehensive maritime law enforcement."[10] The Ningbo Maritime Police Academy faculty asserts that the present situation is intolerable because "China is a country with a large population, and its land-based resources are insufficient. The oceans

Table 1. Pacific Coast Guards Compared

Country	China	South Korea	Japan	United States
Length of coastline (km)	18,000	11,542	30,000	160,550
Large cutters (3,500 tons +)	8	5	11	12
Mid-size cutters (1,500 tons +)	19	9	37	32
Small cutters (500 tons +)	149	66	82	44
Small boats (100+ tons)	304	111	107	258

Source: He Zhonglong et al., "Research on the Building of the Chinese Coast Guard," 142–43.

can replace and supplement for land space and with respect to resources have enormous latent capacity and strategic significance."[11]

By contrast, other Pacific powers, and especially the United States and Japan, wield tremendously strong and effective coast guards. This unfavorable comparison is well documented and understood among Chinese maritime analysts.[12] Indeed, the level of detailed understanding of U.S. and Japanese coast guard capacities is impressive and suggestive simultaneously of envy and admiration.[13] Illustrating the relative weakness of Chinese coast guard capacity, He Zhonglong, for instance, notes that the U.S. Coast Guard (USCG) is equipped with 250 aircraft of different types while the Japanese coast guard has 75. With much less developed aviation forces, Chinese coast guard entities probably field fewer than three dozen aircraft of all types.[14] Aircraft are crucial for both long-range patrol, on the one hand, and complicated rescues, on the other hand. Moreover, the professional requirements to maintain a strong aviation component for a nation's coast guard are considerable. Therefore, these numbers are reflective of the very large gap that separates China from these other major Pacific coast guard forces, a fact duly noted by the Ningbo Academy study.[15] Table 1 illustrates that although People's Republic of China coast guard entities have relatively high numbers of small and very small patrol vessels (under 1,500 tons), Beijing is well behind either Washington or Tokyo in the numbers of medium-sized (1,500–3,000 tons) or large (more than 3,500 tons) cutters. The Ningbo Academy study additionally points out that the Republic of Korea had undertaken a successful unification of disparate maritime enforcement elements in 1996 into a single, powerful "Korea Coast Guard," modeled on the American and Japanese paradigm.

Beijing's impulse to upgrade its coast guard capabilities is clearly related to its overall strategic goal of increasing its maritime forces more generally and is thus quite consistent with China's rapid naval development. Indeed, the national security implications of this initiative for East Asian security are considerable and will be analyzed at the conclusion of this study. The tone of the Ningbo Academy analysis certainly does suggest the significance of the national security factor in Chinese thinking about maritime enforcement capabilities. The authors observe, for example, that "today, cold war thinking still exists in many countries. . . . There are hostile attitudes."[16] Regarding the delicate issue of sovereignty in the South China Sea, the same analysis notes: "On the one hand, China and the ten states of ASEAN signed the code of conduct with respect to the South Sea in Phnom Penh, [but] to some degree, what has happened is that China's sovereignty and interests continue to be seriously encroached upon."[17] This motive is not surprising and is consistent with strong nationalism extant among Chinese intellectuals and policy analysts more generally. However, another strong current is evident in China's buildup of coast guard capacities, representing awareness of globalization and growing interdependence among nations. Present in this current of thinking, also amply evident in the Ningbo Academy analysis by He Zhonglong and colleagues, is the quite sophisticated and encouraging notion that strong coast guards might, by their versatile nature, actually serve as a kind of cushion between navies, helping to mitigate the possibility of interstate conflict in East Asia. Along these lines, it is reassuring when He Zhonglong and colleagues conclude, "Everyone lives together on one planet, and are confronted by common threats, and have common interests."[18] Another Chinese analysis likewise notes that international relationships built with other coast guards have "many times succeeded in foiling transnational criminal activity."[19] The study by the Ningbo Academy faculty ultimately pinpoints the organizational factor in explaining weakness in Chinese maritime enforcement capacity. As He Zhonglong and colleagues write, "The organizational set up of China's maritime governance is not ideal. For a long time, there has been the situation of 'a group of dragons stirring up the water': in every situation there are multiple agencies involved, each with their own competence and scope of jurisdiction overlapping, as well as glaring gaps. Internally, this creates problems with respect to consistent enforcement while externally there is no unity of effort. The result is a situation of a passive, weak, and ineffective force."[20] While this explanation in itself is quite persuasive, this analysis will evaluate some other potential causes of this weakness as well, in addition to evaluating prospects for reform, the potential for developing further international cooperation in maritime security, and the attendant strategic implications for East Asian security.

China's Five Maritime Enforcement Dragons

Altogether, China's "five dragons stirring up the sea," or the five agencies that comprise its maritime enforcement capabilities, amount to roughly forty thousand personnel.[21] The following section briefly describes the organization, missions, and capabilities of each of the so-called dragons. However, with the exception of the Maritime Safety Administration (MSA), which is significantly transparent, the other smaller organizations are less accessible and therefore less well understood by foreigners at this time.

Table 2. Disposition of Chinese Maritime Enforcement Vessels

	Tonkin Gulf	East China Sea	Yellow Sea	Bohai Gulf	South China Sea	Total
Large cutters (3,500 tons +)		4			4	8
Mid-size cutters (1,500 tons +)	2	6	5	1	5	19
Small cutters (500 tons +)	20	30	30	26	43	149
Small boats (100+ tons)	26	95		103	80	304

Source: He Zhonglong et al., "Research on the Building of the Chinese Coast Guard," 142.

Maritime Police of the Border Control Department (BCD)

The China Maritime Police (公安边防海警部门) is a part of the Border Control Department, which is an elite subcomponent of the People's Armed Police under the Ministry of Public Security. The China Maritime Police generally operate speedboats and small cutters. These vessels are often armed with machine guns or small cannons. It is worth emphasizing that this force is armed because several of the other important "dragons" are unarmed, which raises a host of complications.

As for the vessels of the Maritime Police, a current workhorse for the fleet is the Seal [海豹] HP1500-2 high-speed patrol craft. These small vessels are capable of 52 knots, have a range of 250 km, and require a crew of 6 to 9 personnel. Their intended missions include escort, on-the-water marine inspections, and search-and-rescue duties. The new standard small cutter for the Maritime Police is the Type 218. This design is 41 meters in length; displaces 130 tons; and has a beam of 6.2 meters, a top speed of 29 knots, a crew complement of 23, and a single, 14.5-mm machine gun. A large Type 718 patrol cutter for the Maritime Police was apparently launched in 2006. It displaces 1,500 tons, has a length of 100 meters, and has a helicopter landing platform as well as a 37-mm cannon. The Maritime Police also recently took possession of two older PLA Navy *Jianghu*-class frigates (now called 海警 1002 and 海警 1003) after they were overhauled. At this time, the Maritime Police have no aviation assets.[22]

The main training academy for the maritime police is in Ningbo. However, not all the students at the Ningbo Academy are maritime police—students receive a generalized border guard curriculum in their first years and apparently may opt into the maritime specialty about halfway through their education at Ningbo. Training facilities at the Ningbo Academy are impressive, especially the engineering and shiphandling simulators.

With the crime-fighting mission being primary, emergent threats of special concern to the Maritime Police include both terrorism and piracy. Although no cases of maritime terrorism have been reported in or against China, fears have been heightened by the 9/11 attacks against the United States, continued unrest among certain minority populations that have resorted to terrorist tactics, and a naturally heightened consciousness resulting from the 2008 Olympic Games in Beijing. During the Olympic Games, the Maritime Police apparently sortied thirty ships each day and stopped or detained over one thousand vessels in support of security at the games.[23] He Zhonglong and colleagues write: "Our country's cities of Hong Kong, Macau, Shanghai, Guangzhou, and such important cities along the coast . . . could become the major targets of surprise attack by international terrorists."[24] Another China naval affairs analyst observes with similar concern that "armed groups from the Middle East are becoming more and more interested in maritime, surprise terrorist attacks."[25] Indeed, Chinese military and naval analysts have been keen to learn any lessons that have emerged from the November 2008 terrorist attacks against Mumbai that involved insertion by boat teams.

China's maritime history is replete with difficulties arising from piracy, so it is perhaps not surprising to see great interest in the subject as reflected in Chinese maritime publications.[26] Moreover, it is certainly noteworthy that the impetus for the December 2008 counterpiracy deployment of a Chinese navy task force to the Gulf of Aden seems to have originated in part from China's civil maritime sector.[27] Indeed, concern about terrorism has been evident in Chinese maritime writings for some years. One article on the issue emphasizes the proximity of the problem: "Of the 124 incidents of piracy in 2005, 60% occurred in Asia's South Sea triangle [in approximately the area of the South China Sea]."[28] Another recent Chinese analysis of the piracy issue concludes: "The pirates have lots of modern weapons, are equipped with advanced communications equipment, and have secret links with international criminal gangs and even terrorist organizations."[29] Another source observes that Chinese vessels in distant waters have also been victimized by pirates.[30] These conclusions no doubt influenced Beijing's December 2008 decision to send naval ships to the Gulf of Aden to fight piracy, but China's coast guard entities are also likely to be involved in such missions in the future—and in many respects are better trained and equipped for this mission. Thus, it will not be surprising to see various Chinese maritime enforcement elements active in future operations against pirates, perhaps acting in tandem with the PLA Navy.

As the primary armed element among China's maritime enforcement dragons, the BCD (or China Coast Guard) might well be expected to take the lead in confronting such challenges. At present, according to the Ningbo Academy study, the BCD has ten thousand personnel—about one quarter of the aggregate among the five dragons.[31] It is also noteworthy that the BCD has been designated as the lead "dragon" in liaison and exchange with the U.S. Coast Guard—a relationship discussed at length in the final section of this chapter.

The Maritime Safety Administration

The only "dragon" that competes in power and prestige with the BCD (described above) is the Maritime Safety Administration of the Chinese Ministry of Transportation (MOT) (交通部下属的海事局及救打捞局). In terms of manpower, the MSA has twice as many personnel—about twenty-thousand—approximately half of the aggregate total from among the five maritime enforcement agencies. MSA missions include the following: inspection and registration of Chinese and foreign vessels in Chinese ports, investigation of maritime accidents, training and certifying seafarers, supervising marine traffic control, maintaining aids to navigation, implementing domestic and international maritime laws, and conducting maritime search-and-rescue operations. There are fourteen regional MSA offices based mainly in the coastal provinces but also including some inland river transport centers, for example, along the Yangtze River. Each MSA regional office has a rescue coordination center, and many coastal provinces have a variety of additional rescue subcenters.[32]

The author was fortunate to visit the Shanghai Rescue Coordination Center (RCC) in November 2007. As befitting one of the world's busiest ports, Shanghai RCC is equipped with modern and relatively well-integrated ship-management systems. The Shanghai Port relies on at least eleven major radar stations and two vessel-tracking centers in addition to the RCC.[33] These systems are supplemented by the automatic identification system (AIS), which per regulations of the International Maritime Organization, requires vessels more than three hundred tons to automatically report their position, course, and speed via electronic receivers in real time.[34] Such systems have revolutionized ship traffic control, dramatically enhancing maritime domain awareness on all the world's oceans but especially near China's shores, where a major push has been made to set up AIS receiver/tracking stations along the entire length of the busy Chinese coastline.[35] A further vessel-tracking method employed by Chinese authorities is the China Ship Reporting (CHISREP) system. This system requires Chinese-flagged vessels to regularly report their position to a coordination center. Somewhat analogous to the U.S. Coast Guard's AMVER system, which serves as a clearinghouse for merchant vessel positions on a global scale, CHISREP's most obvious significance is in the domain of search and rescue (other applications, e.g., concerning pollution control, are quite conceivable as well). Another important technology on display at the Shanghai RCC was extensive use of closed-circuit television in the port area of the Huangpu River—systems that have no doubt improved port management, safety, and security. Despite this wide variety of reinforcing systems, some problems also seemed evident, especially in the realm of coordination. For example, Shanghai RCC personnel conceded that while their display screens could easily locate the positions of local MSA assets, they could not readily display the positions of BCD/China Coast Guard vessels in the same area.

MSA's important position among China's maritime enforcement dragons is confirmed by evident investments in capital stock: namely, new ships and aircraft. The launching of the relatively large cutter *Haixun 31* (3,000 tons) in 2004 seems to have heralded a turn toward oceangoing rescue vessels. Although the ship reportedly had some problems with communications equipment in particular, the ship was noteworthy not only for its size but also because it was the first MSA vessel to carry an embarked helicopter.[36] Deployment of the vessel to patrol China's exclusive economic zone (EEZ) in the East China Sea was covered widely in the Western press in June 2008.[37] Two successor ships to *Haixun 31* are *Haixun 21* and *Haixun 11*, the latter of which was commissioned in September 2009 and similarly displaces 3,000 tons. It appears *Haixun 11* will be home-ported at Weihai in Shandong Province.[38] Three additional new, large cutters have been commissioned by the MSA, including *Nanhaijiu 101*, *Nanhaijiu 112*, and *Beijhaijiu 111*. These very large cutters—*Nanhaijiu 101* is listed as 6,257 tons—feature a dramatic departure in design from *Haixun 31*, although they are similarly equipped to carry helicopters. With their very prominent foredecks and superstructures, together with extremely low aft decks, they resemble massive tugboats more than their large cutter equivalents in, for example, the Japanese coast guard. They appear to be equipped with very modern features, including for example variable pitch propellers that greatly enhance the maneuverability of large vessels. Current MSA doctrine keeps most ships on station at sea for two weeks, with just one day in port to resupply and then resume position on station. There are apparently two crews per vessel with each crew working two continuous months at sea before taking one month ashore. Crew members are thus at sea about eight months per year.[39]

Yet another innovative design is featured in the recently launched *Beihaijiu 201*. This small cutter is a high-speed catamaran modeled on recent commercial ferry designs.[40] It is worth emphasizing that MSA cutters are unarmed—a clear distinction from the USCG and other coast guards around the world. With respect to small boats, MSA has notably lacked for small, motor surfboats and may have recently purchased some from the United Kingdom.[41] However, attention to smaller cutters is illustrated, for example, by the 2008 launch at Wuhan of a new forty-meter design optimized for Yangtze River rescue operations.[42]

Progress in airborne rescue assets is slower, at least for now. Chinese maritime analysts do appreciate the crucial role of helicopters for contemporary coast guard duties.[43] In the Ningbo Academy study, the authors conclude, "A helicopter operating from a mother ship has enormous value . . . especially in conducting enforcement [operations] in blue water."[44] Nevertheless, airborne search-and-rescue capabilities are being built essentially from scratch. Although a series of MSA flying bases were established in 2004, the service does not appear to currently operate much more than a dozen aircraft.[45] Interestingly, the MSA does already operate a number of Sikorsky helicopters. Some helicopter rescues have reportedly occurred, but night operations are still restricted. According to MSA personnel, the biggest bottleneck preventing a major expansion of the MSA flying service is both pilot and rescue-swimmer training. In both these areas, China has made ambitious proposals for assistance from the USCG (on this relationship, see the final section of this chapter). To date, the People's Republic of China coast guard entities have benefited substantially from training assistance from Hong Kong's capable airborne patrol and rescue service. According to an MSA plan announced in early 2003, the goal is to have effective search and rescue within fifty miles of the coast down to a reaction time of 150 minutes, and by 2020 this time should be improved to less than 90 minutes. The range for search-and-rescue operations is also to be gradually expanded to cover China's entire exclusive economic zone.[46]

China's maritime rescue service has come a long way in a short time. In 1999 the MSA experienced a *"Titanic*-like" tragedy when the ferry *Dashun* went down in bad weather just a few miles offshore in the Yellow Sea. Out of 304 passengers and crew, only 22 survived. The accident, a major national tragedy, helped to galvanize efforts to develop a much more vigorous maritime rescue service. As Captain Bernard Moreland (USCG), posted as a liaison officer at the U.S. Embassy in Beijing, writes: "Less than 10 years after the *Dashun* tragedy, China has a fully-operating professional maritime search and rescue capacity."[47] Indeed, MSA can point to some concrete achievements: reduction in the Tenth Five-Year Plan of maritime accidents by one-third and maritime accident fatalities by one-quarter. A new rescue network was established along the Yangtze River in 2001. During 2002–3, MSA conducted 520 rescue missions involving 1,303 ship sorties and 25 aircraft sorties—of 14,901 persons in danger, 13,997 were saved, including 787 foreign nationals.[48]

A key enabler of enhanced professionalism in China's MSA is the high-quality professional journal *China Maritime Affairs* (中国海事). Of particular note in this journal is the widespread and serious use of the case study method. Accidents are described, dissected, and mined for lessons that can inform future practices.[49] Nor do these cases only describe accidents in Chinese waters. They also address related incidents around the world—for example, the recent sinking of an Egyptian ferry in the Red Sea with great loss of life. Additionally, a major emphasis in this journal is on learning from the experiences and procedures of maritime safety and security in other nations.

Other common themes in this journal include the promulgation of new laws, issues related to toxic spills, typhoon emergency response, newly available technologies, and profiles of service practices in foreign countries. Regarding typhoon response, it is worth noting that China has received high marks in recent years for diligent preparedness and execution of emergency plans for dangerous coastal storms.[50] MSA has played a leading role in establishing Chinese preparedness for the cleanup of oil spills. It was announced in

September 2008 that China was signing an agreement on mutual support for oil spill cleanup among Japan, Russia, South Korea, and China.[51] This agreement followed an incident from December 2007 in which the Hong Kong oil tanker *Hebei Spirit* was involved in a major spill off the Korean coastline, and Beijing's Ministry of Communications (MSA) subsequently dispatched two vessels to assist in the cleanup.

Fisheries Law Enforcement Command

As in fisheries in all areas of the globe, the Chinese fishing industry has been plagued in the last decade by the environmental devastation wrought by overfishing. While growth in aquaculture has mitigated this crisis to some extent, fishermen all along the Chinese coast have experienced a difficult transition. As one Chinese study recently opined: "The fact is obvious that the development of our nation's fishing industry has reached an extremely important juncture. Most—if not all—of the fisheries have been fully exploited, and many are already exhausted."[52] Another study, published in *Marine Policy*, further reveals the scope of the problem. Since the 1960s, fish species in the Beibu Gulf area of the South China Sea have declined from 487 to 238. Stock density reached its lowest level in 1998 at just 16.7 percent of that in 1962, though fish stocks have recovered somewhat in recent years.[53]

Such conditions have increased pressure on fisheries enforcement institutions and personnel because of the imperative to strictly enforce new regulations in order to replenish fish stocks. A "zero growth" plan was initiated in 1999. By 2004, 8,000 fishing vessels had been scrapped and there is an effort to bring down China's total fishing fleet to 192,000 vessels by 2010. Summer moratoriums now exist for almost all of China's coastal areas.[54] The task is made even more complicated by the fact that overlapping exclusive economic zones are extensive in the Western Pacific, and by the wide-ranging migratory patterns of regional fish stocks.[55]

With a total haul of 17 million tons in 2007, China's fishing take is four times that of the nearest competitor.[56] Official figures suggest that China currently has about 297,937 motorized fishing vessels and approximately 8 million fishermen. Among finfish, Chinese are largely catching anchovy, Japanese scad, hairtail, and small yellow croaker; nets, line and hooks, and purse seines are also used. The East China Sea accounts for the largest catch, followed by the South China Sea and then the Yellow Sea. Among these sea areas, only the South China Sea region has seen increasing catches of late. Of China's major marine industries, marine fisheries and related industries are ranked as the largest sector. Guangdong and Shandong are the leading provinces measured by fishing output, though Fujian and Zhejiang are close behind.[57]

China's Fisheries Law Enforcement Command (FLEC, 农业部下属的渔政部门) is part of the Ministry of Agriculture; it apparently has just one thousand personnel.[58] The strategic implications of China's fisheries enforcement capabilities were suggested in early 2009, when Chinese fishing or fisheries vessels were involved in a variety of international incidents with both regional neighbors and the United States.[59] Hints of ineffectiveness and inefficiency are revealed by the Ningbo Academy study, which cites fisheries enforcement as an example of confusion among the five dragons. Thus, He Zhonglong and colleagues describe,

> [There is] the "have jurisdiction, but cannot find, or can find, but do not have jurisdiction" phenomena. . . . The fisheries enforcement department has the function of escorting fishing vessels, but because they are unarmed, they lack enforcement deterrence and coercion capabilities, and thus have trouble dealing with situations that suddenly arise. . . . The public security maritime police though having the police function, and being equipped with all types of weaponry, and possessing an advantage in any circumstances involving escort of fishing vessels, because of limitations on jurisdiction can only play a supporting role, and are in an awkward position. The country's maritime rights and interests, as well as the national honor is difficult to protect in such circumstances.[60]

One further aspect of fisheries is important to consider when evaluating the implications of Chinese maritime enforcement capabilities. In addition to policies encouraging aquaculture, Beijing has also pushed to develop a long-distance fishing fleet in recent years. By 2006 this fleet had grown to almost two thousand vessels operating on the high seas and the EEZs of thirty-five countries.[61] The authors reference this development in the Ningbo Academy study, for example, asserting: "If our country seeks to resolve the food question internally, then it is necessary to exploit the sea's bounty, through . . . developing the deep sea fishing industry."[62] Chinese fishing vessels are now a common sight in the waters of Africa and Latin America, for example, a phenomena that has brought about considerable controversy. From the Chinese perspective, there has been some question as to how Chinese fishermen can be protected, for example against pirate attack, in such distant locations.[63] This question invites maritime analysts to consider whether Chinese maritime enforcement capabilities will expand to a global presence that is commensurate with its global maritime commercial interests—and how such a new mission will mesh with China's emerging naval strategy, which has already embraced the counterpiracy mission. An even more sensitive question arises regarding fishing practices proximate to Chinese waters. As stocks have declined, a sense of fishing nationalism has emerged around the region. Indeed, a recent Chinese fisheries analysis concludes: "Although our country has signed one after another fishing agreements with neighboring states, the number of fishing industry security incidents involving foreigners has unceasingly increased. . . . Some [countries] even send warships to bump and sink our side's fishing boats."[64] Tensions flared in the summer of 2009 as multiple Chinese maritime enforcement agencies patrolled against foreign violators of strict, new fishing regulation in the sensitive South China Sea area.[65] If, as has been suggested recently, a major buildup is under way of large, helicopter-capable cutters for the south sea component of the FLEC, Beijing's fishing policies in the region could well become more assertive.[66]

General Administration of Customs

China's status as an international trade juggernaut raises commensurately the prestige of the Chinese General Administration of Customs (GAC, 海关总署下属的缉私部门). The vast amount of international commerce taking place in China's ports and in its coastal waters determines the important role of China customs in maritime enforcement. Among the chief missions of China customs are (1) compilation of foreign trade statistics; (2) revenue collection; (3) customs control (declarations, etc.); (4) antismuggling measures; and (5) port control.[67] The latter two missions are most relevant to maritime enforcement capabilities.

According to the China Customs 2007 annual report, "[the GAC represents] the competent anti-smuggling authority of the Chinese government, which takes up most, if not all, of the responsibility for combating smuggling."[68] The total of significant smuggling cases prosecuted by the GAC in 2007 was 1,190, which amounted to more than US$1 billion, and up 4.3 percent from the previous year. Of this number, there were some 356 major drug busts that netted almost 500 kg in assorted illegal drugs.[69] It is not clear what percentage of these interdiction activities occurred in the maritime sphere, but some preliminary evidence suggests that a portion of China's drug trade does take place in seaborne vessels. Thus, a 2007 article in the journal of the Fujian Senior Police Academy suggested, "In the last few years, criminals with drugs passing through the port of Xiamen's water transport routes have been using fishing vessels to smuggle drugs."[70] Similar concerns about maritime drug enforcement have been noted in Chinese naval publications.[71] The Ningbo Academy study also notes the importance of the antidrug mission for the future development of China's maritime enforcement capabilities.[72] This is perhaps not surprising because China Customs has been working in coordination with the Ministry of Public Security to form "joint anti-smuggling forces" since 1998.[73]

China Customs also plays a leading role in Chinese port management. The GAC is proud that "ocean going imports and exports can usually be released within 24 hours."[74] China's ambitious "E-port" initiative, outlined by the State Council in 2006, aims to smooth out port operations by harnessing information technology—for example, by allowing online payment of taxes and various charges. China Customs holds the vice-chair of the National E-Port Steering Committee, which also has representatives from the other maritime enforcement dragons, including the BCD and the MSA. According to the Ningbo Academy study, GAC maritime enforcement personnel amount to about two thousand. Thus, the GAC is one of the smallest dragons as measured by personnel.

State Oceanic Administration

With personnel estimated to number about six thousand, the State Oceanic Administration's (SOA) China Maritime Surveillance (海洋局下属的中国海监) constitutes a medium-sized dragon, between the large MSA and the much smaller customs and fisheries enforcement agencies.[75] Major missions for the SOA include environmental protection, scientific research, and enforcement of EEZ rights and interests.

The rising profile of environmental protection in China has increased attention to coastal environmental issues, in particular. The SOA has played an important role in realizing the extent of current problems. In 2006 a major SOA study concluded that "China faces severe ocean pollution."[76] It seems the 2008 Beijing Olympics also spurred a new interest in improving coastal water quality, in particular in conjunction with the sailing events at Qingdao. SOA research centers were active in monitoring and forecasting water quality for that prestigious event.[77] Along with curbing the runoff of pollutants discharged from factories on land, another major concern is coping with spills of oil and other toxic substances that are carried in Chinese waters in huge quantities.

Corresponding with its mission to patrol China's EEZ, SOA has a relatively extensive fleet of ships and aircraft. In 2006 it was reported that SOA itself had twenty-one ships displacing between one thousand and four thousand tons.[78] A recent report on SOA's South China Sea flotilla suggested that this division had eleven ships, six of which are reported to be more than one thousand tons in displacement. This South China Sea division of SOA is said to be equipped with one helicopter and two fixed-wing aircraft.[79] A 2008 report said that CMS had a total of nine aircraft and more than two hundred patrol vessels.[80] Of late, SOA has received at least three new, large cutters including *Haijian 46, Haijian 51*, and *Haijian 83*. According to a 2009 report, the latter is SOA's largest cutter at 98 meters in length. This 3,400-ton cutter, built at Jiangnan shipyard, is said to have cost about US$22 million and is assigned a helicopter.[81]

Though MSA operates some aircraft for search-and-rescue purposes, SOA's allotment of aircraft clearly separates it from the other large dragon, the BCD (China's coast guard, the Border Control Department), which has no aircraft. However, like the BCD, SOA has recently taken over some retired Chinese Navy vessels.[82] Reportedly *Haijian 20* and *Haijian 32* are converted from PLA Navy subchasers and will patrol in the Bohai Sea.[83] With respect to SOA's mission of patrolling China's EEZ, the Ningbo Academy study states bluntly that the agency falls short of requirements: "At this point, maritime enforcement patrol ships are only sufficient to patrol territorial and adjoining sea areas with any frequency, and cannot be responsible for missions within the EEZs or continental shelf areas."[84] According to another report, SOA was directed by China's State Council to initiate patrols of the East China Sea in 2006. These elevated surveillance activities apparently involved daily patrols by four aircraft and six ships operated by SOA in the East China Sea.[85] A 2009 report suggests that CMS initiated regular patrols of the southern part of the South China Sea in 2007.[86] In aggregate, CMS reported between the period of 2001 to 2007 that fifteen thousand cases of illegal activities were detected in China's EEZ, of which about ten thousand cases were apparently prosecuted. According to one 2006 report, SOA is already closely collaborating with the China BCD in the Tonkin Gulf (Beibu Wan) area and is looking to do so elsewhere as well.[87] SOA sources candidly describe close coordination with the Chinese military.[88] Indeed, during a public statement in October 2008, CMS deputy director Sun Shuxian, declared that "the [CMS] force will be upgraded to a reserve unit under the navy, a move which will make it better armed during patrols . . . the current defensive strength of CMS is inadequate."[89] A similar message emerges from a September 2009 Chinese report that documented multiple interactions between SOA and U.S. surveillance vessels. This report suggested that SOA vessels required better sensors and electronic warfare technology to cope with U.S. surveillance ships.[90] Photos of small new CMS cutters that surfaced in April 2010 did suggest that CMS was indeed moving to arm its new cutters—a significant departure from past practices.

SOA is also leading China's oceanographic research effort. According to the official SOA Web site, the agency has no fewer than sixteen discrete research centers and institutes. The agency is a major funder of research projects at

China Ocean University in Qingdao and likely many other university centers as well. In 2005 an SOA research vessel capable of drilling cores from the sea bottom at depths in excess of three thousand meters made a circumnavigation of the globe to advance China's oceanographic research across the world's oceans. SOA has also launched a series of maritime observation satellites. China's recent mission to Antarctica to establish its third base there was organized by SOA and demonstrates the ambitious research agenda that the agency maintains.[91]

The Sixth and Mightiest Dragon?
The Chinese Coast Guard and the Chinese Navy

Among coast guard–like entities, it is natural and proper to consider how roles and missions, not to mention resources, are allocated between coast guard forces, on the one hand, and navies, on the other. Sea power theorist Geoffrey Till explains that overlap is inevitable and logical but that there is a spectrum of coast guard models, all of which entail a different kind of relationship with national navies. Till additionally observes: "With the widening of the concept of security, accelerated perhaps by the events of 11 September, the extent of potential overlap is increasing in ways which raise issues over who should be responsible for what." As he further explains, some countries have had navies and coast guards that have dramatically different tasks while in other countries (often smaller or lesser developed ones) the navies have often themselves functioned essentially as coast guards, involved principally in coastal patrol, management, and search-and-rescue missions.[92]

Chinese analysts have duly noted that other coast guards around the world, including the USCG, have been critically involved in national security policy. One Chinese maritime analyst, for example, notes that Japan's powerful coast guard serves as vital reserve force for the Japanese navy.[93] As the authors of the Ningbo Academy study observe, "The United States explicitly calls its Coast Guard one of the five armed services, many times employing it for combat missions."[94] The same analysts are quite candid in this regard, outlining an important role for China's coast guard entities in any future military conflict: "In wartime, under the command of the navy, [China's coast guard elements] would escort maritime transport, would assist in controlling maritime transport and also with amphibious ships, execute anti-submarine missions, protect ports, secure wharves, provide crews for some portion of the navy's fleet and assist in completing national mobilization."[95] Another expert analyst from China's National Defense University argued similarly in June 2009 that large

Chinese coast guard cutters could be easily converted for use in "far seas" combat while small- and medium-sized coast guard vessels could support coastal defense, undertaking such missions as laying defensive minefields.[96] It is perhaps not surprising to see elements of the Chinese maritime enforcement community taking a hard line on sovereignty and maritime claims issues: "Taiwan is in most respects still dominated by a few foreign powers. . . . From this perspective, Taiwan island forms the strategic core deciding the future fate of the Chinese nation. . . . On the sea, there are many neighboring countries that have island and ocean territorial disputes with China. These contradictions are relatively extensive, and this has a major impact on room for maneuver in Chinese politics, foreign policy and military affairs."[97]

Nevertheless, it would be a mistake to see China's developing coast guard entities as simple adjuncts to the PLA Navy. A cosmopolitan outlook is actually quite evident in the Ningbo Academy study: "The initiation of armed conflict or even limited war would severely impact the whole region and international system, and does not conform to the nation's circumstances of development."[98] Moreover, because the Ningbo Academy is part of the BCD, one of a few armed elements among China's coast guard entities, one might logically presume the unarmed elements (e.g., the powerful MSA) to be even less inclined toward quasi-military activities. Also evident in the Ningbo Academy study is a sense that coast guard entities may actually be in competition with the Chinese Navy for finite resources. These specialists, for example, observe with evident frustration that "internally, many scholars believe that maritime power means maritime military power, and maritime military power means the navy."[99] A crucial question that arises is what the disposition of the Chinese navy and the PLA more generally will be toward improving maritime enforcement capabilities. Preliminary evidence in the form of an article from a June 2008 issue of the official and prestigious *China Military Science* (中国军事科学) suggests that the PLA supports this endeavor, as the author from Chinese NDU emphatically calls for stronger maritime enforcement capabilities as a crucial component of a new Chinese maritime strategy.[100] In July 2009 a significant search-and-rescue exercise was undertaken in the vicinity of the Pearl River Delta. The coorganizers of the exercise were the PLA Navy's South Sea Fleet and the Guangdong provincial government. Thirteen agencies, twenty-five vessels, and two helicopters took part in the exercise, which was termed a "three-dimensional military, coast guard, and civilian" (立体军警民) exercise. A navy publication describing the exercise notes that China has set up a new and robust search-and-rescue system but laments that the military regions are not well integrated into that structure—thereby underscoring the need for such exercises.[101]

In reconsidering Till's two alternative models of either wide bifurcation or extensive overlap, it is worth noting that China clearly has emerged from the latter tradition. For much of the Cold War, its navy was not much more than an elaborate coast guard. Today more bifurcation is occurring as China's navy emphasizes technology intensive warfare. Conversely, the PLA is also more and more interested in issues that have often concerned coast guards, including search and rescue, environmental protection, and piracy—as illustrated by the December 2008 deployment to the Gulf of Aden, which suggests that a strict bifurcation of roles is simply not practical for China in the near and medium term.

Explaining the Weakness of China's Coast Guard

This chapter has prioritized an objective and detailed rendering of the current status in development of various Chinese coast guard entities, but it is also important to lay a foundation for explaining the central phenomenon at issue: China's relative weakness in its present coast guard capacities. A recent article by Richard Suttmeier titled "China, Safety, and the Management of Risks" is extremely helpful in this regard. Three related explanations are examined below in turn: modernization processes, economic issues, and institutional structural issues. No doubt these different explanations have complex linkages, but there is still value in focusing on different segments of the various causal links.

Suttmeier explains that conventional wisdom posits a strong relationship between modernity and safety. He writes, "The wealth and power expected from 'modernization' have long been seen in China—and elsewhere—as risk-reducing, safety-enhancing developments."[102] Wealth and education can bring about China's "sixth modernization"—enabling Beijing "to manage environmental and technological risk."[103] Suttmeier's analysis looks at the example of civil aviation in China, suggesting that "China's performance on safety issues . . . attracted and maintained high-level political and managerial attention . . . which permitted the introduction of redundancy."[104] The essential argument here, then, is that China's coast guard entities could not function effectively until China became a modern society—it simply lacked the wherewithal. Besides, many other priorities took precedence, not least economic and political survival. At certain points during the "Century of Humiliation" or the Cold War, such fundamental aspects of development could not be taken for granted. Having secured China from existential threats and moved the country out of poverty, Beijing can now turn to second-order priorities such as effective maritime governance and even the relatively new concept of valuing individual lives. However, Suttmeier does ask the provocative question of whether the "sixth modernization" can proceed without further political liberalization that would support "transparency in China's risk management strategies" by empowering "activist civil organizations that have autonomy and . . . resources."[105]

An alternative explanation prioritizes economic factors, in particular, and may be more amenable to Beijing's current mode of thinking. Suttmeier calls for a "science-based regulatory regime that is also sensitive to market forces."[106] He explains: "China needs multiple mechanisms of risk management and governance that address the incentives and disincentives operating on individual economic decision-makers."[107] According to this explanation, order in China's coastal waters is simply a requirement of the rapidly developing coastal economy. Powerful corporate entities are demanding the orderly management of ports and the safe, reliable passage of ships (and the goods they carry). Maritime disasters like the *Dashun* ferry tragedy in 1999 injured the victims, obviously, as well as national pride, but the disaster also hurt business, reflecting poorly on Chinese technical quality and organizational efficiency. The safety and security culture may flow from corporate entities outward.

A final explanation has been a recurrent theme of this chapter and is the central theme of the important Ningbo Academy study of 2007, namely, that the balkanization of maritime enforcement entities in China has severely inhibited the coherent development of Chinese coast guard entities. The so-called dragons duplicate one another in certain functions, fail to coordinate effectively in others, and are of themselves too weak to achieve fundamental breakthroughs in maritime governance—for example, in developing strong long-range search-and-rescue capabilities. Suttmeier also addresses this problem, noting that "responsibility for regulation is often fragmented with the result that no one agency in the central government has control."[108]

Future Prospects and Strategic Implications

The 2007 Ningbo Academy study, discussed at length in this analysis, offers an important window into the current thinking and evident frustration of those charged with contemporary Chinese maritime governance. The authors of that study make a strong case that "our current maritime law enforcement forces . . . are not commensurate with our status and image as a great power. . . . Unification of maritime enforcement agencies would strengthen our flexibility in maritime conflicts . . . exert pressure on Taiwan separatists . . . and would not damage the nation's strategic opportunity at the beginning of the 21st century."[109] Still, the solution of unifying the various maritime enforcement dragons seems to remain largely theoretical at this point. The MSA, the largest of the maritime enforcement agencies by far, could be a logical leader, but others have promoted the SOA because of its broader strategic vision. There is little clarity regarding the way forward.[110] The BCD authors of the Ningbo Academy study themselves ask pointedly, "Who will lead?"[111]

At least three possible strategic implications can be drawn from the foregoing analysis. Most obviously, stronger Chinese coast guard entities will no doubt serve to strengthen China's extensive maritime claims. More and better ships and aircraft at Beijing's disposal will likely increase Beijing's confidence in maritime disputes with its neighbors. As stated clearly in the Ningbo Academy study, China will continue to "build up its military maritime power, developing the power to safeguard its national territorial and maritime rights and interests."[112] And yet there is also the practical consideration that "relying on the navy . . . makes it easier for certain other countries to use the excuse of 'the China threat theory.'"[113]

A second major implication is that stronger Chinese coast guard entities are likely to give further impetus to China's rapidly growing "soft power," both in the Asia-Pacific and around the globe. Thus, in June 2008, the Ningbo Academy hosted a maritime law enforcement workshop for forty-two senior maritime officials from Asia and Africa.[114] Such activities are likely to grow in size and scope in future decades, reaching a level more in line with China's major role in international maritime commerce.[115] No doubt, rescuing sailors from foreign (and often neighboring) nations helps to burnish China's emerging prestige in the arena of maritime safety and security.[116]

A third strategic implication may be even more important and emphasizes that coast guards are a distinctively different form of power from navies. As explained by the authors of the Ningbo Academy study: "Naturally, in the course of the struggle for national interests, contradictions are inevitable. The real question is what means are used to settle these disputes. Giving full play to the government's capabilities, deploying the navy cautiously and strenuously trying to limit the conflict's scope to among the civil maritime authorities, can avoid a resort to escalation of the crisis."[117] Thus the authors articulate a vision of coast guards serving as a kind of buffer between states in crisis, circumventing the intensification of crises that may result from rapid naval deployments. Till also makes this point in his classic treatise on contemporary sea power: "Coastguard ships are often more acceptable politically . . . the involvement of grey-painted warships is often seen as unhelpfully escalatory."[118] This is an encouraging line of reasoning. The same Chinese analysts also highlight Deng Xiaoping's prescription to "maintain sovereignty, but shelve rivalry, and pursue joint development." For them, Deng's formulation represents a new way for China to act as a responsible great power that seeks peaceful resolution of maritime disputes.[119] By supporting such reasoning and facilitating stronger and more coherent Chinese coast guard capabilities more generally, the realization of China's emergence as a "responsible maritime stakeholder" in the twenty-first century may become more feasible. U.S.–China coast guard cooperation can serve as the vital foundation for this important endeavor.

Notes

1. Choe Sang-hun, "Desolate Dots in the Sea Stir Deep Emotions as South Korea Resists a Japanese Claim," *New York Times*, 31 August 2008, http://www.nytimes.com/2008/08/31/world/asia/31islands.html.

2. Richard J. Samuels, "New Fighting Power: Japan's Growing Maritime Capabilities and East Asian Security," *International Security* 32, no. 3 (Winter 2007–8): 84–112.

3. M. Taylor Fravel, "Securing Borders: China's Doctrine and Force Structure for Frontier Defense," *Journal of Strategic Studies* 30, nos. 4–5 (August–October 2007): 709.

4. Some of the most important books written about Chinese naval development include Bruce Swanson, *Eighth Voyage of the Dragon: A History of China's Quest for Seapower* (Annapolis, MD: Naval Institute Press, 1982); John Wilson Lewis and Xue Litai, *China's Strategic Seapower: The Politics of Force Modernization in the Nuclear Age* (Stanford, CA: Stanford University Press, 1994); and Bernard D. Cole, *The Great Wall at Sea: China's Navy Enters the 21st Century* (Annapolis, MD: Naval Institute Press, 2001). Some government reports are also useful, especially: Ronald O'Rourke, "China Naval Modernization: Implications for U.S. Navy Capabilities—Background and Issues for Congress," *Congressional Research Service*, 9 April 2010; and *The People's Liberation Army Navy: A Modern Navy with Chinese Characteristics* (Suitland, MD: Office of Naval Intelligence, July 2009).

5. This term is employed to describe the major function of coast guards in Geoffrey Till, *Seapower: A Guide for the Twenty-First Century* (London: Frank Cass, 2004), 333.

6. It is worth noting that the problem of competing bureaucracies in the maritime domain is not unique to China. Even in the United States, the Customs and Border Protection, the National Marine Fisheries Service, and the National Oceanic and Atmospheric Administration also operate vessels for coastal management and research. However, the primary difference is that the U.S. Coast Guard clearly functions as the nation's "center of gravity" for maritime policy and enforcement. For a detailed discussion of the organizational differences, see Captain Bernard Moreland (USCG), "U.S.-China Civil Maritime Engagement," Draft paper presented at the 3rd Annual Conference of the China Maritime Studies Institute, U.S. Naval War College, Newport, RI, 6 December 2007, 1–2.

7. Samuels, "New Fighting Power," 99–102. This analysis reveals the impressive capabilities of the Japan coast guard but also some distinct limits (e.g., antisubmarine warfare or projecting power ashore).

8. 何忠龙, 任兴平, 冯水利, 罗宪芬, 刘景鸿 [He Zhonglong, Ren Xingping, Feng Shuili, Luo Xianfen, and Liu Jinghong], 中国海岸警卫队组建研究 [*Research on the Building of the Chinese Coast Guard*] (Beijing: Ocean Press, 2007), hereafter referred to as the "Ningbo Academy study." The importance of this book is reinforced by the fact that a large number of articles by the same or nearly the same authors have appeared in a wide variety of civil and military maritime professional journals on the subject of Chinese coast guard development. For example, the following articles were published in the journal of the State Oceanic Administration: 何忠龙, 任兴平, 冯水利 [He Zhonglong, Ren Xingping, and Feng Shuili], "我国海上综合执法的特点及对策" ["Our Country's Comprehensive Maritime Enforcement: Characteristics and Solutions"], 海洋开发与管理 [*Maritime Development and Management*] 25, no. 1 (2008): 100–102; 何忠龙, 任兴平, 冯永利 [He Zhonglong, Ren Xingping, and Feng Yongli], "我国海岸警卫队组建模式探讨" ["Inquiry into Building Our National Coast Guard"], 海洋开发与管理 [*Maritime Development and Management*] 23, no. 6 (June 2006): 112–13. This is particularly significant insofar as it means that thinkers in one agency in the Chinese government are reaching outside their organization and speaking to a broader community of maritime policymakers.

9. Ningbo Academy study, 69.

10. Ibid., 145.

11. Ibid., 3.

12. See, for example, 白俊丰 [Bai Junfeng], "中国海洋警察建设构想" ["Conception Regarding the Building of China's Maritime Police"], 海洋管理 [*Maritime Management*], March 2006, 35.

13. Li Peizhi, 美国海岸警卫队 [*The United States Coast Guard*] (Beijing: Social Science Academic Press, 2005) is an authoritative Chinese study of the U.S. Coast Guard. On the Japan coast guard, see, for example, 候建军 [Hou Jianjun], "日本第二支海上力量: 海上保安厅" ["Japan's Second Maritime Force: The Maritime Security Agency"], 舰船知识 [*Naval & Merchant Ships*] (October 2006): 24–28.

14. Discussions with Maritime Safety Administration and State Oceanic Administration personnel, Qingdao, China, April 2008.

15. Ningbo Academy study, 36.

16. Ibid., 14.

17. Ibid., 13.

18. Ibid., 14.

19. Bai, "Conception Regarding the Building of China's Maritime Police," 38.

20. Ningbo Academy study, 4.

21. Ibid., 37.

22. This information is mostly derived from 陈光文 [Chen Guangwen], "中国海上警备力量" ["China's Coast Guard Capabilities"], 兵器知识 [*Ordnance Knowledge*] (May 2009): 50–51.

23. Interviews, Beijing, April 2008.

24. Ibid., 57. Terrorism is also cited as a concern for China's future coast guard in Bai, "Conception Regarding the Building of China's Maritime Police," 36.

25. 烽火 [Feng Huo], "海上保安战: 近海反恐与安全战术" ["The Battle for Maritime Security: Tactics for Littoral Counterterrorism and Security"], 现代舰船 [*Modern Ships*] (June 2008): 20.

26. See, for example, "话说海盗" ["About Piracy"], 中国海事 [*China Maritime Affairs*], (November 2006): 63–65; and "海盗: 国际航运的难去之痒" ["Piracy: A Disruption of International Shipping that Is Difficult to Eliminate"], 中国船检 [*China Ship Survey*] (May 2006): 48–50.

27. "交通部国际合作司长透露海军护航决策由来"   ["Head   of   International Cooperation Department of Ministry of Transportation Reveals Origins of Decision on Naval Escort"], 三联生活周刊 [*Sanlian Life Weekly*], 16 January 2009.

28. 杨翠柏   [Yang Cuibai],   "亚洲打击海盗及武装抢劫船只的地区合作协定评价" ["Evaluation of the Regional Cooperation Agreement on Combating Piracy and Armed Robbery Against Ships in Asia"], 南洋问题研究 [*South East Asian Affairs*], no. 4 (2006): 29.

29. [Wu Weiqing], "浅谈知何预防盗劫" ["A Simple Discussion on Prevention of Pirate Attacks"], 中国水运 [*China Water Transport*] 7, no. 6 (June 2007): 183.

30. [Lu Xianchen], "现代海盗的威胁和防范" ["The Threat and Precautions against Modern Pirates"], 现代舰船 [*Modern Ships*] (October 2006): 26–29.

31. Ningbo Academy study, 37.

32. "十五'海事成果辉煌和谐发展还看令朝" ["Great Maritime Achievements during the Time of the Tenth Five Year Plan and Harmonious Development Now and in the Future"], 中国海事 [*China Maritime Affairs*] (January 2006): 11.

33. *Shanghai MSA* (Shanghai: 2005), 13.

34. For discussion of AIS integration in China, see, for example, 赵海波, 张英俊 [Zhao Haibo and Zhang Yingjun], "中国北方海区AIS应用研究" ["Study on the Application of AIS in the Northern Sea Region of China"], 大连海事大学学报 [*Journal of Dalian Maritime University*] 35 (December 2007): 81–86.

35. Interview, Shanghai MSA director, November 2007.

36. [Cheng Biao], "海巡31号船通导设备安装调试问题的分析及解决方案" ["Analysis and Resolution of the Equipment Debugging Aboard the Vessel *Haixun 31*: A Pathbreaking Project for the Communications Ministry"], 广船科技 [*Guangdong Shipbuiding Science &Technology*] (February 2005): 88.

37. See "China Sends Patrol Fleet to East China Sea," *China Radio International*, 1 July 2008, http://english.cri.cn/2946/2008/07/01/65s375372.htm.

38. 林红梅 [Lin Hongmei], "我国最大最先进的海事巡视船 '海巡11' 列编" ["Our Country's Largest and Most Advanced Maritime Patrol Ship 'Haixun 11' Joins the Fleet"], Xinhua, 28 September 2009.

39. Interviews, Beijing, April 2009.

40. The design of this catamaran is very similar to that of the PLA Navy's Type 022 fast attack craft—one of the few surface vessels that has entered serial production with the Chinese navy.

41. Author's discussions with Captain Bernard Moreland, USCG Liaison Officer of U.S. Embassy Beijing, November 2007.

42. "CSC All-Weather Patrol Rescue Ship Launched," 国际船艇 [World Ships & Boats] (May 2008): 6.

43. The high level of Chinese interest in this subject is evident, for example, in 张显库, 尹勇, 金一丞 [Zhang Xianku, Yin Yong, and Ji Yicheng], "海上搜救模拟器的直升机悬停鲁棒控制" ["Robust Control for Helicopter Hovering in Marine Search and Rescue Simulator"], 中国航海 [Navigation of China] 31, no. 1 (March 2008): 1–5.

44. Ningbo Academy study, 111.

45. According to the U.S. Coast Guard Liaison Officer posted at the U.S. Embassy in Beijing, China MSA and the Rescue and Salvage Bureau currently operate eleven helicopters. Moreland, "U.S.-China Civil Maritime Engagement," 10.

46. "China to Expand Maritime Administration Scope," Xinhua, 12 February 2003, http://www.china.org.cn/english/China/55774.htm.

47. Moreland, "U.S.-China Civil Maritime Engagement," 10.

48. "Great Maritime Achievements," 11.

49. See, for example, "'富山海' 轮 与 'Gdynia' 轮碰撞事故调查," ["Investigation in the Collision Involving M/V 'Fushanhai' and M/V 'Gdynia'"], 中国海事 [China Maritime Affairs] (March 2006): 18–21.

50. See, for example, the assessment by Ramsey Rayyis, International Red Cross representative in China, as quoted in Jaime FlorCruz, "People, Politics Ease China's Disaster Evacuation Efforts," CNN.com, 9 October 2007.

51. 林红梅 [Lin Hongmei], "中日俄朝立起油事故互相援助机制" ["China, Japan, Russia, and South Korea Establish an Oil Accident Mutual Support Mechanism"] on the Web site of 人民网 [People's Daily], 3 September 2008, http://www.people.com.cn.

52. 慕永通 [Mu Yongtong], 渔业管理: 以基于权利的管理为中心 [Fisheries Management: Focusing on a Rights-Based Regime] (Qingdao: Ocean University Press, 2006), 292.

53. Yunjun Yu and Yongtong Mu, "The New Institutional Arrangement for Fisheries Management in the Beibu Gulf," Marine Policy 30 (2006): 251.

54. "Fishery and Aquaculture Country Profiles: China," http://www.fao.org/fishery/countrysector/FI-CP_CN/en, 3.

55. Regarding the role of fishing rights in complicating the East Sea gas field dispute between Beijing and Tokyo, see for example, "Maritime Dispute between China

and Japan Involves Fishing Boats," 19 April 2006, available at http://www.fishupdate.com/news/fullstory.php/aid/4334/Maritime_dispute_between_China_and_Japan_involves_fishing_boats.html.

56. *The State of the World Fisheries and Aquaculture 2008* (Rome: United Nations Food and Agriculture Organization, 2009), 11, http://www.fao.org/docrep/10250e/i0250e00.HTM.

57. This paragraph draws upon information from "Fishery and Aquaculture Country Profiles: China," http://www.fao.org/fishery/countrysector/FI-CP_CN/en; and 李德水, 王曙光 [Li Deshui and Wang Shugang], 中国海洋统计年鉴2004 [*China Marine Statistical Yearbook 2004*] (Beijing: Ocean Press, 2005), xi–xvi.

58. Ningbo Academy study, 37.

59. On this subject, see Lyle Goldstein, "Strategic Implications of Chinese Fisheries Development," Jamestown *China Brief* 9, no. 16 (5 August 2009), available at http://www.jamestown.org/programs/chinabrief/.

60. Ningbo Academy study, 40.

61. Guifang Xue, "China's Distant Water Fisheries and Its Responses to Flag State Responsibilities," *Marine Policy* 30 (2006) 653.

62. Ningbo Academy study, 12.

63. 吕贤臣 [Lu Xianchen], "现代海盗的威胁和防范" [The Threat and Precautions Against Modern Pirates], 现代舰船 [*Modern Ships*] (October 2006): 26–29.

64. Li Zhujiang ed., 海洋与渔业: 应急管理 [*The Ocean and the Fishing Industry: Emergency Management*] (Beijing: Ocean Press, 2007), 299.

65. 王旭 [Wang Xu], "我南海海警依法驱逐外籍渔船20余艘" ["Our South China Sea Maritime Police Acting in Accordance with the Law Expel 20 Foreign Fishing Boats"], 2 August 2009, availabel at http://www.cctv.com.

66. Hai Tao and Qi Fei, "PRC Building Civilian 'Law Enforcement' Fleet for South China Sea," *International Herald Leader*, 20 March 2009, OSC# CPP20090324671007.

67. "China Customs Annual Report 2007," 1, GAC Web site, http://www.customs.gov.cn/publish/portal0/.

68. Ibid., 4.

69. "Chinese Customs Uncover 1,190 Smuggling Cases in 2007," *Renmin Wang*, 10 January 2008.

70. 卢文辉, 叶信鹄 [Lu Wenhui and Ye Xinhu], "厦门市涉台毒品犯罪问题研究" ["Research on the Platforms Used in the Xiamen City Illegal Drug Problem"], 福建公安高等专科学校学报 [*Fujian Police Senior Academy Journal*] (March 2007): 12.

71. [Wang Yisheng], "濒海作战舰载雷达" ["Shipborne Radar for Inshore Combat"], 当代海军 [*Modern Navy*] (December 2005): 54.

72. Ningbo Academy study, 38.

73. "China Customs Annual Report 2007," 4.

74. Ibid., 9.

75. Ningbo Academy study, 27. A higher number of personnel, eight thousand, is given in different sources, including 孙书贤 [Sun Xuxian], "中国海监: 护卫国家海洋权益"

["China Maritime Surveillance: Protecting the Nation's Oceanic Interests"], 中国国防报 [*China National Defense Report*], 5 May 2008, 21.

76. "China Faces Severe Ocean Pollution," *China Daily*, 11 January 2006.

77. Web site of the North China Sea Marine Forecasting Center, http://www.nmfc.gov.cn/.

78. 白俊丰 [Bai Junfeng], "中国海洋警察建设构想" ["Conception Regarding the Building of China's Maritime Police"], 海洋管理 [*Maritime Management*] (March 2006): 37.

79. Report of 1 July 2008 on SOA's official Web site at http://www.soa.gov.cn/.

80. "Sea Patrol Force to Get More Muscle," *China Daily*, 20 October 2008, http://www. chinadaily.com.cn/china/2008-10/21/content_7123436.htm.

81. 陈光文 [Chen Guangwen], "中国海上警备力量" ["China's Coast Guard Capabilities"], 兵器知识 [*Ordnance Knowledge*] (May 2009): 51–52. See also "List of China Marine Surveillance Vessels," at *China Defense Today*, http://www.sinodefence. com/navy/marine-surveillance/ship.asp.

82. 22 July 2008 report on SOA's official Web site, http://www.soa.gov.cn/.

83. Chen, "China's Coast Guard Capabilities," 52.

84. Ningbo Academy study, 145.

85. 孙书贤 [Sun Xuxian], "中国海监: 护卫国家海洋权益" ["China Maritime Surveillance: Protecting the Nation's Oceanic Interests"], 中国国防报 [*China National Defense Report*], 5 May 2008, 21.

86. Chen, "China's Coast Guard Capabilities, 57.

87. 白俊丰 [Bai Junfeng], "中国海洋警察建设构想" ["Conception Regarding the Building of China's Maritime Police"], 海洋管理 [*Maritime Management*] (March 2006): 38.

88. 孙书贤 [Sun Xuxian], "进一步增强使命感和责任感奋精神, 开拓进取不断开创海监工作的新局面" ["Further Enhance the Sense of Mission and Responsibility and Constantly Foster New Work Initiatives for China Sea Surveillance"], 海洋开发与管理 [*Maritime Development and Management*] (March 2008): 11–16; 苏宸 [Su Chen], "雾航: '中国海监18' 船船长亲历东海维权" ["Foggy Patrol: The Captain of 'China Maritime Surveillance Boat 18' Upholds Sovereign Rights in the East Sea"], 海洋世界 [*Ocean World*] (April 2008): 52–53.

89. Sun Xiaohua, "Sea Patrol Force to Get More Muscle," *China Daily*, 21 October 2008, http://www.chinadaily.com.cn/china/2008-10/21/content_7123436.htm.

90. "中国海监跟踪美间谍船详情: 美舰无视中方警告" ["Detailed Description of China Maritime Surveillance Trailing a U.S. Spy Vessel: The U.S. Vessel Defies China's Warning"], 新华网 [Xinhua Net], 15 September 2009.

91. On this recent mission to Antarctica, see, for example, 崔晓龙 [Cui Xiaolong], "亲历 '雪龙' 号远征南极" ["Intimate Look at the 'Snow Dragon's' Expedition to the South Pole"], 舰船知识 [*Naval & Merchant Ships*] (July 2007): 22–25.

92. Till, *Seapower*, 343–46.

93. Bai, "Conception Regarding the Building of China's Maritime Police," 35.

94. Ningbo Academy study, 4.

95. Ibid., 221. Bai Junfeng also asserts that a future Chinese coast guard would support the Chinese navy in wartime. This analysis lists as possible wartime missions: "supporting and participating with the navy in combat operations, escorting maritime commerce, protecting ports, securing wharves, and supporting the full mobilization of citizens." Bai, "Conception Regarding the Building of China's Maritime Police," 38.

96. 田承基 [Tian Chengji], "专家呼唤 '中国海岸警卫队' 保海洋权益" ["Expert Calls for a 'Chinese Coast Guard' to Protect Maritime Rights and Interests"], 人民网 [*People's Daily Net*], 21 June 2009.

97. Ningbo Academy study, 9.

98. Ibid., 14. A similar idea is articulated in Bai, "Conception Regarding the Building of China's Maritime Police," 38.

99. Ningbo Academy study, 213.

100. 孙景平 [Sun Jingping], "新世纪新阶段海上安全战略断想" ["Notes on Maritime Security Strategy in the New Period for the New Century"], 中国军事科学 [*China Military Science*] (June 2008): 77–78.

101. 菖学军 [Chang Xuejun], "黄金水道: 上演立体大搜救" ["The Golden Sea Route: Presenting Multidimensional Search and Rescue"], 当代海军 [*Modern Navy*] (August 2009): 8–14.

102. Richard Suttmeier, "China, Safety, and the Management of Risks," *Asia Policy* 6 (July 2008): 133.

103. Ibid., 131.

104. Ibid., 141.

105. Ibid., 143.

106. Ibid., 142.

107. Ibid., 143.

108. Ibid., 142.

109. Ningbo Academy study, 69–70.

110. Discussions with MSA- and SOA-affiliated personnel, Qingdao, China, November 2007.

111. Ningbo Academy study, 212.

112. Ibid., 16.

113. Ibid., 69.

114. "China Holds Workshop for Asian, African Maritime Officials," Xinhua, 4 June 2008.

115. Regarding other international maritime security initiatives, see for example, 许艳, 刘政 [Xu Yan and Liu Zheng], "中国与东盟加强海事合作" ["Maritime Cooperation Between China and ASEAN Strengthened"], 中国海事 [*China Maritime Affairs*] (September 2007): 60–62.

116. See, for example, 郝光亮 [Hao Guangliang], "海事部门成功救助朝鲜籍'君山'轮上 21名遇险船员" ["China Maritime Authorities Successfully Rescued 21 Seafarers from

the Korean Vessel M/V *Jun Shan*"], 中国海事 [*China Maritime Affairs*] (November 2007): 18–20.

117. Ningbo Academy Study, 15.

118. Till, *Seapower*, 343, 347.

119. Ningbo Academy study, 14.

Bernard Moreland

U.S.–China Civil Maritime Operational Engagement

THE U.S. COAST GUARD'S ENGAGEMENT with civil maritime counterparts in China has grown rapidly since 2006. The civil maritime relationship has expanded on every front, with bilateral and multilateral efforts in port security, search and rescue, fisheries law enforcement and other areas. Several times over the past three years, U.S. and Chinese maritime command centers coordinated control of ships, aircraft, and law enforcement agents in real-time twenty-four-hour operations to save lives or enforce the law on the high seas. U.S. Coast Guard (USCG) port security inspectors have been granted access to Chinese ports, and Chinese port security inspectors have accepted the same courtesy to inspect the security in U.S. ports.

The United States' and China's civil maritime interests are converging, spurring ever-increasing cooperation. The USCG in 2006 established permanent liaison with agencies in four Chinese ministries in Beijing to enable that cooperation, resulting in the rapid expansion of civil maritime contacts. This chapter summarizes these developments.

Why Is the U.S. Coast Guard Engaged with China?

China has an enormous civil maritime sector with interests that overlap those of the U.S. civil maritime sector, and the USCG is the operational core of United States' civil maritime sector. The USCG is in China because the United States and China can better extend their respective civil maritime interests by cooperating. Simply put, we get more maritime governance for less money when we work together, and the USCG is in China to enable that engagement.

To understand this relationship, it is important to first understand the nature of the USCG. The USCG is more than a domestic rescue organization; it is the center of gravity for the United States' civil maritime operations. The USCG has broad authority over virtually every area of U.S. federal civil interests at sea, including safety, security, mobility and protection of natural resources and the environment.[1]

Other U.S. civil agencies have ships, boats, and airplanes, but the USCG has the largest capacity as well as the most extensive capabilities. The National Oceanic and Atmospheric Administration (NOAA) has 19 ships totaling about 27,000 tons, and 12 aircraft.[2] The National Science Foundation leases 2 icebreakers. Customs and Border Patrol has more than 250 aircraft focused on the land borders and 200 boats.[3] The USCG, in contrast, has 250 commissioned cutters more than 65 feet long, totaling about 200,000 tons, and 1,700 boats less than 65 feet long. The USCG's air wing has more than 200 maritime aircraft.[4]

Distinct from the other civil maritime elements noted, the USCG is a military force with more than 39,000 active-duty military officers and troops. The USCG is not a navy, but its count of active-duty personnel puts it in league with the navies of Britain, Japan, Indonesia, Vietnam, and Italy.[5] In addition to the active-duty armed force, the USCG has more than 50,000 civilians, reservists, and auxiliarists, broadening its technical competencies and giving the USCG the ability to surge in a crisis.

One reason the USCG has such scale compared with other U.S. maritime agencies, or even compared with other nations, is the extraordinary scope of its responsibilities. Most federal agencies with maritime components have narrowly defined missions and purpose-built maritime resources to pursue them. The USCG, conversely, is a broadly multimission organization. The USCG is the principal U.S. federal maritime security agency at home and abroad. It enforces all law within U.S. maritime borders as well as international law and high seas conventions globally. It is also the principal U.S. federal maritime safety agency, regulating vessel construction, crewing, and navigational standards. In ensuring maritime safety, it is perhaps most recognized for its excellence in search and rescue. Further still, the USCG establishes and maintains waterways systems for navigation, regulates and enforces standards to prevent maritime pollution, and responds to maritime pollution incidents when they occur. It enforces regulations that protect living marine resources, enables commerce in ice-covered waterways, and represents U.S. interests in the Arctic and Antarctic. The USCG is not the only element of the U.S. government with maritime responsibility and authority, but it is a stakeholder, enforcer, or operating partner in nearly every U.S. civil maritime interest.

What adds significantly to the USCG's scope of maritime authority and capacity is the established practice of using the service to "act" in areas of policy and standards it does not "own." For instance, the Department of State leads U.S. international maritime policy but USCG commanders execute the subsequent maritime agreements. The Department of Transportation establishes the rules governing hazardous material in U.S. ports, and the Transportation Safety Administration of the Department of Homeland Security is in charge of securing all modes of U.S. transportation, but USCG officers in the ports execute their directives and regulations. The National Science Foundation conducts polar research, but the USCG operates polar icebreakers that make such research possible. The Drug Enforcement Administration and the Immigration and Customs Enforcement investigate and penetrate smuggling organizations, and armed USCG boarding teams frequently seize trafficking ships at sea as part of their cases. Customs and Border Patrol is responsible for U.S. borders and has small boats, but the USCG has the operational capability to carry uniform border enforcement nationwide to the Arctic Ocean, Bering Sea, Pacific Ocean, Atlantic Ocean, and Gulf of Mexico. The National Marine Fisheries Service studies and regulates our living marine resources, but the USCG extends United States' enforcement to the farthest fishing grounds in the Pacific.

The USCG further pursues U.S. civil maritime interests through close cooperation with the U.S. Navy, a relationship dating back to 1797 when Congress established the U.S. Navy with an act that also authorized the president to augment the U.S. Navy with revenue cutters when needed.[6] Today, U.S. Navy–USCG cooperation extends U.S. drug interdiction, fisheries regulation, and rescue capabilities beyond the organic capabilities of the USCG.

The USCG has a natural overlap of interests with China, a global leader in civil maritime industry. More than 1,800 merchant ships fly the Chinese flag.[7] Only Panama and Liberia have more ships registered, but virtually none is owned by those nations. Another 1,400 Chinese-owned ships are registered under foreign flags.[8] Five of the world's top ten ports, when measured by cargo volume, are in China.[9] China has 210,000 fishing boats, and 1,700 of them are registered for high-seas fisheries.[10] They are found from the Southern Ocean all the way up to the North Pacific.

China for over a decade was the world's third-largest shipbuilder, behind Japan and South Korea, but China's highest governing body, the State Council, has laid plans for China to become the world's largest shipbuilder, and they are closing fast.[11] China's shipbuilding capacity grew by 40 percent per year in recent years, quadrupling from 2002 to 2005.[12] China's shipbuilding growth "slowed" to 30 percent in 2007, with China's shipbuilders grabbing 42 percent of the world's new orders.[13] New orders for ships fell off sharply in late 2008 and 2009 with the global recession, but have rebounded sharply in 2010 with China leading the world in deadweight tonnage of ships produced in the first quarter of this year.[14]

Any nation with civil maritime interests will find these interests overlapping with those of China. For the United States, the USCG is at the operational center of civil maritime interests. U.S. port security begins in the factories and ports where cargo is loaded in China for shipment to America. U.S. maritime environmental and resource interests are impacted by Chinese resource extraction. The United States and China share coastal borders on the Pacific Ocean. Chinese ships are in U.S. ports and waters. U.S. ships are in China's ports, waters, and shipyards.

Multimission, Multiministry Engagement

China has no civil maritime operational center of gravity like the USCG, so several different Chinese agencies execute China's substantial civil maritime operations. In Chinese maritime governance, policy control extends directly to operational control.

For example, the USCG acts as an operational and enforcement "front end" for U.S. domestic fisheries policy, which is managed by the Department of Commerce, as well as for high-seas fisheries agreements, which are managed by the Department of State. In China, however, the Ministry of Agriculture supervises the fishing industry and is responsible for industry management, control, safety, and enforcement. The Chinese Ministry of Agriculture fisheries cutters enforce Chinese fisheries law. In contrast with the United States, the Chinese Ministry of Agriculture "at the top" has its own International Cooperation Department, which represents China at international fisheries conferences, and "at the bottom" has seventeen of its own cutters, ranging from three hundred tons to four thousand tons, for both domestic and high seas patrols.

China's other maritime interests are similarly organized. A single bureaucratic component will control all aspects of a national interest, from "high level" policy down to "deck plate" capability and enforcement. With that in mind, China has eight departments in four ministries and ministry-level organizations that have substantial civil maritime interests and operational capabilities. They overlap USCG interests in the following mission areas.

Law Enforcement

The People's Armed Police (PAP) is a collective term for militarily trained and organized law enforcement departments and special units in various central government ministries and provincial governments.[15] The PAP's Border Control Department (BCD) is subordinated to the Ministry of Public Security. BCD guards most of China's land and sea borders.[16] With 103,000 troops, the BCD is the second largest of the PAP's eight service arms, which collectively number 660,000 troops.[17]

About 10 percent of the BCD's resources are assigned to China's maritime borders. The BCD operates a fleet of patrol boats but has no air wing. The maritime units are subordinated to regional commanders largely organized along provincial lines; those same commanders are also in charge of land borders as well as land, sea, and air ports of entry.

The BCD in 2007 acquired the first of two new "thousand-ton cutters," about the size of a USCG medium-endurance cutter. In addition, the PLA Navy transferred two frigates to the BCD.

The BCD marks its cutters as "China Coast Guard" (CCG). However, the CCG is not a mirror image of the USCG—there are several important differences. The USCG is a singular organization with a command pyramid leading to the commandant. The CCG is not a separate maritime organization within the BCD. Instead, CCG units are under regional commanders that also control land-oriented units. There is no single CCG commander. The CCG does not have the USCG's broad authority; it does not often act as the "operational front end" for other organizations. There are exceptions; for instance, the CCG patrol boats are often called upon by China's maritime rescue command centers to perform search-and-rescue missions, and sometimes execute boardings at sea on behalf of the China Narcotics Control Department.

However, the CCG also has many similarities to the USCG. The CCG is armed, and its boats and a handful of PAP-operated China Customs' cutters are the only cutters among China's array of civil maritime government vessels that display and use deck-mounted weapons in the executions of their normal missions.[18] The USCG and the CCG's PAP troops are both militarily trained, organized, and disciplined. The Chinese Constitution recognizes the PAP as part of the armed forces of China in a manner similar to the way U.S. law establishes the USCG as part of the armed forces of the United States.[19] Both the CCG and the USCG are maritime armed forces that lie outside their country's respective defense departments or ministries but are available to them for national defense.

Because of these organizational and cultural similarities, the BCD is a good "fit" to act as the primary counterpart to the USCG in China. Senior USCG visitors to China must meet with a variety of Chinese organizations, but the BCD has taken the role of facilitator and host for those visits.

The BCD hosted the visits of USCGC *Rush* to Qingdao in 2006 and Shanghai in 2009, and USCGC *Boutwell* to Shanghai in 2007. The USCG and the CCG conducted their first combined law enforcement operation in December 2009, cooperating in the seizure of the cocaine-trafficking fishing vessel *Jingyu 1*. The Ministry of Public Security has stated in official media its intention to "merge with the international maritime law enforcement community," and CCG senior leaders have been forthright in crediting the USCG with helping them align their maritime law enforcement practices with international standards of safety, presumption of innocence, and humane treatment of those arrested.[20]

Fisheries

In 2007 the United States and China, aided by Japanese, Russian, and Canadian aerial surveillance and intelligence, significantly increased enforcement of the U.N. General Assembly's 1991 resolution against driftnet fishing on the high seas.[21] The USCG and similar agencies in Japan and Canada coordinated long-range maritime air patrols to support cutter patrols by China, Russia, Japan, the United States, and Canada. The cooperation was coordinated under the authority of the North Pacific Coast Guard Forum, a venue to foster multilateral cooperation through the sharing of information on matters related to combined operations, exchange of information, illegal drug trafficking, maritime security, fisheries enforcement, illegal migration, and maritime domain awareness. The current membership includes agencies from Canada, China, Japan, South Korea, Russia, and the United States. Beijing's cooperation was essential to the international fisheries protection effort because China also launched investigations ashore against the illegal high-seas driftnet industry, and enforcement officers in both China and the United States agree that shore-side enforcement must supplement at-sea enforcement to successfully suppress illegal driftnet use. In 2007 the USCG and the China Ministry of Agriculture's Fisheries Law Enforcement Command, with maritime patrol support from other North Pacific nations, seized ten Chinese illegal high-seas driftnetters. An additional three were fined. These seizures are in addition to confiscations resulting strictly from China's own domestic enforcement efforts.

The seizure of *Lu Rong Yu 6007* is an illustrative example of seizures resulting from international cooperation. The USCGC *Boutwell* on 28 August 2007 embarked a China Fisheries Law Enforcement Command (CFLEC) officer in Yokosuka, Japan, and on 3 September entered what Chinese, U.S., Japanese, and Canadian reports suggested would be an optimal area and time window for enforcement of the 1997 U.N. driftnet resolution.[22] The next day, Japan aerial surveillance photographed four possible driftnetters of various nationalities on the high seas. CFLEC headquarters confirmed from e-mailed photographs that one of the vessels, *Liao Dong Yu 6215*, looked like a Chinese fishing boat and bore markings consistent with Chinese registration. However, *Liao Dong Yu 6215* was not in CFLEC's registry database.

The USCGC *Boutwell*, with the CFLEC shiprider aboard, intercepted. The Chinese officer boarded the suspect fishing boat on 5 September, supported by a *Boutwell* boarding team. The master, claiming Chinese registry, initially attempted to deny the USCG's request to board until he realized a Chinese officer was leading the team. Even though its name was not registered with CFLEC, the Chinese fisheries officer determined that there was enough evidence to presume the vessel was Chinese and to continue investigation. After boarding, the Chinese fisheries officer quickly determined from engineering documents that the vessel was in fact the China-registered *Lu Rong Yu 6007.* The ship's holds were full of squid and tuna, caught by the fishing boats' seven and a half kilometers of driftnet. CFLEC Headquarters authorized the seizure of the ship on behalf of China, and two days later, on 9 September, dispatched the fisheries cutter *Yu Zheng 118* from Yantai to Tsugaru Straits, a round-trip journey of 2,400 miles, to rendezvous with *Boutwell* and take custody of *Lu Rong Yu 6007* on 13 September. The Chinese government confiscated the ship and its catch, and fined the owners, master, and crew. Remarkably, this pattern was repeated five more times as the USCG/CFLEC team jointly pursued the North Pacific illegal driftnet fleet in the most successful year of U.S.–China high-seas driftnet enforcement to date. Illegal driftnet fishing by Chinese-flagged vessels dropped off sharply in the North Pacific Ocean in subsequent years.

Port-State Control

The USCG exercises United States' port-state authorities to protect the environment, safety, and security of U.S. ports. The USCG's Chinese counterpart for this mission is China Maritime Safety Administration (MSA), which conducts port-state inspections of foreign ships in China. In a manner similar to the way that the Transportation Safety Administration assesses foreign airports as being in compliance with U.N. International Civil Aviation Organization standards and as being secure enough to send passenger aircraft to the United States, the USCG is required to certify foreign seaports as being in compliance with U.N. International Maritime Organization's International Shipping and Port Security (ISPS) standards.[23] The USCG sends teams of officers to Chinese ports to discuss the requirements and exchange security practices. The MoT Department of Ports and Waterways hosts the visits, which take less than a week, and sends similar teams to ports in the United States. The ISPS exchanges add another layer of defense to the web of freight security programs administered by CBP, TSA, and Department of Energy. Collectively these programs protect the integrity of America's supply lines.

In addition, USCG and China Ministry of Transportation MSA port-state control officers conduct multilateral and bilateral exchanges and seminars, from working level to senior level, to ensure international coordination of port-state control practices.

Flag-State Control

USCG officers have traveled to China to inspect U.S.-flagged merchant ships there since U.S. shipowners started sending their ships to Chinese shipyards in 1980.[24] Increasing numbers of U.S.-flagged vessels are being serviced in China. USCG marine inspectors based in Tokyo and Singapore conduct almost forty certifications and inspections in China per year.

Just a few years ago, USCG marine inspectors required at least thirty days' notice and numerous visits to the Chinese embassy to obtain a visa for a single marine inspection in China.[25] The Chinese Ministry of Foreign Affairs now grants multiple entry visas to USCG inspectors, enabling them to respond to inspection requests within days, saving money for U.S. shipowners and Chinese shipyards. USCG marine inspection officers are rare among nondiplomatic U.S. government officials in enjoying this privilege.

The United States extends similar consideration to Chinese flag–state ship inspectors. China Classification Society (CCS) is warranted by the Chinese government to inspect Chinese-flagged vessels for compliance with Chinese and International Maritime Organization standards, in a manner similar to the way American Bureau of Shipping inspects ships on behalf of the U.S. government. The CCS was once part of MoT but has since been spun off into a self-funding quasi-governmental organization. CCS officers inspect China's registered ships in ports around the world. CCS offices in New Jersey and California dispatch inspectors to U.S. ports to inspect China-registered vessels in the United States. USCG officers maintain regular contact with the CCS, as well as with several major shipping companies with hubs in China, to ensure they understand the port-state expectations of the United States.

Polar Icebreaking

The State Oceanic Administration (SOA) of China is in the Ministry of Land and Natural Resources. SOA has a number of subordinate organizations with various research, survey, meteorological, and surveillance responsibilities. Most of their functions are mirrored in the functions of NOAA; as a result, NOAA considers SOA to be their counterpart in China.[26] Like NOAA, SOA has oceangoing research ships. Their subordinate, China Marine Surveillance (CMS), is responsible for monitoring China's exclusive economic zone. They have a number of TurboPanda twin-engine medium-range surveillance airplanes, similar to the twin-engine CASA HC-144A that the USCG is purchasing in its Deepwater acquisition program. In most cases, there is little operational overlap between SOA and the USCG, and the USCG has not developed a relationship with CMS or the oceanographic departments of SOA.

However, SOA is in charge of the China Arctic and Antarctic Administration as well as the Polar Research Institute of China, which operates China's single polar icebreaker, the research vessel *Xue Long* (*Snow Dragon*). The USCG operates America's two commissioned polar icebreakers, the Coast Guard cutters *Healy* and *Polar Sea*. To date, while Chinese and U.S. icebreakers have carried each other's scientists, the USCG has not conducted any direct polar operational coordination with SOA or R/V *Xue Long*.

Search and Rescue

The MoT leads China's maritime search-and-rescue efforts and runs an interagency Maritime Rescue Center (MRC) in Beijing to coordinate requests for resources across ministries. Although it is a national-level interministry organization, most MRC staff officers come from the MSA, a department of the MoT.

The Beijing MRC has operationally subordinate to it a string of rescue coordination centers along China's coast and major waterways. They are often colocated with MSA headquarters offices and vessel traffic systems. Shanghai

MSA also manages China Ship Reporting System, or CHISREP, a database that tracks the location of PRC-flagged vessels around the world. It is thus a flag-state control instrument.

The United States has a similar instrument, AMVER, but with a different purpose. The USCG's Automated Mutual Vessel Rescue system, or AMVER, is a database that tracks any vessel that elects to participate—any flag, on any voyage. AMVER is not used for flag-state control; AMVER's purpose is to support search and rescue. When mariners are in distress at sea, any rescue coordination center around the world can query AMVER for the location of the nearest registered ships that could possibly render assistance. More than seventeen thousand ships from 155 nations have volunteered to be part of this international safety-at-sea system, but Chinese-flagged vessels are underrepresented with only about three hundred ships registered. The USCG and MoT have had a series of discussions about increasing Chinese participation and developing links between AMVER and CHISREP, which would allow AMVER to query CHISREP to locate ships for rescues.

The power of AMVER to save lives was demonstrated to China twice in 2007. In March the Panamanian-flagged merchant vessel *Unicorn Ace* with nineteen crew, all Chinese citizens, was sailing from Shanghai to Malaysia to embark lumber for Taiwan when it encountered severe weather in the South China Sea. Hong Kong MRC called on the USCG's AMVER system, which located the Indian freighter *Prahuh Yuvika* nearby. M/V *Unicorn Ace* capsized and sank, but the Hong Kong MRC coordinated *Prahuh Yuvika* and search aircraft to locate and rescue eleven Chinese sailors, and they recovered the remains of one other. The South China Sea is not a USCG patrol area. The distressed vessel and rescuing vessel were not U.S. registered or owned, and their crews were not Americans. The command center that coordinated the rescue was not a USCG command center. But the USCG's AMVER was the link that enabled the rescue.

In July 2007 the commander of Coast Guard's 14th District in Honolulu, Hawaii, coordinated a more complex case that illustrated how AMVER and other resources work together within the USCG as well as globally. The Panamanian-flagged motor vessel *Hai Tong 7*, with twenty-two Chinese crew on board, was carrying lumber from Papua New Guinea to Dalian, China, when it encountered Typhoon Man-yi more than three hundred miles northwest of Guam. After a two-day battle against damage and flooding, the ship listed to 30 degrees, submerging its lifeboats, and began to sink. The master activated his emergency position-indicating radio beacon and ordered the crew to abandon ship directly into the water, since the lifeboats could not be launched. The USCG-led Joint Rescue Coordination Center in Honolulu, Hawaii, received notification through COSPAS/SARSAT satellites, a search-and-rescue system operated by a consortium of Russia, Canada, France, and the United States.[27]

The survivors could only live about three days without freshwater and were scattered by the typhoon across thousands of square miles of ocean. The U.S. Navy dispatched two P-3 patrol aircraft from Kadena, Japan, and located the first survivors before the hurricane had even passed. The USCG dispatched two additional C-130 maritime search aircraft from Honolulu to Guam.

Ships have limited open-ocean search capability, but are the only resource that can recover survivors from the water far from shore. AMVER located and called upon ten volunteer merchant vessels bearing flags of five countries to respond to the sinking of the M/V *Hai Tong 7*, and the USCG sortied two cutters to join the effort.[28] Working together, they located and saved thirteen of the twenty-two Chinese sailors, and recovered the remains of three others. The USCG remained in constant contact with China MRC throughout the case, providing updates and coordinating the delivery of remains. China MRC assisted by providing timely information on the rescue equipment on *Hai Tong 7* and debriefing the survivors by radio-telephone for information to support operational planning of the search.

China MRC and the USCG have cooperated in other rescues since then. However, China is currently unable to join mid-ocean searches (except by registering vessels with AMVER) because its civil maritime agencies lack long-range maritime search aircraft. Closer to shore, the China Rescue & Salvage Bureau (CRSB)—another department of MoT—trains, equips, and mans a force of helicopters, boats, and ships dedicated to maritime rescue in China's coastal regions. However, without long-range search aircraft, they are limited to cases where the location of the vessel in distress is known. Nonetheless, CRSB's coastal rescue capability is impressive; it claims to have saved or assisted 3,849 persons and US$6.5 billion in property in 2006, the first year after their new helicopter rescue arm reached its full operational capability.

The CRSB established this capability in a remarkably short time. Before 2003, CRSB's dedicated rescue arm did not exist. Until the *Dashun* ferry disaster in 1999, China organized for rescue as an ad hoc part of its salvage capabilities, and China's salvage organizations received no resources to support dedicated rescue capabilities. When ferry *Dashun* caught fire and sank, 291 persons perished, many succumbing to exposure while awaiting rescue overnight. The tragedy happened within sight of shore.

Reacting to this event, China, in its next Five-Year Plan, reorganized its rescue and salvage capabilities and provided substantial funds to develop an operational rescue capability. CRSB rescue forces are now fully operational. Command centers, rescue ships, and boats along China's coast maintain twenty-four-hour vigilance, and a fleet of eleven helicopters at three air stations is available for daylight rescue operations. The CRSB keeps rescue ships under way constantly in China's busiest waterways to be able to quickly respond to distress calls. Only a decade after the *Dashun* tragedy, China has a fully operating professional maritime search-and-rescue capacity.

Other cases have been more complex, involving a range of U.S. and Chinese national maritime interests. The USCG's multimission flexibility and core competence in interagency coordination has allowed it to broadly negotiate successful outcomes with Chinese counterparts. For instance, the 2007 rescue of M/V *Tong Cheng* started as a search-and-rescue case with a combined USCG–U.S. Navy salvage effort, saving the ship and twenty-three Chinese mariners in the North Pacific, but quickly turned into a negotiation to balance U.S. coastal state rights of port-state control with China's flag-state right for its ships to seek a port of refuge without being unduly subject to U.S. port regulation in Honolulu. The U.S. Ambassador to China, Clark Randt credited the USCG for its sophisticated interagency coordination of the customs, environmental, and safety issues, calling it "the international incident that didn't happen" because of USCG management.

In a similar fashion, in 2010 the USCG and U.S. Navy, together with the help of M/V *Orient Pacific*, saved F/V *Minpuyu* with all hands near Guam in a rescue that began as an illegal migration case. China Border Control Department and Maritime Rescue Center contacted the USCG Honolulu Rescue Coordination Center to provide information critical to the successful resolution of the case.

In April 2008 an unidentified cargo ship en route the high seas from Shanghai ran down the Chinese F/V *Lu Hai Yu 5652*, killing two fishermen. By the following month, the USCG, China Fisheries Law Enforcement Command, China MSA, and Los Angeles Police Department officers had identified and located the fleeing ship, M/V *Fair Sky*, in the Port of Los Angeles, allowing China to resolve the liability with the flag-state, Panama. The breadth of USCG missions and competencies allows USCG and Chinese maritime authorities to address complex interagency maritime issues in a manageable manner.

How Far Will U.S. Coast Guard Engagement with China Go?

The USCG is tightly constrained in resources and has not allocated international engagement funding in its budget, so all USCG engagements with China must serve authorized USCG missions unless funded by an outside agency. The single USCG liaison officer (CGLO) in Beijing is organized under the Department of Homeland Security section of the U.S. embassy; the CGLO does not sit within the Defense Attaché Office. The CGLO in Beijing has no funding for social engagement with Chinese counterparts, and there is no desk officer at any level in the USCG dedicated solely to supporting China engagement. China maritime organizations have invited the USCG to participate in many important engagements, but the USCG is unable to support all the invitations and must prioritize. The CGLO to China examines every potential engagement for three criteria to determine whether the Coast Guard's limited resources can be allocated to it: Is the engagement potentially operational and productive? Do the United States and China have common interests in the issue? Does the engagement align with U.S. law, policy, and the interests of other U.S. government agencies, particularly the State Department and the Department of Defense?

Is Engagement Potentially Operational and Productive?

USCG visits to China, and Chinese maritime agencies' visits to the United States, are warm and well received, but every engagement should have a productive operational potential. In other words, safety should be improved, lives should be saved, laws should be better enforced, resources should be protected, and so on. Although USCG engagements may have a side benefit of "increasing transparency" or "building trust," those elements are not criteria for evaluating an engagement. That the USCG and China's maritime agencies do similar things is not sufficient reason for engagement; the objective of engagement must be to do common tasks together more efficiently than doing them separately.

Do the United States and China Have Common Interests in the Issue?

With so many potential engagements and so few resources to execute them, the USCG does not have the means to pursue activities with the PRC where the Chinese leadership does not have commitment and interest. The CGLO looks for areas where China wants what the United States wants. Negotiating how to execute a mutual interest takes far fewer resources than an adversarial negotiation to find a middle ground. This "low-hanging fruit" strategy avoids more difficult issues in U.S.–China engagement.

Does the Engagement Align with U.S. Law, Policy, and the
Interests of Other U.S. Government Agencies, Particularly the
State Department and the Department of Defense?

The USCG is small. U.S.–China engagement is large. The USCG will align
with and support other U.S. government departments in areas where the service has unique national responsibilities, rather than attempt to carve out a
separate sphere of diplomatic activity within the U.S. government.

The USCG engagement strategy with China is therefore often focused on
lesser U.S. national priorities, but this avoids difficult or politically charged
issues. The USCG is pleased to work with China on important but less political
priorities, such as saving lives at sea, protecting ocean resources, and securing
the supply chain and ports.

The United States' and China's Converging Civil Maritime Interests

China is a signatory to the U.N. Convention on Law of the Sea. The United States
has signed but not ratified the Convention. However, since both the United States
and China are major maritime nations, the U.S. administration and China's leadership both support norms that balance freedom of the seas with coastal state
interests, and both support coastal states' rights to protect themselves.

The two countries' desired balances of port-state versus flag-state rights are
converging. Fifty years ago, the United States had a massive navy and merchant
marine dwarfing those of other nations, including China. America's shores were
relatively unreachable by casual threats. As a result, the United States was sharply
biased towards flag-state rights versus coastal state rights. China, nestled in a historically aggressive and unstable neighborhood, was obsessed with its land and
maritime borders and for the most part denied the existence of flag-state rights.

Today, China has the world's largest civil maritime interests and the second-largest navy. Furthermore, as the world's factory, China has become accustomed to accommodating flag-state rights for exporting ships. The United
States, conversely, has over the past decades become focused on environmental protection of its littoral seas and resources, and since 11 September 2001 has
developed an intense interest in port security. The ratio of foreign flags to U.S.-
flagged merchant ships in U.S. ports is six-to-one;[29] the United States can only
protect its ports through port-state rights. The United States insisted on replacing the old system of allowing merchant mariners ashore with seaman's papers
with a more restrictive new system requiring visas. The United States encour-

aged the IMO to adopt the international shipping and port security codes. The United States has become more interested in coastal states' rights while China has developed more interest in flag-state rights, and the two nations' perceived ideal balance of rights is converging.

The civil maritime operational cooperation has grown quickly in the last three years because, over the past decades, the two nations' interests converged faster than engagement channels grew to accommodate them. There were many potential areas of mutual cooperation waiting to be exploited by U.S. and China civil maritime authorities, and when the USCG and China's civil maritime counterparts opened the dialogue, the engagements rapidly expanded.

Applying the USCG–China Model to Work through Other Issues

USCG engagement with China has grown so successfully and rapidly in the last few years that observers often ask whether the model can be duplicated in other engagements. In the author's opinion, lessons can be learned, but the model is limited in application.

The model hinges on identifying areas where the United States and China both want the same thing. The United States and China both want safe, clean oceans, sustainable and responsible use of marine resources, and security from seaborne transnational and criminal threats, but core national interests will continue to be at the center of U.S.–China engagement, and more peripheral maritime interests will not change the positions on those core issues.[30] However, to some extent this model has already spread as the U.S. Navy and PLA Navy have since 2009 found ways to deconflict efforts to suppress piracy in the Gulf of Aden, in spite of their differences on other issues. As another example of how this model of pragmatic maritime cooperation is spreading, the North Pacific Coast Guards Forum was emulated in 2007 with the establishment of the North Atlantic Coast Guards Forum.

While the cooperation of the USCG and China's civil maritime agencies is unlikely to solve the larger differences of their respective nations, the USCG and its counterparts in China can continue to serve their nations' and the world's oceanic interests cooperatively and with mutual benefit, building shared experiences and lines of communication that assist in resolving issues at the lowest level and facilitating peaceful and secure global trade.

Notes

1. U.S. Code, Title 14, Section 89: "The Coast Guard may make inquiries, examinations, inspections, searches, seizures, and arrests upon the high seas and waters over which the United States has jurisdiction, for the prevention, detection, and suppression of violations of laws of the United States."

2. NOAA Marine Operations Web site, www.moc.noaa.gov/.

3. "Office of Air and Marine Overview," U.S. Customs and Border Protection Web site, www.cbp.gov/xp/cgov/border_security/air_marine/.

4. "Aircraft, Boats, and Cutters," U.S. Coast Guard Web site, www.uscg.mil/datasheet/.

5. "Navy Personnel (Most Recent) by Country," NationMaster.com, www.nationmaster. com/graph/mil_nav_per-military-navy-personnel. NationMaster states that its data come from a compilation of data from the *CIA Factbook*.

6. Act of July 7, 1797 (1 Stat. L. 523,525).

7. "Merchant Marine Total (Most Recent) by Country," NationMaster.com, http://www. nationmaster.com/graph/tra_mer_mar_tot-transportation-merchant-marine-total.

8. "Merchant Marine Registered in Other Countries (Most Recent) by Country," NationMaster.com, http://www.nationmaster.com/graph/tra_mer_mar_reg_in_oth_ cou-merchant-marine-registered-other-countries.

9. "Port Industry Statistics," American Association of Port Authorities, "World Port Ranking 2005," available at http://www.aapa-ports.org/Industry/content.cfm?ItemNu mber=900&navItemNumber=551.

10. China Fisheries Law Enforcement Command, as stated informally to CGLO Beijing.

11. "China's Ship Industry Strives for No. 1 Spot," 14 February 2007, Embassy of the PRC in the United States of America Web site, http://www.china-embassy.org/eng/xw/ t297829.htm.

12. "China Maps out Ambitious Goals for Shipbuilding Industry," 25 September 2006, Xinhua.net.

13. "China Mulls Cooling Shipbuilding Industry," 15 September 2007, Xinhua.net; and "China's Shipbuilding Tonnage up 30% in 2007," 8 March 2008, Xinhua.net.

14. China Knowledge, "China's New Ship Orders Skyrocket in Q1," 14 April 2010, www. chinaknowledge.com.

15. "People's Armed Police Internal Troops," SinoDefence.com, http://www.sinodefence. com/army/organisation/pap-internal.asp; "The People's Armed Police," ChinaDefense. com, http://www.china-defense.com/oped/pap/pap_1.html.

16. Some remote and contentious border areas are under control of the People's Liberation Army.

17. Information Office of the State Council, People's Republic of China, "China's National Defense in 2006," 29 December 2006, http://english.chinamil.com.cn/site2/special-reports/2007gfbps/index.htm.

18. There is at least one other exception. Some Chinese fisheries cutters in the South China Sea are armed for self-protection against pirates. They are not authorized to use their batteries for fisheries enforcement.

19. U.S. Code, Title 14, Section 1: "The Coast Guard . . . shall be a military service and a branch of the armed forces of the United States at all times."

20. Fang Yibo, "美国海岸警卫队专家首次为中国海警官兵讲学" ["U.S. Coast Guard Experts Team Visits and Gives Lectures to the Officers and Men of the China Coast Guard for the First Time"], Xinhua Net, 20 June 2007, available at www.news.cn.

21. UNGA Resolution 46/215 of 20 December 1991.

22. Technically, it was not the U.N. resolution that was being enforced. Many member nations, including China and the United States, have enacted domestic laws prohibiting their flag-state fishing vessels from use of driftnets on the high seas. It is these flag-state laws that are being enforced.

23. The International Civil Aviation Organization (ICAO), a UN organization, establishes standards for airport security and conducts voluntary audits of its member nations. The Department of Homeland Security's Transportation Safety Administration (TSA) separately assesses compliance, a function formerly carried out by the Federal Aviation Administration. If the TSA finds that a foreign airport is not meeting ICAO's recommended standards, it will typically keep the findings confidential and give the airport ninety days to correct problems. The Federal Aviation Administration has in the past issued travel advisories on noncompliant airports, such as Athens in 1985 and Lagos from 1993–99. In the Maritime Transportation Safety Act of 2004, Congress mandated a USCG/IMO security relationship modeled on the successful TSA/ICAO airport security relationship.

24. Nicholas Carron, "U.S. Coast Guard Activities in China," *Proceedings of the Marine Safety Council* (January–March 2003): 36.

25. Ibid.

26. See "NOAA, China State Oceanic Administration Sign Agreement on Marine and Fisheries Science and Technology," *NOAA Magazine*, www.noaanews.noaa.gov/stories2007/s2850.htm. NOAA refers to SOA as its "sister agency in China."

27. China, though not a member, has sent observer delegations to the COSPAS/SARSAT Consortium meetings.

28. The United States, Singapore, Hong Kong, Japan, and the Bahamas also responded.

29. CWO2 A. J. St. Germain, in his 7 November 2007 briefing to the Shanghai International Maritime Forum, pointed out that in 2006 the USCG "Annual Report on Port State Control" identified 8,178 distinct arrivals that were of SOLAS convention applicability. That is to say 8,178 ships that were more than five hundred gross tons or carrying more than twelve passengers on an international voyage called once or more in a U.S. port. By comparison, using current information from USCG databases, the size of the U.S.-inspected fleet subject to SOLAS is 1,414. The ratio is about 5.8 foreign-flagged vessels to 1 U.S.-flagged vessel.

30. Lyle Goldstein, "China, a New Maritime Partner?" U.S. Naval Institute *Proceedings* 133, no. 8 (August 2007): 27.

PART III

Maritime Legal Issues and Humanitarian Operations

Guifang (Julia) Xue

China and the Law of the Sea
A Sino-U.S. Maritime Cooperation Perspective

CHINA PARTICIPATED IN ALL THE SESSIONS of the third UN Conference on the Law of Sea during 1973–82 (UNCLOS III), and China signed the UN Convention on the Law of the Sea (UNCLOS) on 10 December 1982. However, it was only on 15 May 1996 that China ratified the UNCLOS. Over the intervening years, China made considerable effort in adjusting national legislation to prepare for the UNCLOS ratification while building capacity to safeguard sovereign rights and interests in the ocean domain. Against this background, this chapter reviews the major factors that affected China's ratification progress and implementation practice on the UNCLOS, examines the gradual changing of attitude toward international marine affairs, and investigates the potential for and benefits of broader maritime cooperation with the United States.

Introduction

A land power, China's traditional maritime interest was long confined primarily to the sea along its coasts. Except for a very few occasions in the long history of the great land empire, China did not devote sufficient attention to the sea or sea power. This resulted in China's weak maritime defense against foreign invasions.[1] Having suffered from bitter experiences, China today regards maritime security as its major concern. This position is reflected in its national legislation on maritime zones and enforcement practices, which will be discussed later.

Since returning to the United Nations in late 1971, China participated in all the sessions of the Third United Nations Conference on the Law of the Sea (UNCLOS III). For the first time, China contributed to the creation of a new international convention—the UNCLOS.[2]

Participation in UNCLOS III and the maritime practices of its neighbors kindled China's interest in the seas.[3] China was an ardent supporter of the exclusive economic zone (EEZ) regime during the negotiation of the UNCLOS and voiced its stand on many occasions.[4] China took it as the most important legal framework for the use and management of the ocean and its resources.[5] However, when the EEZ was approved under international law, China faced a dilemma. China signed the UNCLOS on 10 December 1982; as a signatory to the UNCLOS, China was keen to embrace the new regime and enjoy the maritime rights and interests.[6] At the same time, China was not satisfied with some of the UNCLOS provisions, including those on innocent passage for warships through territorial seas, the definition of "continental shelf," the boundary delimitation of the EEZ and continental shelf, and the international deep-seabed regime.[7]

Issues that Affected China's Ratification of the UNCLOS

The unsatisfactory provisions, combined with some practical issues, made it a very difficult decision for China to ratify the UNCLOS. A brief discussion of some major factors that affected China's national practice regarding the UNCLOS is offered below.

Concerns for Maritime Security

Article 17 of the UNCLOS provides that "ships of all states . . . enjoy the right of innocent passage through the territorial sea." This requirement posed a major constraint on China's ratification of the UNCLOS. Since China's early statehood, due to its deep concern for maritime security, China established a navigational policy that no right of innocent passage would be granted for warships through its territorial seas. This was accomplished by the "Declaration of the Government of the People's Republic of China (PRC) on Territorial Sea" (1958 Declaration), announced in September 1958.[8] As the basic legal document establishing China's territorial sea regime, this general position has remained unchanged for decades and has been effectively applied to matters concerning China's territorial seas.

Article 11 of the Maritime Traffic Safety Law of the PRC also provides that "no military vessels of foreign nationality may enter the territorial seas of the People's Republic of China without being authorized by the Government thereof."[9] This Chinese practice was reaffirmed in the Law of PRC on Territorial Sea and Contiguous Zone, adopted in 1992 (1992 TS/CZ Law).[10] This law maintained the principles of the 1958 Declaration, and the prior approval requirement regarding innocent passage of warships was reiterated.[11] In addition, jurisdictional control on security issues in the contiguous zone was adopted.[12] Article 33 of the UNCLOS provides coastal states with rights to control in contiguous zones only for fiscal, immigration, sanitary, or customs purposes.

This legislation shows that the security issue is of great concern to China. China's domestic legislation is a reflection of the practices of other states and is based on China's special circumstances.[13] However, restricting military vessels transiting through the territorial sea and the extension of security interests beyond the territorial sea and into the contiguous zone is obviously inconsistent with the UNCLOS. It may be expected that in the future China might amend its legislation on these issues to make them consistent with the provisions of the UNCLOS.

Complex Maritime Disputes

China is interested in the legal and economic aspects of the UNCLOS as well as the political consequences it brings about; however, as a coastal state bordering three semi-enclosed seas, China found itself disadvantaged in enjoying full entitlement under the UNCLOS.[14] In contrast to the worldwide acceptance of the EEZ regime, China hesitated to implement it.

China is adjacent to or opposite eight neighboring countries surrounding the Yellow Sea, the East China Sea, and the South China Sea: North Korea, South Korea, Japan, Vietnam, Malaysia, the Philippines, Brunei Darussalam, and Indonesia. These states vary greatly in size, geographical configuration, social and cultural structures, and economic and political systems, but many of them have contested sovereign rights or sovereignty claims to different parts of the seas and islands.[15]

China has to deal with various unilateral claims made by its maritime neighbors opposite or adjacent to its own coast and within 400 nm.[16] Nowhere in the Yellow Sea does the distance from one end to the other reach 400 nm. Most of the East China Sea is less than 400 nm in width. Any unilateral claim of a full EEZ, or continental shelf, creates substantial overlaps. The overlaps trigger disputes between the states opposite each other, especially in areas with economic potential.

Further complicating the disputes were issues of sovereignty over some offshore islands (rocks) that are valuable to the owners because of their location rather than their physical usefulness.[17] The state that claims the islands would gain enormous jurisdictional rights over the surrounding seas by establishing an EEZ.[18] China has maritime disputes regarding the ownership of the Diaoyu (Senkaku) Islands with Japan and the Xisha (Paracel) Islands and the Nansha (Spratly) Islands with Vietnam.[19] These disputes overlap maritime claims, boundary issues, and competing interests on natural resources (living and nonliving) with its neighbors. Of the disputed claims, the status of the Spratly Islands has been the most serious one and has resulted in several clashes involving military action in recent years, particularly between China and Vietnam.[20] Prompted by the problems of maritime disputes with the adjacent and opposite maritime neighbors in the Yellow Sea, East China Sea, and South China Sea, China found itself very disadvantaged in setting up its maritime zones entitled by the UNCLOS.

China and Japan border the East China Sea. China and South Korea are neighbors in both the Yellow Sea and the East China Sea. The three states have different views regarding the boundary of continental shelf. The essential problem stems from the differences between the parties concerning the principle of international law to be employed in delimitation as well as the geophysical nature of the seabed at issue.[21] South Korea argues for the median line in the Yellow Sea and part of the East China Sea but relies on the doctrine of natural prolongation in the northeastern part of the East China Sea because it extends 200 nm beyond the baseline of its territorial sea.[22]

China's fundamental position on the issue is based on the UNCLOS provision that the continental shelf is the natural prolongation of the coastal state.[23] By virtue of this principle, a coastal state may define, according to its specific geographical conditions, the limits of the continental shelf under its exclusive jurisdiction beyond its territorial sea or economic zone. The maximum limits of such a continental shelf may be determined among states through consultations. Ostensibly, the Okinawa Trough terminates the natural prolongation of Japanese territory; thus it constitutes a natural boundary between Japan, on one hand, and China and Korea, on the other. However, Japan denies this characteristic and insists instead on the application of the equidistance principle.[24]

Except for the two agreements signed with Vietnam, no other agreement has been concluded regarding the settlement of maritime disputes between China and its neighbors.[25] This owes largely to the fact that the relevant territories are claimed by more than one state, or because of the political relationship between the states involved.[26] China is facing tremendous challenges in resolving maritime disputes with its neighbors in the bordering seas.

Enforcement Challenges

Korea and Japan both ratified the UNCLOS in 1996.[27] To safeguard its maritime interests, China had to follow suit without delay. Regardless of the concerns for maritime security and disputes with its neighbors, and in spite of dissatisfaction with some of the UNCLOS provisions and innumerable implementation challenges, China ratified the UNCLOS on 15 May 1996 and formally announced the establishment of its EEZ.[28]

The ratification of the UNCLOS provided China with opportunities to safeguard its marine rights and interests according to the UNCLOS regime for the establishment of maritime zones, including a 200-nm EEZ. It also provided China with the impetus and pressure to adjust its marine laws and policies in accordance with the "Ocean Constitution" because China was facing challenges regarding its management capacities.

To prepare for legislation and enforcement based on the UNCLOS requirements, China needed to transfer the international effects of the UNCLOS to national policies.[29] China also needed to build up the legal and physical capacity to manage its oceans and seas. During the 1990s China adopted or amended a series of national laws and regulations concerning various aspects of marine affairs:

- Law of the PRC on the Protection of Marine Environment, adopted in 1983, amended in 1999[30]
- Fisheries Law of the PRC, adopted in 1986 and amended in 2000[31]
- Regulations of the PRC on Management of Foreign-related Marine Scientific Research, adopted in 1996[32]
- Decision of the Standing Committee of the National People's Congress of the PRC on the Ratification of the United Nations Convention on the Law of the Sea, announced in 1996[33]
- Declaration of the Government on the Baselines of the Territorial Sea of the PRC, announced in 1996[34]
- Law of the PRC on the Exclusive Economic Zone and the Continental Shelf, enacted in 1998 (1998 EEZ/CS Law)[35]

Of these laws and regulations, the 1998 EEZ/CS Law contains important elements of China's policy adjustment in an effort to respond to UNCLOS entitlement and requirements, and it merits a detailed discussion.

The proclamation of its EEZ in 1996 enabled China to declare sovereign rights over a significant ocean domain, guaranteed its growing interests in ocean-related activities, and provided an impetus for China to focus more on the sea and resources bordering its landmass. China finalized its law on the EEZ and continental shelf by adopting the 1998 EEZ/CS Law.[36] This law ensures, with its sixteen articles, China's sovereign rights and jurisdiction over its EEZ and continental shelf and safeguards China's national interests.[37] It provides a legal framework to manage China's marine resources according to the requirements of the UNCLOS.[38]

Article 2 of the 1998 EEZ/CS Law stipulates that the overlapping EEZ claims between China and its maritime neighbors shall be determined by agreement in accordance with the equitable principle of international law. Although China has taken steps to settle fisheries disputes by signing bilateral fisheries agreements pending the delimitations of overlapping EEZ boundaries, it remains to be seen what measures could be taken between China and its maritime neighbors to resolve the unspecified EEZ claim.[39]

Regarding EEZ enforcement, there is great variation in the national regimes that coastal states have put in place.[40] Article 12 of the 1998 EEZ/CS Law makes it clear that China may take such measures as boarding, inspection, arrest, detention, and judicial proceedings over foreign vessels in its EEZ to ensure compliance with Chinese laws and regulations. This provision echoes Article 73 of the UNCLOS without specifying any operational procedures. The lack of specific operational regulations leaves the 1998 EEZ/CS law incomplete and difficult to implement.

Overall, the 1998 EEZ/CS Law signified China's formal establishment of its maritime zones entitled by the UNCLOS.[41] China has taken an important step in building up its capacity and institutional framework to implement the UNCLOS as a coastal state and in bringing its national actions in line with the provisions of the UNCLOS.[42] The 1998 EEZ/CS law makes China stand ready for maritime cooperation with other coastal states based on a compatible legal system. However, the 1998 EEZ/CS Law is very brief and contains only skeleton provisions. It would be difficult to implement the legislation without detailed regulations. China needs to develop more detailed regulations to improve its EEZ enforcement.

Policy Adjustment and Implementation Practice

In addition to the modification of existing regulations to adapt to the changed situation and the adoption of new national laws to address emerging marine issues, China has taken concrete measures to safeguard its sovereign rights and interests, and to improve its overall legislative and administrative system for ocean management by lining up with the UNCLOS framework. Meanwhile, the state practice of China has also shown a strict control of its EEZ and active participation in international cooperation on marine affairs.

First, China pays greater attention to its oceans and seas. The land power has gradually come to realize the strategic importance of the ocean and seas. Along with the development of EEZ activities in the seas, China has attached greater attention to its bordering seas and has made a move away from its previous practice; that is, more effort has been applied in the domain of marine affairs to improve the compatibility between its domestic and international legal and policy framework. As discussed earlier, China's laws and policies have been enhanced to deal with marine issues, including the basic management principles. China absorbed many up-to-date requirements promoted by international instruments into its domestic practice. The harmonization of national policies according to the universal instruments indicates the beginning of a new regime in China.

Second, China adopts strict domestic measures to control the activities of other states in its EEZ.[43] Based on the UNCLOS regime, the EEZ is an area of shared rights and responsibilities between coastal states and foreign states.[44] Within this regime the UNCLOS has maintained balanced rights and duties in the EEZ between developing coastal states and maritime powers. Maritime powers emphasize the principle of freedom of the seas and hope to maximize the freedom while developing coastal states stress sovereignty and security.[45] Because security interest is always given first consideration in the formulation of China's marine policy, China has made an effort to develop its EEZ enforcement forces. China holds the view that the EEZ is subject to a special regime, and that a coastal state is entitled to control its EEZ.[46] It is neither a territorial sea nor the high seas.[47] China considers that its EEZ serves as a buffer zone for defense.[48] This position is demonstrated by the amendment of the Law of the PRC on Surveying and Mapping.[49] This law provides that any survey and mapping activities cannot involve state secrets or harm state security. This is a departure from its previous policy, which granted all states "freedom of navigation in and flight over" its EEZs as long as they comply with international law and Chinese law.[50] China has also updated laws and regulations to manage various aspects of foreign survey activities within its jurisdictional waters, including the EEZ. For example, the "Regulations of the People's Republic of China on the Management of Surveying and Mapping Results" (adopted at the 136th Meeting of the State Council on 17 May 2006 by the No. 469 Decree of the State Council, and put into effect on 1 September 2006) supersedes the law adopted on 21 March 1989. On 19 January 2007 China adopted the "Temporary Management Measures on Surveying and Mapping Activities Conducted by Foreign Organizations or Individuals in China."[51] To improve capability for enforcing China's jurisdictional waters, China has allocated more revenue to build up its maritime surveillance forces in recent years.[52]

Third, China is actively participating in international marine affairs. Over the past two decades, economic reform and a policy of opening up to the outside world has brought remarkable improvement to the national economy of China. With a rapid upgrade of its overall national strength, China shows increasing interests in international affairs and its spheres of influence. A sense of responsibility as a big nation, itself a natural result of China's rapid expansion of its own interests, has led China to adopt a more proactive role by committing to international cooperation on marine issues. This includes the involvement of various sessions of the UN Open-ended Informal Consultative Process on Oceans and the Law of the Sea discussions on safety of navigation, protection of vulnerable marine environments, and international cooperation and coordination on marine affairs.[53] The participation of China in the International Seabed Authority is universally recognized.[54] This has provided China with a broader view of state practice toward the UNCLOS and the general trend in the quest for the management of the world's oceans.[55]

Having realized that cooperation is a better way to achieve a win–win situation, China also participates more actively in the Workshop on Managing Potential Conflicts in the South China Sea and discussions concerning Malacca Strait security issues, and China enhances relations with ASEAN.[56] China regularly attends international forums, signs statements, and conducts consultations on the law of the sea issues with its maritime neighbors. The combination of firm territorial claims, economic and political strength, an uncompromising diplomatic stance, and demonstrated determination in pursuing its objectives makes China an important player regarding marine affairs in the region.[57]

Prospects for Sino-U.S. Maritime Cooperation

The obligations for cooperation are imposed on states by international instruments, particularly the UNCLOS, which emphasizes cooperation on most issues it addresses within its framework.[58] However, the UNCLOS does not provide any mechanism for cooperation or specify what form the cooperation might take.[59] This has made it challenging for countries to initiate maritime cooperation within the UNCLOS framework, particularly in the case of China and the United States.

Although the need for bilateral cooperation between China and United States has always been at the top of the agenda, a wide variety of issues makes cooperation between the two states a complex and a difficult process. The two countries differ greatly in their cultural background and level of economic development. They have different political systems and a great disparity in their respective national strength. Noticeably, fundamental differences exist between the two countries in dealing with some Law of the Sea issues.

Different UNCLOS Stances

The United States, as a unique superpower, has been a world leader in most areas of global affairs. It is not only far superior in terms of its overall national strength, but it also maintains a forceful rising momentum in various fields. In the ocean domain, the United States is also full of vigor as a world leader and has been very active in marine affairs. The United States has contributed immense effort to the establishment of legal regimes that govern the world oceans, including the convening of the UNCLOS; however, it has been very selective in determining its national actions vis-à-vis the "Ocean Constitution." Whether the United States should ratify the UNCLOS has been debated in Washington since 1982.[60] Now more than two and a half decades have passed, and the UNCLOS has been ratified by 160 parties, including the European Union, making it a nearly universal legal document.[61] However, the United States is still outside of this convention as a member of a distinct minority that has not signed. It may not be appropriate to compare China to the United States in this respect because they sit in totally different geopolitical situations and marine environments. Yet this does indicate how selective and vigilant the United States can be while honoring its treaty obligations and international customary law against any potential risks to its national interests.[62]

With the support of the U.S. Navy, the United States has been expanding and strengthening its maritime partnership globally to ensure its national interests. Some large military vessels have global reach and have operated for significant periods, conducting missions through multiple regions. The U.S. military vessels operating in the EEZ of China in recent years have caused some arguments.[63] Of these, the "*Impeccable* Incident" constitutes the most serious friction between China and the United States since the collision of the EP-3 military aircraft near Hainan Island in April 2001.[64]

Both China and the United States have vital interests in marine resources and keen concerns about maritime security and navigational safety. The fundamental problem between them is that they cannot agree on a number of key issues, especially those related to the balance of coastal state and international rights in the EEZ.[65] China and the United States face some outstanding issues including marine scientific research, which has emerged as the most delicate problem between the two countries over the years.[66]

A Rising China and a Rival

With the expansion of an interconnected global system, the prosperity of many countries and their continued growth may create increasing competition for resources and capital with other economic powers. This competition may encourage big countries such as the United States and China to pay greater attention to the world oceans, waterways, and natural resources. The United States has long been a maritime power while China is undergoing a profound and a long-term transformation in the economic, cultural, and political arenas. The outside world, including the United States, has demonstrated mounting concerns over the growth of China's invisible power and its influence in many parts of the world. The United States, as the world's largest trading nation, has the greatest concern regarding free movement around the world oceans and is anxious about the impact of China on the international order. For instance, the maritime claims of China to its surrounding seas, particularly the South China Sea, and EEZ enforcement interfere with the freedom of American navigation and other marine interests. The United States is concerned about asking permission from China to transit the vital international waterway. To some extent, China is considered a direct challenge to America's interest in keeping these strategic sea lines of communications open and unobstructed.

Promotion of Sino-U.S. Maritime Cooperation

Since the 1990s, the maritime power of the world has been undergoing a process of transition. Along with the increasing political, economical, and military interdependence among states, the development of cooperative mechanisms between China and the United States needs to be promoted.

Maintaining World Peace and Security

The variety and complexity of the problems between China and the United States will not allow political obstacles to stand in the way of cooperation. The major forces that promote the development of cooperation between China and the United States and that promote the major contents of their bilateral relations are constantly changing.[67] There are many opportunities for deriving new solutions for the two countries to establish a cooperative framework. Promotion of Sino-U.S. strategic and mutually beneficial relations is not only in the interests of the two countries and peoples but also conforms to the common aspiration and the general expectation of the international community.

Recent years have seen a rise in crimes at sea in the region such as terrorism, smuggling, piracy, and robbery as well as a marked increase in incidents of natural disasters. No one nation has all the resources required to address the maritime challenges and to provide safety and security throughout the entire maritime domain. As the largest developed country and the largest developing country, the United States and China bear special responsibility for safeguarding world and regional peace, stability, and security by suppressing common threats such as piracy, terrorism, weapons proliferation, drug trafficking, and other illicit activities. Meanwhile, as major powers in the world, China and the United States share many common interests in international affairs; thus they shoulder common responsibility in promoting regional and world peace and development.

Supporting Common Interests

In recent years, China–U.S. contacts and exchanges have increased in various fields. Both countries have expressed their desire to increase contacts, enhance mutual understanding, broaden consensus, and promote cooperation with positive and constructive approaches. Major conflicts within bilateral relations have been relieved to some extent, and strategic relations have been strengthened. Both sides have indicated that they attach great importance to the development of bilateral relations and would continue to make a concerted effort to build toward a constructive strategic partnership. Jointly developing a "constructive strategic partnership" represents positive cooperation.

The challenges facing China over the next decade or so include the sustainability of long-term economic growth, national health and education, and the future place of China in the world; that is, where it is heading as a nation and its relevant policy responses. China needs to increase its engagement with the world. The large maritime domain of China is important to its future security and prosperity. The continued prosperity of the U.S. economy requires free access to the markets and producers in Asia. To secure its smooth transit in the world ocean, the United States needs to further build its cooperative mechanism.

In this respect, positive signals are reflected in the newly created Maritime Strategy of the United States titled, "A Cooperative Strategy for 21st Century Seapower," produced by the maritime forces of the United States, namely, the Navy, Marine Corps, and Coast Guard.[68] It is the first maritime strategy to shift from a narrow focus on sea combat toward one that emphasizes the use of "soft power" to counter terrorism and deliver humanitarian assistance. The strategy stresses preventing conflict as much as winning wars and recognizes that no one nation can secure the world's waters against terrorism and other threats. This new approach marks a departure from the last U.S. maritime strategy in the 1980s. In the new strategy, soft power and the humanitarian as well as economic efforts have been elevated to the same level as high-end warfare. The new U.S. Maritime Strategy indicates that the United States has become more forward-leaning on international cooperative activities, which will accelerate the pace of cooperation in the maritime realm between the United States and its partners.

Despite the political obstacles between China and the United States, there have been clear common interests to bring the two countries together. The two sides will be able to allay their fundamental differences to achieve breakthroughs in areas affecting political sensitivity and security. It is possible to avoid political and institutional complacency, and to shelve delicate issues and maintain a stable basis for cooperation.

To promote closer cooperation between maritime forces of the two countries, some sort of forum aimed at fostering maritime cooperation needs to be set up to deal with threats at or from the sea, including mitigating the effects of maritime natural hazards. Maritime teams may also be dispersed to carry out humanitarian missions as well as to counter terrorism, weapons proliferation, piracy and other illicit maritime activities. Also required will be the establishment of standard operating procedures and doctrine, and the creation of a common data link for shared and improved situational awareness.

To build up the Sino-U.S. cooperative relationship, mutual understanding and trust must be continuously promoted so that the strategic interests of the partners are respected. An increased focus needs to be placed on capacity-building, humanitarian assistance, and regional frameworks for improving maritime

governance and enforcement. Concrete actions are needed to conduct cooperative activities, and more conversations at a variety of levels and in both formal
and informal settings need to be held about national objectives and about how
best maritime forces can contribute to the realization of the cooperation.

Conclusions and Recommendations

Despite a host of security challenges and maritime disputes, China ratified the
UNCLOS and accelerated the establishment of its maritime administrative system for the urgent improvement of capacity for EEZ enforcement. Upon formally promulgating national laws on territorial sea, contiguous zone, exclusive
economic zone, and continental shelf, China has redefined its maritime zones
(consisting of a 12-nm territorial sea with straight baseline and part of the outer
limit from the outset, a 24-nm contiguous zone, and 200-nm EEZ and continental shelf). Nonetheless, the Chinese legislation on the law of the sea is still
incomplete because it has not adopted operational regulations regarding specific EEZ enforcement issues.

China has encountered some difficulties in EEZ enforcement. This reflects
the fact that the EEZ is a relatively new regime in international law, and its
precise nature and the full conceptualization of coastal states and rights and
responsibilities of other states in the EEZ are still evolving.[69] In this process, two
trends in China's practice are noticeable. The first was the enclosure of the maritime zones in the form of national control and jurisdiction. The second was
an accommodation of competing interests and an appropriate balance between
the rights and obligations of states. Since the late 1990s China and Japan have
conducted consultations on their maritime disputes in the East China Sea.[70]
Meanwhile, China and South Korea have maintained fairly progressive consultations concerning the boundary delimitation and other Law of the Sea issues.

Although the United States is a nonparty to the UNCLOS, as customary
international law, UNCLOS is also applicable to the United States. The legal
framework of the UNCLOS provides a common regime and guidelines for
China and the United States to address their maritime issues and to facilitate
bilateral cooperation on maritime issues of common concern in a larger area.

The U.S. anxiety over the rise of China is not necessary. Despite considerable advances, a rising China does not have to pose a military, economic, and
political challenge to the United States. However, in its own interest, the United
States must be willing to bear a significant part of the burden of resolving issues
relating to maritime activities in Chinese waters. In addition, in order to lead

the world, the United States has to face and accept certain changes brought by China's entering into the current international system.

To become a major player in world affairs, a rising China also has to consider and deal with various difficulties brought by U.S. policies. Given China's rapid development as a rising economic giant, China will be facing more or less the similar situation as the United States.[71] Thus, it may be necessary for China to alter its stance on some of the Law of the Sea issues. It may also be necessary for China to structure a national maritime development strategy. Such a strategy should emphasize the sustainable development of marine resources and environments, and should consolidate national strength to safeguard its maritime interests. Such a policy should be structured with the priorities of establishing enforcement mechanisms and international cooperative frameworks for medium- and long-term goals.

For big countries such as China and the United States, mutual respect for each other's basic interests and emotions is indispensable. Only by resolving contradiction and conflict can both sides gradually build up a framework that can stabilize bilateral maritime cooperation. It is important to design and create an effective institutional mechanism to keep track of the prevailing "social temperature," and to close any "gaps in perspectives" that may open between the two states. It is also necessary to initiate some joint research projects in the legal sphere to explore the potential for detailed cooperation and to enhance intensive dialogue for confidence building.

Although there are many problems and unseen difficulties lying ahead, the need for improved maritime cooperation between China and the United States is obvious and urgent. Conversely, cooperation is not a magic process, nor can it rely on a single state. Both states have to make a common effort and do the utmost in the formation of this cooperation.

Notes

The views expressed here are solely those of the author, and do not necessarily reflect those of the Chinese government. Research funding was provided by the National Foundation for Social Science (05BFX048), the Grant for Key Research Bases for Humanity and Social Science of the State Education Ministry (SEM) of PRC (5JJDZH24), and the Scientific Research Foundation for the Returned Overseas Chinese Scholars, SEM of the PRC. The author may be reached at the Institute for the Law of the Sea, Ocean University of China, 238 Songling Road, Qingdao, 266100, PRC. Tel: 0086-532-66782330; fax: 0086-532-66781851; email: juliaxue@ouc.edu.cn.

1. In its long history, China has been invaded more than one hundred times, and the major invasions all came from the sea. See C. Park, "Oil under the Troubled Waters: The Northeast Asia Sea-bed Controversy," in *East Asia and the Law of the Sea* (Seoul: Seoul National University Press, 1983), 16. See also T. Wang, "China and the Law of the Sea," in *The Law of the Sea and Ocean Industry: New Opportunities and Restraints*, Proceedings of the Law of the Sea Institute, Sixteenth Annual Conference, ed. D. M. Johnston and N. G. Letalik (Honolulu: University of Hawaii, Law of the Sea Institute, 1982), 582.

2. The UNCLOS was signed on 10 December 1982 and entered into force on 16 November 1994. See "Oceans and Law of the Sea," UN Web site, http://www.un.org/Depts/los/reference_files/chronological_lists_of_ratifications.htm# for a list of ratifications.

3. C. Park, "The Sino-Japanese-Korea Sea Resources Controversy and the Hypowork of a 200-Mile Economic Zone," in *East Asia and the Law of the Sea* (Seoul: Seoul National University Press, 1985), 107. For China's participation of the UNCLOS III and its practice toward the UNCLOS, see J. Greenfield, *China's Practice in the Law of the Sea*, Oxford Monographs in International Law (Oxford: Clarendon Press, 1992), 193, Appendixes 2, 3, and 4. See also Z. Gao, "China and the LOS Convention," *Marine Policy* 15, no. 3 (1991): 199.

4. See Greenfield, *China's Practice*, 231.

5. Wang, "China and the Law of the Sea," 584.

6. China's basic stance toward this convention is optimistic and it considers it reasonable and acceptable to the majority of the states and the establishment of a new legal order of the world oceans. See Gao, "China and the LOS Convention," 199–209.

7. See the Statement of the Chinese delegation in the UNCLOS III in Appendixes, in Greenfield, *China's Practice in the Law of the Sea*, 231.

8. For the Chinese and English versions, see State Oceanic Administration (SOA), *Collection of the Sea Laws and Regulations*, 3rd ed. (Beijing: Ocean Press, 2001), 1–2, 197–98. The 1958 Declaration defined the application of China's sovereignty (paragraph 1 states that China's sovereignty applies to some islands separated from the mainland and four large groups of archipelagoes in the South China Sea); established a 12-nm breadth territorial sea measured by straight baselines; claimed internal waters including the Bohai Sea and Qiongzhou Strait; and required foreign warships to obtain permission before passing through China's territorial sea. See the 1958 Declaration, para. 1, 2, and 3.

9. It was adopted by the Standing Committee of the National People's Congress in 1983 and was put into effect in January 1984. For the Chinese and English versions, see SOA, *Collection of the Sea Laws and Regulations*, 35–42, 251–63.

10. The TS/CZ Law was adopted by the Standing Committee of National People's Congress in 1992. For the Chinese and English versions, see SOA, *Collection of the Sea Laws and Regulations*, 4–6, 201–15. For discussions, see L. Wang and P. Pearse, "The New Legal Regime for China's Territorial Sea," *Ocean Development and International Law* 25 (1994): 434; M. Herriman, "China's Territorial Sea and the Contiguous Zone Law and International Law of the Sea," *Maritime Studies* (January–February 1997): 15–20; and Y. Song and K. Zou, "Maritime Legislation of Mainland China and Taiwan: Developments, Comparison, Implications, and Potential Challenges for the United States," *Ocean Development and International Law* 31 (2000): 303–45.

11. The 1992 TS/CZ Law retains the 12-nm breadth territorial sea, straight baselines, prior approval of foreign warships, and sovereignty over China's archipelagoes and islands claimed in the 1958 Declaration. See Articles 2, 3, 6.

12. See the 1992 TS/CZ Law, Articles 4 and 13. It is worth noting that Article 13 provides that China exercises control in the contiguous zone to prevent and impose penalties for activities violating Chinese laws and regulations on *security* customs and fiscal, sanitary, or entry-exit control within its territory, internal waters, or territorial sea.

13. See X. Ni and A. Zhao, *A Introduction to Territorial Sea and Contiguous Zone* (Beijing: China Ocean Press, 1993), 84. J. R. Morgan is of the view that the security zones claimed by China and North Korea in the Yellow Sea, although not sanctioned by the UNCLOS, appear to contribute to the stability of the region. See J. R. Morgan, "Maritime Zones in the Yellow Sea and Their Effects on SLOC Security," in *The Regime of the Yellow Sea: Issues and Policy Options for Cooperation in the Changing Environment*, ed. C. Park, D. Kim, and S. Lee (Seoul: The Institute of East and West Studies, 1990), 59–61.

14. Article 2 of the 1992 TS/CZ Law specifically mentions the name of the claimed islands in the East China Sea and the South China Sea, in particular, the Diaoyu (Senkaku) Islands. Some countries of East Asia expressed concern over this announcement. See, "Testing the waters," *Far Eastern Economic Review*, 12 March 1992, 9; and L. G. Cordner, "The Spratly Islands Dispute and the Law of the Sea," *Ocean Development and International Law* 25 (1994): 65.

15. Eight parties presently claim sovereignty over the South China Sea islands. China, both mainland and Taiwan, and Vietnam contest ownership of the Paracels Islands. Six claims are asserted on the Spratly Islands: China, both mainland and Taiwan, and Vietnam claim the entire archipelago while the Philippines, Malaysia, and Brunei claim sovereignty over certain portions of the area. These disputes concern the ownership of some mid-ocean islets, most of which are rocks without much value, but the owner of the islets will be entitled to sovereign rights of vast waters around them and interests in the natural resources of these islets. See C. Joyner, "The Spratly Islands Dispute: Rethinking the Interplay of Law, Diplomacy, and Geo-politics in the South China Sea," *International Journal of Marine and Coastal Law* 13 (1998): 195. See also S. B. Kaye, "The Spratly Islands Dispute: A Legal Background," *Maritime Studies* (September–

October 1998): 14–25. For a discussion on the influence of the islands in the South China Sea, see A. G. O. Elferink, "The Islands in the South China Sea: How Does Their Presence Limit the Extent of the High Seas and the Area and the Maritime Zones of the Mainland Coasts?" *Ocean Development and International Law* 32 (2001): 169–90.

16. See G. Ji, "Maritime Jurisdiction in the Three China Seas: Options for Equitable Settlement," in *UN Convention on the Law of the Sea and East Asia*, ed. D. Kim, C. Park, S. H. Lee, and J. H. Paik, (Seoul: Yonsei University, Institute of East and West Studies, 1996), 87.

17. For an overall study of boundary issues, see J. M. V. Dyke, "The Republic of Korea's Maritime Boundaries," *International Journal of Marine and Coastal Law* 18, no. 4 (2003): 509–40.

18. There were tough negotiations over the issues of straight baselines and territorial claims of islands such as Diaoyu (Senkaku) in the East China Sea and the Dokdo/Tokto (Takeshima, Liancourt Rocks) in the Sea of Japan. See T. Okuhara, "The Territorial Sovereignty over the Senkaku Islands and Problems on the Surrounding Continental Shelf," *Japanese Annual of International Law* 15 (1971): 97–106. See also K. Taijiudo, "The Dispute between Japan and Korea Respecting Sovereignty over Takeshima," *Japanese Annual of International Law* 12 (1968): 1–17.

19. The two are also in dispute over the continental shelf of the East China Sea, which is overlapped by three unilateral proclamations of sovereign rights. The dispute has existed since 1969. See Park, "Oil under Troubled Waters," 34–39.

20. For a comprehensive discussion on China's claims and action in the South China Sea, see C. Park, "The South China Sea Disputes: Who Owns the Islands and the Natural Resources?" *Ocean Development and International Law* 5, no. 1 (1978): 30; and G. Austin, *China's Ocean Frontier: International Law, Military Force and National Development* (Canberra: Australian National University, 1998).

21. China and Japan had held more than twenty consultations on the boundary delimitation. China insists on the principle of natural prolongation of China's continental shelf to the Okinawa Trough and on the sovereignty of the Diaoyu (Senkaku) Islands, whereas Japan stresses its proposition on the median line. See Ministry of Foreign Affairs, "China's Maritime Demarcation and Bilateral Fisheries Affairs."

22. For update information, see the Web site of Ministry of Foreign Affairs of China, http://www.fmprc.gov.cn/eng.

23. Article 76, the UNCLOS.

24. For an in-depth survey of the Chinese and Japanese legal positions concerning this dispute, see P. Dutton, "Carving up the East China Sea," *Naval War College Review* 60, no. 2 (Spring 2007): 49–72. See also C. Park, "China and Maritime Jurisdiction: Some Boundary Issues," in *East Asia and the Law of the Sea* (Seoul: Seoul National University Press, 1983), 255–62.

25. The two Sino-Vietnamese agreements are the "Agreement between the Government of the PRC and the Government of the Socialist Republic of Vietnam on the Delimitation of the Territorial Seas, Exclusive Economic Zones, and Continental Shelves of the Gulf of Tonkin" (Sino-Vietnamese Boundary Agreement), and the "Agreement between the

Government of the PRC and the Government of the Socialist Republic of Vietnam on Fisheries Cooperation for the Gulf of Tonkin" (Sino-Vietnamese Fisheries Agreement). They are available from G. Xue, *China and International Fisheries Law and Policy* (Leiden: Martinus Nijhoff Publishers, 2005), 306–16.

26. For China's boundary issues, see Park, "China and Maritime Jurisdiction," 245–70.

27. See "Oceans and Law of the Sea," UN Website, for more details; http://www.un.org/Depts/los/reference_files/chronological_lists_of_ratifications.htm. Except for North Korea, all of the coastal states surrounding China have ratified the UNCLOS. Japan, 20 June 1996; South Korea, 29 January 1996; and Vietnam, 25 July 1994.

28. See "Decision of the Standing Committee of the National People's Congress of the People's Republic of China on the Ratification of the United Nations Convention on the Law of the Sea," adopted on 15 May 1996. For the Chinese and English versions, see SOA, *Collection of the Sea Laws and Regulations*, 3, 199–200.

29. The general approach of China toward the international conventions and agreements it has ratified is to incorporate them into its national laws. In the event of any inconsistency, international law prevails, except where there is clear legislative intent to the contrary. For instance, see Article 46 of the Law of PRC on Environmental Protection and Article 40 of Law of PRC on the Protection of Wildlife. The latter is available in Fisheries Management Body (FMB), *Complete Collection of Fisheries Law and Regulation*, vol. 1 (Beijing: China Law Press, 1999), 8–12, at 12.

30. For the Chinese and English versions, see SOA, *Collection of the Sea Laws and Regulations of the PRC*, 15–34, 216–50.

31. For the Chinese and English versions, see ibid., 43–52, 264–80.

32. For the Chinese and English versions, see ibid., 80–83, 328–33.

33. For the Chinese and English versions, see ibid., 3, 199–200. Para. 1 of this decision provides that "China shall enjoy sovereign rights and jurisdiction over an EEZ of 200 nm and the continental shelf." Para. 2 states that "China will effect, through consultations, the delimitation of maritime boundaries with the states whose coasts opposite or adjacent to China respectively on the basis of international law and in accordance with the equitable principle."

34. For the Chinese and English versions, see ibid., 7–10, 206–9.

35. The 1998 EEZ/CS Law was approved by the Standing Committee of NPC in 1998. For the Chinese and English versions, see ibid., 11–14, 210–15.

36. It is obvious that this legislative action was stimulated by its neighboring states' legislative move on the same subject. Japan and South Korea promulgated their EEZ and continental shelf in 1996.

37. See the Law of the People's Republic of China on the Exclusive Economic Zone and the Continental Shelf, 1998, Article 1. The UNCLOS grants coastal states sovereign rights to the natural resources of their EEZs and jurisdiction over certain activities. See the UNCLOS Article 56.

38. China employed the relevant provisions of the UNCLOS to define its EEZ and sovereign rights. See Article 2 of the 1998 EEZ/CS Law and Articles 55 and 57 of the UNCLOS.

39. China has signed fisheries agreements with Japan in 1999, and with Korea and Vietnam in 2000. For details, see G. Xue, "Bilateral Fisheries Agreements for the Cooperative Management of Shared Resources of the China Seas: A Note," *Ocean Development and International Law* 36 (2005): 369–81; and G. Xue, "Improved Fisheries Cooperation: Sino-Vietnamese Fisheries Agreement for the Gulf of Tonkin," *Marine and Coastal Law* 21, no. 2 (2006): 217–34.

40. See the Official Records of the 134th Plenary Meeting of the Resumed Ninth Session of the Third United Nations Conference on the Law of the Sea, 25 August 1980, vol. XIV, page 15 (1982).

41. China has established a 12-nm territorial sea, a 24-nm contiguous zone, and an EEZ and a continental shelf. Both the EEZ and continental shelf extend up to 200 nm measured from the baseline of China's territorial sea. China announced part of straight baseline coordinates of territorial sea, but some of the outer limits are still not clear.

42. The provisions of the 1998 EEZ/CS Law indicate that China's implementation practice is consistent with the general principles of the UNCLOS provisions. For instances, Articles 2, 3, and 5 of the 1998 EEZ/CS Law are virtually verbatim copies of Articles 56 (1) and 77 (1) of the UNCLOS. Article 10 of the 1998 EEZ/CS Law specifies that China is to prevent and control marine pollution.

43. See M. J. Valencia, "Summary of the Bali Dialogue," *Marine Policy* 28, no. 1 (2004): 7–12.

44. The UNCLOS provides coastal states sovereign rights and jurisdiction over natural resources whereas foreign states retain certain freedoms such as navigation and overfly. See UNCLOS Article 58.

45. Yi-zhou Wang, *International Politics* (Shanghai: Shanghai People's Press, 1995), 80.

46. See China's working papers submitted to the UNCLOS III; and Greenfield, *China's Practice in the Law of the Sea*, Appendixes. See also Morgan, "Maritime Zones in the Yellow Sea," 58. China is of the view that the use of the EEZ for nonpeaceful purposes, such as military and electronic intelligence gathering, is illegal. See X. Cheng, "A Chinese Perspective on 'Operational Modalities,'" *Marine Policy* 28, no. 1 (2004): 25–27.

47. For a supporting view: "EEZ is subject to a 'special regime.' The regime is specific in the sense that the legal regime of the EEZ is different from both the territorial sea and the high seas. It is a zone which partakes of some of the characteristics of both regimes but belongs to neither." See United Nations, *The Law of the Sea: National Legislation on the Exclusive Economic Zone, the Economic Zone and the Exclusive Fishery Zone* (New York: UN Publication, 1986), 13.

48. Morgan, "Maritime Zones in the Yellow Sea," 61.

49. The Law of PRC on Surveying and Mapping was adopted in December 1992. It was promulgated by President Decree No. 66 and effective on 1 July 1993. See SOA, *Collection of the Sea Laws and Regulations*, 64–70, 300–313. The announcement of this new law

followed the confrontation with the U.S. Navy's ocean-survey ship USS *Bowditch* with Chinese military patrol aircraft and ships in September 2002. See B. Gertz, "China Enacts Law Extending Its Control," *Washington Times*, 27 January 2003, 1.

50. See the surveying and mapping law, Article 19. This has been considered by the United States as posing a threat to U.S. Navy survey operations, such as ocean mapping and environmental monitoring. See Gertz, "China Enacts Law," 1.

51. For details of the laws and regulations related to survey and mapping activities, see 国家测绘局 [State Bureau of Surveying and Mapping of the People's Republic of China], http://www.sbsm.gov.cn.

52. For instance, the maritime rescue and research capabilities of China, among others, have improved dramatically. To expand the administrative scope of its EEZ of 200 nm, China's MSA increased its input in science and technology and further improved its maritime administrative methods. More vessels and aircraft of different models will be made in the coming years, to be used for tridimensional inspection and control over the sea, and an Internet Vessel Reporting system will also be put into use. See "China to Expand Maritime Administration Scope," 12 February 2003, Xinhua News Agency, China.org Web site, http://www.china.org.cn/english/China/55774.htm.

53. For China's participation and relevant Chinese views, see "The Key to the Chinese Delegation for Ocean Affairs and Law of the Sea at the United Nations Informal Consultative Process on the 8th Meeting," at http://china-isa.jm.chineseembassy.org/chn/xwdt/t366165.htm.

54. For details, see the Web site of China Ocean Mineral Resources R&D Association: http://www.comra.org/.

55. China has also been dispatching ships to battle Somali pirates. In March 2010 China sent the fifth task force to the Gulf of Aden for escort operations. See 胡光曲 [Hu Guangqu], "中国海军第五批护航编队首次独立护航" ["The Chinese Navy's Fifth Task Force Conducts Independent Escort for the First Time"], Huaxia.com, 23 March 2010, http://www.huaxia.com/zt/js/08-069/1805355.html.

56. For more details, see the full text of Premier Wen Jiabao's speech at the ASEAN-China Commemorative Summit: "Join Hands to Create a Better Future for China-ASEAN Relations," available from http://www.caexpo.org/eng/Info_Centre/3rd_review/leaders/t20070327_70903.html.

57. One noticeable action is the path-breaking participation of Chinese scholars in the very first Vietnamese-hosted international symposium on the South China Sea in November 2009. Although not official engagement, it is indicative of China's attitude toward maritime disputes. For more details, see "越南首召开南海问题国际研讨会中国学者到场" ["Vietnam Convenes an International Forum on South China Sea Issues for the First Time, Chinese Scholars Are Present"], 2 December 2009, http://news.ifeng.com/mil/1/200912/1202_339_1458763.shtml.

58. As compared with the 1958 Geneva Conventions, the UNCLOS has developed much more fully the framework for cooperation, although this framework has been criticized as being excessively general and lacking operational guidance. See A. F. Vysotsky, "Maritime Regionalism and Cooperation Prospect in the Yellow Sea," in *The Regime*

of the Yellow Sea: Issues and Policy Options for Cooperation in the Changing Environment, East and West Studies Series, ed. C. Park, D. Kim, and S. Lee (Seoul: Institute of East and West Studies, 1990), 71.

59. The preamble of the UNCLOS emphasizes cooperation, and the first paragraph instructs that all issues relating to the UNCLOS should be settled "in a spirit of mutual understanding and cooperation."

60. In January 1982, President Ronald Reagan rejected the UNCLOS because of some unacceptable elements of the deep-seabed mining regime, see Ronald Reagan, "Statement on United States Participation in the Third United Nations Conference on the Law of the Sea," 29 January 1982, available from www.reagan.utexas.edu/archives/speeches/1982/12982b.htm.

61. See "Oceans and Law of the Sea" for a list of ratifications. As of 1 March 2010, 160 states, including the European Union, were parties to the UNCLOS.

62. The UNCLOS was rejected for ratification by the United States on the ground that it remains a threat to American interests and it undermines U.S. sovereignty. See Reagan, "Statement on United States Participation."

63. The U.S. Navy ships, such as *Bowditch, Sumner, Mary Sears*, and others, have conducted missions in the EEZ of China and have corresponded with the enforcement vessels of China Maritime Surveillance. For more details on this account, see "U.S. Ships Had Chinese Military Reconnaissance and Anti-reconnaissance Exploration Contest Launched," 10 April 2007, http://www.chinanews.com.cn/gj/news/2007/04-10/912056.shtml. For detailed discussions, see M. J. Valencia and K. Akimoto, eds. "Military and Intelligence Gathering Activities in the Exclusive Economic Zone: Consensus and Disagreement II," *Marine Policy* 29, no. 2 (March 2005): 95–187.

64. For a fuller account, see, Ji Guoxing, "The Legality of the '*Impeccable* Incident,'" *China Security* 5, no. 2 (Spring 2009): 16–21.

65. See, for instance, "Spokesman Zhu Bangzao Gives Full Account of the Collision between U.S. and Chinese Military Planes," Ministry of Foreign Affairs, People's Republic of China, 4 April 2001, http://www.fmprc.gov.cn/ce/ceindo/eng/xwdt/t87158.htm; and "Foreign Ministry Spokesman on U.S. Navy Ships in the Exclusive Economic Zone Activities," *China Daily*, 26 September 2002, http://www.chinadaily.com.cn/gb/doc/2002-09/26/content_28136.htm.

66. For a detailed discussion on a Chinese view of marine scientific research, see H. Zhang, "The Conflict between Jurisdiction of Coastal States on MSR in EEZ and Military Survey," in *Recent Developments in the Law of the Sea and China*, ed. M. H. Nordquist, J. N. Moore, and K. Fu (Leiden: Martinus Nijhoff Publishers, 2006), 317–31; and C. Lee and C. Park, "Joint Marine Scientific Research in Intermediate/Provisional Zones between Korea and Japan," The 7th Conference of Science Council of Asia Conference, http://www.scj.go.jp/en/sca/pdf/7th_weepark.pdf.

67. For a review on Sino-U.S. bilateral relations, see "Bilateral Relations," Ministry of Foreign Affairs of the People's Republic of China, http://www.fmprc.gov.cn/eng/wjb/zzjg/bmdyzs/gjlb/3432/3433/default.htm.

68. Available from GlobalSecurity.org, http://www.globalsecurity.org/military/library/policy/navy/maritime-strategy_2007.htm.

69. China's EEZ enforcement practice may also suggest that international law is determined not as much by conventions as by the practice of states. With the changed global political dynamics, the international legal framework needs to develop to be consistent with the current context. For a summary of states' EEZ legislation and practice, see UN, *Law of the Sea*, 9–13. See also M. Valencia, "The Regime of the Exclusive Economic Zone: Issues and Responses," A Report of the Tokyo Meeting February 2003, available from http://www.EastWestCenter.org.

70. For recent developments between China and Japan, see "Hu Jintao Meets with Japanese Party Leaders," 7 May 2008, Ministry of Foreign Affairs, People's Republic of China, http://asean-chinasummit.fmprc.gov.cn/eng/zxxx/t432834.htm.

71. China is said to be emerging as "the next global power in-the-making"; S. Singh, *Continuity and Changes in China's Maritime Strategy*, available at Food and Agriculture Organization of the United Nations, http://fao.org/DOCREP/005/Y2257E/y2257e04.htm.

Peter A. Dutton

Charting the Course
Sino-American Naval Cooperation to Enhance Governance and Security

> *Suppose there were no cooperation bringing countries together on the issue of maritime transportation security; even if it possessed its own strong naval power, a country might not be able to guarantee the security of long sea lines of communication. . . . China is currently a regional maritime security bystander; it must mature into an important regional maritime participant.*
>
> —*PLA Senior Colonel Feng Liang and Lieutenant Colonel Duan Tingzhi*

Introduction

In December 2004 the president of the United States issued a National Security Presidential Directive that called upon the agencies of the federal government to enhance U.S. security and global security in the maritime domain by, among other measures, "enhancing international relationships . . . [and the] global maritime security framework to advance common security interests, [and] ensuring seamless, coordinated implementation of authorities . . . relating to the security of the Maritime Domain."[1] With these statements, the president called forth the substantial American law enforcement and national security capacities and directed utilization of the full measure of law enforcement and national security authorities to improve maritime security.

Similarly, in December 2008, Chinese leaders announced that the People's Liberation Army Navy (PLA Navy) would join the antipiracy efforts off the Horn of Africa pursuant to UN Security Council resolutions authorizing the international community to enter Somali territorial waters and even its sovereign territory. This shift reflected recognition that China's increasing interests in global affairs are threatened by nontraditional security concerns, including the piracy that caused increasing disruption to shipping traffic in the critical sea lines of communication that run through the Gulf of Aden and connect oil and commercial trade routes between Europe, the Middle East, and Asia.[2]

However, despite China's rapid rise across all dimensions of maritime power and corresponding increased interest in security and stability on the seas, China's unique perspectives on international law authorities, grounded in its long history and current strategic interests, make it difficult to find direct avenues for cooperative maritime security efforts with the United States. Despite China's ongoing participation in counterpiracy operations in the Gulf of Aden, this continues to be especially true of international military efforts to provide security in other states' exclusive economic zones (EEZ)—the nonsovereign maritime zones in which coastal states have sovereign rights to resources and jurisdiction to enforce resource-related laws. This difference of perspective on legal authorities has kept China from contributing to such activities as the Proliferation Security Initiative and Combined Task Force 150; indeed, Chinese officials and scholars have publicly questioned the legal rationales behind them. Conversely, China has been more supportive of direct state-to-state cooperative efforts such as its cooperation with the United States on the Container Security Initiative and antipiracy actions sanctioned by the United Nations. To see more clearly why China is willing to participate in some international efforts to enhance maritime security but not others, it is helpful first to reflect on the maritime environment to which both China and the United States are reacting, then to compare American and Chinese perspectives on the legal authorities legitimately available to achieve security at sea, and finally to reflect on the different maritime strategies from which each country's legal perspectives take shape.

Strength and Weakness in the Southeast Asian Maritime Commons

The United States and China both rely on the stability of the same global system of maritime trade and the security of oceanic and coastal sea-lanes. Beginning in 1989 global merchandise export trade began to expand rapidly from a steady value of about 2 trillion U.S. dollars throughout the 1980s to just under 14 trillion dollars in 2007.[3] China's rapid economic rise during this period was a major contributor to the overall increase in global trade: the value of China's exports increased from just over 50 billion dollars in 1989 to 970 billion dollars in 2006.[4] These statistics only tell part of the story. As one scholar puts it, "The relocation of a factory from one part of the world to another can be considered as a zero sum game from a production standpoint, but from a trade standpoint it results in additional flows. Trade has consequently grown at least three times as much as production between 1950 and 2005. Economies are consequently increasingly interdependent and industrial production [assumes] a global dimension."[5] To accommodate this trade, China alone has 1,870 vessels of one thousand gross tons or larger under its flag, by far the world's largest national fleet, with an additional 296 such vessels under registry by Chinese Hong Kong.[6] Thus, given the volume and value of trade between the United States and China and considering the additional dependent trade generated by these two economic giants, the stakes for security in the world's sea-lanes are enormous.[7] Sea-lane chokepoints, such as the Strait of Malacca and the Sunda Strait, are especially vulnerable to disruptions. Coastal state instability is of course a concern, congestion and collisions pose a hazard, but perhaps the most difficult challenges are presented by protean threats such as piracy, organized crime, and terrorist activity.[8] Through international cooperation, Indonesia, Malaysia, and Singapore have achieved notable success in decreasing the number of attacks by pirates against vessels at sea, but even as the overall number of attacks is decreasing, those attacks that continue to occur are becoming more violent.[9]

In addition to the threat to commercial activity posed by piracy, there is persistent concern over links between attacks against vessels at sea and the rise of transnational terrorism.[10] Although this particular threat seems to have subsided in recent years, as two energy security analysts noted in 2004, "the scourges of piracy and terrorism are increasingly intertwined: piracy on the high seas is becoming a key tactic of terrorist groups."[11] Indeed, the highly predictable pattern of the activities of commercial ships in part makes them attractive targets. This is especially true in waters with restricted maneuvering room, such as those throughout Southeast Asia's archipelagoes and straits, in which commercial vessels often move at low speed, in congested traffic patterns, and with little maneuvering space to avoid shallow water.[12]

The International Maritime Bureau's 2007 piracy report details some attacks against such vulnerable commercial vessels in the Southeast Asian waters by very well organized, supplied, and financed groups. These attacks are clearly not the work of amateurs or petty criminals. For instance, on 14 March 2007, a Honduran-flagged product tanker, the *Ai Maru*, was attacked and boarded while steaming thirty nautical miles east of Bintan Island in the Indonesian archipelago. Ten heavily armed pirates using two speedboats mounted a coordinated attack, boarded the vessel, took control, and held the crew at gunpoint before tying them up and blindfolding them. The pirates stole as much onboard valuable property as they could gather before smashing all of the ship's communication equipment and escaping in the speedboats.[13] Perhaps the most disconcerting reported incident, however, was a coordinated attack by ten speedboats filled with gun-wielding attackers against a Hong Kong–registered cargo vessel, the *Pacific Discoverer*, at anchor in the port of Lombok, Indonesia.[14] These attacks and others make clear that the international shipping system is at risk in this critical region because coastal states with long coastlines, few resources, and plentiful havens for criminals and terrorist organizations cannot provide the necessary level of governance and security on their own. The result is that in some parts of the world, including some Southeast Asian waters, the oceans represent an ungoverned "territory" every bit as enticing to criminals and transnational terrorists as bases of action as are the territories of failed and failing states such as Somalia and Sudan.

The Legal Framework for Governance and Security on the Seas

International authorities to address these instabilities were once clear. Prior to 1945, when coastal states began to assert jurisdiction over the resources of the seabed and coastal waters beyond the historic three-mile territorial sea limit, the world's oceans beyond these narrow territorial seas were entirely international in character. There was no sovereign authority on the high seas; outside a narrow band of territorial seas, the oceans were in a sense a zone of anarchy in which each vessel was responsible for its own protection once it left the relative safety of sovereign waters. The lack of governance at sea had its benefits— it fostered unfettered commercial communication, it enabled effective use of the oceanic resources by those best positioned to exploit them, and it enabled great maritime powers to create a global trade system by dominating and pacifying the seas without offending the sovereignty of coastal states.

Nonetheless, there were a number of drawbacks to this *"mare liberum"* approach to the oceans. Piracy and commerce raiding were at least as persistent a problem then as they are today, especially during periods when no naval power was sufficiently strong to suppress them.[15] Accordingly, a number of legal constructs developed out of early state practice that enabled sovereign states to assert the extraterritorial authority necessary to keep order on the oceans. To solve the problem of jurisdiction over activities on board vessels at sea, for instance, state practice required that all vessels—not just those belonging to the sovereign itself—carry the flag of the state from which they emanated. Vessels flying a state's flag carried with them the state's exclusive jurisdiction to regulate the activities on board while the vessel plied the high seas as if the vessel were a globally mobile piece of that state's territory. In addition to flag-state authority, a second legal construct, universal jurisdiction, was developed to enable the international community to assist in confronting these challenges to order at sea, which often occurred outside the reach or view of a vessel's flag state or were conducted by vessels that did not recognize the authority of any state.

Universal jurisdiction allowed all states to use their naval forces to suppress piracy, to capture offending vessels, to assert prosecutorial authority over piratical crews, and to try crew members according to the captor's domestic law.[16] Similarly, vessels found to be at sea without nationality—that is, without sufficient connection to a sovereign state—were subject to the imposition of jurisdictional authority by the naval forces of any other state. Thus, the legal constructs of flag-state authority and universal jurisdiction served to provide some fundamental policing authority by sovereign states in the maritime commons beyond their own borders. In combination with the universally recognized right of coastal states to use their policing powers to apply sovereign law within their own coastal margins, these collective authorities in international waters enabled sufficient maritime governance to be provided for maritime trade to flourish during peacetime.

During times of armed conflict, pursuant to a state's inherent right of self-defense, additional authorities developed under international law that enabled belligerent maritime powers to intrude upon the sovereign authority of the vessel's flag state. Of course, as an extension of national self-defense, naval and merchant vessels alike had the authority to repel aggressors with the use of force and to seize or destroy the aggressor ship.[17] Additionally, the blockade of an enemy's ports, as an extension of the right of siege under the law of land warfare, was a legitimate means of compelling an enemy to subdue. Under the law of blockade, with a few exceptions for humanitarian purposes, a belligerent could prevent, with force if necessary, any ship regardless of its nationality from entering or leaving an enemy's port.[18]

Other less blunt customary authorities also developed. For instance, to solve the substantial challenge presented by neutral international maritime trade in support of an enemy with minimum intrusion upon commercial interests, international consensus developed that navies could stop neutral merchants and inspect their cargo to ensure the vessel was not trading in supplies that would support the war-making activities of the enemy.[19] Known as "visit and search," this wartime authority provided an efficient mechanism to enable belligerents to control the inflow of war materials into a theater of war without unduly disrupting innocent trade. Thus, a set of authorities to lawfully interfere with other vessels at sea developed under international law in support of national self-defense. With the introduction of the UN treaty regime after World War II, two new powers were added to the customary law authorities: the obligation of states to comply with Security Council resolutions under Article 41 (calling for measures short of the use of force) and Article 42 (calling for measures including the use of force).[20]

Over time, three basic sources of law developed to provide order on the oceans: national law applied in the sovereign territorial waters along the coastal margins and on board vessels flagged by the coastal state, international policing authority in waters beyond the territorial sea, and international law related to national and collective self-defense. Fundamentally preserved in the United Nations Convention on the Law of the Sea, this remains the basic framework of maritime law and reflects the enduring interests and values that the community of states has in the global maritime commons—sovereign law and international law, which continue their long history of coexistence as overlapping sources of authority to balance the interests of coastal states and the international community at sea.[21]

National Law

The law of a sovereign authority, applied within the zones of its exclusive jurisdiction, is the strongest and most legitimate method of providing governance at sea.[22] Because the territorial sea is a zone of sovereignty, for instance, some coastal state law can be applied to ships passing through this zone. For instance, although coastal states should not exercise jurisdiction to board a foreign ship in passage through the territorial waters unless the consequences of the crime have an impact on the coastal state (such as those involving drug trafficking) or unless assistance from the coastal state's authorities is requested by the ship's master, in practice coastal states remain relatively free to define those crimes that impact their sovereignty.[23] Additionally, although the contiguous zone is not a zone of sovereignty, coastal states nonetheless have authority to extend limited jurisdiction over matters related to fiscal, immigration, sanitation, and customs interests.[24] Likewise, in the EEZ, coastal states have no sovereignty, but because they have sovereign rights to the resources, they are accorded the right to exercise jurisdiction to protect them.[25]

Many states have, for various reasons, entered into reciprocity agreements with other states to enforce their own domestic law on their behalf. States entering into such agreements tend to be those with strong maritime interests but weak enforcement capacity, partnering with states that possess stronger enforcement capacity. On 12 May 2004, for instance, Panama and the United States signed a reciprocal maritime ship-boarding agreement as an amendment to an existing bilateral maritime law enforcement assistance arrangement to allow U.S. naval ships and law enforcement cutters to enforce Panamanian domestic law aboard Panamanian-flagged civilian vessels.[26] Panama has global interests: it is the world's largest ship registry with 5,764 flagged vessels of more than one thousand gross weight tons, 4,949 of which are foreign owned. But Panama has no naval forces and no maritime law enforcement capacity capable of operating beyond its coastal waters.[27] Thus the assistance of outside powers is critical to enforcement of Panama's regime of domestic laws.

Figure 1. Chart Displaying Maritime Zones

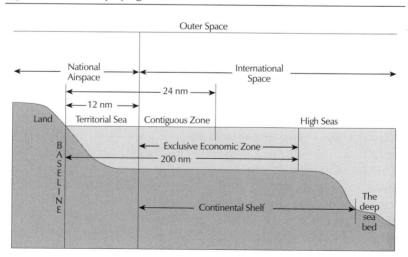

Similar bilateral agreements to enforce counterproliferation laws have been signed between the United States and the Bahamas, Belize, Croatia, Cyprus, Liberia, Malta, the Marshall Islands, and Mongolia.[28] Even where states have not entered into reciprocal law enforcement agreements, a flag state may, on a case-by-case basis, provide consent for the law enforcement authorities of another state to assert some form of jurisdiction over one or more of their vessels.[29] For a graphic representation of different legally significant maritime zones, see figure 1 (previous page).

International Law

Generally a vessel's flag state has exclusive jurisdictional authority when that vessel is on the high seas, and the flag state retains concurrent jurisdiction even in the coastal zones of other states.[30] However, international law provides all states the authority to enforce some basic measures of governance outside the sovereign territorial waters of other states. This fundamental international authority to police the global maritime commons forms the basis of the activities of international coalitions, such as the antipiracy measures taken by ships off the Horn of Africa to suppress seriously disruptive activities at sea largely emanating from Somalia and the southern Arabian peninsula. The policing authority of the international community in nonsovereign zones has as its intellectual foundation the international community's need to impose order where no sovereign authority otherwise exists to do so, in other words, on board a private, unregistered, or unflagged vessel in international waters. Such vessels are beyond flag-state jurisdiction and outside the territorial law enforcement authority of any state. As such, authority exists under customary and treaty law to "approach" civilian vessels at sea to determine the flag state and, if reasonable grounds exist to suspect one or more of the following four illegal activities, to "visit" or board the vessel to inquire further, and finally, to assert national law enforcement authority over the vessel, if necessary.[31]

Crimes of Universal Jurisdiction. Piracy is any illegal act of violence committed for a private purpose by the crew or passengers of a private ship on the high seas or in any other place outside the jurisdiction of any state (including the EEZ, since coastal state jurisdiction in that area is limited to resource and environmental preservation matters) against the crew or passengers of another private ship.[32] International law allows—indeed requires—the commanders of sovereign warships to act against piracy without the need to seek consent from any other sovereign.[33] Accordingly, in June 2007, the United States issued the Policy for the Repression of Piracy and Other Criminal Acts of Violence at Sea, which recognizes that piracy is a crime of universal jurisdiction and poses a continuing threat to the security interests of many states, undermines international economic security and freedom of navigation, threatens regional security, and contributes to the destabilization of weak coastal states. The policy recognizes that piracy may occur in combination with other unlawful and harmful activities, such as illegal fishing, smuggling, terrorism, and proliferation of weapons of mass destruction, and calls upon the international community to support the suppression of piracy.[34] Under the policy, all ships engaged in piracy and other vessels that similarly sail without the jurisdictional supervision of a flag state are subject to being boarded by the sovereign authorities of the United States and having American jurisdiction imposed over them in the interest of maintaining the security of the global maritime system.[35]

◆ ◆ ◆

In addition to crimes of universal jurisdiction, several international conventions also provide a framework for cooperation on matters of policing powers based upon the consent of the relevant sovereign in at least three additional areas that are critical to security at sea: drug trafficking, human trafficking, and international terrorism.

Drug Trafficking. Unlike piracy and slave trade, which are international crimes of universal jurisdiction on the high seas, drug trafficking remains a crime solely under state jurisdiction. That said, UNCLOS and the UN Convention for the Suppression of Illicit Traffic in Narcotic Drugs and Psychotropic Substances articulate strong international norms to provide full cooperation in the suppression of these activities and provide mechanisms for flag-state consent to cooperate with international law enforcement efforts.[36]

Human Trafficking. Human trafficking at sea is of particular concern because it has been linked to international terrorism. In July 2002, for instance, Canadian and French forces cooperated off the Horn of Africa to stop three small, high-speed boats suspected of human smuggling. One of the boats was found to be carrying ten Afghanis, two of whom were arrested as terror suspects.[37] Building on the foundation of broad international cooperation that led to including slave trade as a crime of universal jurisdiction under the Law of the Sea, the UN Convention against Transnational Organized Crime (TOC) and its related protocols were negotiated to gain international consensus for cooperation to suppress human trafficking using a framework similar to that designed to halt the illegal drug trade.[38] The TOC entered into force in September 2003 and as of June 2008 had 147 signatories and 144 state parties.[39] In part because of the threat posed by human smuggling involving transnational terrorists, the TOC's "Protocol against the Smuggling of Migrants by Land, Sea and Air" specifies that states should cooperate "to the fullest extent possible to suppress the smuggling of migrants by sea, in accordance with international law of the sea."[40] As in cases of drug smuggling, flag-state consent is required for law enforcement procedures to be undertaken by another state unless another provision of international law applies, such as the universal jurisdiction applied to vessels without nationality.[41]

International Terrorism. There are thirteen major conventions and protocols dealing with terrorism developed under the auspices of the United Nations.[42] From the perspective of maritime security, perhaps the most important of these is the 1988 Convention for the Suppression of Unlawful Acts against the Safety of Maritime Navigation, and especially its 2005 protocols.[43] The Convention expresses the conviction of the state parties that there is an "urgent need to develop international cooperation . . . [for the] prevention of unlawful acts against the safety of maritime navigation."[44] The 2005 protocols provide a means of international cooperation to suppress the use of vessels to carry out terrorist attacks, to transport terrorists, or to transport cargo destined to aid the development of unlawful programs of weapons of mass destruction. Authority to enforce the protocols' provisions, as is the case with illegal drug and human trafficking discussed earlier, is based primarily on coordination with and consent from the vessel's flag state.[45] Although the protocols have not yet entered into force, eighteen states, including the United States, have signed the protocols and two have ratified them; the protocols will come into force when twelve states have completed ratification.[46]

Fundamentally, this framework of national and international law allows the international community to better cooperate to regulate security at sea, to safeguard commerce, and to ensure the overall stability of the global maritime system. Nevertheless, stability at sea remains under assault in some parts of the world. Piracy, black-market trading, smuggling, human trafficking, weapons trafficking, and other sources of maritime instability threaten critical sea-lanes in portions of the Atlantic, Indian, and Pacific oceans. Additionally, portions of the South China Sea and the waters around the Indonesian archipelago have long harbored pirates that prey on merchant vessels passing through the narrow chokepoints that control the sea-lanes between Asia and the Middle East. Even with stepped-up, coordinated antipiracy patrols by Singapore, Malaysia, and Indonesia, the International Maritime Bureau reported that more attacks on vessels occurred in the waters around Indonesia in 2007 than in any other part of the world.[47] In 2008 and 2009, sharp increases in piracy attacks occurred in the Gulf of Aden, contributing substantially to rising global rates of piracy; however, a significant number of piracy attacks continued to be reported in the Malacca and Singapore straits, the South China Sea, and to a lesser extent in the waters surrounding the Indonesian archipelago.[48] To deal with such threats, and to take advantage of increasing international support for cooperative efforts to achieve security using the broad powers of both national and international law, the U.S. Navy in October 2007 promulgated a new strategy that recognizes that no one country can alone provide the full measure of maritime security required for the health of the global system.

The U.S. Maritime Strategy and East Asian Security Concerns

Since the end of World War II, the United States has maintained unchallenged freedom of action on the world's oceans. This fact has enabled the U.S. Navy to operate globally at will in pursuit of American interests, to provide American armed forces unchallenged space for strategic maneuver and operational reach, to use sea space to project power ashore without serious concern of disruption, and to ensure that most threats to American interests remain far from North American shores. After the Cold War, however, U.S. naval strategy shifted from preparation for global war at sea against the Soviet navy to focusing on regional stability. In the 1994 document "Forward . . . From the Sea," the secretary of the Navy and the chiefs of the naval services stated that "the purpose of the U.S. naval forces [is] to project the power and influence of the nation across the seas to foreign waters and shores in both peace and war."[49] This followed the 1992 document ". . . From the Sea," which was the first articulation of the maritime component of the U.S. national security strategy that represented a shift away from global confrontation to a new focus on regional challenges and opportunities.[50] It reoriented the Navy "toward projecting power and influence across the seas in response to regional challenges"[51] to "preserve the strategic position [that the U.S.] won with the end of the Cold War."[52]

What neither the 1992 nor the 1994 strategic documents adequately foresaw, however, was that the post–Cold War growth of the global system, including the rapid integration of new economies and the explosive expansion of maritime trade, would pose the sort of challenges to security and stability at sea not seen in nearly two centuries. These changing world conditions, in combination with the depletion of American fiscal resources, which caused "an imbalance between our readiness for future global missions and the wars we are fighting today," led the U.S. maritime forces—this time, for the first time, including the U.S. Coast Guard—in October 2007 to articulate a fundamentally new Maritime Strategy based on cooperative efforts between maritime states to achieve stability and peace on the oceans.[53]

"A Cooperative Strategy for 21st Century Seapower," while continuing to acknowledge the need for naval power to fight and win wars, recognizes that many of the chief threats to U.S. vital interests in the maritime domain come from "a hybrid blend of traditional and irregular tactics . . . and nonstate actors using both simple and sophisticated technologies in innovative ways."[54] This strategy recognizes that U.S. vital interests require more than maritime military supremacy; it also requires the capability to provide the necessary governance on the oceans to ensure sufficient security and stability at sea to enable the global system to function and thrive. "No one nation," it acknowledges, "has the resources required to provide safety and security throughout the entire maritime domain . . . and partnerships of common interests are required to counter . . . emerging threats."[55]

In support of the cooperative strategy outlined by the U.S. maritime services, then–chief of naval operations Admiral Michael Mullen, in talks with the chief of the PLA Navy, Vice Admiral Wu Shengli, in Washington in April 2007 called for a "Global Maritime Partnership" as the operational expression of his earlier one-thousand-ship navy concept.[56] The fundamental concept of the Global Maritime Partnership is to combine the maritime capacity of all willing coastal states so coordinated action can be undertaken to address threats to security and stability in the maritime commons.[57] The global system thrives not only because willing states are able to restore stability at sea once unstable areas such as the Horn of Africa develop but also because united action occurs to prevent instability from arising in the first place.[58] This requires cooperative efforts to build partner capacity, enhance goodwill in critical regions of the world, gain access to regional partners, and strengthen regional approaches to instability.[59]

In Asia, the United States hopes to forge closer ties to improve security at sea. For that purpose, each of the 2007 bilateral Cooperation Afloat Readiness and Training (CARAT) exercises between the United States and Brunei, Malaysia, the Philippines, Singapore, and Thailand (some phases of which also included observers from Vietnam) focused on enhancing maritime security among other objectives.[60] At the invitation of host countries, U.S. Navy and Coast Guard units exercised with their regional counterparts to improve overall security in the Sulu Archipelago, the Gulf of Thailand, the waters north of Java, the Singapore Strait, and the South China Sea.[61] Operations were conducted in host-nation ports, territorial waters, and other national waters as well as in maritime zones of international freedoms. Even though CARAT exercises between 2007 and 2009 retained their traditional bilateral nature, because transnational maritime threats require multinational responses, the vision of the Global Maritime Partnership is to foster more multinational exercises to develop cooperative regional action.[62]

The U.S. perspective is that all regional states have a shared stake in international commerce, safety at sea, and freedom of navigation at sea and should be welcomed into regional partnership activities designed to enhance security at sea.[63] Collaborative efforts to quell piracy and other nontraditional threats at sea are a good first step toward building a long-term U.S.–China relationship based on cooperation between powerful countries rather than competition and confrontation.[64] One senior policy advisor to President Hu Jintao agreed, stating in a 2005 speech at the Brookings Institution that China's "peaceful rise" policy is meant in part to achieve for China a role as "a responsible big power playing a constructive [part] in the international community" and that China has an interest in "joint efforts to maintain international order" and recognizes that there is "a high degree of convergence of [U.S. and PRC] national interests and mutual needs in the age of globalization." In order to best protect mutual interests, therefore, "cooperation in response to increased nontraditional security threats" will be necessary.[65] Unfortunately, however, initial reactions by Chinese leaders to the Global Maritime Partnership concept and to the new U.S. Maritime Strategy were guarded, leading U.S. Navy leaders to be only "cautiously optimistic" about the possibility of cooperative maritime action between the two countries.[66]

Chinese Perspectives on International Law of the Sea and Constabulary Maritime Power

Chinese reluctance to participate directly with U.S. maritime security operations is due in part to divergent interpretations of international law of the sea that reflect China's strategic concerns as a coastal state with irredentist offshore claims and historically weak naval forces with which to achieve its strategic objectives. Throughout the negotiations of the Law of the Sea Convention and since, China has exercised leadership among a group of countries—loosely described as "developing countries"—that sees the availability of freedom of navigation to maritime powers as a means of maintaining hegemonic powers.[67] Although China was not fully satisfied with the final compromise text of the Convention in this regard, it became a party in 1996.[68] Nonetheless, Chinese positions on international law of the sea deviate in many ways from more normative interpretations of the law. A comparison of the authorities that the United States and China claim in the major maritime zones is offered in figure 2.

Figure 2. Chart Depicting Maritime Zones and Comparing US and Chinese Authorities Within Them

UNITED STATES	CHINA
• **Territorial Sea:** Innocent passage for *all* ships, including warships.	• **Territorial Sea:** Innocent passage for all ships, *except* warships.
• **Contiguous Zone and EEZ:** Coastal state has sovereign rights to resources and *limited* resource-related jurisdictional authorities.	• **Contiguous Zone and EEZ:** Coastal state has sovereign rights to resources and *broad* jurisdictional authorities, including security interests.
Coastal states can only regulate foreign information-gathering *related to resources*.	Coastal states can regulate *all* foreign information-gathering activities.
All traditional high seas freedoms to conduct military activities are permitted, but must take into account coastal state resource concerns.	*No* traditional high seas freedoms to conduct military activities are permitted— *except passage*.
Universal jurisdiction and related constabulary authorities apply without additional approvals required.	Policy on universal jurisdiction and related constabulary powers unclear; may apply only with UN Security Council approval.

Territorial Sea

China's domestic legislation concerning its territorial sea reflects the international standard that requires coastal states to accept the innocent passage of foreign vessels through a coastal state's territorial waters, but in opposition to the historical norm and the current practice of most coastal states, China expressly excludes warships from exercising the right of innocent passage without its prior consent.[69] Normally the Chinese position on innocent passage is of little consequence to overall maritime security because presumably a coastal state will develop and maintain sufficient law enforcement capacity to maintain governance within this zone of sovereignty.

The Contiguous Zone and the Exclusive Economic Zone

The Chinese dispute the American perspective that coastal state authorities over these zones is limited to the specified rights enumerated in the text of UNCLOS, which is of significant consequence to international efforts to cooperatively achieve security at sea. The Chinese perspective is that coastal states should be allowed to enforce a much broader set of legal authorities in the EEZ; they point to UNCLOS provisions that require maritime users to "refrain from any threat or use of force" against coastal states.[70] Furthermore, the Chinese believe that, when operating in the exclusive economic zone of another state, maritime users may undertake only "internationally lawful uses of the sea" related to navigation.[71] As two Chinese scholars noted, "many developing coastal States insist that [military and intelligence gathering] activities are an abuse of 'freedom of navigation and overflight' and 'other internationally lawful uses of the sea' and are 'non-peaceful,' having encroached on the national security interests of the coastal States. . . . These activities undermine the peace, tranquility and good legal order in their exclusive economic zones and thus, violate their sovereign rights and exclusive jurisdiction."[72] China's Contiguous Zone Law reflects similar concerns with security. Going beyond the specified limits recognized under international law and articulated in Article 33 of UNCLOS, the Contiguous Zone Law states that "this Law is enacted for the People's Republic of China to exercise . . . control over its contiguous zone . . . to safeguard its national security."[73] Although China's Exclusive Economic Zone Law does not specify additional security interests beyond the contiguous zone, it contains the statement, "The provisions in this law shall not affect the historical right that the People's Republic of China enjoys."[74] This is widely viewed as an attempt to codify the Chinese perspective that coastal states may claim special security interests and related legal rights in their EEZ.

Chinese representatives to international conferences dedicated to Law of the Sea continue to argue that the American approach to freedom of navigation and use for military purposes of the EEZ represents a "frozen agenda" set by major maritime powers and enforced for too long without consultation with weaker coastal states.[75] These discussions, they argue, should seek to establish a "new balance" that protects what they see as the unique role of the EEZ in protecting national sovereignty and security when dealing with nontraditional threats. Specifically, the Chinese seek to define as "hostile"—and therefore contrary to both UNCLOS and the UN Charter—"any action that would infringe upon the national security interests of coastal countries . . . [including] carrying out military activities or employing forces in a foreign EEZ; carrying out close observation or simulated attack in a foreign EEZ; without permission of the coastal state, the entrance of submarines into the EEZ or their carrying out a simulated attack therein; carrying out electronic military reconnaissance activities in a foreign EEZ; this is interpreted as an electronic invasion and a threat to the coastal state."[76] In support of their argument that international law of the sea authorizes coastal states to ban foreign military activities in the EEZ, Chinese scholars argue that, although Article 56 requires that "in the exclusive economic zone, the coastal State shall have due regard to the rights and duties of other states," Article 58 requires in return that the international community "have due regard to the rights and duties of the coastal State and shall comply with the laws and regulations of the coastal State." The Chinese further point out that Article 59 requires that "conflict [between these two 'due regards'] should be resolved . . . taking into account the respective importance of the interests involved to the parties."[77]

In prioritizing China's interests over those of the international community, Chinese scholars argue that in the EEZ, UNCLOS affords the coastal state sovereign rights over resources, jurisdiction to manage them, and responsibility to protect and preserve the environment, and that because coastal states have additional national security interests off their coasts, it is self-evident that in the balance of "due regards" there is no room for international military activities in the EEZ without the coastal state's express consent.[78] This perspective, of course, makes nearly impossible Chinese acceptance of the application of international law authorities by U.S. Navy ships, at least in the 40 percent of the world's oceans that comprise the EEZs of other states, even for the important purpose of preventing the spread of weapons of mass destruction.[79]

Clearly, China holds very different views on international law of the sea authorities from those held by the substantial majority of states, including the United States. These differing views have significant implications for opportunities for cooperation between the two countries to achieve security at sea. For instance, the very foundation of the success of Combined Task Force (CTF) 150 is that countries as different as the United States, Denmark, and Pakistan were able to join their naval capacities and to apply an agreed-up framework of authorities based on the international law of policing powers at sea to enhance international sea-lane security in the EEZs of Somalia, Oman, Yemen, and Kenya off the Horn of Africa. Under the Chinese framework of international law, CTF 150's successes could not have occurred, which is especially significant because as much as 40 percent of the world's oceans are covered by waters claimed or claimable as coastal state EEZs. Were the restrictive Chinese approach to become accepted as the international standard, it would severely inhibit the ability of the international community to effectively apply the international law authorities discussed above in many critical ocean spaces unless the coastal state expressly consented.[80]

Chinese Strategies to Achieve Sea Security

Chinese perspectives on the Law of the Sea reflect its long history of invasion from the sea and its weakness as a maritime power for most of the past several centuries. Even today, unlike the United States, which has focused since 9/11 on sending its maritime forces worldwide to counter protean transnational threats far from American shores, China's most serious maritime security concerns remain close to home. China's naval capacity has been developed for the primary purpose of consolidating its claim to sovereignty over the islands not yet under its full control, beginning, of course, with Taiwan but also the Diaoyu (Senkaku) Islands in the East China Sea and the Spratlys and other islands in the South China Sea. Additionally, with a burgeoning shipping industry, a major stake in maritime trade, increasing reliance on seafood to feed its large population, an imperative to develop offshore hydrocarbon resources and expanded responsibilities to provide governance over its large EEZ, China has focused its coast guard capacity-building on consolidating control over the littoral water space necessary to develop and protect these interests.[81]

China's navy remains primarily a defensive force structured to provide maximum strategic antiaccess capability. In contrast to the expeditionary nature of U.S. strategies to achieve national security, for China national security from the sea is seen first and foremost as defense of its littoral periphery.[82] Chinese strategists and scholars are acutely aware that "China has repeatedly suffered grave threats from the sea," in part because China's coastline is hemmed in by a series of island chains that make it easily blockaded and that prevent easy access to the open ocean.[83] Additionally, China shares a sea border with seven neighbors and has maritime boundary or island sovereignty disputes with each of them. For centuries, China's maritime focus has—with varying degrees of success—centered on defending its long coastline from external threats to allow it to use its military strength to face continental foes and to consolidate political power within traditional national boundaries.

Since the beginning of the Communist era, China has clearly articulated only two fundamental sea strategies. The first strategy, best translated as "near-coast defense," was articulated shortly after the PLA ousted the Nationalist forces from the mainland onto Taiwan and was the organizing maritime strategy for more than three decades. Near-coast defense was a purely defensive strategy designed to articulate the navy's role in ensuring that Nationalist forces could not launch a counterattack back onto the mainland. As the cross-strait situation stabilized, the most serious security threat facing the Communist leadership was potential attack by the Soviets, quite possibly from the sea. Under either scenario, the role of the PLA Navy was to defend a narrow band of coastal waters in coordination with ground forces to protect important coastal cities, to control access to a few narrow strategic straits (Bohai, Taiwan, and Qiongzhou), and to attack the logistical vulnerabilities of aggressor forces.[84]

By the late 1970s China's strategic position was significantly stronger, and the twin strategic objectives of reunifying Taiwan and other outlying territories while deterring and defending against foreign intervention became realistic organizing principles. The new strategy to achieve these objectives, which remains China's fundamental maritime strategy today, is called "defend actively and operate in the near seas," also known as the "near seas strategy." This, too, is a defensive strategy under which the area of focus for the navy expanded from the narrow coastal waters to encompass the entire Yellow Sea, East China Sea, and the South China Sea. These seas are bounded to the east and south by a series of islands, stretching from the Kuriles in the northeast to the Indonesian archipelago in the south, which the Chinese call the first island chain. The PLA Navy's tasks in support of this strategy are to capture and maintain sea control within the first island chain to allow other forces freedom of action to coerce Taiwan, to control critical sea lines of communication within and around the first island chain, and to prevent outside forces from interfering. One method frequently discussed for achieving their strategic aim of Taiwanese reunification is blockade and isolation, and much attention has been paid by Chinese legal and strategic scholars to harmonizing China's approach to international law of the sea with its aim of achieving reunification with Taiwan by gaining, if necessary, military control over the full breadth of China's adjacent seas.[85]

Thus, defense of its vulnerable coastline—either close-in or from the littoral seas—and consolidation of control over island territories has historically provided the primary focus of maritime security for China. This has resulted in a very different set of naval interests, policies, and strategies from those developed by the United States over its long history of expeditionary maritime power operating on exterior lines and for which the maximum freedom of global navigation is required. It is from China's need to defend its coastline and coastal seas against Nationalist, Soviet, and American intervention that China's perspectives on international law of the sea have sprung. As negotiations over the text of UNCLOS proceeded throughout the 1960s, 1970s, and early 1980s, Chinese and American interests at sea were particularly sharply divergent. The Chinese have sought to use international law as an adjunct to their military forces to achieve antiaccess maritime objectives by advocating interpretations of international law of the sea that delegitimize foreign military activities in the EEZs of other states and simultaneously maintaining the widest possible maritime claims over the East and South China seas.[86]

Contrary to these historical trends, however, China is increasingly becoming a global maritime "user state" in addition to its traditional role as a "coastal state" and there is evidence that strategists, recognizing this growing convergence of changing national interests, have begun to articulate strategic concerns quite similar to those of the United States. As some Chinese military scholars have noted, "China's harbors import and export more than any in the world . . . and China is connected to all the regions and seas of the world. . . . [Accordingly] China's increasing economic development demands maritime regional security."[87] China's views on its maritime interests have begun to broaden to include concern about acts by international terrorist organizations to disrupt the global economic order from the sea, the protection of the oceans as a "vehicle for mutual commerce," the protection of China's enterprises overseas, and its dependence on overseas supplies of raw materials.[88] China and the United States now share these and many other security concerns. Both, for instance, want to preserve a peaceful international environment and both agree that the further spread of nuclear weapons would be a grave danger.[89] Nonetheless, direct U.S.–Chinese cooperation at sea remains elusive.

Comparative Chinese Maritime Security Decisions

In assessing where future opportunities lie for cooperation between the United States and China, it is helpful to consider cases in which the two countries achieved cooperation and cases in which they did not in order to discern the components of interaction that are more likely to bring a reluctant China on board. Five programs will be considered—the Container Security Initiative, the North Pacific Coast Guard Forum, the Proliferation Security Initiative, Combined Task Force (CTF) 150, and the Gulf of Aden counterpiracy operations. From the Chinese decisions regarding these programs, it will be apparent that China prefers to cooperate where it has equal power to shape the effort and where it can be sure that its sovereign prerogatives will be fully protected.

Container Security and Coast Guard Operations—Opting In

At home, Chinese strategists are cognizant that more than 5.8 billion tons of cargo valued at more than $4 trillion move annually in international maritime trade and that Shanghai and Hong Kong rank second and third, respectively, behind Singapore in annual port volume.[90] Not surprisingly, therefore, as a critical component of the global maritime trading system, China is under pressure from other user states to enhance the security of the global economic trading system by providing secure ports and stability in the roughly 3 million square kilometers of water claimed by China as under its sovereignty or jurisdiction.[91]

As Andrew Erickson explains in his chapter in part II of this volume, the U.S. Container Security Initiative seeks to enhance maritime and port safety by enforcing national regulatory and security standards for the contents of the more than 108 million cargo containers carrying the vast majority of seaborne trade each year. As is the case in the United States, Japan, and the United Kingdom, China's import and export economies are critically reliant on the security of containerized cargo. With the enormous volume of trade between China and the United States—in 2006, 21 percent of all Chinese exports went to the United States, a total value of approximately $250 billion (approximately $211 billion in 2009)—the mutual interest in security is evident.[92] The critical difference between the enforcement mechanisms of the Proliferation Security Initiative and the Container Security Initiative, and the factor making the latter generally palatable to the Chinese, is that the Container Security Initiative is entirely a product of port-state domestic law and therefore fully respectful of port-state sovereignty.

Under the auspices of Container Security Initiative, unarmed officers of the U.S. Customs and Border Protection Service are stationed in key ports around the world to work with host nation counterparts to administer nonintrusive inspections and radiation screening of all containers bound for the United States that pose a potential threat before they leave the host nation ports. The Container Security Initiative is truly a bilateral program: port states have a reciprocal right to send their customs officers to major American ports should they so choose, and the U.S. Customs and Border Protection Service shares relevant information with partner states. Additionally, although the United States has the right to reject the shipment of any container to a U.S. port, only the customs law of the exporting state governs whether a violation has been committed. Accordingly, law enforcement remains fully in the hands of and under the control of the port state and therefore fully respects the sovereignty of the port state. Currently two mainland Chinese cities—Shanghai and Shenzhen— are full participants, which may provide some competitive advantage to trade since prescreened cargo can be received expeditiously in U.S. ports.[93]

Another similarly successful law enforcement relationship exists between the coast guards of the United States and the People's Republic of China. Cooperation has been achieved in enforcement of the national fisheries laws of both countries through joint patrols and coordinated law enforcement against illegal driftnet fishing vessels under the North Pacific Coast Guard Forum.[94] Pursuant to this program, Chinese law enforcement officers have actually sailed on board U.S. Coast Guard cutters to enforce Chinese domestic fisheries law against Chinese fishing vessels on the high seas beyond the reach of most Chinese maritime law enforcement vessels. Chinese officers have also attended a Coast Guard fisheries enforcement school in Alaska. Cooperation has been excellent for nearly three decades in allowing U.S. Coast Guard inspectors access to Chinese ports to inspect U.S.-flagged vessels and to inspect port security requirements.[95] This program, too, has been successful because it relies fully on reciprocal enforcement of each state's domestic law and is therefore free of the barriers posed by the difficulties of interpretation of the scope of legitimate international law authority that continues to plague hopes of wider Sino-American cooperation in other areas.

United Nations–Sponsored Counterpiracy Activities—Opting In

At the United Nations, China voted in favor of international military action in the territorial waters of a coastal state that has insufficient capacity to prevent its waters from being used as safe haven for pirates attacking international shipping. When Somalia's transitional federal government sent a letter of request to the Security Council for international assistance in fighting pirates sheltering inside Somalia's territorial sea, China voted in favor of Security Council Resolution 1816 authorizing members of the international community to "enter the territorial waters of Somalia for the purpose of repressing acts of piracy and armed robbery at sea."[96] China's statement of support for the resolution underscores the importance of Somalia's consent. International assistance "should be based on the wishes of the [Somali] Government and be applied only to the territorial waters of Somalia."[97] The continuing consent of the Somali government remains important to the Chinese government today, fully three years after the UN Security Council Resolution was passed.[98]

The decision by China's leaders to send a small flotilla of ships to join the antipiracy effort has been described as an "adjustment" in China's maritime strategy. Given China's historically defensive maritime posture, this is probably an accurate assessment even though prominent Chinese analysts have taken pains to insist that China's "naval strategy will still focus on off-shore defense."[99] Nonetheless, this change was long presaged by the architects of China's Peaceful Rise and Peaceful Development policies, who called for a greater role for China as a permanent member of the UN Security Council in multilateral operations to enhance international security.[100] Repudiating balance of power realism and power transition theory, these thinkers have attempted to articulate a "new security concept" based on "mutual trust, mutual benefit, equality, and cooperation."[101]

Accordingly, in justification of its decision to send forces abroad prepared to engage in naval operations for the first time since the voyages of Zheng He during the Ming dynasty, the stated Chinese strategic rationales behind the decision were that (1) clear national interests were at stake since six Chinese-flagged vessels were attacked in the region during 2008, the year that Chinese deliberations about the mission took place, and seventeen crew members of a captured Chinese fishing vessel were in captivity; (2) a series of UN Security Council resolutions called upon the international community to take action; (3) UN Secretary-General Ban Ki-moon gave his support for the Chinese mission; (4) through the United Nations, the Somalia government requested the support of the international community, even in Somalia's territory, territorial waters, and sovereign airspace if necessary; and (5) "the West" supports it and the decision did "not stoke the China threat theory."[102]

Given China's preoccupation with nonintervention in what it characterizes as the domestic affairs of other states and its criticism of "hegemons" who use power to bully smaller states, the key rationales from this list of China's bases for participation in antipiracy efforts are the request to the Security Council by the Somali government for assistance and the unanimous decision of that body to provide it.[103] Indeed, shortly after the Chinese ships arrived in the region, the Xinhua News Agency prominently featured a report from Mogadishu noting that "both officials and ordinary people" expressed support for China's efforts.[104] That the provisional government of Somalia requested international assistance and openly supports international antipiracy efforts in its coastal waters is not only critical to China's perception of the efforts as politically legitimate, but it is also fundamental to the Chinese government's view that they comport with international law. Because it is the position of the Chinese government that the international community does not have the right to undertake military activities in the EEZ of another state without its consent, the Legal Affairs Bureau of the Central Military Commission has officially stated that the lawfulness of the PLA Navy antipiracy operations in the Gulf of Aden rests on three grounds: the relevant UN Security Council resolutions authorize it; the government of Somalia requested international support and consented to naval operations by the international community in its territorial sea and exclusive economic zone; and the UN Convention on the Law of the Sea, to which China is a signatory, allows antipiracy operations "in sea areas beyond territorial waters . . . [and] *which have been authorized by that government*" (emphasis added).[105]

However, even given these expressions of the political and legal legitimacy of the operations, China's leaders walk a narrow line. In undertaking antipiracy activities, the Chinese navy must be perceived as contributing to global governance without threatening status quo powers to avoid a possible backlash of balancing behavior from other Asian states concerned about China's growing military prowess.[106] Accordingly, Chinese leaders have prescribed a narrow set of missions for the deployed naval forces: to deter piracy by their presence, to safeguard vessels carrying humanitarian supplies for the people of Somalia, to escort Chinese-flagged merchant vessels (including Hong Kong-, Macau-, and Taiwanese-flagged vessels upon request), to provide information to other merchant vessels about potentially dangerous areas, and to provide "necessary rescue services" to merchant ships that find themselves under attack.[107] Notably, even though UN Security Council Resolution 1851 allows it, the Chinese admiral in command of the PLA Navy flotilla specifically stated that his authority does not include undertaking missions that require his personnel to disembark and go ashore.[108]

Perhaps recognizing a historic opportunity, senior American naval leaders welcomed China's decision to participate in counterpiracy operations in the Gulf of Aden and pledged to work closely together. They began an interagency review of opportunities for closer cooperation and coordination between American and Chinese forces in the region, including sharing relevant intelligence and establishing lines of communication.[109] This is a good omen because it reflects American respect for China's interests and a willingness to accept a role for China in providing regional stability beyond East Asia. As one senior Chinese official put it, "No country, not even a powerful country like the United States, can tackle all the challenges and problems alone. . . . Our countries have common views on more and more strategic issues. . . . [But to] realize greater growth of U.S.-China relations, it is essential for China and the United States to show mutual support [and to] treat each other as equals."[110] This statement provides some insights into why and how China and the United States are able to find room to cooperate in antipiracy operations off the coast of Somalia. In terms of mutual support, independent but coordinated action allows each participant the freedom to define the scope of its participation according to its capacities, and each participant is likewise free to define the scope of authorities it views as legitimate to employ. Thus, China can freely pursue its own interests alongside the United States and other members of the international community without having to compromise its perspectives on the limits of international law. Additionally, in terms of treating each other as equals, that the Somali operations were debated and directed from the UN Security Council ensured that China, as a permanent member, could have a framing influence equal to the other states that also sit as permanent members.

Combined Task Force 150—Opting Out

Conversely, China has never provided direct support for similar operations long carried out by Combined Task Force 150 (CTF 150). Even before piracy emanating from Somali ports became the serious international concern that it did in 2008, the waters off the coast of the Horn of Africa in the critical sea-lanes connecting the Arabian Sea with the Red Sea and the Mediterranean Sea were some of the most dangerous in the world. Fishing vessels, chemical tankers, cargo ships, cruise liners, and other vessels were all the target of attacks in recent years, causing serious disruption to free navigation in this major international sea-lane.[111] To address this source of instability and maritime disruption, a coalition of willing countries with capable naval forces established CTF 150 to police the international waters in this area.[112] Although the primary mission of the task force is to "deny the use of the sea by terrorists," the coalition also works to "prevent piracy, [and] reduce illegal trafficking of people and drugs."[113] To do this it employs the full range of international law policing authorities to suppress piracy and stateless vessels, but it also operates under post-9/11 national self-defense authorities.[114] To accomplish these objectives, the navies of CTF 150 have combined their capacities to enhance international security for civilian vessels in these troubled waters, assisting ships flagged by Panama, Japan, South Korea, Taiwan, the Comoros Islands, and North Korea in the month of November 2007 alone.[115]

The activities of CTF 150 reflect the evolution of oceans governance from its history in international competition to a much stronger model based on international cooperation. However, the strength of its operations lies in the ability to make use of a broad set of international law authorities to use force to suppress crimes of universal jurisdiction and to achieve national and collective self-defense. Contrary to the Chinese approach to international law at sea, CTF 150 members accept these legal authorities as a matter of sovereign right, without need for recourse to the United Nations or need for coastal state consent. These premises are fundamentally unacceptable to China, of course, which has never participated in the activities of CTF 150 despite the fact that the task force has long been operating to protect many of the same interests that China is currently protecting with its own flotilla in the Gulf of Aden.

Another sticking point for China is the chain of command under which CTF 150 operates. CTF 150 was established shortly after initiation of Operation Enduring Freedom (Afghanistan) and in conjunction with the basis of those operations in national and collective self-defense. It operates in a correspondingly large area of operations—the Gulf of Aden, the Gulf of Oman, the Arabian Sea, the Red Sea, and the Indian Ocean all fall within its scope. Most critical is the fact that although CTF 150 has been commanded by British, Canadian, Danish, Dutch, French, German, and Pakistani naval officers, the task force commander reports directly to the American admiral in charge of the U.S. Fifth Fleet in his capacity as commander of the Combined Maritime Forces.[116] These factors are obviously incompatible with China's perspective on the political and legal legitimacy of maritime security operations and run afoul of its insistence that China must operate fully as an equal to all other participating states for it to join an international effort.

The Proliferation Security Initiative—Opting Out

Despite China's port-security cooperation under the Container Security Initiative, China remains reluctant to join more informal international efforts to achieve security at sea such as the Proliferation Security Initiative (PSI). The PSI is described by the U.S. government as "a global effort that aims to stop trafficking of weapons of mass destruction (WMD), their delivery systems, and related materials to and from states and non-state actors of proliferation concern."[117] Not a treaty organization, PSI is simply a loose affiliation of like-minded states that agree on a basic set of principles, articulated in a document known as the Statement of Interdiction Principles, in order to "involve in some capacity all states that have a stake in nonproliferation and the ability and willingness to stop the flow of such items at sea, in the air, or on land. The PSI also seeks cooperation from any state whose vessels, flags, ports, territorial waters, airspace, or land might be used for proliferation purposes by states and non-state actors of proliferation concern."[118] The interdiction principles call upon states to interdict the transfer of weapons of mass destruction and related materials to state and nonstate actors of proliferation concern, to facilitate rapid exchange of information, to strengthen national legal authorities and relevant international law frameworks, and to employ national and international law to interdict and seize proliferation cargoes.

Nine states have chosen to cooperate with U.S. nonproliferation efforts by entering into ship-boarding agreements that facilitate a process by which the flag state can consent to board one of its vessels for the purpose of enforcing nonproliferation laws.[119] The PSI intentionally lacks a defined international organizational structure in order to allow the widest latitude of cooperation as each state sees fit. By helping to enhance national and international nonproliferation legal frameworks, the PSI seeks to decrease proliferation activities across the board. But when a case of suspected proliferation is identified, the PSI seeks to maximize the flexibility of response options by allowing for the coordination of an ad hoc response by states with the will, the authority, and the capacity to intervene. Currently, ninety-one countries have expressed public support for the Statement of Interdiction Principles.[120] China is not among them.

Chinese scholars lodge three basic objections to the PSI. They view the interdiction principles as lacking a "solid basis in international law" and perhaps even in violation of "existing international legal instruments"; they object to the lack of a direct role in PSI activities for the United Nations Security Council; and they question whether "interdiction operations [will be] conducted based on accurate, unbiased, and non-politicized intelligence."[121] The first objection reflects a consistent Chinese preference for narrow interpretations of international law authorities that make it difficult for strong maritime powers to overcome flag state and coastal state jurisdictional authorities. The second objection reflects China's preference for international cooperation through the UN Security Council, where China has a voice and vote equal to each of the other major powers. The third objection, like the first, reflects Chinese mistrust of broad international law authorities that might enable states to act on inaccurate or less than certain evidence of proliferation activity—as occurred in the 1993 Yin He incident.[122] This incident deepened China's fundamental lack of trust in the U.S. approach to enforcement of international nonproliferation norms and resulted in a renewed Chinese commitment to protect the sovereign interests of flag states against what it perceived as "abusive" American practices.[123]

Nonetheless, many Chinese officials and scholars recognize the need for cooperative action. As one researcher at the PLA Naval Military Academic Institute recently put it: "Maritime security represents both the common interest of the concerned nations and the common responsibility of the international community. For instance, antiterrorism and counterpiracy issues in one nation may involve the sea waters of other nations, which can hardly be resolved merely by independent actions or law enforcement strength of a single nation. In this situation, the involvement of military strength becomes inevitable and the cooperation on international maritime security becomes very necessary."[124] This researcher's advice was to primarily undertake cooperative efforts on the high seas beyond the EEZ or other nonsensitive areas in order to avoid offending the sovereign sensibilities of some coastal states by performing military activities in their exclusive economic zones. This approach has some merit in that it could facilitate information-sharing and thereby allow pressure to be applied on states to suppress proliferation activities on vessels under their flag, especially in cases involving long transit times that allow for the necessary exchange of information, diplomatic coordination, and preparation of a naval response. However, this approach avoids whole categories of very effective measures that enable more timely and efficient responses, such as those based on principles of universal jurisdiction, national self-defense, and ship-boarding agreements.

Examining these four examples of opportunities for U.S.–China maritime cooperation reveals that the two successful avenues for future cooperative action with China are mutual state-to-state enforcement of sovereign law, as in the Container Security Initiative and the North Pacific Coast Guard Forum, and assistance under the direction of the UN Security Council at the request of the receiving state, as in recent antipiracy operations in Somalia. These may provide some very real reason to hope for a future of broader cooperation between the United States and China—even under the rubric of the PSI, since time and experience have taught cooperating states that the most effective and efficient means of counterproliferation is through strict enforcement of domestic customs laws, import–export licensing laws, immigration laws, and other national authorities that prohibit transportation of materials that are ultimately intended to be used to create weapons of mass destruction.

The Future of Maritime Security and Governance

A fundamental basis for the restraint expressed by both U.S. and Chinese leaders concerning the potential for increased maritime cooperation appears to be the implicit recognition that even in circumstances in which common interests exist, the capability to provide governance on the oceans is more than simply a function of bringing together physical capacity—ships, aircraft, trained personnel, communications and information systems, and so on—but also of achieving at least a fundamental level of common agreement on the bases of authority on which to employ that physical capacity. In other words, building combined capacity to provide policing power is of little use unless the policing capacities perceive a common authority to act.[125] However, coordinating independent national actions, based on national perspectives of international law authorities, can still be an effective mechanism to achieve maritime security.

The current operations in the Gulf of Aden, in particular, demonstrate the critical role played by coordinating the actions of various maritime arrangements—national and international—to preventing disruption at sea. Indeed, international will to find avenues to cooperate—or at least to achieve common maritime security goals through loosely coordinated, independent activities— has perhaps never been higher. But it is increasingly evident that the capability to achieve maritime security is more than a function of the sum total of national capacities alone. To bring the maximum amount of global maritime security capacity to bear, flexible pathways to combined or coordinated action must be developed to accommodate divergent views on the legitimacy of various authorities to use that capacity.

What is also increasingly evident, however, is that even as the drive toward maximum participation will require states that favor strong international powers to act at sea to find avenues for collective action that accommodate less expansive views of the law, the availability of the full measure of traditional international law authorities must be preserved for states willing to create order at sea in cases where the political will to cooperate is slow to develop or in fact never develops at all. These authorities allow for a rapid international response to destabilizing activity in coastal zones in which some states have insufficient organic capacity to provide order. In short, they help to prevent ungoverned spaces at sea that provide a sanctuary for disruptive elements. As demonstrated by the inability of local and regional governments in the Horn of Africa to effectively provide governance at sea without the intervention of the forces of other states and the resulting rise in disruption caused by piracy, smuggling, and other illegal activities, ungoverned space at sea is just as dangerous to the global system as ungoverned space on land.

Looking beyond the Horn of Africa, three broad areas of agreement between the United States and China chart a clear course toward greater maritime security cooperation. First, both countries should work together to prevent the growth of ungoverned maritime space. Additionally, today's counterpiracy and antiterrorism operations in the Horn of Africa are a direct result of the implosion of Somali governance nearly two decades ago. Accordingly, broad agreement between China, the United States, and other members of the Security Council will be essential in the future to effectively strengthen the capacity of failed and failing states over their territories at sea as well as on land. Building on the broad cooperation achieved by the Security Council in 2008, this work should continue and expand to other regions of maritime instability. Strengthening governance in maritime spaces where current maritime capacity is weak, such as in some areas of the South China Sea, can be an area of future cooperative focus.

Second, China and the United States should agree to strengthen the capacities of coastal states to enforce their own sovereign law. Even as international authorities must remain strong to enable maritime governance to exist where coastal state capacity is weak, the most effective and legitimate means of building maritime governance is to strengthen the sovereign forces of the coastal states to effectively police their own waters. Global regional capacity-building is critical in such areas as maritime Southeast Asia, where the Indonesian and Philippine archipelagoes form two of the four longest coastlines of any country.[126] Cooperation to provide economic support, training, information-sharing and, when asked, direct support is therefore a critical component of future maritime stability in the important sea-lanes of the South China Sea and a potential area for enhanced American and Chinese cooperation.

Finally, the United States and China should work to strengthen communication at all levels. Open dialogue and the exchange of views between the government, military, commercial, and academic communities of both China and the United States is essential to developing a productive partnership. Too often, the result of disagreement has been to shut off interaction. This has been an unproductive practice in the U.S.–China relationship. It has stunted the growth of improved mutual understanding that in turn can lead, if not to the convergence of perspectives, at least to cooperative solutions to provide the maritime governance. With coordinated actions that respect each other's sovereignty, that are based on mutual interest, and that are founded on relationship between equals, the United States and China can work together toward the common goal of stability at sea.

Notes

Epigraph: Senior Colonel Feng Liang and Lieutenant Colonel Duan Tingzhi, "Characteristics of China's Sea Security Strategy in a New Century," *Zongguo Junshi Kexue* [*China Military Science*], January 2007, 22.

1. National Security Presidential Directive NSPD-41, Maritime Security Policy, 21 December 2004.

2. Wu Jiao and Peng Kuang, "Sailing to Strengthen Global Security," *China Daily*, 26 December 2008, www.chinadaily.com.cn/china/2008-12/26/content_7342612.htm.

3. World Trade Organization Statistics Program, available at www.wto.org.

4. Ibid. Corresponding to the overall rise in the value of trade during the last two decades is a rise in the volume of trade between the United States and China, in addition to the rise in value of sea trade. In 2006 China was the world's third-ranking importer and exporter while the United States ranked second in exports and first in imports by value. To carry this burgeoning trade, the total deadweight tonnage of the world's merchant fleet expanded by 8.6 percent in 2006 to just over 1 billion tons, following a 7.2 percent growth in 2005. (UNCTAD Secretariat, "Review of Maritime Transport 2007," UN Conference on Trade and Development [New York and Geneva: United Nations, 2007], x–xii, http://www.unctad.org/en/docs/rmt2007_en.pdf.) This fleet was called upon in 2006 to carry international seaborne trade comprised of crude oil, oil products, and dry bulk goods of more than 7.4 billion tons, about double the tonnage of similar materials carried in international seaborne trade in 1989 (ibid., 5).

5. Jean-Paul Rodique, "Transportation, Globalization and Trade," http://people.hofstra.edu/geotrans/eng/ch5en/conc5en/ch5c2en.html.

6. The United States trails a distant third (behind Russia) with 847 flagged vessels. UNCTAD Secretariat, "Review of Maritime Transport 2007," 32.

7. For instance, the U.S. Department of Energy estimates that more than fifty thousand vessels transit the Strait of Malacca each year, and by other estimates the number surpassed seventy thousand per year as early as 2000. Energy Information Administration, Country Analysis Briefs, "World Oil Transit Chokepoints," January 2008, available at www.eia.doe.gov; and Donna J. Nincic, "Sea Lane Security and U.S. Maritime Trade: Chokepoints as Scarce Resources," in *Globalization and Maritime Power*, ed. Sam Jo Tangredi (Washington, D.C.: National Defense University Press, 2002), ch. 8, p. 6.

8. In 2007 there were more than 260 reported instances worldwide of piracy and armed robbery against ships, about a 10 percent increase over the previous year. Jessica Stern, "The Protean Enemy," *Foreign Affairs* 82, no. 4 (July–August 2003): 27–40. Asia, east of the Indian subcontinent, accounted for 80, or just over 30 percent, of 2007's total. In large part due to cooperative efforts among Indonesia, Malaysia, and Singapore, the 2007 figures for piracy and attacks at sea are down from a staggering regional total of 189 in 2003. (International Maritime Bureau, "Piracy and Armed Robbery against Ships: Annual Report," London: ICC International Maritime Bureau, 2008, http://www.intertanko.com/upload/WeeklyNews/IMBPiracy.pdf, 5. Hereafter, IMB Report.) Indonesia alone, in 2003, with 121 attacks against vessels in waters off its coasts, accounted for 27 percent of the reported attacks against vessels globally. In 2007

that figure dropped to 16 percent, but for a maritime country with territory bordering some of the world's busiest straits and sea-lanes, the persistent danger to international shipping presented by attacks against vessels is of special concern. This is magnified by the fact that 81 percent of all attacks against ships in 2007 were against various types of commercial cargo vessels (49 percent of all attacks) and tanker vessels (32 percent of all attacks). Ibid., 16. The term "reported" instances of piracy is used because International Maritime Bureau acknowledges that "a number of incidents go unreported each year due to various problems." Ibid., 25.

9. The International Maritime Bureau reports that guns are being increasingly used by pirates who "are better armed and [show] no hesitation in assaulting and injuring the crew." Ibid., 24.

10. For instance, for several years after 9/11 there were concerns that al-Qaeda owned or controlled as many as fifteen cargo ships worldwide with which it could launch attacks from the sea. J. Ashley Roach, "Initiatives to Enhance Maritime Security at Sea," *Marine Policy* 28 (2004): 41.

11. Gal Luft and Anne Korin, "Terrorism Goes to Sea," *Foreign Affairs* (November–December 2004): 61, 62–64. In particular, these authors warned of destabilizing security conditions created by increasing connections in Southeast Asia between armed thugs-for-hire and Islamic terrorist groups who see piracy as a means of raising cash in the face of efforts by the international community to deny terrorists access to financial support, and operation of "phantom ships" as a means of operating outside national jurisdiction and the scrutiny of national law enforcement systems. See also, John C. K. Daly, "Terrorism and Piracy: The Dual Threat to Maritime Shipping," *Terrorism Monitor* 6, no. 16 (15 August 2008), available at www.jamestown.org, which details terrorist attacks at sea and draws parallels to piracy in the Gulf of Aden, including material from a jihadist Web site linking piracy with "the global campaign to restore the Islamic Caliphate and to rule the world through it." Compare with Joshua Kucera, "Coalition Patrols Step Up Efforts against Pirates," *Jane's Defense Weekly*, 16 February 2006, which reports that to date only an indirect link exists between piracy and terrorism but that current maritime security operations are designed to ensure a direct link does not develop.

12. James Jay Carafano, "Small Boats, Big Worries: Thwarting Terrorist Attacks from the Sea," *Backgrounder*, no. 2041, The Heritage Foundation, 11 June 2007, 2.

13. IMB Report, 43. Similarly, on 21 April 2007, ten masked pirates armed with pistols and long knives boarded the tanker *Majullah Jasmine* as it steamed just 2.5 miles off the coast of Malaysia. They stole cash and the crew's personal property and escaped in a speedboat. The chemical tanker *Qasidah* was similarly attacked while steaming 3.5 miles off the coast of Malaysia; pirates tied up the crew, seized cash and personal belongings, and escaped. Ibid., 44, 49.

14. Ibid., 77.

15. See, for example, "The Mariana Flora," 24 U.S. 1, 26 March 1826. Available at Justia. com, http://supreme.justia.com/us/24/1/case.html.

16. Alfred P. Rubin, *The Law of Piracy* (Newport, RI: Naval War College Press, 1988), 144, discussing the U.S. congressional decision in 1819 to assert jurisdiction over any person

who, having committed a crime of piracy on the high seas, was later brought within U.S. territorial jurisdiction.

17. Yoram Dinstein, *War, Aggression and Self-Defence*, 4th ed. (New York: Cambridge University Press, 2005), 176: "The legal notion of self-defence has its roots in interpersonal relations, and is sanctified in domestic legal systems since time immemorial."

18. Louise Doswald-Beck, ed. *San Remo Manual on International Law Applicable to Armed Conflicts at Sea* (Cambridge: Cambridge University Press, 1995), 176–80; and Lance E. Davis and Stanley L. Engerman, *Naval Blockades in Peace and War: An Economic History since 1750* (New York: Cambridge University Press, 2006).

19. R. R. Churchill and A. V. Lowe, *The Law of the Sea*, 3rd ed. (Manchester, UK: Manchester University Press, 1999), 208–11.

20. See e.g., Judith A. Miller, "Commentary," in *Legal and Ethical Lessons of NATO's Kosovo Campaign, International Law Studies*, vol. 78, ed. Andru E. Wall (Newport, RI: Naval War College, 2002), 107–12.

21. Chinese maritime theorists are giving considerable attention to the nature of international and coastal state interests in the maritime domain and providing a Chinese perspective on how international and sovereign law should be balanced to meet the interest of both. See, for example, Zhang Wei, "Exploring National Sea Security Theories," *Zhongguo Junshi Kexue* [*China Military Science*], 1 January 2007, 84; and Ren Xiaofeng and Cheng Xizhong, "A Chinese Perspective," *Marine Policy* 29 (2005): 139.

22. By the terms of the Convention, sovereign waters include internal waters (Articles 10[4], 35[a], and 50), the territorial sea (Articles 2 and 3), and archipelagic waters (Article 49). Outside sovereign waters, high seas freedoms apply (Articles 58[1] and 87), including international policing power to impose minimum order and security, such as the right of approach and visit to suppress piracy, sailing without nationality, engaging in slave trade, and, a relative newcomer, engaging in unlawful broadcasting (Article 110). See also Mackenzie M. Eaglen, James Dolbow, Martin Edwin Anderson, and James Jay Carofano, "Securing the High Seas: America's Global Maritime Constabulary Power," *Special Report SR-20*, The Heritage Foundation, 12 March 2008, 3.

23. "United Nations Convention on the Law of the Sea" (UNCLOS), Article 27(1), http://www.un.org/Depts/los/convention_agreements/texts/unclos/unclos_e.pdf.

24. UNCLOS, Article 33.

25. UNCLOS, Articles 56(1) and 73.

26. "Proliferation Security Initiative Logs Varied Activities in Two Years," 2 May 2005, available at www.usinfo.state.gov.

27. CIA, *The World Factbook*, https://www.cia.gov/library/publications/the-world-factbook.

28. Shipping Board Agreements," U.S. Department of State, http://www.state.gov/t/isn/c27733.htm.

29. See, for example, 46 U.S. Code, ch. 705, sec. 70502(c)(1)(c); and *UNITED STATES of America v. Mohammad Waheedullah KHAN; Muhammad Hanif; Abdul Karim; and Abdul Rasheed*, 35 F.3d 426 (1994), in which a U.S. Coast Guard law enforcement

detachment on board two U.S. Navy ships intercepted the M/V *Lucky Star*, registered in St. Vincent, British West Indies, and carrying a Pakistani crew, in international waters off the coast of Hawaii. The master gave the Coast Guard team authority to board and search the vessel, during which a cargo of hashish was found on board. St. Vincent later gave its permission to prosecute the crew under U.S. law. Additionally, in some limited cases, the master of a vessel may consent to subject the vessel to the law enforcement jurisdiction of another state. 46 U.S. Code, ch. 705, sec. 70502.

30. Churchill and Lowe, *Law of the Sea*, 208–9.

31. UNCLOS, Article 110; see also A. R. Thomas and James C. Duncan, *Annotated Supplement to the Commander's Handbook on the Law of Naval Operations, International Law Studies*, vol. 73 (Newport, RI: Naval War College, 1999), 221.

32. UNCLOS, Articles 101 and 58(2).

33. UNCLOS, Article 105.

34. George W. Bush, "Maritime Security (Piracy) Policy," Memorandum from the President, 14 June 2007, available at www.whitehouse.gov.

35. UNCLOS, Article 110(1) (d).

36. UNCLOS, Article 108; and "United Nations Convention against Illicit Traffic in Narcotic Drugs and Psychotropic Substances," Vienna, 20 December 1988, entered into force 11 November 1990, available at http://www.unodc.org/pdf/convention_1988_en.pdf.

37. Roach, "Initiatives to Enhance Maritime Security," 41, 53.

38. The Convention and its Protocols are available at http://www.unodc.org/unodc/en/treaties/CTOC/index.html.

39. "Signatories to the United Nations Convention against Transnational Crime and Its Protocols," http://www.unodc.org/unodc/en/treaties/CTOC/signatures.html.

40. TOC, Article 7.

41. TOC, Article 8(2) and (7).

42. For a comprehensive list of UN treaties and protocols related to terrorism, see UN, "UN Action to Counter Terrorism," http://www.un.org/terrorism/instruments.shtml.

43. The text of the SUA Convention can be found online at http://cns.miis.edu/inventory/pdfs/aptmaritime.pdf. The text of the 2005 Protocol can be found at http://www.state.gov/t/isn/trty/81728.htm.

44. UN Treaty Series, vol. 1678, I-29004, 223.

45. For the provisions of the 2005 protocols, see the International Maritime Organization Web site, www.imo.org.

46. Testimony before the Senate Foreign Relations Committee of Patricia A. McNerney, Principal Deputy Assistant Secretary of State, International Security and Non-Proliferation, 7 May 2008, http://foreign.senate.gov/testimony/2008/McNerneyTestimony080507p.pdf.

47. IMB Report; and Katherine Houreld, "Pirates Terrorize Ships Off Somali Coast," *Washington Times*, 6 December 2007, 13.

48. "2009 World Piracy Figures Surpass 400," *Maritime Executive Magazine*, 14 January 2010, http://www.maritime-executive.com/article/2009-worldwide-piracy-figures-surpass-400/.

49. "Forward . . . From the Sea" (Washington, D.C.: Department of the Navy, 1994), available at http://www.dtic.mil/jv2010/navy/b014.pdf.

50. ". . . From the Sea" (Washington, D.C.: Department of the Navy, 1992), Introduction, available at http://www.navy.mil/navydata/policy/fromsea/fromsea.txt.

51. "Forward . . . From the Sea," Introduction, 1.

52. ". . . From the Sea," Introduction, 1.

53. Statement of Michael G. Mullen, Chairman, Joint Chiefs of Staff, Committee on Senate Armed Services Hearing on Fiscal 2009 Defense Authorization, 6 February 2008, http://www.jcs.mil/speech.aspx?id=1321.

54. "A Cooperative Strategy for 21st Century Seapower" (Washington, D.C.: Department of the Navy, October 2007), http://www.navy.mil/maritime/MaritimeStrategy.pdf, 2.

55. Ibid., 3.

56. P. Parameswaran, "U.S. Asks China to Help Maintain Global Maritime Security," Agence France Press, 10 April 2007, available at http://www.terradaily.com.

57. Phil Mercer, "U.S. Navy Calls for Increased Maritime Cooperation to Combat Threats at Sea," *Voice of America*, 1 February 2008.

58. Ann Roosevelt, "U.S. Joint Forces Command Works Toward Capabilities for Preventing Destabilization," *Defense Daily*, 24 January 2008.

59. Ibid.

60. Ed Early, "U.S. Navy, CNO's Vision of '1,000-ship Navy' Tested by CARAT Exercise," *Navy Newsstand*, 26 June 2007.

61. Ibid.

62. Ibid; see also Dan Meaney, "Thailand Phase of CARAT 2008 Exercises Underway," *Navy News Service*, 14 June 2008, http://www.navy.mil/search/display.asp?story_id=37855; Bill Larned, "CARAT 2009 Marks 15 Years of Enhancing Maritime Cooperation," *PACOM Headlines*, 22 May 2009, http://www.pacom.mil/web/site_pages/media/news%20200905/20090522-CARAT2009.shtml; and Zachary M. Peterson, "Keating: 1000-Ship Navy Possible for China," *Navy Times*, 24 July 2007.

63. Early, "U.S. Navy, CNO's Vision."

64. Bill Owens, "Closer Ties between China and America Are Crucial," *Financial Times*, 19 February 2008.

65. Zheng Bijian, *China's Peaceful Rise: Speeches of Zheng Bijian 1997–2005* (Washington, D.C.: Brookings Institution Press, 2005), 10–11.

66. Peterson, "Keating"; 杨晴川 [Yang Qingchuan], "美国海上力量 '三巨头'—海军作战部长拉夫黑德,海军陆战队司令康韦和海岸警卫队司令艾伦共同出现在罗得岛州纽波特海军战争学院举行的 国际海军演讨会上,向与会的１００多个国家和地区的海军首脑降重推出美国新版的 海上战略" ["The 'Three Magnates' of U.S. Sea Power—Adm. Gary Roughead, Chief of Naval Operations; Gen. James T. Conway,

Marine Corps Commandant; and Adm. Thad W. Allen, Coast Guard Commandant, Presented the Strategy to Maritime Leaders from More Than 100 Countries Attending the International Seapower Symposium at the Naval War College, Newport, R.I."] *International Herald Leader-Beijing*, 17 October 2007, available at www.chinesenews net.com. Translation by Danling Cacioppo and Nan Li.

67. Mingjiang Li, "China's Gulf of Aden Expedition and Maritime Cooperation in East Asia," *China Brief* 9, no. 1 (12 January 2009): 4.

68. UN, "Oceans and Law of the Sea," http://www.un.org/Depts/los/convention_agree ments/convention_declarations.htm.

69. Law of the People's Republic of China on the Territorial Sea and the Contiguous Zone, Adopted at the 24th Meeting of the Standing Committee of the Seventh National People's Congress on 25 February 1992, Article 6.

70. Ibid., Article 301.

71. Ibid., Article 58(1).

72. Ren and Cheng, "A Chinese Perspective," 139.

73. Law of the PRC on the Territorial Sea and the Contiguous Zone, Articles 1 and 13,

74. Law of the People's Republic of China on the Exclusive Economic Zone and the Continental Shelf, 26 June 1998.

75. See, for example, Cheng Xizhong, "A Chinese Perspective on 'Operational Modalities,'" *Marine Policy* 28 (2004): 25, 26.

76. Ibid.

77. It should be noted that this legal interpretation diverges from the perspective of the substantial majority of member states and from the U.S. position. Additionally, Tommy T. B. Koh, who represented Singapore and served as the president of the Third United Nations Conference on the Law of the Sea, said, "Nowhere is it clearly stated [in the 1982 Convention] whether a third state may or may not conduct military activities in the exclusive economic zone of a coastal state. But, it was the general understanding that the text we negotiated and agreed upon would permit such activities to be conducted." Jon M. Van Dyke, ed., *Consensus and Confrontation: The United States and the Law of the Sea Convention* (Honolulu: University of Hawaii, Law of the Sea Institute, 1985), 303–4.

78. UNCLOS, Article 56(1)(a); 56(1)(b); 56(1)(b)(iii). For a detailed articulation of these arguments by Chinese scholars, see, for example, Ren and Cheng, "A Chinese Perspective," 139–46. Dr. Ren, it should be noted, is on the faculty of the China Institute for International Strategic Studies in Beijing.

79. The Chinese legal argument concerning the primacy of coastal state security interests in the EEZ over international navigational freedoms—including military freedoms— is based on a clever though erroneous intellectual sleight of hand. It takes the language of Article 58 regarding the responsibility of the international community to give "due regard to the *rights* of . . . the coastal state" in the EEZ and inserts a coastal *interest* in its place. The *rights* referred to, of course, are those enumerated in Article 56 and elsewhere in UNCLOS concerning sovereign coastal state rights to the resources. What has

been substituted in the Chinese argument is the state's security *interest*—not protected in the EEZ by UNCLOS but by international law related to national self-defense.

80. Churchill and Lowe, *Law of the Sea*, 162.

81. David Rosenberg and Christopher Chung, "Maritime Security in the South China Sea: Coordinating Coastal and User State Priorities," *Ocean Development and International Law* 39 (January 2008): 51, 52.

82. Xu Qi, "21世纪初海上地缘战略与中国海军的发展" ["Maritime Geostrategy and the Development of the Chinese Navy in the Early 21st Century"], 中国军事科学 [*China Military Science*] 17, no. 4 (2004): 75–81, trans. Andrew S. Erickson and Lyle J. Goldstein, *Naval War College Review* 59, no. 4 (Autumn 2006): 46–67.

83. Feng Liang and Duan Tingzhi, "Characteristics of China's Sea Security Strategy in a New Century," *Zongguo Junshi Kexue*, 1 January 2007, 22.

84. This paragraph is based largely on the research of Dr. Nan Li as addressed in Nan Li, "The Evolution of China's Naval Strategy and Capabilities: From 'Near Coast' and 'Near Seas' to 'Far Seas,'" *Asian Security* 5, no. 2 (May 2009): 144–69.

85. Ibid.

86. Liu Qia and Liu Yu, "Breaking Through the Fog: In-Depth Analysis of Sino-Japanese Competition over Maritime Rights," *Modern Ships*, February 2006, 17; and Bai Yanlin, "World Navies from the Island Chains: Island Chains and the Chinese Navy," *Modern Navy*, October 2007, 17.

87. Feng and Duan, "Characteristics of China's Sea," 22.

88. Ibid.

89. See, for example, "Speech by Hu Jintao at the United Nations 60th Anniversary Session," 22 September 2005, http://www.fmprc.gov.cn/ce/cehu/hu/xwdt/t213375.htm; and Chas W. Freeman Jr., *The Promise of Sino-American Relations*, Barnett-Oksenberg Lecture, 21 February 2008, reprinted in *Notes: National Committee on United States-China Relations* 38, no. 1 (Winter/Spring 2008): 21.

90. B. C. Kessner, "International Maritime Security Conference Aims to Boost NATO Initiatives," *Defense Daily*, 15 May 2008; and "China's Marine Sector on Rampage," *Maritime Executive*, 13 March 2008.

91. Sun Zhihui, "Strengthening Ocean Administration and Composing Blue Brilliance," *Seeking Truth*, 16 September 2009, no. 18. This documents the Chinese claim to 3 million square kilometers of sea space (not 4.7 million). See also Rosenberg and Chung, "Maritime Security in the South China Sea," 51, 59; and Feng and Duan, "Characteristics of China's Sea," 22.

92. CIA, *World Factbook*, www.cia.gov.

93. U.S. Customs and Border Protection Service Fact Sheet, 2 October 2007, available at www.cbp.gov.

94. Li, "China's Gulf of Aden Expedition," 3.

95. Lyle J. Goldstein, "China: A New Maritime Partner?" U.S. Naval Institute *Proceedings* 133, no. 8 (August 2007): 26, 30.

96. UN Security Council, "Security Council Condemns Acts of Piracy, Armed Robbery Off Somalia's Coast, Authorizes for Six Months 'All Necessary Means' to Repress Such Acts," 2 June 2008, http://www.un.org/News/Press/docs/2008/sc9344.doc.htm.

97. Ibid.

98. "Sailing into the Storm: International Praise for Chinese Escort Fleets Protecting Merchant Ships against Somali Pirates," *Beijing Review*, 19 April 2010, http://bjreview.com.cn/quotes/txt/2010-04/19/content_264275.htm.

99. Zhang Jingwei, "China Adjusts Its Maritime Power Strategy at the Right Moment," *Hong Kong Ta Kung Pao*, 29 December 2008. The quote reflects the words of Beijing defense analyst Peng Guangqian published in, "Sailing to Strengthen Global Security," *China Daily*, 26 December 2008.

100. See generally the comments on China's global role as a "major country," China's interest in suppressing nontraditional security threats, pacification of "hot spots," and participation in joint efforts to maintain international order found in Zheng, *China's Peaceful Rise*; Tao Shelan, "Rear Admiral: Chinese Navy Provides 'Public Good' to International Community with Its Fight against Pirates," *Beijing Zhongguo Xinwen She*, 24 December 2008; and "China to Bolster Image as Responsible Big Nation," *People's Daily*, 24 December 2008.

101. Zheng, *China's Peaceful Rise*, 35.

102. See, for example, Zhang, "China Adjusts Its Maritime Power Strategy"; Li Ta-kuang, "Chinese Navy Has Capacity to Fight against Piracy," *Wen Wei Po*, 25 December 2008; and "Discreet Naval Development Proves Shared Responsibility of World Peace (Commentary)," Xinhua Economic News Service, 29 December 2008.

103. See, for example, "Faced with Myanmar Protests, China Reaffirms Nonintervention," Associated Press, 25 September 2007.

104. Abdurrahman Warsameh, "Somalis Express Support for China's Naval Operation against Piracy," Xinhua, 8 January 2009; Sun Zifa, "Chinese Navy Escort Fleet Adopts Three Modes of Actions in Providing Escort," *Beijing Zhongguo Xinwen She*, 3 January 2009; and "Somali FM Welcomes Possible Naval Escort Operations by China," Xinhua, 17 December 2008.

105. Bai Ruixue and Zhu Hongliang, "Central Military Commission Legal Affairs Bureau Official Says for Chinese Warships to Protect Ships in Somalian Waters Is Entirely Legal," Xinhua, 20 December 2008.

106. It is worth noting that after the Chinese began to seriously discuss sending a group of navy ships to the Gulf of Aden, East Asian rival Japan began public discussions about reinterpreting constitutional restrictions on expeditionary operations to potentially allow a Japan Maritime Self-Defense Force vessel also to proceed to the Gulf of Aden to escort Japanese-flagged vessels. "MSDF May Get Antipiracy Duty off Somalia," *Kyodo News*, 26 December 2008.

107. "Naval Escort Fleet to Protect 15 Chinese Merchant Vessels from Pirates," Xinhua, 6 January 2008.

108. "PRC Fleet Commander Rear-Admiral Du Jingcheng on Escort Tasks off Somalia," Xinhua, 26 December 2008; and Margaret Besheer, "UN Security Council Approves Anti-Piracy Measure," *Voice of America*, 16 December 2008, http://www.voanews. com/english/2008-12-16-voa62.cfm.

109. Donna Miles, "U.S. Welcomes Chinese Plans to Fight Piracy, Admiral Says," American Forces Press Service, 18 December 2008. In response, a spokesman for the Chinese Ministry of National Defense stated that China is "willing to cooperate with . . . other countries, including the U.S., in strengthening informational and intelligence sharing." Cary Huang, "Warships Will Also Protect Taiwanese Vessels, Crews; Navy Fleet Sent to Somalia to Cooperate with U.S., Says Beijing," *South China Morning Post*, 24 December 2008.

110. Dai Bingguo, "Address at the Dinner Marking the 30th Anniversary of the Establishment of China-U.S. Diplomatic Relations Hosted by the Brookings Institution," Washington, DC, 11 December 2008 (translation), http://www.brookings. edu/~/media/Files/events/2008/1211_china/1211_china_dai.pdf.

111. See, for example, UN Security Council Resolution 1816 (2008), which expresses "grave concern" for the safety of commercial vessels in the waters off the coast of Somalia and for vessels bringing humanitarian aid to Somalia. See also, "Cruise Ship Repels Somali Pirates," *BBC News*, 5 November 2005, http://news.bbc.co.uk/2/hi/africa/4409662.stm; "Chinese Fishing Boat Hijacked by Somali Pirates," Xinhua, 14 November 2008, http:// news.xinhuanet.com/english/2008-11/14/content_10359203.htm; and "Pirates Capture Saudi Oil Tanker," *BBC News*, 18 November 2008, available at http://news.bbc.co.uk/2/ hi/africa/7733482.stm.

112. Combined Maritime Forces Web page, http://www.cusnc.navy.mil/cmf/150/index. html. CTF 150 has been commanded variously by naval officers from the United Kingdom, the Netherlands, Pakistan, Germany, and France.

113. "CTF 150: Maintaining a Lawful Maritime Order," U.S. Naval Forces Central Command Public Affairs Press Release, 31 May 2008.

114. "Pakistan to Assume Anti-terror Coalition Naval Task Force Command," *Deutsche-Presse-Agentur*, 1 August 2007. The task force was established in December 2001 in response to the attacks of 11 September 2001 and pursuant to UNSC Resolution 1373, which calls upon states to cooperate in the suppression of international terrorist activities.

115. Andrew Scutro, "Pirates!" *Navy Times*, 12 November 2007, 8; Houreld, "Pirates Terrorize Ships," 13.

116. Carolla Bennett, "Pakistani Admiral Becomes First Regional Commander of Maritime Task Force," Commander, U.S. Naval Forces Central Command Press Release, 24 April 2006. For description of the relevant chain of command, see http://www.cusnc.navy. mil/leadership/leadership.html.

117. U.S. Department of State Fact Sheet, "Proliferation Security Initiative," available at http://www.state.gov/t/isn/c10390.htm.

118. U.S. Department of State, Fact Sheet, "Proliferation Security Initiative Frequently Asked Questions (FAQ)," 26 May 2005.

119. Ibid.

120. "Shipping Board Agreements," U.S. Department of State, http://www.state.gov/t/isn/c27733.htm.

121. Ye Ru'an and Zhao Qinghai, "The PSI: Chinese Thinking and Concern," *The Monitor,* University of Georgia Center for International Trade and Security 10, no. 1 (Spring 2004): 22–24, http://www.uga.edu/cits/Resources/Monitor/monitor_sp_2004.pdf.

122. "Statement by the Ministry of Foreign Affairs of the People's Republic of China on the 'Yin He' Incident," 4 September 1993, the Nuclear Threat Initiative Web site, http://www.nti.org/db/china/engdocs/ynhe0993.htm; "China Says Cargo Ship Will Anchor Off Oman," *New York Times,* 15 August 1993; and "Saudis Board a Chinese Ship in Search for Chemical Arms," *New York Times,* 28 August 1993. Acting on intelligence reports that apparently turned out to be erroneous, the U.S. government accused the Chinese vessel *Yin He* (*Milky Way*), bound for Iran, of carrying thiodiglycol and thionyl chloride, two chemicals agents used in chemical warfare. The Chinese government provided assurances to the United States that the vessel was not carrying such materials, but the United States insisted that the vessel submit to inspection. An inspection was arranged in a Saudi port by Saudi officials in the presence of Chinese officials and American observers. No chemicals were located.

123. Li, "China's Gulf of Aden Expedition," 4.

124. "PRC Military Expert on International Maritime Security Cooperation," *Zhongguo Xinwen She* [*China News Service*], 3 July 2007.

125. See. e.g., Li, "China's Gulf of Aden Expedition," 4, in which the author describes Chinese skepticism of PSI and the Global Maritime Partnership as American "grand schemes" as "aggressive" and "coercive" mechanisms tied to the U.S. "pre-emptive strategy" and "unilateralism."

126. The Philippines has the fourth-longest coastline of any state, at 36,289 kilometers, and Indonesia's is second, at 54,716 kilometers. Canada's, at 202,080 kilometers, is the longest, and Russia's, at 37,653, ranks third. Comparatively, the length of the U.S. coastline is 19,924 kilometers. *The World Factbook,* Central Intelligence Agency, available at www.cia.gov/library/publications/the-world-factbook.

Su Hao

Maritime Aspects of China's Humanitarian Operations Policy

"HUMANITARIAN OPERATIONS," a new policy concept and diplomatic practice in China's foreign policy, is emerging on China's diplomatic agenda. The Chinese government views humanitarian operations as an important part of international security cooperation. Maritime humanitarian assistance, in particular, has been playing an increasingly vital role in China's international maritime security cooperation practices. In the series of maritime bilateral security cooperation activities that China has launched, "maritime humanitarian search and rescue" has been put at the core. It has become a significant part of China's diplomatic and security policies to strengthen China's maritime humanitarian aid capacity and to conduct all kinds of cooperation practices with other countries. This chapter will analyze this emerging trend.

China's Maritime Humanitarian Policies for Search and Rescue

The term "humanitarianism" is rarely used in traditional Chinese diplomacy. This is because the Chinese government is concerned that some Western countries would interfere in other country's domestic affairs under the banner of "humanitarian intervention" and in the name of "human rights." Besides this political implication, "humanitarianism" seems to have a military connotation, referring to international humanitarian efforts in a war to protect the nonmilitary public and give assistance to relieve their casualties. For instance, the Chinese government is very much concerned about the issue of injuries to the public caused by explosives that remain from World War II, and about the chemical weapons the Japanese army left behind in China following the conflict. In internal affairs, China has viewed "humanitarianism" as an issue of domestic social security, and links it with "helping the wounded and saving the dying" in medical relief. However, these three aspects seem discrete from each other.

For Chinese diplomacy today, humanitarianism is defined as having direct links with the aforementioned three aspects. In 2005 the Chinese government issued "China's Progress in Human Rights in 2004," noting clearly that "the Chinese government regards the safety of its people high above anything else."[1] Ensuring the right to survival is an essential part of China's human rights. There are other issues calling for the use of military measures, such as the post–Cold War nontraditional security concerns to China and the world at large, including transnational security issues, terrorism, piracy, illegal migration, drug trafficking, and smuggling. Moreover, these issues require cross-border cooperation. There are also natural disasters such as pandemics, tsunamis, cyclones, and sand storms, whose threats are also cross-border and lead to international cooperation for assisting the victims under the concept of humanitarianism. Therefore, in today's Chinese diplomacy, cooperation on humanitarian issues is essential to promote cooperation in nontraditional security areas. This type of cooperation is in the interest of China to safeguard national security, and is in the interest of the world as trust and cooperation among countries are enhanced. Therefore, for today's Chinese diplomacy, humanitarian issues have emerged not as a root of confrontation but as a basis of cooperation.

Meanwhile, as China implements international humanitarian cooperation, the policy of "humanitarian assistance" is gradually playing an important role. In February 2006 People's Republic of China (PRC) assistant minister of commerce Chen Jian introduced the cause of China's humanitarian assistance in the year of 2005. He emphasized four basic points for China's humanitarian assistance: First, China is a responsible country that has the duty to assist victims of natural disasters around the world. Second, Chinese people are kind and generous to help others. We have a tradition of promoting friendship with other countries. Third, we should realize that natural disasters do not only strike a single country. They are an enemy and a challenge for human beings as a whole. Therefore, we have the duty to confront them together. Fourth, considering that every country needs help when facing difficulties, no matter how strong the country is, our help is mutual.[2]

Li Baodong, permanent representative of the PRC to the United Nations office in Geneva and other international organizations in Switzerland, addressed the 30th International Conference of the Red Cross and Red Crescent on 27 November 2007. He proposed four points to further the development of the international humanitarian cause: First, seek peace and promote development; second, seek unity and strengthen cooperation; third, adhere to principles and emphasize spreading of international humanitarian law; and fourth, put emphasis on mechanisms and action. Li added, "China has attached great importance to the international humanitarian cause and has participated actively in international humanitarian cooperation. Over a long period of time, China has provided support . . . to other countries."[3]

China is a major shipping power that has a vast maritime territory and abundant resources for navigation of inland rivers. China has become increasingly connected with the external world by sea. Therefore, maritime humanitarian assistance is increasingly important for China. Maritime humanitarian search and rescue is a very important part of international maritime security cooperation. As the Chinese government increasingly participates in international maritime security affairs, it has put forward a policy concerning maritime search and rescue under the guidance of which specific laws and rules, as well as management methods and regulations, have come into force. Especially after the Indian Ocean tsunami disaster in Southeast Asia and the Indian Ocean in 2004, the Chinese government has clearly realized the need for multilateral international cooperation to cope with transnational maritime natural disasters. It is thus clear that the Chinese government has realized the need for a strong assistance program and the cooperation of the international society in the process of disaster relief.[4]

The Chinese government has promulgated specific regulations on maritime humanitarian search and rescue. In January 2006 the Chinese government issued the National Maritime Search and Rescue Contingency Plans. It was the first time that the Chinese government systematically implemented the policy on maritime humanitarian assistance for the sake of "establishing a national maritime search and rescue contingency mechanism; organizing maritime contingency activities rapidly, orderly and effectively; rescuing victims of maritime accidents; controlling the extension of contingencies; and reducing the number of casualties and loss of property as much as possible."[5]

China's government has stipulated that search and rescue have different functions. Definite plans are needed for search, which should then be executed precisely. All activities should be undertaken with relevant equipment, such as distress alerting, receiving, and exploring communication and monitoring devices on ships. Following the search activities, rescue must be undertaken. To realize maritime rescue, it is necessary to combine ship and aircraft assistance. Cooperation between professionals responsible for rescuing victims and administering medical treatment is likewise important. Finally, the causes of the accidents must be carefully analyzed to determine responsibility and put forward advice for preventing such problems from happening again.

It can thus be seen that humanitarian assistance has become an important part of Chinese foreign policy as well as a significant field to promote maritime security cooperation with relevant countries.

China's Legal System for Search and Rescue at Sea

The law of humanitarian search and rescue should conform to both civil and international laws, especially to the bilateral and multilateral international laws to which China has officially acceded. China has developed a relatively integrated legal system based on civil law. To standardize search and rescue at sea; to deal with emergent events at sea swiftly, systematically, and effectively; and to decrease the casualties and loss of property to the fullest extent possible, the State Council issued the "Advance Plans to Deal with Emergency Events and Organizing Search and Rescue at Sea," which was drafted by the Ministry of Transportation in 2006.[6] The government has improved the ability to handle abruptly emerging events and the ability to carry out search and rescue at sea by establishing a series of mechanisms to ensure the security of the life and property at sea: the process of prediction, the system of reporting dangerous situations, the mechanism of ensuring search and rescue, and the mechanism of making scientific strategy and improving the supporting system of search and rescue. In addition, "The Project of Chinese Search and Rescue Center for Emergent Management to the Dangers at Sea" and "The Project for Emergency Management of the Overflow of Petroleum in Chinese Territorial Waters" were drawn up so that the work of search and rescue has become standardized and regularized.

The Ministry of Transportation has also drawn up the PRC's "Regulations of Search and Rescue for Human Life at Sea" (it is pending ratification) according to the requirements in a series of laws and conventions such as the Maritime Traffic Safety Law of the People's Republic of China, Production Safety Law of the People's Republic of China, Regulations of the People's Republic of China on Administration of Traffic Safety in Inland Waters, Radio Administering Regulations of the People's Republic of China, and the Master State Plan for Rapid Response to Public Emergencies.[7] It was based on the International Convention on Maritime Search and Rescue of 1979 and some other international laws. The Chinese Ministry of Transportation intends to standardize the organization, command, coordination, and supply in the process of search and rescue at sea in the form of law.

China has officially joined in or concluded some international conventions and treaties, and it has fulfilled the corresponding international humanitarian obligations. The following are some of the relevant international conventions: the Geneva Convention, UN Convention on the Law of the Sea, the 1974 International Convention for the Safety of Life at Sea, the International Civil Aviation Convention, and the 1979 International Convention on Maritime Search and Rescue. The Chinese government has also made some bilateral achievements, such as the Agreement on Search and Rescue at Sea between China and the United States and the Agreement on Search and Rescue at Sea between China and Korea. All of these obligations have become the legal basis for China to participate in the international security cooperation at sea. Therefore, China has become involved in the international mechanism of security administration more generally as well as in important specific aspects of search and rescue at sea.

China Has Established a Maritime Search-and-Rescue System

In terms of international cooperation, China has been part of international institutions relevant to the maritime search and rescue. According to the requirement of these international regulations, the China Maritime Search and Rescue Center is responsible for directing and coordinating the handling of dangerous ships in distress.[8] As a whole, China's maritime search-and-rescue system has been established at the request of the International Convention on International Cooperation. Chinese domestic coordination among the various departments as well as local governments at all levels form an organizational mechanism. Therefore, China has become an important country in the global maritime search-and-rescue system.

The Maritime Affairs Bureau, a department of China's Ministry of Transportation, is responsible for organization, coordination, and guidance of marine search and rescue, and in charge of the routine business of the Chinese Maritime Search and Rescue Center. The latter's mission entails running a work system based on continuous shifts, establishing contingency plans, and handling contact and cooperation requirements.

The Bureau of Maritime Affairs also performs information service work for maritime search and rescue. It established the China Ship Reporting (CHISREP) system to locate ships and coordinate their rescue. In addition, the Maritime Bureau, in collaboration with the China Maritime Search and Rescue Center, has established the Data for Search and Rescue Experts and developed the Ship Identification Code Retrieving system, the Shipping Transport of Dangerous Goods Tracing system, and the Disaster Statistical Analysis and Tracing system to ensure scientific decision making.

The Maritime Safety Administration and the Center for Maritime Search and Rescue under the Transportation Ministry of the People's Republic of China assumes the special duty of organizing the conduct of "integrated maritime patrol and rescue," promoting the establishment of a network of professional assistance, improving the efficiency of disaster relief, and coordinating the operations of nearby ships to support disaster relief.[9] The State Oceanic Administration is responsible for issuing warnings and forecasts of ocean disasters and for marine environmental monitoring. The administration has established a marine weather information retrieval system, and has provided information for maritime search and rescue.[10] The strengthening of meteorological services and sharing of information resources enable meteorological data to reach all agencies at all levels quickly, thereby improving the service levels for weather forecasting.

The China Coast Guard, under the leadership and administration of the Border Control Department of Ministry of Public Security, is primarily responsible for maritime security. Its forces include a twenty-person marine armed police detachment.[11] The China coast guard is currently equipped with high-speed patrol boats and the most advanced satellite positioning navigation system.[12] In addition to maritime search-and-rescue work, the China coast guard is responsible for providing maritime security, handling criminal cases, enforcing maritime law, and safeguarding the country's maritime rights and interests.

To ensure that marine disasters are addressed rapidly and effectively in accordance with international standards, in 1989 the State Council and the Central Military Commission jointly issued documents declaring the establishment of the China Maritime Search and Rescue Center. This center is responsible for overall organization and coordination for national disaster relief at sea. Its daily work is undertaken by the Maritime Safety Administration, and the relevant State Council departments, such as the State Oceanic Administration and

Public Security Ministry, and military sectors, such as the People's Liberation Army (PLA) Navy and military police troops, must support the work of this center. Its functions include two aspects: search and rescue. More specifically, on 22 May 2005, China established the Inter-Ministerial Joint Maritime Search and Rescue system, which is responsible for coordinating various departments and is composed of the relevant ministries of the State Council and the military departments. Its office—China Maritime Search and Rescue Center—is responsible for organizing, coordinating, and directing search-and-rescue operations. The members of the ministerial units, marine units, individuals, and enterprises of all types have the relevant resources, thereby constituting the country's maritime search-and-rescue forces.

As for the technical means for conducting the search-and-rescue affairs, China has formed aircraft, ship, submarine, and communications networks and a series of other methods. Professional rescue helicopters, advanced cruise ships, professional fire-fighting vessels, and the most advanced professional rescue boats are all involved in searching. Together they permit three-dimensional search and rescue. By relying on advanced charts systems, the CHISREP automatic ship identification system, satellite F stations, videoconferencing systems, multiple functional communication emergency command vehicles, and other information means, the Maritime Search and Rescue Center can collect, process, and disseminate all types of information concerning dangerous situations in such areas as meteorology, oceanography, fisheries, public security, health, and civil aviation. To ensure rapid handling of emergencies, more than ten governmental departments are involved in such operations.

A New Role for China's Navy

The current situation in international security is complicated and changeable. Nontraditional security issues, including natural disasters and maritime incidents, have assumed a place of greater importance on the security agenda. Regarding the shipwrecks caused by disasters at sea, the requirements for emergency management are constantly increasing. As a part of China's government, the PLA Navy should play an important role in ensuring the proper functioning of search and rescue. China's maritime sector must coordinate with the navy to conduct maritime search and rescue. Therefore, maritime search and rescue is an important task of the Chinese navy. During air, land, and sea rescue exercises, military forces should strengthen their abilities of coordination and cooperation with the local relief force.

As an important supplementary means for search and rescue at sea, the hospital ship plays an efficient role in accomplishing this task. In its earlier coastal defense policy, China did not recognize the importance of constructing hospital ships because the medical treatment could be conducted on land. Because Chinese marine forces are now going to the blue oceans to meet the needs of search and rescue at sea, the Chinese navy has been facing the challenge of a shortage of capacities of medical care at sea. The Chinese navy has a hospital ship, *Nankang*, which is registered to the International Red Cross.[13] The Chinese navy's capacity for disaster relief at sea has been enhanced by the launching in August 2007 of a well-equipped type-920 hospital ship, *Peace Ark*.[14] It will take some time for Chinese marine forces to have a strong ability for the relief activities in blue water, however, because the number of hospital ships is still quite limited.

China should establish foreign joint meetings with the various ministries, establish a military liaison mechanism with other relevant governmental sectors, and strengthen coordination, communication, and cooperation with the relevant ministries and departments of the military. All types of available resources, including the professional capabilities and social forces, the army, and local governments, should integrate different kinds of sectors related to the marine forces. Today, the power for managing maritime affairs has been decentralized into several branches of government. As for the marine forces, there are marine surveillance, marine affairs, fishery administration, customs, and marine military police (now called the coast guard), all of which are controlled by the different governmental sectors, and their functions have always overlapped.[15] These forces share some kind of semimilitary capacity to enforcing maritime law, which results in some problems in the mutual collaboration and even contradiction with each other. This embarrassing situation makes China lack efficiency in countering challenges at sea. Consequently, the Chinese government will likely try to integrate those semimilitary forces and could eventually establish a consolidated coast guard with unified management and command.[16]

Participation in civil search-and-rescue activities increases the navy's function. The PLA Navy must not only address traditional security threats but also deal with maritime disasters, humanitarian crises, and other nontraditional security threats. As nontraditional threats to security grow, the functions of the PLA Navy must be more comprehensive; this is a major international naval development trend.

China's Participation in International Humanitarian Relief Cooperation at Sea

In recent years China has carried out many maritime humanitarian relief activities with other countries in the world. This has promoted maritime security cooperation between China and its neighboring countries and other maritime powers and has increased mutual understanding and trust between China and its partners who share common concerns on maritime security. Through this cooperation, China has strengthened its ability to conduct search and rescue at sea, has protected maritime security for Chinese citizens, and has brought great benefits to its neighbors in term of enhancing their maritime safety.[17]

Maritime Search and Rescue Exercises between China and Other Countries

Since the start of the new century, PLA Navy warships have executed search-and-rescue military exercises many times with vessels of foreign countries from all over the world. These exercises are summarized in the following:

Southeast Asia. On 13 December 2005, the Chinese and Thai navies held joint search-and-rescue exercises in the Gulf of Thailand, code-named "Sino-Thai Friendship 2005," the first exercise between the PLA Navy and the Thai navy in the field of nontraditional security. This joint exercise involved communications, sea-air search and rescue, and cooperative supply. In focusing on nontraditional security fields, this joint maritime military exercise differed from traditional military exercises. The joint search-and-rescue exercise was not directed against any third country but was instead designed to help combat piracy, eliminate terrorism, and fight against natural disasters, all of which can safeguard the security of Southeast Asia. During this exercise the scope of search and rescue was not limited to military vessels but also included RMS, merchant ships, and passenger ships, all of which may be involved in search and rescue in the event of an emergency.[18]

Sino-Japanese. On 13 March 2007, under the guidance and coordination of the Chinese Maritime Search and Rescue Center and Shanghai Maritime Search and Rescue Center in cooperation with the Japanese Coast Guard Search and Rescue Center in Kagoshima, the "2007 Sino-Japanese Maritime Search and Rescue Exercise on Communication" was held successfully. To enhance the level of collaboration and ensure that the two agencies were coordinated, bilateral communication was open in accordance with the framework of the 1979 International Convention on Maritime Search and Rescue. Through this exercise, Chinese and Japanese maritime search-and-rescue departments have strengthened exchanges and cooperation. Notably, the Shanghai Maritime Search and Rescue Center had the opportunity to participate in exchange directly with a foreign counterpart. The two sides thus promoted mutual understanding and enhanced the level of search-and-rescue operations at sea.

Indian Ocean. On 22 October 2003 PLA Navy warships held a joint search-and-rescue exercise code-named "Dolphin 0310" with visiting Pakistani naval vessels in the East China Sea near Shanghai. This is the first time that the Chinese navy held joint exercises with a foreign navy on the nontraditional security field. This exercise greatly helped the PLA Navy to expand participation in the nontraditional security field and accumulate experience in joint exercises.

On 1 December 2005 a PLA Navy surface group composed of the missile destroyer *Shenzhen* and the comprehensive supply ship *Weishan Lake* held a joint search-and-rescue exercise code-named "China-India Friendship 2005" with the Indian navy in the northern Indian Ocean. The exercise had two areas: joint fleet formations and rescue. This is the second time that the Chinese navy held an exercise with the Indian navy in the nontraditional security field. On 14 November 2003 the PLA Navy held its first joint exercise with the visiting Indian navy in the East China Sea.

Europe. On 25 September 2007 a Chinese visiting naval fleet composed of the missile destroyer *Guangzhou* and the comprehensive supply ship *Weishan Lake* held the joint military exercise "Sino-French Friendship 2007" with the French navy in the Mediterranean Sea after rigorous training and a long voyage. During the joint military exercise, the two sides exchanged observers to learn from each other and test the quality of the exercise. This first Sino-French naval exercise in the Mediterranean deepened exchanges and cooperation, enhanced international military contacts, and deepened the PLA Navy's learning and understanding of foreign militaries.

China's Contribution to International Rescue Operations

Over the past decade, China has played an important role in safeguarding its own citizens and personnel from the neighboring countries in adjacent seas. China's contributions to maritime search and rescue have created a security umbrella in the sea around China to protect the victims of shipwrecks.

In the late 1990s, China's Bureau of Maritime Affairs established a Chinese center for the system of shipping reports, and promulgated the Regulation for Managing the System of Shipping Reports, which established CHISREP. This regulation requires that all foreign ships over 300 tons on the international sea-lanes and Chinese ships over 1,600 tons on the sea-lanes in the adjacent seas should join this system when they are sailing within an area up to latitude 9° north and west to longitude 130° east (with the exception of those operating in other countries' territorial waters). Thousands of Chinese and foreign ships have already registered with CHISREP. Statistics compiled by China Maritime Search and Rescue Center indicate that from 1998 to mid-2004, the center organized search-and-rescue operations at least 2,189 times, and saved 36,745 personnel, including 1,608 foreigners. The ratio of successful operations has reached 90 percent, almost equal to the level of developed countries.[19] In 2004 alone, the China Maritime Search and Rescue Center conducted operations to help 400 wrecked ships and saved more than 2,000 persons, including 60 foreigners.[20]

In recent years, China Maritime Search and Rescue Center has assumed responsibility for multilateral coordination and organizing command and run several important cases of search and rescue. In November 2005 the grounded vessel *Panama* received assistance and fifteen sailors were rescued. In November 2006 China conducted the largest international rescuing operation in its history. As for the disaster of typhoon, more than fifteen Vietnamese fishing ships were saved successfully when they were in danger in South China Sea.[21] At almost the same time, twenty North Korean shipmen were rescued, for which Pyongyang sent its appreciation to Beijing. China rescued several ships from ASEAN countries in 2007, among which twenty-three Indonesian shipmen and Philippine sailors were rescued in East China Sea and South China Sea.

Following the Indonesian tsunami disaster of 2004, China made its largest-scale humanitarian assistance to foreign countries to date. China donated up to 1.3 billion RMB, and even the Chinese Defense Ministry was directly involved in providing this kind of humanitarian assistance.[22] Despite offering considerable financial aid to Indonesia, China was unable to provide directly human resources and material with its limited marine forces. In contrast, the United States made an influential impact in this disaster relief by means of tangible material assistance offered by its strong blue water navy and former leaders' condolatory visit via military transportation. This experience made China aware of the shortages of its navy's delivery capacity as compared with that of the U.S. Navy. China's navy realized that strengthening its capabilities would increase China's capabilities to help its neighbors when they encounter natural disasters. By offering humanitarian assistance (such as search-and-rescue operations) with other partners, China is aware that it has to share more responsibilities to safeguard its adjacent seas.

Sino-American Cooperation on Maritime Search and Rescue

The United States and China are both important sea powers in the Asia-Pacific region. As the world's sole superpower, the United States has the dominant naval force in the Pacific; as a developing country with rapidly growing overseas interests, China is assuming increasing responsibility for maintaining the safety in its adjacent seas and dealing with natural disasters. Because of convergence of maritime interests, China and the United States should explore this new field for cooperation. Joint efforts to enhance maritime search-and-rescue capabilities could be a key area for the further cooperation in the field of nontraditional security.

China and the U.S. Navy already share common interests in maritime cooperation. In late 2006 some important events laid the foundation for cooperation in maritime search and rescue. After a successful military exchange, the third visit by PLA Navy warships to the United States in September of that year, a Chinese warship formation with the missile destroyer *Qingdao* and the comprehensive refueling tanker *Hongzehu* participated in a joint search-and-rescue exercise northwest of Naval Base San Diego. Ships from the two navies conducted exercises and both sides' sailors worked together directly in a search-and-rescue training session. It was the first time for the two countries to have a military operation for this purpose. They practiced how to save a third ship from fire and flooding while evacuating casualties.[23] At the request of the American navy, this joint exercise incorporated Codes for Unalerted Encounters at Sea (CUES) and Experimental Tactics (EXTACS). Two of these regulations were designed by the member states of the Western Pacific Naval Symposium.[24]

An even more important exercise was conducted when the U.S. Navy made a reciprocal visit to China in December 2006. As agreed by Chinese and U.S. military leaders, the event was the second phase of the first-ever joint Sino-American search-and-rescue exercises. This exercise involved China's guided missile destroyer *Zhanjiang*, its fuel tanker *Dongting Lake*, the USS *Juneau* (LPD-10), and the missile destroyer USS *Fitzgerald*. Commanding different stages of the exercise in the South China Sea, the two navies jointly located a ship in danger and salvaged it. The assumption for this operation was that a ship was being shipwrecked and that the Chinese side asked for an American warship passing by to help in searching for and rescuing the victims. Unlike previous Chinese operations with foreign countries, nothing had been set in advance, which made it more like a real accident.

On 11 July 2007 a ship sank in the northwest Pacific. Almost all of the crew was from China's Fujian Province. The U.S. Coast Guard initiated a search and informed the China Maritime Search and Rescue Center. China's Ministry of Transport immediately ordered implementation of the National Maritime Search and Rescue Contingency Plans to keep in close communication with the U.S. Coast Guard and conduct the search and rescue. Eventually, among twenty victims, three were found dead and seven were missing, but twelve were saved. This case is a good illustration of close Sino-American civil maritime cooperation.

These military search-and-rescue exercises have laid a milestone for maritime security cooperation between China and the United States. They have demonstrated the importance of joint search-and-rescue cooperation and the two nations' ability to do so effectively. The author would argue that humanitarian search and rescue could be the main field for maritime security cooperation between China and the United States.

Conclusion

China is not only a land power but also a sea power playing a positive role in the world by sharing its tradition of managing maritime affairs. Along with its rapid economic development, China increasingly depends on the sea to maintain its strong global linkages. In this process of involvement in international society, China has adopted many universal norms and common behaviors, and humanitarianism has assumed an important and positive role in China's decision making. By now the concept of humanitarianism has become a focal point in China's domestic and foreign policy. The Chinese government stresses the guiding principles of making the people a starting point for the government and managing the governmental affairs for the people first, within which humanitarianism has imbedded its special implication. The practice of humanitarian assistance in society, including activities of search and rescue, narrows the gap to some extent between official leaders and ordinary people, and it enhances the legitimate foundation for the government.

One of the important fields for the practice of humanitarian policy is maritime search-and-rescue operations, which offer a feasible means of safeguarding Chinese civilians on the sea, and of providing a new cutting-edge means of strengthening China's cooperation with its neighbors and even maritime partners overseas. By helping to save victims from shipwrecks and other maritime disasters, China brings the benefits to its neighbors. Thus, China has improved its image and evaporated the so-called China threat theory in the region. As a positive side effect, participating in search-and-rescue operations with other countries enhances China's ability to manage maritime affairs and its navy's capacities. Of particular importance, maritime search-and-rescue cooperation between China and the United States has become a valuable platform for bilateral dialogue under the rubric of humanitarian assistance. Both countries have gained benefits from maritime search and rescue, and mutual understanding and trust have been enhanced in this way. Consequently, humanitarian assistance, particularly maritime search and rescue, could create good conditions for Chinese–American maritime cooperation in the long term.

Notes

1. State Council Information Office of People's Republic of China, *China's Progress in Human Rights in 2004* [中国的人权状况] (Beijing, April 2005).

2. "中国为何援助美国" ["Zhongguo Weihe Yuanzhu Meiguo"; "Why China Assists the United States"], Southeast Express Web site, 8 February 2006, http://news.qq.com/a/20060208/000849.htm.

3. "中国就发展人道主义事业提出四点主张" ["Zhongguo Jiu Fazhan Guoji Rendaozhuyi Shiye Tichu Sidian Zhuzhang"; "China Puts Forward Four Points on the Development of the Humanitarian Cause"], Phoenix Television, 27 November 2007, http://news.phoenixtv.com/mainland/200711/1127_17_313289.shtml.

4. "中国支持社会协调对海啸受灾国的援助" ["Zhongguo Zhichi Guoii Shehui Xietiao Dui Haixiao Shou Zaiguo de Yuanzhu"; "China Supports the International Community's Coordination on Assistance to Countries Affected by the Tsunami"], China.com Web site, 19 March 2005, http://www.china.com.cn/chinese/zhuanti/ydyhx/815374.htm.

5. Chen Xiande, 国家海上搜救应急预案贯彻实施指南及相关法律法规汇编 [*Guojia Haishang Soujiu Yingji Yu An Guanche Shishi Zhinan Ji Xiangguan Fa Lv Fagui Huibian; Guidelines to Implement a National Maritime Search and Rescue Emergency Advance Plan and Compilation of Related Laws and Regulations*] (Beijing: China Transportation Press, 2005).

6. "国家海上搜救应急预案" ["Advance Plans to Deal with Emergency Events and Organizing Search and Rescue at Sea"], http://www.chnlaw.net/chinalaw/HTML/chinalaw_2851.htm.

7. Some of these laws can be read in a series of books edited by the Bureau of Legislative Affairs of the State Council of the People's Republic of China: 中华人民共和国涉外法规汇编 [*Laws and Regulations of the People's Republic of China Governing Foreign-related Matters*] (Beijing: China Legal System Press, 1990–2005).

8. See the Web site of the China Maritime Search and Rescue Center, en.msa.gov.cn/msa/features/root/01/0104/1224130115740.

9. "交通部海事局" ["Introduction to Maritime Safety Administration of the People's Republic of China"], Maritime Safety Administration Web site, http://www.msa.gov.cn/Jgjj/Hsj.aspx?category_id=1.

10. See the Web site of 国家海洋局 [the State Oceanic Administration], http://www.soa.gov.cn/hyjww/index.htm.

11. See the Web site of 公安部边防管理局 [the Border Control Department of the Ministry of Public Security], http://www.mps.gov.cn/n16/n80254/index.html.

12. Since 2002 China launched two satellites, Haiyang 1-A and Haiyang 1-B, which have improved China's capacity to survey the maritime situation.

13. Liu Dian, "Navy Flag on Life Boat," 中国海洋报 [China's Oceanic Affairs], 28 January 2003.

14. "New Hospital Ship," VME Web site, http://www.chinavme.com/viewthread.php?tid=6415.

15. "中国海上执法力量分析" ["Analysis on the Chinese Marine Forces"], China.com Web site, 8 July 2008, http://military.club.china.com/data/thread/1011/2090/86/18/3_1.html.

16. He Zhonglong and Ren Xingping, 打造我国海洋综合执法力量: 中国海岸警卫队组建研究 [Forging Chinese Comprehensive Marine Force for Enforcing Law: A Study on the Establishment of a Chinese Coast Guard] (Beijing: China Ocean Press, 2007), ch. 3 and 4.

17. Information Office of the State Council, People's Republic of China, "China's National Defense in 2006," 29 December 2006, http://english.chinamil.com.cn/site2/special-reports/2007gfbps/index.htm.

18. RMS is an acronym referring to reliability, maintainability, and supportability related to the ship's weaponry system.

19. Zhang Wenjin, "前进中的中国搜救事业," ["Qianjin zhong de Zhongguo Soujiu Shiye"; "China's Search-and-Rescue Affairs Moving Forward"], 中国海运 [China Water Transport], no. 10 (2004): 13–14.

20. "Help to Salvage 400 Wrecking Ships by China Center for Search-and-Rescue," http://www.people.com.cn/GB/channel1/10/20000526/78860.html.

21. "我国最大国际海上救援行动成功救助330名越南渔民" ["China's Biggest Search and Rescue Action Saves 330 Vietnamese Fishermen"], People's Daily, 22 May 2006.

22. "中国国防部决定为海啸受灾国提供资金援" ["China's Defense Ministry Decides to Offer Funds to Countries Destroyed by Tsunami"], Liberation Army Daily, 4 January 2005.

23. Michael R. Gordon, "To Build Trust, U.S. Navy Holds a Drill with China," New York Times, 23 September 2006.

24. "中美海军首次海上联合搜救演习纪实" ["A Record of the First-Ever Joint Search-and-Rescue Exercise between the Chinese and American Navies"], China Youth Daily, 2 September 2006. CUES are a subset of signals proposed by the WPNS charter members to be used when encountering other West Pacific Naval Symposium vessels at sea to provide a means of communication for basic information such as course, speed,

vessel name, and so on. EXTACS is the larger publication from which CUES were originally derived. EXTACS has since been replaced by the Multi-National Tactical Publication (MTP 1D) Multi-National Maritime Tactical Instructions and Procedures. E-mail interview, Captain Mark Manfredi, USN, COMPACFLT (N51), 17 February 2009.

Eric A. McVadon

Humanitarian Operations
A Window on U.S.–China Maritime Cooperation

ARE U.S.–PEOPLE'S REPUBLIC OF CHINA (PRC) relations, as they continue to hover over a strange threshold between excellent and uncertain, stable enough to bring a halt to the all-too-familiar rollercoaster ride for military ties? Are those ties, severed by China in October 2008 and again in January 2010, then ready for further advances in military cooperation such as the Chinese navy's joining the U.S. Navy in providing disaster relief?[1] A glance at the past offers insights and background for the examination that follows of the problems and prospects of both limited cooperation in humanitarian operations and broader maritime cooperation.

A Retrospective: Lessons from the History of PRC–U.S. Military Relations

In the late 1980s but before the tragedy in and around Tiananmen in June 1989, U.S.–China military-to-military relations were good—even excellent by some measures, especially given the profound differences between the two countries and the two militaries. For example, Secretary of Defense Harold Brown visited China in January 1980—a first.[2] By the end of the 1980s there had been several other senior visitors, and at least four major foreign military sales (FMS) cases had been approved for the People's Liberation Army (PLA). The U.S. Air Force flight demonstration team, the Thunderbirds, had flown over the Great Wall in 1987. The PLA Navy training ship *Zheng He* visited Hawaii in 1989, the first visit by a PLA Navy ship to the United States. The ship moored at the Pearl Harbor Naval Station; the U.S. Navy host was Captain Bernard Cole, Commander Destroyer Squadron 35, with considerable "assistance" from the commander of the U.S. Pacific Fleet, Admiral David Jeremiah, whose executive assistant was then-Captain Dennis Blair.[3] The atmosphere was conducive to both symbolic and substantive cooperative undertakings, although many doubted the appropriateness of that sort of relationship with the PRC, as some do now.

Colonel Frank Miller, who headed the Northeast Asia section of J-5 in the U.S. Joint Staff, addressed a prestigious conference in Washington on 24 October 2007. He described the state of, and the rationale for, military relations with China during the 1980s:

> In the early period, 1980 to 1989, the relationship transitioned from one of mutual suspicion regarding Taiwan to recognition of the need to collaborate on the Soviet issue. For the U.S., the SALT treaties needed a means of verification, which China's proximity to the Soviet testing centers provided. In return, the Chinese, by all accounts, needed a hedge to their ongoing border demilitarization negotiations with Moscow. But it took a U.S. delegation to Beijing to broker the deal.
>
> Engagements were divided into three "pillars"—senior-level exchanges, functional exchanges and technology transfers. The senior exchange pillar is simple enough, and technology transfers refer of course to the military equipment sales begun prior to June 1989, though final deliveries extended into the mid-'90s. Covering all three services, the U.S. transferred a total of nearly $290 million worth of military and dual-use equipment to China in this period. Functional Exchanges included intelligence, logistics, professional military education, and observations of combined arms training.[4]

Thus, early in the relationship a matter of great sensitivity but one that served mutual interests—the monitoring of Soviet nuclear testing from sites in China—became a component of bilateral relations. Perhaps this example can put in perspective questions about whether it is premature now to commence cooperation in humanitarian operations and disaster relief.

All was not rosy during this period in the 1980s. With respect to technology transfer, the Chinese wanted a better antisubmarine homing torpedo than was offered; they were also denied a cutting-edge jet engine for a fighter aircraft, as the author recalls from his job as deputy director for policy on the Navy Staff at the time. All those FMS cases and the military-to-military relationship itself were terminated or suspended as a result of the sanctions Washington imposed after the 4 June 1989 events in and around Tiananmen Square. The author, as defense attaché at the U.S. embassy in Beijing from 1990 to 1992, dealt with the angry aftermath.

In the fall of 1993, Assistant Secretary of Defense Charles W. Freeman traveled to Beijing and proposed to the Chinese some cooperative military endeavors—rudimentary exercises. The PLA, twice burned (by the Soviets three decades earlier in the schism and by the Americans in 1989), did not accept the proposal. But the ice had been broken. Nevertheless, it remained common for both sides to deny or ignore requests and queries. Some success was achieved in 1990–92 in reestablishing communication at the flag-officer level of the defense attaché and the Foreign Affairs Bureau of the Ministry of National Defense. In an August 1994 secret (now declassified) memo for the secretaries of the Army, Navy, and Air Force, with a copy to the chairman of the Joint Chiefs of Staff, Secretary of Defense William Perry, confirming the author's personal recollections and looking to the future, wrote:

> The Department of Defense had a robust military relationship with the People's Liberation Army (PLA) in the mid-80s. That relationship halted abruptly in June 1989. Now that it has been revived, I want to use this opportunity to give you my views on where we are now going with the PLA.
>
> Since the Tiananmen crackdown of 1989, there has been a dramatic change of the global strategic situation, and last year, the President decided on a comprehensive engagement policy with respect to China, and that policy includes the resumption of military contacts. . . .
>
> . . . Our security posture dramatically improves if China cooperates with us. In order to gain that cooperation, we must rebuild mutual trust and understanding with the PLA. . . .
>
> Last November, Assistant Secretary Chas Freeman went to China to re-open senior level defense dialogue.[5]

Secretary Perry expressed well the value of relations with the PLA. Nevertheless, over the next several years U.S.–China military relations had ups and downs stemming from such things as China's 1995–96 launches of ballistic missiles impacting near Taiwan and the American reaction thereto of positioning two carrier battle groups in the vicinity of Taiwan. There was, despite interruptions, a brisk exchange of senior military or defense visitors as well as some success in institutionalizing the relations through defense consultative talks and the military maritime consultative talks. Late in the 1990s concerns grew among some in Washington about what the United States was revealing to senior Chinese military visitors. The Fiscal Year 2000 National Defense Authorization Act included a rider that imposed limits on military exchanges with China and curtailed contacts with the PLA.[6] (It should be noted, however, that subsection 1201[c] states that the limitation "does not apply to any search-and-rescue or humanitarian operation or exercise." Humanitarian assistance and disaster relief operations and exercises are permissible.)

The Current Situation

"The Chinese government [now] views [humanitarian operations] as an important part of international security cooperation."

—*Su Hao, China Foreign Affairs University*[7]

The exchange of visits by senior officers and officials continued until the October 2008 disruption of military exchanges by Beijing following a Washington announcement of prospective arms sales to Taiwan. Notably, Secretary of Defense Donald Rumsfeld, clearly not a "panda-hugger," visited in 2005. In 2007 the chairman of the Joint Chiefs of Staff (CJCS), General Peter Pace, visited China; the heads of the two navies, Admirals Wu Shengli and Michael Mullen, exchanged visits—just before Mullen replaced Pace as the top U.S. military officer; Admiral Timothy Keating, the U.S. Pacific commander, visited China in 2007 and again in early 2008.[8] U.S. Marine Corps commandant General James Conway also visited in early 2008. Visits resumed in 2009. Chief of Naval Operations Admiral Gary Roughead was among the many international guests in Qingdao for celebration of the PLA Navy's sixtieth anniversary. In October 2009 General Xu Caihou, vice chairman of the Central Military Commission, visited Washington and various U.S. military bases and invited Secretary of Defense Gates to visit China in 2010.[9] Although it does not normally get placed in the category of a military visit, U.S. president and commander-in-chief Barack Obama visited China and met with Chinese president and chairman of the Central Military Commission Hu Jintao in mid-

November 2009. The rollercoaster ride took another dip with the January 2010 disruption of military ties, once again linked to U.S. arms sales to Taiwan. It was said by the PRC to include a halt of military exchanges; however, U.S. secretary of defense Robert Gates' conspicuous continuing expectation of visiting later in 2010 was mentioned in a report by Xinhua, the official Chinese news agency, seeming to offer tacit confirmation.[10] This and other similar developments point to the likelihood that this rupture is another serious and determined attempt to register objection to U.S. arms sales to Taiwan but will not harden into a permanent barrier to military relations.

Humanitarian Assistance and Disaster Relief

PLA Navy senior captain Li Jie of the PRC Ministry of National Defense, speaking in October 2007 at the aforementioned Washington conference on the topic of enhancing bilateral military relations, said, in answering a question from the author, that a U.S. military delegation had visited China recently and discussed the prospects for U.S.–China cooperation in humanitarian assistance and disaster relief or response (HA and DR).[11] Lieutenant Colonel Eric Barto, then in the office of the U.S. Joint Staff in the Plans and Policy Directorate (J-5), headed by Colonel Miller, confirmed to the author that the idea of bilateral cooperation on HA and DR is not new. The original concept, Barto explained, was introduced in an exchange between presidents Bill Clinton and Jiang Zemin. This is apparently reflected in a 1998 document provided by the PRC embassy in Washington, which includes the following: "Thirdly, the functional exchanges between our two militaries have been rather active. Both sides have agreed to carry out exchanges in the fields of military training, logistics, military academies, military history and justice. Besides, both sides have agreed to share information and discuss issues related to their respective experiences in the areas of humanitarian assistance and disaster relief."[12] Efforts began at the headquarters of U.S. Army Pacific before 2000 on an exchange on HA and DR. The Belgrade embassy bombing and the F-8 and EP-3 air collision incidents caused delays. The program, said Lieutenant Colonel Barto, finally started in 2005 with a U.S. delegation visiting Chengdu, and there have been at least three exchanges so far. (The author discovered evidence of an earlier exchange. The deputy secretary of defense in 2001 advised Congress of, among many other items, PLA participation in the Humanitarian Affairs Disaster Relief Sandtable Planning team visit to the United States, 10–18 October 2000.)[13] In connection with the 2006 U.S. visit of China's senior military officer, General Guo Boxiong, vice chairman of the Central Military Commission (chaired by China's president), the PRC embassy in Washington provided an information document that included the following: "The defense departments [the U.S. Department of Defense and the PRC Ministry of National Defense] of the two countries have restored a series of consultation mechanisms on maritime security, humanitarian disaster relief and military environmental protection."[14] Senior-level support for U.S.–China cooperation in the area of humanitarian exercises and operations appears ample, but the focus has not been on naval or maritime cooperation.

U.S. major general Darryll Wong, in concert with the office of the deputy undersecretary of defense for installations and environment, has engaged in these exchanges with China and states that they reflect a very positive attitude in the PLA toward participation in humanitarian assistance activities, including further international use of an urban rescue team demonstrated to the visiting Americans. General Wong said the earnest approach with respect to cooperation in environmental protection efforts reflects a readiness in the PLA to undertake other cooperation.[15]

Lieutenant Colonel Barto participated in the first two of these recent exchanges as assistant army attaché at the U.S. embassy in Beijing. He thought these were possibly the best exchanges being undertaken between the two militaries.[16] Both sides were very comfortable with the topic. The PLA was uncharacteristically open in describing its efforts and answering questions. The U.S. Army Pacific hosted the Chinese in 2006 in Hawaii, and a U.S. delegation was in China in August 2007. Barto added that this topic is used by senior leaders on both sides as an example of an area in which we can continue substantive cooperation, as corroborated by the Department of Defense 2006 annual report to Congress on the Chinese military, which states: "The Chinese government is still adapting to its role as an emerging power by taking on greater regional and international responsibilities. Positive steps include increasing participation in regional and global fora and in peace operations, humanitarian assistance, and disaster relief."[17] Also, Deputy Undersecretary of Defense Richard Lawless testified to the House Armed Services Committee in June 2007: "We are also making progress in cooperative efforts to address transnational and non-traditional security challenges, including humanitarian assistance and disaster relief."[18] From Lieutenant Colonel Barto's perspective, as conveyed in discussion with the author, we are "establishing the foundation of what is going to be a real success story in our mil-to-mil engagements." However, these exchanges on humanitarian operations have not included naval cooperation, as confirmed by Wong and Barto.

Naval Cooperation in Humanitarian Operations:
A Promising Prospect

This lack of attention to prospective naval participation in humanitarian assistance and disaster relief exercises is not surprising. Because of distrust and the friction in U.S.–China relations, and with considerable wariness on both sides, bilateral exercises between the two navies have been an elusive objective. In 2006, however, there was something of a breakthrough. During a visit to Pearl Harbor and San Diego, a PLA Navy destroyer and replenishment ship carried out the initial phase of a two-part exercise with the U.S. Navy that involved rudimentary communications and passing exercises in waters off Hawaii and a search-and-rescue exercise off Southern California. The final phase occurred in waters near China during the late-2006 visit there of U.S. admiral Gary Roughead, who at the time commanded the U.S. Pacific Fleet and now heads the U.S. Navy as chief of naval operations, yet another indicator of senior support for cooperation.[19]

As a practical matter, the stage seems to be set for a move toward the conduct of HA and DR exercises—potentially including naval exercises. As "icing on the cake," the U.S. Pacific commander spoke at the October 2007 conference in Washington and said that U.S.–China military relations are developing.[20] He said the level and complexity of bilateral and multilateral exercises should be enhanced. The author asked Admiral Timothy Keating about the prospects for naval cooperation with the PLA Navy with respect to HA and DR, noting that Chinese interlocutors had said China may not be ready for such operations and may not be invited. Keating cautioned that the multilateral process was sometimes bureaucratically complicated but that he would favor inviting Chinese participation and that exercises in HA and DR should be conducted. (The previously explained specific exemption of humanitarian assistance exercises from the limitations imposed by the FY 2000 National Defense Authorization Act would seem to be an aid to overcoming some of the bureaucratic hurdles to which Admiral Keating may have been alluding.) In light of two late-2008 developments, China's decision to join international counterpiracy efforts off Somalia and the previously described disruption by Beijing of military relations, Admiral Keating said the PLA Navy's joining the counterpiracy operation "augured well" for reestablishing military ties.[21] The signs that the early-2010 disruption is more a gesture concerning arms sales to Taiwan than an enduring barrier is also somewhat encouraging if not altogether reassuring.

The Concept of Global Maritime Partnership— A Possible Catalyst?

"The Thousand Ship Navy [concept] serves many . . . Chinese and U.S. interests."

—Rear Admiral Yang Yi, director, Institute for
Strategic Studies, PLA National Defense University[22]

Thousand-Ship Navy Concept May Boost HA and DR Effort but Is Not Essential

When military relations are fully restored or possibly during the antici-pated visit by Secretary Gates, U.S.–China maritime cooperation seems ripe for raising. There seem to be two roads that hold promise, and pursuing one course of action does not necessarily preclude a foray down the second. The first would be, as Admiral Keating implied, simply to let the next level of PLA Navy–U.S. Navy exercises become one involving HA and DR operations. The second involves the more complex issue of possible Chinese participation in the Global Maritime Partnership (GMP) initiative, more popularly known as the thousand-ship navy (TSN). Put another way, humanitarian exercises and operations involving the PLA Navy and U.S. Navy do not, and should not be allowed to, hinge on China's participation in TSN-GMP. However, if China elects to participate, HA and DR operations and exercises (bilateral and mul-tilateral) are a logical component of the TSN-GMP concept. In either case, the issue of possible Chinese participation has lain fallow too long. The idea should be rekindled either under the GMP rubric or as part of a broader attempt to establish sweeping maritime cooperation ties with China, as discussed below.

Because TSN-GMP is a potential facilitator or, alternatively, a source of complication for HA and DR exercises and cooperation between the two navies, providing an explanation of the concept is appropriate. In April 2007 the commander of the People's Liberation Army Navy (PLA Navy), Vice Admiral Wu Shengli, visited Washington. Admiral Michael Mullen, then head of the U.S. Navy (the chief of naval operations, or CNO), described to Admiral Wu the concept of the aforementioned Global Maritime Partnership or thousand-ship navy. The U.S. CNO explained this transnational network of navies as a free-form voluntary grouping that China could certainly be a part of, if willing. Admiral Wu expressed interest pending further discussion. The two admirals again discussed the topic when Admiral Mullen visited China before moving up to become the chairman of the Joint Chiefs of Staff. Beijing is moving with caution, wary of the possible implications, and is seeking a fuller understanding of the concept, as elaborated below.

U.S. Concerns

Those on the American side have raised a number of red flags regarding a move toward such cooperation. The United States is concerned about the ongoing modernization of Chinese naval, air, and missile forces, China's antisatellite test in January 2007, and other efforts that have changed the power balance across the Taiwan Strait. First, there is a growing concern over where all of this is headed: What is the endgame for the PLA Navy and the whole of China's military? What are China's strategic intentions? Second, even if China's intent is benign, as it has often stated, that could change. In an uncertain future, there is the perception of the risk that through maritime cooperation the United States could be inadvertently helping a Chinese navy that could one day be used against American interests or even against the United States directly.

Reciprocity and Transparency Issues

Central to these concerns is the familiar complaint about the PLA's lack of transparency (an assertion with which this author does not agree; see below) and reciprocity with respect to the extent and intention of China's military buildup. In the past, China has failed to show American visitors installations and equipment comparable to what PLA visitors are shown in the United States. There are, indeed, many issues regarding China's military modernization efforts that have yet to be clearly understood. The suspicion and uncertainty, well founded or not, have amplified the concerns of the more skeptical voices as to military-to-military cooperation.[23] Although progress has not yet satisfied U.S. critics of the military relationship, there have been improvements; for instance, American requests to see previously denied facilities and ships and aircraft have on occasion been approved.[24]

Lack of Transparency or Not Liking What We See?

Beijing has argued that, contrary to complaints from Washington, its intentions and actions are transparent. Both to assure neighbors and promote regional stability as well as to respond to pressure by the United States, China has published several defense white papers. While this official documentation has limited utility in this respect, on a broader scale, no serious PLA-watcher can fail to understand that China's intention is to have the ability to deter or defeat Taiwan independence moves and to thwart U.S. intervention. Beijing has even enacted the March 2007 Anti-Secession Law, which provides a legal basis to use military force against Taiwan if necessary to prevent separation. In this respect, China's strategic intent is clear. Beyond the sovereignty issues of Taiwan and the East China Sea and the South China Sea, Beijing asserts that it has no expansionist or aggressive intent. The scope and character of China's modernization in naval, air, and missile forces—while significant and a matter of profound concern—is quite transparent and illustrates China's limited regional strategic goals.

The 2007 Hong Kong Speed Bump Put Behind Us

The prospects for U.S.-PRC maritime cooperation were briefly complicated in November 2007 by several denials by Beijing of U.S. requests for ship and aircraft visits to Hong Kong.[25] Beijing was displaying its objections, as it did in 2008 and 2010, to announced U.S. arms sales to Taiwan as well as to a prestigious award by the U.S. Congress to the Dalai Lama.[26] This unexpected hitch in the relationship could have conceivably proved to be an obstacle of significance. Beijing, for example, could have escalated the matter by linking it to demands for the lifting of either the restraints on U.S. interaction with the Chinese military imposed by Congress almost a decade ago, or to the sanctions on technology transfer imposed by Washington after the 1989 events at Tiananmen Square. However, other important elements of the bilateral relationship, such as trade issues, the Senior Dialogue and Strategic Economic Dialogue (in the Bush administration), the Strategic and Economic Dialogue (as it has been dubbed in the Obama administration), other military relations and cooperation in the Six-Party Talks concerning North Korea (even if unsuccessful in returning Pyongyang to the talks) have so far remained on track.[27] Perhaps most important, U.S. Navy ship visits to Chinese ports have resumed with visits to Shanghai and Hong Kong. Both sides long ago put the Hong Kong port-visit denial issue behind them. A U.S. Navy guided-missile destroyer took part in the international fleet review in 2009 to celebrate the sixtieth anniversary of the founding of the PLA Navy.

The United Nations Question

Concerning other perceived problems, the Chinese asked Admiral Mullen during his visit in 2007 how GMP would fit with undertakings directed by the United Nations and regional organizations. The UN secretary-general, as well as representatives from many countries, have, this author was told, provided to the U.S. Navy enthusiastic responses to the idea.[28] Beijing is not likely to qui-

etly accept this response and is more likely to insist on receiving a fuller explanation of the relationship between GMP activities and UN prerogatives. China
shows little "give" with respect to sacrificing or jeopardizing its UN leverage.
The United Nations has long provided a mechanism for Beijing to control certain U.S. undertakings with which China disagrees—notably, in recent years,
issues involving Iran and Iraq.

PRC Concerns Enumerated

Rear Admiral Yang Yi, who was then the director of the Institute for
Strategic Studies at China's National Defense University, emphasized at the U.S
Naval War College conference in December 2007 that critical questions had to
be addressed before Beijing (not the PLA) could decide "whether to join this
program." These questions include "What is the deeper U.S. strategic intention of the TSN program in addition to the declared purpose of fighting global
terrorism? Does it fit with China's foreign policy to participate in such a program? How will participation impact China's national security interests? Can
China open its ports and provide logistic support to the U.S. Navy?" On a case-
by-case basis, Chinese participation may hinge on adherence to the following
principles: "All activities should be strictly within the framework of UN authorization and consistent with international laws; the sovereignty and territorial
integrity of other countries must be respected and the use of force in order to
intervene in a country's internal affairs shall be avoided; the target of activity
should be nontraditional security threats such as terrorism, religious extremism and national separatism."

This seems a good list for the United States to work from to answer Chinese
questions and clear up misconceptions; for example, the U.S. Navy may not be
contemplating an opening of Chinese ports and the seeking of logistics support. Of course, pitfalls insidiously placed in this list, such as the mention of
combating national separatism, must be avoided. The UN issue seems to be
worded a bit more softly, more as a reminder than a reason for not participating. (This author has heard raised the added concern that this seems so far
a U.S. Navy idea; Chinese leaders will need to know that GMP is a concept
approved by the U.S. government more broadly.)

PRC Naval Attaché's Views

In March 2008 the author asked the PRC naval attaché in Washington
about the status of bilateral maritime cooperation initiatives. With respect to
the GMP concept, he said that his navy favors cooperative undertakings, both

bilateral and multilateral; but some senior officers remain apprehensive about the concept, fearing, for example, that it both implies obligations for the PLA Navy and means dominant U.S. leadership of the effort everywhere around the globe. Evidence to the contrary was brought to his attention, in particular the article in the October 2007 U.S. Naval Institute *Proceedings* by Captain Gordan Van Hook, then executive director of the CNO Executive Panel, as well as articles by the author and PLA Navy Rear Admiral Yang Yi in the Autumn 2007 journal *China Security* that cover all angles of the issue of U.S.–PRC maritime cooperation.[29] The concern about a domineering U.S. role in GMP is more pronounced, the naval attaché said, because the United States is now viewed as all-too-frequently using military force to excess to secure its objectives. He thinks that no one in China believes an answer is due or any other step is pending with respect to the GMP concept discussed by Admirals Mullen (then CNO) and Wu (commander of the PLA Navy). He said, however, that there is receptivity to the sorts of cooperative efforts suggested in the new U.S. Maritime Strategy (described below).

While American engagement in the Western Pacific is generally welcomed by regional countries—including China, to some extent—there are indeed whispers of ulterior motives and hidden intentions of containing China or infringing on its sovereignty. Chinese analysts see the potential imposition of U.S. leadership—even dominance or hegemony—where it is not desired. PLA Navy senior officers continue to suspect that, although GMP might contribute to making the Strait of Malacca safer, the unintended consequence could be to put it under U.S. control. The U.S. Navy has by far the dominant naval presence in the region, but the Malacca and other relevant straits are generally policed—albeit imperfectly—by littoral countries. Captain Van Hook, in his article in *Proceedings*, responded directly to these concerns. He cautioned against a heavy American hand, urging that the United States avoid arrogance and be more sympathetic to other parties' concerns regarding U.S. influence. He contends that regional security arrangements have competent leaders with shared cultural ties and strategic interests. It remains to be seen if, when this is explained to the Chinese, their concerns over undue U.S. Navy influence will be significantly diminished.[30]

These concerns must be kept in perspective. For example, a mindset persists within the Chinese military that, because China is the weaker power compared to the United States, a degree of secrecy is appropriate, particularly with regard to specifics. China's military transparency undoubtedly needs improvement, particularly with respect to visibility of programs for systems and capabilities, as U.S. secretary of defense Donald Rumsfeld noted in 2005 after

visiting Beijing. For example, Beijing has not fully cleared up the mystery surrounding its plans with respect to aircraft carrier development. However, the
United States should see that there is much about the PLA that is transparent,
and Washington might also accept a limited measure of persistent PLA secrecy
as essentially inevitable.

In April 2008 an additional query by the author to a knowledgeable PLA
interlocutor suggested that, despite lack of progress, there is genuine interest in
the concept of bilateral or multilateral maritime cooperation, even enthusiasm
by PLA Navy commander Admiral Wu Shengli. However, China was said to be
awaiting more information about the details. Although not directly associated
with the response concerning maritime cooperation, complaints were voiced
at the same time about U.S. arms sales to Taiwan, the congressionally imposed
constraints on U.S.–China military relations, and the annual U.S. Department
of Defense report to the Congress on the PLA.

Confrontation in the South China Sea

Only good luck, and maybe some skillful ship-handling, kept the intense harassment of U.S. surveillance ships by Chinese ships and aircraft from becoming a
sequel to the dangerous and deadly collision of an intercepting PLA Navy F-8
fighter and a reconnoitering U.S. Navy EP-3 aircraft nine years earlier.

Differences over More than EEZ Rules

There are strong objections by Beijing, the PLA, and Chinese citizens to the
presence of U.S. military survey, surveillance, and reconnaissance ships and
aircraft near the coast of China. China does not want intelligence collection
activities in its exclusive economic zone (EEZ—generally two hundred nautical miles from the coast). The United States, on the other hand, insists on the
right to conduct such activities in and over international waters—waters that
are not the territorial sea of another country (generally twelve nautical miles
and farther from the coast). Unspoken is that this intelligence collection activity is especially important and produces valuable results that would make U.S.
actions against the PLA, were it to attack Taiwan, more effective and decisive.

In early 2009 the USNS *Impeccable* and USNS *Victorious* were sequentially
operating near Hainan, the large Chinese island that reaches down into the
South China Sea and serves as China's Hawaii with respect to tourism and as a
major basing complex for China's South Sea Fleet. This includes most prominently a new base for nuclear submarines, featuring tunnels that swallow the

submarines, just as at the long-established North Sea Fleet nuclear submarine base near Qingdao.

The U.S. Navy wants to collect acoustic signatures from the PLA Navy's new submarines, and the PLA Navy objects. Chinese fishery vessels and at least one small armed ship and PLA Navy maritime patrol aircraft have come too close, flown too low, acted too aggressively (even attempted to cut the tow cable to the towed sonar array), violated international rules for preventing collisions at sea and in the air, made threats, obstructed maneuvers, and created a dangerous environment.

Many observers have focused on this confrontation as a manifestation of differing interpretations of permissible activities in an EEZ. China does tend toward treating the EEZ as an extension of territorial waters and went so far as to register that conviction when it became a party to the United Nations Convention on the Law of the Sea (UNCLOS), the document that establishes the EEZ concept. The United States and most other countries assert that UNCLOS' drafters made a careful distinction between these zones and territorial waters—a very important distinction that permits even the laying of underwater cables and pipelines. Some countries are sympathetic to the Chinese position. There is disagreement between China and the United States on this interpretation of international law, but the disagreement would exist precisely as it does now if EEZs ceased to exist. China, understandably from its perspective, wants the intelligence activities to stop; the United States, understandably from its perspective, insists on intelligence collection in accordance with international law against a country that threatens Taiwan, that will not renounce the option to use force against the island, and that has in force an antisecession law that codifies its intent to deter or defeat Taiwan and goes so far as to legitimize domestically the use of force against Taiwan if the possibilities for a peaceful reunification should be completely exhausted.

Implications for U.S.–China Relations

General Xu Caihou, vice chairman of China's Central Military Commission, spoke at the Center for Strategic and International Studies in Washington on 26 October 2009. I asked General Xu about the prospects for U.S. Navy–PLA Navy disaster relief exercises and operations (suggesting, as I do in this chapter, that "for the next disaster, the U.S. Navy and PLA Navy should show up as a team"). General Xu said China–U.S. military-to-military relations are proceeding in a positive direction. The two presidents agreed on this direction for the relationship in April in London, and certainly that will include more cooperation between our navies, he said. There have already been several search-

and-rescue exercises between our navies, and there are contacts and exchanges in the counterpiracy operations in the Gulf of Aden off Somalia. The theme of the sixtieth anniversary of the PLA Navy, to which many navy leaders were invited (including the U.S. chief of naval operations), was a harmonious ocean. However, to be frank, General Xu said, the incidents that occurred in March in China's EEZ were the result of intensive reconnaissance missions by U.S. naval ships—referring to confrontations off Hainan with U.S. acoustic intelligence ships. He said it was encouraging that both sides recognize that we do not wish incidents such as this to interfere with state-to-state and military-to-military relations, as reflected in the recent MMCA consultations in Beijing. Neither side wishes the incidents to recur, and both sides desire for the two navies to proceed in a spirit of friendship and mutual understanding, China's senior general concluded in Chinese, as I heard it interpreted. Other Americans in the audience, hearing it in Chinese, agreed that it was particularly significant that General Xu had not made future naval cooperation contingent on a change in U.S. actions with respect to the intelligence collection missions but had instead emphasized the mutual desire to keep such incidents from disrupting the important bilateral relations.

There had been, however, something of a happy ending to the March confrontation, although it appeared right up to the end that both sides would escalate the incident by sending more forces.[31] Instead the two governments, at very high-level, concluded that issues such as North Korea, climate change, and resolving the global economic crisis depend on Sino-U.S. cooperation and take priority.[32] The confrontation abruptly was brought to a halt. However, we have not resolved the underlying differences over Taiwan, surveillance, permissible actions in an EEZ, and rules to avoid collisions at sea and in the air, as well as human rights, trade, intellectual property rights, and currency revaluation. With respect to a way to prevent collisions and escalation of EEZ confrontations, there is available the 1998 Military Maritime Consultative Agreement for use as a vehicle to discuss how to proceed.[33] To have an expectation of success, it would be necessary for the delegates from both sides to be under a mandate from a very high level, possibly presidents Obama and Hu, to set aside or accept the existing differences and work from that point forward—agree to disagree. It seems clear that neither side is going to change its mind about Taiwan, the EEZ, or conducting surveillance; however, we need to look beyond the differences and establish rules—a bilateral agreement—that will avoid a collision between our ships and aircraft or escalation. The appearance, undenied by Washington and Beijing, that the decision to call a surprisingly abrupt end to the confrontation involving USNS *Impeccable* was reached at the highest level, possibly Obama and Hu personally, in order to get on with global concerns offers the prospect that such intervention is conceivable with respect to negotiations. This is important because the militaries of both countries may lack the motivation and vision to understand that the United States and China may have to agree to disagree on the matter of the intelligence collection missions. The unproductive efforts of the MMCA to date on this matter illustrate this need for direction from on high to reach an agreement to preclude dangerous activities in these encounters.

The Need for an Agreement to Avoid Incidents at Sea and in the Air

An agreement to avoid incidents at sea and in the air might resemble the 1972 Incidents at Sea Agreement with the Soviet Union that continues today as an agreement between the United States and Russia. Whether or not there was bilateral presidential intervention in 2009 at some levels of both the U.S. and PRC governments, there must be recognition that there are now—urgently— bigger fish to fry than the operations of USNS *Impeccable* and other collection activities, the Chinese military's demands for ceasing or curbing the collection activities, and reaffirming Chinese indignation.

Views of Incidents at Sea Agreements and Military Maritime Consultative Agreements Differ

In pursuing with the PRC naval attaché related matters in the area of bilateral naval cooperation, the author was told that China does not want to enter into an Incidents at Sea Agreement (INCSEA) with the United States (as the Soviet Union did) because it does not see itself as resembling a Cold War adversary. He went on to say that the United States and China view the 1998 U.S.–PRC Military Maritime Consultative Agreement (MMCA) through different lenses. The United States considers these agreements as means to protect its sailors and airmen from injury and its ships and airplanes from damage— a means to avoid accidents or collisions, with the potential for disrupting the globally crucial U.S.–PRC bilateral relationship or even escalation of conflict between nuclear powers. China, on the other hand, sees the MMCA primarily as a means to make known its objections to U.S. operations near China and Chinese operational units, that is, the U.S. conduct of surveillance flights and similar missions by ships, including flying and steaming through China's exclusive economic zone (EEZ).

The Form of an Agreement between the United States and China

Interlocutors from both sides, the United States and China, have expressed opposition to essentially replicating the U.S.–Soviet 1972 INCSEA agreement because that agreement was clearly between adversaries, as the PRC naval attaché observed. However, a new direction might be taken. It appears not only desirable but also feasible to incorporate additional and modified provisions and a change in language and tone to avoid these undesirable hostile or adversarial implications and associations.

In essence, an agreement with China might be conceived as prescribing procedures for coordination (in place of the emphasis on incidents). These procedures might collectively be called a Military Maritime Coordination Procedures Agreement (MMCPA). CPA is already a term widely familiar both at sea and in the air; it stands for closest point of approach, or the minimum distance calculated when a ship or aircraft is approaching another ship or aircraft. A minimum CPA for ships while conducting surveillance could be agreed upon. A similar minimum distance could be prescribed for aircraft. Additionally, the agreement could become a coordination method that, to a far greater extent than INCSEA, employs real-time, ongoing communications between the units involved as an additional buffer (beyond the written rules) to avoid collisions or other incidents. For instance, a vessel or aircraft about to commence surveillance would reveal its presence, and then both sides would keep each other apprised of movements of interest.

With respect to language or tone, the agreement with China, in line with the coordination theme, could replace the confrontational thrust generally associated with INCSEA with a collegial and professional quality. Moreover, the wording, as compared to that of INCSEA, should be amplified and updated to reflect technological advances, and the scope might be broadened to include vessels and aircraft of government agencies other than the armed forces since such vessels have been involved in recent events.

MMCPA would cover the activities of military, government, and auxiliary ships and aircraft on the high seas and in the airspace above. Approaching vessels and aircraft would announce by radio maneuvers of interest to the other country. The agreement would, like INCSEA, prohibit interference with naval formations and require special consideration for maneuvers in areas of heavy sea traffic. Also like INCSEA, MMCPA would envision the negotiation of minimum distances for closure and prohibit simulated attacks and the use of strong lights or lasers to illuminate ship bridges and aircraft cockpits. Whatever form the agreement might take, it lies with Beijing and Washington to resolve or put aside their differences and reach agreement on means to avoid collisions and other dangerous activities—and, in so doing, acknowledge that potentially escalatory actions must be avoided.

A Closer Look at the Global Maritime Partnership Initiative

Returning to an examination of the concept of global maritime cooperation, foremost among the purposes of TSN-GMP is the protection of ocean commerce (sea-lane security including combating piracy, smuggling, terrorist acts, and weapons proliferation). However, also readily included in the concept are humanitarian assistance, disaster relief, fishing and other extraction of ocean and seabed resources, maritime safety, oceanography, hydrography, port and container security, and coast guard and other law-enforcement responsibilities in a more dangerous world. Antipollution efforts, ship construction, and scientific activities such as weather and sea forecasting, climate research, and tsunami detection also represent the kind of constructive engagement across many fronts that, if applied to China, would reinforce what will undoubtedly be America's most important strategic relationship in the twenty-first century.

Explaining the Global Maritime Partnership

Many questions persist concerning the GMP concept. Two senior U.S. Navy staff strategists, Vice Admiral John G. Morgan and Rear Admiral Charles W. Martoglio, envisioned in 2005 what was then commonly referred to as the thousand-ship navy concept as a way to meet new worldwide challenges, including "piracy, smuggling, drug trading, illegal immigration, banditry, human smuggling and slavery, environmental attack, trade disruption, weapons proliferation including weapons of mass destruction, political and religious extremism, and terrorism."[34] Admirals Morgan and Martoglio assert that no nation alone, not even the United States, can deal with transnational threats. Cooperation between like-minded nations is required to cope with transnational threats.[35] This multinational cooperation would also apply to other areas including humanitarian assistance and disaster relief operations.

GMP, although currently a somewhat neglected idea, is envisioned to be a combination of national, international, and private-industry efforts to provide platforms, people, and procedures to afford security at sea. It foresees voluntary development of a network of sensors (from simple radars to sophisticated methods of detection of illicit activities) and responders (rapid-reaction capabilities such as ships, interdiction teams, and aircraft) capable of ensuring maritime security. It is within the reach of virtually every nation to contribute in some way, whether through combatant ships, the provision of sensors at sea, or maritime law enforcement—whatever fits each entity or country's commercial or national capabilities and interests.[36]

The proposed GMP is a new concept in yet another way. It focuses on the management of shared security interests of all maritime nations—interests essential to the global economy. A hierarchical organizational model typical of naval forces is not implied; individual regions could establish their own arrangements, absent U.S. leadership—an elastic concept in which those most capable, suitable, or competent navies would shore up the less capable. No one would necessarily be in charge. Traditional structured command and control (C2) could be replaced, where appropriate, with a new C2 of cooperation and coordination. In some cases there might be an ad hoc collective relationship among participants, perhaps with only advisory control over each other. No single solution must necessarily fit and constrain the various arrangements because each country would participate in accordance with its own national policies.[37]

On Balance, Good for Both Countries

The GMP would allow a smaller U.S. Navy to meet both its traditional and its new missions in a world of changing challenges. Also important, the GMP would foster ties between countries with maritime interests, including between the United States and China—a country emerging as a major maritime power. If the GMP concept stalls, then, on a bilateral level but with elements borrowed from the GMP concept, perhaps China and the United States could achieve broad maritime and naval cooperation, even partnership. The effort seems warranted.

To examine the other side of the coin, advocating naval and other forms of maritime cooperation between the United States and China strikes some as unwise, given the historic and systemic national differences. For example, how do we cooperate without revealing military secrets? Some fear that the United States, as the far superior force and more advanced partner, would be taking undue risk. Even if this were true, however, it would not remain that way; as China's capabilities increase over time, it will have more to risk. It might also be argued that China, as a weaker country, is also more vulnerable and arguably faces comparable or greater risk through any collaboration. There is undoubtedly some risk in cooperation, but it is shared by both sides.

In any case, the concept of GMP readily accommodates prohibiting or controlling access to classified or sensitive information or equipment. The level or intensity of cooperation and operations can be modulated as desired.

Under GMP, the U.S. Navy, for practical reasons and for the protection of classified information, would almost certainly not initially engage in anything approaching high-tempo combat operations with the PLA Navy. Nevertheless, this would in no way preclude operating with other navies under different circumstances involving classified and sensitive areas and combat operations. In short, the GMP concept inherently allows selectivity and flexibility in the form of operations and the level of information revealed.

A GMP acceptable to China would be modulated in other ways. It would not incorporate known problems associated with previous maritime security overtures to China, particularly the Proliferation Security Initiative (PSI). Although Chinese leaders are generally now in concert with their American counterparts on the dangers of proliferation of nuclear and other materials for weapons of mass destruction, they are concerned about the methods likely to be employed to execute PSI missions, reminding the United States that these are actions that North Korea has labeled acts of war.[38] Beijing has gone so far as to declare that it will prohibit the transit of illegal material through its airspace and seaports, but Beijing is reluctant to accept the practice of checks on the high seas. Boarding ships too, the Chinese assert, is a violation of international law because the nature of material aboard could not be determined before the actions were taken. China would therefore undoubtedly avoid any role in GMP activities related to PSI implementation at sea. It may not be easy in all cases to isolate PSI actions from other GMP activities, but China's role in the maritime partnership could exclude actions related directly to PSI activities. This does not imply a semantic circumvention of an important issue but rather a use of the flexibility inherent in the GMP concept. A senior PLA Navy officer familiar with this issue opined that the PSI problem could be finessed more readily than a number of the other factors discussed in this chapter.

China retains the attitude of a developing country to the degree that it is instinctively wary of wealthier, more powerful countries. Chinese leaders perceive risks in becoming entangled or dependent on others, particularly the United States. There is worry that if China joins in on crucial maritime security areas, Washington and its friends and allies will take advantage of or abandon China. There is also concern that Chinese cooperation in maritime security could serve to constrain—whether by domestic budget battles or international pressures—the continuing development of the PLA Navy. These fears seem largely unfounded—red herrings. The GMP would not necessarily affect a country's naval forces. Beijing's fears of falling further behind could simply be hedged by its acquiring and maintaining sufficient forces for its national security needs. Undertaking a cooperative effort in sea-lane security and other areas of naval cooperation, viewed objectively, seems a risk worth taking for China.

Chinese Counterpiracy Operations off Somalia Undertaken in Late 2008

Beijing seems to have agreed with this author's assessment concerning the value to China of cooperative sea-lane security. To the considerable surprise of many, including some Chinese observers, Beijing announced in December 2008 that the PLA Navy would send three ships to the Indian Ocean to deter piracy and emphasized the international aspects of the decision—but did not mention its October 2008 severance of military ties with the United States, which offered optimists a chance to portray this as a step toward restoration of military relations. (The 2010 disruption would, right from the start, appear to be a temporary severance.) Professor Zhang at the National Defense University in Beijing, identified as also a senior figure in the PLA Navy, described the motivation for China's reportedly unprecedented dispatch of combatant ships to waters so far from China. Zhang said:

> It is also a very good opportunity to rehearse sea rescue tasks and telecommnications with other military forces. . . . Our future military cooperation with other countries will still be limited to attacking pirates and terrorists or non-battle tasks such as medical service and rescue work. . . . Before, China didn't have an externally oriented economy, so the Chinese navy just needed to stay in Chinese waters. Now, the externally oriented economy has developed so well, the sea interests of China have expanded to other places, so the power of the Chinese navy should reach those places, too.[39]

This statement expresses a Chinese interest in noncombat cooperative maritime operations that clearly seems to include humanitarian operations and exercises. Equally important, there is affirmation in the statement of a new and expanding role of the PLA Navy, as explained elsewhere in this chapter, as a protector of ocean commerce vital to the Chinese economy. For the leadership of China and the PLA Navy, the tenets of Alfred Thayer Mahan have clearly moved from academic to operational. The Chinese decision followed considerable cause for consternation and direct affront to China, as widely reported in the press. Reportedly, more than 100 attacks on shipping occurred in these waters off the Horn of Africa in 2008, with 60 of these in the Gulf of Aden and as many as 400 people and 19 ships, including a Chinese vessel and 17 or 18 people, reportedly being held. *China Daily* asserts that in 2008 a fifth of

1,265 Chinese ships transiting Somali waters "faced piracy" and that 7 of the ships were attacked.[40] The Chinese ship *Zhenhua 4* was rescued by a multinational force firing at the pirates from hovering helicopters.[41] This was one of the Chinese ships that had been attacked.[42]

Nevertheless, it was a surprise to many that this decision was made, and made so firmly and publicly. The author had, days before the announcement, raised the prospect of PLA Navy–U.S. Navy cooperation with a senior Chinese foreign service officer currently working in the prestigious Beijing think tank China Institute of International Studies (CIIS). He had quickly responded that China would not send ships to the waters off Somalia, suggesting that it was simply too distant to permit logistic support and alluding to the political sensitivity of such actions by the PLA Navy in the Indian Ocean. He said waters closer to China were more likely for such PLA Navy operations and did not mention the current interruption of bilateral military ties. This story serves as a reminder that, for China and the PLA Navy, this dispatch of naval combatant forces to the far-western Indian Ocean is indeed an unexpected, remarkable undertaking—and one that has been sustained for well over a year.

The news of the policy decision broke in New York in mid-December 2008 and, unsurprisingly, quickly spread around the globe.[43] Chinese vice foreign minister He Yafei, speaking at a mid-December ministerial meeting of the UN Security Council, which had unanimously authorized international land operations against armed pirates sheltering in Somalia, made the statement. He said, according to China's official news agency: "China is seriously considering sending naval ships to the Gulf of Aden and waters off the Somali coast for escorting operations in the near future."[44] Another CIIS think-tanker with expertise in this area said that this would be the first time in modern history that the nation's navy carried out a mission outside Chinese waters.

This Chinese move raised questions ranging from the strategic to the practical; that is, how will regional and other nations react to a Chinese combatant force, typically composed of two destroyers and a resupply ship, transiting the Indian Ocean and operating off Somalia? How will replenishment of fuel and other resupply be accomplished over time? Will Chinese ships be supported by the existing arrangements for multinational naval forces conducting counterpiracy operations since October 2008, or will replenishment over the long term be accomplished in regional ports, conceivably, Gwadar—a port developed with Chinese aid and feared by some to be a potential overseas base for the PLA Navy? Will this move "augur well" for restoration of bilateral military ties, as Admiral Keating suggested?[45]

Extensive coverage in the government-sponsored *China Daily* of the deployment decision addresses some of these questions.[46] The mission is referred to as the unprecedented deployment of vessels on a potential combat mission, as a major shift in mindset over security issues, and as a move that could have far-reaching consequences. The director of the antiterrorism center at the prestigious think tank China Institute of Contemporary International Relations is quoted as describing the decision as "a huge breakthrough in China's concepts about security" and asserting that this signals a change in how the country is dealing with its perceived threats, noting that this is focused on a nontraditional threat from a nonstate actor, a form of threat that is increasingly imperiling Chinese interests. It is acknowledged that coordination and cooperation with other navies in surrounding areas remain major obstacles for China's inexperienced navy, and anxiety in Japan and India is mentioned. In an apparent attempt to appear magnanimous, there is a statement that ships from Taiwan desiring a counterpiracy escort "could ask" the mainland's naval force; indeed, many have done so and have been escorted.[47] It is suggested that the decision to deploy and the practical aspects of sustaining such an operation will accelerate reform of the PLA Navy, and the resulting requirements for adequate logistics, intelligence, and communications are noted. Nevertheless, in summing up the implications, a Beijing military strategist contends that China's naval strategy will still focus on "near seas" defense and that the PLA Navy cannot be considered a blue water navy, although that does not mean China cannot venture afar. Such operations are said not to contradict China's near-sea defense policy, which should further develop as a vanguard of the country's modernization program. Thus there seems to be full awareness of the implications and potential ramifications of this decision to join a distant battle against a nontraditional foe.

With respect to long-standing concerns about prospective Chinese overseas bases in the Indian Ocean, the Gulf of Aden deployments kindled a debate in China over the prudence of continued adherence to the policy of no overseas bases.[48] A Chinese Air Force colonel openly advocated the development of overseas bases to "safeguard commercial interests and world peace," arguing that such facilities are required not only to protect China's growing global economic interests but also to enable PLA participation in peacekeeping activities, ship escort deployments, and humanitarian assistance, and disaster relief operations.[49] By calling to mind this rather noble rationale, he seemed to be attempting to preempt the objections that some Americans and others might raise. In late 2009 a retired but officially involved senior PLA Navy officer publicly mentioned the possible need for a permanent base in the Gulf of Aden area to support the continuing counterpiracy operations. Retired rear admiral Yin Zhuo, a senior researcher at the PLA Navy's Equipment Research Center, noted that a base there would facilitate persistent Chinese counterpiracy efforts in the region.

In the unsurprising next development, the idea of a base in the region was dismissed—consistent with repeated Chinese denials to this author over the years concerning the prospect of overseas bases. In March 2009 the retired rear admiral and active researcher said China will not seek to establish any overseas military bases: "China's escort frigates only need supply stations, not overseas military bases. We are not going to establish overseas bases like the U.S. did in Singapore," Admiral Yin said.[50]

The PLA Navy forces in the Gulf of Aden have used commercial ports for resupply and port calls but, as this author was told privately by senior U.S. Navy officers very knowledgeable about the international and Chinese counterpiracy operations in the region, Gwadar, the Pakistani port developed with Chinese funding, has not been used—a consequence of a tacit understanding that it would not be used for military purposes.

As with other alarms since at least the early 1990s, including the "string of pearls" assertions (allegations that China is establishing a string of bases across the Indian Ocean), the concern that the PLA Navy deployments to the Gulf of Aden would bring about Chinese basing in the area seems not to have substance. Beijing's long-standing declared policy against forces and bases on the territory of another country prevails. Additionally, Beijing recognizes that there is concern by India and others about this prospect and has elected to take into account those concerns. Moreover, with no bases or forces in other countries, China can take the moral high ground, as it is wont to do, and point a finger at U.S. activities that it wants to criticize—as retired Admiral Yin did in referring to Singapore.

Unmentioned are the factors of cost and complexity. As the U.S. global experience illustrates, it is exceedingly costly and practically and politically complex to establish overseas bases that can truly support operational forces, even to the extent of readiness to rearm ships that have expended major items of ordnance; can carry out routine and battle-damage repairs; can refuel ships with high rates of consumption in combat steaming; and can provide other resupply, logistical, and administrative support that a force far from its home ports requires.

Nevertheless, the internal debate has not ended. One salvo to come to this author's attention was an op-ed piece by the very forthright Professor Shen Dingli of the prestigious Fudan University in Shanghai. Shen is not hesitant to puncture American balloons, and the thrust of the op-ed is opposition to U.S. hegemony. Shen's conjectural piece is not a substantive step in PLA strategic thinking but rather another effort to lay out his objections to U.S. policies and practices.[51] In sum, the PLA Navy is unlikely to acquire U.S.-style overseas "bases" anytime soon but may rather pursue access to some form of "places."

Another pertinent question is what this decision by Beijing portends for Chinese participation in the GMP or for bilateral (U.S.–PRC) or trilateral (including Japan) naval cooperation—assuming, of course, that Sino-American military relations can be reestablished without extended delay. Evidence is scant, but the words of Vice Minister He at the United Nations can be parsed. He's remarks included the following selected extracts:

> This meeting and the resolution just adopted once again fully demonstrate the commitment and confidence of the international community to come together and fight against piracy. . . .
>
> Piracy off the coast of Somalia has become increasingly rampant and is now an international menace posing a grave threat to international shipping, maritime trade and security at sea. . . .
>
> The long-term delay in settlement of the Somali issue is posing a serious threat to international peace and security. . . .
>
> China welcomes international cooperation in the fight against piracy off the coast of Somalia and supports the efforts of relevant countries to send warships to the region to crack down on pirates pursuant to Security Council resolutions. . . .
>
> First, give full play to the important role of the United Nations . . . , especially its Security Council. . . .
>
> The international community should cooperate on the basis of the United Nations Convention on the Law of the Sea [UNCLOS] and the Security Council resolutions. . . .
>
> The international community should take the fight against piracy seriously.[52]

As can be seen in these extracts, Vice Minister He repeatedly emphasizes the international aspects, using the word "international" at least seven times in a brief statement. This surely suggests that China is not opposed to multinational cooperation in protection of the sea-lanes. Early in his remarks, He advocated the coming together of the international community to combat piracy—seemingly a good argument for China to become part of the GMP, if it is established, and certainly for bilateral to multilateral cooperation. Very directly, He said China supports international cooperation in the fight against piracy. However, there is also emphasis on the UN role, seeking to preserve the leverage China exercises in the Security Council on decisions to conduct such operations. With respect to the express commitment to UNCLOS, China was careful to avoid actions it considers EEZ violations by obtaining permission from the government of Somalia—regardless of how weak and unstable it might be.

On 26 December 2008, about ten days after the initial announcement, the anticipated PLA Navy force of two of China's most modern destroyers and a replenishment ship got under way from a South Sea Fleet base on the island of Hainan en route to the Gulf of Aden to combat piracy in waters off Somalia. The three-ship flotilla was said to be ready for a prolonged commitment.[53] The three ships headed for what was described as the escort mission off Somali are among the most advanced ships of the Chinese navy, all built within the last several years. The flagship, *Wuhan* (DDG-169), displaces 7,000 tons, and is equipped with antiship missiles, surface-to-air missiles, a close-in weapons system, and a helicopter. *Haikou* (DDG-171), the newer of the two destroyers, was built in 2003, is almost as large as *Wuhan*, and is equipped with China's first generation of phased-array radar and a vertically launched long-range air defense missile system. Unlike the point defense capabilities of earlier PLA Navy ships, it can provide a measure of area air defense for the task group. Both ships have a typical destroyer maximum speed of about 30 knots, fast enough to respond promptly to distant threats and to outrun many craft that might be used by pirates. The supply ship, *Weishanhu* (hull number 887), of the navy's *Qiandaohu* class, displaces 23,000 tons, can carry two helicopters, and has a maximum speed of 19 knots. It is the largest indigenously produced multiproduct replenishment ship. Although its primary role is supply, it is armed with eight 37-mm guns.

All three ships are assigned to the South Sea Fleet, the closest fleet to the Indian Ocean, arousing curiosity about how command will be exercised.[54] The options might include receiving tactical orders directly from Beijing or by the fleet or military region commander under Beijing's direction.

The stunningly quick but orchestrated deployment suggests a quick process of identification of the components of a surface-combatant and support force ready to respond more rapidly and remain in the deployed location longer than many might have expected. This further suggests the possibility either that there is a standing task group or list of ships ready to be called upon if an urgent reaction is required, or that there were advance planning and preparations for this specific effort. The reported presence onboard of a special forces unit of sixty people further illustrates that this deployment was assigned a high degree of importance. All in all, the several impressive aspects of this deployment (modern ships, prompt reaction, declared readiness to stay in the region for a prolonged period, and incorporation of a sizable SOF capability) could be indicators that Beijing is ripe to receive overtures concerning PLA Navy–U.S. Navy cooperation or the GMP, and is amenable to cooperation with the Japanese Maritime Self-Defense Force (JMSDF)—an issue to be examined next. In any case, China has sustained the counterpiracy naval force off Somalia, periodically replacing the combatant and replenishment ships, thereby demonstrating political will, force readiness, and the ability to support and sustain the operation without a regional base.

The Japanese Maritime Self-Defense Force Factor

The author asked PLA Navy officers whether China would have serious reservations about participating in the GMP with the JMSDF. The two officers consulted replied that this would not be a significant problem. Nonetheless, at least initially, the PLA Navy and JMSDF need not be forced to operate together more than they desire—once again altogether feasible because of the flexibility of the GMP. The combination of historical animosity and current Sino-Japanese disputes over sovereignty and extraction of oil and gas dictate that the United States should be cautious and not, for example, make cooperative efforts with the JMSDF a central feature of any propositions to the PLA Navy and Beijing concerning participation in the GMP. Instead, the focus might be on the ongoing efforts of responsible leaders in Japan and China to ease tensions and build bilateral ties.

The Specter of Taiwan

Despite the concerns previously described, the GMP concept may, on balance, have great appeal to a China concerned with energy security (primarily oil and natural gas shipping) and the protection of ocean commerce more generally (an essential element of the Chinese economy). However, there is a factor that might spoil the deal: the highly likely Chinese rejection of the opportunity to participate in TSN-GMP if Taiwan were to be a participant, or a even potential participant. Reportedly, some PLA Navy officers have talked of a way around the problem, if it arises, as has been done with the Olympic Games and the World Trade Organization. This might take the form of a "formula" allowing the PRC and Taiwan both to be involved in one way or another. (These views have not been offered as Beijing's official position but only as conjecture by the author's interlocutors.) The March 2008 election of a Taiwan president more amenable to improved relations with Beijing than his predecessor (whose term ended in May 2008) offers improved prospects for finding solutions to problems in cross-strait relations, and the GMP could conceivably be folded in if the concept regains momentum. Nevertheless, the potential of Taiwan issues to become obstacles must not be underestimated, as illustrated by Beijing's previously described reactions to Washington's late 2008 and early 2010 announcements concerning arms packages for Taiwan.

Although the United States should be aware of the potential problem (and possible solution) and should avoid the appearance of negotiating or being influenced by Beijing's reported concern, Taiwan participation may not be an issue. Given the absence of exercises and operations between the U.S. and Taiwan militaries and the self-imposed prohibition of visits to Taiwan by senior U.S. defense officials and flag officers, Taiwan simply may not be considered as a candidate for the TSN-GMP concept. Another alternative has already been suggested. Bilateral and multilateral maritime cooperation, specifically HA and DR exercises and operations, could be conducted between the U.S. Navy and PLA Navy and simply not associated with TSN-GMP. In short, cooperation in humanitarian operations need not founder because of either the limitations imposed on U.S. military activities with the PLA by Congress or problems that could arise with respect to Chinese participation in TSN-GMP. The way is clear for HA and DR.

Bilateral Maritime Cooperation as a Goal

While the general concept of bilateral maritime cooperation, not necessarily associated with the GMP concept, has been discussed openly in only the broadest terms, senior U.S. naval officers have expressed support for the idea in various ways. There is the important prospect that such cooperation could serve in the long term to improve military relations between China and the United States. Retired admiral Dennis Blair, four-star commander of U.S. forces in the Pacific from 1999 to 2002 and recently director of national intelligence (2009–10), has publicly expressed frustration over the state of military dialogue between the United States and China. The GMP or maritime cooperation independent of that concept would foster what he calls "habits of cooperation," helping to allay suspicion. This could begin with search-and-rescue exercises (as it indeed has) and could move up to peacekeeping, humanitarian, antiterrorism, and counterpiracy exercises.[55]

The Chairman of the Joint Chiefs of Staff Favors Serious Engagement and Necessary Hedging

Admiral Michael Mullen, in his capacity as chairman of the Joint Chiefs of Staff, was asked by this author on 15 April 2008 about engaging China in such activities as cooperation in humanitarian assistance. He persisted in favoring military-to-military cooperation and engagement—while cautioning about the problems. Admiral Mullen recalled that he was encouraged during his visit to China by the positive Chinese attitude toward cooperation between the U.S. Navy and the PLA Navy. It was clear that Mullen has taken with him to the top U.S. military job the conviction that it serves U.S. interests to engage China in the military arena and to conduct exercises and cooperative undertakings, yet to ensure a readiness to deter or cope with the Chinese forces in combat if circumstances require such a course of action. This might be phrased: "Engage seriously; hedge seriously." And such counsel would apply to Beijing as well as to Washington.

This concept of U.S.–PRC maritime cooperation on a bilateral basis (or trilateral with Japan, for example) could be either a temporary or lasting substitute for the GMP, if that concept becomes stalled or is abandoned. It need not be limited to naval cooperation but would provide broad opportunities for cooperation in areas of nontraditional security. Thus, the concept would make possible cooperative arrangements not only between the two navies and coast guards but also between maritime commerce and other oceanic interests. The implications for the Sino-U.S relationship could be significant and could assist in the building of what will undoubtedly be America's most important strategic relationship in the twenty-first century.

Ongoing Coast Guard Cooperation May Point the Way

U.S.–PRC maritime cooperation offers, in another form, an encouraging example for cooperation in both humanitarian assistance operations and Chinese participation in the GMP or bilateral maritime cooperation. Tangible, practical forms of maritime cooperation between the United States and China are already under way between the U.S. Coast Guard (USCG) and the PRC Maritime Safety Administration.[56] Over a period of several years, the USCG has been engaged with several Chinese ministries and other entities in a relationship that encompasses both exchanges ashore and operations at sea.[57] Chinese officers have been students in relevant courses at the USCG Academy and the fisheries enforcement school in Alaska, and surprisingly served temporarily on U.S. cutters during periods when the cutters were carrying out enforcement actions against Chinese fishing boats in the North Pacific. Furthermore, China became active in the North Pacific Coast Guard Forum, a body that is described as the only maritime security organization in East Asia. The forum is said to provide opportunities for international coast guard leaders to interact regularly, and it reportedly initiated at-sea combined exercises that began in 2005.[58] Together participating coast guards are working to curb oceanic pollution, enhance maritime safety, promote sustainable and equitable extraction of resources, and provide security from threats at sea and in harbors.

USCG captain Barney Moreland, the Coast Guard representative at the U.S. embassy in Beijing, reported in December 2007 at the CMSI annual conference that visits to Chinese ports by USCG cutters have created opportunities for "professional exchanges culminating in demonstrations of practice boarding scenarios." He said the type of fisheries cooperation (as described above) has been extensive as well, and there have been "U.S. and Chinese maritime command centers [coordinating] control of ships [and] aircraft . . . in real-time 24-hour operations to save lives." Beijing, he said, is eager to expand cooperative initiatives with the USCG. In March 2007 Chinese authorities made a formal request to send pilots, rescue aircrew, rescue swimmers, and rescue boat coxswains to USCG training schools. There are, unsurprisingly, complications in the U.S. government. For example, the request to train Chinese pilots on the same helicopter that is a first-line U.S. combat helicopter was rejected. The request had to be evaluated in light of existing U.S. constraints on such activities, but the USCG has provided a list of training options available—most of which would be conducted in China. Five cadets from the Chinese Maritime Academy were scheduled to come to the United States for a summer training program. Regardless of how extensive the training program becomes, there is the reasonable prospect that the coast guard component in U.S.–China relations could prove to be the first step toward a broader joint maritime security enforcement program that could encompass enhanced naval cooperation.

The Energy Security Imperative

Another compelling argument for maritime cooperation between China and the United States is the issue of energy security. In the view of many people who are dubious about the prudence of U.S. engagement with China, the growing demand in both countries (and globally) for limited resources of energy (mainly oil but also natural gas), which is met primarily through transport by sea, will inexorably lead to disruptive competition and, according to some, conflict between the United States and China.[59] Looked at another way, this mutual interest in energy security might be seen as a compelling reason for cooperation. Professor Jonathan Pollack of the U.S. Naval War College characterizes China and the United States as confronting a situation of "mutual assured dependence" in their growing and ineluctable demand for energy.[60] PLA Navy rear admiral Yang Yi used the same expression (almost certainly, for both men, harking back to the Cold War strategic-nuclear term "mutual assured destruction") in late 2007 to characterize the close U.S.–China economic relationship that is so heavily dependent on ocean commerce. Admiral Yang's comment usefully repeats a reminder that the mutual interests in sealane security are not derived solely from energy security considerations but also from an enormous volume of other forms of ocean commerce.

Encouraging Assertions that China Is Not a Threat

Regarding whether the future will see conflict or cooperation between the United States and China, Chinese leaders should be encouraged by the rest of the world when they make pronouncements that China will not be a threat. China is not inexorably on a path to become an aggressive power in the region; Chinese arguments that it is not an expansionist nation should also be reinforced. Washington should skillfully and yet subtly take into account that U.S. policies will also influence the outcome for emerging China and the shaping of its intentions. With respect to the matter of maritime cooperation—specifically the existing and increasing mutual need for a reliable flow of energy, the interests of the United States and China are altogether common, if not identical. Chinese and U.S. interests fully converge in the need to secure the sealanes for transport of the energy that fuels their respective economies and for other ocean commerce. Even those Americans who are highly distrustful of China and pessimistic about bilateral relations between a superpower democracy and an authoritarian megastate are likely to agree that there is a convergence of interests in this regard and that there is every reason to find ways to cooperate rather than forecast or contemplate conflict.

Viewed broadly, energy security and protection of ocean commerce indeed present a compelling rationale for bilateral collaboration in maritime security. The United States would not, of course, pursue such cooperation if national security concerns or risks vis-à-vis China were heightened thereby; however, it is similarly ill advised and unnecessary to pursue strategic goals to the exclusion of cooperation. Despite doubts and concerns among Americans about Chinese strategic intentions, the energy security issue is something that Washington and Beijing should undertake together, without regard to differences over Taiwan, for example. The two countries have clearly adopted this approach with respect to combating terrorism and curbing proliferation. On these issues Washington and Beijing diverge significantly in approach and even to a certain extent on the desired final result; yet cooperation has prevailed precisely because it is perceived as serving the interests of both. The same reasoning applies to maritime cooperation.

Is Helping China Wise?

Some people are concerned that China would benefit unduly from cooperation with the United States in oceanic security and other maritime areas. China's crucial ocean commerce would indeed be better protected. An argument can be made that U.S. interests are not best served thereby, and that the United States should not abet China's progress. Perhaps the United States should focus instead on ensuring that it is readily able to disrupt the flow of oil to China. Pursuing this argument, as some do: maritime cooperation would further China's growth and military modernization. U.S. efforts would add to China's already growing soft power and confer on China further prestige and legitimacy as a regional, even global, player. Bilateral maritime cooperation could directly and indirectly contribute to China's rise and expansion of its military capabilities.

These are real concerns, but cooperation may be the solution rather than the problem. It is prudent to balance against these concerns the optimistic possibilities and the opportunities to alter worst-case scenarios. To begin, maritime cooperation would have a limited, not definitive, role in overall Chinese economic and military developments. China's regional and global emergence depends to a much greater extent on its own national development decisions than on any particular collaborative effort. One has only to observe the surge that is taking place today in what has been termed China's "oceanic economy" to appreciate that collaboration with the United States is not a definitive factor. Short of domestic economic and political upheaval, China's progress is likely to be self-sustaining. Washington's concerns might more realistically be directed on the long-term undesirable consequences of a U.S. policy that fostered a hostile atmosphere or seemed to oppose Chinese progress and ignored the positive aspects of a more open and prosperous China—which we have repeatedly said serves U.S. interests.

A Window on China

U.S. engagement with China on maritime issues would provide a vehicle for gaining a better understanding of China's strategic ambitions and perhaps even favorably influence their direction. The United States might be able to shape China's decisions about its future without appearing judgmental, accusatory, or suspicious of China's proclaimed intent. (Although U.S. policy documents use the word "shape," "influence" seems a better word with less hubristic baggage.) China and the United States are highly interdependent and inextricably linked with respect to economic and social affairs—and increasingly so with respect to strategic and regional security affairs. Americans might want to give more thought to the wisdom of the proclaimed policy of the U.S. government that a secure and prosperous China does greatly benefit the United States.

Military Advantages

Although the United States will have continuing concerns with regard to the Taiwan issue and China's advances in antiaccess capabilities, U.S. interests lie overwhelmingly in support of cooperation over competition. In their presentation therein, the organizers of the U.S. Naval War College conference that gave birth to this book concluded in summary: "Therefore, as the maritime commercial relationship becomes even more dynamic, it is essential that the military and security partnership develop in a manner that complements this trend." Maritime cooperation with China would give the U.S. Pacific fleet an added opportunity to establish operational and administrative ties in the region—and the prospect that bilateral ties would lead to trilateral relationships that could fold in Japan and the Republic of Korea and lead to easing of tensions between these countries and China. It would also serve as an additional link for frequent, practical communication and exchanges in a sensitive arena: PLA Navy modernization and intentions. Most important, it will, at this favorable juncture in cross-strait relations with a more conciliatory Taiwan president in office, advance the proposition that, regardless of residual differences and frictions, China and the United States have common interests beyond the Taiwan issue. U.S. insistence on a peaceful solution for Taiwan (and support for the island's democracy) and Beijing's threat of the use of force to keep Taiwan from becoming independent are important issues; however, they are not the whole story. The bigger picture, examined more thoroughly at the end of this chapter, encompasses many areas of strategic alignment and cooperative efforts on profound international security issues.

The New Maritime Strategy Supports Humanitarian Assistance Cooperation

The new U.S. Maritime Strategy, "A Cooperative Strategy for 21st Century Seapower," was warmly endorsed by several Chinese participants at the conference. One Chinese participant said he "fundamentally agreed with the content of the New Maritime Strategy."[61] Humanitarian operations are repeatedly and prominently mentioned in "A Cooperative Strategy for 21st Century Seapower." One slightly cynical explanation for this is the enormous success and favorable coverage of the U.S.-led effort in aiding Indonesia and other regional countries following the devastating 2004 tsunami. The acclaim for the U.S. Navy and the good work done would indeed warrant special attention in the new Maritime Strategy. However, that is not the whole answer. It is best to examine what the document states to ascertain why the new strategy affords HA and DR such conspicuous and repeated mention. Here are brief, pertinent extracts from the new Maritime Strategy. Amplifying comments by the author are in brackets following each extract.

> Persistent, mission-tailored maritime forces will be globally distributed in order to contribute to homeland defense-in-depth [and to] foster and sustain cooperative relationships. . . . From fostering critical relationships overseas, to screening ships bound for our [U.S.] ports or rapidly responding to any threats . . . maritime forces will promptly support civil authorities in the event of a natural disaster on our shores. [Support by maritime forces of DR is part of the role maritime forces play in the concept of homeland defense in depth.]
>
> Expanded cooperative relationships with other nations will contribute to the security and stability of the maritime domain. . . . Trust and cooperation cannot be surged. They must be built over time . . . while mutual understanding and respect are promoted. . . . Building and invigorating these relationships . . . requires an increased focus on . . . humanitarian assistance. . . . When natural or man-made disasters strike, our maritime forces can provide humanitarian assistance and relief. . . . By participating routinely and predictably in cooperative activities, maritime forces will be postured to support other joint or combined forces to mitigate and localize disruptions. [Participation in humanitarian operations builds trust with other nations and facilitates other employment of maritime forces.]
>
> Building on relationships forged in times of calm, we will continue to mitigate human suffering as the vanguard of interagency and multinational efforts. . . . Human suffering moves us to act, and the expeditionary character of maritime forces uniquely positions them to provide assistance. [Maritime forces arrive promptly with needed capability.][62]

Humanitarian operations thus have merit not only because they provide relief and do good but also because they build trust and goodwill, act as a catalyst for cooperation, and facilitate employment of forces. These operations have earned their way into these several parts of the new Maritime Strategy.

Rear Admiral Yang praised the new U.S. Maritime Strategy during his December 2007 visit to the United States. He saw the new strategy as largely "congruent with China's goal of pursuing a harmonious world" and suggested that it holds promise particularly in the areas of humanitarian operations and disaster relief. He added the caution that the described U.S. efforts to deter major war could "backfire" by making China feel it was the target. Admiral Yang's combination of upbeat and cautionary words illustrate well the seemingly contradictory state of U.S.–PRC relations: both countries seek cooperation in areas such as maritime security and humanitarian operations but must also seek to deter each other and be able to cope with a conflict if circumstances demand.

U.S. Navy Capabilities for Humanitarian and Disaster Relief Operations

Dr. Su Hao said the December 2004 tsunami and the rapidly assembled, impressive relief efforts made "China aware of the limitations of its navy's capacities to delivery, compared with the U.S. Navy."[63] U.S. Navy strike, expeditionary, and logistic forces (combatant, amphibious, and support forces, including hospital ships) along with the Marine Corps and the Coast Guard have forces deployed to many areas of the world and can readily move a majority of those assets even closer to the location of a disaster or crisis. Capabilities include the ability to transport a seemingly endless list of relief materials, skilled helpers and advisors, and equipment and technological items. Ships with large flight decks (carriers and large amphibious ships) or with the capability of operating helicopters (destroyers, frigates, fast combat support ships, hospital ships) have the ability amid chaos and widespread destruction of infrastructure to reach well inland using fixed-wing, rotary-wing, and VSTOL aircraft. Relief assistance can take every form from medical personnel, to food, to blankets and shelter, and much more. Other aid might encompass the provision of experts in diverse areas from public health (e.g., expertise in the provision of clean water) to repair and construction of roads, runways, and structures; from communications and air traffic control to food preparation; and from electrical power specialists to nurses, medical technicians, and psychological counselors.

The commander of the U.S. Pacific Fleet, desiring to draw attention to U.S. capabilities in humanitarian operations, took the opportunity of the beginning of a deployment of the hospital ship *Mercy* to explain the diverse capabilities, far beyond a floating first-aid station, of this ship:

> Almost 900 feet long, the *Mercy* left San Diego on the 24th of April [2006] for a five-month deployment and mission in humanitarian assistance to Southeast Asia. . . . She carries a U.S. medical team . . . from our Army, our Navy and our Air Force. She will have onboard two H-60 helicopters . . . and Navy construction engineers. . . . She will have representatives of the U.S. public health service aboard and also several members of nongovernmental organizations. So they comprise an interagency, international, and multi-specialized team of medical professionals capable of providing a wide range of services onboard and ashore.
>
> The medical capability that *Mercy* will bring to the region includes basic medical evaluation and treatment, dental and optometry screenings, eyewear distribution, preventive medicine treatment, general and ophthalmology surgery, public health services and even veterinary services. Together the *Mercy* team is prepared to administer to medical and humanitarian assistance needs through medical, dental, civic and construction action projects. It's an unprecedented group of volunteers and professionals, civilian and military men and women. They are dedicated to saving lives and restoring hope and spreading goodwill.
>
> The *Mercy* deployment is a demonstration of U.S. commitment to the region and . . . the people of the region with whom we share common bonds as stakeholders in the Pacific. Because we are a Pacific nation, we have strong links to the Pacific.[64]

As seen in this example of the hospital ship, the diverse forces outlined here can put ashore by aircraft, boat, landing craft, or moored ship the right mix of people, equipment, and technical wherewithal—and sustain that force without producing a burden on the locale that is being assisted. Much attention has justifiably been given to the monumental assistance effort, headed by a three-star U.S. Marine Corps general, after the December 2004 tsunami that severely affected Sumatra and other Southeast and South Asian areas. Less attention has been given to other significant efforts since that time including a major effort after the earthquake in Pakistan in 2005, headed by U.S. Navy rear admiral Michael A. LeFever commanding Expeditionary Strike Group One, and the assistance provided in 2007 by the amphibious warfare ship USS *Wasp* (LHD-1) when Hurricane Felix struck Nicaragua.

Bangladesh 2007 Tsunami Redux: Heavy U.S. Role; Minimal PRC Role

In the fall of 2007, the U.S. Navy–Marine Corps team once more rapidly geared up to provide relief for victims of deadly Cyclone Sidr in Bangladesh on 17 November. The large amphibious ships USS *Essex* and USS *Kearsarge* (LHD-2 and -3), each carrying twenty helicopters and hovercraft and equipped with hospital facilities, were dispatched even before receipt of a formal request for help from the Bangladesh authorities. There was a potential role for the PLA Navy to play in Bangladesh relief and the potential for the United States to encourage and facilitate that involvement. *China Daily* on 18 November 2007 had the following revealing sentences: "The government [of Bangladesh] deployed military helicopters, naval ships and thousands of troops to join international agencies and local officials in the rescue mission following Tropical Cyclone Sidr. The U.S. and other countries also offered assistance."[65] While the U.S. role was noted, there is the conspicuous absence in this official outlet of the PRC government of any consideration of a prompt Chinese role. The PRC government and the PLA Navy, as best as could be ascertained, did not respond, reflecting a likely continuing weakness in crisis management and decision making and revealing, as further discussed in the following, a mind-set (and the self-fulfilling reality) that China, in general, and the PLA Navy, in particular, cannot respond promptly and effectively.

The United States has encouraged the PLA (in general, not the PLA Navy directly) to be more participatory in HA and DR operations, such as occurred in Bangladesh in 2007. This came after U.S. relief supplies were quickly airlifted into China following 2007–8 winter floods. The PLA response was that they (the PLA) had shipped via commercial means US$5 million worth of relief supplies to the United States following Hurricane Katrina. The PLA thereby revealed the lack of ability to rapidly ship this material and the need to employ a commercial (even if government-sponsored) airline. Thus PLA leaders were once again reminded of the need to develop and exercise such capabilities if they are to be employed promptly after a disaster. In addition, Washington and U.S. Pacific Command should keep in mind that the U.S. capability is seen as so overwhelming that other nations, including China, may be intimidated and reluctant to initiate action—an additional good reason for moving forward as soon as possible with conducting at least a bilateral humanitarian assistance exercise that brings in the PLA Navy and relieves anxiety, and with testing the waters on Chinese participation in the GMP.[66]

The Tsunami Example

The U.S. effort in Bangladesh in 2007 was effective; however, the extensive 2004–5 tsunami-relief operations depict more fully the capabilities of the U.S. armed services and agencies in either a national or international effort. Extracts from an article by Dr. Ralph Cossa, president of the Pacific Forum CSIS, describe those capabilities:

> "The military role is to provide its unique capabilities and significant capacity to provide immediate relief and save lives." This simple sentence, by Admiral Thomas Fargo, commander of the U.S. Pacific Command, sums up the very complicated mission undertaken by U.S. forces in response to the horrific December 26, 2004, earthquake and tsunami that left some 300,000 people dead or missing, with upwards of a million more displaced, in 11 South and Southeast Asian nations and Africa. . . .
>
> At the height of the relief effort, some 16,000 U.S. military personnel were deployed throughout the areas most affected. . . . More than two dozen U.S. ships (including an aircraft carrier battle group, a Marine amphibious group, and the hospital ship USNS *Mercy*, which remained after the main . . . forces departed) and over 100 aircraft were dedicated to the disaster relief effort. . . . Significant . . . was the availability of almost 60 U.S. helicopters, which flew over 2,200 missions, shuttling relief supplies from U.S. ships and other staging areas to hard-hit towns and villages.
>
> In Indonesia . . . the first fresh water many survivors saw was delivered by U.S. military units that rushed to the region even before the full extent of the damage was known. All told, through mid-February the U.S. military had delivered over 24 million pounds of relief supplies and equipment. Six Maritime Preposition Ships from Guam and Diego Garcia. . . provide[d] critical drinking water: each can store about 90,000 gallons of fresh water and is capable of producing 36,000 gallons daily. . . .
>
> U.S. ships were given orders to begin deploying to the region within hours of the tragedy . . . in order to be there if and when called upon. Within 24 hours, U.S. Navy P-3 Orion reconnaissance aircraft began flying missions over the affected areas to help assist in the search and rescue effort and to assess the extent of the damage. . . .
>
> [An] invaluable U.S. contribution focused around another Defense Department unique capability: command, control, communications,

and coordination. . . . Within 48 hours of the tragedy . . . the U.S. Pacific Command was already establishing a joint task force to coordinate and conduct humanitarian assistance and disaster relief operations. . . . As Deputy Secretary of Defense Paul Wolfowitz subsequently testified, "the ability of the Department of Defense to respond so quickly would not have been possible without the relationships developed over many years with the militaries of countries in the region. . . ." Three days after the tsunami struck, Combined Support Force 536, . . . was already playing a key role in coordinating the U.S. and initial international effort. . . .

U.S. military personnel . . . worked closely with their local military counterparts, in some cases overcoming years of suspicion, and once again demonstrating the value of routinizing military-to-military contacts to allow for more effective cooperation during periods of crisis. As Admiral Fargo noted, "one of the reasons [we] have been able to respond effectively is because we have established these habits of cooperation together over many years."[67]

Haiti 2010 Earthquake

In response to the catastrophic earthquake that struck Haiti on 12 January 2010, the nuclear-powered aircraft carrier USS *Carl Vinson*, steaming at maximum speed, arrived on 15 January with 600,000 emergency food rations, 100,000 ten-liter water containers, and an enhanced wing of 19 helicopters; 130,000 liters of drinking water were transferred to shore on the first day. The helicopter carrier USS *Bataan*, with three large dock-landing ships and two survey/salvage vessels, created a "sea base" for the rescue effort. On 16 January, the hospital ship USNS *Comfort* and the guided-missile cruiser USS *Bunker Hill* left the United States for Haiti.

The role of the U.S. Navy in providing relief in the 2010 earthquake disaster in Haiti reaffirmed what has been described earlier in the Asian examples, the part of the world where the PLA is more likely to be engaged, at least initally.

PLA Navy Increasingly Able to Make a Valuable Contribution— If Encouraged

"The PLA Navy could gain experience and build confidence in the region by exercising with the U.S. and other navies to be better prepared for operations in response to future humanitarian crises."

—Dr. Michael Green, CSIS and former senior director
for Asian affairs at the National Security Council,
statement at the CMSI conference.

Could the PLA's Penchant to Aid the People of China Extend to PLA Navy Relief Operations Abroad?

The author commented to the PRC naval attaché in Washington in October 2007 that there was a bad joke going around: China secretly hopes for another major tsunami in its part of the world so it can do better than it did last time, when the United States played a starring role. Senior Captain Liu Hongwei smiled and replied that for "the next tsunami," the PLA Navy will think differently, that is, aspire to be more helpful. The Bangladesh storm could have provided an opportunity on an appropriate scale. However, it became another missed opportunity, raising the question of how to improve the chances for cooperation between the U.S. Navy and PLA Navy in the future.

PLA Navy HA and DR Capabilities and Shortcomings: Views of Three PRC Specialists

Senior Captian Liu confirmed that the PLA takes seriously the first word in its name: People's. The PLA supports both socialist economic construction and humanitarian assistance and is very experienced with humanitarian assistance missions in China (natural disasters). This experience, he opined, could be extended abroad, but the PLA Navy remains limited in capabilities and knowledge. Consequently, he asserted, this would be a good field for a PLA Navy–U.S. Navy exercise so the PLA Navy could gain experience and knowledge—a good area for bilateral cooperation.

Queries by the author to a prominent Shanghai think-tanker and a PLA Navy flag officer brought the following responses:

- The main problem is the inadequacy of PLA Navy equipment and experience. Moreover, Beijing and the PLA Navy may feel that China is not welcome or has not been invited.

- The PLA Navy has a new concept (not explained further by the flag officer) and is making an effort to improve the capabilities to fulfill the new missions.
- The PLA Navy is more experienced in domestic HA and DR than the U.S. military and is less capable than the U.S. military in overseas HA and DR operations.
- There is in China strong support for HA and DR exercises and operations with the U.S. Navy and bilaterally or trilaterally with the JMSDF.
- China will be very active in participating in the next major disaster in the region but will not be enthusiastic to take the lead.
- With respect to examples of U.S.–China HA and DR cooperation in the last decade, there have been such exchanges but only in a very limited way. The two sides had some cooperation in South Asia disaster relief; for example, U.S. helicopters transported Chinese troops (in civilian dress) and relief materials.
- HA and DR exercises with other countries were not recalled by either person. But there also was no recollection of problems that would preclude the conduct of such exercises.
- Concerning a central office for managing such operations and the prospects for a central point of contact for U.S.–China efforts in this area, this was described as a "dark area." Beijing's crisis management contact office might be the central office of foreign affairs, but the think-tanker suspects its scope does not include HA and DR. These matters, he suggested, are "too trivial."

Additional Positive Considerations for the PLA Navy

From the author's perspective, several factors, in addition to the positive perspectives of the naval attaché, think-tanker, and flag officer as described above, suggest good prospects for future PLA Navy cooperative contributions to humanitarian operations. Beijing's new foreign policy is more active and progressive; China wants to be seen as a responsible member of the community of nations and welcomes the opportunity to help in response to a disaster. Beijing's policy of pursuing good relations with Washington will help overcome reservations about undertaking such exercises and operations with the U.S. Navy.

Bilateral and Multilateral Exercises

China lacked confidence and pride in its navy until recent years. With respect to getting started in the conduct of exercises with other countries, the PLA Navy has been intentionally slow and cautious. There was apprehension that a backward PLA Navy would be an embarrassment when its shortcomings were revealed to advanced navies. Moreover, there was concern that vulnerabilities and weaknesses would be exposed. Beijing's significantly greater confidence in its navy now is reflected in the bold steps the PLA Navy has taken since its first bilateral exercises with the Pakistani and Indian navies in 2003. Exercises since then have been coincident with the PLA Navy visits abroad, or other navies' calls at Chinese ports. With the modernization of the PLA Navy, China can now be justifiably proud of many of its new ships and other assets. The naval attaché put it this way: exercises with other countries demonstrate that China is confident in the results of its defense buildup—an illustration that China can accomplish this complex undertaking.

Following those first bilateral exercises with Pakistan and India in 2003, China's list of bilateral exercise partners has grown long; it now includes the United States, United Kingdom, France, Spain, Australia, Vietnam, Philippines, and Russia.[68] As for multilateral exercises, two events are particularly noteworthy: A PLA Navy frigate in May 2007 participated in a Western Pacific Naval Symposium (WPNS) exercise.[69] Although China is a founding member of the two-decade-old U.S.-and Australia-inspired WPNS, this was the first time the PLA Navy engaged in a live exercise.[70] More than twenty warships from twelve countries were included in the six-day exercise. Two months before, according to the official news agency Xinhua, a Chinese frigate commanded the four-day sea phase of an exercise called "Peace-07" in the Arabian Sea that included ships from nine navies.[71] As a result of all of this, a step into participation in HA and DR exercises with the U.S. Navy and other navies would not now seem for the PLA Navy like stepping into an altogether strange world.

What Significant Contribution Might the PLA Navy Make?

Regarding PLA Navy capabilities for humanitarian operations, China has a large, capable, modern navy with many ships and aircraft that could, in one way or another, contribute to a humanitarian assistance or disaster relief undertaking. Nevertheless, as we have seen, there is a feeling in China that the PLA Navy is not in a position to make a contribution of value. It appears to be time to change that mindset. China has had for some time a significant number of medium and large amphibious ships called LSTs, some of which can carry helicopters. China has undertaken in this decade an expansion of its amphibious warfare fleet. This has included the addition of as many as two dozen new amphibious warfare ships.[72] Significantly, this expansion includes a new, large amphibious warfare ship. The new ship, which is estimated to be from 17,600+ tons in displacement, can carry four hovercraft (air-cushion landing craft) and two helicopters.[73] Based with the South Sea Fleet in Zhanjiang, this LPD could operate far from China, engaging in a humanitarian operation several thousand miles from its home port. Moreover, there is ample space for additional communications equipment and other items. Consequently, the Type 071 LPD could provide, among other valuable capabilities, a platform for helicopters to fly on humanitarian missions and evacuate casualties and refugees from the area.[74]

Additionally, the PLA Navy launched in August 2007 and made operational in 2008 a hospital ship with helicopter capability. The newly constructed ship, according to *Jane's Fighting Ships*, displaces 23,000 tons, is almost 600 feet long, 25 meters wide, has a beam of more than 80 feet, and draws 29.5 feet.[75] This new ship could add the ability for the PLA to bring advanced medical care to a disaster area as well as a capability to treat a significant number of injured or ill victims. There is uncertainty with respect to actual current medical capabilities. It may be that some of the medical equipment as well as personnel would be placed aboard when needed. There are also questions about the ability to treat critically wounded or ill patients.[76] However, the author was able to confirm through a knowledgeable and reliable Chinese colleague that the ship is operational, with at least basic medical equipment and personnel permanently aboard, and has already accomplished several missions.

On the issue of the rationale for PLA Navy acquisition of a hospital ship, the PRC naval attaché in March 2008 said he knew nothing of its size or its place in the organization. He chuckled when told that the Japanese and Koreans ask why China is building a hospital ship and pointed out that a conflict over Taiwan would be waged within a short distance of many hospitals ashore. He dismissed the idea that a power projection aspiration is implied by acquisition of such a capability. He said the PLA Navy has a history of employing small ships suitable for service as medical facilities when manned under special circumstances by doctors, nurses, and technicians. He surmised, looking at the description of the hospital ship taken from the Web, that this reportedly much larger hospital ship (more than twenty thousand tons) would likely have been approved or ordered by Beijing because of a recognized inability to carry out the rescue from foreign soil of Chinese citizens—especially if many had suffered injuries from a natural disaster or from being subjected to attacks during times of tumult, citing Indonesia some years ago as an example.

When pressed on this issue of the purpose of a large hospital ship, he said that in situations where Chinese citizens abroad had been in danger or injured, the government had been forced to resort to calling upon COSCO (China Ocean Shipping [Group] Company)—hardly an optimum capability, he suggested. He went on to discuss PLA acquisition strategy, asserting that building a hospital ship was easy and cheap. It would, of course, be a natural extension of the described purpose of the PLA Navy hospital ship to employ it in humanitarian and disaster relief roles whether Chinese citizens were involved or not.

Other plausible reasons for PLA Navy acquisition of a hospital ship come to mind. China may wish to mimic the enormous success the United States has achieved in what can be termed medical diplomacy. Absent a disaster, specific or general medical treatment can be brought to areas where medical care is primitive or largely unavailable. This might be envisioned for areas of Africa, where it is also possible that Chinese citizens pursuing China's interests in any of several African countries could be in need of medical care because of injuries or illnesses stemming from some chaotic development. There is also likely chagrin at its navy's failure to aid in the Indonesian tsunami and Burmese storm relief. All of these can bolster national confidence in China as a more capable country and more compassionate member of the community of nations. They foster pride in the PLA Navy in the international arena in the same way that PLA troops take great pride in aiding the people of China in domestic disasters. There is no reason to believe that any one of these was necessarily the dominant factor in the decision to acquire the hospital ship. Several or all may have been factors. And, of course, combat scenarios from the East China Sea to the Gulf of Aden, however unlikely they may currently seem, can be envisioned where such a capability would be an asset.

It is clear that PLA Navy ships would be welcomed as part of the force for future humanitarian operations; the PLA Navy should take part in exercises that rehearse such operations. In many instances, the U.S. Navy will have the preponderance of forces and capabilities, but even when that is clearly the situation, Chinese and American leaders should ensure that China's role is substantive and appropriate. There should be no hint of competition as to which country contributed the most or played the larger role. In place of competition there might be a sense of accomplishment or national and navy pride in consistently being a contributor—a party to the described "habits of cooperation" idea originated by Admiral Blair when he was the U.S. Pacific commander.

Humanitarian and Maritime Cooperation Could Also Enhance Trust and Confidence

"Needless to say, the Chinese and American armies [militaries] are both making military preparation for worst-case scenarios in the Taiwan Strait. So, at present, it is unrealistic for the PLA and the U.S. military to engage in substantial military cooperation."

—*Rear Admiral Yang Yi, statement made at the CMSI conference*

"While there is renewed momentum in U.S.–China maritime cooperation, reciprocity is falling short of expectations."

—*Dr. Michael Green, statement made at the CMSI conference*

"The emphasis of the new U.S. Maritime Strategy on disaster relief offers opportunities for the U.S. and China to cooperate and build mutual trust."

—*Prof. Zhuang Jianzhong, statement made at the CMSI conference*

The Bigger Picture

The first two quotations above demonstrate the obstacles that need to be overcome or perhaps, alternatively, the perceptions that should be changed to avoid a seeming impasse in the U.S.–PRC relationship. China and the United States arguably have already entered a period of maturity and stability in their relationship. A GMP-like initiative or bilateral maritime cooperation and humanitarian operations or exercises, if executed, would constitute a positive factor to help consolidate ties by enhancing trust, understanding, and confidence. As Professor Zhuang implies, bilateral ties and the commonality of both countries' interests are ripe for a deeper maritime security relationship.

As has been explained, U.S. Navy–PLA Navy cooperative efforts in humanitarian activities are favored by both governments and by others who represent to some extent China's strategic thinkers. Many of those who favor these forms of naval cooperation see success here as its own reward. However, there is a bigger picture. The bilateral relationship has progressed to the point where both broad maritime cooperation and particularly humanitarian operations and exercises could serve the dual goals of doing good in the world and building trust and confidence—even influencing Chinese decisions and providing the United States with better understanding of Chinese thinking. This additional trust and confidence could serve to stabilize relations and make less likely disruptions such as the severance of military contacts in October 2008.

While U.S. strategic interests may dictate cooperation with mainland China, implementing it could be complicated and could face severe political resistance. The GMP concept is broad and includes opportunities to engage in activities beyond naval forces, including commercial, international trade, and security activities: free-form maritime cooperation. Senior U.S. Navy officers explain, "The world needs not just gray hulls flying the U.S. or any other nation's flag, but a network of international navies, coast guards, port operators, commercial shippers, and local law enforcement all working together to increase security."[77] Some of this could require the lifting of the congressionally imposed constraints. However, the specific authorization by Congress of humanitarian operations and exercises in the National Defense Authorization Act of 2000 (which lists the prohibited activities) would seem to be an excellent opening to avoid the prohibitions of that act and move forward with HA and DR: clearly permissible elements of U.S.–PRC maritime cooperation.

A Solid Bilateral Foundation to Build On

With respect to the question posed at the beginning of this chapter concerning readiness of the bilateral relationship to support expansion in these areas, relations between Washington and Beijing need no longer be viewed as dangerously fragile—despite the 2008 and 2010 disruptions. The United States and China might even be seen as limited strategic partners. Their cooperation in the Six-Party Talks concerning North Korea's nuclear program is the most impressive example of this partnership, bolstered by the agreement in early November 2007 to establish a military hotline (in spring 2008) between the capitals.[78] Washington and Beijing have compatible views on terrorism and proliferation. Beijing disagreed with the U.S. invasion of Iraq but has kept quiet and now sees stability in Iraq as an important goal. China has not been vociferous about U.S. military activities in the Central Asian states that border China. China does not attempt to undermine the presence of U.S. forces in Asia, and many Chinese agree that the United States has brought stability and resultant economic progress to the region and even to China.

Beijing is concerned about what its sees as excessive and misguided U.S. support of Japan and more widely active Japanese military forces, but it has recently couched the concern in terms of inadequate U.S. recognition of China's constructive actions while being overly absorbed with Japan. The November 2007 statements by then–Japanese prime minister Yasuo Fukuda and U.S. secretary of defense Gates make this appeal by Beijing all the more interesting. Fukuda talked of narrowing the focus of Japanese foreign policy to Asia, particularly North Korea and China, and Gates said in Tokyo that Japan should shoulder more global security responsibilities. Meanwhile, eight years of JMSDF oilers' refueling ships in support of military operations in Afghanistan ended abruptly in January 2010 when Prime Minister Yukio Hatoyama refused to renew the law authorizing the mission. Considerable tension over security issues developed between Washington and the government of Prime Minister Yukio Hatoyama during his recent term (September 2009–June 2010). This is not to suggest that this foretells doom for the U.S.–Japan alliance, but Washington may wish to listen more closely to Beijing's appeal to the United States to better balance its relations with Japan and China—all the while preserving the alliance.

Regardless of the persisting important areas of disagreement, Beijing and Washington now refrain from calling each other names (a habit of the past) and seem to have largely abandoned the conviction that the other is appropriately viewed and dealt with as an outsider or incorrigible troublemaker—even if some vociferous figures in both countries persist in these views. Washington goes so far as to look to Beijing to take the lead on security issues concerning North Korea. This is a dramatic change from just a few years ago when Washington saw Beijing primarily as a persistent problem and sometimes proliferator. This development is all the more remarkable because both capitals fully appreciate that they must still hedge against possible confrontation with one another. The relationship has been transformed, and its foundation seems strong enough to build on—even as the two countries appreciate fully that, while they exhibit signs of strategic partnership, the Taiwan issue has produced an ongoing problem and could still (but is now less likely to) put them into conflict and human rights issues still produce friction.

This apparent, but understandable and manageable, contradiction of simultaneous strategic alignment and hedging has become a characteristic of the U.S.–China relationship. The juxtaposition suggests that serious engagement and fulsome hedging are not mutually exclusive courses of action. We may be simply acknowledging the modus operandi that has evolved for the relationship, and it is in this context that a cooperative maritime security initiative should be viewed. It would not exist in isolation of other cooperative arrangements between the two countries but alongside them and with the potential to be a catalyst for further consolidating cooperative relations.

Cooperation in areas beyond the talks about North Korea and economic matters has the potential for developing understanding and building confidence and trust that can make conflict less likely. Just as partnership in the thousand-ship navy is not essential to U.S.–China cooperation in humanitarian operations, final resolution of the Taiwan issue (particularly with a Taiwan president not inclined to exacerbate cross-strait tensions) is not essential to fostering improved U.S.–China military relations. The specific area of humanitarian assistance and the broader area of fulsome maritime cooperation, notably including counterpiracy operations, can serve to improve relations while bringing aid to the distressed, devastated, threatened, and victimized. These forms of U.S.–China navy and maritime cooperation are an idea whose time may well have come.

Notes

1. Alan R. Romberg, "U.S. Arms Sales to Taiwan—Beijing Reacts Sharply," *Stimson Publications* (Washington, DC: Henry L. Stimson Center, February 2010), 1, http://www.stimson.org/pub.cfm?id=%20927; and Jacquelyn S. Porth, "United States Eager to Team with China to Deter Pirate Attacks," America.gov, U.S. Department of State, 23 December 2008, http://www.america.gov/st/peacesec-english/2008/December/200 81222172545sjhtropo.5483972.html. The article describes the 2008 disruption of U.S.–China military-to-military relations as follows: "China severed U.S. military contacts after Washington announced a $6.5 million arms sale to Taiwan in October."

2. This historic visit was the second to a communist country by a U.S. secretary of defense. The author, working in the Office of the Secretary of Defense during 1977–80 as country director for the Soviet Union, Yugoslavia, and Spain, made preparations and accompanied Brown on the first trip to a Communist country by a sitting secretary of defense: Yugoslavia in 1977.

3. Now Professor Cole is a recognized specialist on the PLA at the U.S. National Defense University. Admiral Blair served as commander of U.S. forces in the Pacific and was chosen to be the director of National Intelligence in the Obama administration.

4. The author was present for the speech and obtained a copy of the text from Colonel Miller.

5. Secretary of Defense William J. Perry, Memorandum for the Secretaries of the Army, Navy, and Air Force, "U.S.-China Military Relationship," August 1994, http://www.gwu.edu/~nsarchiv/NSAEBB/NSAEBB19/12-01.htm.

6. U.S. Congress, Public Law 106-65 National Defense Authorization Act for Fiscal Year 2000, "Section 1201: Limitation on military-to-military exchanges and contacts with Chinese People's Liberation Army," http://frwebgate.access.gpo.gov/cgi-bin/getdoc.cgi?dbname=106_cong_public_laws&docid=f:publ065.106.

7. Statement at the 3rd Annual China Maritime Studies Institute (CMSI) Conference, "Defining a Maritime Partnership with China," 5–6 December 2007, U.S. Naval War College.

8. The author followed the planning and conduct of the 2007 visits because he was consulted informally by both sides, which were often expressing concern about the prospects for a successful visit. Reciprocity remains a big issue based on the complaints by the U.S. side that Chinese visitors see far more military platforms and facilities than Americans are shown. As to the January 2008 visit by Admiral Keating, see the Pacific Command report of a press roundtable, http://www.pacom.mil/speeches/sst2008/080115-keating-china.shtml.

9. The author has personal knowledge of the Roughead and Xu visits based on contact with the two principals.

10. "China's Position on Suspending Military Visits with U.S. 'Unchanged': Spokesman," Xinhua, 28 February 2010, http://eng.mod.gov.cn/Press/2010-02/25/content_4126529.htm.

11. The conference, attended by the author, was sponsored by the Scowcroft Institute of International Affairs and was called the "China–U.S. Security Forum: Evolving and Enhancing Military Relations," 24 October 2007.

12. PRC Embassy in Washington, "China-U.S. Military Exchanges and Agreements Reached since the Visit by Chinese Defense Minister General Chi Haotian to the U.S. in Dec. 1996," http://www.china-embassy.org/eng/zmgx/zmgx/Military%20Relationship/t35738.htm.

13. Deputy Secretary of Defense Paul D. Wolfowitz, Letters to the chairmen of the Armed Services Committees, Senator Levin and Congressman Stump, covering an attachment listing exchanges with the PLA during 2000, 8 June 2001, http://www.defenselink.mil/news/Jun2001/d20010626m2m.pdf.

14. PRC Embassy in Washington, "China's Top General Departs for U.S., Boosting Military Ties (07/17/06)"; available at http://www.china-embassy.org/eng/xw/t263531.htm.

15. Conversation on 15 November 2007 with Major General Darryll D. M. Wong, who is the commander and chief of staff of the Hawaii Air National Guard. He coordinates the development and implementation of Hawaii Air National Guard policies and is responsible for developing strategic and contingency plans.

16. Lieutenant Colonel Barto's opinions are especially pertinent because he was working in a Joint Staff office that is engaged in U.S.–China policy matters, has served as an attaché at the U.S. embassy in Beijing (including specific experience with HA and DR), and is a specialist on China and its military.

17. Office of the Secretary of Defense, "Annual Report to Congress on the Military Power of the People's Republic of China 2006," chapter 2: "Understanding China's Strategy," http://www.globalsecurity.org/military/library/report/2006/2006-prc-military-power02.htm.

18. Richard P. Lawless, "China: Recent Security Developments," 13 June 2007, http://armedservices.house.gov/pdfs/FC061307/Lawless_Testimony061307.pdf.

19. "U.S. Pacific Fleet Commander Visits China," Story Number: NNS061113-20, U.S. Pacific Fleet Public Affairs Navy Newsstand, 13 November 2006, http://www.news. navy.mil/search/display.asp?story_id=26570.

20. This conference, cited previously, was sponsored by the Scowcroft Institute of International Affairs and was called the China–U.S. Security Forum: Evolving and Enhancing Military Relations, 24 October 2007.

21. Porth, "United States Eager to Team with China."

22. Statement at the December 2007 CMSI conference at the U.S. Naval War College.

23. These problems brought about the described provisions in the fiscal year 2000 National Defense Authorization Act limiting Chinese access and requiring an annual reporting to Congress by the secretary of defense on military interaction with the PLA.

24. For example, General Richard Myers, while chairman of the Joint Chiefs of Staff, became the first foreigner to visit the Beijing Aerospace Control Center; see Jim Garamone, "Myers Is First Foreign Visitor to Chinese Space Center," American Forces Press Service, 14 January 2004, http://www.defenselink.mil/news/newsarticle .aspx?id=27502. Admiral Michael Mullen told CBS News that he had been given unprecedented access to China's navy during his visit and indicated he would continue to nurture ties after taking over as President George W. Bush's main military advisor and leader of the Army, Navy, Air Force, and Marines. Mullen said his trip had included a speech to midshipmen at a naval academy and the observation of naval exercises from on board a Chinese warship. "There were several things that I did that I was told had not been done before," Mullen said. "To get under way on a destroyer and to see an exercise that included air, submarine and surface exercises" was a first for a U.S. Naval officer, he said. Brian Montopoli, "Incoming Joint Chiefs Chair Visits China," CBS News, 21 August 2007, http://www.cbsnews.com/stories/2007/08/21/poli tics/main3188954.shtml.

25. Several Hong Kong port visit requests were denied by Chinese authorities in November 2007; such requests are generally routinely approved. The first was a request for a fueling stop for two minesweepers during a time of bad weather—an extraordinary denial given the jeopardy of the two craft, low on fuel in poor weather. (The author heard Chinese and American observers, concerned with bilateral relations but not directly involved in the visit denials, suggest that the minesweepers were not in immediate jeopardy from the weather. The Chinese seemed to be suggesting that their government's conduct had not been egregious—even if impetuous. The Americans, discussing the matter in early December, were hopeful that the issue could be quickly gotten past.) Another request was for a Thanksgiving holiday visit to Hong Kong by the carrier *Kitty Hawk* and escort ships—with hundreds of family members awaiting the ships' arrival. The reversal of the *Kitty Hawk* denial, said to be for humanitarian reasons, came too late, and the crews and families were not together for the holiday; the ships returned to Japan where, coincidentally, a PLA Navy ship was making an unprecedented port visit. A New Year's holiday port visit for a frigate and a cargo plane stop in Hong Kong were also denied.

26. Associated Press, "China: Cancellation of Navy Visit Was No Misunderstanding," *USA Today*, 30 November 2007, 4A.

27. Ann Scott Tyson, "U.S. Protests China's Denial of Port Entry," *The Wall Street Journal Asia*, 30 November 2007, 10.

28. The author raised this issue with Vice Admiral Morgan in late September 2007 and received this response.

29. Gordan van Hook, "How to Kill a Good Idea," U.S. Naval Institute *Proceedings* 33, no. 10 (October 2007), 32–35; Eric McVadon, "China and the United States on the High Seas," *China Security*, no. 8 (Autumn 2007), 3–28, http://www.chinasecurity.us/images/stories/CS8_1.pdf; and Yang Yi, "Engagement, Caution," *China Security*, no. 8 (Autumn 2007), 29–39, http://www.chinasecurity.us/images/stories/CS8_2.pdf.

30. Some of the potential problems with and prospects for U.S.–PRC maritime cooperation presented in this chapter represent refined ideas that appeared previously in the author's articles: Eric McVadon, "China and the United States on the High Seas" in *China Security*, Autumn 2007, http://www.wsichina.org/cs8_1.pdf; and McVadon, "U.S.-PRC Maritime Cooperation: An Idea Whose Time Has Come?" in the Jamestown Foundation's *China Brief*, 13 June 2007, http://jamestown.nvmserver.com/124/?no_cache=1&tx_ttnews%5Btt_news%5D=4229.

31. "Sino-U.S. Sea Standoff Appears to Have Ended," *China Daily*, 20 March 2009, http://www.wsichina.org/morningchina/archive/20090320.html.

32. Jane Macartney, "China Ends Naval Stand-off and Credits Barack Obama," *Times Online*, 21 March 2009; http://www.timesonline.co.uk/tol/news/world/asia/article5942562.ece.

33. The NTI Research Library entry for MMCA states: "The agreement provides for operator level exchanges to discuss issues of maritime safety and communication; the accord also expands cooperation in a number [of] related areas including search and rescue at sea, and humanitarian assistance. The first annual MMCA meeting took place in Beijing in July 1998." "Military Maritime Consultative Agreement (MMCA)," Nuclear Threat Initiative (NTI), http://www.nti.org/db/china/mmcaorg.htm.

34. John G. Morgan and Charles W. Martoglio, "The 1,000-Ship Navy: Global Maritime Network," U.S. Naval Institute *Proceedings* 131, no. 11 (November 2005): 15.

35. Ibid., 14–17. Nevertheless, serious questions are asked about the scope of the threat to sea-lanes today, including asking why there is this sudden furor when the disruption of oil shipments is hardly a pressing current concern.

36. Ibid., 15–16.

37. Gordan Van Hook, "How to Kill a Good Idea," U.S. Naval Institute *Proceedings* 133, no. 10 (October 2007): 32–35. Captain Van Hook is currently the executive director of the CNO Executive Panel, a prestigious advisory group charged with advising the head of the U.S. Navy on emerging technologies and policy issues. Captain Van Hook's insights, published in October 2007, are especially valuable because of his unique position at the time and association with the chief of naval operations and other senior leaders of the U.S. Navy.

38. PSI is a U.S.-initiated multinational initiative to curb the transfer of WMD-related material.

39. Quoted in Maureen Fan, "China to Aid in Fighting Somali Pirates," *Washington Post*, 18 December 2008, A-20.

40. Wu Jiao and Peng Kuang, "Sailing to Strengthen Global Security," *China Daily*, 26 December 2008, available at http://www.chinadaily.com.cn/china/2008-12/26/content_7342612.htm.

41. "Chinese Ship Rescued in Gulf of Aden, Pirates Retreat," Xinhua, 17 December 2008, http://www.chinadaily.com.cn/china/2008-12/17/content_7315328.htm.

42. The author received from various colleagues around the world reports, comments, and snippets of news stories from Reuters, Xinhua, and Agence France Press, all around 17 December 2008. The *Zhenhua 4* story is from the Xinhua report (ibid.) and the *Washington Post* article by Maureen Fan, "China to Aid in Fighting Somali Pirates."

43. Ibid.

44. The PRC foreign ministry reported He's words as follows: "China welcomes international cooperation in the fight against piracy off the coast of Somalia and supports the efforts of relevant countries to send warships to the region to crack down on pirates pursuant to Security Council resolutions. China is seriously considering sending naval ships to the Gulf of Aden and waters off the Somali coast for escorting operations in the near future." This extract is from "Remarks by Vice Minister He Yafei at the UNSC Ministerial Meeting on Counter Piracy off the Coast of Somalia," http://www.fmprc.gov.cn/eng/zxxx/t526519.htm.

45. Porth, "United States Eager to Team with China."

46. Wu and Peng, "Sailing to Strengthen Global Security."

47. "Taiwan Ships 'Can Ask for Mainland Escorts' off Somalia," Xinhua, 29 December 2008, http://www.chinadaily.com.cn/china/2008-12/29/content_7351367.htm.

48. Michael S. Chase, and Andrew S. Erickson, "Changes in Beijing's Approach to Overseas Basing?" *China Brief* 9 no. 19 (24 September 2009), http://www.jamestown.org/programs/chinabrief/single/?tx_ttnews%5Btt_news%5D=35536&tx_ttnews%5BbackPid%5D=25&cHash=1e7c04ad8f.

49. "Colonel: China Must Establish Overseas Bases, Assume the Responsibility of a Great Power," *Global Times*, 5 February 2009, http://www.chinareviewnews.com/doc/7_0_100877861_1.html.

50. Zhao Chunzhe, "China not to Establish Overseas Military Base: Researcher," *China Daily*, 4 March 2010; http://www.chinadaily.com.cn/china/2010npc/2010-03/04/content_9536135.htm.

51. Shen Dingli, "Don't Shun the Idea of Setting up Overseas Military Bases," China.org.cn, 28 January 2010; http://www.china.org.cn/opinion/2010-01/28/content_19324522.htm.

52. The PRC Foreign Ministry report of He's full statement is available at http://www.fmprc.gov.cn/eng/zxxx/t526519.htm.

53. Cui Xiaohuo and Wang Hui, "Chinese Navy Ready for Prolonged Mission in Somalia," *China Daily*, 26 December 2008, http://www.chinadaily.com.cn/china/2008-12/26/content_7341963.htm.

54. "Chinese Navy Sends Most Sophisticated Ships on Escort Mission off Somalia," *Window of China*, www.chinaview.cn, 26 December 2008, http://news.xinhuanet.com/english/2008-12/26/content_10565179.htm.

55. Wendell Minnick, "'Habits of Cooperation': Former PACOM Chief Calls for U.S., Chinese Militaries to Work Together More," *Defense News*, 30 April 2007.

56. Lyle Goldstein, "China: A New Maritime Partner," U.S. Naval Institute *Proceedings* 133, no. 8 (August 2007): 26–31.

57. Ibid., 27.

58. Ibid., 30.

59. See, for example, Dan Blumenthal and Joseph Lin, "Oil Obsession," *Armed Forces Journal*, June 2006, http://www.armedforcesjournal.com/2006/06/1813592.

60. Jonathan Pollack, "Energy Insecurity with Chinese and American Characteristics: Realities and Possibilities," in *China's Energy Strategy: The Impact on Beijing's Maritime Policies*, ed. Gabriel Collins, Andrew Erickson, Lyle Goldstein, and William Murray, 437–55 (Annapolis, MD: Naval Institute Press, 2008).

61. Zhuang Jianzhong, Shanghai Jiaotong University, statement at CMSI conference.

62. Department of the Navy, "A Cooperative Strategy for 21st Century Seapower," http://www.navy.mil/maritime/MaritimeStrategy.pdf.

63. Statement at the CMSI conference.

64. Admiral Gary Roughead, Commander, U.S. Pacific Fleet, "Deployment of Hospital Ship 'Mercy' and Current Pacific Command Operations," Foreign Press Center Briefing, 10 May 2006, http://2002-2009-fpc.state.gov/66063.htm.

65. "Over 2,200 Die in Bangladesh Cyclone," *China Daily*, 18 November 2007, http://www.chinadaily.com.cn/world/2007-11/18/content_6262172.htm.

66. Colonel Frank Miller, chief of the Northeast Asia section of the J-5 directorate of the U.S. Joint Staff, told the author on 14–15 April 2007 of the U.S. overture to the PRC Ministry of National Defence and the PLA's employment of a commercial airline to accomplish delivery of the aid material for victims of Hurricane Katrina.

67. Ralph A. Cossa, "South Asian Tsunami: U.S. Military Provides 'Logistical Backbone' for Relief Operation," *eJournalUSA, Foreign Policy Agenda*, November 2004, http://www.america.gov/st/washfile-english/2005/March/20050304112100dmslahrelleko.5331537.html.

68. "In 2003, the PLAN conducted its first joint maritime search-and-rescue exercises during separate visits by vessels from Pakistan and India. Since then, it has conducted similar exercises with French, British, and Australian vessels. The PLAN also conducted search-and-rescue exercises during its ship visits to the United States, Canada, and the Philippines in late 2006," Office of Naval Intelligence, "China's Navy 2007," 116, http://militarytimes.com/static/projects/pages/20070313dnplanavy.pdf. See also Qian Xiaohu and Zhu Guangyao, "Chinese Naval Vessels Wrap up European Visit and Long-Voyage Training," *PLA Daily*, 19 October 2007, available at www.english.chinamil.com.cn.

69. The WPNS is a forum initiated in 1988 for naval professionals. It aims to increase naval cooperation in the Western Pacific by providing a forum for discussion of professional issues, generating a flow of information and opinion leading to common understanding.

70. Lu Desheng and Li Gencheng, "'Xiangfan' Returns in Triumph after Joining Maritime Exercise of WPNS," *PLA Daily* (in English), 24 May 2007, http://english.pladaily.com. cn/site2/news-channels/2007-05/24/content_825510.htm.

71. "Sea Phase of 'Peace-07' Exercises Ends," *Xinhuanet*, 12 March 2007, http://big5.cctv. com/english/20070312/101407.shtml.

72. Bernard D. Cole, *Sea Lanes and Pipelines: Energy Security in Asia* (Westport, CT: Praeger Security International, 2008), 139–40.

73. "Yuzhao (Type 071) Class," *Jane's Fighting Ships*, 28 June 2008, available at www.janes. com.

74. "Type 071 Landing Platform Dock," *China's Defense Today*, http://www.sinodefence. com/navy/amphibious/type071.asp.

75. "China/Auxiliaries," in Stephen Saunders, ed., *Jane's Fighting Ships, 2008–2009* (Alexandria, VA: Jane's Information Group, 2008), 154. The author thanks Leah Averitt for this and related research support.

76. Interview with a U.S. naval expert.

77. Van Hook, "How to Kill a Good Idea," 32–35.

78. Edward Cody, "China and U.S. to Establish Military Hotline," *Washington Post*, 6 November 2007, A16.

Lyle J. Goldstein and William S. Murray

Submarine Rescue and the Potential for U.S.–China Naval Cooperation

LIKE ALL THE WORLD'S SUBMARINE POWERS, the PLA Navy has suffered major submarine accidents. Integrating the PLA Navy into cooperative international submarine rescue programs and exercises would improve the Chinese navy and could also serve as an effective confidence building measure to the benefit of Asia-Pacific security.

This study reveals that China's submarine rescue capabilities are modest and notes that the PLA Navy recognizes the need to increase its efforts in this area. These efforts present an opportunity for greater PLA Navy involvement in international cooperative naval programs. Further integrating the Chinese navy into the International Submarine Escape and Rescue Liaison Office (ISMERLO) could create a pattern of cooperation between the Chinese and other regional navies. Such cooperation would build on the momentum established by recent bilateral naval exercises and thereby reinforce efforts to achieve regional security.

Policy implications that flow from this analysis include the following:

- Given the disparity between China's increasingly modern submarine force and its antiquated submarine rescue capabilities, the Chinese navy would benefit by vigorously pursuing submarine rescue technology, doctrine, and training.

- Beijing should increase its level of participation in ISMERLO, which was established in response to the loss of the Russian navy submarine *Kursk*.

- The United States and other Asia-Pacific maritime powers should encourage the PLA Navy to more fully integrate into the maritime security architecture of the Asia-Pacific region, including specifically multilateral submarine rescue exercises.

Introduction

China is emerging as a significant maritime power. Its shipbuilding sector is extremely dynamic. Beijing is also investing heavily in oceanographic research and ocean resource exploitation. Sovereignty concerns along China's maritime periphery combine with these maritime commercial tendencies to create the impetus for an ambitious program of naval modernization. At the center of China's naval modernization is the submarine force, which was simultaneously building four classes of submarines within the past decade while also acquiring a significant number of submarines from abroad. This rapid naval modernization, with its obvious emphasis on undersea warfare, has aroused the suspicions of regional states as well as those of the traditional East Asian maritime powers, including the United States.

Underlining the imperative for greater cooperation between the U.S. and Chinese navies, in October 2006 a Chinese submarine operated in close proximity to the U.S. Navy's *Kitty Hawk* battle group. Commenting on this incident, Admiral William Fallon, then commander of U.S. Pacific Command, underlined the possible risks of such unscripted encounters between warships observing, "if this Chinese sub came in the middle of [an ASW exercise], then it could have escalated."[1] To envision an alternative future of cooperative security and not rivalry, it is worthwhile to consider how cooperation in submarine rescue could help to spur a larger vision in which U.S. and Chinese fleets cooperate together within a global thousand-ship navy—or a maritime partnership—to protect the shared interest in a global commons.[2]

China has long been a continental power; its emergence as a maritime power necessarily raises profound questions for the stability and security of the Asia-Pacific region. Most particularly, can the United States, the most dominant Pacific power, find a modus vivendi with a rising China given Beijing's evident maritime aspirations? The potential for extended naval rivalry is obvious, but to avoid this dangerous future, an agenda for positive maritime cooperation must be developed. The small-scale but historically significant bilateral search-and-rescue exercises conducted by Chinese and U.S. ships in late 2006 should form the beginning of an expanded naval cooperation agenda. This chapter explores how increased cooperation in submarine rescue is one potential avenue for expanded maritime cooperation between the established and the emergent naval power in the Asia-Pacific region. While the promise of such cooperative initiatives should not be exaggerated and cannot be expected to alter potentially conflicting national interests, such mechanisms may facilitate greater trust and transparency in addition to having an impact on the worldview of decision makers in sensitive national security positions.[3]

Submarine rescue may be regarded as more sensitive than other Asia-Pacific maritime cooperation initiatives such as multilateral oceanographic research, fisheries management, and coast guard cooperation. After all, the details of submarine operations and capabilities comprise some of the most closely held secrets of nations that operate such warships. Nevertheless, the value of international cooperation in submarine rescue is a concrete and incontestable fact that can be measured in lives saved—as the August 2005 rescue of the Russian submersible AS-28 *Priz* by a team from the United Kingdom's Royal Navy vividly demonstrated. Meanwhile, the increased domestic and international attention given to China's submarine fleet and its accidents suggest that submarine rescue capabilities will become much more important to the People's Republic of China (PRC). The tragic loss of an entire Chinese submarine crew in 2003 powerfully underlines this imperative. Cooperation among submarine forces in the Pacific may be more challenging than other aspects of regional naval and maritime cooperation, but the consequences for mutual confidence could be much more profound as elite (and, hence, influential) military organizations are drawn into cooperative activities. A considerable consensus in Washington coalesced around former deputy secretary of state Robert Zoellick's articulation of the "stakeholder" concept for U.S.–China relations. The naval component should not be neglected in this and following efforts to encourage Beijing to exercise its new power in order to "sustain, adapt, and advance the peaceful international system that has enabled its own success."[4]

This analysis is composed of three sections. The first examines China's record of submarine accidents, focusing on the most recent tragedy of *Ming 361*. A second section places China's record in a larger context, illustrating that all submarine powers have inevitably suffered disastrous accidents. This section also discusses in some detail two recent disasters, the loss of *Kursk* and the rescue of AS-28 *Priz*, which have together created strong momentum behind submarine rescue initiatives. The third section surveys the multinational, institutional basis for submarine rescue, and the conclusion presents policy recommendations.

China's Experience with Submarine Accidents

China has suffered many submarine accidents. Perhaps the most notorious of Beijing's underwater mishaps is the April 2003 loss of the *Ming*-class submarine *361*, in which the entire crew of seventy officers and sailors perished while operating in relatively shallow water near the entrance to the Bohai Gulf.[5] Some reports suggest that local fishermen found the vessel floating in a semi-submerged condition with its air induction mast and periscope raised above the surface of the water.[6] Another report says that the entire crew perished so quickly that "the positions of all 70 officers and sailors were 'very peaceful.' Some were lying in bed. Some were at work positions. There was no single trace of [struggle]."[7]

The exact cause of the disaster is not known outside of the Chinese navy; however, it was publicly declared to be the result of a "mechanical problem" that occurred during "valve testing."[8] A logical explanation that fits with the majority of reported features of the accident is that the ship operated its diesel engines without opening the air induction valve. With no air entering the ship, the ship's atmosphere became rapidly depleted of oxygen (since the ship is quite small and the engines have a voracious appetite) and the crew suffocated.

The loss of the *Ming 361* resulted in an unprecedented political-military dynamic within the Chinese leadership. It is noteworthy how quickly this event became public, perhaps because of the difficulty of containing information in an age of the Internet and increasing globalization, and because of the public relations disaster that had befallen the Russian government during the *Kursk* tragedy several years prior.[9] Shortly after the accident, Central Military Commission (CMC) chairman Jiang Zemin and vice chairman Hu Jintao were shown on television inside the recovered submarine. Those in the military chain of command deemed ultimately responsible, including the PLA Navy commander and political commissar, and the North Sea Fleet (NSF) commander and NSF political commissar, were publicly dismissed.[10] The message, it would appear, was that PLA Navy commanders would be held personally accountable for preventable accidents. This is a hallmark of an increasingly professional organization.

The *Ming 361* incident left no opportunity for rescue. But this has not been the only accident that China has suffered. Like other submarine powers, China has a long history of submarine accidents. There is a report of the loss of a large group of prospective submarine captains when a *Romeo*-class submarine sank in 1993.[11] Another possible loss of a *Ming*, with all hands, is said to have occurred in the Yellow Sea in the 1980s, allegedly after the submerged submarine collided with a merchant ship.[12] Rumors exist of another accident that killed ten in the 1980s, and of an even more serious incident in the 1960s in which there was only one survivor.[13] At some point, the Chinese may have even lost an additional *Ming* to a fire.[14] There is likewise speculation regarding a second *Xia*-class ballistic missile submarine that might have been "lost in a fire before it went to sea."[15]

Beijing continues to operate a large fleet of submarines, half to one-third of which are relatively obsolete, in the relatively shallow waters around the South Sea, East Sea, and North Sea fleet submarine bases. These waters are becoming increasingly crowded with merchant shipping as China's export economy expands. This combination of ever-growing merchant ship activity, the continued obsolescence of some proportion of the PLA Navy submarine force, and often young and inexperienced crews practically guarantees further accidents. Indeed, the Japanese newspaper *Yomiuri Shimbun* recently reported that another *Ming*-class submarine suffered a fire at sea in May 2005 and had to be towed back to its South Sea Fleet port.[16] A PLA Navy corvette was severely damaged in a collision with a large merchant ship in late June 2006. Thirteen Chinese officers and men were reported missing in this accident.[17] Submarines operating in these intensely congested waters face the same risk of collision and sinking, especially while operating on the surface.

China might be able to execute an effective submarine rescue by drawing solely on indigenous naval assets. In fact, one source suggests that successful escapes from stricken submarines by PLA Navy sailors were made through the torpedo tubes during incidents in 1959 and in 1987.[18] China continues to train its submariners in that method of escape but also has some additional submarine rescue capabilities. The PLA Navy operates *Dajiang*-, *Hudong*-, and *Kancha*-class support vessels, all of which have some ability to facilitate submarine rescue operations. The Chinese navy also has two deep submergence rescue vehicles (DSRVs). The PLA Navy DSRV was first tested in 1986. It is capable of conducting "wet rescue" at depths up to two hundred meters. Deployed from the above salvage vessels and with a capacity to carry six survivors, these rescue vessels are equipped with underwater cameras, high-frequency active sonar, and a manipulator arm.[19] In late 2008 China greatly improved its underwater rescue potential when it took delivery from Great Britain of an LR 7 submarine rescue vehicle. This vessel, presumably contracted for in the aftermath of the *Ming 361* disaster, can bring to the surface up to eighteen sailors at a time from stricken submarines, and can operate at depths exceeding five hundred meters.[20] PLA Navy submarine rescue exercises are becoming more common, but according to Chinese sources, the first major submarine rescue exercise occurred in 2004.[21] In September 2006 the PLA Navy successfully conducted a joint exercise employing a diving bell for submarine rescue. The 解放军报 (*Liberation Army Daily*) report on this exercise, which was conducted by the North Sea Fleet, suggests that the exercise demonstrates that China is aiming to reach international standards in this arena.[22] China's evident lack of significant experience in this aspect of naval development suggests that Beijing could benefit from studying foreign submarine accidents and, more importantly, from interacting with foreign navies that have much more experience with submarine rescue.

Submarine Accidents and Factors Influencing Rescue

Although China is the most recent country to lose a submarine crew due to a peacetime accident, all of the other permanent members of the UN Security Council have suffered similar fatal submarine disasters. Russia has the sad distinction of experiencing the most.

The United Kingdom lost four diesel-powered submarines during the Cold War. France lost two *Daphne*-class diesel submarines, both with all hands. The United States suffered two submarine losses in the 1960s, the USS *Thresher*, a nuclear-powered attack submarine sinking during sea trials in the Gulf of Maine in 1963, and the USS *Scorpion*, which was lost near the Azores in 1967, most probably due to an internal explosion. Altogether, since 1945 at least twelve countries have lost submarines and their crews due to accidental causes in peacetime.[23]

Potentially catastrophic submarine accidents are more common than is usually realized. The Canadian submarine HMCS *Windsor*, for example, recently suffered a small electrical fire.[24] This would never have been reported in the newspapers had not the HMCS *Chicoutimi* suffered a fire and the death of a crew member only thirteen months earlier.[25] Other accidents, however, avoid becoming major disasters by the narrowest of margins. USS *Dolphin*, formerly the U.S. Navy's only diesel submarine, suffered major flooding in May 2002 and was almost lost. More widely known is the collision in 2001 between USS *Greeneville* and a fishing school vessel in which nine Japanese students were killed. There was one fatality when the USS *San Francisco* struck an undersea mountain in January 2005 while operating submerged at high speed several hundred miles south of Guam.[26]

An example of a relatively minor submarine accident that had the potential to be a major disaster occurred in September 2005 when the USS *Philadelphia* was struck by a Turkish freighter while the submarine was operating on the surface as it entered Bahrain. The nature of the damage, though relatively minor, suggests the submarine could just as easily have been sunk.[27] Another potential disaster was narrowly averted when the USS *Hartford* suffered severe damage to its sail after colliding while submerged with the USS *New Orleans* near the Strait of Hormuz in March 2009. One has to conclude that submarining is simply a dangerous business, even for the most accomplished practitioners of undersea warfare. As the professionalism of China's navy increases, therefore, submarine accidents will remain a major concern. Accidents involving the *Kursk, Thresher, Scorpion, Ming 361, Dakar,* and many other submarines occurred with the loss of all hands, but less fatal submarine accidents also occur relatively frequently. This discussion also illustrates that, unlike air crashes, submarine accidents frequently have survivors, so that the imperative to develop rescue capabilities is acute.

To effect a rescue of stranded submariners, the time delay between the accident and rescue attempt must be short. Hypothermia and asphyxiation from the buildup of carbon monoxide or noxious gasses from fires or chemical reactions between seawater and battery acids generally kill their victims within seventy-two hours. HMS *Thetis*' ninety-nine-member crew, for example, succumbed during rescue efforts while trapped in their stranded vessel in 1939.[28] Two crucial elements have a direct impact on the time to rescue.

First, there is the problem of accurately determining the stranded vessel's location. Occasionally this task has been simple, as in 1923 when the U.S. submarine *O-5* sank following a collision and was quickly lifted off the thirty-foot-deep bottom near the entrance to the Panama Canal. The water was so clear that the submarine could be easily seen from the surface.[29] Similar accidents are quite possible to this day, perhaps including in the extensively shallow waters of China's littoral. Unfortunately, locating the stricken submarine is rarely as easy as in the case of the *O-5*, even in shallow waters. To help solve this problem, many submarines—China's included—are equipped with lighted or radio beacon buoys that can be released from a stranded submarine. These buoys, painted yellow and located in the bow and stern, are plainly visible in photos of contemporary PLA Navy submarines. Submarines also carry flares that can be launched to attract attention.

A second factor crucial for rescue, of course, is for adequate rescue forces and machinery nearby. The crew of the USS *Squalus* was rescued in 1939 from waters off the New Hampshire coast by a rescue bell lowered and raised by cables onto the hatch of the submarine from the rescue vessel USS *Falcon*, which had fortuitously been ready to sail from Groton, Connecticut. Unfortunately, even the close proximity of rescue forces cannot guarantee a successful rescue outcome, as two recent cases from the Russian navy illustrate. It is worth dwelling on these two cases in particular because they demonstrate the strong imperative to develop international cooperation in this sphere.

The *Kursk* Tragedy

On 12 August 2000 the Russian navy's five-year-old Oscar II–class guided missile submarine *Kursk* became disabled by an internal explosion and plunged to the bottom of the Barents Sea. The vessel lay trapped at a depth of 108 meters, approximately 85 miles off the Russian port of Severomorsk. Up to 23 crew members trapped in the submarine's rear compartments may have survived until approximately 15 August.[30] Repeated attempts by the Russian navy to reach the submarine and save the surviving crew members ended in failure. Thus, the *Kursk*'s entire crew of 118 sailors and officers perished.

On the day following the accident, 13 August, the submarine was located by the sonar of the cruiser *Pyotr Veliky*, and Russian submersibles already may have been diving on the site later that evening.[31] On 14 August Moscow revealed the submarine accident to the world. During the same day, foreign navies from Norway, the United Kingdom, and the United States all offered assistance to the Russian navy. However, these offers were initially rejected. Russian deputy prime minister Ilya Klebanov commented on 15 August: "We have all the necessary technology to carry out the [rescue] operation."[32] Meanwhile, numerous Russian navy attempts to dock *Priz*-class rescue vehicles with *Kursk* failed—perhaps partially due to a storm that passed through the area.[33] By 15 August Russian sources reported that there were no longer any signs of life aboard *Kursk*.

The increasingly desperate situation finally pushed Russian leaders to explore the possibilities of international assistance. However, these efforts appear to have been somewhat half-hearted in nature. For example, a British submersible was flown into Norway, instead of to any of the Russian naval bases that were much closer to the stricken submarine.[34] Moreover, when international aid from the United Kingdom and Norway did finally arrive on site on 19 August, more time was expended on negotiations concerning how the countries intended to cooperate during the rescue operation.[35] Norwegian deep-sea divers succeeded in opening the *Kursk's* rear escape hatch by 21 August, just one day after beginning their operations.[36]

An April 2006 series that appeared in the Chinese naval journal 舰船知 识 (*Naval and Merchant Ships*) provides a detailed examination of the *Kursk* accident. The analysis cites the belief initially held in the Russian navy that the incident was triggered by a collision with a U.S. Navy submarine, noting the frequency of such undersea collisions in the Barents Sea. However, the Chinese author states unequivocally that the discovered cause of the accident was a faulty Russian torpedo. Moreover, this analyst pulls no punches in blaming Russian navy leaders for their reluctance to accept international assistance, which was offered immediately after the accident was made public by Russian authorities.[37]

Rescue of AS-28 *Priz*

Almost exactly five years after the *Kursk* tragedy, the AS-28 *Priz* submersible deployed on a training mission in the waters of Beryozovaya Bay, approximately fifty miles south of Kamchatka's capital, Petropavlovsk. The propeller of the minisubmarine appears to have become ensnared by a discarded fishing net or by Soviet-era surveillance equipment lying on the sea bottom.[38] Trapped at 190 meters (about 625 feet)—significantly deeper than the wreck of the *Kursk*— the AS-28 *Priz* was too deep to allow the crew to simply abandon ship and swim to the surface. The following day, 5 August, Russian ships appeared on the scene and attempted to free the submarine by dragging it along the bottom. When this was unsuccessful, the Russian navy, out of options, wisely opted to call for international assistance at an early point in the developing crisis.[39]

Within twenty-four hours, help was on its way from the United Kingdom, the United States, and Japan. In Scotland, a Royal Navy remotely controlled *Scorpio* minisubmarine capable of cutting through steel cables 70-mm thick, was put aboard a military transport aircraft and began the long flight to the Russian Far East.[40] The same day, a similar U.S. Navy *Scorpio* submersible was loaded on a C-5 *Galaxy* transport to make the same journey.[41] Meanwhile, a flotilla of Japanese navy ships including *Chiyoda*, a submarine rescue mother ship, readied to sail for the waters of Kamchatka.[42]

On 6 August, foreign assistance began to arrive in Kamchatka. While U.S. Navy elements, including deep-sea divers, provided valuable assitance, the Royal Navy contingent led by Commander Jonty Powis spearheaded the international rescue effort, freeing the *Priz* on 7 August. Thanks to the efforts of the international rescuers but also the difficult and brave decision to invite foreign assistance, the entire seven-man crew of the *Priz* escaped from the episode unharmed.

The November 2005 issue of 当代海军 (*Modern Navy*), China's premier naval publication, carried an extensive story related to the *Priz* rescue. Oddly, the focus of the article was not on the rescue itself but rather on a remarkably detailed survey of the operational history of Russia's Project 1855 *Priz*-class rescue submersibles. Although it does not directly relate the compelling details of the rescue, the discussion is nevertheless noteworthy in that it honestly identifies that the United States, the United Kingdom, and Japan all took actions to assist the Russian navy with the rescue effort. It also minces few words in criticizing the Russian navy: "This accident once again demonstrates that the condition of Russian Navy undersea rescue equipment allows for little optimism."[43] This may reflect an internal PLA Navy debate, for another article from this same official PLA Navy journal (December 2004) expresses some evident reluctance with regard to asking for foreign assistance with respect to submarine rescue.[44]

Another Chinese article on the *Priz* rescue was published in September 2005 issue of 舰船知识 (*Naval & Merchant Ships*). Like the article described earlier, it does not address the facts of the actual incident but rather explores the technical and doctrinal aspects of the "NATO submarine rescue system." This article begins with the assertion, particularly applicable to the circumstances of China's naval development, that the vast majority of submarine accidents have occurred in waters shallow enough to feasibly undertake rescue. Most encouraging for the purposes of the present study, this article highlights the major efficiency benefits of submarine rescue activities that are international in scope.[45] Highlighting China's interest in submarine rescue issues, an article from the October 2005 issue of the same journal actually shows a sequence of underwater photos of the Royal Navy *Scorpio* systems at work in cutting the *Priz* free from the cables that were trapping it.[46]

This survey of historical accidents leads to some inescapable conclusions. Despite the best efforts of every country involved, future submarine accidents are a certainty, and some of these will present the opportunity for rescue. In some future cases, it may be that the crews will be able to leave the ship on their own accord using individual rescue gear.[47] But history shows that more often stranded submariners will perish without external assistance. To affect a successful rescue, a submarine's location must be quickly determined and the vital equipment and expert personnel must reach the scene in a timely manner. As illustrated here, the *Kursk* offered an opportunity for rescue, and the consequent failure underlines the requirement to develop faster and more effective cooperative mechanisms for submarine rescue. The *Priz* example of successful international submarine cooperation stands in stark contrast to the *Kursk* tragedy. Evidently some vital lessons have been learned by the international community.

Opportunities for China in International Submarine Rescue

China's "new diplomacy" features a variety of bold and almost unprecedented (in the Chinese context) multilateral initiatives—for example, the Shanghai Cooperation Organization—but has also encompassed bilateral naval exercises on a limited but growing basis. Perhaps in part spurred by China's increasing stature as a global trade juggernaut, Chinese commercial aircraft and ships have adjusted to global operating and safety standards. In the context of U.S.–China relations, this process has been manifested in a variety of new initiatives and agreements. For example, China has led other nations in cooperating with the U.S. Container Security Initiative (CSI) so that new port security measures do not significantly hinder the efficiency of maritime trade.[48]

With respect to military-to-military cooperation, a Military Maritime Consultative Agreement (MMCA) was signed between Beijing and Washington in 1998. The MMCA is designed to raise "measures to promote safe maritime practices and establish mutual trust [such] as search and rescue, communications procedures when ships encounter each other, interpretation of the Rules of the Nautical Road and avoidance of accidents-at-sea." The agreement provides for annual meetings and for working groups of naval professionals to discuss specific topics.[49] Despite this clearly positive step, the overall military relationship was gravely damaged by the so-called EP-3 incident of April 2001, after which many cooperative activities were suspended. In 2005, however, Admiral Fallon spearheaded efforts to reengage with the PLA—an initiative that led to the fall 2006 bilateral naval search-and-rescue exercises. During one of these events recently, the PLA Navy deputy chief of staff spoke of a desire to add "momentum" to the relationship.[50] In spite of some recent tensions—for example, those related to the January 2007 Chinese antisatellite test and to China's reactions to U.S. arms sales to Taiwan—Admiral Fallon's initiative generally has set the tone for enhanced U.S.–China navy-to-navy cooperation.

From a submarine-rescue perspective, the *Kursk* tragedy has served as a strong impetus for the world's various submarine powers to accelerate cooperative submarine rescue initiatives. These initiatives have been concentrated among traditional alliance partners, but the subsequent founding in September 2004 of ISMERLO offers the potential for significantly widening the scope of international cooperation in this sphere. The opportunities for enlarged Chinese participation in these activities need to be taken seriously, especially in Beijing and Washington, if China is to develop as a "responsible maritime stakeholder."

An especially significant international submarine rescue exercise, dubbed "Sorbet Royale," occurred near Taranto, Italy, in June 2005. During this NATO exercise, four submarines from Italy, Spain, the Netherlands, and Turkey rested on the bottom of the Mediterranean Sea. Rescue vehicles from the United States, Italy, France, and the United Kingdom practiced "rescuing" sailors from these submarines and were supported by vessels, divers, and medical support personnel from France, the Netherlands, Israel, Italy, Spain, and the United Kingdom. Significantly, despite the secrecy traditionally associated with submarines, forces from Russia and the Ukraine also participated in the exercise. This proved to be of particular importance less than two months later when the rescue of the *Priz* described earlier was strongly facilitated by international efforts.[51]

Similar efforts have been undertaken in the Asia-Pacific region, where major biannual submarine rescue exercises have been under way since 2000. In Pacific Reach 2004, held in the waters off Cheju Island in South Korea, five participating countries conducted submarine rescue exercises involving three submarines and three surface ships. The priority that Washington placed on this event was demonstrated when a Russian heavy transport was contracted to deliver the U.S. Navy's DSRV *Mystic* because U.S. Air Force transports were committed to ongoing operations in the Middle East. According to Captain Russell Ervin of the U.S. Navy's Submarine Development Squadron 5, "From arctic to tropical waters, from reef and shoal-littered littorals to the deepest blue water in the world . . . navies operating in Asian waters contend with the most challenging operating theater on the planet. Asian navies are emerging as submarine rescue thought leaders and have a great deal to offer the international community. . . . In Asia, especially due to the distances and limited rescue assets, we depend on one another more than other areas of the world."[52] China was among the eight countries that sent observers to Pacific Reach 2004. In fact, a major article in *Modern Navy* discusses Pacific Reach 2004, and highlights China's observer status in that event.[53] China again sent observers to Pacific Reach 2006. This development may be a signal of Beijing's increasing inclination to realize the benefits of international submarine rescue cooperation.

The founding of a new and unprecedented international organization, ISMERLO, is a broader initiative that supports international cooperation in submarine rescue. According to the organization's sophisticated and well-maintained Web site, ISMERLO will "establish endorsed procedures as the international standard for submarine escape and rescue using consultation and consensus among submarine operating nations." ISMERLO "is the international hub for information and coordination on submarine rescue, acting as the liaison office between the nation that has a disabled submarine and the rest of the submarine escape and rescue community."[54] According to the organization's coordinator, Bill Orr, "We look at the availability of rescue assets out there, provide notice for urgent requirements for rescue, and post that information on our web site. The nation that lost the submarine, as well as nations that can respond, can see that information and identify the best possible assets to respond to the disabled submarine."[55] While perhaps the organization's colocation with major U.S. Navy facilities in Norfolk, Virginia, could be objectionable to certain states, it is still logical given the U.S. Navy's long history in the realm of submarine rescue.[56]

This young international organization has already amassed an impressive record in submarine rescue, playing a vital role in the successful outcomes of both the *Chicoutimi* and *Priz* incidents. In the former case, ISMERLO information enabled the rapid location of a suitable towing vessel, which proved crucial.[57] In the latter instance, ISMERLO played an important coordinating function, for example helping to locate a U.S. "K-loader" in Japan that was necessary for off-loading of the Royal Navy's rescue equipment in Kamchatka.

China has already joined ISMERLO and provided some limited information including, for example, points of contact within the PLA Navy. Unfortunately, according to ISMERLO's Web site, "no details [regarding rescue systems] have been received from the People's Liberation Army (Navy)." This source speculates that Chinese submarine rescue systems may conform to Russian specifications; hence, PLA Navy "submarines with a docking seat can receive a Submarine Rescue Vehicle (SRV) fitted with a NATO STANAG rescue skirt."[58] Obviously, the level of cooperation from the Chinese navy in this regard is disappointing, and there is ample room for improvement.

It should be recognized that more robust membership for China in ISMERLO and greater participation in international submarine rescue activities more generally may come at some cost to Beijing, particularly when considered in the context of China's traditional tendency toward secrecy. The Chinese military has long resisted Western-style transparency in an effort to hide its deficiencies and protect military secrets. This is less and less true today, however, and the PLA has made substantial progress in this realm. Submarine rescue information, in any case, is relatively benign, consisting of data such as rescue vehicle mating surface and hatch dimensions. Neither of these engineering issues is relevant to war fighting. Besides, the United States and China both possess high-quality pictures of the relevant hull exteriors, so this should also not be a major concern.[59] It is worth noting that all other major submarine powers, including Russia, have shared this sort of information with each other through ISMERLO. Moreover, any rescue operation involving a Chinese submarine would take place in direct collaboration with Chinese naval officers, implying that they could strictly control access to the stranded vessel, thus protecting any secrets in the submarine's interior. The Chinese leadership should consider that more robust submarine rescue cooperation could become a positive example of the Chinese Navy's willingness to address transparency—even with respect to some of its most advanced platforms.

Because the two recent submarine accidents detailed in this chapter involved Russia, it is natural that much submarine rescue attention has focused on Europe and especially enhanced NATO cooperation with Russia in this realm. Nevertheless, it would be wrong to neglect the Asia-Pacific region, wherein a variety of powers, including Australia, Canada, India, Indonesia, Japan, Malaysia, North Korea, Pakistan, Singapore, and South Korea, in addition to China, continue to invest significantly in submarine capabilities. Chinese naval analysts have observed the important role that NATO has played in the submarine rescue arena, and it is possible that multilateral forums will be most appropriate for addressing these issues in the Asia-Pacific region as well.[60] Indeed, Beijing's special interest in undersea warfare provides an opportunity for drawing this rising power into a nascent but growing web of cooperative relationships among "maritime stakeholders" that could bind Asia-Pacific states together for the twenty-first century and beyond. Greater participation by China in ISMERLO could also lead to a situation in which China's recently acquired LR7 rescue vehicle could save the crew of another nation's stranded submarine. Presumably, this scenario would only enhance China's prestige and lend credibility to its adherence to the tenet of a "harmonious ocean."

Conclusion

Beijing should honor the memory of the crew that perished in the 2003 *Ming 361* tragedy by pursuing submarine rescue technology, doctrine, and training with full vigor. This imperative is underlined by three fundamental factors: (1) the expanding pace and sophistication of Chinese submarine operations; (2) the shallow littoral regions surrounding China that are amenable to rescue operations; and (3) the immense amount of merchant traffic off the Chinese coasts that increase the risks to submarines. These factors combine to virtually guarantee future accidents. Preparing for these incidents through increased participation in ISMERLO, and taking advantage of international rescue capabilities during future rescue operations will save lives, reduce distrust, and establish momentum toward greater integration of the PLA Navy into other international maritime initiatives.

If the PLA Navy becomes a more active partner in ISMERLO, it would enjoy numerous benefits, not least the benefit of exchanging views on submarine rescue with the world's foremost submarine powers. Full participation in submarine rescue exercises would help to "operationalize" U.S. Navy and PLA Navy confidence-building measures above and beyond the search-and-rescue exercises recently held, and would increase the personal exposure between elite segments of the two sides' officer corps. Such a policy of enhanced military-to-military engagement and increased participation in international organizations would increase transparency, demonstrate a Chinese commitment to becoming a stakeholder in an important arena, and be wholly consistent with recent developments in Chinese foreign policy. For example, China has been steadily increasing its contribution to UN peacekeeping operations, offering up to one thousand troops in September 2006 for service in Lebanon. China's navy is also increasingly active in worldwide military diplomatic initiatives such as the AMAN 2007 multilateral exercise in March 2007 with naval forces from Pakistan and the United States, among others.[61]

Washington and other Western states should encourage these developments and warmly welcome the PLA Navy more fully into multilateral submarine rescue exercises such as Sorbet Royale and Pacific Reach. Since the April 2001 E-P3 incident, when U.S.–China relations reached a new nadir and military-to-military relations were suspended, the situation has improved and both sides appear ready to enhance U.S.–China military cooperation. There seems to be a broad recognition in Washington that, although China has a different political system, this rising power must be treated with due regard so that new power will in turn breed new responsibility. Nowhere is this process more important than in the maritime domain. It is incumbent on the naval analytic community in both countries and throughout the Asia-Pacific region to elaborate further opportunities for naval cooperation, such as submarine rescue.

Notes

A preliminary version of the present argument was published as "International Submarine Rescue: A Constructive Role for China?" *Asia Policy*, no. 5 (January 2008): 167–83.

1. Quoted in Audra Ang, "U.S. Admiral Says China Submarine Incident Not Dangerous," *San Diego Tribune*, 17 November 2006.

2. On the thousand-ship navy concept, see John Morgan Jr. and Charles Martoglio, "Global Maritime Network," U.S. Naval Institute *Proceedings* (30 November 2005), http://www.military.com/forums/0,15240,81652,00.html, See also the ideas of a global maritime partnership as expressed in "A Cooperative Strategy for 21st Century Seapower" (Washington DC: U.S. Departments of the Navy and Homeland Security, 2007), http://www.navy.mil/maritime/MaritimeStrategy.pdf.

3. See, for example, Benjamin Self and Yuki Tatsumi, eds., "Confidence-Building Measures and Security Issues in Northeast Asia," Report no. 33 (Washington DC: Henry L. Stimson Center, 2000).

4. "Deputy Secretary Zoellick Statement on Conclusion of Second U.S.-China Senior Dialogue," U.S. Department of State, 8 December 2005, http://www.america.gov/st/washfile-english/2005/December/20051208165226ajesromo.4026758.html.

5. Wang Chine-min, "Story Behind the Truth of Submarine No. 361," *Yazhou Zhoukan*, 12 May 2003, OSC# No. CPP20030513000070.

6. Nanfang Wang, "Mystery Surrounding No. 361 Submarine Accident Remains Unsolved, Outdated Equipment Become Potential Danger for National Defense," *Jianghuai Chenbao*, 6 May 2003, OSC# CPP20030506000139.

7. Wang Jianmin, "Military Family Revealed Inside Secret," *Yazhou Zhoukan*, 26 May 2003, 48–49, OSC# CPP20030619000201.

8. Ibid; and "CMC Chairman Jiang Zemin Denounces PLA Navy for Errors Behind Submarine Accident," *Kuang Chiao Ching* [*Wide Angle*], 15 August 2003, 15, OSC# CPP20030815000047.

9. A similar phenomenon appears to have been at work when it was revealed rather quickly that China had lost one of its experimental early warning aircraft (KJ-200) in an air crash during June 2006.

10. "Enforce Strict Discipline to Avoid Repeat of Tragedy," *Ta Kung Pao*, 16 June 2003, OSC# CPP20030616000032.

11. Joseph S. Bermudez Jr., Sean Boyne, Paul D. Buell, James Foley, and John Hill, "China and Northeast Asia, Navy," *Jane's Sentinel Security Assessment,* 19 November 2002, available at www.janes.com.

12. Wang, "Story Behind the Truth."

13. Ma Ling and Li Ming, "Why Did China Make Public the Submarine Accident?" *Ming Pao*, 9 May 2003, OSC# CPP20030509000043.

14. "Ming Type 035," Federation of American Scientists Web site, http://www.fas.org/man/dod-101/sys/ship/row/plan/ming.htm.

15. Bernard Cole, *The Great Wall at Sea: China's Navy Enters the 21st Century* (Annapolis, MD: Naval Institute Press, 2001), 196n46.

16. See Qiu Yongzheng, "U.S., Japan, Taiwan Work Together to Forge Antisubmarine Chain," *Qingnian Cankao*, 9 June 2005, OSC# CPP20050609000045. This article disputes the *Yomiuri Shimbun*'s account, and relays a PRC foreign ministry explanation that the submarine was instead engaged in "emergency rescue training."

17. "Hong Kong Ship Rams into Missile-Carrying Vessel, Leaving 13 People Missing," *Tung Fang Jih Pao*, 26 June 2006, OSC# CPP20060627710002.

18. From the Web site of the International Submarine Escape and Rescue Liaison Office (ISMERLO), http://www.ismerlo.org.

19. Stephen Saunders, ed., *Jane's Fighting Ships, 2005–2006* (London: Jane's, 2005), 149. The Chinese navy's first deep-diving manned submersible, 鱼鹰-1 (Osprey-1), was completed by Institute 705 in 1969. This submersible was not created for submarine rescue, however, but rather primarily for salvage tasks associated with torpedo development. For an extensive discussion of this system, see 郑楚 [Zheng Chu], "将沉雷打捞出水" ["A Deep Water Torpedo Salvage Vessel Goes to Sea"], 舰船知识 [*Naval & Merchant Ships*] (October 2006): 10–13.

20. "One of the World's Most Advanced Rescue Subs Takes to the Water in Scotland," *Big Partnership*, 10 September 2008, http://www.yourindustrynews.com/news_item.php?newsID=10094.

21. "The Chinese Navy Conducts a Large-Scale Submarine Rescue Exercise for the First Time," *Zhongguo Xinwen* [China News], 1 June 2004, OSC# CPP20050601000107. Another recent report on Chinese submarine rescue exercises is Li Gengcheng and Li Bingzheng, "South Sea Fleet Successfully Organizes Submarine Rescue Drill," *Jiefangjun Bao* [Liberation Army Daily], 28 July 2005, OSC# CPP20050826000230.

22. 张建 [Zhang Jian], "海军救生钟首次援潜成功" ["Navy Lifesaving Bell Successfully Rescues Submarine for the First Time"], 解放军报 [*Liberation Army Daily*] (21 September 2006): 12. See also "PLA Navy North China Sea Fleet Organizes Underwater Submarine Rescue Training Exercise Involving Warships, Helicopters, Divers in Yellow Sea Area," *Jiefangjun Bao*, 21 September 2006, OSC# CPP20060921711001. Another article suggests that rescue bells were developed for the Chinese navy in the 1980s and first successfully tests in 1989. See 王龙起 [Wang Longqi], "潜艇艇员水下脱险—全记录" ["A Insider Account of Submarine Crew Undersea Escape"], 当代海军 [*Modern Navy*] (November 2004): 44–45.

23. Smaller countries have also suffered submarine accidents and losses. Peru lost the *Pacocha* in 1988 and Israel the *Dakar* in 1968. Turkey lost the *Dumlupinar* in 1953 and Spain the C4 in 1946. Edwyn Gray, *Disasters of the Deep* (Annapolis, MD: Naval Institute Press, 2003), 282–89.

24. Kelly Toughill, "Blaze Damages Navy's Last Working Submarine," *Toronto Star*, 1 November 2005.

25. "Canadian Dies of Injuries from Submarine Fire," CBC News, 7 October 2004, http://www.cbc.ca/canada/story/2004/10/06/saunders041006.html. This incident was reported upon in China's most important naval publication: see 刘琳琨 [Liu Linkun],

"从俄加潜艇救援失败看潜艇救援" ["Examining Submarine Rescue from the Perspective of the Recent Russian and Canadian Submarine Rescue Failures"], 当代海军 [*Modern Navy*] (December 2004): 58–59.

26. The USS *San Francisco* accident was covered extensively in the Chinese military press. See, for example, 葛立德 [Ge Lide], "从'旧金山'号海底触礁看美国核潜艇" ["The U.S. Nuclear Submarine Fleet in the Wake of USS *San Francisco*'s Collision with the Sea Bottom"], 中国军网 [*China Military Net*], 19 January 2005, http://www.chinamil. com.cn/site1/xwpdxw/2005-01/19/content_117477.htm.

27. Robert A. Hamilton, "Sources: Sub Not at Fault in Collision," *New London Day*, 7 September 2005. See also Robert A. Hamilton, "Damage to Groton-Based Sub is Worse Than Expected," *New London Day*, 10 September 2005.

28. Delays in first locating the stricken submarine and in getting personnel to the accident site with adequate equipment that could cut a hole through the exposed stern of the vessel contributed to the severity of this disaster. Gray, *Disasters of the Deep*, 162–71.

29. The entire eighteen-member crew was saved in this rapid rescue operation; ibid., 117.

30. A thorough chronicle of the *Kursk*'s foundering and subsequent steps to rescue and recover the crew is available at "The Kursk Accident" section of the Center for Non Proliferation Studies Web site, http://cns.miis.edu/reports/kursk.htm. A note later found on the recovered body of a crew member stated that a total of twenty-three men survived the initial explosion and waited in vain for rescue in the aft section of the vessel. See "Kursk Bodies Recovery Planned," *BBC News*, 22 August 2000, CNN.com, http://news.bbc.co.uk/2/hi/uk_news/scotland/891320.stm.

31. "The Kursk Disaster: Day By Day," 24 August 2000, *BBC News*, http://news.bbc. co.uk/1/hi/world/europe/894638.stm; and "Project 1855 Deep Submergence Rescue Vehicle," Global Security.org, http://www.globalsecurity.org/military/world/russia/ 1855.htm.

32. "Russian Submarine Rescue Bid Under Way," 14 August 2005, CNN, http://archives. cnn.com/2000/WORLD/europe/08/14/russia.submarine.06/index.html.

33. "Project 1855 Deep Submergence Rescue Vehicle."

34. "U.S. Analysis Suggests Crew Died Early," 17 August 2000, CNN.com, http://archives. cnn.com/2000/WORLD/europe/08/16/russia.submarine.04/.

35. "UK 'Underwater Helicopters' Arrives to Help Entombed Russian Sub," CNN.com, 19 August 2000, http://archives.cnn.com/2000/WORLD/europe/08/19/russian. submarine.03/.

36. "Norwegian Divers Open Hatch of Stricken Nuclear Sub," *People's Daily*, 21 August 2000, english.people.com.cn/english/200008/21/eng20000821_48656.html.

37. 王新森 [Wang Xinsen], "库尔斯克号祭 (一)" ["In Memoriam: The *Kursk* (1)"], 舰船知识 [*Naval & Merchant Ships*], no. 318 (March 2006): 46–49; and 王新森 [Wang Xinsen], "库尔斯克号祭 (二)" ["In Memoriam: The *Kursk* (2)"], 舰船知识 [*Naval & Merchant Ships*], no. 319 (April 2006): 54–58.

38. "Project 1855 Deep Submergence Rescue Vehicle," Global Security.org, http://www. globalsecurity.org/military/world/russia/1855.htm.

39. It is worth noting, however, that the decision to seek international assistance was still opposed by some quarters within the Russian military. Thus, Admiral Eduard Baltin, commander of the Russian Black Sea Fleet, stunned observers on 5 August—particularly in light of the *Kursk* tragedy—when he said that asking NATO countries for help was a mistake because the region in question was "filled with [Russian] military secrets." See Anna Arutunyan, "Scorpio's Subprize," *Moscow News*, http://english.mn.ru/english/issue.php?2005-30-1.

40. Michael Thurston, "Britain Trumpets Role in Rescuing Russian Sailors," *Defense News*, 8 August 2005, http://www.defensenews.com/story.php?F=1019711&C=navwar.

41. "Russian Mini-Submarine Rescue Efforts in the Pacific," Moscow News.com, http://www.mosnews.com/images/p/9956.shtml.

42. Iain Ballantyne and Yoshiharu Fukushima, "Happy Outcome for International Sub Rescue," *Warships IFR*, http://www.warshipsifr.com/pages/signal.html.

43. 靳涛 [Jin Tao], "前苏联和俄罗斯: 海军潜水器发展回顾" ["The Former Soviet Union and Russia: A Review of Diving Capability Development"], 当代海军 [*Modern Navy*], no. 146 (November 2005): 48–51. In this rendering of the operational history of the *Priz*-class rescue submersibles, it is mentioned that these platforms were used to investigate the crash site of the Korean airliner shot down by a Soviet fighter in 1983.

44. Here it is explained that "the U.S. and the former Soviet Union, these two maritime powers, themselves experienced serious accidents in the course of various patrols, and even when confronting the peril of destroyed vessels and lost crew members, still declined the assistance of foreign military forces." Liu, "Examining Submarine Rescue," 58.

45. 曾志荣 [Zeng Zhirong], "水下救生新锐: 北约潜艇救援系统" ["New Spirit for Undersea Rescue: NATO's Submarine Rescue System"], 舰船知识 [*Naval & Merchant Ships*], no. 312 (September 2005): 28–30. The analysis discusses the different advantages and disadvantages of both manned and unmanned rescue systems. It concludes that submarine rescues must generally be completed in fewer than seventy-two hours to be successful and in that regard describes the importance of air mobility for rescue submersibles. The author additionally points out that rescue submersibles can also perform nonmilitary tasks, such as retrieving the so-called black boxes from aircraft crash sites.

46. The U.S. Navy and Royal Navy *Scorpio*s are different platforms. The British *Scorpio* did the cutting that freed the *Priz*. The British rescue team arrived in Kamchatka two hours before its U.S. counterpart, and, in the interest of time, the U.S. team assisted the British team rather than unloading its gear. [Zhi Ge], "'天蝎'-45与LR5救生艇" ["The Heavenly Scorpion and the LR5 Rescue Vehicle"], 舰船知识 [*Naval and Merchant Ships*] (October 2005): 20–21. Interestingly, the authors have not encountered these photos in any other venue, either on the Web or in any Western naval publication.

47. Apparently, the Chinese navy regularly practices self-rescue via torpedo tube, using special breathing apparatus. See Wang, "An Insider Account," 44–45. There is some evidence that the PLA Navy is undertaking submarine rescue exercises with its newest classes of submarines. See Qian Xiaohu and Yu Zifu, "Submarine Probes Ways of Turning New Armament into Fighting Power," *Liberation Army Daily*, 21 August 2006.

48. For background on this cooperative initiative, see "China Implements Container Security Initiative at Port of Shanghai to Target and Pre-Screen Cargo Destined for U.S.," 28 April 2005, U.S. Customs and Border Protection, http://www.cbp.gov/xp/cgov/newsroom/news_releases/archives/2005_press_releases/042005/04282005.xml.

49. See Charles A. Meconis, "U.S.-China Confidence-Building More Important than Detargeting," *Global Beat Issue Brief*, no. 39, 14 July 1998, http://www.bu.edu/global beat/pubs/ib39.html.

50. Adam R. Cole, "Juneau, 31st MEU Arrive in Zhanjiang," *Marine Corps News*, 15 November 2006.

51. Phil Maguinn, "ISMERLO Comes to Aid of Disabled Russian Submarine," *Undersea Warfare* (Fall 2005), http://www.navy.mil/navydata/cno/n87/usw/issue_28/perfect.html.

52. Quoted in Kyung Choi, "Pacific Reach 2004, U.S. Foreign Navies Practice Submarine Rescue, Foster Cooperation, and Improve Interoperability," *Undersea Warfare* (Summer 2004), http://www.navy.mil/navydata/cno/n87/usw/issue_23/reach2004.htm. The primary mission of Submarine Development Squadron 5 (San Diego) is submarine rescue.

53. 赵宇 [Zhao Yu], "美日朝新澳举行潜艇救援演习" ["The US, Japan, Korea, Singapore and Australia Conduct a Submarine Rescue Exercise"], 当代海军 [*Modern Navy*] (July 2004): 44–45.

54. See the International Submarine Search and Rescue Liaison Office Web site at http://www.ismerlo.org/.

55. Mark O. Piggott, "ISMERLO Put into Action for Submarine Rescue Exercise," *Navy News Stand*, 15 June 2005, GlobalSecurity.org, http://www.globalsecurity.org/military/library/news/2005/06/mil-050615-nns01.htm.

56. The U.S. Navy's long history with submarine rescue has been noted in the Chinese military press. See, for example, 张艳明 [Zhang Yanming], "S-5死里逃生记" ["A Memoir of the S-5's Narrow Escape"], 环球军事 [*Global Military Affairs*], no. 28 (2004): 17–19.

57. HMCS *Chicoutimi* was disabled by a fire, which killed one officer, and was stranded in heavy seas in the North Atlantic without power. Absent ISMERLO's quick identification and dispatch of a towing vessel, the submarine would have sunk with significantly larger loss of life.

58. See the ISMERLO Web site at http://www.ismerlo.org/.

59. There are hundreds of detailed photos of Chinese submarines on the Internet; for example, see the Web site of the SinoDefence Forum at http://www.sinodefenceforum.com/.

60. See, for example, Liu, "Examining Submarine Rescue," 59; and Zeng, "New Spirit for Undersea Rescue," 28–30.

61. "AMAN 2007: Nations United against Maritime Terrorism," *Asia-Pacific Defense Forum*, no. 3 (2007), http://forum.apan-info.net/2007-3rd_quarter/aman/1.html.

Andrew S. Erickson

Prospects for Sino-U.S. Naval Cooperation against Avian Influenza

THIS CHAPTER SEEKS TO INCREASE AWARENESS among scholars, analysts, and policymakers concerning the potential danger posed by an outbreak of avian influenza and concerning Sino-American efforts thus far to militate against such a contingency. It is based on the author's preliminary examination of Chinese news reports, technical papers, and public statements. The study begins by explaining the unique importance of China, the Asia-Pacific's largest developing member and home to 800 million people who live in close contact with more than 15 billion poultry, to avian influenza prevention efforts. It then surveys a range of relevant Chinese domestic and cooperative initiatives. Avian influenza poses a particularly significant threat to residents of the Pacific Basin, including some three hundred thousand U.S. forces and their dependents. The strategic planning goals formulated by the U.S. Pacific Command (PACOM) to respond to a pandemic outbreak in the Asia-Pacific region are therefore outlined. Given the importance of cooperation between countries in combating a pandemic, the chapter also explores the challenges and opportunities inherent in Sino-American cooperation to combat avian influenza. This may be a particularly productive area of cooperation for the U.S. and Chinese militaries, perhaps especially their navies, which possess significant resources and expertise yet historically have had difficulty cooperating because of differences in political systems and national interests. The global threat of avian influenza may be one area in which Sino-American collective security interests are so great as to outweigh these competing concerns.

China as a Major Stakeholder

Avian influenza (禽流感 in Chinese), which has the potential to assume pandemic proportions, poses a large and growing threat to international security. The Severe Acute Respiratory Syndrome (SARS) outbreak of November 2002–July 2003 infected more than eight thousand in thirty-seven nations, killed roughly eight hundred, and reduced China's 2003 GDP by 0.7 percent.[1] According to the World Bank, an avian influenza pandemic could have an adverse economic impact of $2 trillion.[2] Experts estimate that an influenza pandemic in 1918 killed as many as 50 million individuals across the world.[3] While ten pandemics have erupted in the past three centuries, the eleventh will be the first to occur in an instantly interconnected world.[4]

No nation is safe from the pandemic influenza threat, and every nation is essential to defense efforts. In one indication of the importance of such efforts to international economic stability, Robert R. Morse, Citicorp's Asia-Pacific head, has stated, "We do not view the possibility of avian flu as an Asian issue, we view it as a global issue."[5] In response to this worldwide challenge, important progress has been made already.[6] At a major international conference to combat avian influenza, China's vice foreign minister Qiao Zonghuai noted that "our destinies are interconnected. In the fight against avian influenza, no country can stay safe by looking the other way."[7] Cooperation is vital to defend against pandemic influenza. Robust partnerships involving the United States, Japan, South Korea, Australia, New Zealand, Association of Southeast Asian Nations (ASEAN) member states, other Asia-Pacific allies, and nations around the world will be critical.[8]

However, several factors make China worthy of particular focus for U.S. policymakers and medical experts. China will likely be at the center of a pandemic influenza crisis. China possesses 20 percent of the world's population and more than 14 percent of its disease burden.[9] It is home to some 800 million people who live in close contact with more than 15 billion poultry, and it thus possesses a potential reservoir for the incubation of avian influenza that is perhaps unequaled anywhere in the world.[10] China also has "1,332 species of migratory birds, over 13 percent of the world's total."[11] The persistence of conditions analogous to those detailed above over decades explains why "most flu pandemics in recorded history originated in South China" (including, possibly, the 1918 Spanish Flu, as well as the 1957 Asian flu, and 1968 Hong Kong flu).[12] Since 2003 at least fourteen people have died from avian influenza in China.[13] China's massive scale and vulnerable populations thus give it a unique importance in disease control measures. Despite continuing challenges in relations between the United States and China, therefore, no effort to stem the spread of infectious disease will be complete without cooperation between what are respectively the world's largest developed and developing nations.

As two Asia-Pacific nations potentially threatened by pandemic influenza, the United States and China have significant shared interests in the area of the prevention of large-scale outbreaks of devastating infectious disease. The two nations also share a strategic interest in fighting other unconventional threats such as terrorism.[14] Thanks to its largely apolitical and nonreligious nature, the combating of pandemics, even more than counterterrorism, offers common ground upon which to build a basis for bilateral and multilateral cooperation. Given the important work that remains to be done before effective cooperation between the United States and China can be fully realized, however, this chapter will be devoted to demonstrating the extent to which the two great powers share an interest in combating avian influenza, and suggesting how robust collaboration toward this end can more fully be realized.

China's Current and Potential Contributions

Dr. Jilan Liu, special advisor for Center for Health and Aging, National Bureau of Asian Research, assesses that "China experiences sporadic cases of avian influenza every year, but seems to track, handle, and isolate the cases well."[15] Dr. Liu explains: "China's overall preparedness for disaster and epidemic response has improved enormously since 2003. Many people in the world still have fresh memories of China's initial ineffective response to SARS in 2003. But most people do not know how quickly and effectively the Chinese government learned from it and put that learning to good use in building a very good disaster response system. Disaster planning has been beefed up considerably."[16]

China has already allocated more than $246.6 million for domestic efforts to control avian influenza.[17] These efforts include building a network of monitoring stations to track transmission of avian influenza by migratory birds and its infection of humans.[18] Chinese officials are simultaneously working to raise awareness, coordinate preventative measures including extensive poultry vaccination, and build a more efficient reporting system between provinces.[19] The last is an attempt to address the fact that, particularly in recent years, interprov-ince coordination has posed a particular challenge for Beijing. The $100 mil-lion China Information System for Disease Control and Prevention (CISDP) is "currently the largest in the world for reporting infectious disease cases." CISDP uses Web-based, real-time data reporting on thirty-seven diseases (includ-ing high pathogenicity avian influenza and SARS).[20] China is also working to reform its overall healthcare policy and infrastructure, which faces challenges in the areas of "population size and diversity; disparities in economic welfare between rural and urban China; insufficient or inconsistent medical education and training; misaligned incentives for primary care and early health activities; and a lack of standards within and among health institutions."[21] Although it still has some improvements to make, China has made rapid progress in using health information technology, on which it already spends $700 million annu-ally. The 2003–10 Ministry of Health guidelines for health information tech-nology development in China "call for the introduction of EHRS [electronic health records] and regional health information networks to be implemented throughout the country."[22]

China has been similarly proactive in the international arena. Beijing has a significant history of health diplomacy on which to draw, having sent 6,500 health workers to aid 72 million people in forty-two countries from 1963–82.[23] Since 2001 China's Yunnan Province has participated formally in the Mekong Basin Disease Surveillance (MBDS) network, which has been credited with facilitating a coordinated regional response to the 2003 SARS crisis. The scal-able nature of MBDS offers the potential to expand it to cover additional nations.[24] Since 2002 Beijing has organized high-level health dialogue mech-anisms with Washington, Moscow, London, and Tokyo. In reflection of the special importance that it attaches to avian influenza as a nontraditional secu-rity threat in Southeast Asia, China has also done so with ASEAN, organizing in 2004 a "China-ASEAN special meeting on the control of avian influenza, which committed all parties to implement the meeting's recommendations," and subsequently a China-ASEAN Public Health Fund to finance relevant ini-tiatives.[25] In 2005 China adopted the World Health Assembly's International Health Regulations (IHR 2005). As part of a larger opening up post-SARS, this facilitated the sharing of information on communicable diseases with the World Health Organization and foreign scientists.[26] That November, in a welcome contrast to Indonesian claims of "viral sovereignty," China accepted WHO requests to deliver additional avian influenza virus samples to facilitate international research.[27] In April 2006 Dr. David Nabarro, UN system coor-dinator for influenza, met with Chinese officials "to discuss China's role in the international control of avian influenza and preparation for dealing with any possible influenza pandemic."[28] During that same month, China hosted the "Asia-Pacific Economic Cooperation Symposium on Emerging Infectious Diseases." Other relevant forums in which China participates include the ASEAN+3 Summit, the East Asia Summit, and the Asia Europe Meeting.[29]

Chinese universities, government research institutions, and corporations have responded to the growing challenge of avian influenza by conducting what official Chinese media sources report to be cutting-edge research in the prevention and treatment of infectious diseases.[30] A wide variety of research is being conducted by students and faculty members at academic institutions all over China, apparently with particularly prolific contributions from the Chinese Academy of Agricultural Sciences (中国农业科学院), China Agricultural University (中国农业大学), Shandong Agricultural University, (山东农业大学), and Yangzhou University (扬州大学).[31] Academic conferences have been held periodically in China to disseminate research results.[32] In December 2005 China's Ministry of Agriculture announced that Harbin Veterinary Research Institute had developed the "world's first live vaccine against bird flu."[33] In 2005 China's State Food and Drug Administration implemented a fast-track approval process for pandemic influenza vaccines.[34] "A major advantage of China's research into the bird flu virus is our technical reserve and capacity to meet emergencies," Vice Science Minister Liu Yanhua concludes. "They are powerful resources."[35]

Having played a significant role in the handling of the 2003 SARS crisis, China's People's Liberation Army (PLA) can claim valuable experience with regard to infectious disease control measures.[36] In 2004 the PLA published a practical pamphlet on techniques for dealing with avian influenza.[37] In fact, due to its large network of high-level hospitals and research facilities, the PLA holds jurisdiction over a crucial element of China's disease prevention responsibility and expertise. Academy of Military Medical Sciences researcher Li Song recently reported that his team had "completed clinical experiments" concerning a new Chinese drug similar to Tamiflu "and find it is more effective on humans than Tamiflu."[38] While little data are available in the West concerning the specifics of such achievements, the PLA is so central to China's medical infrastructure that it would probably be difficult to engage deeply with China in the prevention of avian influenza without also engaging with elements of the PLA.

U.S.–China Cooperation to Date

In domestic, bilateral, and international forums, the United States and China have already made considerable, if preliminary, progress in combating avian influenza. In April 2005, for instance, the U.S.-China Global Issues Forum began to discuss such matters as public health.[39] In October 2005 Chinese minister of health Gao Qiang signed an agreement with the U.S. Department of Health and Human Services to enhance cooperation on avian influenza and other infectious diseases.[40] On 19 November 2005, the United States and China announced a "Joint Initiative on Avian Influenza," through which the countries' respective ministries of health and agriculture will "strengthen cooperation" concerning vaccines, detection, and planning.[41] Such bilateral measures could offer a model for U.S. cooperation with other nations.[42]

At the January 2006 Ministerial Pledging Conference for Avian Influenza, attended by seven hundred representatives of more than one hundred nations, including the United States, Chinese premier Wen Jiabao stated that "China will continue to actively participate in international cooperation in avian influenza prevention and control, share our experience with related countries and help them fight avian influenza."[43] Paul Wolfowitz, president of the World Bank, emphasized, "By hosting this event in Beijing, the Chinese Government is sending a powerful message . . . that we urgently need a global commitment to share information quickly and openly, and to find ways to work together effectively."[44] Such information exchange has already been facilitated by a draft agreement signed on 20 December 2005, affirming China's intention to share "virus samples isolated from human H5N1 cases" with the World Health Organization.[45] At the end of the conference, representatives matched their words with substantive actions. The World Bank agreed to contribute $500 million; the Asian Development Bank, $470 million; the United States, the largest national share at $334 million; and China, $10 million (in addition to its significant relevant domestic spending, as detailed earlier).[46] As of October 2006, virtually all the $1.9 billion granted at the Pledging Conference had been committed.[47]

In September 2006 presidents George W. Bush and Hu Jintao agreed to establish a Strategic Economic Dialogue.[48] Five meetings were held between 2006 and 2008. Health and food and drug safety issues were discussed in two subforums: by the U.S. Department of Health and Human Services and Chinese Ministry of Health in a U.S.–China Health Care Forum, and by the U.S. trade representative and the Chinese vice premier responsible for trade under a Joint Commission on Commerce and Trade. Drawing on these improved contacts, in November 2008, the U.S. Food and Drug Administration officially opened offices in Beijing, Shanghai, and Guangzhou to help ensure the safety of Chinese exports to the United States.[49] Since April 2009 these efforts have continued via U.S.-China Strategic and Economic Dialogue, established by presidents Barack Obama and Hu Jintao.[50] On 6 May 2009 Hu telephoned Obama to express "sincere condolences" for two recent American H1N1 influenza fatalities and to express China's determination to "maintain communication with the World Health Organization, the United States, and other parties, as well as strengthen cooperation, to jointly deal with this challenge to human health and safety."[51]

Other examples of Sino-American cooperation regarding pandemic preparedness include the Joint Science Academies' statement on avian influenza and infectious diseases, whose signatories include Lu Yongxiang of the Chinese Academy of Sciences and Ralph Cicerone of the U.S. National Academy of Sciences. Noting that SARS caused as much as $30 billion in economic damage, and affirming the accomplishments of the Beijing ministerial pledging conference, the statement calls for "coordinated actions on a global scale by a whole spectrum of stakeholders including governments, scientists, public health experts, veterinary health experts, economists, representatives of the business community, and the general public."[52] To ensure that these recommendations are carried out, however, it is necessary to explore in depth the potential roles of the U.S. and Chinese militaries in combating avian influenza. No pandemic disease-prevention efforts will be complete without the robust involvement of these two powerful and influential organizations. Given the U.S. military's strong presence throughout the Asia-Pacific region as well as the abundance of relevant information thanks to its relative transparency, its potential role in such efforts will now be examined in detail.

The U.S. Pacific Command's Role and Contributions

The United States and China share a tremendous interest in preventing outright, or at least containing and mitigating the effects of, an outbreak of pandemic influenza. Like Beijing, Washington has a strong interest in maintaining a global environment that is safe for economic development and trade. In contrast to China, however, the United States in recent decades has had both the capability and the willingness to use its military to further such goals on a global scale. The U.S. military is thus often used to provide security for the benefit of not only American citizens but also those of other nations around the world, as when the U.S. Navy secures the economically vital global maritime commons against criminal activities, piracy, terrorism, or even the actions of hostile states that might seek to disrupt it. One potential instrument for securing the global health environment in the event of a medical crisis, therefore, is the U.S. military. Yet to provide such public goods effectively, the U.S. military must first be able to protect its own personnel and equip them to perform their duties even under the most adverse conditions.

In light of its substantial global responsibilities, the U.S. military cannot afford to be immobilized by pandemic influenza. Yet the widespread deployment of U.S. forces and the sheer scope of their military operations illustrate the difficulties inherent in guarding against this contingency. This challenge has been recognized, and extensive preparations have already been made. The Department of Defense and the Department of Veterans Affairs are envisioned as a critical foundation. According to the U.S. federal government's official Web site for information related to avian and pandemic influenza: "We currently have pandemic influenza plans in place that address how we would take care of DOD [Department of Defense] and VA [Veterans Administration] patient populations and others, as well. DOD and VA are authorized by several laws and policies to provide care to persons who are not their usual patients in the event of national or local emergencies or disasters."[53]

Within the U.S. government, efforts to prepare for pandemic influenza are apportioned as follows: the Department of Homeland Security has overall responsibility, the Department of Health and Human Services oversees domestic efforts and medical issues, the Department of State manages public diplomacy (and most overseas issues), and the Department of Agriculture manages issues relating to animals, including birds.[54] A variety of other agencies also cooperate in these efforts.[55]

PACOM, due to its scope of operations and interactions with regions in Asia known to be potential incubators of avian influenza, is also on the front lines of the pandemic influenza threat.[56] Although not itself a lead agency in avian influenza prevention efforts, PACOM is preparing to support the U.S. government in its effort to combat domestic and international outbreaks of influenza.

In the event of pandemic influenza, PACOM must be prepared to maintain the operational capabilities of U.S. forces and to protect military troops, civilians, and dependents as well as PACOM's military bases and facilities. This will be a difficult task: PACOM's area of operation spans 169 million square kilometers over sixteen time zones (roughly half the Earth's surface) and encompasses thirty-six nations that are collectively home to more than half of the world's population, the world's six largest armed forces, five of the seven U.S. mutual defense treaties, and 35 percent of U.S. trade (more than $550 billion).[57] The dimensions of PACOM's responsibilities are extended by the fact that about 350,000 U.S. troops (one-fifth of the total U.S. armed forces) are based in the region.

Given the potential for pandemic influenza to spread rapidly and to inflict devastation on human societies, PACOM must develop coordinated capabilities that can rapidly respond to, address, and continue to ensure the function of relevant organizations during such an outbreak. Because this is a task that no nation can accomplish alone, proper prevention and treatment will hinge upon multilateral cooperation. Effective information sharing will thus be essential to the success of such a broad-based effort. Because of the potential need to actively involve law enforcement agencies and even militaries from many countries in the Asia-Pacific region and around the world, significant mutual trust is essential if preparation efforts are to succeed.

U.S. Preparations to Protect Troops, Dependents, and Asian Neighbors

To assist U.S. forces, military dependents, and citizens of other countries as they prepare for an influenza pandemic, PACOM has developed a set of planning goals to address all foreseeable contingencies. These goals involve regional cooperation, preparation and prevention, containment, and recovery.

PACOM is currently seeking to improve the regional security environment by cooperating with Asia-Pacific nations. PACOM is well aware that preparations for avian influenza have been more thoroughly tested in some Asian countries than in the United States, which thus far has been fortunate not to have suffered from H5N1 avian influenza. The United States has much to learn from experts in the countries that have experienced clusters of H5N1 infection.[58] To facilitate this learning process, the United States plans to build a Pacific region coordination center that will "allow rapid communications, coordination, and information sharing among the 43 [Pacific] nations, their militaries, international organizations, and U.S. interagency representatives active in the Pacific."[59] It is hoped that this effort will forge a positive basis for collective health security.

Two additional aspects of current operations to shape the health security environment involve preparation and prevention.[60] Toward this end, in October 2005 PACOM sponsored the Public Health Emergency Officer Influenza Seminar in Pearl Harbor, Hawaii.[61] Information awareness is an essential component of security maintenance. For this reason, the Military

Medical Laboratories Syndromic Surveillance Network is actively monitoring more than thirty sites in Southeast Asia for the eruption of infectious diseases. In the event of an actual outbreak, laboratories in Indonesia and Thailand will help both the host nation and WHO's Surveillance Network for Influenza to better track the spread and evolution of the disease so that appropriate countermeasures can be taken in a timely manner. In a recent issue of *Nature*, medical experts urged that this existing network of rapid response laboratories should be enhanced in collaboration with WHO to emulate U.S. Naval Medical Research Units, which were established after World War II to protect U.S. troops overseas.[62] To minimize the chances that U.S. forces and related personnel will contract and transmit avian influenza, the U.S. Department of Defense has been stockpiling the drug Tamiflu at PACOM bases. As of February 2006, 6 million doses had been stored.[63] In November 2005 PACOM held a "Tabletop Exercise" to test preparations for a pandemic. PACOM has used a variety of venues including ASEAN, Chiefs of Defense meetings, and Noncombatant Evacuation Operations planning meetings to help provide forums for discussions on pandemic influenza and to share planning ideas with a number of foreign government and military leaders.

In the event of a pandemic, PACOM would support the relevant U.S. agencies as they worked with Asia-Pacific nations and WHO to contain the outbreak. Given the potential of the United States to provide substantial aid, the U.S. government would also likely work to support any recovery efforts that might ensue because of the outbreak. Potential regional challenges stemming from an avian influenza outbreak in the Asia-Pacific region might include damage to the regional economy and threats to domestic stability.[64] Economic threats could involve the disruption of transnational supply chains as well as reductions in foreign direct investment and local spending. During the 2003 SARS outbreak, for instance, "110 out of the 164 countries with which China had diplomatic relations placed at least some restrictions on travel to China."[65] "International travel to affected areas fell by 50 to 70 percent, hotel occupancy dropped by more than 60 percent, and businesses in tourism-related areas failed."[66] This caused between $50 and $100 billion in economic damage.[67] The Asia-Pacific region alone is estimated to have borne $40 billion of this cost.[68] Threats to domestic stability could occur in those Southeast Asian nations that rely heavily on poultry production as well as in those Pacific island states that might be particularly vulnerable were a significant portion of their relatively small populations to be threatened with infectious disease. At a panel discussion at the Asia Society in New York City in 2006, senior UN system influenza coordinator Dr. David Nabarro stated that the U.S. government had made commendable efforts to prepare for pandemic influenza but that far more international cooperation was needed to address the threat.[69]

PLA Preparations

China's government has organized a comprehensive disaster response system relevant to combating avian influenza. Dr. Liu explains:

> China's disaster preparedness planning process is led by the central government (the State Council), and all ministries, (with the Ministry of Health and Chinese Disease Control and Prevention in an important position). It has a clear command and control structure penetrating all levels of government throughout the entire country. The roles and responsibilities of all the hospitals and other sectors are clearly defined. The supply chain connects directly with manufacturers (with built in just-in-time production mechanisms) and transportation companies. The coordination and communication mechanisms have the capacity to reach large populations pretty much anywhere in the country, involving not only the formal structure to connect all the organizations, but also the media and internet to connect volunteers and population at large. China's surveillance system is now perhaps the most sophisticated in the world.[70]

The PLA has an important role to play as part of this larger structure and process. All elements of the Chinese armed forces engage in societal activities (e.g., disaster relief and some infrastructure development). An unknown number of civilians (technical specialists, administrative and custodial staff, administrative contractors, and local government-paid staff) also support PLA operations. The PLA is developing in a fashion that promises to better support such nontraditional missions as combating avian influenza. In the fall of 2008, a PLA officer at the Academy of Military Science outlined the following trends: new laws and regulations have greatly facilitated PLA capacity building in humanitarian assistance and disaster relief. China's National Defense Act has made disaster relief one of the PLA's major tasks. The State Council and the Central Military Commission (CMC) promulgated relevant regulations in June 2005. In October 2006 the CMC issued a disaster relief contingency plan that discusses in detail guiding principles and specific measures for implementation and regulates coordination between civil and military authorities. When a serious disaster occurs, the State Council will set up leading committees, with the participation of leading agencies, to which the PLA will send representatives (including from the General Staff). Local governments will establish disaster relief committees, invite military officers of equivalent rank to attend discussions, and task the PLA with disaster relief work if necessary. If the situation is urgent, local military forces should get to work immediately and report to the senior command. The PLA's combat operations command system supports disaster relief work. All army coordination work is overseen by an emergency response officer under the General Staff Department. New operational sectors above the regimental level have been established for humanitarian assistance and disaster relief work. Because China constantly suffers from natural disasters, the PLA is strengthening relevant training and making preparations. Under the 2008 guidelines for military training, disaster relief training has become daily routine training for military units. Troops also conduct exercises with local governments. Equipment has been improved for professional relief teams.

An excellent example of the PLA's significant ability to respond to natural disasters within China is its rapid response to the tragic Great Sichuan Earthquake of May 2008. In Dr. Liu's assessment,

China's 2008 Beichuan earthquake was a major test of its disaster preparedness system. It responded very promptly, very effectively overall. All of those major elements were tested and they scored very well. Of course, some issues were identified. With an earthquake of that magnitude, nobody can respond perfectly. But it was as good as any country could have pulled together, much better than America's response to Hurricane Katrina. I feel very confident about China's disaster preparedness, based on their response to the earthquake. A response to an outbreak of avian influenza would have some different elements and resource management, but the response to this major earthquake demonstrated that China has its domestic disaster response system pretty much worked out, including their communicable disease surveillance system, and their CDC's response mechanism. China's disaster response system, including its pandemic response system, is probably as good as any nation has currently.[71]

China has begun small-scale, low-level military cooperation with ASEAN regarding humanitarian assistance and disaster relief. For now, in one PLA officer's opinion, "the political significance exceeds the practical significance." China–ASEAN cooperation is a good model for China–U.S. cooperation, but cooperation should be increased among Asia-Pacific nations as well. Because this kind of cooperation is less sensitive, it can be implemented in three ways: (1) promoting exchanges between and among different nations' military academies; (2) conducting joint exercises and training and sending small teams of officers to other countries for training to improve their capabilities; and (3) enhancing cooperation between defense sectors, particularly at the higher levels, to "learn from experiences." The officer clearly stated his opinion that "if disaster relief cooperation stops at the academic level, it is not meaningful."

U.S.–China Military Medical Cooperation: Challenges and Opportunities

The fight against avian influenza has proven fertile ground for enhanced levels of U.S.–China cooperation overall. There is now potential for both countries to build upon this success in the area of military medical information exchange. Military medical information and related technology lacks direct application to offensive warfare for the United States and China, both parties to the Biological Weapons Convention, and is abundantly available in both countries.[72] China's substantial experience and expertise concerning avian influenza, particularly within its military, raises the possibility of both China and the United States benefiting substantially. Concerns that such mutual benefit could not be achieved, in part because of differing conceptions of transparency, has frustrated previous military exchanges. Perhaps there is now a chance to bridge that gap. Admiral William J. Fallon, former commander of PACOM, has already extended an invitation to the Chinese military to engage in a discussion concerning avian influenza.[73] In March 2006 a PACOM medical team met with medical leaders in the PLA to discuss pandemic influenza planning efforts and opportunities for the U.S. military and the PLA to work together. If the United States and China can engage in military exercises, surely they can cooperate to combat avian influenza, a mutual enemy that spares no one on the basis of nationality.

To be sure, progress must be made in several areas for this goal to be realized. First, the overall strategic situation will likely influence Beijing's willingness to participate. A prominent Chinese academic has told the author that the 2003 Joint Statement of the ASEAN+3 Labour Ministers Meeting in Mataram, Indonesia, and the March 2004 China-ASEAN Joint Declaration on Dealing with the Avian Influenza Crisis were positive steps, but that the ASEAN forum is "inefficient in crisis."[74] At the same time, traditional security issues and historical issues impose limits on cooperation. For instance, the United States held the Pacific Military Management Seminar in Hawaii to discuss cooperation in non-traditional security fields, including how to establish a cooperative mechanism and structure. China wanted to attend but cancelled because of U.S. arms sales to Taiwan. Choosing the appropriate counterparts with whom to raise the possibility of cooperation is also important. A PLA officer has told the author that the subject of avian influenza is too specialized for many PLA officers to address, and suggests that the General Logistics Department and the Health Ministry have the most relevant expertise.

Perhaps most importantly in terms of specific challenges, the timely flow of information must be improved. A challenge common to the CISDCP and MBDS networks is a lack of integration between surveillance, data sharing, and response between the animal and human health sectors.[75] Minister of Health Zhu Chen, for instance, has advocated increasing surveillance of animal health. This may help to bridge the gap and align prevention efforts more closely with the needs of developing societies that cannot easily afford to lose farm animals to zoonotic viruses.[76] International cooperation faces challenges stemming from both the Chinese domestic political landscape and concerns that Chinese scientists receive proper credit for their research overseas.[77] Aside from domestic politics, one major reason for the minimization of U.S.–China military contacts has been U.S. concern that military transparency and cooperative benefits will be asymmetric. This discrepancy might be partially addressed, however, by first determining which areas demand an absolute equality of exchange, and which disparities might be compensated for by alternative areas of comparative advantage and willingness to share information and other resources. Cooperation undertaken in response to the mutual threat of avian influenza could be an excellent place to begin efforts to improve overall military relations between the United States and China.

During the 2003 SARS crisis, which has been described as "the most severe social or political crisis encountered by China's leadership" since Tiananmen, Premier Wen Jiabao told fellow officials that "the health and security of the people, overall state of reform, development, and stability, and China's national interest and image are at stake."[78] Yet there is a widespread perception, both inside and outside China, that Beijing's attempts to control information backfired, thereby hampering international response efforts and undermining domestic public confidence.[79] Recently, however, there appears to be growing official recognition that transparency is essential to good governance and public safety. An October 2005 *China Daily* opinion editorial underscores the importance of increasing transparency in furthering China's own national interests:

> Unlike the SARS . . . outbreak in 2003, when the nation was in panic . . . [and] the authorities' initial foot-dragging left the public nervous . . . we can see a substantial change in the government's response this time around. The response has been prompt. . . . More importantly, information sharing with international health institutions appears to be timely, smooth and comprehensive. These are some of the lessons learnt from the fight against the SARS epidemic. . . . A better-informed and thus better-prepared public is conducive to its own safety in the face of a life-threatening epidemic. . . . There is no harm if people are honestly informed about what is happening and what is at stake. And there obviously is room for improvements regarding transparency. Also, we find it imperative to upgrade our involvement in international efforts to cope with bird flu.[80]

Although the *China Daily* typically contains content that is different from official domestic Chinese-language media sources in order to influence a Western audience, the outlook expressed here is refreshingly realistic and positive, in marked contrast to previous silence or even questionable statements concerning this issue. In any case, it is clear that, in the words of Liu Depei, Chinese Academy of Medical Sciences, "China has learned a great deal from its experience with SARS."[81]

Furthermore, as unexpected challenges surrounding America's own highly disappointing Hurricane Katrina relief efforts in October 2005 demonstrate, responding to large-scale natural disasters is inherently difficult and requires substantial preparation, coordination, and learning from previous problems.[82] Avian influenza, which has the potential to inflict far greater human suffering with far fewer warning signs, could challenge government response efforts unlike any other natural disaster. At the same time, however, preventative and emergency measures can drastically reduce the impact of a potential pandemic. As the policy measures and official leadership and media statements listed earlier suggest, Beijing is to be commended for its continued, and apparently strengthening, efforts in this regard.

The United States and China are now at the point where their common challenges outweigh their differences. Dr. Liu offers a major example:

> One of the issues that China faces, and the entire world faces, would be the size of its stockpile of vaccines, in the event of an outbreak of avian influenza. The fact that it takes quite long to produce vaccines for the specific string makes just-in-time production difficult. Ideally, it should have enough H5N1 vaccines for the 1st (and 2nd) dose for

a large population. For a small-scale outbreak, China should have enough vaccines and medication, plus a strong system of isolation to bring it under control; for a larger outbreak, it is more uncertain. But this is an issue for the entire world.[83]

A Logical Place to Begin

Cooperation against the threat of avian influenza could build mutual confidence and generate momentum for initiatives in other areas. As Dr. Liu explains, "There is already considerable collaboration between China and the U.S.: some very successful, some less so. The most effective areas for cooperation are narrowly defined fields of science and research, and of course, in commerce."[84] In addition to enhancing communication, the building of more robust and extensive bilateral contacts could give both sides a healthy respect for each other's capabilities, thereby reducing the chance of dangerous miscalculations. Ongoing tensions in U.S.–China relations are based in part upon differences in national interests that are likely to endure. A positive bilateral military relationship alone will not resolve those tensions. But such a relationship could offer realistic first steps that might serve to outline and safeguard mutual interests and thereby provide incentives to avoid unnecessary escalation and avert serious crises as the two nations seek to realize stable, if competitive, coexistence. China, situated at the potential epicenter of an avian influenza outbreak, has a particularly vital role to play in infectious disease control. Already, according to Dr. David Nabarro, Asia as a whole has made substantial progress in preparation for an influenza pandemic.[85]

One way to increase mutual understanding and goodwill would be for Chinese and U.S. researchers to translate unclassified Chinese documents— starting with those concerning avian influenza and related public health threats—into English and to facilitate their wider distribution among Western experts. Such dissemination could increase Western knowledge of Chinese advances in disease prevention and control, which are reportedly numerous and rapid—particularly in specific technological areas. This might help to set the stage for follow-on medical research—perhaps supported with an innovative combination of government and private sector funding—that could exploit the synergy between U.S. technology and analysis and Chinese ability to conduct large-scale experiments and biotechnological production in a cost-effective manner and without an excessive regulatory burden in areas that do not pertain directly to human health. Moreover, Western analysts and scholars could use knowledge of China's disease prevention efforts and security challenges to augment their understanding of China from a broader perspective.

It must be emphasized that a more robust and nuanced spectrum of U.S. analyses of China, such as could be facilitated by greater transparency concerning Chinese military medical progress, is in China's own national interest. After all, like its counterparts around the world, the U.S. military is duty bound to anticipate and prepare for worst-case scenarios. But more optimistic projections and positive-sum suggestions produced by other analysts who are free from such responsibilities are extremely important as well. Such analyses could further elucidate the great benefits that the United States and China might derive from effective cooperation in a wide range of areas. Otherwise, exclusive focus on the possibility of conflict could negatively influence U.S.–China relations by overshadowing these other vital areas.

At very least, the origins and purposes of military medical and other analyses should be made transparent where possible by their authors and kept in proper perspective by those who consume them. This can be facilitated by efforts on both sides of the Pacific, even in the absence of explicit intergovernmental cooperation. There is substantial room for improvement in both nations. American analysts must strive to better understand important nuances of increasingly robust (though often still somewhat opaque) Chinese policy debates in order to differentiate between official government policy and opinionated reports from China's ever-livelier media. This effort would be greatly facilitated if more Americans would develop their often-inadequate language skills—Beijing can be surprisingly transparent *in Chinese*. Chinese analysts, who already tend to be far more capable linguistically than their American counterparts and quite sophisticated in their ability to trace political debates, would do well to document their assertions with ample specific references, such as footnotes, to explain where they obtained their information. While slowly improving and already achieved by some highly advanced journals such as the Chinese Academy of Social Sciences' *American Studies* (美国研究), the overall dearth of such citations in both Chinese scholarship and official government reports makes it extremely difficult even for foreigners fluent in Chinese to assess the quality of data being presented. This is particularly true in the exacting fields of science and medicine, in which a vaccine's efficacy must be proven in a manner that is replicable by experts around the world, not simply announced without supporting evidence.

These significant challenges should not distract us from the larger issues at stake: that a significant threat to humanity can be, and must be, averted. This collective responsibility requires cooperation across national boundaries regardless of political differences. A sense of humility and respect is vital for effective cooperation to be realized in practice, however. As Dr. Liu observes,

> Both China and [the] U.S. have the capacity to play leadership roles in the response to pandemic outbreak. The U.S. and China need to build infrastructure for cooperation and coordination if joint leadership and response is needed. At present, there are lots of exchanges; avian influenza experts in the West already collaborate with their Chinese counterparts, and vice versa. But it needs to be broadened and deepened. Again, if joint leadership and response is expected, ongoing scientific collaboration needs to be applied to policy and command structures. A superiority complex on the part of any country could jeopardize effectiveness when it comes to working together. Under time pressure, the negative effects of such an attitude would be intensified.[86]

In this spirit, through translation and analysis of Chinese sources, I have endeavored to increase awareness among Western scholars, analysts, and policymakers of important Chinese developments and their potential relevance to Sino-American cooperation against avian influenza. The bottom line is that differences in other national interests should not prevent the United States and China—or, for that matter, all other nations—from recognizing their growing collective interests in combating emerging threats such as that of pandemic influenza. As Admiral Michael Mullen stated in 2005 as U.S. Chief of Naval Operations, "in today's interconnected world, acting in the global interest is likely to mean acting in one's national interest as well. In other words, exercising sovereignty and contributing to global security are no longer mutually exclusive events."[87] And as a Chinese proverb cautions, "disasters know no boundaries" (水火无情).

Notes

The views expressed in this study are solely those of the author as a private individual. This study is based only on publicly available sources and does not represent the official position or analysis of the U.S. Navy or any other organization of the U.S. government. A previous version of this chapter appeared as Andrew S. Erickson, "Combating a Truly Collective Threat: Sino-American Military Cooperation against Avian Influenza," *Global Health Governance: The Scholarly Journal for the New Health Security Paradigm* 1, no. 1 (January 2007), http://ghgj.org/Erickson_1.1_Combating.htm. The author is grateful to Stephanie Black, Robert Goldstein, Yanzhong Huang, and Jilan Liu for their helpful comments and suggestions. Particular appreciation is due to Claire Topal for her extensive insights and assistance throughout the course of this research project.

1. Yanzhong Huang, "Pursuing Health as Foreign Policy: The Case of China," *Indiana Journal of Global Legal Studies* 17, no. 1 (Winter 2010): 115.

2. Carin Zissis, "The Potential Avian Flu Pandemic," Council on Foreign Relations, 21 November 2006, http://www.cfr.org/publication/12061/.

3. Ibid.

4. "An Analysis of the Potential Impact of the H5N1 Avian Flu Virus," Food Industry QRT Pandemic Analysis, August 2005, http://www.cidrap.umn.edu/cidrap/files/47/panbus plan.pdf, 3, 6.

5. "Bird Flu Tops Agenda at APEC CEO Summit," *China Daily*, 18 November 2005, available at http://www.chinadaily.com.cn/.

6. See, for example, "Japan-WHO Joint Meeting on Early Response to Potential Influenza Pandemic," Tokyo, Japan, 12–13 January 2006, WHO Web site, http://www.wpro.who.int/sites/csr/meetings/mtg_20050112-13.htm; Shigeru Omi, "Opening Remarks," http://www.wpro.who.int/NR/rdonlyres/2FFE9F2B-1369-44C4-9281-761747BF8A95/0/RDSpeech.pdf; and "Asian Countries Commit to an Early Response to the Threat of an Influenza Pandemic," Manila, 16 January 2006, http://www.wpro.who.int/media_centre/press_releases/pr_20060116.htm.

7. Zhao Huanxin, "World Meet Seeks Funds to Combat Epidemic," *China Daily*, 18 January 2006, available at http://www.chinadaily.com.cn/. For an expression of similar sentiments, see "Nations Must Rally to Combat Avian Flu," *China Daily*, 18 January 2006, available at http://www.chinadaily.com.cn/; and Zhang Feng, "WHO Calls for Pandemic Preparation," *China Daily*, 18 January 2006, available at http://www.china daily.com.cn/.

8. See, for example, "Japan-WHO Joint Meeting on Early Response"; Shigeru Omi, "Opening Remarks"; "Asian Countries Commit to an Early Response."

9. Huang, "Pursuing Health as Foreign Policy," 106.

10. Jim Fisher-Thompson, "U.S. Officials Praise China for Efforts to Combat Bird Flu Prompt Investigation, Reporting of Suspected Cases Key to Preventing Epidemic," *Washington File*, Bureau of International Information Programs, U.S. Department of State, 2 March 2006.

11. Liang Chao, "300 Stations to Prevent Epidemic," *China Daily*, 2 December 2005, available at http://www.chinadaily.com.cn/.

12. Christine Loh, "Lessons for SARS: Spread of Virus Shows China and Hong Kong's Growing Pains," YaleGlobal, 9 April 2003, formerly available at http://yaleglobal.yale.edu/article.print?id=1308.

13. "China Confirms One New Human Case of Bird Flu," Xinhua News, 10 January 2007, http://news.xinhuanet.com/english/2007-01/10/content_5587731.htm.

14. For further support of this assertion, see Jonathan D. Pollack, ed., *Strategic Surprise? U.S.-China Relations in the Early Twenty-First Century* (Newport, RI: Naval War

College Press, 2003). Washington, however, does not accept Beijing's expansive definition of terrorism, which includes political activities.

15. Dr. Liu also serves as a consultant, Joint Commission International, headquartered in Chicago; and as visiting professor, Renmin University in Beijing.

16. Dr. Jilan Liu, e-mail interview with author, 12 February 2009.

17. Zhao Huanxin, "2b Yuan Earmarked to Control Epidemic," *China Daily*, 3 November 2005, available at http://www.chinadaily.com.cn/.

18. Liang, "300 Stations to Prevent Epidemic"; Wu Jiao, "Network Built to Monitor Migrant Birds," *China Daily*, 2 March 2006, available at http://www.chinadaily.com.cn/; and Zhang Feng and Zhao Huanxin, "Monitoring Increases to Fight Flu," *China Daily*, 21 November 2005, available at http://www.chinadaily.com.cn/. See also Zhang Feng, "Early Detection of Human Cases Vital in Treatment," *China Daily*, 18 November 2005, available at http://www.chinadaily.com.cn/.

19. See, for example, Liu Li and Shao Xiaoyi, "Expert: Bird Flu to Affect More Regions Globally," *China Daily*, 6 March 2006, available at http://www.chinadaily.com.cn/; Bao Daozu, "Local Authorities Launch Awareness Campaign," *China Daily*, 28 February 2006, available at http://www.chinadaily.com.cn/; Wang Zhenghua, "Delays over Treatment Blamed for Death Rate," *China Daily*, 11 February 2006, available at http://www.chinadaily.com.cn/; "Human Role in Spread of Flu Must Be Faced," *China Daily*, 26 January 2006, available at http://www.chinadaily.com.cn/; "China Calls for Enhanced Efforts to Prevent Avian Flu in China," Xinhua, 23 January 2006; Zhang Feng, "Poor Surveillance Led to Human Infections," *China Daily*, 11 January 2006, available at http://www.chinadaily.com.cn/; "China Demands Quick Action to Prevent, Control Human Infection of Bird Flu," Xinhua, 7 November 2005; Wang Zhenghua, "Local Authorities Step up Surveillance," *China Daily*, 31 October 2005, available at http://www.chinadaily.com.cn/; Zhao Huanxin, "Defences Prepared in Virus Battle," *China Daily*, 29 October 2005, available at http://www.chinadaily.com.cn/; "Nation Must Stand up to Bird Flu Threat," *China Daily*, 26 October 2005, available at http://www.chinadaily.com.cn/; Guo Nei, "Beijing Steps up Efforts to Combat Spread of Bird Flu," *China Daily*, 24 October 2005, available at http://www.chinadaily.com.cn/; Wang Zhenghua, "Efforts Stepped up in Bird Flu Fight," *China Daily*, 21 October 2005, available at http://www.chinadaily.com.cn/; Zissis, "The Potential Avian Flu Pandemic"; and Dr. David Nabarro, "How Should Asia Prepare for the Next Great Pandemic?" Panel, Asia Society, New York, 10 October 2006.

20. Long-De Wang, Yu Wang, Gong-Huan Yang, Jia-Qi Ma, Li-Ping Wang, and Xiao-Peng Qi, "China Information System for Disease Control and Prevention (CISDP)," National Bureau for Asian Research, 2007.

21. National Bureau of Asian Research, "Pandemics: Working Together for an Effective and Equitable Response," A report from the Pacific Health Summit, Seattle, USA, 12–14 June 2007, 18.

22. Grace Yu, "China HIT Case Study," in *Health Information Technology and Policy Lab HIT Briefing Book*, ed. Claire Topal and Kaleb Brownlow (Seattle, WA: National Bureau of Asian Research, 2007).

23. Huang, "Pursuing Health as Foreign Policy," 108–9.

24. "Mekong Basin Disease Surveillance (MBDS) Network," National Bureau for Asian Research.

25. Huang, "Pursuing Health as Foreign Policy," 121, 131.

26. Ibid., 122.

27. Ibid., 123.

28. "China's Role in Tackling Avian Influenza Discussed with Senior UN Officials," United Nations Development Programme, 4 April 2006, http://en.news2u.net/release. php?id=00000222.

29. Huang, "Pursuing Health as Foreign Policy," 124.

30. Important Chinese governmental organizations in this field include Harbin Institute of Veterinary Medicine, www.hvri.ac.cn; Chinese Academy of Sciences (CAS) Shanghai Institute of Materia Medica, www.simm.ac.cn; CAS Biophysics Institute, www.ibp. ac.cn; and CAS Shanghai Institute for Biological Sciences, www.sibs.ac.cn. Major private-sector partners include Beijing Sinovac Biotech Co. Ltd., www.sinovac.com.cn. For more information on Sinovac's role in vaccine research and production, see Zhang Feng, "Vaccine Team Prepared if Virus Mutates," *China Daily*, 17 November 2005, available at http://www.chinadaily.com.cn/.

31. Dissertations published in 2005 alone include the following: 薛霖莉 [Xue Linli], "禽流感病毒（H5N1）NA基因的克隆与序列分析" ["Molecular Cloning and Sequencing of NA Gene of Avian Influenza Virus"] (diss., 山西农业大学 [Shanxi Agricultural University]); 袁建琴 [Yuan Jianqin], "H9（N2）型禽流感病毒HA基因的克隆与序列分析" ["Cloning and Sequence Analysis of HA Gene of H9 (N2) Avian Influenza Virus"] (diss., 山西农业大学 [Shanxi Agricultural University]); 孙博兴 [Sun Boxing], "H9N2亚型禽流感非结构蛋白NS1A基因的克隆，表达及其诱导Hela细胞凋亡的研究" ["Study on Cloning and Expression of NS1A Protein of H9N2 Avian Influenza Virus and Inducing Apoptosis in Hela Cells"] (diss., 吉林大学 [Jilin University]); 余丹丹 [Yu Dandan], "两株H5N1亚型禽流感病毒诱导的细胞凋亡研究" ["Apoptosis Induced by Two H5N1 Avian Influenza Viruses"] (diss., 南京农业大学 [Nanjing Agricultural University]); 金英杰 [Jing Yingjie], "抗禽流感病毒H5亚型血凝素单克隆抗体的研制" ["Preparation of Monoclonal Antibodies against the H5 Haemagglutinin of Avian Influenza Virus"] (diss., 中国农业大学 [Chinese Agricultural University], 1 June 2005); 曹振 [Cao Zhen], "禽流感病毒H5亚型血凝素单克隆抗体的制备及捕获ELISA方法的建立" ["Preparation of Monoclonal Antibodies against Hemagglutinin of Subtype H5 Avian Influenza Virus and Establishment of Capture ELISA"] (diss., 中国农业大学 [Chinese Agricultural University], 1 June 2005); 李呈军 [Li Chengjun], "中国H9N2亚型禽流感病毒进化分析与H5N1亚型禽流感病毒标记疫苗的研究" ["Evolution of H9N2 Influenza Viruses in China and Study on H5N1 Influenza Marker Vaccine"] (diss., 中国农业科学院 [Chinese Academy of Agriculture], 1 June 2005); 李宝全 [Li Baoquan], "H9亚型禽流感病毒抗独特型抗体的研制与其免疫原性的初步分析" ["Preparation for Anti-idiotypic Antibodies to Avian Influenza Virus Subtype H9 and Primary Analysis to Their Immunogenicity"] (diss., 山东农业大学 [Shandong Agricultural University], 1 June 2005); 马仲彬 [Ma Zhongbin], "抗H9N2亚型禽流感病毒单克隆抗体杂交瘤细胞的建立及快速检测试纸条的研制" ["Establishment of Hybridoma Cell

Lines Secreting Monoclonal Antibodies against H9 Subtype Avian Influenza and Application in the Rapid Diagnosis Strip"] (diss., 河南农业大学 [Henan Agricultural University], 1 June 2005); 陈素娟 [Chen Sujuan], "用不同鸡痘病毒载体构建单表达或双表达抗H5和H9亚型禽流感的重组疫苗及其免疫效力" ["Development of Recombinant Vaccines against H5 and/H9 Subtype AI with Different Fowlpox Virus Insertion Vectors and Their Protective Efficacies"] (diss., 扬州大学 [Yangzhou University], 30 May 2005); 郝贵杰 [Hao Guijie], "抗H5亚型禽流感病毒血凝素蛋白特异性单克隆抗体的研制及初步应用" ["Development and Application of the Monoclonal Antibodies against Hemagglutinin of H5 Subtype Avian Influenza Virus"] (diss., 扬州大学 [Yangzhou University], 1 May 2005); 徐忠林 [Xu Zhonglin], "共表达NDV F 基因与H9亚型AIV HA基因的重组鸡痘病毒及其免疫效力" ["A Recombinant Fowlpox Virus Co-expressing the F Gene of NDV and the HA Gene of H9 Subtype AIV and Its Protective Efficacy"] (diss., [Yangzhou University], 1 May 2005); 高璐 [Gao Lu], "MPAIV与较低致病性禽源E.coli的协同致病作用及不同感染途径对MPAIV致病性的影响" ["Study on the Synergistic Pathogenesis between MPAIV and Avian E. coli with Low Pathogenicity and the Impact of Different Inoculation Routines on the Pathogenicity of MPAIV Evaluated in Chickens"] (diss., 扬州大学 [Yangzhou University], 1 May 2005); 孙学辉 [Sun Xuehui], "高效表达H5亚型禽流感病毒HA基因的重组鸡痘病毒的构建及其免疫效力" ["Construction of Recombinant Fowlpox Virus Vaccines Expressing Hemagglutinin Gene of H5N1 Avian Influenza Virus and Their Protective Efficacy"] (diss., 扬州大学 [Yangzhou University], 1 May 2005); 黄楷 [Huang Kai], "南宁H5N1型禽流感病毒分子流行病学研究" ["Molecular Epidemiological Studies on H5N1 Influenza Viruses from Poultry in Nanning"] (diss., 广西医科大学 [Western Medicine University of Science & Technology], 1 May 2005); 周凯 [Zhou Kai], "禽流感H5N1病毒的RNAi研究" ["RNA Interference Research on Avian Influenza H5N1 Virus"] (diss., 河北师范大学 [Hebei Normal University], 1 May 2005); 焦凤超 [Jiao Fengchao], "减毒沙门氏菌运送的H5亚型禽流感病毒口服DNA疫苗的免疫效力研究" ["The Immune Efficacy of Oral DNA Vaccines against H5 Subtype of Avian Influenza Virus Delivered by Attenuated Salmonella Typhimurium"] (diss., 扬州大学 [Yangzhou University], 1 May 2005); 刘丽平 [Liu Liping], "减毒沙门氏菌运送的H9亚型禽流感病毒DNA疫苗及其免疫效力" ["DNA Vaccines against H9N2 Subtype of Avian Influenza Virus Delivered by Attenuated Salmonella and Their Immune Efficacy"] (diss., 扬州大学 [Yangzhou University], 1 May 2005); 杨旭芹 [Yang Xuqin], "检测新城疫病毒和禽流感病毒的双重RT-PCR方法的建立" ["Detection of Avian Influenza Virus and Newcastle Disease Virus by Duplex RT-PCR Technique"] (diss., 扬州大学 [Yangzhou University], 1 May 2005); 李东燕 [Li Dongyan], "高致病性禽流感随进口禽类及其产品传入的风险 分析" ["The Risk Analysis of Highly Pathogenic Avian Influenza Incidentally Introduced into China with Imported Bird and Its Products"] (diss., 中国农业大学 [Chinese Agricultural University], 1 May 2005); 胡青海 [Hu Qinghai], "鸡IL-2, IL-18, IFN-?和CpG DNA在减毒沙门氏菌运送H5亚型禽流感核酸疫苗中的佐剂作用及鸡CD4和CD8分子单克隆抗体的研制" ["Effect of Co-expressing Chicken IL-2,IL-18, IFN-? or Built CpG DNA in the Plasmid Backbone as Adjuvants on DNA Vaccines against H5 Subtype Avian Influenza Delivered by Attenuated Salmonella and Production of Anti-Chicken CD4 and CD8 Monoclonal Antibodies"] (diss., 扬州大学 [Yangzhou University], 1 May 2005); 陈凤梅 [Chen Fengmei], "鸡常

见呼吸道病诊断基因芯片的研制与应用" ["Research and Application of Diagnostic Assay for Poultry Respiratory Syndrome with Macroarray Techniques"] (diss., 山东农业大学 [Shandong Agricultural University], 18 May 2005); 霍惠玲[Huo Huiling], "抗禽流感疫苗与野毒感染的抗体区分方法的初步建立" ["Establishment of the Method to Distinguish the Anti-Avian Influenza Virus Antibody between Vaccinated and Infected Chickens"] (diss., 吉林大学 [Jilin University], 25 April 2005); 邱美珍 [Qiu Meizhen], "禽流感核酸疫苗免疫保护性研究" ["Protection against Avian Influenza Virus by Immunization with DNA Vaccines"] (diss., 湖南师范大学 [Hunan Normal University], 1 April 2005); and 杨彩然 [Yang Cairan], "禽源H3, H4亚型流感病毒的序列分析及对鸡的致病性研究" ["Studies on Sequence Analysis and Pathogenicity for Chickens of H3 and H4 Subtype Avian Influenza Viruses"] (diss., 内蒙古农业大学 [Inner Mongolian Agricultural University], 1 April 2005).

32. Conferences held recently in China include: 国际实验动物专题研讨会 [International Experimental Animal Specialty Forum], 中国实验动物学会 [China Experimental Zoological Association], Beijing, China, 2005; and 2005年浙江省呼吸系病学术年会 [Zhejiang Province Respiratory Illness Science 2005 Annual Meeting], 浙江省医学会呼吸系病分会 [Zhejiang Province Medical Science Respiratory Illness Branch], Jiaxiang, Zhejiang Province, China, 2005.

33. Zhao Huanxin, "China Develops First Live Vaccine," *China Daily*, 26 December 2005, available at http://www.chinadaily.com.cn/.

34. National Bureau of Asian Research, "Pandemic Influenza Vaccines Workshop: Building a Platform for Global Collaboration," 28–30 January 2007, Beijing, 5.

35. Li Jiao, "Experts Step up Fight against Bird Flu," *China Daily*, 2 December 2005, available at http://www.chinadaily.com.cn/.

36. See, for example, 范顺良, 周猛 [Fan Shunliang and Zhou Meng], "全军防治禽流感工作电视电话会议召开" ["Army-Wide Avian Flu Prevention and Control Work Television Teleconference Convenes"], 解放军报 [*Liberation Army Daily*], 6 February 2004; 陶智平 [Tao Zhiping], "群防群控坚决打好防治禽流感硬仗" ["Group Defense and Crowd Control for Preventing and Curing Avian Flu"], 人民军队报 [*People's Armed Forces Daily*], 7 February 2004, 1; and 殷飞 [Yin Fei], "依法做好高致病性禽流感防治工作" ["Conduct Effective Avian Flu Prevention and Cure Work on the Basis of Law"], 解放军报 [*Liberation Army Daily*], 15 February 2004.

37. 金宁一 [Jin Ningyi], 禽流感白问白答 [*Avian Influenza: 100 Questions and Answers*] (人民军医出版社 [People's Military Medical Press], 2004). See also 杜新安 [Du Xinan], 曹务春 [Cao Wuchun], 生物恐怖的反对与处置 [*Bioterrorism Countermeasures and Management*] (人民军医出版社 [People's Military Medical Press], 2005).

38. Yu Zhong, "Treatment for Human Infection Developed," *China Daily*, 27 December 2005, available at http://www.chinadaily.com.cn/. See also "China Develops Vaccine against Human Infection," *China Daily*, 15 November 2005, available at http://www.chinadaily.com.cn/; and Zhang Feng, Wu Yong, and He Nan, "China Develops Vaccine against Human Infection," *China Daily*, 15 November 2005, available at http://www.chinadaily.com.cn/.

39. "Newly Launched U.S.-China Global Issues Forum Proves Productive: Focus on Cooperative Efforts on International Issues, Stronger U.S.-China Ties," America.gov, 14 April 2005, http://www.america.gov/st/washfile-english/2005/April/20050414110048ajesrom4.512966e-03.html.

40. Fisher-Thompson, "U.S. Officials Praise China."

41. U.S. Department of State, "United States-China Joint Initiative on Avian Influenza," 19 November 2005, http://merln.ndu.edu/archivepdf/china/State/57157.pdf. See also Xing Zhigang: "Leaders Highlight Common Interests," *China Daily*, 21 November 2005, available at http://www.chinadaily.com.cn/.

42. In fact, when I explained these measures to an audience at the Asia Society in New York in October 2006, officials from several foreign consulates approached me and expressed interest in having their nation conclude a similar agreement with the United States.

43. Zhao Huanxin, "World Meet Seeks Funds to Combat Epidemic," *China Daily*, 18 January 2006, available at http://www.chinadaily.com.cn/; and "Address by Premier Wen Jiabao at the Opening Session of the International Pledging Conference on Avian and Human Pandemic Influenza," Beijing, China, 18 January 2006, http://web.world bank.org/WBSITE/EXTERNAL/PROJECTS/0,,contentMDK:20765611~menuPK:207 7305~pagePK:41367~piPK:51533~theSitePK:40941,00.html. Wen had earlier convened a State Council executive meeting to assess China's strategy for dealing with avian influenza. See Xinhua, 2 November 2005.

44. "Paul Wolfowitz Remarks to the International Pledging Conference on Avian and Human Influenza" (statement made via videoconference to the International Pledging Conference on Avian and Human Influenza, Beijing, China, 18 January 2006), http:// web.worldbank.org/WBSITE/EXTERNAL/COUNTRIES/EASTASIAPACIFICEXT/ CHINAEXTN/0,,contentMDK:20788677~menuPK:318973~pagePK:2865066~piPK:2 865079~theSitePK:318950,00.html.

45. Zhang Feng and Zhao Huanxin, "China, WHO Sign Virus Co-Op Deal," *China Daily*, 21 December 2005, available at http://www.chinadaily.com.cn/.

46. Zhao Huanxin, "Countries Show Sense of Urgency," *China Daily*, 19 January 2006, available at http://www.chinadaily.com.cn/; and Zissis, "The Potential Avian Flu Pandemic."

47. Nabarro, "How Should Asia Prepare."

48. "Fact Sheet: Creation of the U.S.-China Strategic Economic Dialogue," Press Room, U.S. Department of the Treasury, 20 September 2006, http://www.ustreas.gov/press/ releases/hp107.htm.

49. "HHS Opens Offices of the Food and Drug Administration (FDA) in China," Press Office, U.S. Department of Health & Human Services, 18 November 2008, http://www. dhhs.gov/news/press/2008pres/11/20081118a.html.

50. "U.S.-China Strategic and Economic Dialogue," U.S. Department of the Treasury, http://www.ustreas.gov/initiatives/us-china/.

51. "Hu Jintao and U.S. President Barack Obama with a Telephone," Xinhua, 6 May 2009, http://news.xinhuanet.com/newscenter/2009-05/06/content_11325709_1.htm; op. cit. Huang, "Pursuing Health as Foreign Policy," 125.

52. "Joint Science Academies' Statement: Avian Influenza and Infectious Diseases," InterAcademy Council, http://www.interacademycouncil.net/?id=10854.

53. "Summary of Progress," National Strategy for Pandemic Influenza Implementation Plan, December 2006, http://www.flu.gov/professional/federal/stratergyimplementa tionplan.html. Information is available in Chinese at http://chinese.pandemicflu.gov/ pandemicflu/enzh/24/_www_pandemicflu_gov/chinese.html.

54. See *National Strategy for Pandemic Influenza* (Washington, DC: Homeland Security Council, November 2005), http://www.flu.gov/professional/federal/pandemic-influ enza.pdf. See also, for example, Thierry M. Work and Renee Eismueller, "2006/2007 Avian Influenza Surveillance Report for the Pacific Islands, An interagency collabora tion between U. S. Fish & Wildlife Service, U. S. Geological Survey, U. S. Department of Agriculture, State of Hawaii Department of Land & Natural Resources, American Samoa Department of Marine & Wildlife, and Palau Conservation Society," http:// www.nwhc.usgs.gov/hfs/Globals/HotTopic/AIPacificReport2007.pdf.

55. See, for example, "Avaian and Pandemic Influenza: Preparedness and Response," USAID Web site, http://www.usaid.gov/our_work/global_health/home/News/news_ items/avian_influenza.html.

56. "Pandemic Influenza Phases," Department of Defense Pandemic Influenza Watchboard, http://fhp.osd.mil/aiWatchboard/DoDPhases.jsp.

57. Headquarters, U.S. Pacific Command, "USPACOM Facts," http://www.pacom.mil/ web/site_pages/uspacom/facts.shtml.

58. Bob Brewin, "Pacom Leads Military in Pandemic Planning," Government Health IT, 8 February 2006, previously available at http://www.govhealthit.com/article91626-12- 06-05-Web.

59. R. D. Hufstader, "Avian Flu Preparations and Role with State of Hawaii Agencies," Testimony to Joint House Committee Hearing of Hawaii State Legislature, 18 November 2005, http://www.pacom.mil/speeches/sst2005/051118hufstader-flu.shtml.

60. "DoD's Pandemic Flu Web Site Goes Live," American Forces Press Service, 7 November 2005, http://www.defense.gov/news/newsarticle.aspx?id=18367.

61. Tim Meyer, "PACOM Sponsors Influenza Seminar," U.S. Pacific Command Public Affairs, http://www.pacom.mil/articles/articles2005/051027story1.shtml.

62. "'Military-Style' Flu Network Call," *BBC News*, 1 March 2006, http://news.bbc.co.uk/2/ hi/health/4763224.stm; and J. P. Chretien, J. C. Gaydos, J. L. Malone, and D. L. Blazes, "Global Network Could Avert Pandemics," *Nature* 440 (2 March 2006): 25–26.

63. Audrey McAvoy, "Hawai'i Forces Take Aim at Bird Flu," *Honolulu Advertiser*, 13 November 2005, http://the.honoluluadvertiser.com/article/2005/Nov/13/ln/ FP511130340.html/?print=on.

64. U.S. Congressional Budget Office, "A Potential Influenza Pandemic: Possible Macroeconomic Effects and Policy Issues," 8 December 2005, http://www.cbo.gov/ ftpdocs/69xx/doc6946/12-08-BirdFlu.pdf.

65. Huang, "Pursuing Health as Foreign Policy," 115.

66. David L. Heymann, "The Sovereignty of Disease," YaleGlobal, 6 June 2006, http://yaleglobal.yale.edu/content/sovereignty-disease.

67. Nabarro, "How Should Asia Prepare"; and Heymann, "Sovereignty of Disease."

68. Michael T. Osterholm, "Preparing for the Next Pandemic," *Foreign Affairs*, July/August 2005, http://www.foreignaffairs.org/20050701faessay84402/michael-t-oster-holm/preparing-for-the-next-pandemic.html.

69. Nabarro, "How Should Asia Prepare."

70. Dr. Jilan Liu, e-mail interview with author, 12 February 2009.

71. Ibid.

72. "Parties and Signatories of the Biological Weapons Convention," Bureau of Arms Control, U.S. Department of State, 17 November 2003, previously available at http://www.state.gov/t/ac/rls/fs/2003/26276.htm.

73. Keith Bradsher, "U.S. Seeks Cooperation with China," *New York Times*, September 12, 2005.

74. "Addressing the Impact of Severe Acute Respiratory Syndrome (SARS) in East Asia," Joint Statement of the ASEAN+3 Labour Ministers Meeting, Mataram, Indonesia, 9 May 2003, Association of Southeast Asian Nations, http://www.aseansec.org/14779.htm.

75. See Long-De Wang et al., "Mekong Basin Disease Surveillance (MBDS) Network."

76. National Bureau of Asian Research, "Pandemics," 5.

77. Nicholas Zamiska, "How Academic Flap Hurt World Effort on Chinese Bird Flu," *Wall Street Journal*, February 24, 2006, A1.

78. Osterholm, "Preparing for the Next Pandemic."

79. See, for example, 迟福林 [Chi Fulin], ed., 警钟—中国: SARS危机与制度变革, 中国改革发展研究院2003年转轨研究报告 [*Alarm—China: SARS Crisis and System Reform, Transition Report 2003*] (Beijing: China Institute for Reform and Development, 2003); 尹萍 [Yin Ping], "信息公开与法治政府—从'非典'到'禽流感'的启示" ["Information Publication and Government by Law—Inspiration from 'SARS' to 'Bird Flu'"], 河北法学 [*Hebei Law Science*] 22, no. 11 (November 2004): 147–50.

80. "Bird Flu Requires Better Global Response," *China Daily*, 29 October 2005, available at http://www.chinadaily.com.cn/. For an argument that the issue was not media transparency but rather bureaucratic transparency, see 尹韵公 [Yin Yungong], 中国社会科学院新闻和转播研究所 [News and Broadcast Research Institute, China Academy of Social Sciences], "对'非典'时期新闻转播的科学反思" ["A Scientific Recollection of News Broadcasts during the Period of SARS"], 新闻文摘 [*News Digest*], no. 23 (2006): 152–54.

81. Quoted in National Bureau of Asian Research, "Pandemics," 9.

82. See, for example, *The Federal Response to Hurricane Katrina: Lessons Learned* (Washington, DC: Department of Homeland Security, 2006). In response to the hurricane, China sent the United States $5 million in aid. Jim Garamone, "U.S. Sends Relief Supplies to China," American Forces Press Service, 18 May 2008, http://www.defenselink.mil/news/newsarticle.aspx?id=49920.

83. Dr. Jilan Liu, e-mail interview with author, 12 February 2009.

84. Ibid.

85. Nabarro, "How Should Asia Prepare."

86. Dr. Jilan Liu, e-mail interview with author, 12 February 2009.

87. Michael Mullen, "Remarks as Delivered for the 17th International Seapower Symposium," Naval War College, Newport, RI, 21 September 2005, http://www.navy.mil/navydata/cno/mullen/speeches/mullen050921.txt.

PART IV

Perspectives on Regional Security

Michael J. Green

U.S.–China Maritime Cooperation
Regional Implications and Prospects

IN THIS CHAPTER I CONSIDER THE SIGNIFICANCE of trends in Chinese naval modernization and U.S.–China maritime cooperation for broader regional stability in Asia. I will do so in three parts: first, the impact of China's naval modernization on other regional powers; second, the expectations of the region broadly for U.S.–China maritime cooperation; and third, the agenda for future U.S.–China cooperation.

Regional Responses to China's Naval Modernization

History, culture, and geography all cause different reactions across Asia to China's naval modernization trends. There is no doubt, however, that militaries and governments in the region are watching with interest, if not alarm, as Chinese naval capabilities grow, particularly as the PLA Navy gains new reach beyond its littoral areas. No Asian governments are actively seeking to contain Chinese power, but all of the maritime nations in the region are attentive to the balance of power. While few are engaged in pronounced internal balancing (increasing naval capabilities) in response to China's growing capabilities, there is clear evidence of external balancing (alignment) to ensure that a stable equilibrium is maintained.[1]

Japan

Japan's response to China's maritime buildup has been most pronounced, but it would be a mistake to attribute this to historical enmity alone. After all, the architect of Japan's postwar security strategy, Prime Minister Yoshida Shigeru, believed that China would split from the Soviet Union and eventually develop a closer relationship with Japan based on economic interdependence. For Japanese strategists at the end of the Cold War, China appeared to present far more of an opportunity than a threat. With the collapse of East–West competition, many in Tokyo thought that Japan would be able to establish a more balanced relationship with the United States by expanding ties with China. After the Tiananmen Incident, the Japanese government was the first of the G-7 countries to reopen dialogue with China, and Tokyo saw itself in a unique position to serve as a bridge between China and the West.

The sudden reversal in positive Sino-Japanese strategic relations in the mid-1990s had a great deal to do with China's own military policies. Certainly, the collapse of the Japanese economic bubble and the rise of a more assertive and nationalistic generation of politicians in Japan (the so-called Heisei generation) were factors, but it was the Chinese nuclear test at Lop Nor and Chinese missile tests off of Taiwan in 1995–96 that triggered a Japanese reassessment of Yoshida's original assumptions about Japan's ability to manage relations with China based on economics alone. In the lead-up to what became the April 1996 Clinton–Hashimoto Joint Security Declaration, there was hesitation within the ruling coalition in Tokyo over whether to include revision of the 1978 U.S.-Japan Defense Guidelines to cover "situations in the area surrounding Japan that have a direct impact on Japanese security," but after the missile tests bracketing Taiwan, consensus quickly formed that the alliance did have to revise the guidelines. While the American and Japanese governments argued sincerely that the revision was not aimed at any country, there can be little doubt that it was propelled by the PLA's missile tests.

As the PLA Navy has increased its capability to control littoral areas of China, this has only increased the visibility of Chinese military operations in Japan's traditional sea-lanes and propelled Tokyo to pursue closer security cooperation with the United States. The Japanese press has reported on incidents over the past few years that include the circumnavigation of Japan and intrusion in Japanese territorial waters by PLA Navy submarines; the suspected mapping of the underwater seabed between Japan and Taiwan for potential submarine warfare; the deployment of three PLA Navy destroyers around the contested Diaoyu/Senkaku Islands that subsequently trained deck guns on a

Japanese Maritime Self Defense Force P-3C surveilling the area; the January 2007 antisatellite test; the deployment of close to one hundred medium-range ballistic missiles that range Japan; rapid increases in tactical air and surface warfare capabilities; and the 8 and 21 April 2010 events in which, during a ten-vessel PLA Navy exercise west of the Ryukyu Islands, a PLA Navy helicopter reportedly approached within ninety meters of a Japanese Maritime Self-Defense Force destroyer.[2]

It is well known that Beijing has been displeased with Japan's pursuit of missile defense capabilities and particularly resentful of the February 2005 U.S.-Japan "Two-plus-Two" statement that listed stability in the Taiwan straits as a shared "common strategic objective." However, it is worth noting that Japan has not chosen to dramatically increase its own defense spending in response to a Chinese defense budget that has increased an average of 15 percent per year since 1990.[3] Indeed, the Japanese defense budget has been flat or declining in most of the past five years. Japanese external balancing behavior is far less destabilizing than the alternative responses available to strategic planners in Tokyo, such as enhanced offensive capabilities or even nuclear weapons.

Moreover, it is important to note that Japan has sought greater military-to-military cooperation and mutual transparency with the PLA in an effort to enhance stability. In 1998 Japanese defense minister Kyuma visited China where he agreed with Minister Chi Haotian to arrange for reciprocal port visits. The deputy defense ministers also initiated a security dialogue comparable to the U.S.–China Defense Consultative Talks in 2003. However, Japan's interest in expanding military-to-military (and particularly maritime) cooperation with China was derailed because of bilateral tensions over Prime Minister Koizumi's visits to Yasukuni Shrine and collisions between Tokyo and Beijing over other diplomatic issues such as Japan's bid for a permanent seat on the UN Security Council. From 28 November to 1 December 2007, the PLA Navy guided missile destroyer *Shenzhen* finally conducted a port visit to Harumi, Tokyo, and the Japanese Maritime Self-Defense Force (JMSDF) sent the destroyer *Sazanami* to the PLA Navy South Sea Fleet headquarters in Zhanjiang for a reciprocal visit from 24–28 June 2008.[4] Most recently, former Prime Minister Yukio Hatoyama made unprecedented overtures to China, stating repeatedly his hope that "the East China Sea will be a sea of fraternity," even in the face of accusations that his policies have undermined the U.S.–Japan alliance and encouraged Chinese military assertiveness.[5]

The belated launch of Japan–China maritime cooperation is useful, but it could be considered to be too little and too late in light of the increasing operational tempo of the PLA Navy beyond its littoral and the incidents between

Japanese and Chinese aircraft and vessels in recent years. Japan and China could use an effective Military Maritime Consultative Agreement (MMCA, as is discussed more fully in David Griffiths' contribution to this volume) and certainly would benefit if military-to-military cooperation were better insulated against extraneous political and ideological disagreements.

South Korea

The Republic of Korea (ROK) has been far less concerned about the Chinese maritime buildup than has Japan. Recently, the ROK navy has been sizing itself based on a potential JMSDF threat as much as any PLA Navy threat (a sentiment not reciprocated by the Japanese side thus far). The bilateral Japan–ROK dispute over the Tokdo/Takeshima islands and the use of the "Japan" card against conservatives at home by the administration of Roh Moo-hyun (2003–08) certainly contributed to the tensions and the ROK navy's new focus on Japan. In addition, the Korean public has enjoyed something of a honeymoon period with China after normalizing ties in 1992, seeing some of the same opportunities to balance relations with Washington through the China card that Japanese leaders saw in the late 1980s. Moreover, the primary threat to Korean peninsula security remains the Pyongyang government. Now in the throes of an apparent leadership transition from Kim Jong-il to his third son, Kim Jong-un, North Korea was found by an international investigation team to have caused the 26 March 2010 incident in which South Korean navy corvette Choenan, on a routine patrol in international waters, was rent in two by an underwater explosion, killing at least forty sailors.[6]

Despite these other issues, polls show that the Korean public's anxiety about China is now growing. Polls published by the Korean Institute for Defense Analyses in March 2006 listed China as the Korean public's main security concern in the future, well ahead of either Japan or North Korea. Subsequent polling has borne out this new trend. For Korea, the growing sense of threat from China is not focused on the maritime or even the military threat per se but rather on concern that China is increasing its strategic influence over North Korea. This worry is reinforced in the public's mind by Beijing's insistence on teaching that the Koguryo Kingdom (which spanned Manchuria and what is now North Korea) was "Chinese." Korean trade with China has surpassed the ROK's trade with the United States since 2006, but the growing sense of uncertainty about China's rising power has led to a broad consensus in Seoul that alliance with the United States is a critical national interest. This was evident in the 2007 Korean presidential election, in which all three of the leading candidates ran on their records as good stewards of the U.S.–ROK alliance, and the most pro-U.S. candidate, Lee Myung-bak, easily won. Although Lee did run into political trouble in 2008 when the public protested his agreement to open the Korean market to U.S. beef, his unabashed pro-U.S. stance was a real contrast to the anti-American demonstrations that colored the 2003 election and much of the term of his predecessor, Roh Moo-hyun. In terms of China's naval modernization, however, continental Korea is significantly less sensitive than maritime Japan.

Australia

Australia is a major maritime power in Asia and the closest U.S. ally in the region. Prime Minister John Howard expanded Australian defense thinking to the global scale and sized the Australian navy so that it could operate not only in the Pacific but also alongside U.S. forces maintaining international peace and stability as far away as the Persian Gulf. The Howard government was comfortable expanding diplomatic and economic ties with China while simultaneously initiating a U.S.-Japan-Australia Trilateral Security Dialogue (since 2001) and a new Japan–Australia security cooperation agreement in 2007. The current Labor leader of Australia, Kevin Rudd, is well known as a China expert, but he is equally known in Washington as a stalwart supporter of the U.S.–Australia alliance. Some defense intellectuals close to Labor have argued that Australia must rebalance its strategic relations between Washington and Beijing, and Rudd's foreign minister announced during a press conference with visiting Chinese foreign minister Yang Jiechi in February 2008 that Australia would not participate in proposals for a U.S.–Japan–Australia–India quadrilateral summit, sparking further speculation that Rudd was leaning toward China. However, it is far more likely that Rudd will continue to deepen Australia's defense interoperability with U.S. forces even as he builds a constructive diplomatic relationship with China. The Australian public is far less worried about China's rise than the publics in Japan or even Korea, and the Rudd government will be unlikely to imply any military commitment from Australia to Taiwan. But, at the same time, Australian governments have always been careful to help sustain active U.S. presence and thereby maintain a strategic balance of power in Asia. The new Australian Defense white paper will be read carefully for signs of this commitment, and all indications are that it will contain an unmistakable focus on maritime security in the Asia-Pacific region with the subtext of China's naval modernization driving that strategic logic. It is also a safe bet that Canberra will want to see more transparency from the PLA Navy as it expands capabilities, and it will continue to focus more—not less—on interoperability with the U.S. Navy and other navies in the region if the PLA Navy continues expanding into blue water capabilities.

India

Under Prime Minister Manmohan Singh, India has sought to stabilize all of its external relations, particularly with China. India is focused on achieving its own version of a "peaceful rise" and has little to gain from aggressive strategic competition with China or a renewal of the criticism of PLA modernization once famously articulated by Defense Minister George Fernandes. However, the Indian navy is deeply concerned about the potential for a Chinese naval presence in the Indian Ocean, through basing arrangements with either Pakistan or Myanmar/Burma; such concerns have been heightened in some quarters by China's ongoing counterpiracy deployments in the Gulf of Aden. The Indian navy has increased its maritime cooperation with the United States and Japan, with several full paragraphs of the August Abe-Singh joint summit statement dedicated to India–Japan naval cooperation issues. The Indian navy is careful not to let its growing relationship with the United States and Japan cause a Chinese backlash. On the margins of U.S.–Japan–India trilateral Malabar exercises in March 2007, for example, the Indian navy vessels engaged in symbolically important (though less operationally significant) exchanges with the PLA Navy.

Association of Southeast Asian Nations (ASEAN)

While ASEAN recently celebrated its fortieth anniversary with a new charter and sense of purpose, there is no common ASEAN position on China or reaction to Chinese naval modernization. The maritime nations of Singapore, Vietnam, and Indonesia are most acutely sensitive to PLA naval modernization and all three have strengthened military-to-military ties with the United States in recent years. Vietnamese ships have come under fire from PLA patrol boats around the disputed Spratly Islands. Singapore's focus on external balancing is evident in the 2005 U.S.–Singapore Strategic Framework Agreement, which expanded U.S. logistical support in Singapore as well as intelligence and technology collaboration. By contrast, the continental states of Cambodia and Laos do not seem particularly concerned about the PLA Navy. Thailand and the Philippines are focused on internal challenges and not the PLA Navy. Malaysian leaders seem to find China's rise a useful political card to stress Asian exceptionalism in the way that Mahathir used the rise of Japanese power in the 1980s, though Defense Minister Najib and others do maintain a focus on balance of power and the U.S. and Malaysian navies have a good history of cooperation.

What can be concluded from this brief survey of regional reactions to Chinese naval modernization? First, that those maritime powers closest to China are most acutely sensitive to Chinese naval modernization (Japan and Vietnam) but that other powers are growing more concerned as PLA maritime reach expands (India, Singapore, Indonesia). Second, that the response to PLA naval modernization is primarily to engage in some form of external balancing (with the United States or secondarily with Japan or India)—but not to match PLA Naval spending increases dollar for dollar (or yen for renminbi)—although Japan, Korea, and Australia have all launched impressive new platforms, such as the JMSDF's helicopter carriers and the ROKN's TBMD-capable destroyers. Third, that few Asian states (other than Japan) see any advantage in openly criticizing China's military buildup, even as they explore strategies to balance it. Fourth, that all of the maritime powers in Asia seek closer cooperation, confidence-building, and mutual transparency with the PLA Navy.

U.S.–China Maritime Cooperation and Regional Security

There is one other perspective on Chinese naval modernization that may be common across Asia: all of the powers seek a stable U.S.–China relationship. When the United States and China proved briefly incapable of resolving the EP-3 incident in 2001, there was alarm not only in Washington but also in Tokyo, Singapore, Canberra, and Bangkok. Indeed, it may have been the regional reaction more than any steps taken by the Bush administration that led Beijing to soften its stance.

President Bush agreed in his first summit meeting with President Jiang Zemin after the EP-3 incident that U.S.–China military-to-military cooperation and transparency had to increase, but there was resistance from both the PLA and the civilian leadership in the Pentagon. Secretary of Defense Rumsfeld's visit to China in October 2005 helped to propel U.S.–China military contacts in the direction President Bush had sought back in 2001, and Secretary Gate's recent visit in November 2007 made headlines with the agreement to establish a U.S.–China military "hotline." PACOM under Admirals William Fallon and Timothy Keating has also increased the pace of Sino-U.S. maritime contacts and cooperation, though these efforts have slowed subsequently with recent suspensions of bilateral military relations.

However, if the rest of Asia was concerned in April 2001 about the inability of the United States and China to manage a military crisis, is there any more reason today for confidence? U.S.–China relations have certainly improved, based in large part on the growing personal trust established between presidents Bush and Hu. The defense exchanges, dialogue on nuclear issues, and agreement to establish a hotline are all manifestations of that more trusting relationship. Yet U.S.–China military-to-military cooperation is still far short of achieving the levels of transparency, communication, and understanding that would be necessary to negotiate another crisis like the EP-3. And the trajectory of bilateral military relations remains unclear under presidents Obama and Hu.

Three problems are particularly striking. First, maritime cooperation is not insulated against capricious political actions. It is particularly worrisome that the Thanksgiving 2007 Hong Kong port call of the USS *Kitty Hawk* was cancelled in apparent retaliation for the visit of His Holiness the Dalai Lama to Washington. Until recently, Washington and Beijing have been careful not to retaliate in one sector for actions taken in another sector. The United States never resorted to arms sales to Taiwan in frustration over China's inaction on North Korea, for example. Beijing was careful not to retaliate over human rights by blocking investment. Both governments recognized the need to keep each critical component of our relationship compartmented. Breaking down those compartments is extremely dangerous to the overall relationship. The fact that China did so this time suggests either the heightened sensitivity of the Tibet issue or increased confidence in China that such steps can be taken with impunity (although PLA Navy and foreign ministry officials seem to have recognized after the fact how damaging the move had been for their own interests in stable U.S.–China relations).

Second, paper agreements like the MMCA are not exercised or tested. The agreement on a hotline may prove easier to implement and test than the MMCA, but it is prone to bureaucratic delay and cannot replace well-rehearsed "rules of the road" in theater. Third, U.S. congressional frustration with lack of reciprocity is a continuing danger. As the Congressional Research Service noted in a report in 2007, Congress has an oversight responsibility for U.S.–China military-to-military contacts based on a range of legislation, and it continues to find that U.S. defense officials report inadequate cooperation from the PLA. While PACOM has significantly more latitude today to engage in maritime cooperation with the PLA Navy, voices in Washington continue to argue that civilian Department of Defense and congressional oversight of PACOM's cooperation are insufficient. In other words, while there is renewed momentum in U.S.–China maritime cooperation, reciprocity is falling short of expectations for some political and policy actors in Washington.

Expanding the Agenda for Maritime Cooperation

As a baseline for further progress, the United States and China will need to do more to insulate maritime cooperation from capricious political retaliation, to test and strengthen agreements like the MMCA, and to increase reciprocity.

There is also much that can be achieved by expanding the agenda of maritime cooperation to focus on practical problems in the Asia Pacific region. The 2004 tsunami led to unprecedented cooperation among Asia Pacific navies, centered on the U.S.-Japan-India-Australia Regional Core Group. The PLA Navy could gain experience and build confidence in the region by exercising with the U.S. Navy and other navies to be better prepared for operations in response to future humanitarian crises. The trend is for the U.S., Japanese, Indian, and Australian navies to increase interoperability in these areas. Beijing has expressed concern about proposals for a quadrilateral U.S.–Japan–India–Australia dialogue or consortium in Asia. The best way to ensure that such a grouping is not aimed at Beijing would be for the PLA Navy to be more open to maritime cooperation.

There may also be a need to trilateralize the MMCA to include Japan, given the incidents at sea and in the air around the Diaoyu/Senkaku Islands. The United States and Japan do not have a full understanding of how to manage a Sino-Japanese incident at sea, and there is obviously even less of a framework for managing such an incident between Tokyo and Beijing. The U.S. government remains neutral on the question of whether China or Japan has sovereignty over the Diaoyu/Senkaku Islands but has clearly stated that under Article V of the 1960 U.S.-Japan Treaty of Mutual Security, there is an obligation to help Japan defend territories it administers, which includes the disputed islands. Retreating from this commitment would be extremely damaging to U.S.–Japan relations, particularly in the wake of North Korea's nuclear expansion and Japanese concerns about China's military modernization. Yet the traditional division of U.S. and Japanese "roles and missions" is no longer a useful framework for preventing the United States from becoming entrapped in a Sino-Japanese escalation, since Tokyo now considers "retaking" its own territories as an appropriate Japanese mission (the traditional division was that Japan did defense and the United States did counteroffense in any attack on Japan). This ambiguity should be addressed bilaterally in the U.S.–Japan roles and missions dialogue, but it is also in the United States' interests to press China to be more responsive to Japanese interest in Sino-Japanese CBMs.

Finally, the U.S. Navy and the PLA Navy should not lose sight of the fact that both are warfighters, not "engagers." Cooperative engagement can only go so far in building trust and confidence if it does not lead to a better understanding of doctrine and intentions. It is critical that this process not be left in the military-to-military channel. The civilian leaders ultimately manage the U.S.–China relationship at the strategic level. One of the lessons of the EP-3 incident was how difficult it was for Chinese leaders to manage a crisis involving the PLA. It appeared quite clear to the White House that the U.S. president had far more information available from the Pentagon and PACOM than did President Jiang from the PLA. U.S.–China military-to-military cooperation must therefore also strengthen the ability of civilian leaders in both capitals to manage military incidents.

Notes

1. The terms "external balancing" and "internal balancing" are used by theorists to describe how states respond to rising powers or threats in their external environment. Internal balancing involves an increase in indigenous military capabilities to maintain balance of power vis-à-vis the rising power. When internal balancing is not possible or practical because of limited resources, domestic political constraints, or a desire to avoid tension with the rising power, then states will choose external balancing; that is, alignment (either formal alliances or increased cooperation) with other states that are similarly threatened by the rising power. In the case of Japan, the evidence of external balancing is more pronounced, particularly in Tokyo's March 2007 security cooperation agreement with Australia and its October 2008 agreement with India.

2. Hideki Kawasaki and Toshimitsu Miyai, "China Actions Due to Govt Weakness," *Yomiuri Shimbun*, 1 May 2010, http://www.yomiuri.co.jp/dy/national/T100430004385.htm.

3. Information Office of the State Council, People's Republic of China, "IX. Defense Expenditure," in "China's National Defense in 2006," 29 December 2006, http://www.fas.org/nuke/guide/china/doctrine/wp2006.html.

4. "Chinese Naval Warship Arrives in Tokyo for Visit," 28 November 2007, Xinhua, http://english.people.com.cn/90001/90776/90883/6310911.html. Chinese Foreign Ministry spokesman Liu Jianchao stated, "This visit will promote exchanges between the defense departments of the two countries and will help ship the assistance materials to the earthquake-hit area in China. This will also help enhance the friendship and mutual trust between the two countries." "JMSDF Destroyer Makes First Port Call in China," *China Daily*, 24 June 2008.

5. Hideki and Toshimitsu, "China Actions Due to Govt Weakness."

6. Sunny Lee, "South Korea Confirms Torpedo Sank Its Warship," *The National*, 25 April 2010, http://www.thenational.ae/apps/pbcs.dll/article?AID=/20100426/FOREIGN/704259850/1015.

Wu Shicun

Opportunities and Challenges for China–U.S. Cooperation in the South China Sea

The Current Situation in the South China Sea

In the South China Sea (SCS) there are disputes regarding sovereignty claims over islands and reefs as well as maritime jurisdiction. The disputes involve six nations and seven parties: China, Vietnam, the Philippines, Malaysia, Brunei, Indonesia, and Taiwan. Indonesia is not involved in any sovereignty dispute, but its exclusive economic zone (EEZ) claim falls partially within China's U-shaped line.

The most heated issue concerning the SCS is the sovereignty over the Spratly Islands and the marine jurisdiction that flows from sovereignty. The issue first arose in the 1950s. The government of the Philippines used Franklin M. Meads' establishment of "the Kingdom of Humanity" and Tomas Cloma's "discovery" of Kalayaan to raise its claims over parts of the Spratly Islands. This was met with strong protests from mainland China, Taiwan, Vietnam, France, and the United Kingdom. Facing these strong objections, the Philippine government relaxed its support for Cloma's claims based on *res nullius*.

Vietnam traces its claim to the Spratlys back to French colonial times. In 1933 France occupied nine of the Spratly Islands. The Chinese government challenged the French occupation from the very beginning, which resulted in the French retreat from those islands following the Geneva Accords of 1954.

Therefore, South Vietnam's claim over the islands based on "accession" of French rights was invalidated. During the same period, high-level government officials in North Vietnam repeatedly affirmed their support for China's claim of sovereignty over both the Paracel and Spratly islands. The discovery of oil in the late 1960s and the ratification of the 1982 United Nations Convention on the Law of the Sea (UNCLOS) have sparked a new round of South China Sea disputes. According to unilateral explanation of relevant provisions of UNCLOS, some Southeast Asian countries have made their claims over territorial seas, contiguous zones, continental shelves, and EEZs. In spite of the signing of the Declaration on the Conduct of Parties in the South China Sea (DOC) in 2002, these countries still reinforce their occupation and sovereignty claims in one way or another. The actions include exploring for and exploiting oil and gas with foreign companies in disputed waters, developing tourism on occupied islands, setting up administrative schemes for those occupied islands, furthering construction of military facilities including military-used airport runways, and strengthening law enforcement on illegal, unreported and unregulated (IUU) fishing in disputed waters.

At present, the Spratly Islands are occupied by different countries: thirty islands, islets, and reefs by Vietnam; nine by the Philippines; and five by Malaysia. Brunei has declared sovereignty over Louisa Reef but has not stationed any troops on it. As the real Sovereignty State of the Spratly Islands, China (including Taiwan) has control over eight islands, islets, and reefs. In addition to military occupation, all claimant countries declared their unilateral EEZ claims from 1977 on, resulting in large overlapping claims in the SCS. The situation is complicated by historical or treaty lines. Although the 1998 map (below) misses the only maritime boundary between China and Vietnam in the Tonkin Gulf, it gives a general picture of the overlapping claims in the South China Sea.

China's position on the SCS issue is that China has always been the sovereign over the Spratly Islands from both historical and legal perspectives. This statement is supported by ample evidence of historical records and maps.[1] China discovered the island groups in the South China Sea. The Chinese people have occupied and developed the islands since a long time ago.[2] Since the 1970s, coastal countries, particularly Vietnam, the Philippines, and Malaysia, have claimed their sovereignty over the islands, islets, and reefs of Spratly Islands. Vietnam's sovereignty claims are based on historical records and maps from precolonial time and from the French colonial period. Vietnam maintains its position that the "Feudal Vietnamese State" effectively controlled the two archipelagoes since the seventeenth century according to international law

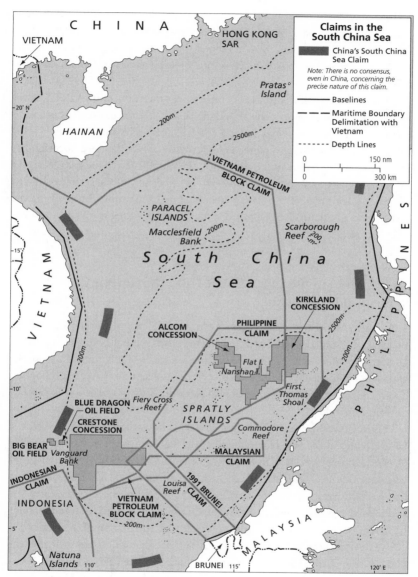

Map 1. Claims in the South China Sea

requirements. Vietnam also relies on documentation from the former Republic of Vietnam to substantiate its claims. Brunei's claim to Louisa Reef seems to be based on its location within the continental shelf area claimed by Brunei. Malaysia's claim to parts of the Spratlys seems to be based on the fact that these features are located within the continental shelf area claimed by Malaysia. The Philippines' claims are based on the notion of discovery as well as adjacent and effective occupation.[3]

The claimants' efforts to assert control over the features in the SCS stems from their desire to exploit the abundant oil and natural gas resources and to control the critical sea-lanes linking the Indian Ocean and the west Pacific Ocean. Due to the changed pattern of international relations and uncertainties in Asia's security system after the end of Cold War, the SCS issue has assumed a prominent position in Asia's security system, especially in the security strategy of relevant countries. The SCS has become one of the most disputed marine areas in the world, involving many disputants and covering the largest overlapping sea area.

The Position of the United States and Its Interests in the South China Sea

The United States showed its presence in the SCS shortly after its founding. In 1784 a fully loaded U.S. merchant vessel, the *Chinese Empress*, arrived in Guangzhou via the SCS. After its occupation of the Philippines in 1899, the United States gained its foothold in the SCS for the first time. As the Philippines became a base for U.S. entrance of East Asia, the SCS served as a U.S. gateway to China's mainland.

During World War II, the intensified conflicts between Japan and the United States in the SCS region led to a war for dominance in the west Pacific Ocean. Although the United States won the war, the quick rise of the socialist camp and the emergence of the Cold War were deemed as a major threat to the Western world. In this context, the containment of the socialist camp led by the former Soviet Union became the dominant strategic U.S. foreign policy doctrine. The SCS region was critical for the implementation of this policy.

With the emergence of the South China Sea as a regional hot spot after the Cold War, the United States has gradually changed its neutral and nonintervention position in the SCS disputes. Many sources indicate that the United States had switched from a policy of "active neutrality" to one of "active concern" by 2000 and was moving in the direction of becoming willing to intervene in sovereignty questions.[4] The United States started to see the SCS issue as a "threat to the security of sea lanes of communication," which may lead to large-scale military conflicts.[5] On 26 July 1994, during the ASEAN Post-Ministerial Conference, U.S. deputy secretary of state Strobe Talbott stated that the challenge facing Southeast Asia was in the SCS.[6] When mentioning the threats to the stability of East Asia in an address before the National Press Club on 6 August 1994, then–U.S. ambassador to Japan Walter Mondale pointed out that "competing territorial claims in the South China Sea . . . cannot be ignored."[7] In his address at China's National Defense University in October 1994, U.S. secretary of defense William Perry stated that the third challenge in Asia was in the South China Sea. He added that "if disputed territorial claims to the Spratly Islands erupt into conflict, it could be a devastating blow to regional security and could threaten sea lines of communication vital to the United States and other countries of the world. Inflammatory statements and military deployments help keep tensions high. They also prevent the development of natural resources which might help reduce tensions. That is why I am encouraged by the stated desire of China and Vietnam to avoid conflict."[8]

All of these statements by high-level U.S. officials showed the Clinton administration's "active-concern" about SCS issues.[9] With respect to the conflict between China and the Philippines over the Mischief Reef, under pressure from the media and some congressional representatives, the U.S. government changed its "neutrality" stance and started to show its support to the Philippines. The U.S. statement of 10 May 1995 on its policy on the South China Sea clearly referred to China, albeit indirectly.[10] Later, on 16 June 1995, while talking to reporters in Tokyo, Joseph Nye, then U.S. assistant secretary of defense for international security, said, "if military action occurred in the Spratlys and this interfered with the freedom of the seas, then we would be prepared to escort and make sure that navigation continues."[11] This was the first time that a U.S. high-level official expressed the possibility of U.S. military intervention on the SCS issue on the basis of its interference with navigation.[12] When addressing the Institute for International Relations in Hanoi in August 1995, U.S. secretary of state Warren Christopher expressed that one of the key issues for the stability in Southeast Asia was the South China Sea: "It is a vital sea lane through which one-quarter of the world's ocean freight passes. The United States will continue to urge countries with competing claims to resources there to resolve their disputes through dialogue."[13]

Because the sea-lanes of the SCS are vital for the United States and its allies, regional stability and the freedom of navigation in the SCS are of fundamental interest to the United States. In addition, the United States has to consider its economic interest in Southeast Asia because the latter is an important overseas market and absorbs substantial U.S. investments. After the Cold War, with the rapid economic growth in the Asia-Pacific region and new development of regional economic cooperation, U.S. influence in East Asia has declined. Beginning in 1993, the "China Threat Theory" began to form in the United States, which holds that China's rapid economic growth will lead it to become another major U.S. adversary. The geopolitics and disputes of the SCS provide a useful instrument for a U.S. containment policy toward China. In Washington's view, strengthening military links with Southeast Asian countries can help the United States achieve its strategic objective of restricting China's military expansion in the SCS.

Based on these considerations, the United States has overtly intervened in the SCS disputes. First, although the United States refrains from taking any stance regarding SCS sovereignty claims, U.S. experts have described Chinese jurisdiction claims in the SCS as excessive.[14] Second, the United States has been seeking to master and reform relevant multilateral security dialogue mechanisms, such as the ASEAN Regional Forum. Third, the United States has stepped up its military collaboration with South China Sea littoral countries in the form of joint military exercises, arms sales, and the lease of military bases. Fourth, the United States continues to strengthen its military presence in the Western Pacific, expanding its military base in Guam and collecting information about the South China Sea issue. Fifth, U.S. oil companies often jointly explore oil resources with Southeast Asian countries in the disputed waters. In July 2008 a U.S. oil company signed an agreement with VietPetro on oil exploration inside China's U-shaped claim line. These intervening activities, on one hand, strengthen the U.S. presence in the SCS both militarily and economically and, on the other hand, further its economic interests and its influence on Southeast Asian countries to counterbalance China's influence in this region. Military expansion in Guam and information collection are for the aim of containing China's possible military actions.

Opportunities and Challenges for China–U.S. Cooperation in Traditional and Nontraditional Fields in the South China Sea

Despite the issues described earlier, it is important to consider the prospects for cooperation between China and the United States regarding the SCS. There are several major sources of opportunity. First, the complexity of the sources of regional security threats requires strong cooperation among countries. With the development of globalization and regional integration, nontraditional threats to regional security have increased substantially. The nontraditional threats include terrorism, drug trafficking, smuggling, highly contagious diseases, piracy, illegal immigration, environmental safety, financial stability, and cyber security. Because these problems are transnational, complex, and have associated effects on traditional security threats, it is hard for a single country to deal with them. If not handled well, they can lead to a serious traditional security crisis. Hence, China and the United States should strengthen their cooperation in this regard.

Second, mutual interests require China–U.S. cooperation. As the two leading powers in the Asia-Pacific region, both countries hope to safeguard the peace and stability of the region and to ensure free and safe passage along the sea-lanes through the SCS. A closer cooperation in counterterrorism, counterpiracy, and disaster relief will contribute to the common interests of our two countries.

Traditional political and military security issues are still on the top of the agenda. Threats of these kinds in the SCS mainly come from disputes over sovereignty and marine rights as well as the conflicting interests among great powers such as the United States, China, Japan, India, and Russia. Therefore, cooperation and exchanges in the field of security will enhance mutual trust and understanding. This is beneficial for maintaining peace and stability in the region.

Cooperation between China and the United States can start from the easier and less sensitive areas to combat nontraditional threats in the region. Opportunities for cooperation include exchanges of information on piracy and terrorists, prevention of natural disasters, and search-and-rescue exercises. With increases in mutual confidence, cooperation can be enlarged to military fields to include joint personnel training, setting up information-sharing schemes, and joint military exercises. However, cooperation must take into consideration the concerns of neighboring countries.

Despite these sources of promising potential, a variety of obstacles to cooperation remain. First, worrying about the rise of China is unfavorable to cooperation. Following the collapse of the former Soviet Union, the United States became the sole superpower in the world. Currently, the United States aims to maintain and reinforce its global leadership. However, due to major differences in social system, ideology, cultural background, and historical tradition, China has different views regarding the future international order. With its rapid economic growth, China is enjoying an increasingly high international status. According to a forecast by the RAND Corporation, China will become a regional rival to the United States in many aspects by 2015.[15] Although China's power will not be equal to that of the United States, China can exert direct influence on the neighboring areas and frustrate the U.S. political and military ambitions. The existence of distrust in the United States regarding China's rapid development may adversely affect China–U.S. security cooperation in the SCS.

Second, long-term disputes and complex international relations in the SCS make Sino-U.S. security cooperation sensitive. As the link between the Pacific Ocean and the Indian Ocean, the SCS is of strategic importance. The sea-lanes through the waters around the Spratly Islands are the busiest in the world. However, such sea-lanes pass through the waters where seven parties contend for territorial sovereignty and marine rights. In addition, external regional powers such as the United States, Japan, India, and Russia have complex vested interests in the SCS that will inevitably influence their policies toward East Asia and China. The factors mentioned here make Sino-U.S. security cooperation in the SCS difficult and sensitive.

Future Prospects for the South China Sea Issue

In security cooperation, China and the United States will undoubtedly take into account possible impacts on the sovereignty claims by different countries. The two sides may focus on the following points.

Develop Consensus on Cooperation and Promote Mutual Trust

The essential precondition for Sino-U.S. security cooperation is to build consensus and promote mutual trust. To maintain its global leadership, the United States has to ensure the safe navigation of oil and other strategic materials across the SCS. However, with the development of multipolarization and emerging new powers, the United States may find it more and more difficult to maintain its global leadership; thus, it needs to get support from its allies and other powers. To make security cooperation possible, the United States must understand and support China's strategic interests in the SCS region. Sovereignty disputes are not easy to solve within a short time and shall be solved among related disputants through friendly negotiation according to international law, including UNCLOS. The intervention of outside powers can only further complicate the sensitive issue.

Facilitate Economic and Social Development to Tackle Security Threats at the Root

After Asia's financial crisis in the late 1990s, some Southeast Asian countries were thrown into social disorder, increased poverty, and unemployment. This partly explains the increasing cases of piracy in the SCS. In this regard, there is substantial room for China–U.S. cooperation. China and the United States in particular can make full use of their capital and technological advantages to facilitate economic and social development in this region, improve people's living standards, promote social justice, protect the environment, and realize sustainable development in the region. This can establish a significant foundation to finally eliminate the roots of crimes at sea.

Strengthen Information-Sharing Mechanisms between China and the United States

Sino-U.S. cooperation in tackling nontraditional security threats is less sensitive than tackling traditional security threats and is beneficial to both parties. The following measures offer a positive way forward. First, information sharing should be strengthened. Because terrorist activities, pirate attacks, and cross-border crimes are highly organized and have a high level of mobility, effective information sharing or a common database would avoid double standards and lend itself to combating such crimes. Second, the role of nongovernmental think tanks should be brought into full play. Based on their research, nongovernmental think tanks can provide relevant suggestions for cooperation in the field of nontraditional security.

Shelve Disputes, Pursue Joint Development

Putting aside disputes in favor of joint exploration and development is a realistic choice for the peaceful and final resolution of the SCS disputes. Due to the complexity of disputes over sovereignty claims in the SCS, it would be extremely difficult to find a solution acceptable to all the parties concerned within a short time. To facilitate the peaceful resolution of the disputes, the countries concerned, including China, signed the Declaration on the Conduct of Parties in the South China Sea (DOC) in 2002.[16] This declaration laid down the principles of peaceful resolution. Parties concerned promised to act with restraint and to make no moves that might complicate or expand the disputes or otherwise affect peace and stability in the region. Before the sovereignty and jurisdiction disputes are peacefully settled, the parties concerned promised to explore possible ways of establishing mutual trust in the spirit of cooperation and understanding. Before the disputes are finally resolved, parties concerned may discuss or pursue cooperation. However, some countries have conducted provocative activities in the disputed waters almost every year after the signing of the DOC. Vietnam, for instance, has drawn out bidding areas, carried out oil exploration, and organized tours and local elections.[17] The purpose of these moves was to declare its so-called sovereignty and consolidate its occupation. In 2008 Vietnam signed a contract with a large U.S. oil company for the exploration of oil and natural gas in disputed waters.[18] Such acts violate the spirit enshrined in the DOC and have led to increased tension in the region.

China initiated the proposal of shelving disputes for joint development, which has proved to be consistent with the interests of the parties concerned and beneficial for the final peaceful resolution of the South China Sea disputes. First, the proposal is in line with the spirit of the DOC. Second, it takes into account the interests of all the parties concerned. Third, it has proven to be workable in practice. In this regard, the Agreement on Joint Seismic Survey of the South China Sea signed by China, the Philippines, and Vietnam in March 2005 is a good case in point.[19] Finally, it reflects the aspiration of surrounding countries for peace and development and is in the interest of the whole world. Such an initiative highlights the image of China with a strong sense of responsibility.

Notes

1. For detailed description of the early records and maps that recorded China's discovery and development activities in the South China Sea, refer to Wu Shicun, *A Study on the South China Sea Dispute* (Haikou: Hainan Press, 2005), 22–34. The early books, which recorded the facts that Chinese people discovered the archipelagoes in the South China Sea, include, among others, *The Records of Special Matters in the Southern States* (Nanzhou Yiwu Zhi) by Wan Zhen, *The Records of the Three Kingdoms* (Sanguo Zhi), and *The Book of Liang* (Liang Zhu). All the three writers lived in the Three Kingdoms period (220–65). In the early eighteenth century, a book by a fishermen of Hainan Island, Bo Genglu, recorded in greater detail dozens of features in the South China Sea, including those of the Spratlys. Admiral Zheng He's seven voyages in the Indian Ocean eliminated the pirate activities rampant in the Southeast Asia and promoted maritime trade with and security in the region. *Zheng He's Navigational Map* provides valuable navigational materials for future voyages. Early maps that show the SCS archipelagoes include *Map of Guangyu* (Guangyu Tu) by Luo Hongxian of Ming dynasty (1368–1644), *The Master Map of the Four Seas* (Sihai Zong Tu) by Chen Lunjiong, the map depicted in *The Records of The Maps of the Seas* by Lin Zexun and Wei Yuan, and the map depicted in *The Records of the Journeys by the Central Government* (Guochao

Rouyuan Ji) of the Qing Dynasty (1644–1911). In particular, three maps created during the Qing dynasty include the Spratlys as part of China's territory. They are *Detailed Maps of Provinces under Qing* (Qing Zhisheng Fentu) of 1724, *Detailed Maps of All Provinces under Royal Qing* (Huangqing Ge Zhisheng Feitu) of 1755, and *The Map of the United Great Qing* (Daqing Tongyi Tianxia Tu) of 1817.

2. Wu, *Study on the South China Sea Dispute*, 22–34.

3. Ramses Amer and Nguyen Hong Thao, "Vietnam and the South China Sea in the Border Context of Its Maritime Issues," Paper prepared for "SCS 2008—The South China Sea: Sustaining Ocean Productivities, Maritime Communities and the Climate," a Conference for Regional Cooperation in Ocean and Earth Sciences Research in the South China Sea organized by The Institute of Ocean and Earth Sciences, University of Malaya in Kuantan, 25–29 November 2008; Nguyen Hong Thao and Ramses Amer, "Managing Vietnam's Maritime Boundary Disputes," *Ocean Development & International Law* 38 (2007): 305–24; Wu, *Study on the South China Sea Dispute*.

4. Yann-Huei Song, "The Overall Situation in the South China Sea in the New Millennium: Before and After the September 11 Terrorist Attacks," *Ocean Development & International Law* 34, no. 3 (2003): 229–77.

5. Statement by William Perry, "The Sino-U.S. Relationship and Its Impact on World Peace," U.S. Department of State Dispatch, 31 October 1994, http://findarticles.com/p/articles/mi_m1584/is_n44_v5/ai_15967997?tag=content;col1.

6. Statement by Deputy Secretary Strobe Talbott at the Six-plus-Seven Open Session of the ASEAN Post-Ministerial Conference, Bangkok, Thailand, 26 July 1994, U.S. Department of State Dispatch, 8 August 1994, http://findarticles.com/p/articles/mi_m1584/is_n32_v5/ai_15743469?tag=content;col1.

7. Statement by Walter Mondale, "Managing U.S-Japan Relations into the 21st Century," U.S. Department of State Dispatch, 19 September 1994, http://findarticles.com/p/articles/mi_m1584/is_n38_v5/ai_15930213?tag=content;col1.

8. Statement by William Perry, "The Sino-U.S. Relationship"; and Wu, *Study on the South China Sea Dispute*.

9. Yann-Huei, "Overall Situation."

10. U.S. Department of State Daily Briefing, 10 May 1995.

11. Quoted in B. Raman, "Chinese Territorial Assertions: The Case of the Mischief," http://www.southchinasea.org/docs/Chinese%20Territorial%20Assertion%20The%20Case%20of%20the%20Mischief%20Reef.htm.

12. Abram N. Shulsky, "Deterrence Theory and Chinese Behavior," RAND Monograph report 1161, particularly chapter 4, http://www.rand.org/pubs/monograph_reports/MR1161/MR1161.chap4.pdf.

13. Warren Christopher, "U.S.-Vietnam Relations: A New Chapter," U.S. Department of State Dispatch, 14 August 1995, http://findarticles.com/p/articles/mi_m1584/is_n33_v6/ai_17443513?tag=content;col1.

14. Yann-huei Song, "The U.S. Policy on the Spratly Islands and the South China Sea," *The Indonesian Quarterly* 25, no. 3 (1997): 316–34. For characterizations of Chinese SCS

jurisdiction claims as excessive, see Peter A. Dutton, "Testimony before the U.S.–China Economic and Security Review Committee Hearing on the Implications of China's Naval Modernization for the United States," 11 June 2009, especially pp. 3, 5, http://www.uscc.gov/hearings/2009hearings/written_testimonies/09_06_11_wrts/09_06_11_dutton_statement.php; James Kraska, *Seapower, Statecraft and the Law of the Sea* (Oxford, UK: Oxford University Press, 2010); James Kraska, "China Set for Naval Hegemony," *The Diplomat*, 6 May 2010, http://the-diplomat.com/2010/05/06/china-ready-to-dominate-seas/; and James Kraska, "The Legal War Behind the Impeccable Incident," *World Politics Review*, 16 March 2009, http://www.worldpoliticsreview.com/articlePrint.aspx?ID=3449.

15. Charles Wolf Jr., *Straddling Economics and Politics: Cross-cutting Issues in Asia, the United States and the Global Economy* (Santa Monica, CA: RAND, 2002), ch. 18, http://www.rand.org/pubs/monograph_reports/2006/MR1571.pdf.

16. "Declaration on the Conduct of Parties in the South China Sea," ASEAN Web site, http://www.aseansec.org/13163.htm; Web site of Foreign Ministry of the People's Republic of China, http://www.fmprc.gov.cn/eng/wjb/zzjg/gjs/gjzzyhy/2608/2610/t15311.htm.

17. "越南在南沙群岛举行'国会选举'宣示'主权'" ["Vietnam Congress Holds Election in Nansha and Declares 'Sovereignty'"], 世界新闻报 [*World News Report*], http://news.hsw.cn/2007-06/15/content_6347625_2.htm; and "Vietnam Holds Congress Election in Nansha and Plunders Gas and Oil Resources," *TianshuiNet*, http://www.tianshui.com.cn/news/guoji/2007061507150948122.htm.

18. "China Protests the U.S. Petro Giant's Oil Exploration in the South China Sea," *Global Times*, 21 July 2008, http://news.sina.com.cn/c/2008-07-21/084715968739.shtml; and "Tussle for Oil in the South China Sea," *South China Morning Post*, 20 July 2008, http://www.viet-studies.info/kinhte/Tussle_for_oil_SCMP.htm.

19. "All-Win Rational Choice," *People's Daily*, 18 March 2008 (English Language Bulletin), http://english.peopledaily.com.cn/200503/18/eng20050318_177391.html.

Zhu Huayou

Enhancing Sino-U.S. Maritime Security Cooperation in Southeast Asia

The Status of Regional Security in the South China Sea Area

The South China Sea (SCS), which is a politically and economically open geographical unit, is heavily relied upon by countries and regions around it since the sea is crucial for their development and even their survival. Consequently, the maritime security of the SCS is connected not only to geographical factors but also to the political, economic, and social development in the area. The Association of Southeast Asian Nations (ASEAN) has formed a political and economic unit to pursue open regionalism and to promote the mutual development of its members. However, due to the great difference in political systems and economic levels among the ASEAN member countries, many challenges have been and will still be encountered in the process of regional integration. Because the SCS connects the Pacific Ocean with the Indian Ocean, it is of great geographical and strategic interest. Furthermore, the SCS is of great significance to the social and economic development of the surrounding countries and region. These two factors together endow the maritime security on the SCS with an obvious feature of regionality.

In the process of regional integration and economic globalization, the maritime security of the SCS should accordingly be understood in the context of globalization. As a commercial logistics channel, the sea has become an important factor affecting the global economy and a key medium of the global sea route system. The regional maritime economy has also become very conspicuous with its dynamism and influence on the Asian economy and even the global economy. The vicissitudes in political and economic patterns in this area also reflect the adjustment of the international political and economic orders. For all these reasons, regional nations seek international cooperation to maintain regional security; furthermore, powers outside the area also try to get involved in the regional issues to pursue their strategic and vital interests. This adds a global dimension to the maritime security of the SCS.

Interaction of Traditional and Nontraditional Security Issues

Although there has been a trend of weakening traditional security threats since the end of the Cold War, traditional security threats will still be a very important part of national security together with changes and adjustment of geopolitical and economic patterns. In particular, we can see that some military alliances outside the SCS area are strengthening instead of weakening and are being readjusted, which will influence the development of traditional forces in the area to some extent. In the meantime, nontraditional security issues—piracy, maritime terrorism, and maritime ecosecurity, in particular— have emerged as new challenges. The intertwinement of traditional and nontraditional security has brought us new understanding of the intervention of traditional security forces into nontraditional security problems. A new trend has emerged.

The Concomitance of Both Positive and Negative Factors

A consensus has been established among the related countries and regions that the maritime security of the SCS plays a significant role in the regional and even the global economy. With the increase of exchanges in economy, culture, and human resources, there are more and more positive factors that affect and even decide maritime security cooperation. Thus, a consensus of sharing interests and taking the responsibility of guaranteeing security should be established as well. Of course, there are still many negative factors affecting maritime security and maritime security cooperation. At the macroscopic level, the lack of strategic mutual trust may constitute one important factor due to the problems inherited from history and the clashes of real national interests. At the microscopic level, due to such factors as limitations in funding and technology, the means to guarantee maritime security still lag behind.

At present, maritime security cooperation in the SCS area mainly takes the form of cooperation on nontraditional security issues such as counterterrorism and counterpiracy. Because there may be some strategic considerations of traditional security behind the nontraditional security cooperation, regional crisis management is kept at a low level with limited effects.

There is a trend toward increased, strengthened bilateral and multilateral nontraditional security cooperation. The projected "ASEAN Security Community" has been organized to combat terrorism and piracy. The ministers of defense of the "Five Power Defense Arrangements" have discussed new cooperation mechanisms to strengthen cooperation in providing humanitarian assistance and disaster relief. The Five Power Defense Arrangements support Malaysia's proposal of setting up a regional relief center to strengthen the coordination of disaster relief. The Regional Cooperation Agreement on Combating Piracy and Armed Robbery against Ships in Asia (ReCAAP) took effect in 2006, and an information-sharing center was established in Singapore with the objective of facilitating the sharing of piracy-related information. The Philippines has decided to improve its ability to combat and counter any biological weapons attack made by terrorists.

Nontraditional security cooperation among the ASEAN member countries is also promoted by countries outside the Southeast Asian region. The seismic sea wave warning apparatus developed by Indonesia, when combined with the tsunami warning systems developed by Germany and the United States, can increase warning time markedly. The Philippine government received help from the United States in the raid against the Abu Sayyaf camp, and a mechanism of military cooperation, a security engagement board, has been established to complement the existing military cooperation between the two countries. In 2006 Malaysia signed the Treaty on Mutual Legal Assistance in Criminal Matters with the United States to enhance the cooperation between the two countries to combat transnational crime, including international terrorism. On behalf of ASEAN, Malaysia and Canada signed a Joint Declaration for Cooperation to Combat International Terrorism in July 2006. Several training exercises to enhance the capacity of enforcement personnel from the ASEAN member countries in dealing with various aspects of drug production and trafficking have been held in collaboration with Australia. Vietnam and Russia signed an agreement to strengthen cooperation on counterterrorism. In addition, Japan and India have strengthened cooperation with ASEAN on counterterrorism.

Initial success has been achieved. According to annual reports, "Piracy and Armed Robbery against Ships," compiled by the International Maritime Bureau, there has been a decrease in the number of reported incidents of piracy and armed robbery against ships. In 2006, a total of 239 incidents were reported all over the world, 88 of which happened in waters of SCS. Of these incidents, 50 were reported in Indonesian waters (dropping from 79 in 2005), 11 in the Malacca Strait, and 10 in Malaysian waters. The drop in the number of reported attacks shows that the attempts by the international community to combat piracy and armed robbery against ships have yielded good results.

Multilateral and nontraditional security cooperation between China and Southeast Asian countries is becoming much more frequent. In August 2006, the ASEAN-China Seminar on Maritime Law Enforcement Cooperation was held in Dalian, China. The seminar was the first one cohosted by the two sides, symbolizing a concrete step forward for cooperation on maritime law enforcement and enhancing the law enforcement cooperation in the field of nontraditional security issues. China signed the "Memorandum of Understanding on Maritime Affairs Cooperation" and the "Memorandum of Understanding on Maritime Cooperation" with Malaysia and Indonesia, respectively, thereby enhancing cooperation with the ASEAN member countries on anti–money laundering and guaranteeing maritime security in the Malacca Strait. China, Singapore, and Norway signed the "Memorandum of Understanding on Maritime Research Development, Education and Training" to further strengthen cooperation in maritime and shipping research among the three countries. China also joined the ReCAAP. During the commemorative summit marking the fifteenth anniversary of ASEAN–China dialogue relations in 2006, Chinese premier Wen Jiabao and leaders of ASEAN members signed a joint statement to strengthen cooperation and information sharing in nontraditional security areas; to promote cooperation on criminal justice and law enforcement, including in anticorruption efforts; to encourage exchange of defense/security officials; and to work together in ensuring maritime security in the region.

In conclusion, the maritime security cooperation of the SCS is part of the regional security cooperation. The cooperation is constantly expanding and deepening; the methods that the powers inside and outside the region use to combine resources and cooperate offer some new features. The security cooperation mechanism or crisis handling mechanism that covers the whole SCS, however, is still under formation. Because the strategic interests and safety boundaries of the related powers overlap and sometimes collide with each other, crisis management is still limited to a sort of "soft constraint."

Rationale for China and the United States to Enhance Maritime Security Cooperation in the Asia-Pacific Region

Maritime security cooperation is in the interests of both parties. In recent years, China and ASEAN countries, based on their close geographical location, have established reciprocal and mutual beneficial partnerships for win-win cooperation in both political and economic areas. It is now the trend to establish the China-ASEAN Free Trade Area to further boost cooperation in all respects in this region. As a major investment partner and export market, the United States serves as an important driver for the rapid growth of the ASEAN economy. The United States is not only ASEAN's top trade partner; much more significantly, it remains ASEAN's most important security partner. It is in the strategic interests of both China and the United States to enhance maritime cooperation to safeguard the economic prosperity, political stability, security, and peace in the Asia-Pacific region.

The settlement of traditional and nontraditional security issues relies on Sino-U.S. maritime cooperation. Along with economic globalization and Asia's economic growth, the political security situation in the Asia-Pacific region is now undergoing profound changes. In addition to traditional security problems, nontraditional security issues such as terrorism, proliferation of weapons of mass destruction, environmental pollution, and sea-lane security are increasing, thereby affecting economic development and social progress in the region. To deal with such challenges, bilateral and multilateral security cooperation is increasingly active, and cooperative mechanisms of various forms are taking shape. However, uncertainties persist. The ultimate settlement and management of these issues cannot be achieved without Sino-U.S. cooperation, especially Sino-U.S. maritime cooperation. China and the United States should carry out cooperation based on mutual understanding of each other's interests because it is of great significance to maintain peace and stability in the Asia-Pacific and Southeast Asia region.

The Pragmatic Possibility of Sino-U.S. Maritime Cooperation in the Region

Both China and the United States are willing to enhance regional security cooperation. Since the normalization of Sino-U.S. diplomatic relations, both countries are willing to enhance cooperation in the security area. The United States realizes that China, as a major regional power, one of the five permanent members of the UN Security Council, and a major nuclear power, plays an inevitable role in its security interests both in the region and around the world. Conversely, China strives to maintain a secure surrounding environment by means of security cooperation to ensure its peaceful development. It is the common will of both countries to work together to eliminate conflicts caused by misjudgment. This creates the ground for their possible enlargement of cooperation.

Increased mutual understanding is the fundamental condition for Sino-U.S. maritime cooperation. Along with the changing international strategic environment and increasingly active contacts, China and the United States have greatly enhanced mutual understanding. In recent years, U.S. elites have gradually realized a consensus on China. Deputy Secretary of State Robert B. Zoellick described China as a "stakeholder" in 2005, a designation that was further reflected in documents of the State Department, the Pentagon, and the White House. The Bush administration followed a policy of engagement with China. The Armitage Report II in 2007 ("The United States and Japan: Getting Asia Right through 2020") presented a much more positive judgment toward China than had previous documents because it regarded China as a key factor for regional stability and it emphasized the need for the United States to cooperate and coordinate with China in Asian affairs. The Chinese government also attaches great importance to Sino-U.S. relations, stressing the need to "enhance trust, reduce trouble, develop cooperation, and avoid confrontation." China is convinced that the enhancement of Sino-U.S. security cooperation and the sound development of Sino-U.S. relations can play a significant roll in alleviating its security predicament and maintaining world peace.

The existing security cooperation mechanism serves as a framework or platform for maritime cooperation. Besides bilateral cooperation, both China and the United States are actively engaging in multilateral security cooperation. It is believed that the existing security cooperation mechanism provides an excellent platform for further security cooperation and maritime security cooperation. Sino-U.S. interactions in Asia-Pacific Economic Cooperation (APEC), the ASEAN Regional Forum (ARF), and other mechanisms also offer some useful experiences and practices for cooperation and thus enhance mutual understanding, trust, and the expansion of common benefits.

Moreover, China and the United States have laid a good foundation for maritime cooperation. In 1998 the two countries signed the Agreement on Establishing and Strengthening Maritime Military Security Consultation Mechanism, thereby intensifying maritime security consultation. The formation of the Sino-U.S. Maritime Security Consultation Mechanism, the

Annual Defense Affairs Consultation Mechanism, and the Sino-U.S. Joint Maritime Search and Rescue Exercises help to increase mutual understanding and decrease security barriers. After the 9/11 attacks, China and the United States have strengthened the bilateral and regional cooperation in nontraditional security areas. The Container Security Initiative signed by the two countries has also enhanced maritime security cooperation and helped to prevent the proliferation of weapons of mass destruction. The cooperation on nontraditional security areas has not only increased mutual understanding between two countries but has also laid a foundation for further synergy. In recent years, Sino-U.S. maritime cooperation has made additional progress. For further details on events in 2006, see table 1 (below).

Table 1. Sino-U.S. Maritime Cooperation in Relevant Sea Areas in 2006

Time	Events	Participating Countries	Sea Areas
May	Joint serial maritime defense exercise for the first time	China, U.S., Japan, Russia, Canada	Northeast Asia
September	Maritime telecommunication exercise	China, U.S.	Hawaii
September	Joint maritime search-and-rescue exercise	China, U.S.	San Diego
November	Joint maritime search-and-rescue exercise	China, U.S.	South China

Suggestions for Strengthening Sino-U.S. Marine Security Cooperation in the South China Sea Area

Professionals and dialogue between related research institutes should be actively exchanged. Such exchanges can be carried out in three aspects. First, the two countries can exchange scholars, on either a regular or an irregular basis, for sharing updated research on issues such as regional security and maritime cooperation. Second, workshops, training courses, and conferences can be designed to foster connections between universities and research institutes and to enrich the dialogues. Third, a regular exchange of visits by scholars is likely to help expand the cooperative opportunities for Sino-U.S. regional maritime security.

Less sensitive topics such as Sino-U.S. maritime search and rescue should be addressed and are feasible areas for Sino-U.S. cooperation. For instance, with respect to threats to property and pass-by vessels and the loss of lives of fishermen caused by bad weather or pirates, if a Sino-U.S. joint rescue mechanism on the sea is created, lives and property vulnerable at sea may be better secured, and trust between the United States and China may be cemented. The latter is of significance for further cooperation on future maritime security issues. In addition, other nonsensitive subjects such as maritime environmental protection and maritime climate study can also be taken into consideration.

More Sino-U.S. maritime cooperation mechanisms should be explored. Based on Sino-U.S. cooperation in less-sensitive areas including maritime search and rescue, the issue of regularizing and standardizing joint maritime cooperation could be discussed. For example, exchanging information on maritime terrorism, maritime environmental protection, maritime search and rescue, and the fight against pirates will all help build a solid foundation for closer ties and the safeguarding of regional security.

James R. Holmes and Toshi Yoshihara

China and the United States in the Indian Ocean

An Emerging Strategic Triangle?

Prospects for a Strategic Triangle

Today the Asian seas are witnessing an intriguing historical anomaly: the simultaneous rise of two homegrown maritime powers against the backdrop of U.S. dominion over the global commons. The drivers behind this apparent irregularity in the Asian regional order are, of course, China and India. Aspirations for great-power status and, above all, their quests for energy security have compelled both Beijing and New Delhi to direct their gazes from land to the seas. While Chinese and Indian maritime interests are natural outgrowths of impressive economic growth and the attendant appetites for energy resources, their entries into the nautical realm also portend worrisome trends.

At present some strategists in both capitals speak and write in terms that anticipate rivalry with each other. Given that commercial shipping must traverse the same oceanic routes to reach Indian and Chinese ports, mutual fears persist that the bodies of water stretching from the Persian Gulf to the South China Sea could be held hostage in the event of crisis or conflict. Such insecurities similarly animated naval competition in the past, when major powers depended on a common nautical space. Moreover, lingering questions over the sustainability of American primacy on the high seas have heightened concerns about the U.S. Navy's ability to guarantee maritime stability, a state of affairs that has long been taken for granted.[1]

It is within this more fluid context that the Indian Ocean has assumed greater prominence. Unfortunately, much of the recent discourse has focused on future Chinese naval ambitions in the Indian Ocean and potential U.S. responses to such a new presence. In other words, the novelty of the Indian Ocean, as it currently stands, stems from expected encounters between extraregional powers. But such a narrow analytical approach assumes that the region will remain an inanimate object perpetually vulnerable to outside manipulation. More importantly, it overlooks the possible interactions arising from the intervention of India, the dominant regional power. Indeed, omitting the potential role that India might play in any capacity would risk misreading the future of the Indian Ocean region.

There is, therefore, an urgent need to bring India more completely into the picture as a full participant, if not an arbiter, in the region's maritime future. To add depth to the existing literature, this study assesses the longer-term maritime trajectory of the Indian Ocean region by examining the triangular dynamics between the United States, China, and India. To be sure, the aspirational nature of Chinese and Indian nautical ambitions and their current capabilities precludes attempts at discerning potential outcomes or supplying concrete policy prescriptions. Nevertheless, exploring the basic foundations for cooperation or competition among the three powers could provide hints at how Beijing, Washington, and New Delhi can actively preclude rivalry and promote collaboration in the Indian Ocean.

As a first step in this endeavor, this chapter examines a key ingredient in the expected emergence of a "strategic triangle": the prospects of Indian sea power. While no one has rigorously defined this international relations metaphor, scholars typically use it to convey a strategic confluence of interests among three nation-states. In this initial foray, we use the term fairly loosely, using it to describe a pattern of cooperation and competition among the United States, China, and India. It is our contention that Indian Ocean stability will hinge largely on how India manages its maritime rise. On the one hand, if a robust Indian maritime presence fails to materialize, then New Delhi would essentially be forced to surrender, leaving a strategic vacuum to the United States and China. On the other hand, if powerful Indian naval forces are one day used for exclusionary purposes, then the region would almost certainly become an arena for naval competition. Either undesirable outcome would be shaped in part by how India views its own maritime prerogatives and how

Washington and Beijing weigh the probabilities of India's nautical success or failure in the Indian Ocean. If all three parties foresee a muscular Indian naval policy, then a more martial environment in the Indian Ocean would likely take shape. If the three powers view India and each other with equanimity, then the prospects for cooperation would brighten considerably. Capturing the perspectives of the three powers on India's maritime ambitions is thus a critical analytical starting point.

To provide a comprehensive overview of each capital's estimate of future Indian maritime power, we gauge the current literature and forecasts in India, the United States, and China on Indian maritime strategy, doctrine, and capabilities. We then conclude with an analysis of how certain changes in the maritime geometry in the Indian Ocean might be conducive to either cooperation or competition.

India's Self-Assessment

While Indian maritime strategists are not ardent followers of Alfred Thayer Mahan, they do use Mahan to underscore the importance of the Indian Ocean. A Mahan quotation of doubtful provenance commonly appears in official and academic discussions of Indian naval power. "Mahan, the renowned naval strategist and scholar had said over a century ago 'whosoever controls the Indian Ocean, dominates Asia. In the twenty-first century, the destiny of the world will be decided upon its waters,'" declared an official Indian press release in 2002.[2] Rear Admiral R. Chopra, then the head of sea training for the Indian Navy, offered a somewhat less-bellicose-sounding but equally evocative version of the quotation at a seminar on maritime history: "'Whoever controls the Indian Ocean controls Asia. This ocean is the key to the Seven Seas.'"[3]

Quibbles over history aside, India clearly sees certain diplomatic, economic, and military interests at stake in Indian Ocean waters. In particular, shipments of Middle East oil, natural gas, and raw materials are crucial to India's effort to build up economic strength commensurate with the needs and geopolitical aspirations of the Indian people. Some 90 percent of world trade, measured by bulk, travels by sea. A sizable share of that total must traverse narrow seas in India's geographic neighborhood, notably the straits at Hormuz, Malacca, and Bab el-Mandeb. Shipping is at its most vulnerable in such confined waterways.

Strategists in New Delhi couch their appraisals of India's maritime surroundings in intensely geopolitical terms—jarringly so for Westerners accustomed to the notion that economic globalization has rendered power politics and armed conflict passé. Robert Kaplan has rendered a service by returning geography to its rightful place at the center of Asian politics. In a much-debated 2009 article in the journal *Foreign Policy*, Kaplan opines that, far from transcending geography, "globalization is reinforcing it." He enjoins practitioners and scholars of international relations to reclaim the older tradition of geopolitics embedded in the works of thinkers such as Fernand Braudel, Sir Halford Mackinder, and Alfred Thayer Mahan.[4] In a 2010 *Foreign Affairs* article, he applies geopolitical logic to China, implying strongly that China's surging economy and growing military reach is bringing peripheral areas—maritime and terrestrial—under the sway of a Greater China.[5] While geography is not fate, then, it still sets the bounds within which international politics plays out.

None of this comes as a surprise to Indians, who voice views that hark back to the age of Mackinder and Mahan. New Delhi now eyes important geographic features worriedly and has set out to build up Indian diplomatic, economic, and military power as a counterweight to Chinese power. The Indian economy has grown at a rapid clip—albeit not as rapidly as China's—allowing an increasingly confident Indian government to yoke hard power, measured in ships, aircraft, and weapons systems, to a foreign policy aimed at primacy in the Indian Ocean region.[6] If intervention in regional disputes or the internal affairs of South Asian states is necessary, imply Indian leaders, India should do the intervening rather than allow outsiders any pretext for doing so. New Delhi envisions remaining on the strategic defensive for the foreseeable future, but it apparently foresees fulfilling defensive aims through offensive ways and means.

The threat environment, then, helps explain the tenor of Indian strategic pronouncements. While certain past U.S. actions at sea inspire misgivings in New Delhi—as recently as the late 1980s, the Indian military waged counterinsurgent operations on Sri Lanka to prevent the U.S. Navy from obtaining basing rights at Trincomalee—Indians generally welcome the American presence in South Asian waters. One Indian naval officer, in fact, declared that the Indian Navy had scrutinized the 2007 U.S. Maritime Strategy (discussed below) and found "not a word out of place."[7] To be sure, retired Indian officials with greater liberty to speak their minds have voiced qualms about certain aspects of U.S. strategy in the Indian Ocean.[8] On balance, official opinion nonetheless seems to regard the real advantages of dominant U.S. sea power as outweighing whatever hypothetical drawbacks there might be.

Again, China is another story. A robust Chinese naval presence in the Indian Ocean would likely prompt robust countermeasures on New Delhi's part, manifest in an accelerated buildup of the Indian Navy and, perhaps, a decision to expand the Indian naval presence in regions such as the South China Sea and the Horn of Africa. A recently retired Indian flag officer told an audience at the U.S. Naval War College that forward-deployed Chinese nuclear submarines would cross an Indian red line for naval competition.[9] In late 2007, voicing a view common among Indian strategists, one Indian officer told the United Services Institute, New Delhi, that China would remain a "potent threat" to regional security because of its ties to Pakistan and a host of unresolved disputes with India. By contrast, the United States could create problems for India through any inability to vanquish terrorism in Afghanistan or calm the nuclear dispute with Iran.[10] The upshot: any problems created by the United States would be an inadvertent by-product of U.S. actions elsewhere in the region while China and its growing maritime presence in the Indian Ocean could bring about a direct clash of interests between New Delhi and Beijing.

In light of this, any Indian doctrine aimed at regional preeminence will clearly have a strong seafaring component to it. In 2004, accordingly, New Delhi issued its first public analysis of the nation's oceanic environs and how to cope with challenges there. Straightforwardly titled "Indian Maritime Doctrine," the document describes India's maritime strategy largely as a function of economic development and prosperity:

> India's primary maritime interest is to assure national security. This is not restricted to just guarding the coastline and island territories, but also extends to safeguarding our interests in the [exclusive economic zone] as well as protecting our trade. This creates an environment that is conducive to rapid economic growth of the country. Since trade is the lifeblood of India, keeping our SLOCs [sea lines of communication] open in times of peace, tension or hostilities is a primary national maritime interest.[11]

The trade conveyed by the sea-lanes traversing the Indian Ocean ranks first among the "strategic realities" that the framers of the "Indian Maritime Doctrine" discern. Roughly forty merchantmen pass through India's "waters of interest" every day. An estimated $200 billion worth of oil transits the Strait of Hormuz annually, while some $60 billion transits the Strait of Malacca en route to China, Japan, and other East Asian countries reliant on energy imports.[12]

India's geographic location and conformation rank next in New Delhi's hierarchy of strategic realities. Notes the Indian Maritime Doctrine: "India sits astride . . . major commercial routes and energy lifelines" crisscrossing the Indian Ocean region. Outlying Indian possessions such as the Andaman and

Nicobar islands sit athwart the approaches to the Strait of Malacca while the Persian Gulf is near India's western coastline, conferring a measure of influence over vital sea communications to and from what amounts to a bay in the Indian Ocean. While geography may not be destiny, the document states bluntly that "by virtue of our geography, we are . . . in a position to greatly influence the movement/security of shipping along the SLOCs in the IOR provided we have the maritime power to do so. Control of the choke points could be useful as a bargaining chip in the international power game, where the currency of military power remains a stark reality."[13] The Indian Maritime Doctrine prophesies a depletion of world energy resources that will make the prospect of outside military involvement in India's geographic environs even more acute than it already is. Modern economies' dependence on the Persian Gulf region and Central Asia "has already invited the presence of extra-regional powers and the accompanying Command, Control, Surveillance and Intelligence network. The security implications for us are all too obvious." Sizable deposits of other resources—uranium, tin, gold, diamonds—around the Indian Ocean littoral only accentuate the factors beckoning the attention of outside maritime powers to the region.[14]

Indian leaders, then, take a somber view of the international security environment. In the "polycentric world order" that New Delhi sees taking shape, economics is "the major determinant of a nation's power." While "India holds great promise" owing to its size, location, and economic acumen, its "emergence as an economic power will undoubtedly be resisted by the existing economic powers, leading to conflicts based on economic factors." The likelihood that competitors will "deny access to technology and other industrial inputs," combined with "the shift in global maritime focus from the Atlantic-Pacific combine to the Pacific-Indian Ocean region," will only heighten the attention major powers pay to the seas.[15]

A buildup of Indian maritime power represents the only prudent response to strategic conditions that are at once promising and worrisome in economic terms. Maritime threats fall into two broad categories in Indians' reckoning. First, judging from official pronouncements such as the 2004 and 2009 Indian Maritime Doctrine and the 2007 Maritime Military Strategy, New Delhi is acutely conscious that nontraditional threats such as seagoing terrorism, weapons proliferation, or piracy could disrupt vital sea-lanes. Cleansing Asian waters of these universal scourges has become a matter of real and growing concern.[16]

Second, Indians are wary of not only banditry and unlawful trafficking but also rival navies. While Indian strategists exude growing confidence, increasingly looking beyond perennial nemesis Pakistan, they remain mindful of the Pakistani naval challenge, a permanent feature of Indian Ocean strategic affairs. Over the longer term, a Chinese naval buildup in the Indian Ocean, perhaps centered on Beijing's much-discussed "string of pearls," would represent cause for concern.[17] This is the most likely quarter from which a threat to Indian maritime security could emanate over the long term, once China resolves the Taiwan question to its satisfaction and is free to redirect its attention to important interests in other regions—such as free passage for commercial shipping through the Indian Ocean region.

But Indians remain acutely conscious that the U.S. Navy rules the waves in Asia, as it has since World War II. Despite closer maritime ties with the United States, Indian officials bridle at memories of the U.S. Seventh Fleet's intervention in the Bay of Bengal during the 1971 Indo-Pakistani war. They also remain ambivalent about the U.S. military presence on Diego Garcia, which they see as an American beachhead in the Indian Ocean region. As one Indian scholar observes, Diego Garcia and the Bengal naval deployment have "seeped into Indians' cultural memory—even among those who know nothing about the sea."[18] Whatever the prospects for a U.S.–Indian strategic partnership, such memories will give rise to a measure of wariness in bilateral ties. On balance, the factors impinging on Indian and U.S. strategic calculations will make for some form of partnership—but perhaps not the grand alliance some Americans seem to assume. This is not a sure thing, and sustaining it will require painstaking work on both sides.

Historical Models for Indian Sea Power

Given the challenges New Delhi perceives as it surveys its surroundings, and given the novelty of Indian pursuit of sea power, New Delhi has consulted Western history. That Indians would look to *American* history rather than European history for guidance, however, may come as a surprise. Given their skepticism toward American maritime supremacy—the residue of Cold War ideological competition as well as a product of geopolitical calculations—nineteenth-century American history represents an unlikely source for lessons to inform Indians' efforts to amass maritime power.

There is a theoretical dimension to India's maritime turn as well. Many scholars of "realist" leanings assume that the sort of balance-of-power politics practiced in nineteenth-century Europe will prevail in Asia as the rise of China and India reorders regional politics.[19] If so, the coming years will see Asian statesmen jockey for geopolitical advantage in the manner of a Bismarck or a Talleyrand. And there is merit to objections to the notion that strategic triangles and similar metaphors are artifacts of nineteenth-century thinking—but many Indians and Chinese think in geopolitical terms reminiscent of that age. Other scholars deny that European-style realpolitik is universal, predicting instead a revival of Asia's hierarchical, China-centric past.[20] Chinese diplomats have skillfully encouraged such notions, hinting that a maritime order presided over by a capable, benevolent China—and excluding predatory Western sea powers such as America—would benefit all Asian peoples, now as in bygone centuries.[21]

Indians more commonly look for insight to a third model: the Monroe Doctrine, the nineteenth-century American policy declaration that purported to place the New World off-limits to new European territorial acquisitions or an extension of the European political system to American states they did not already control. James Monroe and John Quincy Adams, the architects of the Monroe Doctrine; Grover Cleveland and Richard Olney, who viewed the doctrine as a virtual warrant for U.S. rule of the Americas; and Theodore Roosevelt, who gave the doctrine a forceful twist of his own, may exercise as much influence in Asia—particularly South Asia—as any figures from European or Asian history.

Soon after independence, Indian statesmen and pundits took to citing the doctrine as a model for Indian foreign policy. It is not entirely clear why Indians adopted a Western paradigm for their pursuit of regional preeminence rather than some indigenous model suited to South Asian conditions. India's tradition of nonalignment surely played some role in this. For one thing, Monroe and Adams announced their doctrine in an era when American nations were throwing off colonial rule, while India's security doctrine had its origins in the post–World War II era of decolonization. Thus the United States of Monroe's day, like the newly independent India, positioned itself as the leader of a bloc of nations within a geographically circumscribed region, resisting undue political influence—or worse—from external great powers. This imparts some resonance to Monroe's principles despite the passage of time and the obvious dissimilarities between American and Indian histories and traditions.

Thus the diplomatic context was apt—especially since Indian statesmen intent on effective "strategic communications" designed their policy pronouncements to appeal to not only domestic but also Western audiences. Prime Minister Jawaharlal Nehru's speech justifying the use of force to evict Portugal from the coastal enclave of Goa is worth quoting at length:

> Even some time after the United States had established itself as a
> strong power, there was the fear of interference by European pow-

ers in the American continents, and this led to the famous declaration by President Monroe of the United States [that] any interference by a European country would be an interference with the American political system. I submit that . . . the Portuguese retention of Goa is a continuing interference with the political system established in India today. I shall go a step further and say that any interference by any other power would also be an interference with the political system of India today. . . . It may be that we are weak and we cannot prevent that interference. But the fact is that *any attempt by a foreign power to interfere in any way with India is a thing which India cannot tolerate, and which, subject to her strength, she will oppose. That is the broad doctrine I lay down* [our emphasis].[22]

Parsing Nehru's bracing words, the following themes are worth noting. First, while a European power's presence in South Asia precipitated his foreign policy doctrine, he forbade *any* outside powers to take any action in the region that New Delhi might construe as imperiling the Indian political system. This was a sweeping injunction indeed. Second, he acknowledged realities of power but seemingly contemplated enforcing his doctrine with new vigor as Indian power waxed, making new means and options available. And third, Nehru asked no one's permission to pursue such a doctrine. While this doctrine would not qualify as international law, then, it was a policy statement to which New Delhi would give effect as national means permitted. India did expel Portugal from Goa in 1961—affixing an exclamation point to Nehru's words.

Prime ministers Indira Gandhi and Rajiv Gandhi were especially assertive about enforcing India's security doctrine.[23] From 1983–90, for example, New Delhi applied political and military pressure in an effort to bring about an end to the Sri Lankan civil war. It deployed Indian troops to the embattled island, waging a bitter counterinsurgent campaign—in large part because Indian leaders feared that the United States would involve itself in the dispute, in the process obtaining a new geostrategic foothold at Trincomalee, along India's southern flank. One commentator in *India Today* interpreted New Delhi's politico-military efforts as "a repetition of the Monroe Doctrine, a forcible statement that any external forces prejudicial to India's interests cannot be allowed to swim in regional waters."[24]

India's security doctrine also manifested itself in 1988, when Indian forces intervened in a coup in the Maldives, and in a 1989–90 trade dispute with Nepal. Western scholar Devin Hagerty sums up Indian security doctrine thus: "The essence of this formulation is that India strongly opposes outside intervention in the domestic affairs of other South Asian nations, especially by outside powers whose goals are perceived to be inimical to Indian interests. Therefore, no South Asian government should ask for outside assistance from any country; rather, if a South Asian nation genuinely needs external assistance, it should seek it from India. A failure to do so will be considered anti-Indian."[25] This flurry of activity subsided after the Cold War as the strategic environment appeared to improve and New Delhi embarked on an ambitious program of economic liberalization and reform. Even so, influential pundits—even those who dispute the notion of a consistent Indian security doctrine—continue to speak in these terms.

Indeed, pundits and strategists seemingly take the concept of an Indian Monroe Doctrine for granted. C. Raja Mohan, perhaps India's foremost commentator on foreign policy, routinely uses this terminology, matter-of-factly titling one op-ed column "Beyond India's Monroe Doctrine" and in another exclaiming that "China Just Tore Up India's Monroe Doctrine."[26] "This Indian variation of the Monroe Doctrine, involving spheres of influence, has not been entirely successful in the past," Mohan allows, "but it has been an article of faith for many in the Indian strategic community."[27] Speaking at the U.S. Naval War College in November 2007, Admiral R. Chopra vouchsafed that India should "emulate America's nineteenth-century rise" to sea power. As Indian naval capabilities mature, matching ambitious ends with vibrant means, its need to cooperate with outside sea powers will diminish. Declared Chopra, New Delhi might then see fit to enforce "its own Monroe Doctrine" in the region.[28] The doctrine has entered into India's vocabulary of foreign relations and maritime strategy. Again, using nineteenth-century U.S. history as a proxy, we can discern three possible maritime futures for India:

Monroe the "Free-Rider"

Indian statesmen animated by Monroe's principles as originally understood would take advantage of the maritime security furnished by a dominant navy—Great Britain's Royal Navy then, the U.S. Navy now—dedicating most of their nation's resources and energies to internal development. Limited efforts at suppressing piracy, terrorism, and weapons trafficking—the latter-day equivalents to the slave trade, a scourge the U.S. and Royal navies worked together to suppress—would be admissible under these principles, as would disaster relief and other humanitarian operations intended to amass goodwill and lay the groundwork for more assertive diplomatic ventures in the future. This modest reading of the doctrine would not forbid informal cooperation with the U.S. Navy, today's answer to the Royal Navy of Monroe's day. In short, the Indian navy would content itself with "free-riding" on American sea power, using the resultant strategic holiday to experiment with new naval platforms, technologies, and tactics.

Cleveland the "Strongman"

In 1895, President Grover Cleveland's secretary of state, Richard Olney, informed Great Britain that the United States' "fiat is law" throughout the Western Hemisphere, by virtue not only of American enlightenment but also American physical might—the Republic's capacity to make good on Monroe's precepts.[29] This hypermuscular vision of the Monroe Doctrine would impel aspirants to sea power to openly avow their desire to dominate surrounding waters and littoral regions. From a geographic standpoint, the Cleveland/Olney model would urge them to make good on their claims to regional supremacy, employing naval forces to project power throughout vast areas. No international dispute would be off-limits when national leaders deemed it a threat to their interests, and they would evince a standoffish attitude toward proposals for cooperation with external naval powers. Like Cleveland's America, India would pronounce itself a regional "strongman."

Roosevelt the "Constable"

Theodore Roosevelt took a preventive view of the Monroe Doctrine, framing "an international police power" that justified U.S. intervention in the affairs of weak American states when it appeared that Europeans might use naval force to collect debts owed their lenders—and, in the process, wrest naval stations from states along sea-lanes vital to U.S. shipping. Roosevelt's interpretation of the Monroe Doctrine, as expressed in his 1904 "Corollary" to the doctrine, called for a defensive posture: Monroe's principles applied when vital national interests were at stake and the would-be dominant power could advance its good-government ideals. These principles would apply within circumscribed regions of vital interest and would be implemented with circumspection, using minimal force in concert with other tools of national power. Cooperation with outside powers with no likely desire or capacity to infringe on the hegemon's interests would be acceptable.[30] Washington, in short, would act as a hemispheric "constable."

◆ ◆ ◆

What form such a doctrine will assume and how vigorously New Delhi prosecutes it will depend on such factors as Indian history and traditions, the nature and magnitude of the security challenges Indians perceive in the Indian Ocean, the vagaries of domestic politics, and the Indian Navy's ability to make more than fitful progress toward fielding potent naval weapon systems.[31] India will pursue its doctrine according to its needs and capabilities—just as each generation of Americans reinterpreted the Monroe Doctrine to suit its own needs and material power. India-watchers can use the doctrine as a measuring stick for Indian grand strategy and naval development.

American Views of Indian Sea Power

Curiously, given the importance they attach to the burgeoning U.S.–Indian relationship and their concerted efforts to forge a seagoing partnership, American policymakers and maritime strategists have long paid scant attention to the evolution of Indian sea power or the motives and aspirations prompting New Delhi's seaward turn. One small example: the Pentagon publishes no Indian counterpart to its annual report on China's military, "The Military Power of the People's Republic of China," despite the growth of Indian power and ambition. To the contrary: U.S. diplomats speak in glowing terms of a "natural strategic partnership" between the world's biggest and the world's oldest democracy while the U.S. military has reached out to the Indian military on the tactical and operational levels, for example, through the "Malabar series" of combined maritime exercises that dates to 1992.[32] Both presidential contenders backed a "league" or "concert" of democracies during the 2008 campaign. But few in Washington have devoted much energy to what lies between high diplomacy and hands-on military-to-military cooperation by analyzing the maritime component of Indian grand strategy.

To be sure, the recently published U.S. Maritime Strategy, titled "A Cooperative Strategy for 21st Century Seapower," proclaims matter-of-factly that "credible combat power will be continuously postured in the Western Pacific and the Arabian Gulf/Indian Ocean," but its rationale for doing so is purely functional in nature: guarding U.S. interests, assuring allies, deterring competitors, and so forth.[33] The multinational context for this pronouncement—how Washington ought to manage relations with regional maritime powers, such as India, on which the success of a cooperative maritime strategy ineluctably depends—is left unexplained. Why New Delhi has rebuffed such seemingly uncontroversial U.S.-led ventures as the Proliferation Security Initiative (PSI), a primarily maritime effort to combat the traffic in weapons-of-mass-destruction-related materiel, will remain a mystery to U.S. officials absent this larger context.[34]

Why the apparent complacency toward India on the part of U.S. officials? Several possible explanations come to mind. For one thing, the United States does not see India as a threat. The Bill Clinton and George W. Bush administrations sought to enlist New Delhi in a "concert of democracies," and, as mentioned before, they viewed India as a natural strategic partner or ally of the United States. The Barack Obama administration has largely followed suit since assuming power in 2009.

For another, other matters have dominated the bilateral relationship in recent years. The Bush administration lifted the sanctions imposed after the 1998 Indian and Pakistani nuclear tests and negotiated an agreement providing for transfers of American nuclear technology to the Indian commercial nuclear sector in exchange for partial international supervision of Indian nuclear facilities. Wrangling in Congress long stalled the "123" agreement, with nonproliferation advocates questioning whether new Indian nuclear tests would terminate the accord and lodging assorted other complaints.[35] Maritime cooperation has been subsumed in other issues. And, more to the point, India was slow to publish a maritime strategy that American analysts could study. Its first Indian Maritime Doctrine appeared in 2004, while a full-fledged Maritime Military Strategy appeared only in 2007—meaning that India-watchers in the United States have had little time to parse its meaning and its implications for U.S.–Indian collaboration at sea, let alone to publish and debate their findings.

For now, absent significant policy attention, any maritime–strategic partnership takes place mainly on the functional level, with "naval diplomacy" filling the void left by policymakers. How Washington will grapple with Indian standoffishness toward the PSI and other enterprises remains to be seen. If New Delhi does indeed embark on a Monroe Doctrine—especially one of the more militant variants identified above—political supervision of U.S. naval diplomacy will be at a premium for Washington. The opportunity to craft a close strategic partnership with New Delhi could be a short-lived one as Indian power grows, especially if Indian leaders take an ominous view of their nation's geopolitical surroundings or irritants to U.S.–Indian relations begin to accumulate.

Chinese Views of Indian Sea Power

Chinese views of Indian sea power are animated by Beijing's increasing concerns about energy security. Given China's insatiable appetite for energy resources to feed its economic growth, the uninterrupted flow of oil and natural gas from the Persian Gulf and the Horn of Africa has assumed a paramount position among China's many strategic requirements. The security of the waterways stretching from the Chinese coastline to the Indian Ocean has thus taken on special policy importance for Beijing.[36] Indeed, some Chinese analysts have already begun to forecast the need to develop an Indian Ocean Fleet as an insurance policy against both accidental and deliberate disruptions to China's energy supplies. According to U.S. observers, "the idea of a Chinese Indian Ocean Fleet represents a radical shift in the [Chinese navy's] response to the SLOC security issue."[37] Such forward-leaning propositions for an independent seagoing flotilla have caught the attention of influential commentators in the West. As Kaplan speculates, "a possible future scenario is a Chinese merchant fleet and naval presence in some form from the coast of Africa all the way around the [Indian and Pacific Oceans] to the Korean Peninsula—covering, in effect, all Asian waters within the temperate and tropical zones, and thus protecting Chinese economic interests and the global maritime system within which those interests operate."[38] It is not surprising, then, that Beijing pays substantial attention to both Indian sea power and New Delhi's potential politico-military responses to a robust Chinese naval presence in the Indian Ocean.

As China casts anxious eyes on the sea lines of communication to its south and southwest, Beijing faces the prospects of a classic two-front dilemma. China's naval modernization for the past decade has been designed primarily to cope with crisis and wartime contingencies related to Taiwan. Chinese strategists are especially preoccupied with potential U.S. military intervention on behalf of the island, which would likely originate from various forward bases across the western Pacific, namely Japan, South Korea, and Guam; as well as in Hawaii and San Diego. Thus, at least for the moment, cross-strait considerations will exert a powerful intermediating effect on any resource and force-structure decisions that look farther offshore toward the Indian Ocean. Conversely, clear indicators that China is embarking on programs more suited for blue water missions would suggest that Beijing is acquiring the confidence and capacity to keep the island in check while posturing itself for the "day after Taiwan."

In any event, if American analysts seem blasé about the intentions and capabilities of their prospective strategic partner, many Chinese analysts depict the basic motives behind India's maritime ambitions in starkly geopolitical terms. Indeed, their assumptions and arguments are unmistakably Mahanian. Zhang Ming asserts in *Modern Ships*: "The Indian subcontinent is akin to a massive triangle reaching into the heart of the Indian Ocean, benefiting anyone from there who seeks to control the Indian Ocean."[39] In an article casting suspicion on Indian naval intentions, the author states, "Geostrategically speaking, the Indian Ocean is a link of communication and oil transportation between the Pacific and Atlantic Oceans and India is just like a giant and never-sinking aircraft carrier and the most important strategic point guarding the Indian Ocean."[40] The reference to an "unsinkable aircraft carrier" was clearly meant to trigger emotive reactions, given that for many Chinese the term is most closely associated with Taiwan.

Intriguingly, some have invoked Mahanian language, wrongly attributed to Mahan himself, to describe the value of the Indian Ocean to New Delhi. One Chinese commentator quotes Mahan without citation as asserting, "Whoever controls the Indian Ocean will dominate India and the coastal states of the Indian Ocean as well as control the massive area between the Mediterranean and the Pacific Ocean."[41] In a more expansive reformulation, two articles cite Mahan as declaring, "Whoever controls the Indian Ocean controls Asia. The Indian Ocean is the gateway to the world's seven seas. The destiny of the world in the 21st century will be determined by the Indian Ocean."[42] (As noted before, a very similar, and likewise apocryphal, Mahan quotation has made the rounds in India—even finding its way into the official Maritime Military Strategy.) Faulty attribution notwithstanding, the Chinese are clearly drawn to Mahanian notions of sea power when forecasting how India will approach its maritime environs.

Zhao Bole, a professor of South Asian studies at Sichuan University, places these claims in a more concrete geopolitical context. Zhao argues that four key geostrategic factors have underwritten India's rise. First, India and its surrounding areas boast a wealth of natural resources. Second, India is by far the most powerful country in the Indian Ocean region. Third, the physical distance separating the United States from India affords New Delhi ample geopolitical space for maneuver. Fourth, India borders economically dynamic regions such as the ASEAN states and China. Zhao quotes Nehru and K. M. Panikkar to prove that Indian politicians and strategists have long recognized these geopolitical advantages and that they have consistently evinced the belief that India's destiny is inextricably tied to the Indian Ocean.[43] However, due to India's insistence on taking a third way during the Cold War superpower competition, New Delhi was content to focus on its own subcontinental affairs.

In the 1990s, though, India sought to shake off its nonaligned posture by increasing its geopolitical activism in Southeast Asia under the guise of its "Look East" policy. According to Zhao Gancheng, New Delhi leveraged its unique geographic position to make Southeast Asia—an intensely maritime theater—a "breakthrough point" (突破口), particularly in the economic realm. In the twenty-first century, Zhao argues, the Look East policy has assumed significant strategic dimensions, suggesting that India has entered a new phase intimately tied to its great-power ambitions. While acknowledging that the underlying strategic logic pushing India beyond the subcontinent is compelling, Zhao worries that Indian prominence among the ASEAN states could tempt the United States to view India as a potential counterweight to China.[44]

To Chinese observers, these broader geopolitical forces seem to conform to the more outward-looking Indian maritime strategy on exhibit in recent years, and they tend to confirm Chinese suspicions of an expansive and ambitious pattern to India's naval outlook. Zhang Xiaoling and Qu Yutao divide the evolution of Indian maritime strategy, particularly with regard to its geographic scope, into three distinct phases: near seas defense (近海防御; from independence to the late 1960s); area control (区域控制; from the early 1970s to the early 1990s); and open-ocean extension (远海延伸; from the mid-1990s to the present).[45]

During the first stage, the navy was confined to the east and west coasts of India and parts of the Arabian Sea and Bay of Bengal in support of ground and air operations ashore. The second phase called for a far more assertive control of the Indian Ocean. Indian strategists divided the Indian Ocean into three concentric rings of operational control. First, India needed to impose "complete or absolute control" over three hundred nautical miles of water from India's coastline to defend the homeland, the exclusive economic zone, and the offshore islands. Second, the navy had to exert "moderate control" over an ocean belt extending some three hundred to six hundred nautical miles from Indian coasts to secure its sea lines of communications and provide situational awareness. Finally, the navy needed to exercise "soft control," requiring power projection and deterrent capabilities, beyond seven hundred nautical miles from Indian shores.[46]

Chinese analysts differ over the extent of Indian naval ambitions in the twenty-first century. But they concur that India will not restrict its seafaring endeavors to the Indian Ocean indefinitely. Most discern a clear transition from a combination of offshore defense and area control to a blue water offensive posture. One commentator postulates that India will develop the capacity to prevent and implement its own naval blockades against the chokepoints at Suez, Hormuz, and Malacca.[47] Unsurprisingly, the prospect that India might seek to blockade Malacca against China has attracted substantial attention. One Chinese analyst, using language that would have been instantly recognizable to Mahan, described the 244 islands that constitute the Andaman-Nicobar archipelago as a "metal chain" (铁链) that could lock the western exit of the Malacca Strait tight.[48] Zhang Ming further argues that "once India commands the Indian Ocean, it will not be satisfied with its position and will continuously seek to extend its influence, and its eastward strategy will have a particular impact on China."[49] The author concludes that "India is perhaps China's most realistic strategic adversary."[50]

While they pay considerable attention to the potential Indian threat to the Malacca Strait, Chinese observers also believe the Indian sea services are intent on

- Achieving sea control from the northern Arabian Sea to the South China Sea;

- Developing the ability to conduct SLOC defense and combat operations in the areas above;

- Maintaining absolute superiority over all littoral states in the Indian Ocean;

- Building the capacity for strategic deterrence against outside naval powers;[51]

- Amassing long-range power-projection capabilities sufficient to reach and control an enemy's coastal waters in times of conflict;

- Fielding a credible, sea-based, second-strike retaliatory nuclear capability; and

- Developing the overall capacity to "enter east" (东进) into the South China Sea and the Pacific, "exit west" (西出) through the Red Sea and Suez Canal into the Mediterranean, and "go south" (南下) toward the Cape of Good Hope and the Atlantic.[52]

Clearly, the Chinese foresee the emergence of a far more forward-leaning Indian Navy that in time could make its presence felt in China's own littoral realm. Moreover, the Chinese uniformly believe that New Delhi has embarked on an ambitious modernization program to achieve these sweeping aims. Interestingly, some have pointed to America's apparent lack of alarm toward India's already powerful navy. This quietude, they say, stands in sharp contrast to incessant U.S. concerns over the People's Liberation Army Navy (PLA Navy), representing a blatant double standard.[53] In any event, Chinese assessments of Indian capabilities and the emerging body of work tracking India's technological and doctrinal advances are indeed impressive. For instance, *Modern Navy*, the PLA Navy's monthly periodical, published a ten-month series on the Indian Navy beginning in November 2005. Articles ranged widely from analyses of platforms and weaponry to basing and port infrastructure.[54] Not surprisingly, given the decades-long debate within China surrounding its own carrier acquisition plans, India's aircraft carriers have attracted by far the most attention.[55]

Despite the alarming projections of Indian ambitions and capabilities, a number of Chinese analysts hold far more sober, if not sanguine, views of India's rise. The former Chinese ambassador to India, Cheng Ruisheng, argues that policymakers in Beijing and New Delhi have increasingly abandoned their antiquated, zero-sum security outlooks. Indeed, Cheng exudes confidence that improving U.S.–Indian ties and Sino-Indian relations are not mutually exclusive; thus, he holds out hope for a balanced and stable strategic triangle in the region.[56] Some Chinese speculate that India's burgeoning friendships with a variety of extraregional powers, including the United States and Japan, are designed to widen India's room for maneuver in an increasingly multipolar world without forcing it to choose sides. As Yang Hui asserts, "India's actions smack of 'fence-sitting.' This is a new version of non-alignment."[57] On balance, then, strategic continuity might prevail over the potentially destabilizing forces of change.

However, even those projecting major changes in the regional configuration of power seem confident that India's rise will neither upend stability nor lead automatically to strategic advantages for New Delhi. To be sure, a small minority believes that an increased Indian presence in the Indian Ocean would generate great-power "contradictions" that could in time lead New Delhi to displace the United States as the regional hegemon, consistent with more forceful conceptions of an Indian Monroe Doctrine.[58] But a far more common view maintains that growing Indian sea power will likely compel Washington and other powers in Asia to challenge or counterbalance New Delhi's position in the Indian Ocean region.[59] And structural constraints will tend to act against Indian efforts to wield influence beyond the Indian Ocean. Zhao Gancheng, for example, argues that China's firmly established position in Southeast Asia and India's relative unfamiliarity with the region will prevent New Delhi from reaping maximum gains from its Look East policy.[60]

On the strictly military and technological levels, some Chinese analysts believe that Indian naval aspirations have far outstripped the nation's concrete capacity to fulfill them. Noting that increases in the defense budget have consistently outpaced India's annual gross domestic product growth rate, Li Yonghua of *Naval and Merchant Ships* derides India's ambition for an ocean-going naval fleet as a "python swallowing an elephant [蟒蛇吞象]."[61] Similarly, Zhang Ming identifies three major deficiencies that cast doubt on India's ability to develop a fleet for blue water combat missions. First, India's current comprehensive national power simply cannot sustain a "global navy" and the panoply of capabilities that such a force demands. Second, India's long-standing dependence on foreign technology and relatively backward industrial base will severely retard advances in indigenous programs—especially plans for domestically built next-generation aircraft carriers. Finally, existing Indian Navy surface combatants are unequal to the demands of long-range fleet operations in both quantitative and qualitative terms. In particular, shortfalls in robust air-defense capabilities constitute the "most fatal problem" for future Indian carrier task forces.[62] Interestingly, key aspects of Zhang's critique apply equally to the challenges facing the PLA Navy today.

This brief survey of Chinese perspectives suggests that definitive conclusions about the future of Indian sea power would be premature. On the one hand, evocative uses of Mahanian language and worst-case extrapolations of Indian maritime ambitions certainly represent a sizable geopolitically minded school of thought in China. On the other, the Chinese acknowledge that India may not be able to surmount the geopolitical and technological constraints it confronts for years to come. Such mixed feelings further suggest that Sino-Indian maritime competition in the Indian Ocean or the South China Sea is not fated. Neither side has the credible capacity—yet—to reach into the other's nautical backyard. At the same time, the broader geostrategic climate at the moment favors cooperation. Until either side acquires naval forces able to influence events beyond its own maritime domain, and as long as New Delhi's and Beijing's extraregional aims remain largely aspirational, there is still ample time to shape mutual threat perceptions through cooperative efforts.

An Uncertain Geometry

This initial inquiry into the maritime geometry of the Indian Ocean region suggests that conditions are auspicious for shaping a mutually beneficial maritime relationship among India, China, and the United States. For now, New Delhi seems at once sanguine about its maritime surroundings and conscious that it lacks the wherewithal to make good on a muscular Monroe Doctrine. While in principle India asserts regional primacy, much as Monroe's America did, it remains content to work with the predominant naval power, the United States, in the cause of maritime security in South Asia. If nothing else, this is a matter of expediency.

There is ample basis on the functional level to construct a maritime partnership. While India and the United States harvested abundant goodwill for their maritime relief efforts following the 2004 tsunami, China remained unable to make a meaningful contribution.[63] The intervening years, however, have seen the PLA pursue capabilities that would allow Chinese forces to operate at longer distances, thereby helping prevent a recurrence of the embarrassment Beijing suffered from its nonparticipation in tsunami relief. If all three seafaring powers are now committed to mutual interests such as disaster relief, humanitarian response, and antipiracy patrols, then New Delhi, Beijing, and Washington have a solid foundation to build upon—if they will. One obvious next step toward a tripartite arrangement would be to expand the annual U.S.-Indian Malabar exercises to include the PLA Navy. If New Delhi or Beijing balks at combined exercises that would make a trilateral maritime partnership a matter of routine, this will provide Washington with an indicator of the strategic triangle's future.

It is worth noting that there is little prospect that India will join the United States to contain Chinese ambitions in the Indian Ocean, as Japan joined the United States to contain Soviet ambitions. India's independent streak, codified in its policy of nonalignment, predisposes New Delhi against such an arrangement. Nor does India resemble Cold War–era Japan, dependent on an outside power to defend it against an immediate, nearby threat to maritime security and indeed national survival. The geographic conformation of Japan's threat environment significantly heightened the urgency of a far more alert strategic posture. The Japanese archipelago closely enveloped Vladivostok, home to the Soviet Union's Pacific Fleet, as well as the naval base from which commerce-raiding cruisers harassed Japanese trade and military logistics during the Russo-Japanese War. Tokyo had to develop the capacity to monitor Soviet hunter-killer submarines lurking in the Sea of Japan and to repel a massive amphibious invasion against Hokkaido. India, by contrast, enjoys two great oceanic buffers—the eastern Indian Ocean and the South China Sea—vis-à-vis China. As a simple illustration, several thousand nautical miles separate the fleet headquarters of China's South Sea Fleet, located in Zhanjiang, Guangdong Province, from Visakhapatnam, the eastern naval command of the Indian Navy. Geography alone, then, constitutes a major disincentive for New Delhi to prematurely enlist in an anti-China coalition.

For its part, Washington has not yet dedicated serious attention and energy to analyzing the future of Indian sea power or the likely configuration of great-power relations in the Indian Ocean. It remains hopeful that a durable strategic partnership with New Delhi will take shape. Should the three sea powers manage to draw other powers with little interest in or capacity to infringe on India's Monroe Doctrine—say, Australia, an Indian Ocean nation in its own right, or Japan, which depends on Indian Ocean sea-lanes for energy security—the regional geometry could become quite complex. But the participation of such powers might also reduce the propensity for competition among the three vertices of the Sino-Indian-U.S. triangle. A wider arrangement, then, warrants study in American strategic circles. Indeed, some U.S. strategists have begun to urge Washington to lead overlapping, ad hoc maritime coalitions in the Indian Ocean that reflect diverse interests in Asian waters.[64]

And, as we have seen, China views India's maritime rise with equanimity for now, doubting both New Delhi's capacity and will to pose a threat to Chinese interests in the region. American hopes and Chinese acquiescence may not add up to an era of good feelings in South Asia, but they may form the basis for cooperative relations in the near- to midterm.

But this inquiry also suggests that the opportunity to fashion a tripartite seagoing entente may not endure for long. If India succeeds at building powerful naval forces, it may—like Cleveland's or Roosevelt's America—set out to make the Indian Ocean an Indian preserve in fact as well as in principle. If so, China would be apt to take a more wary view of Indian naval ambitions, which would seem to menace Chinese economic, energy, and security interests in South Asia. Its hopes for a strategic partnership dashed, the United States might reevaluate its comforting assumptions about a consortium of English-speaking democracies. This too would work against a cooperative strategic triangle.

Maritime security cooperation, then, is by no means foreordained. A host of wild cards could impel New Delhi toward a more forceful security doctrine. Should, say, the United States use the Indian Ocean or the Persian Gulf to stage strikes against Iranian nuclear sites, New Delhi might see the need to expand its regional primacy at America's expense. A failure of the U.S.–Indian civilian nuclear cooperation accord would have unpredictable if indirect impact on the bilateral relationship, fraying Indian patience and potentially loosening this "side" of the strategic triangle. Similarly, if China began deploying ballistic-missile and nuclear-attack submarines to the Indian Ocean, India might redouble its maritime efforts, working assiduously on antisubmarine warfare and its own undersea nuclear deterrent. Competition, not cooperation, could come to characterize the strategic triangle—perhaps giving rise to some other, less benign regional geometry.

Notes

The authors are associate professors of strategy, U.S. Naval War College. The views voiced here are theirs alone. The authors published a different version of this article with the same title in *Naval War College Review* 61, no. 3 (Summer 2008): 40–60.

1. For an assessment of U.S. naval decline, see Seth Cropsey, "The US Navy in Distress," *Strategic Analysis* 34, no. 1 (January 2010): 31–45.

2. Government of India Press Information Bureau, "Guarding the Coastline of the Country," 28 August 2002, http://pib.nic.in/feature/feyr2002/faug2002/f280820021. html.

3. R. Chopra, in Government of India, "A Seminar on Maritime History," *Sainik Samachar* 49, no. 4 (16–28 February 2002), http://mod.nic.in/samachar/html/ch15. htm.

4. Robert D. Kaplan, "The Revenge of Geography," *Foreign Policy* 172 (May–June 2009): 96–105.

5. Robert D. Kaplan, "The Geography of Chinese Power," *Foreign Affairs* 89, no. 3 (May–June 2010): 22–41.

6. For a good recent overview, see Donald L. Berlin, "India in the Indian Ocean," *Naval War College Review* 59, no. 2 (spring 2006): 58–89, http://www.usnwc.edu/getattach ment/cc7b0300-af3a-47be-99c4-4dd3cb9c801a/India-in-the-Indian-Ocean---Berlin,- Donald-L-.

7. Discussions with Indian officials, Naval War College, Newport, RI, August 2008.

8. Ibid., May 2008.

9. Ibid.

10. "India: Article Forecasts Future Geostrategic Changes, Calls for Preparedness," OSC# SAP20080626524003.

11. Government of India, INBR-8, "Indian Maritime Doctrine" (New Delhi: Integrated Headquarters, Ministry of Defence [Navy], 25 April 2004), 63.

12. Ibid., 63–64.

13. Ibid., 64.

14. Ibid., 64–65.

15. Ibid., 65–67.

16. Ibid. See also Indian Navy, Integrated Headquarters, Ministry of Defense, *Freedom to Use the Seas: India's Maritime Military Strategy*, May 2007; Government of India, INBR-8, "Indian Maritime Doctrine" (New Delhi: Integrated Headquarters, Ministry of Defence [Navy], August 2009).

17. Case in point: an opinion piece by a former chief of the Indian Navy. See Arun Prakash, "China's Naval Gazers," *Indian Express*, 5 September 2007, http://www.indianexpress. com/story/214471._.html.

18. Author interview with Indian scholars, University of New Hampshire, Durham, NH, 6 October 2007.

19. Kenneth N. Waltz, "The Emerging Structure of International Politics," *International Security* 18, no. 2 (Fall 1993): 44–79; and Kenneth N. Waltz, *Theory of International Politics* (Reading, MA: Addison-Wesley, 1979). See also Aaron Friedberg, "Ripe for Rivalry," *International Security* 18, no. 3 (Winter 1993–94): 5–33; Richard K. Betts, "Wealth, Power, and Instability: East Asia and the United States after the Cold War," *International Security* 18, no. 3 (Winter 1993–94): 34–77; and Avery Goldstein, "Great Expectations: Interpreting China's Arrival," *International Security* 22, no. 3 (Winter 1997–98): 36–73.

20. David C. Kang, "Getting Asia Wrong: The Need for New Analytical Frameworks," *International Security* 27, no. 2 (Spring 2003): 57–85; David C. Kang, "Hierarchy in Asian International Relations: 1300–1900," *Asian Security* 1, no. 1 (January 2005): 53–79; and Chen Jian, *The China Challenge for the Twenty-first Century* (Washington, DC: U.S. Institute of Peace Press, 1998), 4–8.

21. James R. Holmes and Toshi Yoshihara, "Soft Power at Sea: Zheng He and Chinese Naval Strategy," U.S. Naval Institute *Proceedings* 132, no. 10 (October 2006): 34–38.

22. Jawaharlal Nehru, *India's Foreign Policy: Selected Speeches, September 1946–April 1961* (Delhi: Government of India, 1961), 113–15.

23. Indeed, Indian and foreign commentators use "Indira Doctrine" or "Rajiv Doctrine" interchangeably with "India's Monroe Doctrine." Devin T. Hagerty, "India's Regional Security Doctrine," *Asian Survey* 31, no. 4 (April 1991): 352.

24. Dilip Bobb, "Cautious Optimism," *India Today*, 31 August 1987, 69. See also Hagerty, "India's Regional Security Doctrine," 351–63.

25. Hagerty, "India's Regional Security Doctrine," 351–53. See also Bhabani Sen Gupta, "The Indian Doctrine," *India Today*, 31 August 1983, 20. Even those who deny the existence of an India security doctrine write in these terms. See for instance Raju G. C. Thomas, *India's Search for Power: Indira Gandhi's Foreign Policy, 1966–1982* (New Delhi: Sage, 1984), esp. 292.

26. Mohan, a leading Indian commentator on international affairs, continues to discern such a doctrine behind Indian foreign and security policy. C. Raja Mohan, "Beyond India's Monroe Doctrine," *The Hindu*, 2 January 2003, http://mea.gov.in/opinion/2003/01/02002.htm. See also C. Raja Mohan, "SAARC Reality Check: China Just Tore up India's Monroe Doctrine," *Indian Express*, 13 November 2005, LexisNexis database.

27. C. Raja Mohan, "What If Pakistan Fails? India Isn't Worried . . . Yet," *Washington Quarterly* 28, no. 1 (Winter 2004–5): 127.

28. R. Chopra, "The Indian Navy and Sea Power in the New Millennium," address at Naval War College, Newport, RI, 20 November 2007.

29. Richard Olney to Thomas F. Bayard, 20 July 1895, in *The Record of American Diplomacy: Documents and Readings in the History of American Foreign Relations*, 4th ed., ed. Ruhl J. Bartlett, 341–45 (New York: Knopf, 1964).

30. Theodore Roosevelt, "Message of the President to the Senate and the House of Representatives," 6 December 1904, in U.S. Department of State, *Foreign Relations of the United States, 1904* (Washington, DC: Government Publishing Office, 1905),

xli; Dexter Perkins, *A History of the Monroe Doctrine*, rev. ed. (Boston: Little, Brown, 1963), esp. 228–75; and James R. Holmes, *Theodore Roosevelt and World Order: Police Power in International Relations* (Dulles, VA: Potomac Books, 2006).

31. Andrew C. Winner, "India as a Maritime Power?" in *Asia Looks Seaward: Power and Maritime Strategy*, ed. Toshi Yoshihara and James R. Holmes, 125–45 (Greenwood, CT: Praeger, 2007).

32. See, for instance, R. Nicholas Burns, "America's Strategic Opportunity with India: The New U.S.-India Partnership," *Foreign Affairs*, November–December 2007, http://www.foreignaffairs.com/articles/63016/r-nicholas-burns/americas-strategic-opportunity-with-india; and "Remarks by Geoffrey Pyatt, Deputy Chief of Mission, U.S. Embassy, India, at the Malabar 2006 Exercises Aboard the U.S.S. Boxer, Sunday, October 29, 2006," http://newdelhi.usembassy.gov/pr110106c.html.

33. U.S. Navy, Marine Corps, and Coast Guard, "A Cooperative Strategy for 21st Century Seapower" (Washington, DC: U.S. Navy, October 2007), 9.

34. See James R. Holmes, "India and the Proliferation Security Initiative: A U.S. Perspective," *Strategic Analysis* 31, no. 2 (March–April 2007): 315–37. The article identifies intervening variables in India's strategic calculus with respect to the PSI, showing how domestic politics, lingering resentments toward nonproliferation arrangements that once targeted India, and other factors have induced New Delhi to stay clear of the initiative while endorsing its basic principles.

35. For background on the agreement on civil nuclear cooperation, see Dennis M. Gormley and Lawrence Scheinman, "Implications of Proposed India-U.S. Civil Nuclear Cooperation," July 2005, Nuclear Threat Initiative Web site, http://www.nti.org/e_research/e3_67a.html.

36. James R. Holmes and Toshi Yoshihara, "China's Naval Ambitions in the Indian Ocean," in *China's Energy Strategy*, ed., Gabriel Collins, Andrew Erickson, Lyle Goldstein, and William Murray (Annapolis, MD: Naval Institute Press, 2008), 119.

37. Gabriel Collins, Andrew Erickson, and Lyle Goldstein, "Chinese Naval Analysts Consider the Energy Question," in *China's Energy Strategy*, ed. Gabriel Collins, Andrew Erickson, Lyle Goldstein, and William Murray (Annapolis, MD: Naval Institute Press, 2008), 323.

38. Robert Kaplan, "China's Two-Ocean Strategy," in *China's Arrival: A Strategic Framework for a Global Partnership*, ed. Abraham Denmark and Nirav Patel (Washington, DC: Center for a New American Security, September 2009), 55.

39. 章明 [Zhang Ming], "马六甲困局与中国海军的战略抉择" ["The Malacca Dilemma and the Chinese Navy's Strategic Choices"], 当代舰船 [*Modern Ships*], no. 274 (October 2006): 23.

40. Jian Hua, "The United States, Japan Want to Rope in India Which Cherishes the Dream of Becoming a Major Country," *Ta Kung Pao*, 4 June 2001.

41. 谢值军 [Xie Zhijun], "21世纪亚洲海洋 群雄争霸 中国怎么办?" ["Asian Seas in the 21st Century: With So Many Rival Navies, How Will China Manage?"], 军事文摘 [*Military Digest*], 1 February 2001, 21.

42. 张晓林 屈玉涛 [Zhang Xiaolin and Qu Yutao], "从近海到远洋延伸—印度海军战略的演进" ["From Offshore Defense to Open Ocean Extension: The Evolution of Indian Naval Strategy"], 学习时报 [*Study Times*], 10 October 2007, available at www.studytimes.com.cn; and 崔为耀 [Cui Weiyao], "一路驶来的印度航母" ["Steering the Developmental Path of the Indian Aircraft Carrier"], 舰船知识 [*Naval and Merchant Ships*], no. 330 (March 2007): 37.

43. 赵伯乐 [Zhao Bole], "印度崛起的地缘因素" ["The Geopolitical Roots of India's Rise"], 当代亚太 [*Contemporary Asia-Pacific*] 146, no. 2 (February 2007): 12–13. K. M. Panikkar was probably India's preeminent geopolitical thinker, publishing influential texts such as *India and the Indian Ocean: An Essay on the Influence of Sea Power on Indian History* (London: Allen & Unwin, 1962); and *Geographical Factors in Indian History* (Bombay: Bharatiya Vidya Bhavan, 1955).

44. 赵干城 [Zhao Gancheng], "印度东向政策的发展及意义" ["The Development and Implications of India's 'Look East' Policy"], 当代亚太 [*Contemporary Asia-Pacific*] 146, no. 8 (August 2007): 13.

45. Zhang and Qu, "From Offshore Defense."

46. Lang Chao, "全景扫描印度海军—战略战术及战斗力" ["A Complete Assessment of the Indian Navy: Strategy, Operations, and Combat Capabilities"], 当代海军 [*Modern Navy*], July 2006, 41.

47. Xie, "Asian Seas in the 21st Century," 21.

48. 东安刚 [Dong Angang], "印度海军风风火火走大洋" ["The Indian Navy Energetically Steps Towards the High Seas"], 现代舰船 [*Modern Ships*], no. 267 (July 2006): 17.

49. Zhang, "The Malacca Dilemma," 22.

50. Ibid., 23.

51. 丁皓 [Ding Hao], "转守为攻—印度海军新作战理论简析" ["From Defense to Offense: Analysis of the Indian's Navy's New Warfighting Theory"], 海事大观 [*Maritime Spectacle*], no. 56 (August 2005): 53.

52. Lang, "A Complete Assessment," 41; and Yang Hui, "Experts See U.S., Japan, and India as 'Strange Bedfellows' Despite Holding a Joint Military Exercise," *Zhongguo Tongxun She* [*China News Agency*], 16 April 2007.

53. 丰帆 [Feng Fan], "美散布中国海军威胁" ["U.S. Spreads "China Naval Threat""], 环球时报 [*Global Times*], 5 March 2007.

54. Authored by Lang Chao, the series ran for ten months ending in September 2006. Each in-depth analysis ran at least five pages. It is notable that no other regional navy, including Japan's Maritime Self-Defense Force, received such sustained attention from *Modern Navy*. For the first in the series, see 浪潮 [Lang Chao], "全景扫描印度海军—发展综述" ["A Complete Assessment of the Indian Navy: Overall Analysis of Developments"], 当代海军 [*Modern Navy*], no. 146 (November 2005): 42–47.

55. See 侯建军 [Hou Jianjun], "印度现行航母发展之路" ["The Developmental Path of India's Carriers"], 舰船知识 [*Naval and Merchant Ships*], no. 330 (March 2007): 39–41; 王兵 [Wang Bin], "印度航母的国产化之路" ["The Indigenous Path of India's

Carriers"], 现代舰船 [*Modern Ships*], no. 279 (January 2007): 19–21; and 浪潮 [Lang Chao], "全景扫描印度海军—航空母舰" ["A Complete Assessment of the Indian Navy: Aircraft Carriers"], 当代海军 [*Modern Navy*], no. 147 (December 2005): 56–61.

56. 程瑞声 [Cheng Ruisheng], "论中印战略合作伙伴关系" ["The Sino-Indian Strategic Cooperative Partnership"], 中国与世界专论 [*International Studies*], no. 117 (January 2007): 16.

57. Yang, "Experts See U.S., Japan, and Indian as 'Strange Bedfellows.'"

58. 赵莉 [Zhao Li], "印度不可能成为美国的盟友" ["It Is Impossible That India Will Become a U.S. Ally"], 广角镜 [*Wide Angle*], no. 356 (16 May 2002): 27.

59. Zhao, "Geopolitical Roots of India's Rise," 13.

60. Zhao, "Development and Implications of India's 'Look East' Policy," 16.

61. 李永华 杜文龙 [Li Yonghua and Du Wenlong], "力不从心的远洋进攻" ["The Unreachable Open Ocean Attack"], 舰船知识 [*Naval and Merchant Ships*], no. 335 (August 2007): 28–29.

62. 章明 [Zhang Ming], "从印度洋出发—印度海军的未来航母战略" ["Launching from the Indian Ocean: The Future Carrier Strategy of the Indian Navy"], 国际展望 [*International Outlook*] 568, no. 14 (July 2007): 79.

63. See, for example, Bruce A. Elleman, "Waves of Hope: The U.S. Navy's Response to the Tsunami in Northern Indonesia," Newport Paper no. 28 (Newport, RI: Naval War College Press, February 2007).

64. Robert Kaplan, "Center Stage for the Twenty-first Century: Power Plays in the Indian Ocean," *Foreign Affairs* 88, no. 2 (March–April 2009): 28–32.

PART V

Future Prospects for U.S.–China Maritime Security Cooperation

Nan Li

Similarities and Differences in American and Chinese Naval Education
Implications for Cooperation

WHAT ARE THE MAJOR COMPONENTS of the Chinese naval education system? What are the similarities and differences in American and Chinese naval education systems? What naval education cooperation has taken place between China and the United States and between China and other major naval powers? What are the windows of opportunity for naval education cooperation? How can naval education cooperation facilitate the broader maritime cooperative relationship? These are the major research questions that this chapter intends to address.

Addressing these questions is important because a better understanding of these issues may help to identify the possibilities of future maritime cooperation between the United States and China. Also, the extent to which a professional military education (PME) system has developed is a major indicator of the degree of military professionalization. Because of the increasing technological and organizational complexity of the modern military, for instance, the specialized knowledge and expertise of the profession can be acquired "only by prolonged education and experience," and their "extension and transmission" require "institutions of research and education."[1] A naval education system consists mainly of such institutions. A better understanding of this system in turn should help to gain a better understanding of China's naval modernization.

The chapter has five sections. The first discusses the major components of the Chinese naval education system. The second addresses the similarities in the Chinese and American naval education systems. The third section discusses major differences between the two systems. The fourth shows how these differences are being narrowed. The final section examines issues concerning American and Chinese naval cooperation through education.

Major Components of the Chinese Naval Educational System

The Chinese naval education system consists of two types of schools: advanced (高级)- and intermediate (中级)-level command schools, and primary (初级)-level command and engineering schools. The first type refers to those that mainly provide up to one year of preassignment education to middle- and high-ranking military, political, logistics, and armament commanding officers and staff officers at higher-level headquarters; and offer master's and doctorate degrees in naval military arts and sciences. These schools include Nanjing Naval Command College and Guangzhou Naval Arms Command College (see table 1 for details). Preassignment education of middle-ranking submarine commanding officers, however, is the responsibility of Qingdao Submarine Academy.

The second type refers to those that primarily educate entry-level officer candidates (see table 2 for details). Because these schools offer college degrees, and because some degree programs are not substantially different from those of civilian universities, these schools may consolidate further over time as more education of officer candidates is outsourced to civilian universities.[2] The emphasis of some primary command and engineering schools, for instance, would gradually shift from offering college-degree education (学历教育) to postgraduate preassignment education (任职教育), and others would gradually consolidate into comprehensive universities that primarily offer college degrees.[3]

The principal mission of the naval education system is to educate and train commanding and engineering officers to meet the demand of People's Liberation Army Navy (PLA Navy) modernization. These schools are also responsible for "scientific research" on major strategic, doctrinal, operational, organizational, and technological issues concerning the PLA Navy. As a result, these schools are intended to provide effective "personnel" and "intellectual" support for the long-term, general goal of modernizing China's mil-

Table 1. Advanced and Intermediate Naval Command Schools

	Nanjing Naval Command College	Guangzhou Naval Arms Command College
Student grades	Naval equivalents of regiment- and division-level command-ing officers	Company- and battalion-level commanding officers
Degree programs	Preassignment education; master's and doctorate degrees in naval military arts and sciences	Preassignment education; master's in naval military arts and sciences
Majors	Naval campaign command; naval combined arms (合成兵种) tactical command; naval political work at regiment and division levels; naval aviation tactical command; naval logistics command; naval staff command; faculty education for naval schools	Surface combatant basic-level command; second-level surface combatant tactical command (for aviators); surface combatant tactical command (for ship captains); amphibious warfare/marine corps tactical command; coastal defense missile command; naval combined arms command
U.S. equivalents	Naval War College	Surface Warfare School

Sources: Chen Lijun, "The Highest Institution of Higher Learning for China's Navy: Nanjing Naval Command College," *Dangdai haijun (Modern Navy)*, no. 2 (2003); and Tuo Xinguo, "Get Close to the New-Type Command School of the Chinese Navy: Naval Arms Command College," *Modern Navy*, no. 6 (2005).

itary, and the short-term, specific goal of preparing for "military struggle."[4] While research has been expanded and institutionalized over time, it is generally noted that education and training are probably still more important than "scientific research" for these schools. This is because the PLA Navy, like other services, has separate research institutes that are fully devoted to "scientific research" on naval technological and doctrinal issues.[5] Conversely, to the extent that military schools have the comparative "advantage of high density of talent, knowledge and technologies, they have tremendous potentials for scientific research and development."[6]

Similarities in American and Chinese Naval Education

There are some similarities in the American and Chinese naval education systems. In terms of subjects of study, for instance, both systems would address major strategic, doctrinal, operational, technological, and organizational issues

Table 2. Primary Command and Engineering Schools

	Dalian Naval Combatant Academy	Wuhan Naval Engineering University	Qingdao Submarine Academy	Huludao Naval Flight Academy	Yantai Naval Aviation Engineering Academy
Student grades	Officer candidates	Officer candidates; preassignment training of graduates recruited from civilian universities	Officer candidates; pre-assignment education of company- and battalion-level submarine commanding officers	Officer candidates; preassignment education of lower-level naval aviation commanding officers	Officer candidates; petty officer education at Qingdao Campus
Degree programs	Four-year college (本科, or bachelor's degree); master's	Bachelor's; master's; doctorate	Three-year college/technical education (大专); bachelor's; master's	Three-year; bachelor's	Three-year; bachelor's; master's; doctorate
Departments or majors	Basics; maritime navigation; surface-ship armament; underwater armament; missiles; command, control, and information; oceanic mapping; naval political work; international students' education	Basics; ship engineering; ship diesel turbine; ship gas and steam turbines and nuclear power; ship electrical engineering; ship armament engineering; management engineering; international students' education	Submarine command and engineering; sea search and rescue; submarine crew training; international students' education	Naval aerial flight, command, and staff; ship-born helicopter command	Aircraft engineering; aviation materials engineering; electrical and mechanical engineering and automation; navigation engineering; radar engineering; missile engine, launching, control, and testing engineering; simulation engineering; aircraft, engine and avionics maintenance (three-year)
U.S. equivalents	Naval Academy	Combination of Naval Academy and Naval Postgraduate School	Naval Submarine School	Naval Flight School	No direct equivalent

Sources: "Introduction to Military Schools Recruiting Current Graduates from Ordinary Civilian Senior-High Schools," 2 June 2008, available at http://www.chinamil.com.cn; Liu Haiyang, "Get Close to the Only Comprehensive University of the Chinese Navy: The Latest Story from Naval Engineering University," *Xiandai jianchuan* (*Modern Ships*), no. 12 (2003); "Naval Submarine Academy: Forge the Underwater Steel Great Wall of the Republic," *Modern Navy*, no. 8 (2003); and "Forge Naval Air Vital Force: China's Naval Aviation Academy," *Modern Navy*, no. 4 (2003).

regarding maritime domain and naval operations, as shown in tables 1 and 2. In teaching and learning, both systems are committed to developing effective methods and skills in socializing ideas to deal with maritime and naval issues. This means that both systems are dedicated to developing the appropriate curricula and teaching and learning methods, and enhancing the quality of the teaching and research faculties. The objective for both systems is to produce the best naval talent for their respective navies.

A major driving factor for the similarities has to do with the characteristics of the maritime environment within which both navies have to operate, which can be quite different from those of the environment where other services of the military, such as the army and air force, operate. Both American and Chinese naval education systems, for instance, have to address similar strategic, doctrinal, operational, organizational, and technological issues concerning operations in a similar maritime environment to enhance the security and interests of their respective countries. Therefore, one can argue that in functional and technical terms, both systems are more similar to one another than to the PME systems of the other services of their respective armed forces.

Differences in American and Chinese Naval Education

In spite of these similarities, major differences exist in the American and Chinese naval education systems. Differences are primarily found in scope and demand, in the extent of specialization and integration, in content, and in teaching and learning methods and behavior.

In comparison to its U.S. counterpart, the Chinese naval education system has been more limited in scope and demand, largely due to the underdevelopment of the PLA Navy. A major reason for this underdevelopment was the dominance of the land-based threats to China's security. Since the late 1960s, for instance, the main threat to China's security had been considered to be a possible Soviet invasion of China from the north. The preparation of the PLA against such an invasion had largely been centered on a people's war strategy of "luring the enemy in deep" and then defeating the invaders through attrition. Such a strategy, however, rendered the PLA Navy almost irrelevant because maritime and coastal defense became virtually unnecessary in such a scenario. It was not until after Deng Xiaoping came to power in the late 1970s that a naval strategy of "near-coast defense" ("近岸防御") was endorsed to formally justify the PLA Navy's role in defending China against a possible Soviet invasion from the sea.[7]

By the mid-1980s, however, Admiral Liu Huaqing, then commander of the PLA Navy, had articulated the new naval strategy of "near-seas active defense" ("近海积极防御") to replace the near-coast defense strategy. Endorsed by the party and PLA leadership, such a strategy has expanded China's maritime defensive perimeter from the coastal waters up to and slightly beyond the first island chain, which extends from the Japanese archipelago through Taiwan to the Philippines and possibly southward. Rather than countering the Soviet threat, this strategy aims mainly to restore lost and disputed maritime territories, protect China's maritime resources, and secure major sea lines of communications (SLOCs) in times of war.[8] Such a strategy, however, had not been translated into substantial change in naval capabilities until the early 2000s. The lag between change in strategy and change in capabilities can be explained by several factors.

In spite of the seeming decline of the Soviet threat when the new naval strategy was endorsed, for instance, the territorial dispute that underlies such a threat had not been fundamentally resolved. The sense of a land-based threat was further aggravated by an ongoing border war with Vietnam. In addition, threats from the sea such as the Taiwan issue had not become apparent. Moreover, Deng's policy of reform and opening up had just begun, and the vulnerability associated with the dependence of the Chinese economy on SLOCs for shipment of raw materials and traded goods had not yet been felt. Furthermore, since 1985, Deng had decided to divert limited resources from defense to economic development and as a result, defense spending was cut, and the PLA had to go into business to make up for the shortfalls. Finally, Chinese technologies crucial to naval development were rather backward at the time. All these factors had contributed to the underdevelopment of the PLA Navy.[9] Such underdevelopment had in turn limited the scope and demand of Chinese naval education.

Another major difference between the U.S. and Chinese systems is in the extent of specialization and integration. As table 3 indicates, Chinese naval education emphasizes specialized command, engineering, and technical education for officer candidates as well as more specialized, single-arm command education for intermediate-level officers. It is only at the advanced level that officers receive a more integrated education, and such an education is largely defined by an intraservice combined arms command curriculum. In comparison, American naval education stresses integrated education for officer candidates, mainly in terms of a liberal arts education. At the next level, however, officers receive specialized education. At higher levels, integrated education again becomes the norm (see table 4). But unlike the Chinese system, where

Table 3. Levels of Specialization and Integration in Chinese Naval Education

Integration (naval combined arms command)	Nanjing Naval Command College
Specialization (naval single arm command)	Guangzhou Naval Arms Command College
Specialization	Dalian Naval Combatant Academy, Wuhan Naval Engineering University, Qingdao Submarine Academy, Huludao Naval Flight Academy, and Yantai Naval Aviation Engineering Academy

Table 4. Levels of Integration and Specialization in American Naval Education

Integration (naval and joint operations, interagency coordination and coalitional command)	Naval War College
Specialization	Naval Surface Warfare School, Naval Submarine School, Naval Flight School, Naval Postgraduate School, Officer Candidate School (OCS)
Integration (liberal arts education)	Naval Academy, Naval Reserve Officers Training Corps (ROTC)

intraservice combined arms command education is stressed, the American integrated education at higher levels places emphasis on naval and interservice joint operations, interagency coordination, and coalitional command.[10]

There are several plausible explanations for this difference. The Soviet naval education system, which places strong emphasis on specialized engineering and technical training, clearly has a strong influence on the Chinese system. Furthermore, the PLA Navy has undergone a process of "mechanization," or acquiring heavier naval operational platforms. Under a condition of "imperfect information" for lack of "informatization (developing information technology-based software and networks to enhance situational awareness)," functional and technical specialization is clearly indispensable for better coordination to optimize the combat effectiveness of these platforms. In contrast, the U.S. Navy has already completed "mechanization" and is currently "informatizing" its naval forces and platforms, and "informatization" generally enhances integration due to highly improved situational awareness. Finally, the medium-term goal of China's naval modernization is developing capabilities to achieve local and temporary sea denial or control in the Asia-Pacific region. Also, China has disputes over maritime territories with most of its maritime neighbors. The limited regional goals and significant number of maritime disputes make it unlikely for China to have many naval partners. In contrast, the goal of the U.S. Navy is global, and the United States has almost no disputes over maritime territories with other countries; as a result, it has many naval partners. Soviet influence, difference in levels of naval development, and difference in naval goals and partners may be important variables to explain the difference in the extent and types of specialization and integration between the two systems.

There are some other major differences between the U.S. and Chinese systems. In educational content, for instance, naval political work is a major subject of study in the Chinese system but is absent from the American system. In teaching and learning, lectures and exam-driven (应试) learning seem to constitute the normative behavior in the Chinese system. In comparison, seminar-based discussions and problem-solving are more characteristic of the U.S. system. The difference in the political systems may explain the difference in educational content while a Leninist political structure and a Confucian culture that value hierarchy and conformity may have contributed to the difference in teaching and learning behavior.

Narrowing Differences

In recent years, however, major changes have taken place in China that are narrowing the differences in American and Chinese naval education. First, since the early 2000s, the PLA Navy has received increasing resources for its development. Such a change in resources allocation can be attributed to several factors. China's disputes over land territories with most of its neighbors such as Russia, Vietnam, and the Central Asian countries have been resolved. Threats from the sea, such as the issue of Taiwan and disputes over maritime territories and resources with China's maritime neighbors, by contrast, not only have not been resolved but rather have become more pronounced due to the decline of land-based threats. The sense of vulnerability stemming from the increased dependence of the Chinese economy on SLOCs for shipping raw materials and traded goods has also been felt more acutely. Furthermore, due to rapid economic growth, more resources can be allocated to military modernization, as reflected in the steady increase in defense spending over the years. Finally, partly because of the accumulation of "technological reserves" ("技术储备") over the years and partly because of assimilation of imported technologies and dual-use technologies stemming from the rapidly growing ship-building and information industries, naval technologies in China are more advanced and can better support the development of a modern navy. All these factors have contributed to the relatively rapid naval development in China.[11] This development, in turn, has increased the demand for educated naval talent and, thus, the scope of Chinese naval education.

Moreover, since the late 1990s, the PLA has embarked on a new path of "leap-frogging" ("跨越式") development, shifting emphasis from "mechanization" to "informatization." As a result, Jiang Zemin, then Central Military Commission chair, requires the PLA's PME to educate "new-type military talent," defined mainly in terms of compound (复合式) knowledge structure and synthetic (综合) and innovative (创新) abilities.[12] Such a new policy emphasis implies several changes to the Chinese naval education.

One change is that highly specialized engineering and technical schools would be gradually transformed and consolidated into comprehensive universities. In April 1999, for instance, Wuhan Naval Engineering Academy and Nanjing Naval Electronics Engineering Academy were merged to form the new Naval Engineering University. This university has also enhanced its humanities, social sciences, and management education over time to provide a more well-rounded education.[13] Similarly, Dalian Naval Combatant Academy was designated as the first PLA school to implement an experimental program of "integrated education for basics, and specialized education for upper level" ("基础合训, 专业分流"), in which a student receives four years of integrated education followed by one year of specialized education, leading to two bachelor's degrees.[14] By the same token, naval aviator candidates must spend two and a half years at Yantai Naval Aviation Engineering Academy for basic college education before they spend another year at Huludao Naval flight Academy for specialized flight training.[15] These changes intend to offer a liberal arts–based college education that helps to integrate humanities and sciences, command and technical specialties, and management and engineering at the primary level, thus contributing to developing the "compound knowledge structure" of the officer candidates.

Furthermore, the emphasis of some primary command and engineering schools has been shifting from college-degree education to preassignment specialized education, as has happened to Naval Aviation Engineering Academy–Qingdao Campus.[16] Similarly, the Wuhan Naval Engineering University has become the major naval school to implement a program of "4 + 1" and "2 + 2," where students who have received four or two years of college education from major civilian universities are recruited to receive another one or two years of basic military, political, and specialized education in a military school.[17] These changes aim to create a more specialized education for officer candidates after they have received a more integrated college education but before they are assigned to assume command of a basic-level unit.

In the meantime, higher-level command schools, in addition to their traditional emphasis on intraservice combined arms command, also begin to stress interservice joint operations command. The Nanjing Naval Command College, for instance, has signed contracts with command schools of other PLA services to enhance education in joint operations.[18] This new stress aims to develop the ability of commanding officers to optimize utilities of various services in highly integrated operations, foreseeably enabled by a more improved situational awareness stemming from "informatization" of the PLA.

Changes have also been made to educational content. While military political work remains an integral part of Chinese naval education, the scale of the program has been reduced. Dalian Naval Political Academy, the sole naval political work education institution, for instance, has been eliminated and its programs downsized to a department within the Dalian Naval Combatant Academy in 1999.[19] In the meantime, new content such as new sciences and technologies, international relations and foreign policy, law, psychology, operations research, modern management science, joint operations, and nontraditional security have been integrated into the curricula.[20] For specialized schools, new courses are developed to keep up with new developments in their areas of expertise. Huludao Naval Flight Academy, for instance, has added fresh courses in new types of aircraft engines, global positioning satellite navigation, new radar systems, electronic warfare, stealth technologies, and modern air combat to its curricula.[21] These changes are also intended to enhance the "compound knowledge structure" of the students.

Finally, there have also been changes in teaching and learning. Teachers are now required not only to transmit knowledge through lectures but also to serve as organizer, director, and equal participant in small seminars where critical issues and cases are identified, analyzed, and discussed.[22] To enhance teaching and research effectiveness, faculty members are now regularly sent to major civilian universities or abroad to study or acquire advanced degrees.[23] Faculty members are also assigned deputy positions in operational units to gain empirical experience and knowledge, and military instructors (教官) from operational units who are rich in empirical knowledge have been hired to teach.[24] Combat simulation and war-gaming have been extensively employed. Nanjing Naval Command College, for instance, has established a naval campaign and tactical center lab capable of multilevel war-gaming, and Guangzhou Naval Arms Command College has developed a simulation training complex that integrates tactical training in naval surface warfare, antisubmarine warfare, amphibious warfare, coastal defense, and naval air warfare.[25] Similarly, Qingdao Submarine Academy has developed a submarine warfare simulation center.[26]

Students, conversely, are encouraged to expand their horizon to gain knowledge and to develop problem-solving abilities through hands-on experience. For comprehensive universities, for instance, a more flexible credit-hour system has been adopted so students can take more selective courses in humanities, social sciences, natural sciences, and management. An independent studies program has also been introduced so students can choose the location, content, and mentors for research projects of individual academic interests. Similarly, seniors participate in a collective effort to design a combat ship before graduation. Moreover, students are encouraged to volunteer for assignments in cadet brigades, and they regularly participate in training and exercises involving diving, emergency ship repairs, long-range sampan trips, sailing, sea survival and rescue skills, sea navigation on training ships, and damaged submarine survival.[27]

All these changes in teaching and learning are intended to enhance the "synthetic" and "innovative" abilities of both teachers and students. If successfully implemented, these changes would gradually narrow the difference of American and Chinese naval education.

Implications for Cooperation

So far, except for occasional exchanges involving short visits to each other's naval schools by higher-ranking officers, no institutionalized, longer-term exchange programs exist between the American and Chinese naval education systems. Chinese naval schools, however, do educate and train commanding and engineering personnel from developing countries that receive military assistance from China or have purchased naval hardware from China. The Nanjing Naval Command College, for instance, has graduated more than ten classes of international students over the years.[28] Dalian Naval Combatant Academy has graduated about two hundred international students from eight countries, and three hundred students from more than ten countries have graduated from Wuhan Naval Engineering University.[29] Similarly, in one class alone, the maritime salvation program of Qingdao Submarine Academy has students from more than forty countries, including Ghana, Sri Lanka, Egypt, and Cameroon.[30] None of these countries, however, is a major naval power.

Chinese naval schools also dispatch faculty members and students to study abroad. Nanjing Naval Command College, Guangzhou Naval Arms Command College, Dalian Naval Combatant Academy, Wuhan Naval Engineering University, and Qingdao Naval Submarine Academy all claim to have exchange programs with foreign countries and have sent faculty members and students to study, give lectures, attend conferences, participate in foreign assistance programs and scientific survey expeditions, and visit as naval delegation members in foreign countries.[31] To the extent that most of these foreign tours are not dedicated to residential or degree programs in foreign schools, the number of Chinese naval faculty members and students studying abroad may be somewhat limited.

A major reason for lack of more institutionalized exchange programs may have to do with finance. It seems the PLA Navy is more interested in spending on foreign visits by its ships and higher-ranking officers than on academic exchanges. There are also political constraints. The U.S. Navy, for instance, may have reservations about opening up its schools to Chinese naval officers, stemming from concerns that this may strengthen a PLA Navy that may challenge U.S. naval supremacy in the long term. Nor may the PLA Navy be eager to develop more permanent exchange programs for fear that they might expose vulnerabilities that could be exploited in the future. These relative-gain concerns, however, are largely driven by worst-case scenarios such as a possible military conflict over Taiwan. Tension over the Taiwan Strait has declined substantially as the proindependence Democratic Progressive Party lost the Taiwan presidential election in 2008, and the United States and China do have common maritime interests, so there should be opportunities for cooperation.

Specifically, two major windows of opportunities seem promising for naval education cooperation. One has to do with the content of naval education. As the perceived urgency of the Taiwan issue declines, PLA Navy planners seem to shift their attention to nontraditional security missions, or nonwar military operations, as a major legitimizer and driver for China's naval modernization. Such operations involve conducting at-sea counterterrorism and counterpiracy operations and related exercises; providing emergency relief and humanitarian aid to maritime disasters such as tsunamis and hurricanes; protecting maritime rights and interests; securing SLOCs that are vital to international trade and energy flows; and providing security to overseas national offices and properties and people.[32] The recent deployment of naval ships to escort Chinese merchant ships against pirates in Gulf of Aden is a typical example.

To enhance effectiveness in these operations, PLA Navy planners highlight the need to conduct systematic research on these operations in terms of their targets, space, and domain; characteristics, forms, and trends; types of appropriate force structure, hardware, and command-and-control and support infrastructure; scope and rules of engagement; and impacts on China's strategic environment. There is also the need to socialize and internalize related ideas and concepts through education.[33] The PLA Navy's new emphasis on nonwar military operations opens a window of opportunities for U.S.–China naval education cooperation. Most of these operations address similar issues and concerns as articulated in the new U.S. Maritime Strategy, and related research and learning are likely to take place in the naval institutions of higher learning in both countries.[34]

Furthermore, education is largely about socializing and internalizing ideas and concepts to deal with issues of common concern. As a result, the second window of opportunity for U.S.–China naval education cooperation is to develop joint programs for curriculum, teaching and learning, and faculty development. These programs serve to enhance the effectiveness of socializing and internalizing related ideas and concepts.

How can naval education cooperation facilitate the broader maritime cooperative relationship between the United States and China? A plausible answer to this question is that cooperation on nontraditional security missions may lay the cognitive and interactive basis for further cooperation to mitigate the potential consequences of maritime and naval competition. It is important to note that a major reason for narrowing American and Chinese differences is that China has been trying to imitate the United States through learning and adaptation. This behavior validates the neorealist theory of international politics, one that argues that major powers imitate the most effective country in military organization and technological development. This is because they are concerned about their own survival in an anarchic environment, particularly if they lag behind too far in relative military capabilities. An unintended consequence of such a security competition, as shown during the Cold War, is that major competitors had become more similar to one another over time because of mutual learning and adaptation and, as a result, become more familiar with each other's behavior.[35] Such similarity and familiarity eventually contributed to the similar behavior of these competitors to engage in both maritime conflict reduction and strategic arms limitation and reduction.

While current U.S.–China relations are not comparable to those between the United States and the Soviet Union during the Cold War, there are worrying signs that suggest the possibility of greater competition in the future. These include the 1996 Taiwan Strait crisis, the EP-3 incident in 2001, the close approach to a U.S. aircraft carrier by a PLA Navy nuclear submarine in 2006, the Chinese refusal to allow USS *Kitty Hawk* to visit Hong Kong in 2007, and the *Impeccable* incident in 2009. Because all these instances occurred in the maritime and naval arena, it has become not just desirable but also necessary to explore naval education cooperation as an additional venue for the two countries to become familiarized with each other's behavior. Such a familiarity may in turn help to enhance confidence building and improve crisis management in the future.

Notes

1. Samuel Huntington, *The Soldier and the State* (Cambridge, MA: Harvard University Press, 1964), 8, 11–14.

2. See "Naval Colleges of National Defense Students Have Become 'Military Schools' within Schools of Higher Learning,'" *Jiefang junbao* (*Liberation Army Daily*), 29 January 2009, 1.

3. For transformation of Naval Aviation Engineering Academy–Qingdao Campus from degree to preassignment education, see Su Xiongfeng and Feng Zi, "Realize New Stride in Transformation," Xinhua, 18 September 2008, available at http://www.china mil.com.cn/site1/milschools/2008-09/18/content_1502463.htm#.

4. "Central Military Commission (CMC) Plan on Implementing the Strategic Project Concerning Military Talent," cited in Chen Dongxiang, chief ed., *Weilaixing junshe rencai gouxiang* (*Constituting Thoughts on Future-Type Military Talent*) (Beijing: Liberation Army Press, 2005), 200. "Military struggle" is the People's Liberation Army (PLA) euphemism for a military conflict over Taiwan.

5. 海军装备研究院 (Naval Armament Studies Academy) and 海军军事学术研究所 (Naval Military Art Studies Institute) are the most well known.

6. See, "Overview of Military Schools," 2 June 2008, available at http://www.chinamil.com. cn/site1/milschools/2008-06/02/content_1310696.htm#. The Information Integration Technologies Studies Institute at Yantai Naval Aviation Engineering Academy, for instance, is a leading PLA Navy research institute on target acquisition and evaluation. See Xu Hengtong and Li Wenxi, "Visit People at the Naval Aviation Engineering Academy Who Compete to Occupy the Information Forward Position," *Dangdai haijun* (*Modern Navy*), no. 11 (2006). *Modern Navy* is a publication of the PLA Navy's political department.

7. For detailed discussion of this strategy, see Nan Li, "The Evolution of China's Naval Strategy and Capabilities: From 'Near Coast' and 'Near Seas' to 'Far Seas,'" *Asian Security* 5, no. 2 (Spring 2009), 144–69.

8. See Liu Huaqing, *Liu Huaqing huiyilu* (*Liu Huaqing's Memoirs*) (Beijing: Liberation Army Press, 2004), 432–38.

9. See Li, "Evolution of China's Naval Strategy and Capabilities."

10. See "Educating Tomorrow's Leaders, Defining the Future Navy," Naval War College, Newport, RI, public relations brochure.

11. See Li, "Evolution of China's Naval Strategy and Capabilities."

12. See Jiang Zemin, "Make Great Efforts to Educate and Bring up Large Number of High-quality New-type Military Talent," Speech delivered at the CMC Expanded Conference on 9 April 1999 and collected in Jiang Zemin, *Lun guofang he jundui jianshe* (*On National Defense and Army Construction*) (Beijing: Liberation Army Press, 2003).

13. See Liu, "Get Close to the Only Comprehensive University."

14. See Zhang Wei and Li Gen, "Get Close to Dalian Naval Combatant Academy: Navigating Your Naval Dream," *Modern Navy*, no. 4 (2004), 62.

15. Huang Yuancheng, "Naval Aviation Flight Academy in Takeoff," *Xiandai junshi* (*Modern Military*), no. 12 (2005), 12–13.

16. See Su and Feng, "Realize New Stride in Transformation."

17. See Liu, "Get Close to the Only Comprehensive University."

18. These schools include Beijing Air Force Command College, Wuhan Second Artillery Command College, and Nanjing and Shijiazhuang Army Command Colleges; see "Five Services and Arms Command Colleges Sign Agreement on Joint Education," *Liberation Army Daily*, 19 December 2006, 9.

19. Zhao Yang and Cao Jinping, "The 'Old' School of the Chinese Navy: Dalian Combatant Academy," *Modern Navy*, no. 3 (2003), 43.

20. See "Overview of Military Schools" (note 6).

21. Sun Lixin, Hou Jinsheng, and Wang Ziyong, "Cradle of Sea-Air Brave Eagles," *Modern Navy*, no. 9 (2001), 47.

22. See "Naval Command College Widens Channels to Foster Talent," *Liberation Army Daily*, 4 January 2007, 9.

23. See Tuo, "Get Close to the New-Type Command School"; Liu, "Get Close to the Only Comprehensive University"; and "Naval Submarine Academy."

24. Tuo, "Get Close to the New-Type Command School."

25. Chen Lijun, "The Highest Institution of Higher Learning for China's Navy: Nanjing Naval Command College," *Modern Navy*, no. 2 (2003), 37; and Tuo, "Get Close to the New-Type Command School."

26. See "Naval Submarine Academy."

27. See Liu, "Get Close to the Only Comprehensive University"; and Zhang and Li, "Get Close to Dalian Naval Combatant Academy."

28. Chen, "Highest Institution of Higher Learning."

29. Zhao and Cao, "'Old' School of the Chinese Navy"; and Liu, "Get Close to the Only Comprehensive University."

30. Liu Dai and Liu Jian, "'Thorny' Stories in the 'United Nations': An Account of the International Students Department of the Naval Submarine Academy," *Modern Navy*, no. 12 (2007), 34–37.

31. For details, see Chen, "Highest Institution of Higher Learning"; Tuo, "Get Close to the New-Type Command School"; Zhao and Cao, "'Old' School of the Chinese Navy"; Liu, "Get Close to the Only Comprehensive University"; and "Naval Submarine Academy."

32. See, in particular, Shen Jinlong, "Challenges Faced by Naval Non-War Military Operations and Coping Strategies," *Renmin haijun (People's Navy)*, 1 December 2008. Shen is commander of a PLA Navy North Sea Fleet support base, and *People's Navy* is the newspaper published by the PLA Navy's political department.

33. Ibid.

34. For the new U.S. Maritime Strategy, see *A Cooperative Strategy for 21st Century Seapower*, October 2007.

35. See, in particular, Kenneth Waltz, *Theory of International Politics* (New York: McGraw-Hill, 1979).

Andrew S. Erickson

Chinese Views of America's New Maritime Strategy

THE UNITED STATES AND CHINA are entering a new era of shared stakes in the global maritime commons. How the two nations interact on the high seas will be of enormous import to their respective futures and that of the international system. The United States is forging a new path with the recent promulgation of a new maritime strategy, "A Cooperative Strategy for 21st Century Seapower," which was presented by the chief of naval operations (CNO) and the commandants of the U.S. Marine Corps and U.S. Coast Guard at the International Seapower Symposium in Newport, Rhode Island, on 17 October 2007. China's reaction to the strategy will significantly impact its direction and even perhaps its realization and success.

The new U.S. Maritime Strategy contains a variety of crucial elements that could facilitate enhanced cooperation with China: (1) the emphasis on conflict prevention echoes many elements of Chinese strategic culture and doctrine; (2) the avowed objective of securing the global maritime commons is highly compatible with China's strategic interests; and (3) the new emphasis on humanitarian operations, especially, offers opportunities for bilateral cooperation to build mutual trust.

This chapter describes the new U.S. Maritime Strategy and surveys unofficial Chinese responses to date. Most Chinese analyses laud the strategy's focus on conflict prevention and international cooperation but emphasize that the strategy is not altruistic and instead serves U.S. national interests. Placing the onus on the United States to demonstrate its strategic "sincerity," Chinese observers are waiting for the new Maritime Strategy's ideals to be realized through concrete U.S. actions. This study subsequently reviews cooperative efforts relevant to the strategy before candidly examining major remaining obstacles to enhanced cooperation while also emphasizing the need to more fully explore the new strategy and China's attitude as a maritime stakeholder. While China appears to be maintaining a cautious, hedging approach in its rhetoric, actual maritime cooperation is proceeding quietly.

A Path-Breaking Document

The new Maritime Strategy embodies a historic reassessment of the international system and how the United States can best pursue its interests in harmony with those of other nation-states. The unveiling of the strategy in front of the heads of nearly one hundred navies and coast guards from around the world demonstrated initial global maritime inclusiveness. The new direction for a U.S. Maritime Strategy began with a landmark speech delivered at the 17th International Seapower Symposium, held at the U.S. Naval War College in September 2005, by then–U.S. CNO Admiral Michael Mullen. He called for a series of "Global Maritime Partnerships" spearheaded by a "thousand-ship navy" that would bring the maritime forces of friendly nations together based on their abilities, needs, and interests to provide collective security against a variety of threats in the maritime commons.[1]

Under the leadership of Admiral Mullen and Admiral Gary Roughead—the current CNO—the U.S. government has brought all three of its maritime forces (the Navy, Marine Corps, and Coast Guard) together for the first time to produce a unified strategic document, "A Cooperative Strategy for 21st Century Seapower."[2] This new strategy incorporates the ideas of U.S. military officers, government civilians, and academics.

As former U.S. secretary of the navy Donald C. Winter has cautioned, the United States is "not walking away from, diminishing, or retreating in any way from those elements of hard power that win wars—or deter them from ever breaking out in the first place."[3] But this first major U.S. Maritime Strategy in twenty-five years is based on the premise that "preventing wars is as important as winning wars."[4] The strategy places renewed emphasis on cooperating to protect the global maritime commons (shared international space) on which the security and prosperity of nations around the world depend, as demonstrated by Gabriel Collins in his chapter in this volume. In this new vision, U.S. maritime forces will focus more heavily on participating in collective security efforts that recognize the importance of broad coalitions "in an open, multi-polar world."[5] Long-term engagement with other nations, in the form of maritime law enforcement (e.g., against terrorism, proliferation, and drug trafficking), regional maritime governance frameworks, capacity building, humanitarian assistance, and disaster relief will be emphasized. This is because trust and cooperation, while vital to collective defense against security threats, cannot simply "be surged" to respond to a crisis; they must be painstakingly built and maintained on a permanent basis.[6]

The new U.S. Maritime Strategy represents a significant departure from the last major strategy, as defined by Navy secretary John F. Lehman Jr. in his 1986 "Maritime Strategy."[7] War fighting played a much more prominent role in that policy document: whereas the Soviet Union was the explicit focus of the 1986 strategy, today there is no identified adversary. The new eleven-page strategy document is not detailed, but it does contain a powerful vision. In today's globalized and uncertain world, U.S. maritime forces are committed to working with other states' forces to maintain the security of the global maritime commons. Every nation has the opportunity to participate in this process; no nation is explicitly excluded. Rather, it is only nations and substate actors that actively decide to challenge or disrupt the cooperative process that could become a threat to the existing order and hence trigger countermeasures on the part of the United States and its global maritime partners.

While it is premature to predict the degree to which the new U.S. Maritime Strategy will succeed in shaping and safeguarding the global maritime commons, a variety of indicators should be monitored over the next several years.[8] Within the U.S. Navy, continued CNO support and the appearance of the Maritime Strategy's principles in key navy planning documents as well as national strategy pillar documents will provide important barometers of success.[9] Already, U.S. military planning documents, including the February 2010 Quadrennial Defense Review (QDR)—the Pentagon's guiding strategy document—and the March 2010 Joint Operating Environment (JOE) echo the Maritime Strategy's emphasis on developing and maintaining international partnerships to address shared nonconventional security threats and thereby safeguard the security of the global maritime commons.[10] As in the past, reactions from other military services (e.g., the U.S. Army), Congress, and mass media will signal policy and monetary support for relevant programs. Given U.S. fiscal difficulties, particularly given the global financial crisis, ongoing challenges associated with the wars in Iraq and Afghanistan and the continuing counterterrorism mission, implementation is likely to be subject to budgetary limitations. Cooperation and coordination between the U.S. Navy, Marines, and Coast Guard will be particularly important to the strategy's successful functioning.

Why Chinese Views Matter

A broad acceptance of and participation in the Global Maritime Partnership Initiative by the international community will likewise be essential if the strategy is to fulfill its intended goals. In light of the strategy's focus on building partnerships to better safeguard the global maritime commons, it is vital that U.S. leaders understand clearly the frank and unvarnished views of allies, friends, and potential partners. The new Maritime Strategy generates responses from numerous states.[11] As U.S. leaders work to implement global maritime partnerships in the years ahead, they must carefully study the reactions of the nations and maritime forces with which they hope to work.

Chinese responses to the strategy warrant especially close consideration. China is a key global stakeholder with which the United States shares many common maritime interests. Beijing has not yet made any official public statements on the Maritime Strategy. Yet Chinese opinions on this matter are clearly important, even if they suggest that in some areas the two nations must "agree to disagree." Chinese reactions to the Maritime Strategy provide a window into a larger strategic dynamic, not just in East Asia, where China is already developing as a great power, but also globally, where it is playing an ever-greater role. How the United States can maintain its existing status and role while China continues to rise will be perhaps the critical question in international relations for the twenty-first century.[12]

Elements of the new U.S. Maritime Strategy could further cooperation with China. First, the strategy's emphasis on conflict prevention is compatible with many elements of Chinese strategic culture and doctrine in general, and new missions of the People's Liberation Army (PLA) in particular. The PLA's fourth mission, "play an important role in maintaining world peace and promoting common development," is especially relevant in this regard.[13] Second, the avowed objective of securing the global maritime commons is highly compatible with China's strategic interests. China relies increasingly on the oceans to import tremendous amounts of energy and raw materials, and to ship its finished goods to market. At the same time, while its navy becomes increasingly formidable as a means of asserting influence over Taiwan and contested littoral maritime areas, it has not yet developed the extensive high-end blue water capabilities needed to independently safeguard interests farther afield. The key for the United States will be to attempt to convince China that the goals and intentions of the new strategy are real and not, as many in China fear, merely "window-dressing" or camouflage for "containment" of China. Third, the new emphasis on humanitarian operations offers opportunities for bilateral cooperation to build mutual trust even as Beijing may avoid participating in activities that it deems objectionable.

Complex Reactions

The People's Republic of China (PRC) has a long tradition of informing its policy elites on international affairs through the widespread translation of foreign news and documents. Since the beginning of Deng Xiaoping's reforms in the early 1980s, which opened the way for market forces and more widespread circulation of information (e.g., through an increasingly diverse and lively news media), a "public intellectual complex" has emerged. Members of this community of strategic scholars and policymakers at a variety of private and public institutions engage in vigorous debates; publish widely in specialized and popular journals; make media appearances; and, on occasion, brief policymakers, sometimes even China's senior leadership. Some intellectuals are privy to internal deliberations and a few play a major role in shaping policy, particularly in specialized subject areas. Even when Chinese public intellectuals are not directly involved in the policy process, their views often have substantive impact. Their ideas may inform policymakers indirectly and may even be adopted as policy. They may also play a role in justifying or socializing already-established policies. When politics or bureaucratic maneuvering comes to the fore, they may become caught up in a larger competition of ideas. For all these reasons, the writings of public intellectuals are particularly worth examining for possible insights into Chinese policy debates, even government decision making. Chinese analysts are meticulous students of policy documents from major countries (particularly the United States) and scrutinize their texts in the belief that wording contains specific insights; any such document is likely to receive careful vetting in Chinese publications. In this context, it is hardly surprising that the Maritime Strategy has been subject to Chinese description and evaluation. In the years following the strategy's promulgation, a variety of assessments has emerged.

Early Media Portrayals

The strategy has been covered extensively in China's civilian (and, to a lesser extent, military) press. The vast majority of these articles are brief and descriptive.[14] Some of the more extensive ones touch on the strategy indirectly in discussing more broadly the U.S. military presence in the Asia-Pacific, and several are rather sensational in their obsession with the idea that the United States is attempting to contain China. Still, initial articles and news reports do offer some insight into Chinese assessments of the U.S. Maritime Strategy.

Some analyses evince a desire to better understand the Maritime Strategy and the reasons for its promulgation. An article in China's military affairs press develops the overall theme that the strategy and other U.S. military realignments are "inseparable from the Iraq War" but also states that "there are also different voices within the U.S. Navy."[15] The basic facts of the strategy's promulgation are well covered, and even such details as the influence of "Conversations with the Country" (与国家对话)—efforts to educate the American public about the strategy and incorporate its feedback—are recognized.[16] In October 2007, for instance, an article in *International Herald Leader*, a weekly general affairs newspaper, described a new emphasis on soft power and highlighted the document's balance of preventing war with winning war.[17] While seemingly open to this new approach, the article quotes a U.S. official as stating that the new strategy fails to address critical issues, such as "commercial fleets, industrial bases, polar resources and missile defense."[18] In a theme common to nearly all Chinese articles on the subject, however, the author states, "so-called 'international cooperation' still serves the global deployment of U.S. sea power."[19]

More blatant suspicions of U.S. intent are often on prominent display. Many Chinese observers contend that U.S. military activities are specifically designed to "'encircle' China." In one case, emphasis is expressed with regard to U.S. military activities with the Philippines, which, located in Southeast Asia and so close to Taiwan, is seen by two Chinese reporters as being vital for such "encirclement."[20] This last point, while seeming to ignore the overwhelming rationale for counterterrorism cooperation between Washington and Manila, does underscore the centrality of Taiwan to the U.S.–China relationship. The theme of Chinese "encirclement" is likely to continue to influence bilateral strategic interactions.

Many articles infer ulterior motives for the new U.S. Maritime Strategy with their assessments of the strategy's determination to "contain potential competitors."[21] An October 2007 article on the Xinhua News Web site maintains that while the U.S. public believes that the strategy reflects a new emphasis on coop-eration, in fact "this strategy's basic objective still lies in preserving America's maritime hegemonic status. . . . The U.S. emphasis on so-called 'international cooperation' is for the mission of deploying U.S. sea power globally."[22] A tran-script from China's state television network concurs: "Although on the surface it might appear that the new U.S. Maritime Strategy is not as overbearing as its predecessor, its basic objectives have not changed in the slightest."[23] A People's Liberation Army Navy (PLA Navy) magazine article states, "The latest cover for U.S. sea power is called 'maritime cooperation.'"[24] These strongly expressed sentiments suggest that some Chinese observers at this early stage of the new strategy's application may already believe that U.S. sea power and ambitions remain fundamentally unchanged and continue to challenge China's interests.

A somewhat more balanced account in *China Defense News* opines that "cooperating with other countries is a necessary choice to protect U.S. inter-ests." At the same time, it states that "the [USS *George*] *Washington* [carrier strike group] will undoubtedly further strengthen U.S. military presence in the Western Pacific region."[25] Increasing U.S. focus on deploying forces to the Western Pacific is the subject of several articles.[26] China's military and civil-ian media have been monitoring U.S. military deployments in the Asia-Pacific with concern well before the strategy's promulgation.[27]

Other unofficial sources do articulate the balance of challenges and oppor-tunities for China in the area of maritime strategy. The *People's Daily Online* attempted to place the new document within the larger context of America's strategic conditions.[28] Having previously suffered from a "strategically con-fusing" period with the removal of its Soviet competitor, and having labored mightily to respond to the September 11 terrorist attacks and support the wars in Iraq and Afghanistan, the U.S. Navy, *People's Daily Online* reports, has been too busy to conduct a systematic self-examination of its long-term develop-ment until very recently. The new U.S. Maritime Strategy is thus correctly seen as an attempt to re-create strategic clarity and direction for U.S. maritime forces. In a more positive tone, the article contends that the new U.S. Maritime Strategy is "quite gentle, and it really embodies the lofty ideal of 'coopera-tion,' and regards war prevention as an important mission of U.S. sea power." Moreover, the author notes, "this is the first time that a U.S. official document has put forward the concept [of a] 'multi-polar world,'" a foreign policy goal long championed by Beijing.

Yet the gist of the analysis is consistent with the other analyses in its concern with and suspicion of U.S. motivations. Had Washington not revised its mari-time strategy to emphasize fighting nontraditional security challenges such as terrorism in keeping with changes to the international system following the end of the Cold War, "the mighty U.S. fleet [would] be like a giant that [had] lost its way, a colossus without any merit." Renewed U.S. emphasis on cooperation and humanitarian operations is thus not seen as being altruistic. Rather, it is a utilitarian repackaging of a time-honored power-politics approach. "In this strategic document that emphasizes protecting the global system, there is not a single mention of the role of the United Nations," the author continues. "Will the nations of the world identify with and accept a maritime security system presided over by the United States?" The article concludes, "Americans have recognized the weaknesses of the unilateralism of the last several years . . . What [the strategy] expresses can only be one thing, that is, American hegemony has put on a new cover called 'cooperation.'"

Still, the potential for a significant change in U.S. naval strategy is taken seriously by some analysts. An article by China's Xinhua news agency states that "within the next 15 years, the U.S. Navy's large scope of maritime operations will become smaller and smaller. Far ocean operations are already no longer the U.S. Navy's focal point."[29] While this may raise questions about Washington's long-term influence, it does suggest that the ongoing focus on counterterrorism is being taken seriously. In a possible indication of perception of U.S. weakness, however, other articles raise questions about U.S. ability to persevere in protracted conflicts.[30]

Substantive Analyses

As this volume went to press, three articles have been published openly that stand out from the rest in their focus on the strategy and their detail and sophistication of analysis. Therefore, they have been selected as the focus of this chapter. The respective authors' affiliations with different major institutions suggest that their writing (through variations in coverage) offers windows into how different elements of China's bureaucracy, with their specific interests and perspectives, assess the new U.S. Maritime Strategy. While these informed commentaries are not definitive and should not be overinterpreted, they may be suggestive of the Chinese government's viewpoint and future policy responses.

The first article is by Dalian Naval Vessel Academy emeritus professor Lu Rude.[31] Lu's full-page article appeared in *People's Navy*, the official newspaper of the PLA Navy, which is published by the PLA Navy's political department and provides guidance for PLA Navy officers and enlisted personnel.[32] The second article is by Wang Baofu, researcher and deputy director of PLA National

Defense University's Institute for Strategic Studies.[33] Wang's article appeared in *Study Times*, a journal of the CCP Central Party School. The third article is by fellow contributor Su Hao, who has himself published a full-length Chinese translation of the strategy.[34] Su's article appeared in *Leaders*, a popular magazine on current affairs and policy published in Hong Kong for popular consumption there, as well as for a select mainland audience.

Common Assessments

The three articles give a sophisticated and relatively comprehensive summary of the U.S. Maritime Strategy. They differ in assessing various arguments in its text, and there is some tension between the commonalities that emerge from shared perspectives and those that are products of their following the strategy's original structure. But they share unambiguously several major conclusions.

A New Strategic Direction

All three authors see the new U.S. Maritime Strategy as representing a major shift from the Maritime Strategy of 1986. Each regards the strategies issued in the interim as products of post–Cold War strategic uncertainties, with little lasting influence.[35] They characterize the current strategy as fundamentally different. Su explains that when formulating the 2007 edition, "U.S. Navy theoretical circles were faced with the new situation of international anti-terrorism and the rapid rise of emerging countries." Wang states that the new strategy "not only has new judgments and positions concerning maritime security threats, but more importantly has new thinking regarding how to use military power to meet national security objectives." All emphasize the importance of the subject at hand: in Wang's words, "As a bellwether of world military transformation, U.S. maritime strategic transformation merits scrutiny."

Emphasis on Cooperation and Conflict Prevention

All three analysts describe—with apparent approbation—the strategy's explicit focus on cooperation. Su declares that "it prominently emphasizes maritime security cooperation." Wang states that "the U.S. military's 'maritime strategy' has already taken 'international cooperation' as an important principle. This . . . indicates that the United States security and military strategy will face a major new adjustment." Lu writes, "One can see that the new U.S. Maritime Strategy emphasizes 'military software' such as 'humanitarian rescue missions and improving cooperative relations between the U.S. and every country.'"

The analysts all emphasize that the new Maritime Strategy elevates preventing war to an equal status with winning wars. They interpret war prevention as involving primarily soft power operations, as opposed to deterrence based on war winning capabilities to undergird otherwise cooperative approaches. Wang terms the emphasis on war prevention the strategy's "most prominent feature." Lu describes this "conspicuous new viewpoint" as being a product of "major change" and recognizes the utility of "maritime military operations other than war" and increased "international cooperation and non-combat use of navies," to include humanitarian rescue missions and improved cooperative relations with other regions. Su describes this as a "major bright spot." Chinese analysts implicitly welcome a U.S. Navy more focused than before on such missions vis-à-vis sea control and power projection.

But the Chinese analysts are not prepared to fully acknowledge that war prevention may require substantial coercive capabilities, and they do not endorse U.S. efforts in this area.[36] They quite naturally examine regional maritime security from the perspective of China's national interests. These include emphasizing the use of venues in which Beijing is relatively influential (e.g., the United Nations) to address disputes and limit foreign military influence. In the views of many Chinese, letting other states unduly shape these areas could—in a worst-case scenario—lead to military intervention in a manner that could harm China's regional influence and sovereignty claims.[37] In the analysts' apparent unwillingness to acknowledge that conflict prevention can sometimes rely on coercive capabilities, one can see an effort to emphasize desired elements of the document while deemphasizing or contesting undesired ones—a common practice in both policy analysis and international relations.

Mention of Multipolarity

The analysts also note the Maritime Strategy's reference to a "multipolar" world. Lu describes this as a "first time" shift in U.S. policy documents. In the present author's opinion, however, the term "multipolar" (which is often confused with "multilateral") does not properly describe the current international system, at least from a U.S. scholarly or policy perspective.[38] Moreover, many Chinese audiences regard multipolar (多极) as having a specific meaning akin to: "a world in which there are several major regional powers and no single superpower hegemon."[39] This situation would be realized in the near future only by substantial relative decline in U.S. power to the benefit of other emerging major powers. A small but increasingly influential Chinese school of thought promoting an American "decline theory" (衰落论)—which lost influence after it incorrectly predicted the emergence of multipolarity following the Cold War's end—has recently gained ground with the U.S. difficulties in Iraq and elsewhere.[40] The strategy's very use of the term "multipolar," therefore, appears to validate the Chinese government's vision of the benefits of a decline in American hegemony, which it has described periodically as a threat to its core interests.[41] According to China's Foreign Ministry, "Multipolarization on the whole helps weaken and curb hegemonism and power politics, serves to bring about a just and equitable new international political and economic order and contributes to world peace and development."[42] China's 2008 Defense White Paper judges that "economic globalization and world multi-polarization are gaining momentum."[43] To be sure, directly promoting the erosion of U.S. hegemony on a global scale is not an active policy on the part of China's government, which remains focused on internal development and defense of core interests on China's periphery. And the writings surveyed clearly state that the United States is still hegemonic and thus retains significant deterrence power.[44] However, in the present author's personal view, encouraging the misperception that U.S. power is ebbing risks harming U.S. deterrence capabilities in the longer term.

Together with other apparent instances of the United States recognizing the limitations of its power and influence, the author believes that such a change of attitude is likely to be seen by many Chinese as being inspired not by sudden enlightenment in an altruistic sense but rather by growing recognition of weakness (in light of previously overly ambitious strategic goals). Indeed, the analysts cited here welcome, as Su points out in almost Corbettian fashion, a strategy apparently based on recognition of limitations (i.e., U.S. "ability is not equal to its ambition") and a consequent reliance on cooperation with other international partners. As Su states, paraphrasing the strategy itself, "no country alone has adequate resources to ensure the security of the entire maritime area." In the author's opinion, then, the problematic use of the term "multipolar" potentially risks engendering misinterpretation, miscalculations, and false expectations on the part of Chinese analysts. Or, perhaps even worse, the term may make the strategy's rhetoric seem removed from the reality of U.S. force structure and deployments. Care should be taken in further interactions with Chinese counterparts to counteract any potential misperceptions in this regard.

Appreciation of Domestic Dimensions

The analysts also recognize the interagency aspects of U.S. maritime cooperation and coordination. As Su notes, this is the "first time that the U.S. sea services jointly issued a strategic report." He notes the strategy's injunction that "coordination and cooperation must be strengthened among the maritime forces of each military service and each domestic department." This indicates recognition that cooperation and coordination between the U.S. Navy, Marines, and Coast Guard will be particularly important to the strategy's successful functioning. In Wang's analysis, as will be discussed in more detail, he displays significant understanding of the U.S. defense policy process.

A Special Role for Naval Forces

The analysts see the maritime domain as being vital to many nations' development and recognize the central role that the U.S. Navy has played in the world. Wang contends that "the ability of the United States to become the world hegemon is directly related to its . . . comprehension of sea power, and [its] emphasis on maritime force development." All three note the strategy's own wording that today "the majority of the world's population lives within several hundred kilometers from the ocean, 90 percent of world trade is dependent on maritime transport, [and] maritime security has a direct bearing on the American people's way of life." Lu additionally observes (using wording similar to that of Wang) that naval forces are particularly relevant to fighting terrorism because of such "special characteristics" as "mobility, which gives [them] the ability to advance and withdraw, to deter and fight."

Asia-Pacific Focus

All three scholars identify the Asia-Pacific as a priority area for U.S. naval presence. Lu describes the Middle East as a "powder keg" and acknowledges the status of the Indian Ocean and Arabian Sea—the two other areas specifically mentioned in the strategy—as strategic energy lifelines. But he uses his own interpretation to connect several issues mentioned in the strategy, concluding that "the Western Pacific is determined to be 'a region of high tension' where the U.S. has the responsibility to 'carry out treaty obligations' to its allies and to 'contain potential strategic competitors.'" Wang and Su also take notice of the Maritime Strategy's specific mention of the Western Pacific.

Continued Hegemony

Most important, all three analysts view the strategy as part of a larger U.S. effort to maintain its predominant international power and capabilities for unilateral action. They do acknowledge that the new strategy is far more cooperative than the 1986 version in both concept and rhetoric. Wang states that "overbearing, offensive language is relatively reduced, and there is noticeably more emphasis on 'strategic cooperation.'" Lu notes that "the new Maritime

Strategy is relatively moderate compared to the previous version in its use of words and style." But, he emphasizes, while the strategy "projects the pleasant words of 'peace,' 'cooperation,' and 'war prevention,' hegemonic thinking remains its main thread." The analysts see the United States as being unwilling to abandon the traditional "hegemony" and "sea control" that its capabilities have long afforded it. Wang judges that the United States retains a long-standing "maritime hegemonic mentality," which he traces to Mahanian thought, and remains "the only superpower in the world today." He adds, "Because the U.S. . . . places maritime power above all others, its maritime strategy can be better described as serving its global hegemony rather than safeguarding the world maritime order." Lu charges that "the hegemonic U.S. thinking of dominating the world's oceans has not changed at all." In his view, "what is behind 'cooperation' is America's interests, having 'partners or the participation of allies' likewise serves America's global interests."

The Chinese analysts express concern that the United States retains power to threaten core Chinese interests. These interests include reunification with Taiwan, assertion of sovereignty over disputed islands (and associated resources and air and water space) on China's maritime periphery, and ultimately some form of sea-lane security and regional maritime influence. Chinese concerns in this area offer a useful caution regarding the possibilities of U.S.–China cooperation in the near term.

Diverging Viewpoints

Despite these shared viewpoints, there are identifiable differences in focus and interpretation among the three analysts. By chance, the Maritime Strategy's promulgation has coincided with a vigorous and unprecedented debate within China concerning its own maritime development. The three Chinese assessments of the U.S. strategy, particularly in their judgments about the contours and directions of U.S. strategy, cannot help but influence that debate.

A Model for PLA Navy Development?

Lu's lengthy, complex analysis contains apparent attempts to use the new Maritime Strategy, rightly or wrongly, as evidence of an elevated position of influence for the U.S. Navy. Lu writes that the new U.S. Maritime Strategy demonstrates that the Navy "has been placed in an extremely prominent position" and "continues to serve as the daring vanguard and main force of U.S. global strategy." While the latter point may seem optimistic to some, this does realistically describe the character of U.S. power projection from Lu's strategic vantage point in maritime East Asia. Even in its current fiscal difficulties, the U.S. Navy in terms of capabilities alone must seem very impressive to the PLA Navy. Such a portrayal of U.S. naval power and influence is consistent with his advocacy of rapid, robust Chinese maritime development.

There are several indications that Lu's evaluation, in addition to educating PLA Navy officers about the U.S. Maritime Strategy, may also contain an implicit argument for a similar increase in the PLA Navy's mission from access denial to blue water SLOC defense consistent with China's growing interests as a great power.[45] More than Su and even Wang, Lu appears to believe that "the oceans have become a new domain for rivalry." He notes that "the Western Pacific is the area of most intense competition among nations for maritime sovereignty," "has the highest growth and concentration of the world's naval forces," and "is the sea area where the U.S. military conducts the largest and most frequent maritime exercises with its allies." Lu appears also to hint that PLA Navy development must inevitably be used to balance against U.S. naval power projection. "Some Asian countries are rising rapidly, have abundant economic and technological strength, and possess nuclear weapons," he notes elliptically. "They will directly influence and challenge American hegemonism."

Here Lu may be arguing implicitly for some form of PLA Navy power projection capabilities, perhaps in the form of deck aviation (as might be broadly surmised from the context). In East Asia, he emphasizes, the United States "dispatches carrier battle groups to cruise around in a heightened state of war readiness." Were it operationally feasible, one might infer, China could benefit from having similar capabilities to protect its sovereignty claims. And "by setting up point defenses and carrying out strategic deployment, the U.S. is prepared to act at any time and to intervene" in the Arabian Sea and the Indian Ocean, where China has similar interests in SLOC security and energy access.

In time, at least by Lu's ambitious standards, China might likewise benefit from a navy that could maximize its forward presence while minimizing its international footprint to avoid the tremendous political risk of overseas bases, which the PRC has foresworn since its founding in 1949. This would allow for a Chinese approach to power projection—respecting sovereignty while influencing events ashore. Wang and Su do not appear to share Lu's emphasis or advocacy. But Lu's arguments should not be dismissed as mere naval promotion.[46] While likely reflecting the PLA Navy's bureaucratic interests, naval advocates publishing in official forums such as Lu must defer to the guidance promulgated by China's civilian leadership. A real danger here is that having Chinese naval development inspired by that of the United States, as manifested in internal bureaucratic debates and budgetary battles, risks generating the sort of interaction effects that have triggered previous arms races.[47]

Seeking Explanations in Foreign Policy and Bureaucratic Politics

Where Lu takes a narrow institutional approach, Wang seeks larger strategic explanations. Wang describes the new Maritime Strategy as not only representing a major departure from the tone of previous security documents issued by the Bush administration but also as "one of the most far-ranging adjustments in the last 20 years." He sees it as the logical outcome of three major factors: military setbacks in Iraq; the failures of transformation in that conflict; and the need for the Navy to justify its share of the defense budget.[48] "The '9.11' terrorist attacks produced a tremendous assault on the U.S. security concept," Wang observes, in wording akin to Lu's. "The U.S. maritime strategy changed accordingly." The Iraq War experience, Wang states, is teaching America the importance of combining hard and soft power to develop "rational strength." This strategic rethinking, and the concepts of the thousand-ship navy and Global Fleet Stations, "can only be regarded as a major transformation in [U.S. military] understanding of the application of military force in the realization of national interests, following setbacks in earlier unilateralist and pre-emptive strategy."[49] According to Wang, "As Chief of Naval Operations, [Admiral] Mullen repeatedly suggested that 'the old maritime strategy had sea control as a goal, but the new maritime strategy must recognize the economic situation of all nations, [and] not only control the seas, but [also] maintain the security of the oceans, and enable other countries to maintain freedom of passage.' It is precisely through his promotion that the new 'maritime strategy' was introduced."

Wang's charge of strategic overreach is broadly compatible with Su's less abrasive assessment, but it stands in contrast to Lu's, which focuses more on U.S. capabilities than limitations. Wang's third conclusion is based on a sophisticated understanding of the U.S. defense establishment and its policy processes. "For the maritime forces to obtain a larger share of the future defense spending pie, they must lead strategic thinking and initiatives," Wang maintains. At the same time, like many of his peers, he also alleges that people and "military industrial interest groups have worked together to frequently concoct a 'Chinese naval threat theory.'"

Strategic Coherence

Su's largely descriptive article contains a fairly favorable assessment of U.S. maritime power and intentions. Su sees the United States developing a coherent maritime policy in which the Maritime Strategy and "the so-called

'Thousand Ship Navy' concept currently being deliberated in U.S. Navy circles are two sides of the same coin." Where Lu sees a model for PLA Navy development and Wang sees responses within the U.S. military bureaucracy to changing conditions and failed policies, Su sees a diplomatic message that is carefully calibrated and coordinated.

Issues Not Addressed

A number of key uncertainties are neither mentioned nor explored by the analysts. For all their insights, the three analysts do not address the fact that the new U.S. Maritime Strategy is not a stand-alone document, even in the U.S. domestic bureaucratic context.[50] U.S. Navy modernization goals would have seemed a potential subject for inquiry, especially as the U.S. Navy appears first (in 2005) to have derived a goal of increasing its 281-ship fleet to 313 vessels by 2020, and then developed a strategy for their use.[51] These ambiguities between the ends and means of U.S. policy are not explored.

The Maritime Strategy was issued at the end of the second Bush administration, yet the analysts seem to assume that it will serve as a precursor to future policy regardless of changes in U.S. government leadership. It is portrayed more as authoritative policy than a "trial balloon," yet few indications are given as to how it will actually shape U.S. policy. Most U.S. analysts, by contrast, believe that the specific effects of the document on future U.S. maritime policy are not yet certain.[52]

As in the past, reactions from other military services, Congress, and the media will signal policy and monetary support for relevant programs. Wang does appear to allude to this when he states that a major rethinking of military and foreign policy remains under way: "The U.S. intellectual elite is in the process of comprehensively rethinking the war, and this is beginning to have an impact on policy-making departments." Implementation of the new strategy is certain to be subject to budgetary limitations, particularly given the recent recession and ongoing challenges associated with the wars in Iraq and Afghanistan. From Wang's perspective, by contrast, "whether the Republican Party or the Democratic Party comes to power, adjustments and changes in the U.S. government's foreign policy are inevitable." Wang and Su appreciate the fiscal challenges that may impact U.S. military spending. None of the analysts appears to entertain the idea, however, that funding constraints might constrain the development of nontraditional low-end capabilities to support the Maritime Strategy.

Are the Chinese analysts "mirror imaging," assuming that the strategy is a more authoritative document than it actually is based on their own experience with a more centralized policy process? Perhaps. But the three analysts cannot be expected to address all of its contents and related issues. What is noteworthy is that all three do emphasize a most important point: a broad acceptance of and participation in the Global Maritime Partnership (GMP) initiative by the international community will be essential if the strategy is to fulfill its intended goals. Nevertheless, these collective omissions do suggest that the analyses represent a "first cut" at understanding the strategy and how it may affect China. The goal is apparently to consider some initial implications for maritime development in the United States and China as well as the prospects for future bilateral relations.

Tentative Implications

In the first year and a half since the new U.S. Maritime Strategy's promulgation (during late 2007 and through early 2009), public reaction in China has been relatively muted although substantive commentary has increased over time. There are several likely explanations for this relative reticence. The new strategy may not have been perceived to represent a bona fide shift in U.S. policy— a strategic opportunity for China. Other events, such as cross-strait politics preceding the March 2008 Taiwan presidential election, likely demanded greater attention at the time. Among officials and analysts, lack of direct response may also have represented a deliberate hedging strategy to avoid definitive judgments until the new document could be better understood. On this point, it must be recognized that Beijing may require time and further explanation from the United States before it is ready to issue an official response to the strategy.

These preliminary unofficial Chinese reactions suggest that revising America's maritime strategy alone will not persuade China of positive U.S. intentions. Relative capabilities are important for Beijing, making it hard to believe that the United States will do good with so much power. The Chinese analysts obviously retain major concerns vis-à-vis the goals of U.S. military strategy. Regarding the Maritime Strategy in particular, they worry that beneath a veneer of cooperative rhetoric, they are being asked to tolerate—or even directly acquiesce to—projection of U.S. power in a manner that threatens China's core national interests. In these Chinese views, the new Maritime Strategy recognizes the limits of unilateralism, but a perceived fundamental arrogance of American power is seen as structural and unchanged. Thus, there is a degree of competing perspectives on the future use of U.S. naval power. Here the cooperative implications of the strategy may run against the grain of much Chinese thinking regarding the United States, particularly its armed forces. The initial reaction remains highly circumspect and more will need to be done to overcome Chinese suspicions. In this regard, America's actions must ultimately speak louder than its words. Unilateral military disarmament in selected areas, though convincing in theory, seems unrealistic. In the absence of actual conflict, however, there should be some room to cooperate.

At the same time, many Chinese analysts are heartened by the new U.S. emphasis on cooperation. While retaining concerns about U.S. strategic objectives, they do not dismiss the strategy outright. For Lu, Washington stands at a strategic crossroads: it must demonstrate its true strategic intentions to Beijing. On the one hand, Lu is concerned about the United States conducting frequent "transnational and multinational maritime military exercises" in East Asia, which, he believes, constitutes "evidence that the new U.S. Maritime Strategy has already been put into effect." On the other hand, the new cooperative approach may truly represent "a major change in the U.S. military's maritime strategy," Lu allows. "It must receive the affirmation of all the world's nations."

China's attitude toward the Maritime Strategy can also be gleaned from its assessments of the GMP, previously termed the "thousand-ship navy" (TSN). A number of articles express strong support for the concepts encompassed in GMP, although they do not mention it directly. They include comments by the PRC ambassador to the United States and the PRC minister of foreign affairs, discussion by military commentators, and an example of actual GMP-type cooperation between the U.S. and PRC coast guards.[53] Conversations with Chinese academics and analysts reveal fairly unanimous general approval for the "cooperate to achieve security" concept behind the GMP. Other analyses, such as a recent one in a Chinese military trade publication, are at least even-handed: "strengthening the alliance system and building maritime alliances have been important tasks of the U.S. Navy all along. This is clearly manifested in the U.S. Navy's 'Thousand-Ship Navy' plans, as well as in the New U.S. Maritime Strategy of 2007."[54] But China is not likely to approve of the GMP directly by name since, from its leaders' perspective, to do so would effectively cede control of the international initiative and the framework of cooperative efforts to the United States.

This ambivalence is reflected in two articles published before the Maritime Strategy was issued. The first highlights two benefits the United States can gain from the program: contractual access to ports of partner countries, which benefits U.S. global naval deployment; and partner countries sharing the U.S. burden of fighting terrorism. It also states that the Asia-Pacific/Southeast Asia is the emphasis of the program because of sea-lanes and chokepoints and competing Russian and Chinese influence, but countries of the region may not fully embrace the program.[55] A second article highlights Chinese navy commander Wu Shengli's visit to the United States in early April 2007 and the U.S. proposal for China to join the program. According to an anonymous naval expert from Nanjing Naval Command College, the United States stands to receive strategic benefits in the form of port and logistics accesses. Japan and South Korea likewise strongly support the program because of their dependence on sea-lanes and the Malacca Strait for oil shipment. So does India, to whom the United States has offered such preferential measures as the sale of an amphibious assault ship and joint exercises. But, perhaps in an oblique reference to China, he states that other Asian countries may have reservations because of sovereignty infringement.[56]

There is room for optimism in the sense that the views from Chinese think tanks, policy analysts, and government officials—like those of their U.S. counterparts—as they become publicly available, are likely to be more balanced and pragmatic. They are likely to acknowledge the many potential benefits of more actively cooperating with the United States in the maritime dimension. Here it will be important for U.S. officials and scholars to engage deeply with a wide variety of Chinese interlocutors to explain in great detail the strategy's genesis, intent, word choices, evolution, and potential applications as well as to discuss specifically Chinese concerns and reactions. In this sense, the strategy can serve as a catalyst for much-needed Sino-American strategic dialogue and engagement.

Chinese analysts are encouraged by the strategy's new rhetoric, and encouraging progress has been made in bilateral maritime cooperation already, but at the higher levels of China's military and civilian government, officials believe that the ball is in Washington's court, and are waiting for concrete actions on the part of the United States. Chinese observers will therefore likely wait to see how Washington's initiatives affect Beijing's core strategic concerns. Statements in China's maritime press are guardedly positive, noncommittal, and emphasize the need to carefully consider the implications for China's national interests: "At the present stage, the U.S. has put forward the 'Thousand Ship Navy' plan and invited China to join; we should pay great attention to this, and actively carry out discussion and research."[57] In future discussions with their U.S. counterparts, they will probably continue to probe for U.S. willingness to commit to actions that make China feel strategically assured. They will undoubtedly be watching for the United States to, in the words of a Chinese proverb, "言必信,

行必果" ("be true to its words and resolute in its deeds"). As Lu puts it, "The people of the entire world are glad to see this transformation in strategic think-ing, [but] will wait and see, hoping for genuine actions and practical results."

Growing Cooperation

Amid the suspicious rhetoric of its official media, China is quietly cooperating with the United States on a number of maritime security activities.[58] The prem-ise for these increased activities may be China's 2006 Defense White Paper, which for the first time acknowledges that "Never before has China been so closely bound up with the rest of the world as it is today." China, in this state-ment of national policy, is "committed to peace, development and cooperation" as it seeks to construct "together with other countries, a harmonious world of enduring peace and common prosperity."[59] Looking further into the future, an analysis in *Modern Navy* advocates maritime engagement and cooperation on China's part and goes so far as to declare that "a big and powerful [Chinese] fleet will support a stable supply chain" from which "all oil trading nations benefit."[60]

This new wave of cooperation already extends from the corridors of gov-ernment to the Pacific Ocean. Here the two nations' navies and other maritime services have the opportunity, even the duty, to do what other services have not: establish a new and cooperative relationship. This special maritime role is not a coincidence. Given the unique nature of sea-based presence, port visits, diplomacy, and critical trade relations, maritime forces interact in peacetime differently from other services. For the U.S. and Chinese maritime forces, this generates many compatible and overlapping strategic priorities. Indeed, when seaborne bilateral trade is considered, the two nations already have a major maritime partnership, albeit one in which the military element lags far behind the commercial.[61] This peacetime contact, particularly between the U.S. and Chinese navies, is potentially vital; given the nature of the volatile Taiwan issue, U.S. and Chinese naval forces would also be the most likely to directly engage each other in the unfortunate event of kinetic war. Therefore, there is a strong impetus for the two nations' maritime forces, particularly their navies, to better relations regarding issues critical to both peacetime and times of conflict.

Underscoring the value of the new Maritime Strategy's comprehensive sea service scope, the U.S. Coast Guard has established a working relationship with its Chinese counterparts.[62] As Captain Bernard Moreland documents in his chapter in this volume, Chinese fisheries enforcement officers have served temporarily on U.S. cutters (to interdict Chinese ships fishing illegally). Their patrol boats work with U.S., Japanese, and Russian counterparts annually to prevent illegal driftnet fishing in the North Pacific Coast Guard Forum, East Asia's only maritime security organization, in which China and the United States both play substantive roles.[63] The possible creation of a unified Chinese coast guard organization may provide further opportunities to build on this progress by reducing institutional conflict and confusion, as Lyle Goldstein explains in his contribution to this volume.

Despite its greater sensitivity, cooperation between the U.S. and Chinese navies is expanding as well. A number of substantial visits have taken place. In July 2006 PRC Central Military Commission vice chairman Guo Boxiong became the highest-ranking Chinese military officer to visit the United States since 2001. Then-commander of U.S. forces in the Pacific, Admiral William Fallon, visited China in May and August 2006.[64] During the first visit, he extended to the PLA an unprecedented invitation to observe the June 2006 U.S. Guam-based military exercise Valiant Shield, which was readily accepted. This gesture of transparency demonstrates that the Unites States has nothing to hide from China, even in major military exercises in the Western Pacific. As Nan Li's chapter in this volume suggests, interaction between the nations' institutions of professional military education is also growing.[65]

Building on the foundation of this growing series of exchanges, the United States and China have held a series of unprecedented bilateral exercises. Two decades of cooperative rhetoric were matched with concrete if modest action when a search-and-rescue exercise took place off the coast of San Diego on 20 September 2006.[66] Although a series of port visits had previously occurred and are scheduled to continue, this was the first bilateral military exercise ever conducted between the two nations.[67] A second phase of the exercise was held in the strategically sensitive South China Sea in November 2006.[68] In Xinhua's assessment, "The holding of the joint search-and-rescue exercises indicates that Sino-U.S. military relations are 'moving toward the pragmatic' and carries major significance for the future development of relations between the two militaries."[69]

China has also been invited to cooperate more broadly with the U.S. Navy under the framework of GMP, as set forth in the new Maritime Strategy. While visiting China in November 2006, Admiral Gary Roughead stated to Chinese officials that "our navies can improve the ability to coordinate naval operations in missions such as maritime security, search and rescue, and humanitarian relief."[70] During PLA Navy commander Vice Admiral Wu Shengli's April 2007 visit to the United States, Admiral Mullen asked him to consider "China's potential participation in Global Maritime Partnership initiatives."[71] China's navy is reportedly in the process of considering this proposal.[72] In a subsequent news conference, Chinese Foreign Ministry spokesman Qin Gang declined to elaborate on this point but said that the naval leaders "reached a consensus in many areas."[73] On 17–21 August 2007, Admiral Mullen visited a variety of naval facilities and educational institutions and discussed possibilities for future maritime cooperation with China's top navy officials.[74] As discussed in the introduction, recent naval leadership visits include U.S. CNO Admiral Gary Roughead's participation in the PLA Navy's sixtieth anniversary commemoration in Qingdao in March 2009.

Many of the aforementioned activities would have been unthinkable only a few short years ago when there was not a mutual outreach for cooperation on both sides. However, one could argue that only the easier areas of cooperation have been attempted thus far, while the truly substantive areas have not yet been fully explored. Much remains to be done before both sides can forge a robust maritime partnership that generates any sort of policy momentum. As the two sides must acknowledge (at least in private), several fundamental issues still serve to undermine the bilateral political and military-to-military relationship and thereby limit the possible options for deeper maritime cooperation. The next section reviews these difficult, sensitive issues.

Remaining Obstacles to Enhanced Cooperation

Unfortunately, several core differences between the United States and China—absent significant policy changes—are likely to limit cooperation for the foreseeable future. The inability of Beijing and Washington to reach an understanding concerning Taiwan's status has long been the principal obstacle to improvements in U.S.–China relations, and hence will likely retard some forms of maritime security cooperation.

Since 1949 Beijing has consistently and clearly emphasized the vital importance of reunifying with Taiwan as a central tenet of national policy. To safeguard its interests in East Asia, Washington must firmly honor its commitment not to support Taiwan independence while also honoring its responsibility to protect Taiwan's democracy amid massive geopolitical changes. Economic integration and rising Chinese military strength arguably make the island increasingly indefensible militarily and complicate the status quo that previously prevailed. It is thus essential for the United States to make clear that, in the words of former deputy assistant secretary of state for East Asian and Pacific affairs Thomas Christensen, "Americans will not fight and die to defend a Taiwan that declares constitutional independence from the

Chinese nation. At the same time, America should warn the mainland that a military attack on a Taiwan that is still legally Chinese will meet a U.S. military response."[75] Fortunately, since his election in March 2008, Taiwan's new president, Ma Ying-jeou, has pursued a positive and practical policy of improving relations and economic links across the strait. This is a welcome relief from the counterproductive policies of his predecessor, Chen Shui-bian, who managed to both provoke Beijing and alienate Washington with a seemingly endless stream of ill-considered actions.

Despite these recent improvements, Taiwan's status will remain a sensitive issue. But Beijing must recognize that no U.S. president has the power to change a basic reality: the preservation of Taiwan's democracy is an issue of critical importance to the United States and one that enjoys overwhelming congressional support.[76] For this reason, the question of Taiwan's status must be separated from other issues if robust bilateral cooperation is to be achieved. The ability of Washington and Beijing to agree to disagree regarding their enduring strategic differences will thus determine the degree of their ability to cooperate to safeguard larger commercial, resource, homeland security, and maritime interests.

In addition to their concerns about the sensitive issue of Taiwan's status, Chinese policymakers and analysts also believe that the United States tends to focus unduly on using military means to address problems that may be better addressed by other approaches. Recent efforts by the Obama administration to reinvigorate such organizations as the State Department and pursue a wide range of diplomatic initiatives suggest a broader-based approach that should be welcomed by all who wish the United States well in its efforts to provide public goods in the international system. While this represents realization on Washington's part that hard power wielded unwisely can be disastrous for all concerned, it in no way represents an abdication of "hard power" capabilities. Rather, it also signifies renewed appreciation that "soft power" tools are vitally important as well—a fact that Beijing appears to have recognized in recent years, with considerable benefit to its own foreign relations. Still, a sustainable future can only be realized if both powers recognize the importance of each other's continued contributions to the world system. The United States must continue to acknowledge the reality that China is assuming an increasingly important and interdependent role that produces undeniable benefits. Arguments by some American scholars that extreme and divisive efforts should be made to prevent China's rise are neither realistic nor helpful.[77] And some calls by U.S. pundits for military procurement to counter China have been patently absurd, with one advocating that the United States should deploy "not . . . 280 ships but a thousand; not eleven carriers, but 40, not 183 F-22s, but a thousand; and so on."[78] It will be important to communicate to Chinese policymakers that America is home to diverse discussion and debate, and these perspectives are in no way mainstream views.

There is another side to this story, however. From the U.S. perspective, China's ongoing limitations in military transparency, both in terms of capabilities and intentions, coupled with its rapid increases in defense spending and wide-ranging military modernization, remains another source of great concern. This situation undermines U.S. cooperation initiatives—which are being attempted with increasing willingness—for fear that China is unwilling or unable to reciprocate equitably. A related concern is that China may attempt to exploit U.S. goodwill by imposing ever-larger political demands. Under these conditions, the political reality in Washington circumscribes the evolution of better military-to-military relations with Beijing, something the latter does not seem to fully understand (or accept). Beijing's lack of transparency and reciprocity only strengthens the critics of cooperation. This has led to a wide speculation in the United States and elsewhere concerning China's intentions, much of it inaccurate, unsubstantiated, and worst-case in nature. But the lack of communication from Beijing unnecessarily helps feed this trend in Washington.

Various incidents epitomize this issue of nontransparency and its impact on crisis management between the two nations. Not only have a number of recent events been murky in explanation, there have also been confusing signals about who was making the decision (the PLA, the foreign ministry, or even China's central leadership). The November 2004 incident in which a Chinese Han-class submarine was tracked by the Japanese Maritime Self-Defense Force as the submarine passed submerged through Japanese territorial waters in the Ishigaki Strait was blamed on a navigational error in a manner that does not appear credible to naval experts.[79] In October 2006 a Chinese diesel submarine reportedly surfaced unexpectedly within eight kilometers of the U.S. Navy's Kitty Hawk aircraft carrier as it was operating near Okinawa.[80] China's January 2007 antisatellite test, reportedly the single-greatest human source of satellite-endangering debris in history, has still not been satisfactorily explained despite repeated inquiries by the U.S. government. In November 2007 two U.S. minesweepers and the Kitty Hawk carrier battle group were denied permission, on separate occasions, to make port calls in Hong Kong. This issue raises the larger question as to what degree military-to-military activities will be subject to ever-shifting political winds and strategic disagreement.

There may well be clear explanations for each of the aforementioned events, but unfortunately China's government has thus far been unwilling to provide any. A degree of public clarification is necessary and would do much to allay U.S. concerns, even if it defends China's strategic reasoning, with which the United States may strongly disagree. While official explanations for China's military development and assertions of benign intent may fulfill domestic political and even cultural imperatives, they ultimately do not serve Beijing's interests vis-à-vis the United States because they are not persuasive, or in some cases even comprehensible, to an American audience.

The obstacles to strategic transparency are sobering. As neoliberal institutionalist literature in the field of political science reminds us, the breakdown of cooperation is often a problem of information; the lack of perfect information can lead to mutual defection from agreements. Asymmetric information could be intentional or unintentional. It could stem from a lack of internal coordination (e.g., the military and diplomatic bureaucracies) or intentionally mixed messages. Even the security dilemma could be driven by (mis)perceptions of information.[81] Thus, Chinese provision of vague descriptions of its strategic intentions that fail to explain key behaviors, coupled with a degree of military power and influence on the part of the United States that causes even its more detailed explanations of intent to be held in suspicion, make it more difficult for the two sides to achieve a firm basis for robust maritime security cooperation. At the same time, however, better practices, agreements, and even institutions can help demonstrate commitment and reassurance.[82]

Trans-Pacific Progress?

While China appears to be maintaining a cautious, hedging approach in its rhetoric, low-level yet concrete maritime cooperation is proceeding without great fanfare. The real question is whether this progress has the ability to catalyze greater maritime and naval cooperation, or broader strategic relations. Given the issues at stake, it is time to explore how to take those important steps. This will require presidents Obama and Hu to expand the Bush administration's vision of both the United States and China as global "stakeholders" more fully into the maritime dimension. With the importance of the high seas as an irreplaceable conduit for international trade and energy, maritime security includes both civil maritime and naval cooperation. Forging a relationship through which the two nations can help to secure this global commons and still avoid conflict is the crux of the issue. Once launched, overcoming the many incidents that could scuttle it will require better communication and a high level of interaction.

A wide variety of nonsensitive cooperation areas will remain the most viable starting point and can likely continue regardless of the state of U.S.–China maritime relations. These include tourism, civilian academic conferences and exchanges, Track II diplomacy (i.e., by the Council for Security Cooperation in the Asia Pacific), commercial utilization of new maritime resources and technologies, environmental protection, meteorology (e.g., typhoon and tsunami detection), and scientific research. For these areas, the private sector and nongovernmental organizations can continue to play a major role.

For areas of cooperation that impinge more directly on issues of national security, a more organized and official basis for exchange will be essential. A vital underpinning of both civil maritime and naval cooperation will be the development of robust ties between relevant institutions of professional military education. It is to be hoped that exchanges of faculty and students, currently limited, can grow steadily in the future. The author has been told by Chinese experts that "China still has concerns about some U.S. proposals, and wants to know more about the 'Thousand Ship Navy.'" Exchanges can facilitate fuller explanation of all aspects of the new Maritime Strategy to Chinese officials and subject matter experts, as described earlier, as well as mutual discussion of nonsensitive linguistic, curricular, and technical elements (e.g., best practices and simulation procedures) that could further cooperation possibilities (e.g., in humanitarian operations and disaster relief) under its aegis. A new community of military officers can be trained to be capable of sophisticated interaction and even some degree of interoperability. Development of bilateral academic links will help to provide continuity to the relationship while facilitating the processes and personal interaction that are essential in a Chinese cultural and bureaucratic context. These foundations, in turn, can help support and sustain more robust official events, initiatives, and agreements over the longer term.

Senior Colonel Li Yaqiang, a researcher at the Naval Research Institute (the PLA Navy's strategic think tank in Beijing), has outlined areas of maritime security cooperation that would be acceptable to China. In Li's view, cooperation should occur "mainly in nonsensitive, nontraditional fields to avoid endangering maritime security due to traditional military behaviors." As for location, the appropriate areas include "high seas, international sea areas, nonsensitive sea areas, and waters welcomed or acceptable by concerned countries to avoid taking actions in sensitive sea areas, and waters that are under jurisdiction of other countries, under conflict, not accepted or rejected by concerned countries." Acceptable activities include "friendly exchange, peaceful consultation, and joint operation to avoid abuse of force and unilateral intervention." More specifically, "the naval forces may launch cooperation in the fields of maritime joint law enforcement, anti-terrorism, anti-piracy, maritime navigation safety, and search and rescue in order to frighten and contain the force posing potential threat to international maritime security, stabilize maritime situation of turbulent regions, promote and safeguard ocean shipping security, and eventually establish an effective maritime security safeguarding mechanism."[83]

Given the fundamental interests of both nations, then, cooperation against terrorism, maritime crime, piracy, and trafficking in humans, drugs, and other illegal goods should be able to proceed at a fairly sophisticated level over the next few years. Infectious diseases, environmental safety, and economic issues may also be addressed. As is described more fully in the fourth chapter in this volume, "The Container Security Initiative and U.S.–China Relations," China's participation in the Container Security Initiative (CSI) is a positive development in this area, and it is to be hoped that more Chinese ports will join soon. Cooperating against piracy may be more complicated, depending on the context, given its association with international maritime legal issues on which China tends to have different interpretations from those of the United States. Yet, the interests involved are fundamentally the same here as well, and China's ongoing deployment to the Gulf of Aden offers an encouraging example. In the minds of many Chinese analysts, energy security is connected to scenarios of naval conflict, but commercially viable confidence-building measures can be explored in an effort to remedy this.

With respect to maritime energy security, the United States and China, now the world's two largest oil consumers, share an interest in maintaining secure, stable, and affordable oil supplies. They should consider establishing a joint petroleum inventory reporting system. Their navies should address maritime crises in places far from sensitive areas surrounding China and the United States (e.g., preventing Somali pirates from pirating tankers in the Gulf of Aden). They should also establish a joint threat-reporting database for vital sea lines of communication (SLOCs). Washington should also encourage Beijing to join the International Renewable Energy Agency (IRENA) and the International Energy Agency (IEA) to facilitate closer strategic petroleum reserve (SPR) management cooperation.[84] With the right agreements and incentive structures, technology transfer in clean energy production could likewise go very far in assuaging suspicions while promoting shared economic interests.

In particular, the new U.S. Maritime Strategy can play a crucial role by facilitating a variety of missions that require substantial coordination but are not viewed as inherently sensitive by either side. Much more can be done in terms of humanitarian operations, particularly as China increases its capabilities in this area. Joint search-and-rescue exercises can expand from the current ones between civil maritime and select naval forces to more regular naval cooperation. As Admiral Eric McVadon explains in his chapter in this volume, China's commissioning of its first naval hospital ship in 2008 may have demonstrated an intention to project increased "soft power" in the maritime realm. Already China's largest deck aviation platform, the multirole aviation training ship *Shichang*, which has a hospital module, has supported domestic flood relief efforts and deployed as far away as New Zealand.[85] There is no inherent reason why China's already significant domestic maritime disaster relief capabilities could not be mobilized in the future to provide humanitarian assistance overseas. In fact, China's *Peace Ark* hospital ship is now slated to engage in annual overseas deployments. The first, in 2010, will reportedly involve port calls in the Middle East and Africa.[86] Perhaps in the future *Peace Ark* could work with USNS *Mercy* to further mutual interests in vulnerable areas.

As China's naval modernization continues at a rapid pace and new Chinese aircraft and vessels appear unannounced, American and Chinese military platforms are increasingly encountering each other in or near territorial waters or airspace. As David Griffiths explains in his chapter in this volume, these incidents increase the possibility of tactical incidents escalating into major crises. The U.S.–Soviet 1972 Incidents at Sea and 1989 Prevention of Dangerous Military Activities agreements established specific guidelines for conduct in such situations that have been credited with preventing countless crises. The current U.S.–PRC 1998 Military Maritime Consultative Agreement provides for annual consultations but offers no specific procedures. The two nations could benefit from a new code of conduct—one that stresses the role of early communication between military platforms in an era of advanced communications and sensing technology. This, coupled with more frequent meetings and perhaps some form of confidence building measures, would greatly further a larger effort to improve bilateral communications and crisis management.

What the new U.S. Maritime Strategy alone cannot accomplish is to change China's perception of its fundamental national interests. It will not persuade China to participate in activities with implications that it may deem objectionable. According to Senior Colonel Li Yaqiang, this includes any activities that Beijing believes do not "follow the purpose of the United Nations charter, the well-acknowledged international laws, and the Five Principles of Peaceful Coexistence, respect national sovereignty, safeguard common interests, accept political diversity, take mandatory national responsibilities, fulfill international obligations, abandon cold-war thinking, and give full consideration to strategic interests, values, and social characteristics of each concerned nation."[87] Such activities might include intrusive boardings under the aegis of the Proliferation Security Initiative, which China apparently believes to contravene its oft-stated need for UN-based legitimacy (a point disputed by many Western maritime legal scholars) and complicates its attempts to stabilize the Korean Peninsula. Even areas of concern and disagreement must be discussed in forums related to the Maritime Strategy, however, because the two nations must understand each other's perspectives in a detailed and comprehensive manner. Cooperative partners must be able to have open and candid dialogue on all issues of mutual interest.

Regardless of its exact parameters, building and sustaining a high level of cooperation will require substantial effort and patience. Washington and Beijing will have to live with considerable ambiguity, and should expect occasional setbacks. For the foreseeable future, there will be significant differences in their military capabilities, political systems, and national interests. To guard against the threat of conflict as China, the rising power, gains on the United States, the dominant power today, both sides will likely find it necessary to "hedge"—not only rhetorically, but also economically, politically, and even militarily. This power transition conflict scenario is a natural part of international politics, and will be a highly destabilizing factor at times, particularly when U.S. and Chinese domestic politics are thrown into the mix.

Despite the long-term strategic importance of cooperation, perceptions and misperceptions will continue to wield great influence over its success. Just as what Chinese analysts would term a "China threat theory" continues to maintain a firm grip on many in Washington, many in Beijing construe ulterior motives from virtually any U.S. action (an "America threat theory") as well. American analysts and planners need to look at the big picture, which strongly suggests an overall Chinese desire and need to cooperate with the United States rather than to challenge it. And the renewed American focus on humanitarian operations should be seen by Chinese for what it is, an opportunity for better cooperation and improved relations with the United States. Only time, increased interaction, and concrete efforts at cooperation will ameliorate these knotty problems of perception and trust.

As mentioned earlier, the election of Ma Ying-jeou as Taiwan's president in March 2008 has placed cross-strait relations on an improved trajectory after eight years of instability under the provocative leadership of Chen Shui-bian. Meanwhile, recent developments, such as the continuing deployment of naval vessels to defend against piracy in the Gulf of Aden, suggest that PLA and PLA Navy missions may become increasingly compatible with the Maritime Strategy's focus on humanitarian assistance and disaster relief. At an expanded Central Military Commission conference on 24 December 2004, Chairman

Hu Jintao introduced a new military policy that defines the four new missions of the PLA, including "play an important role in maintaining world peace and promoting common development."[88] PLA and PLA Navy writings are operationalizing both this theme and Hu's recent guidance that China's military should pay attention to "diversified military tasks" (多样化军事任务).[89] Such factors may well support mission convergence and increase strategic space for Sino-American maritime cooperation, although exploiting opportunities will take substantial effort from both sides, and will not be easy.[90]

Despite the challenges before it, maritime security lies at the heart of the survival and prosperity of nations. It is important never to lose sight of the greater perspective: the world's largest developed nation and its largest developing nation stand to reap tremendous benefits by jointly ensuring the safety of the maritime commons. The possibility of conflict will always threaten the U.S.–China relationship, but the objective rationale of national interests overwhelmingly reinforces the need for the world's greatest developed and developing powers to reach an understanding to support a durable, if sometimes competitive, coexistence on the world's oceans.

Notes

The views expressed in this chapter are solely those of the author as a private individual. This study is based only on publicly available sources and does not represent the official position or analysis of the U.S. Navy or any other organization of the U.S. government [在这篇文章的意见完全是写者个人的学术观点，并不代表美国海军或者美国政府的官方看法或者政策]. The author thanks Amy Chang, Peter Dutton, Nan Li, Donald Marrin, William Murray, William Pendley, Jonathan Pollack, Robert Rubel, Michael Sherlock, Frederic Vellucci, and Andrew Winner for their helpful inputs. To give readers the most accurate sense of how the U.S. Maritime Strategy is rendered in Chinese, quotations in this translation have deliberately *not* been synchronized with the English phrases used in the original text, which can be obtained at www.navy.mil/maritime/MaritimeStrategy.pdf. This article draws on earlier research that appeared as "Assessing the New U.S. Maritime Strategy: A Window into Chinese Thinking," *Naval War College Review* 61, no. 4 (Autumn 2008): 36–53; and "New U.S. Maritime Strategy: Initial Chinese Responses," *China Security* 3, no. 4 (Autumn 2007): 40–61, www.wsichina.org/cs8_3.pdf. The latter has been translated into Chinese as 汪北哲译 [Wang Beizhe, trans.], "美 <中国安全>: 中国谨慎应对美海洋战略" ["U.S. 'China Security': China Cautiously Reacts to the U.S. Maritime Strategy"], 环球时报 [*Global Times*], 18 December 2007, http://china.huanqiu.com/eyes_on_china/2007-12/36152.html.

1. Michael Mullen, "The Thousand Ship Fleet," *Pentagon Brief,* 1 October 2005; and "'Global Maritime Partnership' Gaining Steam at Home and with International Navies," *Defense Daily International* 7, no. 42 (27 October 2006).

2. Admiral Mullen is now chairman of the Joint Chiefs of Staff.

3. Peter Dombrowski, "Maritime Strategy Project: Overview and Preliminary Analysis," presentation to author, October 2007.

4. Several maritime strategies have been issued in between, but most analysts evaluate that they have had no lasting legacy. Few outside the U.S. Navy have even heard of them. "A Cooperative Strategy for 21st Century Seapower" (Washington, DC: U.S. Chief of Naval Operations and the Commandants of the U.S. Marine Corps and U.S. Coast Guard, 17 October 2007), http://www.navy.mil/maritime/MaritimeStrategy.pdf, 4.

5. Ibid., 5.

6. Ibid., 11.

7. John Hattendorf, *The Evolution of the U.S. Navy's Maritime Strategy, 1977–1986,* Newport Paper 19 (Newport, RI: Naval War College Press, 2004), http://www.usnwc.edu/Publications/Naval-War-College-Press/Newport-Papers/Documents/19-pdf.aspx.

8. Dombrowski, "Maritime Strategy Project."

9. Key naval planning document include "Navy Strategic Plan in Support of Program Objective Memorandum 08" (Washington, DC: U.S. Chief of Naval Operations, May 2006), http://www.docstoc.com/docs/23263501/Navy-Strategic-Plan; and "Naval Operations Concept 2006" (Washington, DC: U.S. Navy and Marine Corps, 2006), https://www.mccdc.usmc.mil/CIW/ER/Naval%20Operations%20Concept.pdf. National strategy documents include "The National Security Strategy of the United States of America" (Washington, DC: The White House, 2010); "The National Defense Strategy of the United States of America" (Washington, DC: Department of Defense, June 2008), http://www.defense.gov/news/2008%20National%20Defense%20Strategy.pdf; "The National Military Strategy of the United States of America: A Strategy for Today; A Vision for Tomorrow" (Washington, DC: Chairman of the Joint Chiefs of Staff, 2004), http://www.defenselink.mil/news/Mar2005/d20050318nms.pdf; "The National Strategy for Maritime Security" (Washington, DC: Department of Homeland Security, September 2005), http://www.dhs.gov/xlibrary/assets/HSPD13_MaritimeSecurityStrategy.pdf; and "The Nuclear Posture Review Report" (Washington, DC: Department of Defense, April 2010), http://www.defense.gov/npr/docs/2010%20Nuclear%20Posture%20Review%20Report.pdf.

10. *Quadrennial Defense Review Report (QDR) 2010* (Washington, DC: U.S. Department of Defense, 1 February 2010), http://www.defense.gov/qdr/QDR%20as%20of%2026JAN10%200700.pdf; and *The Joint Operating Environment (JOE) 2010* (Norfolk, VA: U.S. Joint Forces Command, 15 March 2010), http://www.jfcom.mil/newslink/storyarchive/2010/JOE_2010_0.pdf. Like the Maritime Strategy, the QDR has been criticized for saying little about the growing challenges posed by the PLA—particularly to U.S. access to the global maritime, air, space, and cyber commons. Yet there are good reasons for taking a relatively indirect approach, rather than enumerating directly a litany of specific Chinese military developments and corresponding threats. These issues

are well known, and well documented in other forums. Given the complex, bifurcated, and uncertain military relationship with China that the above discussion suggests, it makes sense to focus primarily on U.S. access interests. This enables a more constructive focus on U.S. interests and objectives, and thereby—as with the Maritime Strategy—places the onus on all nations (including China) to respect them, rather than automatically assuming that there is no hope for avoiding conflict, which could become a self-fulfilling prophesy in critical aspects.

11. See, for example, Paul D. Taylor, ed., *Perspectivas Sobre Estrageica Marítima: Ensayos de las Américas, La Nueva Strategia Marítima de EE UU y Comentario Sobre: Una Estrategia Cooperativa para el Poder Naval en el Siglo XXI* [Perspectives on Maritime Strategy: Essays from the Americas, the New U.S. Maritime Strategy and Commentary on a Cooperative Strategy for 21st Century Seapower] (Newport, RI: Naval War College Press, 2009).

12. See, for example, Ashton B. Carter and William J. Perry, "China on the March," *The National Interest* 88 (March–April 2007): 16–22; Thomas J. Christensen, "Fostering Stability or Creating a Monster? The Rise of China and U.S. Policy toward East Asia," *International Security* 31, no. 1 (Summer 2006): 81–126; and Aaron L. Friedberg, "The Future of U.S.-China Relations: Is Conflict Inevitable?" *International Security* 30, no. 2 (Fall 2005): 7–45.

13. Chairman Hu Jintao introduced a new military policy that defines the four new missions of the PLA at an expanded Central Military Commission conference on 24 December 2004. The first three missions are (1) serve as an "important source of strength" for the CCP to "consolidate its ruling position"; (2) "provide a solid security guarantee for sustaining the important period of strategic opportunity for national development"; and (3) "provide a strong strategic support for safeguarding national interests." See "Earnestly Step Up Ability Building within CPC Organizations of Armed Forces," 解放军报 [*Liberation Army Daily*], 13 December 2004, http://www.china mil.com.cn/site1/xwpdxw/2004-12/13/content_86435.htm; and "三个提供，一个发挥," ["Three Provides and One Brings into Play"], 解放军报 [*Liberation Army Daily*], http://news.sina.com.cn/c/2005-09-29/08517064683s.shtml.

14. See, for example, 彭立军 [Peng Lijun], "美国推出新的海上战略" ["The U.S. Releases a New Maritime Strategy"], 新华网 [Xinhua Net], 18 October 2007, http://news.xinhuanet.com/newscenter/2007-10/18/content_6898372.htm; "美国新海上战略强调合作和预防" ["The New U.S. Maritime Strategy Emphasizes Cooperation and Prevention"], 新华社电 [Xinhua News Agency Online], 18 October 2007, http://www.ycwb.com/ycwb/2007-10/18/content_1651674.htm; and 杨晴川，王薇 [Yang Qingchuan and Wang Wei], "美国推出新海上战略" ["The U.S. Releases a New Maritime Strategy"], 新华社华盛顿 [Xinhua News Agency, Washington], 19 October 2007, available at http://www.sina.com.

15. 吕德胜 [Lu Desheng], "伊战带给美军的影响" ["The Influence of the Iraq War on the U.S. Military"], 中国民兵 [*Conmilit*], no. 11 (2007), http://www.pladaily.com.cn/site1/zgmb/2007-11/23/content_1030774.htm.

16. "美军: 21世纪海上力量的合作战略" ["The U.S. Military: A Cooperative Strategy for 21st Century Sea Power"], 人民网军事频道 [People's Net Military Channel], 25 October 2007, http://news.ifeng.com/mil/4/200710/1025_342_272411.shtml.

17. 杨晴川 [Yang Qingchuan], "美国海上力量 '三巨头'—海军作战部长拉夫黑德, 海军陆战队司令康韦和海岸警卫队司令艾伦共同出现在罗得岛州纽波特海军战争学院举行的国际海军演讨会上, 向与会的100多个国家和地区的海军首脑降重推出美国新版的海上战略" ["The 'Three Magnates' of U.S. Sea Power—Adm. Gary Roughead, Chief of Naval Operations; Gen. James T. Conway, Marine Corps commandant; and Adm. Thad W. Allen, Coast Guard Commandant, Presented the Strategy to Maritime Leaders from More than 100 Countries Attending the International Seapower Symposium at the Naval War College in Newport, R.I."], 国际先驱导报 [*International Herald Leader*–Beijing], 17 October 2007, available at www.chinesenewsnet.com. Translation by Danling Cacioppo and Nan Li. *International Herald Leader* is published by *Reference News*, a daily with materials translated by the foreign press, carried by China's official news agency, Xinhua. Like a brief Xinhua English-language summary, and a wide variety of other online articles and Internet commentaries to date, it provides some basic facts about the strategy and the circumstances of its roll-out. See also "U.S. Releases Unified Maritime Strategy," Xinhua General News Service, 18 October 2007, http://news.xinhuanet.com/english/2007-10/18/content_6899251.htm.

18. For a similar quotation regarding "omitted" topics, see 未克 [Wei Ke], "美国《国防新闻》: 美军海上战略缺陷多" ["U.S. Defense News: The U.S. Military's Maritime Strategy Has Many Defects"], 新华网 [Xinhua Net], 25 October 2007, http://www.china.com.cn/military.txt/2007-10/25/content_9124389.htm; http://mil.news.sohu.com/20071025/n252858218.shtml. A similar version appeared in a major PRC-funded Hong Kong newspaper: "美媒: 美軍海上新戰略缺陷多" ["U.S. Media: The New U.S. Maritime Strategy Has Many Defects"], 大公報 [*Ta Kung Pao*], 26 October 2007, http://www.takungpao.com/news/07/10/26/YM-814681.htm.

19. This final point may help to explain the reasoning behind the article's contention that "[Admiral] Mullen not long ago aroused great concern from the international community by proposing the so-called '1000-ship Navy.'" It is important to note that this term appears to have been largely replaced by the phrase "Global Maritime Partnerships" in current U.S. Navy parlance.

20. 刘华, 吴强 [Liu Hua and Wu Qiang], "美国通过新海上战略 指导美军重返菲律宾" ["Through the New Maritime Strategy, the U.S. Directs its Military to Return to the Philippines"], 国际先驱导报 [*International Herald Leader*], 24 October 2007, http://www1.chinataiwan.org/xwzx/gj/200710/t20071024_473467.htm. See also 肖亭 [Xiao Ting], "美军变相重返菲律宾企图 '包围' 中国" ["The U.S. Military Covertly Returns to the Philippines in Attempt to 'Encircle' China"], 国际先驱导报 [*International Herald Leader*], 25 October 2007, http://www.chinadaily.com.cn/hqzg/2007-10/25/content_6207471.htm. For a related online posting, see "'中国不造航母行吗' 系列之五 '美国在海上包围中国'" ["'Is It OK for China Not to Build an Aircraft Carrier?' Series No. 5 'The U.S. Encircles China by Sea'"], 新浪论坛 [*Sina Forum*], 24 November 2007, http://s.bbs.sina.com.cn/pview-70-16355.html.

21. 杨晴川, 王薇 [Yang Qingchuan and Wang Wei], "美国推出新的海上战略—遏制潜在竞争对手" ["The U.S. Releases a New Maritime Strategy—Containing Potential Competitors"], 新华网 [Xinhua Net], 18 October 2007, http://www.pladaily.com.cn/site1/xwpdxw/2007-10/18/content_986293.htm. Translation by Andrew Erickson and Nan Li. It must be emphasized that this is not a *Liberation Army Daily* article and did not appear in that publication's print edition. The brief text gives factual information on the strategy; it is the seemingly arbitrary label "containing potential competitors" that is troubling. See also 邱贞讳 [Qiu Zhenhui], "美国海军发布21世纪海权合作战略" ["The U.S. Navy Issues a Cooperative Strategy for 21st Century Sea Power"], 环球网 [*Global Net*], 18 October 2007, http://www.huanqiu.com/www/86/2007-10/13500.html; and 杨晴川 [Yang Qingchuan], "美国海上战略 '由硬变软' 以谋求海上全球部署" ["The U.S. Maritime Strategy Changes 'From Hard to Soft' in the Quest for Global Maritime Deployment"], 国际先驱导报 [*World Herald Leader*], 24 October 2007, http://news.xinhuanet.com/newscenter/2007-10/24/content_6933474.htm.

22. 封长虹 [Feng Zhanghong], "美抛出 '以海制陆' 新战略—多样手段维持霸权地位" ["The U.S. Puts Forward a New Strategy to 'Use the Sea to Control the Land'—Diverse Means to Preserve [Its] Hegemonic Position"], 新华网 [Xinhua Net], 8 December 2007, http://news.xinhuanet.com/world/2007-12/08/content_7217221.htm; and "美军推出海上新战略" ["The U.S. Releases a New Maritime Strategy"], 工人日报 [*Worker's Daily*], 20 October 2007, http://news.sohu.com/20071020/n252754840.shtml.

23. 许钦铎 [Xu Qinduo, reporter], 张鹏飞 [Zhang Pengfei, editor], "美国推出新海上战略" ["The U.S. Releases a New Maritime Strategy"], 中央电视台国际在线 [China Central Television International Online], http://news.cctv.com/world/20071019/103473.shtml; republished as "突破狭隘海洋斗争定义—美军推出新的海上战略" ["Break Through a Narrow Definition of Ocean Combat—The U.S. Releases a New Maritime Strategy"] 云南信息港 [Yunnan Information Portal], http://news.yninfo.com/world/gjjs/200710/t20071020_502850.htm.

24. 顾祥兵 [Gu Xiang Bing], "美国海权的 '最新外衣'—新海上战略透视别国隐私" ["The 'Latest Cover' for U.S. Sea Power—The New Maritime Strategy Scrutinizes Other Countries' Secrets"], 当代海军 [*Modern Navy*], http://news.xinhuanet.com/mil/2008-02/27/content_7609770.htm.

25. 刘江平, 沈基飞 [Liu Jiangping and Shen Jifei], "美海军新战略: 打入全球核心区" ["The New U.S. Maritime Strategy: Infiltrate Global Core Regions"], 中国国防报 [*China Defense News*], 29 November 2007, http://bbs.people.com.cn/postDetail.do?boardId=2&id=84122024.

26. See, for example, "针对台湾与朝鲜问题美军增兵太平洋将不 '太平'" ["The Increase of U.S. Armed Forces in the Pacific to Counter the Taiwan and North Korean Problems Will Not Be 'Peaceful'"], 环球时报 [*Global Times*], 12 November 2007, http://www.sxgov.cn/jstd/jsrd/501023.shtml.

27. 美海军全球作战新概念 ["The U.S. Navy's New Global Concept of Operations"], 解放军报 [*Liberation Army Daily*], 21 April 2005, http://www.pladaily.com.cn/site1/jsslpdjs/2005-04/21/content_188893.htm; and 章华 [Zhang Hua], "美军两大航母东亚演练形成威摄—磨刀霍霍为实战" ["The Drills of the U.S. Armed Forces' Two

Large Aircraft Carriers in East Asia Create Deterrence—Sharpening the Sword for Actual Combat"], 国际先驱导报 [*International Herald Leader*], 20 August 2008, http://www.southcn.com/news/international/gjkd/200408200230.htm.

28. Unless otherwise specified, all quotations from this and the following paragraph were derived from 邢蓬宇 [Xing Pengyu], "美国新海上战略: 以合作之名谋强权之实" ["The United States' New Maritime Strategy: Solidifying Its Might under the Banner of Cooperation"], 人民网军事频道 [*People's Daily Online*: Military Affairs Section], 24 October 2007, http://military.people.com.cn/GB/8221/51756/81282/81532/6422552.html.

29. 周婷 [Zhou Ting], "美海军作战范围从远洋转到近海—催生近海战斗舰" ["The Scope of U.S. Naval Operations Shifts from Far Oceans to the Littoral—Hurrying to Develop the Littoral Combat Ship"], 新华网 [Xinhua Net], 21 February 2008, http://news.xinhuanet.com/mil/2008-02/21/content_7638401.htm.

30. 米兰, 维希 [Mi Lan and Wei Xi], "美海洋战略因缺乏对冲突持续时间的预判可能失败" ["The U.S. Maritime Strategy May Fail Because It Lacks Prediction of the Duration of Sustained Conflict"], 四川新闻网 [Sichuan News Network], 4 March 2008, http://world.newssc.org/system/2008/03/04/010714245.shtml.

31. This article was originally published as 陆儒德 [Lu Rude], "美海上新战略浮出水面" ["The New U.S. Maritime Strategy Surfaces"], 人民海军 [*People's Navy*], 27 November 2007, 3. Lu's home institution is perhaps most similar to the U.S. Naval Academy, although this comparison has significant limitations, in part because Chinese professional military education is dispersed among a wider range of schools than is the case in the United States.

32. See also 陆儒德 [Lu Rude], "在大战略中给中国海权定位" ["Defining Sea Power in China's Grand Strategy"], 人民海军 [*People's Navy*], 6 June 2007, 4.

33. This article was originally published as 王宝付 [Wang Baofu], "美军 '海上战略' 与未来军事转型" ["The U.S. Military's 'Maritime Strategy' and Future Military Transformation"], 学习时报 [*Study Times*], 22 January 2008, http://www.lianghui.org.cn/xxsb/txt/2008-01/22/content_9568776.htm.

34. This article was originally published as 苏浩: 外交学院外交学系教授; 吴兵: 外交学院外交学系博士生 [Su Hao, Professor of Diplomacy, China Foreign Affairs University; Wu Bing, Doctoral Student, China Foreign Affairs University], "美国海上战略新思路—21 '世纪海权的合作战略' 报告评述" ["The U.S. Maritime Strategy's New Thinking—Reviewing the 'Cooperative Strategy for 21st Century Seapower' Report"], 领导者 [*Leaders*], no. 19, December 2007, 29–30. Su's translation of the U.S. Maritime Strategy is 吴兵, 母耕源, 钟龙彪翻译, 苏浩审校 [Wu Bing, Mu Gengyuan, Zhong Longbiao (translator), and Su Hao (proofreader)], "21世纪海权的合作战略—首开历史先河: 21世纪海权的合作战略" ["A Cooperative Strategy for 21st Century Seapower—For the First Time in History: A Cooperative Strategy for 21st Century Seapower"], 领导者 [*Leaders*], no. 19, December 2007, 21–28.

35. For Chinese assessments of these maritime strategies, see 许世勇 [Xu Shiyong], "美海军实施网络反潜新战略" ["The U.S. Navy Implements a New Network Anti-Submarine Warfare Strategy"], 当代海军 [*Modern Navy*], September 2006; and 李杰 [Li Jie], "重视前沿存在, 强调联合作战—十年来美国海军战略的调整变化及

特点" ["Attach Importance to Forward Presence, Emphasize Joint Operations—The Revision, Change and Characteristics of U.S. Naval Strategy Over the Past 15 Years"], 现代舰船 [*Modern Ships*], no. 1 (2003): 13–14.

36. Wang does mention "strategic deterrence theory" and Su notes that the strategy "does not assume conflict, but recognizes the historical reality that peace cannot be automatically maintained."

37. See Peng Guangqian and Yao Youzhi, eds., *The Science of Military Strategy* (Beijing: Military Science Publishing House, 2005), 439–43; and 徐起 [Xu Qi], "21世纪初海上地缘战略与中国海军的发展" ["Maritime Geostrategy and the Development of the Chinese Navy in the Early 21st Century"], 中国军事科学 [*China Military Science*] 17, no. 4 (2004): 75–81; trans. Andrew Erickson and Lyle Goldstein, *Naval War College Review* 59, no. 4 (Autumn 2006): 46–67.

38. See Leif-Eric Easley, "Multilateralism, not Multipolarity: China's Changing Foreign Policy and Trilateral Cooperation in Asia," *JoongAng Daily* (with *International Herald Tribune*), 14 March 2008, 11. As Samuel Huntington explains, "A multipolar system has several major powers of comparable strength that cooperate and compete with each other in shifting patterns. A coalition of major states is necessary to resolve important international issues. European politics approximated this model for several centuries." Nearly two decades after Huntington wrote this, the world is still closer to the "uni-multipolar" system that he described than to true multipolarity. The closest Chinese approximation is 一超多强 ("one superpower and several great powers"). Samuel Huntington, "The Lonely Superpower," *Foreign Affairs* 78, no. 2 (March–April 1999): 35–49, http://www.foreignaffairs.com/articles/54797/samuel-p-huntington/the-lonely-superpower. In a recent alternative interpretation, Richard Haass likewise rejects the idea that the current international system is multipolar: "In a multipolar system, no power dominates, or the system will become unipolar." Richard N. Haass, "The Age of Nonpolarity: What Will Follow U.S. Dominance," *Foreign Affairs* 87, no. 3 (May–June 2008): 44–56, http://www.foreignaffairs.com/articles/63397/richard-n-haass/the-age-of-nonpolarity.

39. For similar wording, see Robert Kagan, "The September 12 Paradigm: America, the World, and George W. Bush," *Foreign Affairs* 87, no. 5 (September–October 2008): 25–39, http://www.foreignaffairs.org/20080901faessay87502/robert-kagan/the-september-12-paradigm.html.

40. For Chinese discussion of U.S. decline, see 王恬 [Wang Tian], "美国衰落与群雄崛起" ["U.S. Decline and the Rise of Other Power Centers"], 人民日报 [*People's Daily*], 30 May 2008, http://world.people.com.cn/GB/1030/7318287.html; 肖刚 [Xiao Gang], "在单极与多极之间: 中国外交的平衡" ["Between Unipolarity and Multipolarity: China's Diplomatic Balance"], 太平洋学报 [*Pacific Journal*], no. 3 (2008), http://scholar.ilib.cn/A-QCode~tpyxb200803003.html; 郑羽 [Zheng Yu], "多极世界是否已经成为国际关系的现实" ["Has a Multipolar World Already Become the Reality in International Relations?"], 中国社会科学院院报 [*Journal of the Chinese Academy of Social Sciences*], 31 January 2008, http://en.chinaelections.org/NewsInfo.asp?NewsID=122477; 李义虎 [Li Yihu], "世界经济多极化趋势将进一步加强" ["The Trend of World Economic Multipolarization Will Further

Strengthen"], 现代国际关系 [*Contemporary International Relations*], no. 12 (2007), http://scholar.ilib.cn/A-QCode~xdgjgx200712005.html; 孟庆龙 [Meng Qinglong], "美国衰落过程的重要地标" ["Footprints of U.S. Decline"], 现代国际关系 [*Contemporary International Relations*], no. 9 (2006): 30–32, http://scholar.ilib.cn/A-QCode~xdgjgx200609016.html; Zhang Wenmu, "Sea Power and China's Strategic Choices," *China Security* (Summer 2006): 28–29, http://www.wsichina.org/cs3_2.pdf; and 裘元伦 [Qiu Yuanlun], "美国 '衰落论' 与 '夏兴论' 之争" ["Contention between 'U.S. Decline Theory' and 'U.S. Revival Theory'"], 了望 [*Outlook*], no. 16, 1989.

41. Denny Roy, "China's Pitch for a Multipolar World: The New Security Concept," *Asia-Pacific Security Studies* 2, no. 1 (May 2003), http://www.apcss.org/Publications/APSSS/ChinasPitchforaMultipolarWorld.pdf; and Yong Deng, "Hegemon on the Offensive: Chinese Perspectives on U. S. Global Strategy," *Political Science Quarterly* 116, no. 3 (Autumn 2001): 343–65.

42. "China's View on the Development of Multi-polarity," Web site of China's Foreign Ministry, 15 November 2000, http://www.fmprc.gov.cn/eng/gjwt/gjzzyhy/2594/2595/t15139.htm.

43. Information Office of the State Council, People's Republic of China, "China's National Defense in 2008," January 2009, www.gov.cn/english/official/2009-01/20/content_1210227.htm.

44. See also 宋国友 [Song Guoyou], "美国衰落的幻象" ["The Illusion of U.S. Decline"], 东方早报 [*Oriental Morning Post*], 24 January 2008.

45. Lu's discussion of the UN Convention on the Law of the Sea (UNCLOS) appears to represent further advocacy of PLA Navy development to support regional stability. Lu refers directly to UNCLOS Article 301's admonition to use the seas only for peaceful purposes—a provision to which, as a nonmember, the United States is not technically bound to observe. Lu's reference would not be readily recognizable to many American readers, and the United States and China disagree about Article 301's meaning in any case. Lu makes a similar reference to UNCLOS Article 197's call for global and regional cooperation to protect and preserve the maritime environment, which would be received in the same manner as the Article 301 reference by most American readers. The author greatly appreciates Peter Dutton's contributions concerning concepts and wording in this and the two following paragraphs.

46. Evidence of Lu's seapower advocacy can be seen in many of his writings. See, for example, 中国走向还海洋 [*China Advances on the Sea*], (海潮出版社 [Sea Tide Press], 1998); "实施海洋强国战略的若干问题" ["A Number of Issues in Carrying out a Strong Sea Power Strategy"], 海洋开发与管理 [*Ocean Development & Management*], no. 1 (2002): 62–63; "创新做大 加快步伐" ["Blaze Great New Trails, Quicken the Pace"], 大连日报 [*Dalian Daily*], 20 April 2006, B04; and "树立海洋战略意识建设海上经济强国" ["Establish a Maritime Strategic Consciousness, Build a Maritime Economic Power"], 中国软科学 [*China Soft Science*] (April 1997): 13–17.

47. For theoretical literature on this subject, see Alastair Iain Johnston, "Is China a Status Quo Power?" *International Security* 27, no. 4 (Spring 2003): 49–56; and Thomas J. Christensen, "China, the U.S.-Japan Alliance and the Security Dilemma in East Asia," *International Security* 23, no. 4 (Spring 1999): 49–80.

48. An article in a popular newspaper similarly highlights the U.S. need for burden-sharing because of the war in Iraq. 严国群 [Yan Guoqun], "美国千舰海军的如意算盘能否实现" ["Can the U.S. Navy's Wishful Thinking about the Thousand-Ship Navy Be Realized?"], 新京报 [*New Capital News*], 27 November 2006, available at http://www.sina.com.cn.

49. According to *Naval Operations Concept 2006*, a "Global Fleet Station . . . is a persistent sea base of operations from which to coordinate and employ adaptive force packages within a regional area of interest."

50. For Chinese sources (most of which precede the strategy's release, and none of which focuses on it) that demonstrate a basic understanding of the relationship between major recent U.S. strategic documents with relevance to naval development, see "美国面向21世纪的国防转变" ["U.S. National Defense Transformation for the 21st Century"], 全球防务 [*Global Defense*], 11 April 2007, http://www.defence.org.cn/article-1-66416.html; 秦大鹏 [Qin Dapeng], "美国海军 '全球作战概念' 构想及未来兵力构成" ["The U.S. Navy's 'Global Concept of Operations'"], 全球防务 [*Global Defense*], 19 February 2007, http://www.defence.org.cn/article-1-64612.html; "美军21世纪海上新战略: 打造 '全能武士'" ["The U.S. Military's New Strategy for 21st Century Seapower: Build 'All-Around Warriors'"], 中国国防报 [*China Defense News*], 6 July 2006, available at http://www.chinareviewnews.com; 艾雨兵, 郑金华, 张文丽 [Ai Yubing, Zheng Jinhua, and Zhang Wenli], 中国船舶重工集团公司第716研究所, 江苏 连云港 [China Shipbuilding Industry Corporation, 716th Research Institute, Lianyungang, Jiangsu Province], "美国海军21世纪战略概念分析 (连载一)" ["Analysis of the U.S. Navy's Strategic Concept for the 21st Century" (Part 1)], 情报指挥控制系统与仿真技术 [*Information, Command Control Systems & Simulation Technology*] 26, no. 3 (June 2004): 1–9; Ai Yubing, Zheng Jinhua, and Zhang Wenli, "Analysis of the U.S. Navy's Strategic Concept for the 21st Century" (Part 2), *Information, Command Control Systems & Simulation Technology* 26, no. 4 (August 2004) 9–20; "U.S. Navy's New Global Concept of Operations," *Liberation Army Daily*, 21 April 2005, http://www.pladaily.com.cn/site1/jsslpdjs/2005-04/21/content_188893.htm; and 李杰 [Li Jie], "看美国海军 '新军事变革' 有何高招" ["A Look at the U.S. Navy's 'New Military Transformation': What are the Brilliant Stratagems?"], 现代军事 [*Modern Military Affairs*], no. 5 (May 2004), http://www.cetin.net.cn/storage/journal/xdjs/xd2004/xd2004-05-1.htm.

51. This "313 Ship Plan" was clearly reported in China's media at the time. See "U.S. Navy Plans to Expand Fleet: Report," Xinhua, 6 December 2005. The order in which the "313 Ship Plan" was issued in relation to the Maritime Strategy does remain unclarified in some Chinese news reports that mention both of them. See, for example, "美海军作战长称美需要更多舰船—313艘是底限" ["The U.S. Chief of Naval Operations States that the U.S. Needs More Warships—313 Hulls Is the Lower Limit"], 新华网 [Xinhua Net], 19 November 2007, http://news.xinhuanet.com/mil/2007-11/19/content_7106284.htm. For detailed Chinese speculation on the relationship between the two events, see 李红军 [Li Hongjun, author/expert], 晓枫 [Xiao Feng, reporter], "专家解读美国海上新战略: 继续走强权路线" ["Expert Analyzes New U.S. Maritime Strategy: Continue to Go the Route of Power and Might"], 兵器知识 [*Weapons Knowledge*], 11 May 2008, available at http://www.wforum.com/gbindex.html.

52. Dombrowski, "Maritime Strategy Project."

53. For the PRC ambassador's comments, see Scott Girard, "Chinese Ambassador Stresses Peaceful Relations with U.S.," *Kansas State Collegian*, 12 February 2008. For the PRC minister of foreign affairs' comments, see Wu Qiang, "Yang Jiechi Makes a Speech at the 14th ASEAN Regional Forum Foreign Ministers' Conference," Xinhua, 2 August 2007, OSC# CPP20070802704004. For discussion by military commentators, see, for example, Liu Demao and Tao Shelan, "Military Expert: The Navy's Function in Strengthening National Maritime Defense and Security Cooperation," *Zhongguo Xinwen She*, 3 July 2007, OSC# CPP20070720530001. For an example of GMP-type cooperation, see Richard Halloran, "Emerging Maritime Security Net," *Washington Times*, 20 August 2007, 15.

54. 付征南 [Fu Zhengnan], "美海军第七舰队迎来 '新舵主'" ["The U.S. Navy's 7th Fleet Welcomes the 'New Helmsman'"], 环球军事 [*Global Military*], no. 180 (August 2008): 53.

55. 李诚文 [Li Chengwen], "美军提出 '千舰海军' 计划　进行全球海军串联" ["The U.S. Navy Puts Forward the 'Thousand Ship Navy' Plan to Advance Global Naval Connections"], 环球时报 [*Global Times*], 24 November 2006.

56. "美邀中国加入'千舰海军' 计划 目的不仅是反恐" ["The U.S. Invites China to Join the 'Thousand Ship Navy' Project: The Purpose Is Not Only Counter-Terrorism"], 国际先驱导报 [*International Herald Leader*], 13 April 2007.

57. 杜朝平 [Du Zhaoping], "与狼共舞: 美国 '千舰海军' 计划与中国的选择" ["The U.S. Navy's 'Thousand Ship Navy' Plan and China's Choices"], 舰载武器 [*Shipborne Weapons*] (December 2007): 23–27.

58. For a positive but realistic exploration of this topic, see Andrew Erickson and Lyle Goldstein, "Hoping for the Best, Preparing for the Worst: China's Response to U.S. Hegemony," *Journal of Strategic Studies* 29, no. 6 (December 2006): 955–86. This section draws heavily on Andrew Erickson, "Combating a Collective Threat: Prospects for Sino-American Cooperation against Avian Influenza," *Journal of Global Health Governance* 1, no. 1 (January 2007), http://ghgj.org/Erickson%20article.pdf.

59. Information Office of the State Council, People's Republic of China, "China's National Defense in 2006," 29 December 2006, 1, 3, available at www.chinaview.cn.

60. 顾祖华 [Gu Zuhua], "维护海上石油安全须有强大海上编队," ["In Order to Safeguard Energy Security, A Massive Naval Fleet Is Necessary"], 当代海军 [*Modern Navy*] (August 2004): 40.

61. Kevin L. Pollpeter, "U.S.-China Security Management: Assessing the Military-to-Military Relationship" (Arlington, VA: RAND, 2004), http://www.rand.org/pubs/monographs/2004/RAND_MG143.pdf.

62. These include the Ministry of Public Security (with its Border Control Department and Maritime Police Division), the Ministry of Communications (with its Maritime Safety Administration and Rescue and Salvage Agency), the Ministry of Agriculture (with its Bureau of Fisheries), and the State Oceanic Administration.

63. "Shanghai Hosts U.S. Coast Guard Cutter *Boutwell* during North Pacific Coast Guard Forum 2007," U.S. Coast Guard Visual Information Gallery, 16 August 2007, http://cgvi.uscg.mil/media/main.php?g2_itemId=159644.

64. For an analysis of agenda items for the May visit, see Qiu Yongzheng, "Four Major Objectives of U.S. Admiral's Visit to China," *Qingnian Cankao*, 12 May 2006, OSC# CPP20060515504001.

65. Xiong Zhengyan, Rong Yan, and Bai Ruishue, "2006: A Year of Most Active Exchanges between Chinese and U.S. Militaries," Xinhua, 27 December 2006, OSC# CPP20061227045002.

66. "Chinese Fleet Visits San Diego," *People's Liberation Army Daily*, 18 September 2006, http://english.pladaily.com.cn/site2/special-reports/2006-09/19/content_591087.htm.

67. Vessels from the U.S. and Chinese navies have previously participated in search-and-rescue exercises in Hong Kong (e.g., in 2003) but did not directly interact in the exercise. "U.S., Chinese Navies Complete SAREX Together," *Navy Newsstand*, 21 September 2006, http://www.navy.mil/search/display.asp?story_id=25702.

68. Information Office of the State Council, PRC, "China's National Defense in 2006," 31–33.

69. Ibid. For a similarly positive analysis, see Li Xuanliang and Xiong Zhengyan, "Sino-U.S. Military Exchange Is Not 'Empty Talk' Anymore," *Liaowang Dongfang Zhoukan* [*Oriental Outlook Magazine*], no. 48 (30 November 2006): 24–25, OSC# CPP20061221710018.

70. "U.S. Pacific Fleet Commander Visits China," *Navy Newsstand*, 13 November 2006, available at www.news.navy.mil.

71. P. Parameswaran, "U.S. Asks China to Help Maintain Global Maritime Security," Agence France Presse, 5 April 2007.

72. P. Parameswaran, "Plea by Pentagon to Top Naval Visitor," *The Weekly Standard*, 6 April 2007, http://www.thestandard.com.hk/news_detail.asp?we_cat=3&art_id=41726&sid=13026608&con_type=1&d_str=20070406.

73. "Transcript of Regular News Conference by P.R.C. Foreign Ministry on Apr. 5, 2007; Moderated by Spokesman Qin Gang," OSC# CPP20070405071002.

74. "中美海军上将握手大洋" ["The Chiefs of the Chinese and U.S. Navies Shake Hands over the Ocean"], 当代海军 [*Modern Navy*], October 2007, title and facing page.

75. Thomas J. Christensen, "Clarity on Taiwan: Correcting Misperceptions on Both Sides of the Strait," *Washington Post*, 20 March 2000, A17.

76. For a cogent summation of U.S. Taiwan policy, see Thomas J. Christensen, "A Strong and Moderate Taiwan," Speech to U.S.-Taiwan Business Council Defense Industry Conference, Annapolis, MD., 11 September 2007, http://www.state.gov/p/eap/rls/rm/2007/91979.htm.

77. See, for example, Bradley A. Thayer, "Confronting China: An Evaluation of Options for the United States," *Comparative Strategy* 24, no. 1 (January–March 2005): 71–98.

78. See, for example, Mark Helprin, "The Challenge from China," *Wall Street Journal*, 13 May 2008, A17.

79. Peter A. Dutton, "International Law and the November 2004 'Han Incident,'" in *China's Future Nuclear Submarine Force*, ed. Andrew S. Erickson, Lyle J. Goldstein, William S. Murray, and Andrew R. Wilson, 162–81 (Annapolis, MD: Naval Institute Press, 2007).

80. "U.S. Confirms Carrier Had Close Brush with Chinese Submarine," *Asian Political News*, 20 November 2006, http://findarticles.com/p/articles/mi_moWDQ/is_2006_Nov_20/ai_n16854183/.

81. See Robert Jervis, *Perception and Misperception in International Politics* (Princeton, NJ: Princeton University Press, 1976).

82. For institutional aspects, see G. John Ikenberry, *After Victory: Institutions, Strategic Restraint and the Rebuilding of Order after Major Wars* (Princeton, NJ: Princeton University Press, 2001). For the ways in which interests can factor into institution-building, see Andrew Moravscik, *The Choice for Europe: Social Purpose and State Power from Messina to Maastricht* (Ithaca, NY: Cornell University Press, 1998). For research on when groups who might otherwise oppose some sort of institutional commitment turn to support such arrangements, see Helen V. Milner, "Trading Places: Industries for Free Trade," *World Politics* 40, no. 3 (April 1988): 350–76. Most of the best institutionalist literature in American political science is in the subfield of international political economy since it is an area where there tend to be more institutions (even though commitment problems, coordination problems, and collective action problems still apply); it is to be hoped that more research will be done in the area of security studies.

83. Quoted in Liu and Tao, "Military Expert."

84. See Andrew S. Erickson and Wei He, "U.S.-China Security Relations," in *Task Force Report—U.S.-China Relations: A Roadmap for the Future*, Center for Strategic and International Studies Pacific Forum *Issues & Insights* 9, no. 16 (20 August 2009): 7–12, http://csis.org/files/publication/issuesinsights_v09n16.pdf; and Carola Hoyos, "China Invited to Join IEA as Oil Demand Shifts," *Financial Times*, 30 March 2010, http://www.ft.com/cms/s/0/0f973936-3beb-11df-9412-00144feabdco.html.

85. Andrew Erickson and Andrew Wilson, "China's Aircraft Carrier Dilemma," in *China's Future Nuclear Submarine Force*, ed. Andrew S. Erickson, Lyle J. Goldstein, William S. Murray, and Andrew R. Wilson (Annapolis, MD: Naval Institute Press, 2007), 254.

86. Senior Captain Duan Zhaoxian, Assistant Chief of Staff, PLA Navy, presentation in "Session 5: Humanitarian Assistance and Disaster Relief," Maritime Security Challenges Conference 2010, Maritime Forces Pacific, Canadian Navy, Victoria, British Columbia, 29 April 2010.

87. Quoted in Liu and Tao, "Military Expert."

88. "Earnestly Step up Ability Building."

89. 韩志庆 [Han Zhiqing], "'能战度'—非战争军事行动新课题" ["Degree of War-fighting Ability—The New Issue of Military Operations Other Than War"], 解放军报 [*Liberation Army Daily*], 24 June 2008, 11; and 霍小勇 [Huo Xiaoyong], "锻造有多样化能力的现代化军队" ["Forging a Modern Army with Diversified Capabilities"], 解放军报 [*Liberation Army Daily*], 24 June 2008, 11; and Michael S.

Chase and Kristen Gunness, "The PLA's Multiple Military Tasks: Prioritizing Combat Operations and Developing MOOTW Capabilities," Jamestown *China Brief* 10, no. 2 (21 January 2010), http://www.jamestown.org/single/?no_cache=1&tx_ttnews%5Btt_news%5D=35931.

90. Tao Shelan, "Military Expert: Military Cooperation in Non-Traditional Security Areas is an Important Approach in China's Peaceful Development," *Zhongguo Xinwen She* [*China News Agency*], 13 December 2007, OSC# CPP20071214136010.

Yu Wanli

The American Factor in China's Maritime Strategy

SINCE THE FOUNDING OF NEW CHINA, Chinese naval strategy has followed a step-by-step process, from coastal defense, to near-seas defense, to new development in the new century. Chinese naval strategy persists in its defensive purpose; its development depends on the needs of national defense strategy and the overall level of national strength, and is subject to the influence of China's traditional land power culture. Although the Chinese and U.S. navies have no areas for direct conflict except for Taiwan, the United States has a far-reaching effect on Chinese navy's strategic thinking, which is reflected in China's dream since modern times to become a sea power. From the debate on China's status as a sea power in recent years, we can see that the Chinese navy's defensive posture and the gap in strength between China and the United States makes it impossible for the two sides to launch a peer competition or arms race. China's national strategy for the "strategic opportunity period" for development and the stakeholder relations between China and the United States call for the two navies to strengthen bilateral exchanges and joint actions in areas such as sea rescue and antipiracy operations. This will help to enhance mutual trust to build bilateral cooperation and facilitate the coordination of naval strategies.

The 1894 Sino-Japanese War completely annihilated what was then called "the number-one navy in the Far East." This incident put an end to the naval dream of the Chinese people. It left China's coastal defenses wide open and all the major powers cruised and fought in China's sea areas, ports, and rivers as they wished. Not having an effective navy for coastal defense, China was trampled upon for half a century. This constituted the basic background of Chinese naval construction after the founding of New China in 1949.

The Evolution of Chinese Naval Strategy

People's Liberation Army Navy (PLA Navy) commenced its development from a low base, which determined the subsequent step-by-step process from small to large, and from weak to strong. The evolution of China's naval strategy has always been constrained by the needs of national defense strategy and comprehensive national strength, from "coastal defense" strategy at the very beginning to "near-seas defense" strategy at the present stage.

Coastal Defense Strategy

The PLA Navy was founded in 1949 and began its slow development with the help of the former Soviet Union. From the beginning to the late 1970s, the operational space of the Chinese navy at sea was extremely small, not only because of the threat from the superpowers but also because of foreign trade blockade and restrictions. It was limited within the range of only about twelve nautical miles. Conversely, under the guidance of "people's war" strategic thinking, the Chinese navy was considered as an extension of the army to the sea. In essence, it was a coastal defense force, and it pursued a strategy of coastal defense during that period.

The first mission required by this strategy was to prevent invasion from the sea. In view of historical lessons, China's basic judgment was that China was menaced by Western maritime powers and imperialism would come from the sea. Therefore, the navy should focus on battles relying on land forces and islands to protect the Chinese mainland from large-scale landing attack and to defend the sovereign waters. At the enlarged meeting of the Political Bureau of the Communist Party of China (CPC) Central Committee on 4 December 1953, Mao Zedong articulated a general policy direction on overall navy building: "In order to eliminate harassment of the sea bandits to protect the safety of sea transport; to reserve forces for recovering Taiwan at an appropriate time to fully reunify the territory; to prepare for the battle against invasion of imperialism from the sea, we need to gradually build a powerful navy in a long period of time, based on the level of industrial and financial development."[1] At an enlarged meeting of the Central Military Commission held in March 1956, China formulated the first national defense strategy for the period of peace and construction after the founding of New China: active defense of the homeland. The Chinese navy also adopted the strategy of "active defense at sea."

Second, such a strategy required that navy development focus on "aircraft, submarines, and fast-attack craft (FAC)." Taking into consideration the situation, tasks, development prospects, and Soviet experience, the Chinese navy worked out the "aircraft, submarines and FAC" development plan at a meeting held in August 1950. This plan was mainly influenced by the Soviet theory of "small fleet, small war." It advocated that the navy and army implement a unified strategy; that the navy coordinates with, and is subordinate to, the army; and that the state sets up a small navy and its main task is to defend the coast, resist foreign invasion, and assist the ground troops to fight on shore. Under this thinking, the navy should neither undertake fighting in the main battlefield nor execute decisive battle with a strong enemy at sea, so it should focus its development on a land-based naval air force, submarines, FACs, and other coastal defense vessels.[2] Partially as a result of this thinking, "aircraft, submarines and FAC" was the basic characteristic of the Chinese naval forces for several decades.

Third, this strategy required the Chinese navy to implement guerrilla tactics at sea. In view of the strength disparity between the two sides, the navy did not aim at seizing command of the sea but rather adopted flexible tactics. The navy would retreat when losing superiority but strike when gaining superiority. A prominent tactic was guerrilla or sabotage operations at sea, which aimed to employ a number of small battle groups to attack the enemy's transport ships, scatter naval vessels, and damage the enemy's lines of communication and base ports that lacked protection. This also helped to consolidate security and represented the application of the people's war strategy in naval warfare.

Near-Seas Defense Strategy

The coastal defense strategy was abandoned by the late 1970s. Chinese leader Deng Xiaoping pointed out in July 1979: "Our strategy [engages in] near-seas operations. We do not reach out everywhere like hegemonic powers do. We build a navy basically for defense. Faced with the powerful navies of hegemonic powers, it does not help without proper force. The force should be useful. We do not need too much, but we need excellent, truly modern things."[3]

According to this principle, the Chinese navy commander Liu Huaqing developed and promulgated the "near-seas defense" strategy in December 1985. Liu believed that the near-seas defense strategy of the Chinese navy was a regional defense strategy; for an extended period the navy's operational area would mainly be bounded by the first island chain, the extended sea areas along it, and the areas within it—the Yellow Sea, East Sea, and South Sea.[4] This area includes both all the waters under the jurisdiction of China according to the International Convention on the Law of the Sea and China's inherent territories such as islands in the South China Sea; the strategic duties of the navy are to safeguard national unity, territorial integrity, and maritime rights and interests; to prepare for local naval battles; and to hold back and prevent aggression from the sea.[5] Since the 1980s, the Chinese navy's near-seas defense strategy has continuously improved and taken in more content.

The first mission of the new strategy is to deal with regional wars at sea. Since the new era of reform and opening-up, China has changed its views on war and peace significantly and believes that world war can be avoided for a long period of time. Large-scale foreign invasion is unlikely in the foreseeable future. It is also impossible for a long-lasting and large-scale land war in the way of "people's war" to break out. However, it is probable that maritime or local border wars and small conflicts may occur. Accordingly, the navy began to take on new national defense strategic tasks, such as preparing for regional wars and conflicts at seas surrounding China.

The second mission of the new strategy is to safeguard maritime rights and interests and national unity, which is included in the navy's strategic objectives. After the Sino-Vietnamese war over the Paracel Islands (Xisha) in 1974, the task of safeguarding China's maritime rights and interests was gradually put on the navy's agenda. In a statement issued by the Chinese government on China's "indisputable sovereignty over Nansha, Xisha, Zhongsha and Pratas Islands" on 11 January 1974, it is clearly stated that "the resources in the waters near the islands all belong to China."[6] In early 1980s China signed and ratified the United Nations Convention on the Law of the Sea (UNCLOS); safeguarding China's maritime rights and interests has become one of the important missions of the navy. With the advent of the struggle against Taiwan independence, safeguarding national unity has also become an important mission of the navy.

Third, the new strategy puts forward the goal of winning informatized warfare. Since the Gulf War in 1991, the trend and impact of new military revolution, which are mainly reflected in the wide application of information technology to the military field, have become increasingly clear. As a result, the idea and outcome of new revolution in military affairs have entered into the naval strategy, that is, to emphasize improving the capability to win informatized warfare. Following the overall objective of winning informatized warfare, new areas for naval development have been set up, including the C4ISR System (command, control, communications, computers, intelligence, surveillance, and reconnaissance); the electronic combat system (the electronic interception, direction, and [anti-]interference and confrontation system); the Internet war system (computer network systems to link scattered ships and air combat units through satellite early warning information assets); and joint combat capability (the capability to form integrated combat systems of the navy, the air force, and the land forces).

Chinese Naval Strategy in the Future

Historically, the near-seas defense strategy is associated with a certain stage of a nation's development and plays an effective role in maintaining national sovereignty and security of the near seas. Contemporary sea powers all adopted this strategy in the early development of the navy. The United States clearly established the near-seas defense strategy in Thomas Jefferson's time but abandoned it by the end of the nineteenth century when the United States realized industrialization. As China continues to industrialize, as its trade with the world continues to develop, and as its maritime rights and interests continue to expand, the near-seas defense strategy has shown its limitations. The changing reality calls for a breakthrough in the near-seas defense strategy.

In the early twenty-first century, the debate on Chinese naval strategy has become heated in academic and strategic thinking circles. In this debate, several new naval strategies have emerged.

Extend Strategic Depth for Near-Seas Defensive Operations This strategy appeared in the 2004 China national defense white paper, which stated that "the navy has expanded the space and extended the depth for near-seas defensive operations. Preparation for maritime battlefield is intensified and improved while the integrated combat capabilities are enhanced in conducting near-seas campaigns, and the capability of nuclear counter-attacks is also enhanced."[7] The defensive depth mentioned here is still within the near seas, and the operations are also defined within the near-seas region.

Far-Seas Defensive Combat Capability, or Far-Seas Mobile Combat Capability Far-seas defensive combat capability, which was first put forward in 2000, requires the navy to develop comprehensive combat capability beyond the first island chain. In the long term, the navy should have far-seas defensive combat capability. Far-seas mobile combat capability, which was put forward in 2004, means that the navy should develop comprehensive combat capability and far-seas mobile combat capability. The two concepts, with more or less the same meaning, represent the trend of maritime defense and naval strategy and have practical significance for the development of the navy and the improvement of naval combat capability in the future. As for the scope of the far seas, it obviously exceeds the first island chain, but the exact scope is yet to be clearly defined.

Regional Navy Strategy According to the regional navy view, the Chinese navy is not only different from the navies of superpowers but also different from those of the third world countries. The distinctive characteristic is that China's maritime interests extend beyond the scope of the near seas; therefore, its naval forces must have some platforms capable of middle- and far-seas operations and with strong maneuvering capability as well as weapons and equipment with middle- and long-range strike power. The coverage of its navy should extend to at least one thousand nautical miles outside the coastal areas. This view suggests that the Chinese navy should be at the same level with those of Britain, France, Italy, Spain, India, and Australia. Their regional characteristics distinguish them from the superpowers such as the United States and, to some extent, Russia.

Near-Oceans Defense Strategy "Near ocean" refers to the Western Pacific, meaning that the navy must have the capability to go beyond the first island chain. With the establishment of the two-hundred-nautical-mile exclusive economic zone, all countries should revise their old sea-defense thinking and move forward their sea-defense lines. The navy should cover all the waters under China's jurisdiction in terms of the international law of the sea, all the subordinate islands of China's sovereignty, and the full scope of the Chinese seas. This, on one hand, will help to protect China's maritime territories, resources, transport, and other maritime development activities. On the other hand, this plan is also conducive to regaining sovereignty over the islands. As the range of naval tactical missiles has surpassed one thousand nautical miles for great powers, multilevel, continuous defense can only be effectively organized to defeat an invasion from the sea when the defense strategic depth is expanded.

The Characteristics of Chinese Naval Strategy's Evolution

Taking a panoramic view of the evolution of Chinese naval strategy since 1949, we can discern the following characteristics. First, Chinese naval strategy is subordinate to mainland defense strategy. For a long time, Chinese naval strategy was not an independent strategy. "Active homeland defense strategy" in the 1950s and 1960s, with the premise of dealing with a large-scale foreign invasion, did not intend to rely on naval forces to stop and destroy the enemy off the coastline. In this strategy, the navy merely offered a means to "trade space for time." The aim of "coastal defense" was to try to disrupt and delay the landing and advance of the invading enemy forces, to cover the strategic shift of the main force from the coast to inland areas. From 1970s on, the navy's areas of operation have extended from the coastal waters to the near seas. The focus of near-seas defense is on deterring Taiwan independence, and it is mainly intended for the navy to act in concert with the landing operations of the army. With the adoption of UNCLOS, the disputes over the islands of South China Sea and East China Sea and maritime rights and interests have given another mission to the Chinese navy, which is limited to local deterrence and conflicts.

Second, Chinese naval strategy is about capacity development. New China's navy began to develop from a low base, without significant equipment, technology, or capacity at the starting point. The Chinese navy at that time also lacked experience in military operations. In spite of the limited help offered by the Soviet Union at the early stage, the Chinese navy was mainly self-reliant in its development. Every step it took in the development process carried great risks. A navy is a complex system of high technologies and multiple arms, and its development depends fundamentally on its nation's level of scientific, technological, and industrial development. That is why the development of the Chinese navy must be gradual. It is difficult to achieve development by leaps and bounds. Strategic planning beyond the current technological level and operational and training skills entails great risks. In the 1980s, the navy put forward the near-seas defense strategy. However, Deng Xiaoping requested that economic development be prioritized over military construction. As a result, resources for military equipment and training were largely restricted, and the navy did not obtain sufficient resources to develop based on this strategy. This created a bottleneck by the twenty-first century. The navy's combat capability is far behind the needs of national defense and diplomacy.

Finally, Chinese naval strategy has always been constrained by land power thinking. As mentioned above, both the Chinese navy's coastal defense and near-seas defense strategies are essentially the extension and accessories of the mainland defense. As China becomes more deeply involved in globalization in recent years, its overseas interests will continue to expand, and the value of the seas in China's security and strategic interests will attract more attention. Many scholars value Alfred Thayer Mahan's thinking on "sea power," which emphasizes achieving control of the sea, particularly in important sea-lanes, through the development of a strong navy, and which defines "dominance of the oceans" as the fundamental purpose of maritime strategy.[8] However, these thoughts still do not represent the mainstream in China's naval strategy. Speaking objectively, the Chinese navy does not have the capability to go beyond the first island chain; speaking subjectively, traditional Chinese Confucian culture and the introversion of the "Middle Kingdom" imply the lack of an impulse to expand. Besides, putting too much emphasis on developing military power at sea is bound to cause tension with existing sea powers and to raise the vigilance of neighboring countries. This may lead to a historical trap in which coastal countries that develop their maritime forces cannot escape the coalitional attack of sea powers and neighboring countries, which precipitates their decline.[9] As a result, there are some new ideas on China's future naval strategy, including far-seas, regional, and near-oceans strategies, but there is no far-oceans strategy. In the foreseeable future, the Chinese navy will not incorporate "oceans" or "dominance of the oceans" into its strategic thinking.

The United States in Chinese Naval Strategic Thinking

Realistically, U.S. influence on Chinese naval strategy is primarily concerned with the Taiwan issue. China's navy plays a key role in the military struggle to deter Taiwan independence. Especially when faced with the threat of U.S. military intervention from the sea, the Chinese navy must ensure the effectiveness of deterrence against Taiwan. At present, technological and operational preparations based on China's near-seas defense strategy all focus on the fight over the Taiwan Strait, with the first island chain as the main combat area. In 1997 Jiang Zemin once again pointed out clearly: "The navy must implement 'near-seas defense' strategic thinking and truly have comprehensive combat capability to carry out the battle within the first island chain."[10]

During the 1996 Taiwan Strait crisis, the U.S. aircraft carriers did not enter the Taiwan Strait but still imposed great pressure on China. Under the current technological conditions, tactical missiles' effective range of attack has reached one thousand nautical miles, which is far beyond the scope of the first island chain. This reality has forced China to consider the depth of its near-seas defense strategy, which constitutes the background of strategic thinkings such as "extending the depth for near-seas defensive operations" and "far-seas defensive combat capability." In his December 2001 speech, Jiang Zemin placed "emphasis on improving far-seas defensive combat capability" to adapt to the characteristics of future sea battle and the needs of improving strategic depth for defense.[11]

It is difficult to make a realistic assessment of the influence the United States poses on China on issues other than the Taiwan issue. China and the United States do not have direct disputes over sea territories. Even on the Taiwan issue, the prospect of conflict depends on the manner and extent of U.S. intervention. However, the United States still has a huge impact, albeit indirect, long-term, and philosophical, on Chinese naval strategy. This impact is not on the strategic planning level but on the strategic thinking level. In Chinese people's awareness and debate of sea power theory since modern times, the United States is a major factor that cannot be ignored.

In 1890 the U.S. Navy captain Alfred T. Mahan published his book *The Influence of Sea Power upon History, 1660–1783*, which laid the theoretical foundation for the modern sea power theory. Ten years later, Mahan's works began to be serialized in the Chinese newspaper *East Asia Times* in Shanghai; this was the first time for Chinese readers to have access to Mahan's theory. At that time, the Chinese nation was on the brink of extinction, and many thinkers were contemplating how to save the country. Mahan's theory soon attracted the attention of Chinese political and military leaders and caused a great impact.

Modern Chinese nationalist leader Dr. Sun Yat-sen particularly respected Mahan's sea power ideology. He believed that the rise and fall of a country is closely related to sea power: "As the world situation changes, national strength rises and falls, which is often caused by sea power instead of land power. The nation with dominant sea power often surpasses others."[12] In an article on Pacific issues, he wrote: "What is the problem of the Pacific? It is the sea power issue among countries. The struggle for sea power moved from the Mediterranean to the Atlantic, and now from the Atlantic to the Pacific. . . . Neither do I know nor do I care about the old issues in the Mediterranean or the Atlantic, but the problem in the Pacific concerns the survival and fate of the Chinese nation. . . . The center of the Pacific is China. The struggle for the Pacific sea power is indisputably the struggle for China's gateway. Whoever holds this gateway gets access to the hinterland and rich resources. Other countries are coveting this, how can we put it aside?"[13]

Influenced by Mahan's sea power theory, Sun Yat-sen advocated placing the building of the navy in an important position of national defense construction: "The navy is the basis for strength and prosperity. As is often said by people in Britain and the U.S., whoever dominates the sea dominates world trade; whoever dominates world trade dominates the Golconda [a location of great wealth]; whoever dominates the Golconda dominates the world. . . . Boost the shipping industry to expand the navy; let our national navy keep pace with the big powers and get into the rank of first-class powers. The only way for China to become prosperous is to develop its military arms."[14]

In times when China was not unified, faced with foreign aggression, and weak in strength and military force, for Sun Yat-sen and strategic thinkers of that era, sea power was just a part of their superpower dream. As the "center of the Pacific," China not only did not have the strength to compete for sea power but also became the target of competing powers. However, the sea power dream, as one of the main driving forces in modern Chinese history, has a far-reaching impact. Chinese communist leaders, from Mao Zedong, Deng Xiaoping, and Jiang Zemin to Hu Jintao, although not explicitly advocating the sea power thoughts, always use "building a powerful navy" as a slogan to incentivize the officers and soldiers of the navy.

In the twenty-first century, with the growth of China's national strength and the rise of its international status, sea power theory once again inspires Chinese strategic thinkers. For the first time since the Sino-Japanese War of 1894–95, the Chinese people truly have the foundation of strength and interests needed to discuss naval strategies. A century's sea power dream has become attainable. Over the past decade, there has emerged a great debate on sea power in China's academic and strategic thinking circles. Some scholars have concluded from the history and experience of other countries that the development of sea power and the establishment of a strong navy are necessary for the rise of China. The following are some representative views.

One view is that sea power is an important factor in the rise and fall of a country. Historically, coastal nations without strong naval and maritime forces have no sea power and therefore no guarantee of their sovereignty.[15] In five large-scale invasions of modern China by the imperialists, their navies played the role of forerunners to control China's coast. The fundamental reason for the failure of the modern Chinese navy is that its development has never been integrated into the development of sea power.[16]

Also, after the emergence of world trade, humans enter into the "era of the oceans." Survival in the future and sustainable development require China to step in big strides toward the sea, and a country that steps toward the sea must have sea power.[17]

Moreover, a country's reliance on seas in an era of globalization is an inevitable cause for developing sea power. Sea power is the lifeline of China's market economy. The basis of China's sea power development strategy in the future should no doubt be "an export-oriented economy dependent on the maritime channels of communication."[18] The civilizational transformation of Chinese society forces us to move from land power to sea power.

Furthermore, from a geostrategic perspective, eight of China's nine maritime neighbors have disputes with China over maritime territories. Maritime security has become a central part of China's national security.[19] The Taiwan issue is also a major issue facing the Chinese navy. Economic globalization cannot exclude the globalization of self-defense means; the ability to defend overseas energy and trade depends on overseas military capability. With the expansion of its overseas interests, China's security boundaries have already far exceeded its territorial boundaries, which requires China to develop the corresponding overseas military capability.[20]

However, many scholars are critical of the "sea power" views stated above. They raise doubts based on geopolitical and overall national strength constraints and the risks of conflict with hegemonic powers and neighboring countries, and they warn that China should avoid falling into the "sea power trap." Xu Qiyu, for instance, has criticized Zhang Wenmu of Beijing University of Aeronautics and Astronautics and other scholars item by item:

- From a historical perspective, it is history that decides sea power, rather than sea power that decides history.

- The logic that economic globalization calls for sea power to protect the international market and resources is to pursue "absolute security" and "absolute self-help" by "absolute means," which is impossible as proved by history and reality.

- The idea that sea power is required for the rise of a power is not only a misunderstanding of history but also ignores the objective conditions to attain sea power because not all countries are able to grow into sea powers.

- The logic that a navy sustains hegemony reverses cause and effect. In short, it is sea power that drives strategy, rather than strategy causing sea power.[21]

Tang Shiping also believes that development of China's military strength is to achieve national strategic objectives instead of realizing China's maritime power dream; to deter U.S. intervention in the Taiwan Strait, China does not need to develop a navy that can compete with that of the United States; missiles, air capability, underwater naval capability, and effective nuclear deterrent are more effective than an expensive naval surface force. One-sided pursuit of an oceangoing navy will only bring China burdens or even disaster, because the United States may think that China is challenging its supremacy at sea, and all the other Asian countries will be anxious about the competition between China and the United States for supremacy at sea. As a land and sea power, China cannot devote too many resources to maritime defense because the navy is much more expensive to build than the army; China must develop a navy according to its ability, and military forces must comply with the overall interests of the country.[22]

Ye Zicheng of Peking University thinks that each country should balance between development of land power and sea power according to its natural endowment, and that the ultimate goal is the long-term development of the nation. From a macrohistorical perspective, the development of land power is more lasting because the maritime space is liquid, uncertain, and unstable, and sea forces converge and disappear fast and are therefore unsustainable. To some extent, human society has the initiative to change certain aspects of nature's limitations, but there is a limit. It will end in failure if one tries to change land to sea or vice versa. Therefore, merely having military power at sea is not enough to be a sea power. The traditional Western concept of sea power may not be appropriate for China's development; it is unlikely that China will become a sea power, and even more unlikely that it will become both a land and a sea power. The only course for China is to become a land power with a strong navy.[23]

Almost all scholars agree that development of Chinese sea power will inevitably result in contradiction and conflict with the existing maritime hegemon—the United States: "The dynamic between China and the U.S. today is closely reminiscent of the 19th century, when Britain attempted to keep a young America under control. . . . As China grows out of its isolation and attains greater influence internationally, there is a very real risk that the U.S. will repeat the mistakes of past great powers, and try to contain China."[24]

It is worth noting that few scholars publicly declare that the development of the Chinese navy aims to challenge U.S. supremacy at sea. Zhang Wenmu once argued that the development of China's sea power can enhance its ability to share maritime interests with major powers such as the United States, but he later revised his view to suggest that China's sea power is limited and does not exceed the sovereignty and scope determined by international law. The development of the navy does not go beyond the purpose of self-defense. Zhang has also stressed that "both unlimited expansion of the Chinese Navy and giving up basic naval modernization are catastrophic for China. We should adhere to the dialectical attitude towards the issue of China's sea power."[25] Most scholars believe that China should take the multiple needs of its own national strategy as the starting point. China should calmly understand the sea power issue in Sino-U.S. relations, make all efforts to avoid a conflict with the United States, further strengthen Sino-U.S. maritime military safety consultation mechanisms, increase mutual understanding and trust regarding security issues to avoid or reduce conflict, and promote the development of sea power with both naval and air forces in a careful and orderly fashion to seek peace through strength.[26]

Conclusion

We can see from the Chinese navy's strategic evolution and debate on sea power among Chinese scholars in recent years that development of the Chinese navy has its own logic and is a gradual process, and that it is not possible to achieve phenomenal progress. As a result, in the foreseeable future, China will not challenge U.S. supremacy at sea unless the loss of control in the Taiwan Strait leads to a direct conflict between China and the United States. China's naval development does not constitute a competition or race with the powerful U.S. Navy.

First, the Chinese navy's strategy is still dominated by the thought of near-seas defense and implies no inevitable conflict with the United States. The Chinese navy's main goal in recent years is to ensure relative security of the seas within the first island chain, deter foreign aggression, intervene in a Taiwan Strait crisis, and defend the sovereignty of islands in territorial waters. The basic posture of this strategy is defensive. The Chinese navy will not fight the U.S. Navy unless events in the Taiwan Strait go out of control or other crises arise, which may lead to the invasion of the U.S. forces into the first island chain and threaten the national security of China.

With the expansion of China's overseas interests and the volatility of the international energy market, China has started to consider its navy's capacity-building beyond the coastal areas in recent years. The concept of "safeguarding national development interests" was first raised in China's 2004 national defense white paper, which proposes higher requirements for the development of the navy.[27] Current interpretation of this concept has some ambiguity and controversy. From my perspective, this concept mainly indicates protecting international sea lines of communication and dealing with the threats to China's overseas interests posed by piracy, terrorism, and regional instability such as protecting the Malacca Strait and other key passages from the threat of piracy or terrorism and protecting and evacuating Chinese nationals when civil strife happens in foreign countries. "Safeguarding national development interests" does not indicate conflict with the U.S. global strategy. In fact, China and the United States have common interests and goals when dealing with the threats mentioned earlier.

Second, capacity is still the main factor that constrains the development of the Chinese navy. The huge disparity in strength between China and the United States makes it impossible for the two sides to launch a peer competition or arms race. The power transition theory developed by A. F. K. Organski says that the possibility of war is quite low before the strengths of the challenging country and the leading country become close. After the rising country overthrows the leading country and establishes its own dominance, the possibility of war will decline. War is most likely to break out at a time when the strength of the rising country becomes close to or just exceeds that of the leading country. Under the last circumstance, the two will enter "the zone of contention and probably war."[28] At present, the great superiority in strength of the U.S. Navy is sufficient to prevent any challenge from China at sea, and there is no possibility of peer competition or arms race. Based on this premise, some scholars suggest the so-called asymmetrical warfare theory, which is about the strategy that the weak side takes to deal with a strong opponent, with the objective of staying undefeated, not winning. This is an effective defense strategy but it is not about offense.[29]

Safeguarding national development interests requires the Chinese navy to develop its oceangoing capability. Currently the Chinese navy is still at its early phase to develop from coastal waters to the oceans in its scope. Based on this premise, the development of an aircraft carrier is brought up on the Chinese navy's agenda. However, a navy is a high-tech, multiarms system. With current resources and technical conditions, the Chinese navy will continue to insist on a gradual development strategy that does not exceed its means. In 2008 rampant Somali piracy seriously threatened the world's oceangoing transportation security. Cargo ships of many countries, including those of mainland China and Hong Kong, were hijacked. Seventeen Chinese crew members were taken hostage. The UN Security Council passed a motion against Somali pirates. France, Russia, India, and other countries sent warships to patrol in nearby waters. Constrained by limited oceangoing sailing and supply capability, the Chinese navy has previously ended up in an embarrassing situation of being reluctant to participate in overseas naval deployments even for humanitarian purposes. This time, however, when voices in China called for the navy to be deployed, a decision was made to send the PLA Navy to support counterpiracy operations in the Gulf of Aden under the aegis of the United Nations.

Finally, the ocean should be a field for Sino-U.S. strategic cooperation in the "strategic opportunity period." At present, China's basic national strategy judgment, as noted in the report of the 16th CPC National Congress, is that "the first two decades of the 21st century are a period of important strategic opportunities, which we must seize tightly and which offers bright prospects."[30] This means that China will commit itself to economic development and construction between now and 2020. The fundamental goal of diplomacy and national defense is to create a conducive international environment for domestic construction. China's "peaceful development" is realized by participating in the existing international system and economic globalization. The "strategic opportunity period" requires maintaining the stability of the existing U.S.-led international order, rather than challenging the U.S. hegemony. As a result, the concept of responsible stakeholder proposed by the Deputy Secretary of State Robert Zoellick received a positive response from China.[31] The development of the Chinese navy should be fundamentally subordinated to the overall national strategy. With the rise of China, the Chinese navy will not only bear the responsibility to defend the sovereignty of the territorial waters but will also contribute to stability and security of the international system.

In recent years, both China and the United States have been faced with the threats of financial crisis, international terrorism, piracy, failed states, and regional instability, which call increasingly for the joint action of the two countries. Sino-U.S. relations have developed from bilateral structural interdependence to global strategic interdependence. If facets of Sino-U.S. relations may be represented by the staves of a wooden barrel, the lowest point of which determines how much water (cooperation) the barrel can hold, military relations remain the shortest stave. This is because they are characterized by suspicion and mistrust and are often interrupted by such issues as U.S. arms sales to Taiwan. As the stronger side, the United States, particularly its navy, should take more initiative to repair this shortest stave. At present, the situation in Taiwan is relatively relaxed, which provides a rare opportunity for positive interactions between the two sides. The navies of China and the United States can promote mutual trust by strengthening bilateral exchanges and joint actions such as sea rescue and antipiracy operations to enhance cooperation and coordination of bilateral naval strategies.

Notes

1. Yang Guoyu, ed., *Dangdai Zhongguo Haijun* [*Contemporary Chinese Navy*] (Beijing: Zhongguo Shehui Kexue Chubanshe [China Social Sciences Press], 1987), 40.

2. Ibid., 41–42.

3. Deng Xiaoping, "Haijun Jianshe Yaojiang Zhenzheng de Zhandouli" ["Naval Construction Should Focus on Battle Effectiveness"], *Deng Xiaoping Lun Guofang He Jundui Jianshe* [*Deng Xiaoping on National Defense and Army Construction*] (Beijing: Junshi Kexue Chubanshe, 1992), 63.

4. The first island chain is generally understood to extend from the Japanese archipelago through Taiwan to the Philippines and possibly southward.

5. Liu Huaqing, "Wo Tichu Zhongguo 'Haijun Zhanlue' Wenti" ["I Raise the Issue of Chinese 'Naval Strategy'"], *Junshi Lishi* [*Military History*], no. 1 (2005).

6. *Dangdai Zhongguo Haijun*, 394.

7. Information Office of the State Council of PRC, "China's National Defense in 2004," December 2004, 24, http://english.peopledaily.com.cn/whitepaper/defense2004/defense2004.html.

8. Alfred T. Mahan, *The Influence of Sea Power upon History, 1660–1783* (Boston, MA: Little, Brown, 1918).

9. Ye Zicheng and Mu Xinhai, "Dui Zhongguo Haiquan Fazhan de Jidian Sikao" ["Some Thoughts on Chinese Sea Power Development"], *Guoji Zhengzhi Yanjiu* [*International Politics Quarterly*], no. 3 (2005).

10. Quoted in Liu Huaqing, *Liu Huaqing Huiyilu* [Liu Huaqing's Memoirs] (Beijing: Jiefangjun Chubanshe, 2004), 434.

11. Chen Xuesong, Du kai, "Zhongguo de Haiquan Yisi yu Haijun Fazhan Jianshe" ["China's Sea Power Consciousness and Navy Development and Construction"], *Junshi Lishi* [*Military History*], no. 4 (2008): 72.

12. Sun Yat-sen, *Guofu de Guofang Xueshu Sixiang Yanjiuji* [*A Collection of Studies on the Founding Father's National Defense Academic Thinking*] (Taipei: Zhongguo Wenhua Yanjiusuo Zhonghua Dadian Bianyinhang, 1996), 321.

13. Ibid., 344.

14. Ibid., 318.

15. You Ziping, "Haiquan Gangjian" ["An Overview of Sea Power"], *Xiandai Jianchuan* (*Modern Warships*), no. 12 (2001): 2–4.

16. Liu Xinhua, "Shilun Zhongguo Fazhan Haiquan de Zhanlue" ["On the Strategy of Chinese Naval Development"], *Fudan Xuebao* [*Fudan Journal*], no. 6 (2001): 69–70.

17. Zhang Shiping, *Zhongguo Haiquan* [*China Sea Power*] (Beijing: Renmin Ribao Chubanshe [People's Daily Press], 1998), 1–12.

18. Ni Lexiong, "Cong Luquan Dao Haiquan de Lishi Biran" ["The Historical Necessity from Land Power to Sea Power"], *Shijie Jingji yu Zhengzhi* [*World Economics and Politics*], no. 11 (2007): 29.

19. Gao Zichuan, "Shixi 21 Shijichu de Zhongguo Haiyang Anquan" ["Analysis on Chinese Maritime Security at the Beginning of the 21st Century"], *Xiandai Guoji Guanxi* [*Modern International Relations*], no. 3 (2006): 27–28.

20. Zhang Wenmu, "Jingji Quanqiuhua yu Zhongguo Haiquan" ["Economic Globalization and China's Sea Power"], *Zhanlue yu Guanli* [*Strategy and Management*], no. 1 (2003): 84–96.

21. Xu Qiyu, "Haiquan de Wuqu yu Fansi" ["Misunderstanding and Retrospection of Sea Power"], *Zhanlue yu Guanli* [*Strategy and Management*], no. 5 (2003): 15–19.

22. Tang Shiping, *Suzao Zhongguo de Lixiang Anquan Huanjing* [Shaping China's Ideal Security Environment] (Beijing: Zhongguo Shehui Kexue Chubanshe, 2003), 223–27.

23. Ye Zicheng, *Luquan Fazhan yu Daguo Xingshuai* [*The Development of Land Power and Rise and Fall of Great Powers*] (Beijing: New Star Press, 2007).

24. Zhang Wenmu, "Sea Power and China's Strategic Choices," *China Security* (Summer 2006): 17–31.

25. Zhang Wenmu, "Jingji Quanqiuhua yu Zhongguo Haiquan" ["Economic Globalization and China's Sea Power"]; and "Lun Zhongguo Haiquan" ["On China's Sea Power"], *Shijie Jingji yu Zhengzhi* [*World Economics and Politics*], no. 10 (2003).

26. Liu Zhongmin, "Haiquan Wenti yu Lengzhanhou de Zhongmeiguanxi: Maodun de Renzhi yu Jiannan de Xuanze" ["The Issue of Sea Power and Sino-U.S. Relations after the Cold War: Awareness of Contradiction and Hard Choices"], *Waijiao Pinglun* [*Diplomacy Review*], no. 6 (2005): 57–59.

27. Information Office of the State Council of PRC, "China's National Defense in 2004,"

28. A. F. K. Organski, *World Politics* (New York: Knopf, 1958).

29. Huo Ke, "Feiduichen Zuozhan yu Zhongguo Haijun Fazhan Zhanlue" ["Asymmetrical Warfare and Strategy for China's Naval Development"], *Jianchuan Zhishi* [*Naval and Merchant Ships*], November 2006.

30. Jiang Zemin, "Report at the 16th Party Congress," http://www.china.org.cn/english/features/49007.htm.

31. Robert B. Zoellick, "Whither China: From Membership to Responsibility?" Remarks to National Committee on U.S.–China Relations, New York City, 21 September 2005.

Yang Yi

A PLA Navy Perspective on Maritime Security Cooperation

An Opportunity Not to Miss

In October 2007 U.S. maritime forces issued their first unified maritime strategy, titled "A Cooperative Strategy for 21st Century Seapower." Many new concepts and perspectives have been put forward and some key paragraphs were encouraging, such as the statement that "maritime forces will be employed to build confidence and trust among nations through collective security efforts that focus on common threats and mutual interests in an open, multi-polar world."[1] From this we can see the strong will of U.S. maritime forces in seeking international cooperation to build global maritime partnerships. In 2005 then–U.S. chief of naval operations Admiral Michael Mullen announced for the first time the "thousand-ship navy" (TSN) proposal at an international symposium on international naval development. As the U.S. Navy explained it, TSN would neither be a traditional fleet of one thousand warships flying the same flag nor a plan of the U.S. Navy to build one thousand more warships. Rather, its purpose would be to address global maritime threats by establishing close partnerships with foreign navies to form an international maritime alliance. Two years later, in April 2007, while China's top admiral and chief of naval operations, Wu Shengli, visited Washington, Mullen proposed that China consider the possibility of joining the Global Maritime Partnership (GMP) Initiative, as TSN is now known.

It is imperative for China to undertake a full-scale, in-depth study of what the TSN program entails and what it would mean for the Chinese military. Only after weighing all the positive as well as negative consequences and ramifications of joining such an initiative should China decide whether to join this program.

We are living in a world of globalization in which events anywhere in the world may have significant positive or negative implications for China's national security interests and development. As has been widely recognized, China's national security and economic strength have strengthened rather than weakened through the implementation of reform and opening-up policies begun by Deng Xiaoping. As a great power that enjoys high levels of economic growth, China relies heavily on international cooperation and globalization. As such, China and the international community are faced with a wide array of security challenges and threats that no single country can possibly cope with singlehandedly. It is always necessary to remain vigilant regarding the challenges of safeguarding national security and development. Therefore, at the present time China must move beyond a "victim mentality" and move toward a more confident and open-minded approach in the face of new ideas such as GMP.

Broadly speaking, China should play a constructive role as a responsible great power and should cooperate more vigorously with foreign countries, including the United States. The same mentality should be applied to an examination of the GMP proposal. Although the United States has already extended the invitation to the People's Liberation Army (PLA) Navy to join the GMP program, the Chinese government and military have yet to officially respond to the invitation.

Some civilian policy analysts and academic scholars, however, have raised a number of concerns. For instance, what is the deeper U.S. strategic intention of the GMP program in addition to the declared purpose of fighting global terrorism? Does it fit in with China's foreign policy to participate in such a program? How will participation impact China's national security interests? Can China open its ports and provide logistical support to the U.S. Navy? These suspicions of U.S. intentions go beyond a few individuals and include a significant group of people in China, for good reasons.

Regardless of these suspicions, China should form a new strategic perspective and take advantage of any positive aspects such a proposal brings while preventing any compromises to its national interests. As for the issue of whether China should open its ports to provide logistics support for the U.S.

Navy in an effort to safeguard regional peace and security, it is not an issue that entails a simple "yes" or "no" response. Further consultations between the two sides will be necessary. Although it is impossible to give any definite answer now, however, China should not hastily slam shut the door on the proposal.

The United States and China Should Transcend "Zero Sum Threat Perceptions"

Whether Chinese and American navies can or should team up under the framework of GMP needs to be closely examined from a greater strategic context. One undeniable fact is that China and the United States harbor strategic suspicions toward each other in the sphere of traditional security. While China suspects that the United States has a strategic intention of containing China, the United States is skeptical of how China will leverage its growing military might and whether China will challenge the dominant position of the United States in the world's power structure.

A number of conditions have set the strategic tone. First, changes in the relative strength of China and the United States have led the United States to develop a sense of strategic uneasiness. The United States still holds an absolute superiority in comprehensive national power, especially military power. In the past few years, however, the United States has been busy with the global antiterrorism war, on one hand, and on the other hand, bogged down in its efforts to restore postwar order in Iraq. The long battle line in the Middle East has stretched the U.S. military so thin that it has impaired the routine building of its defense capability. Furthermore, the rift between the United States and its allies created by the launch of the Iraq War has not yet been fully mended.

Conversely, China is enjoying an increasing international influence as well as political and social stability and economic prosperity. Guided by the military preparations against the Taiwan independence movement, PLA has been noticeably strengthened through the Revolution in Military Affairs with Chinese characteristics, which focused on the two-pronged development of mechanization and "informationalized warfare" capability. Such a shifting in relative strength between the two great powers has made the United States feel uneasy as it continues its effort to consolidate its power and maintain its current global position.

Second, the United States needs a threat like China to maintain its military hegemony. After the end of the Cold War, the United States shifted the focus of its military strategy from competing with the Soviet Union for world hegemony to tackling regional conflicts and preventing the rise of regional powers that might challenge the United States. Russia's military strength has greatly diminished since the Cold War, and it is unlikely that it will regain strategic footing with the United States in the near future. Moreover, Russia—as a major military target—can no longer mobilize the American public and achieve a bipartisan consensus as in the past. Only China can fulfill that role.

"Security Dilemmas" in China's Peaceful Development Road

China's rapid development and expanding national interests require peace and stability not only in Asia but also throughout the world. At the same time, China should, as an important and responsible member of the international community, contribute to safeguarding world peace and promoting progress for all. China's advocacy for building a "harmonious world" is by no means an empty political slogan but rather a serious political pursuit.

China's commitment to peaceful development is sincere. But history has taught the Chinese that peaceful development can never be realized simply by a dint of good intentions. To achieve peaceful development, China must face the profound contradictions associated with its national security strategy and its strategy for economic development. First, there is a contradiction between China's rapidly growing interests and the means to protect those interests. At another level, there is a contradiction between the urgency of strengthening the means of protecting China's expanded national interests and the ever-increasing external constraints for its growth.

China's expanding economic scale has led to rapidly growing interests overseas, where the raw materials, energy resources, and markets necessary for its economic development are spreading globally. The number of Chinese living overseas and their assets are also continually on the rise, and are becoming an increasingly important part of China's national security. Thus, as the Chinese economy and the world economy grow increasingly interdependent, peace and stability in the world, especially within the Asia-Pacific region, are crucial to China's national interests.

Although China's interests around the world are continually expanding, its influence to help safeguard those interests remains insufficient. China lacks the strategic power to actively influence and shape the direction and process of major international affairs. In other words, China's military power lags far behind its political, diplomatic, and cultural power in its ability to better protect the nation's interests in the world. China gravely lacks a military deterrent and real combat capability to effectively address not only traditional security threats but also antiterrorism, counterpiracy, international disaster relief, humanitarian aid, UN peacekeeping operations, and, consistent with international norms, the evacuation of its overseas citizens in the case of a major international crisis. As a responsible great power, China should make larger contributions to the international community. Therefore, it needs to build a powerful military that is commensurate with its international position. This is a necessity to protect both China's interests of national security and development as well as world peace and development of all.

Importantly, however, China's military modernization has created a second contradiction: the need to strengthen the means for the protection of national interests versus the international suspicions that result from doing so. Some countries are fearful of China's military modernization. These doubts and anxieties have been used by some with ill intent to spread and exaggerate the "China threat theory." This has complicated China's security situation and caused greater security pressure on the nation.

Wealth, Not Hegemony; Strength, Not Aggression

Discussion between China and the United States about cooperation—naval cooperation included—is always dominated by the issue of transparency. The Chinese believe that military transparency should be more than just the "technical transparency of hardware," including such things as military budgeting, the size of the armed forces, and the scale of weaponry and armament. More importantly, revealing strategic intention is fundamental to transparency. Military capability cannot indicate whether that military force constitutes a threat or not. The key to that judgment is what strategic intention it has, what policies are implemented, and how it uses its military forces.

The strategic intention of the United States and Japan is not transparent in many aspects. For example, the United States deliberately maintains "strategic ambiguity" with respect to its military intervention in a military conflict across the Taiwan Strait, including under what scenarios and scope a U.S.–Japan alliance would function. The United States has taken advantage of the war against terrorism to seize important strategic points and adjust the deployment of its military forces toward its actual strategic targets. In another example, Japan has exaggerated the "missile threat" and "nuclear threat" of North Korea to create a reason for the political transformation and pursuit of the status of a military great power. The strategic intention of both countries is highly deceitful, making cooperation on the sea difficult.

Whether one country's military buildup constitutes a threat to others can be determined by how it uses such power rather than how powerful it is. The strategic objective of the United States is to maintain its hegemonic position in perpetuity. To this end, it must possess unrivaled power, especially military power. The strategic goal of China is what it says it is: not to seek regional and world hegemony but rather to safeguard and consolidate national territorial integrity and domestic stability, increase national per capita economic development, and achieve and maintain a stable regional environment that supports national development. At the same time, however, China must achieve the means that can match its national position and protect the expansion of its national interests.

China must implement a defensive military strategy. Even though China will become one of the greatest powers in the world, it needs to build a military strength capable of both offensive and defensive operations. This is the legitimate pursuit of any sovereign state. China indeed has no need to develop military power rivaling that of the United States because China's strategic objective is different. The Chinese will be content with a military strength just powerful enough to make anyone think twice before attempting to bully China. The fact that China will not enter an arms race with the United States does not mean that it will not work hard to develop its military power, however. A responsible great power inevitably needs to have a comprehensive strength and the strategy and policies for its rational use thereof.

China calls for the construction of a harmonious world. This means that the use of national strength also needs to be "harmonious" by combining "soft power" with "hard power." China has consistently advocated the "soft" use of hard power to provide more public goods in efforts to achieve greater security in specific regions and the world in general, of which the best example is China's contribution to peacekeeping operations, disaster relief, and humanitarian aid. China's late-2008 decision to deploy naval ships to escort merchant fleets against pirates in the Gulf of Aden is another excellent example.

Mutually Beneficial Military-to-Military Relations

Driven by their political leaders, Chinese and American militaries are gradually deepening their engagement. The military-to-military relationship is the most sensitive and most fragile part of Sino-U.S. relations. It is also one of the most important bellwethers for overall bilateral relations between the two countries. The political leaders of China and the United States have reached a consensus to build productive Sino-U.S. relations as responsible stakeholders and constructive partners. The two countries have made impressive progress in political and economic cooperation. In contrast, their cooperation in the field of security, especially in the field of traditional military security, lags far behind. Is it possible to set up a relationship characterized by stakeholdership and constructive cooperation with strategic mutual benefits between the PLA and the U.S. military? This is indeed a sensitive and difficult question.

From the strategic standpoint of developing stable and sound relations between China and the United States in a general sense, it is both possible and imperative to extend that standpoint to relations between the two militaries. In the least, this should be a goal to pursue boldly. However, we must be sober enough to see that a number of obstacles continue to prevent the two militaries from forming such a relationship, some of which will be difficult to resolve in the near future.

A quick review of recent events makes it clear that suspicions and misperceptions between Chinese and U.S. militaries are unlikely to melt away quickly. In 1996 the United States sent two aircraft carrier battle groups toward the Taiwan Strait, which threw the two militaries into a dangerous face-off. After 1997 the two countries resumed the exchange of visits by senior military officers and military groups. But substantive military cooperation did not rebound to the "peak" level that it had reached in the past. U.S. president George W. Bush's labeling of China as a "potential adversary" early in his presidency, followed by the EP-3 incident in 2001, drove the military-to-military relationship into a deep freeze. In particular, the U.S. National Defense Authorization Act, adopted by the Congress for fiscal year 2000, imposed a number of restrictions on the interactions between the U.S. defense establishment and the PLA. Needless to say, the Chinese and American militaries are both making military preparations for worst-case scenarios in Taiwan Strait. At present, it is unrealistic for the PLA and the U.S. military to engage in substantial military cooperation.

Developing and implementing the road map of U.S.–China military-to-military relations will not be an easy job; there will always be some kinds of obstacles and even some setbacks from time to time. But as long as the top leadership of two countries remains dedicated to strengthening this relationship, we can envision a quite optimistic future. The events of the *Kitty Hawk* battle group being initially denied a port call in Hong Kong and U.S. minesweepers being denied their request to stop there made headlines in 2007, causing people to think about the stability of the U.S.–China military-to-military relationship. Personally, I am confident about relations between the U.S. military and the PLA, and I remain, as always, optimistic about its potential because both the United States and China need a stable and healthy bilateral military relationship. The overall relationship between the United States and China is much more mature and solid than it has ever been and is strong enough to endure significant difficulties.

GMP: A Good Starting Point?

The key to success in developing military-to-military cooperation is to select the appropriate "thin wedge" to initiate it. GMP may well perform that role. Most importantly, this form of cooperation might be attractive to China because it helps to address the great nontraditional security challenges that all great powers face, China included.

No doubt, many conflicts of interest do and will continue to exist between countries, especially great powers, and conflicts may even lead some nations to head-on confrontations. However, unlike in the twentieth century, today the probability of a large-scale military conflict between great powers has been significantly reduced. Instead, interests are increasingly characterized by a common set of nontraditional security threats. Terrorism, religious extremism, and national separatism have become the most dangerous elements imperiling regional peace, stability, and economic prosperity. The proliferation of weapons of mass destruction has elevated these threats to an even more destructive and horrific scale. Cooperation between great powers has already been seen in the joint action taken in the global war on terror, in tsunami relief efforts in Southeast Asia, in the reconstruction of Afghanistan, and, in particular, regarding the nuclear weapon programs pursued by North Korea and Iran.

GMP serves many of these Chinese and U.S. interests. It is congruent with China's goal of pursuing a harmonious world. As a responsible and growing power, China can no longer close its doors and care only about its own affairs. Instead, it should use its own power and provide the world with more "public goods." In addition, however, the challenges that face China at the strategic level should be seen for what they are. From the U.S. side, GMP does not originate from a U.S. intention to seek hegemony in traditional security but rather from its intention to address increasing nontraditional security threats around the world. The fact is, the United States already has a global naval power that remains unmatched, and that will not face a true rival from any country or group of countries for the foreseeable future. The United States can well maintain its hegemony with its current military power.

To view the GMP program as a possible "test-bed" for military cooperation means neither a rejection nor categorical acceptance of the concept. Instead, the GMP program represents an opportunity to begin gradual trust-building and to reduce suspicions and misjudgment. It means an exploration in selective and incremental engagement.

A Cautious but Positive Working Framework

The decisive factor that governs the success of military-to-military exchange between China and the United States is the basis and scope of cooperation as opposed to whether the cooperation is under a multilateral or bilateral framework. Having said that, there are several principles that must be observed: all activities should be strictly within the framework of UN authorization and consistent with international laws; the sovereignty and territorial integrity of other countries must be respected and the use of force in order to intervene in a country's internal affairs must be avoided; the target of activity should be nontraditional security threats such as terrorism, religious extremism, and national separatism; and efforts should be made to increase mutual understanding and promote deeper cooperation with such exchanges. Under these principles, China, as a responsible great power, will be willing to team up with the United States within multilateral and bilateral frameworks. However, China will have difficulty in cooperation if the teamwork involves such sensitive issues as maritime interception, the boarding of vessels for inspection, quarantine, and embargo that are not authorized by the UN Security Council.

Active Attitude and Step-by-Step Approach

As the United States gradually shifts the focus of its military strategy from Europe to the Asia-Pacific region, and as China modernizes its naval power, contact between the two navies will increase. If the two are in a state of serious mutual distrust, "incidents" will never cease to crop up. This will ultimately impact Sino-U.S. relations. The establishment of a Sino-U.S. maritime military security consultation mechanism will help the naval and air forces of both countries prevent accidents, misconception, or misjudgment.

The first step to accomplish this is to strengthen the communication and contact between the PLA Navy and the U.S. Navy, and to conduct joint exercises in which both nations work together to develop practices to prevent accidents and any military operation that may arouse misunderstanding. For example, the two countries could undertake communication exercises, which are an integral part of joint search-and-rescue operations. The United States and the Soviet Union offer a relevant example of the benefits of such cooperation; after signing a maritime security agreement in 1972, the number of maritime incidents between the two countries dropped by 60 percent.

In 1997 the United States and China concluded an agreement to establish a maritime military security consultation mechanism. This occurred after PLA Navy vessels *Harbin* and *Zhuhai* visited the Hawaii and San Diego ports, respectively—the first time a PLA naval fleet visited the homeland of the United States. More recently, in September 2007, the two sides held joint maritime search-and-rescue exercises near China's coastline. The two nations may consider the possibility of more frequent joint search-and-rescue as well as humanitarian aid exercises, and could even explore joint maritime operations at a higher level if the U.S. Congress lifts the laws and decrees that currently restrict exchanges with the PLA.

The gap in strength and capabilities between Chinese and U.S. navies will remain unaltered for a very long time, if not forever. But this should not be an obstacle to greater Sino-American naval cooperation. Other naval powers in Asia that are much smaller and weaker than China's navy conduct exercises and cooperate with the U.S. Navy. Why cannot China? Ultimately, maritime cooperation is primarily a matter of the right political environment and sufficient political will. Political determination will be up to the leadership of both countries. As for the right environment, it is only a matter of time that the PLA Navy and the U.S. Navy will break out of the old mode of thinking and change their strategic perspectives and postures toward each other. Achieving peace, stability, and prosperity in the Asia-Pacific region and beyond will demand it.

Notes

The views expressed herein are personal and do not represent any government agency or department. A previous version of this chapter appeared as Yang Yi, "Engagement, Caution," *China Security* (Autumn 2007): 29–39.

1. "A Cooperative Strategy for 21st Century Seapower" (Washington, DC: U.S. Chief of Naval Operations and the Commandants of the U.S. Marine Corps and U.S. Coast Guard, 17 October 2007), Introduction, http://www.navy.mil/maritime/MaritimeStrategy.pdf.

Abbreviations and Acronyms

AMVER	Automated Mutual Vessel Rescue System
ASEAN	Association of Southeast Asian Nations
BCD	Border Control Department
CBM	confidence-building measure
CBO	Congressional Budget Office
CCG	China Coast Guard
CCS	China Classification Society
CFLEC	China Fisheries Law Enforcement Command
CGLO	Coast Guard Liaison Officer
CHISREP	China Ship Reporting System
CISDP	China Information System for Disease Control and Prevention
CNPC	China National Petroleum Corporation
CRSB	China Rescue & Salvage Bureau
CSI	Container Security Initiative
CTF	Combined Task Force
C-TPAT	U.S. Customs Trade Partnership against Terrorism
CUES	Code for Unalerted Encounters at Sea
DOC	Declaration on the Conduct of Parties in the South China Sea
DSRV	deep submergence rescue vehicle
EEZ	exclusive economic zone
EEZ/CS Law	Law of the PRC on the Exclusive Economic Zone and the Continental Shelf
ETIM	East Turkestan Islamic Movement

EXBS	Export Control and Related Border Security Assistance Program
EXTACS	experimental tactics
FLEC	Fisheries Law Enforcement Command
FMS	foreign military sales
GAC	General Administration of Customs
GDP	gross domestic product
GMP	Global Maritime Partnership
HA and DR	humanitarian assistance and disaster relief
IMO	International Maritime Organization
INCSEA	incidents at sea
INECP	International Nonproliferation Export Control Program
ISMERLO	International Submarine Escape and Rescue Liaison Office
ISO	International Organization for Standardization
ISPS	International Ship and Port Facility Security
JMSDF	Japanese Maritime Self-Defense Force
LNG	liquefied natural gas
MBDS	Mekong Basin Disease Surveillance
MMCA	Military Maritime Consultative Agreement
MoT	Ministry of Transportation
MRC	Maritime Rescue Center
MSA	Maritime Safety Administration
NII	nonintrusive inspection
NTC	National Targeting Center
PACOM	U.S. Pacific Command
PAP	People's Armed Police
PLA	People's Liberation Army
PLA Navy	People's Liberation Army Navy
PME	professional military education
PRC	People's Republic of China
PSI	Proliferation Security Initiative
RCC	Rescue Coordination Center
RFID	radio-frequency identification
ROK	Republic of Korea
SAFE	Security and Accountability for Every Port
SARS	Severe Acute Respiratory Syndrome
SCO	Shanghai Cooperation Organization
SCS	South China Sea

SLOC	sea lines of communication
SOA	State Oceanic Administration
TEU	twenty-foot container equivalent unit
TS/CZ	Law of PRC on Territorial Sea and Contiguous Zone
TSN	thousand-ship navy
TSN-GMP	Thousand-Ship Navy–Global Maritime Partnership
UNCLOS	United Nations Convention on the Law of the Sea
USCG	U.S. Coast Guard
WCO	World Customs Organization
WMD	weapons of mass destruction
XUAR	Xinjiang Uighur Autonomous Region

About the Contributors

MR. GABRIEL B. COLLINS is a private-sector commodity market analyst focusing on China and Russia. He was an OSD/ONA research fellow in the U.S. Naval War College's China Maritime Studies Institute (CMSI) from 2006–8. Collins is an honors graduate of Princeton University (2005, A.B. Politics) and is proficient in Mandarin Chinese and Russian. His primary research areas are Chinese and Russian energy policy, maritime energy security, Chinese shipbuilding, and Chinese naval modernization. Mr. Collins' energy- and shipbuilding-related work has been published in *Oil & Gas Journal, Jane's Intelligence Review, Geopolitics of Energy, Proceedings, Naval War College Review, The National Interest, Hart's Oil & Gas Investor, LNG Observer,* and *Orbis.*

PROF. PETER A. DUTTON is an associate professor of strategic research in the China Maritime Studies Institute (CMSI) at the Naval War College. The focus of his work is the strategic implications for the United States and its navy of Chinese views of international law of the sea. Recent research projects have focused on East Asian flashpoints for conflict, including maritime delimitation disputes, territorial and sovereignty disputes, and contention related to U.S. maritime intelligence flights. Professor Dutton was formerly the Howard S. Levie Chair of operational law on the teaching faculty of the Naval War College's Joint Military Operations Department. Professor Dutton also teaches law of the sea and national security law in the Marine Affairs Institute at Roger Williams University's School of Law in Bristol, Rhode Island. Professor Dutton is a retired Navy Judge Advocate who began his Navy service as a naval flight officer in 1985, flying electronic warfare aircraft until 1990, when he was selected for transition from aviation into the Judge Advocate General's Corps. As a Navy JAG, Professor Dutton served in various positions with the operating forces, including as the legal advisor to commander, Carrier Group Six (*John F. Kennedy* Battle Group). Professor Dutton received his juris doctor degree from the College of William and Mary in 1993. He received a master's in National Security and Strategic Studies, with honors, from the Naval War College in 1999, and his bachelor's degree, cum laude, from Boston University in 1982.

DR. MICHAEL J. GREEN holds the Japan Chair and is a senior advisor at CSIS, in addition to being an associate professor of international relations at Georgetown University. He served as special assistant to the president for national security affairs and senior director for Asian affairs at the National Security Council (NSC) from January 2004 to December 2005, after joining the NSC in April 2001 as director of Asian affairs with responsibility for Japan, Korea, and Australia/New Zealand. His current research and writing is focused on Asian regional architecture; Japanese politics; U.S. foreign policy history; the Korean peninsula, Tibet, and Burma; and U.S.–India relations.

Dr. Green speaks fluent Japanese and spent more than five years in Japan working as a staff member of the National Diet, as a journalist for Japanese and American newspapers, and as a consultant for U.S. business. He has also been on the faculty of the Johns Hopkins School of Advanced International Studies (SAIS), a fellow at the Council on Foreign Relations, a staff member at the Institute for Defense Analyses, and a senior advisor to the Office of Asia-Pacific Affairs in the Office of the Secretary of Defense. He graduated from Kenyon College with highest honors in history in 1983, and received his MA from Johns Hopkins SAIS in 1987 and his PhD in 1994. He also did graduate work at Tokyo University as a Fulbright Fellow and at the Massachusetts Institute of Technology as a research associate of the MIT-Japan Program. He is a member of the Council on Foreign Relations, Institute for International Security Studies, and the Aspen Strategy Group. He is also vice chair of the congressionally mandated Japan-U.S. Friendship Commission and serves on the advisory boards of the Center for a New American Security and Australian American Leadership Dialogue and the editorial board of *Washington Quarterly*.

MR. DAVID N. GRIFFITHS is an independent consulting analyst who specializes in maritime aspects of international confidence and cooperation. A former Canadian naval officer, he spent fifteen of his thirty-one years in uniform at sea in ships and submarines, with the remainder in staff appointments that included personnel policy, project management, operational planning, and doctrine development. For the latter, he received a Maritime Commander's Commendation in 1996. In 1992–93 he was seconded to the European Community Monitoring Mission in the Balkans where he became head of the Coordination Centre responsible for operations in Eastern Herzegovina, Montenegro, and the southern Dalmatian coast of Croatia. Between 1993 and 1996 his duties included serving as a naval advisor to the Middle East Peace Process. Mr. Griffiths left the navy in 1996 to establish Pendragon Applied Research, an independent consultancy that conducts varied projects in Canada, the Middle East, Central Asia, and the Indo-Pacific. He is a resident research fellow at the Centre for Foreign Policy Studies at Dalhousie University and a senior research fellow at the International Centre for Emergency Management Studies at Cape Breton University. He also serves on the executive of the Emergency Management Association of Atlantic Canada and on the Board of Directors of the Canadian Naval Memorial Trust, which preserves the last surviving World War II corvette, HMCS *Sackville*. Mr. Griffiths is a graduate of the Canadian Forces Command and Staff College and holds a master's degree in Marine Management from Dalhousie University.

DR. JAMES R. HOLMES is a Phi Beta Kappa graduate of Vanderbilt University and earned graduate degrees at Salve Regina University, Providence College, and the Fletcher School of Law and Diplomacy at Tufts University. He graduated from the Naval War College with highest distinction in 1994 and, as the top graduate in his class, was the recipient of the Naval War College Foundation Award. Before joining the Naval War College faculty in the spring of 2007, he was a senior research associate at the University of Georgia Center for International Trade and Security, Athens, Georgia; a research associate at the Institute for Foreign Policy Analysis, Cambridge, Massachusetts; and a U.S. Navy surface warfare officer, serving in the engineering and weapons departments on board the battleship *Wisconsin*, directing an engineering course at the Surface Warfare Officers School Command, and teaching Strategy and Policy at the Naval War College, College of Distance Education. His books include *Theodore Roosevelt and World Order: Police Power in International Relations* (Potomac Books, 2006), *Chinese Naval Strategy in the 21st Century: The Turn to Mahan* (Routledge, 2008; coauthor), *Indian Naval Strategy in the 21st Century* (Routledge, 2010; coauthor), and *Red Star over the Pacific: China's Rise and the Challenge to U.S. Maritime Strategy* (Naval Institute Press, 2010; coauthor).

REAR ADMIRAL ERIC A. MCVADON, USN (RET.), concluded his thirty-five years of naval service as the U.S. defense and naval attaché at the American Embassy in Beijing, 1990–92. A consultant on Asian security affairs, he works extensively with the U.S. policy and intelligence communities and the Department of Defense, directly and indirectly; his writing is published widely in the West and Asia. He is also senior advisor and director emeritus of Asia-Pacific Studies at the Institute for Foreign Policy Analysis and a nonresident fellow at the Atlantic Council of the United States. His naval career included extensive experience in air antisubmarine warfare and politico-military affairs, including service as the NATO and U.S. subunified commander in Iceland and assignments on the Navy Staff, Office of the Secretary of Defense, and with the chairman of the Joint Chiefs of Staff. He also commanded a P-3C squadron and the naval station in Iceland. Admiral McVadon, a designated naval aviator, is a 1958 graduate of Tulane University and has a master's degree in international affairs from George Washington University. He is a distinguished graduate of the Naval Postgraduate School, Naval War College (Command & Staff), and National War College. He and his wife, Marshall, both from Baton Rouge, Louisiana, live and work in Great Falls, Virginia.

CAPTAIN BERNARD "BARNEY" MORELAND, USCG, is the senior analyst for the U.S. Navy's Pacific Fleet. As a mobilized Coast Guard Reservist, he served from 2006 to 2008 as the first U.S. Coast Guard Liaison Officer to the People's Republic of China. Prior to that assignment, he was mobilized under arms in Egypt, Thailand, Kuwait, Iraq, and Cuba in the war on terror. As a Coast Guard junior officer, he sailed aboard U.S. Coast Guard cutter *Munro* in the Northern Sea of Japan in 1983 during *Munro*'s search for wreckage and survivors from the Korean airliner destroyed by a Soviet fighter aircraft. From 1985 to 1989, he served as operations director for the National Narcotics Border Interdiction System Western Pacific Region office in Honolulu, coordinating support for the seizure of five ships carrying more than 250 tons of Southeast Asian marijuana. Mr. Moreland earned a BS in oceanography from the U.S. Coast Guard Academy in 1983, an MBA (International) from the University of Hawaii in 1995, and an MA in East Asian Studies from Harvard University in 2000. For his master's thesis, he researched Fujian Province human traffickers. He studied the Chinese language at Peking University in 2000. Captain Moreland married the former Edie Lin in 1987. He still serves as a captain in the U.S. Coast Guard Reserves in Honolulu.

PROF. WILLIAM S. MURRAY is an associate research professor in the U.S. Naval War College's warfare analysis and research department. Professor Murray served as a junior officer and plank owner on the USS *Pittsburgh* (SSN 720), and as the navigator on the USS *Houston* (SSN 713). He conducted overseas deployments in both vessels and is qualified to command nuclear-powered submarines. Professor Murray has served on the operations staff at the U.S. Strategic Command, and as a member of the faculty of the Naval War College's strategic research department. He retired from the Navy in 2003. He has published articles in *International Security, Naval War College Review, Parameters, Comparative Strategy, Proceedings, Jane's Intelligence Review,* and *Undersea Warfare.*

DR. PAUL J. SMITH is an associate professor at the U.S. Naval War College in Newport, Rhode Island, where he specializes in transnational security issues and the international politics of East Asia (with particular emphasis on the People's Republic of China). In addition, he studies the impact of such issues as narcotics trafficking, terrorism, human smuggling, small arms trafficking, and infectious disease on governance and regional security. He has published in *Contemporary Southeast Asia, Fletcher Forum of World Affairs, Harvard Asia-Pacific Review, Jane's Intelligence Review, Orbis, Parameters,* and *Survival.* His chapter contributions have appeared in such books as *Fires across the Water: Transnational Problems in Asia* (Council on Foreign Relations, 1997) and *Tiger's Roar: Asia's Recovery and Its Impact* (M. E. Sharpe, 2001). His edited books include *Human Smuggling: Chinese Migrant Trafficking and the Challenge to America's Immigration Tradition* (Center for Strategic and International Studies, 1997) and *Terrorism and Violence in Southeast Asia: Transnational Challenges to States and Regional Stability* (M. E. Sharpe, 2004). He is author of the book *The Terrorism Ahead: Confronting Transnational Violence in the 21st Century* (M. E. Sharpe, 2007). Dr. Smith frequently provides commentary for national and international news organizations, including the *International Herald Tribune, Christian Science Monitor, Defense News,* and *Japan Times.* He has been a member of the Council for Security Cooperation in the Asia-Pacific (CSCAP) Transnational Crime working group. Dr. Smith has lived and studied in the People's Republic of China, Taiwan, and the United Kingdom and is conversant in Mandarin Chinese. He earned his bachelor of arts degree from Washington and Lee University, his master of arts from the University of London, and his juris doctorate (law) and doctorate (political science) from the University of Hawaii at Manoa.

DR. SU HAO is a professor in the Department of Diplomacy at the China Foreign Affairs University, director of its Center for Asia-Pacific Studies, and a board member in a range of Chinese organizations that focus on security, cooperation, and bilateral exchange. Dr. Su is the acting chairman of CFAU's Diplomacy Department and director of its China's Foreign Relations Section. He is a member of the Chinese Committee, Council of Security Cooperation in the Asia-Pacific (CSCAP); he is a board member of China Association of Arms Control and Disarmament, China Association of Asia-Pacific Studies, China Association of Asian-African Development Exchange, and China Association of China-ASEAN. Dr. Su received his BA and MA in history and international relations from Beijing Normal University and PhD in international relations from China Foreign Affairs University. He pursued advanced studies in the School of Oriental and African Studies (SOAS) at the University of London in 1993–95 and was a Fulbright Scholar in 2001, at both Columbia University's Institute of War and Peace Studies and at the University of California at Berkeley's Institute of East Asian Studies. In 2004 Dr. Su served as a visiting professor in Uppsala University's Department of Peace and Conflict Research (Sweden). He teaches and conducts research on China's diplomatic history, strategic studies and international security, politics, and economy in the Asia-Pacific region. Su has published several books and many articles concerning China's foreign policy, security issues, international relations in the Asia-Pacific region, and East Asian cooperation.

DR. WU SHICUN is president of and a senior research fellow at the National Institute for South China Sea Studies (NISCS). Dr. Wu graduated from Nanjing University in 1984. He has participated in study programs at the School of Advanced International Studies (SAIS), John Hopkins University, and the John F. Kennedy School of Government, Harvard University. He was a visiting scholar for the research program on the dynamics of U.S. foreign policy and regional security sponsored by the U.S. government, and he was a visiting senior research fellow at the Asia-Pacific Center for Security Studies.

Dr. Wu's research interests include the history and geography of the South China Sea, maritime delimitation, maritime economy, international relations, and regional security strategy. His main published works include *Origin and Development of Spratly Disputes, Collection of Literatures on the South China Sea Issues, A Bibliography of Research Documents on the South China Sea, A Study on the South China Sea Disputes,* and *Selective Studies on World Famous Island Economic Bodies.* His published academic papers include "Zheng He's Voyages to the Indian Ocean and the South China Sea," "Historical Background on the 1943 Sino-British New Treaty," "Relativity of Historical Cognition," "The Foundation of Sino-ASEAN Free Trade Zone and Cross-Strait Commercial Relations," "Imperative Task: the Exploitation of South China Sea Resources," "Institutional and Policy Factors Affecting Taiwan's Economic Development," and "South China Sea Issues in the Period of the Republic of China."

DR. GUIFANG (JULIA) XUE is the director and professor of the Law of the Sea Institute, Ocean University of China (OUC). She received her PhD from the Centre for Maritime Policy, University of Wollongong, Australia. Dr. Xue has extensive research interests and practical experiences in the areas of the United Nations Convention on the Law of the Sea (UNCLOS), the state practice of China on the UNCLOS, ocean-related legislation and management, marine environmental protection, international fisheries law and policy, and bilateral fisheries relations between China and its neighboring states. She is actively involved in academic activities at home and abroad and has published widely on these issues.

In addition to the day-to-day functions of the Law of the Sea Institute, Dr. Xue is responsible for funding applications and project operations. She chairs government-funded projects for drafting national marine laws and regulations, provides consultancy to ocean-related ministries and governmental agencies, and conducts training courses for their administrative personnel and enforcement teams. Dr. Xue hosts English courses for international students, and bilingual courses to master's students and doctorate candidates on marine laws, law of the sea international fisheries agreements, and international law of the sea and marine affairs. She also supervises postgraduates in international law, ocean governance, and fisheries management.

REAR ADMIRAL YANG YI was born on 21 September 1949 in Tianjin, China, and joined the Chinese Navy in 1968. In early 2002 Rear Admiral Yang was named director of the Institute for Strategic Studies at the PLA National Defense University after serving as the deputy director general of that institute from late 2000.

In addition to his current responsibilities, Rear Admiral Yang has served in the following positions in the Chinese navy: 1968–72, engineer, Naval Air Arm, South Sea fleet; 1972–79, instructor, Surface Warfare Training Center, East Sea Fleet; 1979–81, naval technical assistance expert to the navy of Cameroon; 1981–83, executive commanding officer, frigate, East Sea Fleet; 1983–85, Staff Officer, PLA Navy Headquarters; 1985–90, director, PLA Navy Foreign Affairs Bureau; 1990–95, deputy director general of the General Office and International Policy

Adviser of the Commander in Chief of the PLA Navy; and 1995–2000, naval attaché, embassy of the People's Republic of China, Washington, DC.

Rear Admiral Yang is a graduate of Peking University and of Laval University in Canada. He studied at the National Defense University and the National Defense Science and Technology University in China. He also studied briefly at the Institut d'Études Politiques de Paris in France. Rear Admiral Yang has a good command of both French and English and is an expert on national security and military strategy, international relations, and foreign policy. He has attended many international conferences and has given a great number of lectures in a wide variety of countries. Rear Admiral Yang is married to Bai Xiangyun and has a daughter named Yang Yalin.

DR. TOSHI YOSHIHARA is an associate professor in the strategy and policy department at the Naval War College, Newport, Rhode Island. Previously, he was a visiting professor in the strategy department at the Air War College, Montgomery, Alabama. Dr. Yoshihara has also served as a senior research fellow at the Institute for Foreign Policy Analysis in Cambridge, Massachusetts. His research interests include U.S. alliances in the Asia-Pacific region, China's military modernization, security dynamics on the Korean Peninsula, Japan's defense policy, and China–Taiwan relations. He is coauthor of *Indian Naval Strategy in the Twenty-first Century* (Routledge, 2009), *Chinese Naval Strategy in the 21st Century: The Turn to Mahan* (Routledge, 2008), and coeditor of *Asia Looks Seaward: Power and Maritime Strategy* (Praeger Security International, 2008). Dr. Yoshihara holds a PhD in international relations from the Fletcher School of Law and Diplomacy, Tufts University; an MA in international relations from the School of Advanced International Studies, Johns Hopkins University; and a BS in international relations from the School of Foreign Service, Georgetown University. Web site: http://www.usnwc.edu/Academics/Faculty/Toshi-Yoshihara.aspx.

DR. YU WANLI is an associate professor at the School of International Studies and a member of the academic committee of the Center for International and Strategic Studies at Peking University. His main areas of expertise include U.S. politics and foreign policy, U.S.–China relations, and the international political economics of globalization. He received a doctorate in international politics from the graduate school of the Chinese Academy of Social Sciences in 2003; a master's degree in international politics from School of International Studies, Peking University in 1998; and bachelor of law from the School of International Relations and Public Affairs, Fudan University, 1995.

Dr. Yu joined the faculty team of the School of International Studies, Peking University in 2006. Before that he worked as a research associate in the Institute of American Studies, Chinese Academy of Social Sciences from 1998 to 2006 and was appointed to deputy director of the U.S. Foreign Relations Section. He was a visiting fellow at the Kettering Foundation in Dayton, Ohio, from June to December 2004. He has published a book, *The Wind Vane of U.S. Politics: On-Site Observation of Presidential Election* 2008. His coauthored books include *Ideology and U.S. Foreign Policy, Chinese Government Rule by Law, Same Bed Different Dream: U.S.-European Strategy*, and *History of China-U.S. Relations: 1949–1972*. He may be reached at yuwanli@pku.edu.cn.

DR. ZHU HUAYOU is vice president of the National Institute for South China Sea Studies. He received his PhD in economics from Nanjing University. Dr. Zhu has presided at or participated in many national and provincial research programs and was twice awarded scientific and research achievement awards by the provincial and national governments. His primary research areas are economic reform and social development, South China Sea resources and their exploitation, and international relations. Dr. Zhu's main published books include *Why China's Reforms Succeed, Theory and Practice of China's Market Economy, The Growth Vitality—Development of China's Non-governmental Economy*, and *The Emerging Market*.

Dr. Zhu has served in a variety of intellectual and leadership positions. Between 2004 and 2007 he was deputy director-general of the National Institute for South China Sea Studies and a member of the research staff. From 1997 to 2004 he was deputy director-general of the Hainan Institute for South China Sea Studies. Between 1993 and 1996 he served as division director of China Reform and Development Research Institute. Dr. Zhu was a professor at Yangzhou University from 1983 to 1992.

PROF. ZHUANG JIANZHONG is currently the deputy director of the Center for National Strategy Studies of Shanghai Jiao Tong University (CNSS). He is also the general secretary of Shanghai Society for Pacific Region Economic Development (SSPRED), a professor at Shanghai Jiao Tong University's School for International and Public Affairs, and a research fellow at the university's Center for RimPac Studies (CPSIS). Professor Zhuang also serves as a standing board member of Shanghai Society of International Relations, an adjunct research fellow at Fudan University's ROK Research Center, and an adjunct professor at Tongji University's Asian Pacific Research Center. He was previously a visiting scholar at Fudan University's Center for American Studies of (1997) and at George Washington University (2001).

Professor Zhuang's main research areas include international politics, U.S.–China relations, the Taiwan issue, the Korean issue, Northeast Asian Security, and nonproliferation. Professor Zhuang joined the People's Liberation Army in 1960 and served in the General Staff as a senior political analyst with the rank of senior colonel before his retirement in 1999, when he transferred to Shanghai Jiao Tong University.

The Editors

DR. ANDREW S. ERICKSON is an associate professor in the strategic research department at the U.S. Naval War College and a founding member of the department's China Maritime Studies Institute (CMSI). He is also a fellow in the Princeton-Harvard China and the World Program, an associate in research at Harvard University's Fairbank Center for Chinese Studies, and a fellow in the National Committee on U.S.–China Relations' Public Intellectuals Program. Erickson previously worked for Science Applications International Corporation (SAIC) as a Chinese translator and technical analyst. He has also worked at the U.S. Embassy in Beijing, the U.S. Consulate in Hong Kong, the U.S. Senate, and the White House. Proficient in Mandarin Chinese and Japanese, he has traveled extensively in Asia. Erickson received his PhD and MA in international relations and comparative politics from Princeton University and graduated magna cum laude from Amherst College with a BA in history and political science. His research, which focuses on East Asian defense, foreign policy, and technology issues, has been published widely in such journals as *Asian Security* (forthcoming), *Journal of Strategic Studies*, *The American Interest*, and *Joint Force Quarterly*. Erickson is coeditor of, and a contributor to, the Naval Institute Press book series, Studies in Chinese Maritime Development: *China Goes to Sea* (2009), *China's Energy Strategy* (2008), *China's Future Nuclear Submarine Force* (2007); as well as the Naval War College Newport Paper *China's Nuclear Modernization*. His recent publications include the coauthored article "Welcome China to the Fight against Pirates," U.S. Naval Institute *Proceedings* 135, no. 3 (March 2009), http://www.usni.org/magazines/proceedings/story.asp?STORY_ID=1809. He may be reached at www.andrewerickson.com.

DR. LYLE J. GOLDSTEIN is an associate professor in the strategic research department of the Naval War College in Newport, Rhode Island. He is the founding director of the Naval War College's China Maritime Studies Institute (CMSI), which was established in October 2006 to improve mutual understanding and maritime cooperation with China. He has also worked in the office of the secretary of defense. Dr. Goldstein earned a PhD from Princeton University in 2001, an MA from Johns Hopkins SAIS, and a BA from Harvard University, and has studied at Beijing Normal University. Proficient in Chinese and Russian, Professor Goldstein has conducted extensive field research in both China and Russia. Dr. Goldstein's first book, which compared proliferation crises and focused particularly on Chinese nuclear strategy, was published by Stanford University Press in 2005. His research on Chinese defense policies, especially concerning naval development, has been published in *Asia Policy, China Quarterly, International Security, Jane's Intelligence Review, Journal of Strategic Studies,* and *Proceedings.* Recently his research focus has been on further development of China's Coast Guard and related cooperation issues. He lectured at the Chinese Coast Guard Academy in Ningbo in 2007 and has published research on Chinese maritime enforcement capabilities in U.S. Naval Institute *Proceedings* and in *China Brief.* His most recent publication on this subject, "Five Dragons Stirring up the Sea: Challenge and Opportunity in China's Improving Maritime Enforcement Capabilities," Naval War College *China Maritime Study* 5 (April 2010), is available at http://www.usnwc.edu/Research—Gaming/China-Maritime-Studies-Institute/Publications/documents/CMSI_No5_web1.pdf.

DR. NAN LI is an associate professor at the China Maritime Studies Institute of the U.S. Naval War College. He received his PhD in political science from Johns Hopkins University and has taught at a number of American universities. He was an Olin fellow and associate at Harvard University during 1993–95, and a senior fellow at the U.S. Institute of Peace during 1997–98. He coordinated the China program for the Institute of Defense and Strategic Studies, Nanyang Technological University in Singapore during 2003–6. Dr. Li has published extensively on Chinese security and military policy. His writings have appeared in *Security Studies, China Quarterly, China Journal, Armed Forces & Society, Issues & Studies,* and many others. He has contributed to edited volumes from the RAND Corporation, the National Defense University Press, Clarendon Press, M. E. Sharpe, U.S. Army War College, and National Bureau of Asian Research. He has also published a monograph with the U.S. Institute of Peace. Li is the editor of *Chinese Civil-Military Relations* (Routledge, 2006). His most recent publication is "Chinese Civil-Military Relations in the Post-Deng Era: Implications for Crisis Management and Naval Modernization,"

Naval War College *China Maritime Study* 4 (January 2010), http://www.usnwc.edu/Research—Gaming/China-Maritime-Studies-Institute/Publications/documents/China-Maritime-Study-No-4-January-2010.aspx.

Index

THE NAVAL INSTITUTE PRESS is the book-publishing arm of the U.S. Naval Institute, a private, nonprofit, membership society for sea service professionals and others who share an interest in naval and maritime affairs. Established in 1873 at the U.S. Naval Academy in Annapolis, Maryland, where its offices remain today, the Naval Institute has members worldwide.

Members of the Naval Institute support the education programs of the society and receive the influential monthly magazine *Proceedings* or the colorful bimonthly magazine *Naval History* and discounts on fine nautical prints and on ship and aircraft photos. They also have access to the transcripts of the Institute's Oral History Program and get discounted admission to any of the Institute-sponsored seminars offered around the country.

The Naval Institute's book-publishing program, begun in 1898 with basic guides to naval practices, has broadened its scope to include books of more general interest. Now the Naval Institute Press publishes about seventy titles each year, ranging from how-to books on boating and navigation to battle histories, biographies, ship and aircraft guides, and novels. Institute members receive significant discounts on the Press's more than eight hundred books in print.

Full-time students are eligible for special half-price membership rates. Life memberships are also available.

For a free catalog describing Naval Institute Press books currently available, and for further information about joining the U.S. Naval Institute, please write to:

Member Services
U.S. NAVAL INSTITUTE
291 Wood Road
Annapolis, MD 21402-5034
Telephone: (800) 233-8764
Fax: (410) 571-1703
Web address: www.usni.org